TAXATION AND THE
DEFICIT ECONOMY

TAXATION AND THE DEFICIT ECONOMY

Fiscal Policy and Capital Formation in the United States

Edited by
DWIGHT R. LEE

Foreword by
Michael J. Boskin

Pacific Studies in Public Policy

PACIFIC RESEARCH INSTITUTE FOR PUBLIC POLICY
San Francisco, California

ISBN 0-936488-03-4 (paper)
      0-936488-13-1 (cloth)

Library of Congress Catalog Card Number 85-63549

Printed in the United States of America

Pacific Research Institute for Public Policy
177 Post Street
San Francisco, California 94108
(415) 989-0833

Library of Congress Cataloging-in-Publication Data

Taxation and the deficit economy.

  (Pacific studies in public policy)
  Bibliography: p.
  Includes index.
  1. Fiscal policy—United States. 2. Saving and investment—United States.
3. Government spending policy—United States. 4. Taxation—United States. I. Lee,
Dwight R. II. Series.
HJ257.2.T385 1986   339.5′2′0973   85-63549
ISBN 0-936488-13-1
ISBN 0-936488-03-4 (pbk.)

PACIFIC RESEARCH INSTITUTE
FOR PUBLIC POLICY

The Pacific Research Institute for Public Policy is an independent, tax-exempt research and educational organization. The Institute's program is designed to broaden public understanding of the nature and effects of market processes and government policy.

With the bureaucratization and politicization of modern society, scholars, business and civic leaders, the media, policymakers, and the general public have too often been isolated from meaningful solutions to critical public issues. To facilitate a more active and enlightened discussion of such issues, the Pacific Research Institute sponsors in-depth studies into the nature of and possible solutions to major social, economic, and environmental problems. Undertaken regardless of the sanctity of any particular government program, or the customs, prejudices, or temper of the times, the Institute's studies aim to ensure that alternative approaches to currently problematic policy areas are fully evaluated, the best remedies discovered, and these findings made widely available. The results of this work are published as books and monographs, and form the basis for numerous conference and media programs.

Through this program of research and commentary, the Institute seeks to evaluate the premises and consequences of government policy, and provide the foundations necessary for constructive policy reform.

CONTENTS

8

Bismarckism

9

The Welfare State, Capital Formation, and Tax-Transfer Politics

10

Credit Allocation and Capital Formation: The Political Economy of Indirect Taxation

11

Union Myopia and the Taxation of Capital
—Dwight R. Lee   297

12

**Commanding Resources: The Military Sector and
Capital Formation**
—Lloyd J. Dumas   323

PART IV   **Taxation and Individual Rights**

LIST OF FIGURES

LIST OF TABLES

ACKNOWLEDGMENTS

I am deeply indebted to Gregory Christainsen who was in a real sense the co-editor of this volume. He worked with me and with most of the contributors, providing us with both his enthusiasm and competence. Charles Baird also has my enduring gratitude for coming up with the idea for the volume, suggesting that I edit it, and providing invaluable assistance getting it off the ground. Finally, I would be remiss if I did not thank Francine Hartman for her cheerful help throughout the development of the book.

Dwight R. Lee

FOREWORD

The United States has the lowest rates of national saving and investment of any advanced economy. This state of affairs, which has existed for decades, was often justified by reference to our higher per capita incomes and the possibility that as economies grew wealthier through time, the incremental value of producing still greater wealth would decline. Yet most of Western Europe has now caught up to the United States in terms of its standard of living, and Japan is close and gaining; yet their rates of saving and investment continue to exceed ours by substantial amounts.

An economy's rates of saving and capital formation reveal much about its values, institutions, and opportunities. These rates reflect the way in which the economic and political systems interact to trade off present consumption versus future opportunities. There can be no doubt that for decades the United States, relative both to its own history and to the rest of the world, has stacked its cards heavily in favor of current consumption. In *Taxation and the Deficit Economy: Fiscal Policy and Capital Formation in the United States,* almost two dozen prominent scholars explore various aspects of the economic and political reasons why our rates of saving and capital formation are persistently so low. From standard economics through public choice analysis of the political process to philosophy and ethics, these authors present theories and evidence documenting their conclusions;

they also present policy proposals to raise the rates of saving and capital formation or to render less potent the political bias toward current consumption.

The relationships among saving, investment, productivity, and economic growth are many and complex. Policies inhibiting or stimulating saving or investment may affect growth, labor productivity, the short-run macroeconomic performance of the economy, the relative efficiency of the allocation of the current capital stock, the efficiency with which society trades off current consumption against future consumption, and intergenerational equity. Each of these concerns has been important in the recent historical experience of the United States. For example, many economists, myself included, place a substantial fraction of the blame for the productivity slowdown from the late 1960s to the present on lower rates of capital formation per worker. What are some of the causes of our low rates of saving and capital formation?

Various pundits argue that (1) deficits help stimulate employment; (2) large deficits are inflationary, (3) deficits shift the composition of output by crowding out investment and net exports, (4) deficits decrease the rate of national saving dollar for dollar, (5) deficit phobia will eventually help control the growth of spending, (6) deficit finance is a primary means for increasing government spending, and (7) deficits simply do not matter (given the level of government spending).

Obviously, deficits cannot do all of these things simultaneously. Deficits do matter, but we must ask how, for what, and under what circumstances they matter. First, some rough numbers. Until recently, the Congressional Budget Office estimates placed the deficit as a fraction of Gross National Product (GNP) at about 5 percent for the remainder of the decade. This amounts to most of domestic private saving. Deficits of between $200 and $300 billion per year for several years double the national debt and, correspondingly, the interest payments necessary to service it.

Before turning to the likely effects of such deficits, the first thing that we must all admit is that this is a virtually unprecedented scenario. We have run deficits of this size in the United States only in the midst of deep recessions or in wartime. The prospect of such deficits when the economy is at relatively full-employment during peacetime is simply unprecedented.

Next, federal government spending is running at over 24 percent of GNP, while tax receipts are running at about 19 percent. Spending has gone up, not down, as a percentage of GNP under President Reagan, despite his efforts to control nonmilitary spending. While defense spending as a fraction of GNP is running one percentage point more than when President Reagan took office, it is approximately at the level he called for in his original March 1981 proposals. Indeed, the recent congressional budget resolutions call for a halt to the defense buildup. The really big increases have been in the interest on the national debt and in middle-class entitlement payments, *which are not related to need*. The most important of these entitlement programs are Social Security and Medicare, only some of whose benefits accrue to low-income elderly individuals. The President has been relatively successful in cutting grants-in-aid to state and local governments and in tightening eligibility for those transfer payments with specific means tests. Of course, we had a substantial three-year phased-in (although partially scaled back) tax cut.

Should we be concerned? Some recent deficit projections have been more sanguine than the 5 percent figure I cited earlier, but such projections assume no recessions or other unwelcome developments. Assuming we should be concerned, what should we do? Can we do anything given our political apparatus? My evaluation of the evidence is that *sometimes* deficits do matter for various economic outcomes. When the economy is at substantially less than full employment, a tax cut or spending increase can produce some small stimulus in aggregate demand. However, it is important to realize that this stimulus is *much less* than textbook Keynesian models predict. This occurs for a variety of reasons, the most important being that we live in an economy very open to both trade and capital flows. This in turn severely limits the possibility of substantial fiscal stimulus, as a deficit produces pressure on interest rates, attracts foreign capital, appreciates the dollar, curtails exports, and stimulates imports. If you believe that the decline in our trade position is not very important, recall that almost half of the decline in GNP in the 1981–82 recession was in our net exports.

Some economists hold that deficits will be offset by increased private saving. Three potential avenues for this effect to occur have been suggested. First, the rise in interest rates should increase saving. I believe this effect to be important but neither large nor rapid enough to offset the effects noted above. Second, it has been argued that the prospect of future taxes to pay higher future interest payments on the larger debt will lead to increased saving to pay those future taxes.

This analysis is intriguing, but the conditions for it to hold are quite restrictive, and there is little empirical support for it. Third, if GNP expands, saving should increase. But to offset the deficit, this would require *both* a marginal propensity to save and an expansion in GNP *many times* our historical experience.

Thus government deficits, properly measured, lead to a decrease in national saving (the sum of household, business, and government saving). Simply put, federal government borrowing is offsetting three-quarters of private saving.

Only simple arithmetic is needed to demonstrate that at full employment, continuing substantial *primary* deficits (deficits net of interest payments) *eventually* will lead to monetization by the Federal Reserve and hence to inflation. This requires substantial deficits run over *many* years to guarantee an inflationary outcome. There is no necessary short-term relationship between deficits and inflation, whether through monetization by the Federal Reserve or otherwise (in the high inflation of the late 1970s, the Fed monetized very little of the deficit). But a substantial primary deficit with real interest rates close to the real growth rate of the economy means a steadily rising ratio of national debt to GNP to levels vastly exceeding the entire net worth of the private economy. This is impossible unless foreigners hold the majority of this huge national debt. Would they be willing to do so? I doubt it. Eventually, their dollar holdings will reach a saturation point as ever higher fractions of their portfolios are denominated in dollars, and they are exposed to greater risks to inflation and other events in the United States.

History knows *no* compelling example of an advanced economy financing its long-term growth by importing foreign capital. The success stories of importing foreign capital to promote growth have related to less developed countries, whether some LDCs today or, for example, the United States in the nineteenth century. Thus, there are only two alternatives: the Federal Reserve buys the bonds, reigniting inflation, or we change our fiscal policy. Thus, large primary deficits are inflationary if continued indefinitely.

Finally, it is very probable that deficits contribute to high interest rates both directly and through uncertainty premiums regarding the manner of their resolution and their likely economic effects. While the empirical evidence is hardly overwhelming, I believe this is primarily because we face an enormously elastic supply of capital from the rest of the world in the short and medium run. When our interest rates rise above those in the rest of the world, we attract saving from the rest of the world and, therefore, limit further interest rate increases. However, the naive view that business investment is crowded out dollar for dollar of the deficit overstates the case. First, as noted above, the interest rate increases attract foreign capital (currently offsetting half of our current deficit), which limits further interest rate increases and supplies capital for investment. Second, it is not only business investment competing for the available supply of capital, but also state and local government projects and residential construction. Perhaps a sensible estimate is that long-run crowding out comes at 50 cents per dollar at the expense of business investment.

Thus, deficits do matter sometimes, and those differences can be very important. Deficits of the order of magnitude we are now running are likely to make it difficult for *real* (inflation-adjusted) interest rates to fall substantially. This may lead to a twist in the composition of output away from investment. Since our investment is already the lowest of any major industrialized country, fiscal policies that hinder investment are a source of major concern to a society urgently trying to restore substantial long-term growth.

So far we have been speaking of deficits, and adopting the convenient shorthand of the officially recorded nominal budget deficit. Official budget deficit numbers can be misleading, for a variety of reasons. Many items are excluded from the budget, and the off-budget borrowing and contingent liabilities committing us to future spending by decisions made today, which do not appear on the books, can be enormous, whether in loan programs (Bennett and DiLorenzo) or Social Security benefit formulas (Flowers). Further, there is no inflation adjustment for the deficit. Inflation erodes the value of the previously issued debt, and even at our current modest rate of inflation (given the large value of the national debt) the first $70 billion of the deficit is really just repaying of this inflation-eroded principal, not additional real debt. A myriad of other accounting difficulties with our budget documents could be cited.

Budget deficits reflect the difference in outlays and revenues (however improperly measured). However, the composition of revenues and outlays can also affect the composition and growth of output and the uses of income. Most important among these issues is the structure of taxation, particularly the structure and size of labor and capital income taxes. A combination of high and rising marginal tax rates (until the early 1980s), the use of historic rather than replacement cost depreciation, and the taxation of nominal interest (and the deduction of nominal interest as well), and other features combine to make the effective marginal tax rates on new investment quite high (Browning, Reynolds, Roberts, Kirzner). Despite the gradual movement to allow people to save at the pretax rather than the posttax return (e.g., by Individual Retirement Accounts, employer prepaid pensions, the inside buildup in life insurance, and the special tax treatment of housing), our income tax system offers a substantial disincentive to save and a strong incentive to borrow in order to consume. Because the structure of taxation in the United States misallocates our capital stock both among investments and between current consumption on the one hand and saving and investment on the other, we have major inefficiencies. The structure of taxation in the United States leads to too little saving and capital formation and too much current consumption. While it is easier to think of one issue at a time, this structure of taxation is particularly pernicious at a time when our economy is running substantial deficits causing the same kind of problems. Thus, while some people think of deficit reduction and tax reform as separable issues, they come together in many ways, the most important of which is their interaction in the incentives they create—or, more accurately under current circumstances, curtail—for saving and investment. Again, the evidence on the extent to which our tax system discourages saving in favor of current consumption and misallocates our capital stock is mixed, but my judgment is that the effects are substantial.

If continued, large primary deficits and an anti-capital-formation tax system combine to shift the composition of output away from capital formation for future growth and to shift the uses of income toward current consumption at the expense of saving for retirement, which would provide the resources for financing our badly needed investment.

These twin problems—large deficits and antisaving and antiinvestment taxation—raise innumerable issues. First, the intergenerational equity considerations of leaving future generations greater public liabilities and less private assets with which to pay them imply a double impoverishing of our children relative to a more neutral tax system and budget balance (Buchanan). Second, the imbalance created in our economy in the early 1980s because of the overvalued dollar depressed our exports, encouraged imports, and worse yet, paved the way for protectionist legislation and a possible trade war with our allies. Again, this reflects the short-time horizon of the political process, which should in fact focus on a new round of GATT talks to promote freer trade, encompass agriculture in the GATT, and eliminate nontariff trade barriers. Our long-term productivity and economic growth, as well as our short-term macroeconomic performance, are threatened by decades of deficits and a continuation of high marginal tax rates on productive saving and investment, work effort, and innovation. The economic answer to these dilemmas is straightforward: lower tax rates on a broader base focused on consumption rather than income (Vedder); eliminate unnecessary government spending and make transfer payment programs much more target-effective and cost-conscious. In many cases, government programs could be privatized (Wagner). Variations on this theme occur throughout the volume, ranging from broad goals to specific implementation. What is unique about this volume is not only the economic analysis, but its enrichment by the political analysis of why these problems persist, despite the general consensus of what should be done about them— in short, the political economy of deficit reduction and tax reform. Surely, economists (myself included) spend much of their time analyzing the effects of current policies and policies that *could* improve the situation. Most of us have never thought out what the comparative advantage was in analyzing why our proposals tend not to be adopted, or in developing proposals that public choice theory suggests are more likely to be adopted, or in examining the preconditions for the adoption of these proposals.

The short-run horizon of our political process is particularly pernicious in dealing with policies that transfer resources across lifetimes and between generations. Our most important policies in this regard are our public debt, Social Security, and capital income taxation. The lack of a vote by unborn generations aggravates the political and ethical dimensions of these policies immensely. Thus, the mixture of economics and public choice theory in this volume is an important, welcome, and overdue addition to the debate concerning fiscal policy and capital formation in the United States.

Michael J. Boskin
Professor of Economics
Stanford University

INTRODUCTION

Dwight R. Lee

Few economic issues are more important today than the issue of capital formation. Unless we maintain our capital base, all other economic issues will be derived from, and secondary to, the problem of restoring the economy's productive capacity. Few political issues are more important today than the issue of taxation. Political concerns over deficits, inflation, and economic growth all come back to the issue of how, and how much, government taxes the productive efforts of its citizens.

Taxation and spending and the effects of fiscal policy on capital have always been important issues. But as a result of the economic stagnation of the 1970s, the political impetus behind, and the economic consequences of, fiscal policy have been subjected to increased scrutiny. That the decade of the 1970s was a period of disappointing economic performance is painfully obvious. Personal income, after adjusting for taxes and inflation, remained almost constant. This is not surprising, given the depressed growth rate in labor productivity that was experienced. Over the period 1973–79 the annual growth in U.S. labor productivity averaged 0.5%, down from both the 1965–73 rate of 1.9% and the 1948–65 rate of 2.6%. Why the decline in productivity growth? As with all economic questions there are many things to consider, but capital is of overriding importance for the productivity of labor and for the performance of the economy as a whole.

And the growth in capital formation slowed appreciably in the United States during the 1970s.

The major reason for the slowdown in capital formation can be explained in a word. That word is taxation—where taxation is broadly defined to cover all government actions that forcibly transfer resources from private control to political control. The tax of inflation, in conjunction with our structure of explicit taxation, discouraged savings and imposed a tremendous burden on the returns to capital investment during the 1970s. The Social Security system imposed tax obligations that reduced people's ability to save, while promising benefits that reduced their incentive to save. Well-intended government regulations imposed on business often failed to achieve their stated objectives, but almost invariably succeeded in reducing the size of the productive capital base. The implicit government taxation of private capital formation, through credit allocation schemes (direct loans, loan guarantees, and credit market rules and restrictions), has increasingly made investment funds responsive to political concerns rather than to productivity concerns. Last but not least, chronic and expanding budget deficits have diverted available savings away from productive business investment and into a vast and relatively unproductive political pork barrel of spending programs.

Despite some progress in reducing the income tax burden under the Reagan administration and the improved economic performance since 1983, and despite Congress's attempt to bring federal deficits under control by passing the Gramm-Rudman-Hollings bill in 1985, it is still widely acknowledged that our fiscal system is, from the perspective of economic efficiency, an abomination. The existing structure of taxes still burdens some economic activities while encouraging others, with no economic rationale whatsoever behind the pattern of incentives that are created. Not only is the tax burden discouraging socially desirable capital formation, but tax incentives are distorting the capital investment commitments that are being made, with tax considerations rather than real value considerations serving as the guideposts for capital formation. There can be no doubt that significant wealth gains could be realized through additional reforms in the tax code.

The issues of taxation, deficit spending, capital formation, and fiscal policy reform are complex, and many crucial questions can best be plumbed by concentrating on strictly economic considerations. But insights obtained in this way can provide us with only part of the story. A full understanding of the problems, and possible solutions, surrounding fiscal issues requires coupling our economic knowledge with a realistic assessment of the political process. It is the purpose of the present volume to do exactly that. The authors of some of the chapters that follow concentrate almost entirely on the economic consequences of fiscal policy, with the focus of their concern being on the consequences for capital formation. Other of the authors, however, devote much of their attention to the *politics* of the fiscal process, with the focus of their concern being the vulnerability of improved fiscal policy and capital formation to prevailing political incentives.

While the analysis of fiscal policy and its consequences is necessarily complex, analyses of politics and its consequences are, all too often, unnecessarily naive. Most people have little difficulty in recognizing that self-interest is the dominant motive in the private market place. The statement that members of Chrysler's board of directors, for example, are primarily concerned with the public interest would be met with widespread mockery. And well it should. Yet, it is still commonly assumed that those in the political sector are motivated by the desire to promote broad social objectives. Even economists, whose understanding of market activity comes from applying the self-interest assumption, have been content to assume, at least implicitly, that the public interest guides government activity. This is particularly true in the case of fiscal policy. Public finance economists have traditionally seen their role as that of determining the best way for taxes to achieve social goals and then advising government of their findings. It has simply been assumed that the government would use these findings to further the public interest. For example, one question that economists have addressed is how to reduce the efficiency loss from raising a given amount of tax revenue. The standard answer is that the government should tax those commodities people find most difficult to consume less of as the price goes up (commodities with inelastic demands). In this way, the argument goes, taxes will do little to distort economic choices. But this only makes sense if we assume that the government will remain faithful to the public interest and not be tempted by opportunities to capture more tax revenue. This is exactly the assumption that public finance economists have traditionally made, despite the fact that they would be appalled at suggestions that a private firm be given monopoly rights over an inelasticly demanded commodity like, for example, drinking water.

Simply on the face of it, there is no reason for believing that people experience some sort of mystical public interest transformation upon leaving the private sector and moving into the public sector. Where is the evidence that public employees are more selfless, socially concerned, and public spirited than their private sector counterparts? It simply does not exist. A sure prescription for misguided policy is to analyze market "failures" under the assumption of self-interest, and then to compare these "failures" to what could be the case if we imposed an "ideal" political solution administered by selfless public servants. Yet it is exactly this wishful innocence that is used to justify a host of government programs, regulations, and taxes that are discouraging and misdirecting capital formation.

In recent years economists have begun developing explicit models of the political process. In doing so, they have been forced to recognize both the theoretical naiveté of applying the public interest assumption to political decision-makers, and the policy errors to which this naiveté leads. The distinguishing feature of this development, known as public choice economics, lies in the willingness to assume self-interest on the part of political decision-makers and to pursue the implications of this assumption to their logical limits. There are no romantic notions here about how government would behave in some ideal world, only realistic predictions and assessments of how the government will behave in the world as it actually is. It is only through such a realistic analysis of the political process that fiscal policy can be understood and sensible suggestions for reform be determined. Many of the chapters that follow are in this public choice tradition. It is in these chapters that we will begin to understand why the political process finds so appealing fiscal policy that, with economic analysis, can be shown to be so detrimental to capital formation and, therefore, so harmful to the long-run interests of us all.

Based on the analysis of the authors of this volume, still-needed policy reforms include the following:

1. Replacement of the current federal tax system with a true flat-rate tax on consumption; accompanied by appropriate spending cuts, such a tax could be set at a sharply reduced rate.
2. A constitutional amendment requiring a balanced federal budget, with all "off budget" spending explicitly included in the total budget.
3. Consideration of a phase-out scheme for the Social Security program (without reducing benefits to current retirees), plus reform or privatization schemes for other transfer programs.

4. Reduction of military spending without compromising national
    security through efficiencies that could be realized in such areas
    as weapons-procurement policies and changes in financial ar-
    rangements with allies.

The Social Security program (including Medicare) currently costs
more than a quarter of a trillion dollars per year. Other transfer programs amount to another $150–$200 billion per year, depending on
the health of the underlying economy. The United States is presently
spending more than $125 billion per year to defend Western Europe
alone, an area with a per capita income level comparable to that of
the United States; almost as much spending goes to the combined
defense of Japan, South Korea, Taiwan, the Philippines, and the Mideast. Furthermore, the Grace Commission and others have documented the enormous costs from waste, duplication, and unnecessary
programs found in military expenditures, totaling at least $165 billion
over the three-year period beginning in fiscal 1984.

It is therefore no exaggeration to say that the authors' proposed
reforms involve potential budget savings that by today's standards
would amount to more than half of the roughly *$1 trillion* budget for
1986. Elimination of federal deficits would also curtail the spiraling
portion of the budget expended to pay interest on federal government
debt (currently about $150 billion per year). If these reforms were
adopted, the proposed flat-rate tax could indeed be set at a sharply
reduced rate—well under 15 percent of total consumption—in fact,
closer to 10 percent. The problem, of course, is that the very process
which brought these programs into existence makes them very difficult to reform or repeal. The arena of public opinion, in which this
book is a participant, is the only place the process of change can
begin.

In the first section of the book the emphasis is on the economic
effects of taxation. In Chapter 1 Edgar Browning considers the effect
of capital taxation on both the formation of capital and the equity of
government policy. Capital accumulation is, of course, of overriding
importance to the long-run vitality of the economy, and without savings there can be no capital accumulation. Unfortunately, there are
several reasons for believing that saving and capital formation are too
low in the United States today, with most of these reasons centering
on the distortions created by government policy. In this regard, it is
the negative impact of taxing capital income that is the primary concern of Browning's chapter. From the perspective of economic effi-

ciency, Browning concludes that capital income is currently being taxed too heavily. Browning also addresses equity concerns, concerns that predispose many to favor increasing the tax on capital. However, once a careful comparison is made between capital income taxation and labor income taxation, it is not at all clear that the former is justified by commonly accepted equity norms. Indeed, Browning concludes that capital income is currently being taxed too heavily from the perspective of both efficiency and equity.

In Chapter 2 Morgan Reynolds reviews the empirical evidence concerning the effects of taxation on capital formation. Reynolds examines the evidence from U.S. history, from interstate comparisons, from comparisons among industries, and finally from data at the international level. There is little question that taxation has a negative impact on capital formation and productivity. It is only the magnitude of this effect that, because of the imprecision of statistical techniques, remains in doubt. Reynolds's underlying theme is that the declining growth in capital formation and productivity has been but one manifestation of a more general problem. The major problem facing the United States, as Reynolds sees it, is the political impulse to respond to every problem, or perceived problem, with policies designed to manipulate economic decision-making. Such manipulation is seldom guided by more than shortsighted political considerations, seldom achieves the desired outcome, and inevitably reduces individual liberty and, in the process, economic well-being.

The next two chapters in this first section concentrate on the crucial role of relative prices in motivating productive decisions, with the emphasis being on the destructive effects high marginal tax rates have on productivity through their distorting impact on relative prices. In Chapter 3 Paul Craig Roberts explains the antisaving and anticapital perversities that result when marginal tax rates increase the price of engaging in productive activities relative to the price of leisure. Evidence is cited that establishes compellingly what economists have always known—that people respond to incentives. The increased incentive to engage in productive effort, saving, and investment resulting from the 1981, 1982, and 1983 reductions in marginal tax rates moved the economy in the right direction. But, as Roberts points out, there is still a long way to go in reducing the antiproductivity bias in our current tax system.

James Gwartney and James Long consider, in Chapter 4, the tax avoidance activities motivated by high marginal tax rates. There is no doubt that, at least until 1981, the marginal tax rates faced by U.S. taxpayers had been increasing. As Gwartney and Long point out, "there were more than thirteen times as many taxpayers confronting marginal tax rates of 28 percent or more in 1979 as was the case in 1965." This has, as straightforward economic theory would predict, caused taxpayers to (1) generate less taxable income than they otherwise would and (2) engage in more tax deductible consumption. The empirical evidence presented by Gwartney and Long indicates that increased marginal tax rates have had a dramatic effect on taxable income in the higher income tax brackets. Indeed, based on 1979 tax returns, there seems little doubt that high marginal tax rates reduced the tax base and tax revenue. The real concern, however, is not that high taxes have been destructive of tax revenue, but that they have been destructive of economic productivity. When taxpayers respond to high tax rates by reducing taxable income, they are also making decisions that reduce capital formation and the economy's long-run productive capacity.

A tax reform that has received recent attention is the "flat rate tax." Richard Vedder examines the case for the flat rate tax in Chapter 5. The primary concern of Vedder's chapter centers on the potential for the flat rate (or nearly flat rate) tax to promote economic growth. Looking at the variations in tax structures across states, Vedder concludes that the flatter and lower the rate the greater the economic growth. At a casual empirical level, Vedder points out that the 13 states with what are effectively flat rate tax systems grew 50 percent more rapidly over the period 1970–1982 than did the 14 states with the most steeply graduated rate structures. This evidence is reinforced by a more sophisticated statistical analysis which finds that the flatter and lower a state's tax structure the greater its economic growth.

In the second section of the book the effect of social spending programs, budget deficits, and other forms of hidden taxation are examined. It is this section that makes most use of the insights provided by public choice. The first chapter in this section, Chapter 6, is by James M. Buchanan who, along with Gordon Tullock (the author of Chapter 8), is credited with founding the field of public choice. Buchanan's concern is with public debt and the destructive impact the escalation of this debt is having on the formation of capital. The standard arguments that public debt has a benign, if not beneficial, effect on the future productivity of the economy are dealt hammer blows. Although Buchanan finds chronic federal deficits unacceptable, he does not find them unexpected. They are seen as the natural consequence of self-interested politicians responding to constituent demands in the absence of effective fiscal restraint. Buchanan argues that the best hope to "stop the bleeding" of continued fiscal irresponsibility is through genuine restrictions on political discretion—restrictions that will be realized only through constitutional reform.

No government program transfers more money and imposes a larger tax than does the Social Security program. The recent press attention given to the possible bankruptcy of the Social Security system has undermined the myth that this is a funded program in which each participant is contributing into his or her own retirement fund. In fact, the "contributions" of current workers are being used immediately to finance the benefit checks of current recipients. In addition to concerns over the viability of the system, the pay-as-we-go approach also raises concern over the system's impact on capital formation. If, for example, individuals reduce their savings in response to Social Security taxes and the promise that their retirement will be financed by future workers, then capital formation will suffer.

In Chapter 7 Marilyn Flowers considers in detail the above argument, along with arguments suggesting that the negative effects of Social Security on savings may not be very pronounced—some have even argued that a nonfunded retirement system may actually increase savings. The question then becomes an empirical one, and Flowers examines the evidence from the major studies on the issue. This empirical evidence has been somewhat clouded by the fact that the best-known study, one by Martin Feldstein, which concluded that Social Security has a large negative impact on private savings, was found to suffer from a statistical flaw that overstated the effect. After correcting for this error, Feldstein still found a significant, though smaller, negative effect. Others have found smaller effects, though none have convincingly documented a positive effect. It is interesting to note that when the Social Security program was enacted, it was widely accepted by economists that it would reduce savings. Indeed, this was considered an important argument in favor of the Social Security Act, given the Keynesian view that savings should be discouraged. Almost certainly the Social Security system does reduce savings and therefore capital formation, although exactly to what extent is difficult to determine with precision. Flowers concludes by noting a way by which the system could be scaled back without reducing benefits going to the current elderly.

To fully understand the prospects for the Social Security system, one has to consider its appeal and viability from a political perspective. In Chapter 8 Gordon Tullock focuses attention on the politics of the Social Security program. The original political motivation for enacting a program like Social Security comes from the fact that when such a system is initiated, it generates a windfall for current voters. The political persistence of such a system comes from the fact that, once in operation, its termination would impose losses on current voters. However, Tullock goes on to argue that the viability of the Social Security system may ultimately depend on whether it can avoid disappointing expectations. If, as seems likely, it becomes widely believed that the system will not be able to fulfill the promises made for it, the confidence upon which any unfunded system depends will be undermined. How long the Social Security system will remain politically viable is, of course, hard to pin down. But one thing appears certain. It will be the impact of Social Security on the distribution of existing wealth, not its impact on the production of new wealth, that will be weighted most heavily by the political process.

Providing assistance to the poor and promoting a more equal distribution of income than would be generated by the market has been used to justify a major portion of the tax burden being imposed on the productive sector of the economy. Transfer expenditures by government now total over 10 percent of the GNP, up from less than 5 percent in 1965. Richard Wagner, in Chapter 9, points out that the additional taxes required to support these transfer payments have discouraged capital formation, both physical and human, and as a consequence have reduced the growth of wealth in the economy. One might feel this reduced economic productivity to be justified had it resulted in genuine help to the less advantaged in our society. However, Wagner points out several reasons for doubting that this has been the case. He cites evidence that public transfers crowd out private charity, that transfer recipients respond in ways that not only reduce their own earning potential but that of their offspring as well, and that some transfer programs increase income inequality above that which would result from strict market forces. When these distorting effects are added to the negative impact transfer programs have on capital formation and the overall wealth of the community, it is not at all clear that the poor have benefited from public "charity." The transfer programs that characterize the welfare state may not only be harmful to capital accumulation and economic growth, they may also be a bad bargain for the very ones they are supposed to help.

Any government policy that substitutes public for private control over resources is a form of government taxation and can (indeed, generally does) have deleterious effects on capital formation and productivity. A particularly harmful, extensively employed, but typically overlooked, form of taxation is federal credit allocation—the topic of Chapter 10 by James Bennett and Thomas DiLorenzo. Through direct loans and loan guarantees, the federal government allocates hundreds of billions of dollars to projects that have failed the market test of economic efficiency but have passed the political test of special interest influence. Not only is federal credit allocation just as inimical to productive capital formation as is more explicit taxation, but it has the more insidious feature of being off budget and therefore largely invisible to those who are paying the bill (all of us). As Bennett and DiLorenzo explain, it is the mirage of a free lunch created by federal credit allocation that makes this form of taxation so popular politically—and such a rapidly expanding source of economic inefficiency.

As has been emphasized before, taxation can take many forms, and Chapter 11 considers a form of capital taxation that is seldom recognized as such. The present author argues in this chapter that government, through its regulation of labor relations, imposes a tax on capital just as surely and perniciously as if capital were being confiscated directly by government. The explanation for this is found in the incentive structure of labor unions, an incentive structure that motivates myopic decisions. Moreover, this incentive structure contrasts in important ways with the incentives built into the structure of private firms and corporations—incentives that are more likely to motivate appropriate attention to the long-run consequences of current decisions. As long as owners and managers of private businesses are free to allocate revenues among capital owners, employees, and capital investment in response to market forces, decisions will be made that promote capital formation and lead to long-run economic growth. Unfortunately, government regulation of labor relations has increasingly usurped business control over decisions relevant to capital investment and has passed that control to union officials. The result has been to substitute economically excessive wages for appropriate capital investment, thus reducing the competitive vitality of major U.S. industries.

In Chapter 12 Lloyd Dumas concludes the second section of the book with a chapter that considers the impact of military spending on capital formation in the private economy. The sheer size of our military establishment, and the expense of maintaining and expanding it, guarantees that military spending will divert significant amounts of resources out of civilian production and capital projects. On the one hand, this reflects little more than the obvious fact that the provision of national security, like the provision of everything else, imposes costs. However, Dumas examines the enormous magnitude and components of the cost imposed by the military and argues that much of this cost reflects politically motivated inefficiency and waste. He observes that huge savings could be realized by appropriate reforms, including changes in relations with allies.

The third section of the book looks at private sector entrepreneurship and public sector entrepreneurship, considering how the latter imposes tax burdens on the former, especially insofar as it diverts resources from creative to politically motivated uses.

While all economists recognize the distorting potential of taxation, much economic analysis suggests that it is possible, and desirable, to search out and impose taxes that have minimal economic effects. Supposedly taxes can be imposed on economic "rents" (returns to an activity in excess of what is needed to make the activity more attractive than the known alternatives) without affecting economic choices. This view is informed by models that depict the economic environment as static, with all alternatives to a particular course of action being known. But as those economists who write in the Austrian economic tradition continue to remind us,[1] this is neither an accurate nor useful way of describing the essence of economic activity.

In Chapter 13 Israel Kirzner, one of the leading economists in the Austrian school of thought, examines the effect of capital taxation on entrepreneurial activity in a world where many opportunities are unknown and economic activity is best described as a discovery process. Even if the taxing authorities were able to identify pure economic rents (an impossibility in the real world of unknown, but discoverable, possibilities) and were able to resist the temptation to tax anything else (highly unlikely), taxation would still distort economic decision-making by dampening the incentive to engage in activities that lead to discovery. And it is this distortion which, in the long run, is more harmful to economic productivity than are those static dis-

1. See, for example, F. A. Hayek, "Competition as a Discovery Procedure," in *New Studies in Philosophy, Politics, and the History of Ideas* (Chicago: University of Chicago Press, 1978).

tortions with which economic analysis is often preoccupied. The productivity of the capital base ultimately depends on discovery, and taxes, even those seen as benign by many economists, distort the productive process of discovery.

In Chapter 14 E. C. Pasour, Jr. complements Kirzner's discussion by addressing the common misconception that the taxation of monopoly profits provides an opportunity to raise tax revenue in an economically neutral way. Pasour first challenges the usefulness of the monopoly concept by emphasizing the dynamic nature of the market process. Like Kirzner, Pasour sees the role of the entrepreneur as crucial to economic progress and points out that no firm can achieve a monopoly position in entrepreneurship. And taxes inevitably depress entrepreneurial incentives, distort the market incentives so crucial to the entrepreneur's function, and, as a consequence, "adversely affect entrepreneurial activity—the key element in capital formation." Kirzner and Pasour are calling for economic realism. The economically neutral tax does not exist, and the search for it can accomplish little beyond providing a rationale for imposing the heaviest tax burden where it may do the most to depress productive capital formation.

A common suggestion for reforming state and local taxation is the creation of regional compacts among states designed to unify tax burdens and to discourage "inefficient" shifting of capital between states. In Chapter 15 Bruce Benson and Ronald Johnson look critically at reforms of this type. Their empirical work suggests strongly that state taxes are important determinants in the location of capital growth, and that tax competition among states promotes capital growth by disciplining the political desire for more tax revenue. If the tax burden in one state gets out of line with that of other states, outflows of capital will serve to forcibly remind state politicians of the benefits derived from maintaining a healthy business climate. Not surprisingly, politicians do not appreciate this constraint on their taxing and spending proclivities, and see regional tax compacts as a way of sheltering themselves against the inconveniences of tax competition. As with all cartel-type arrangements, of course, tax compacts are subject to cheating. Benson and Johnson point out that policies of the federal government, such as deductibility of state and local taxes and revenue sharing, have served to enforce a tax cartel among states and to reduce tax competition. By allowing the combined state and federal tax burden to remain higher than it otherwise would, these policies have discouraged capital formation in all states.

The lagging productivity growth experienced by the U.S. economy in recent years has been seen by some as a justification for yet more government involvement in the economy—a classic case of the "hair of the dog that bit you." The failed policies of the past tend to sell better, however, when they are repackaged and relabeled, and so in recent years we have had government planning advocates masquerading their proposals under the label of "national industrial policy." In Chapter 16 John Baden, Tom Blood, and Richard Stroup consider the implications of a formalized national industrial policy for economic growth and productivity. They present their case in an insightful and entertaining way that goes beyond pointing out that such a policy invariably means more centralized economic control, less informed decision-making, and the substitution of political influence for economic efficiency. The chapter discusses the Melanesian "cargo cults" and the Melanesians' superstitious attempts to create wealth by going through various rituals. As far-fetched as it may first seem, the authors show that there are striking parallels between this approach to economic progress and the approach recommended by the advocates of national industrial policy.

Richard McKenzie continues with attention to national industrial policy in Chapter 17. McKenzie first makes the case that from a political perspective, capital offers an enticing target for taxation. Capital tends to be fixed in the short run and therefore not immediately responsive to the burdens imposed by taxation. In effect, shortsighted politicians can mine capital and ignore many of the adverse consequences, since these consequences will not be realized until the politically distant future. But fixed though capital may be in the short run, given enough time capital owners do respond to heavy capital taxation by letting existing capital depreciate and by moving new capital projects to more hospitable locations. Sometimes this means exporting capital formation to a different state, sometimes to a different country. But capital mobility, whether intranational or international, is a source of frustration to tax-and-spend politicians. It is this frustration that, according to McKenzie, explains much of the political popularity of many policies that fall under the rubric of national industrial policy. As McKenzie sees it, the objective of industrial policy advocates is to "reduce the mobility of capital in order that capital can be more heavily taxed by governments at all levels. . . ."

Since public policy decision-making is not, and should not be, based solely on cost-benefit considerations, the volume ends with a one-chapter section that analyzes the ethical basis of taxation-funding of government services. In so doing, Eric Mack moves us from considerations of economics and politics to those of philosophy. Mack is not primarily concerned with whether taxation promotes or retards economic efficiency but focuses instead on fundamental ethical questions of the justification of the coercive use of taxation to achieve social ends. Even in arguments for limited taxation, Mack finds serious flaws. He concludes that no convincing case for taxation can be made and that fiscal policy should seek maximum tax reductions plus the use of privatization and other voluntary means to finance social services.

Montesquieu, the eighteenth century French philosopher, once asked: "Will the state begin by impoverishing the subjects to enrich itself? Or will it wait for the subjects to enrich it by their own prosperity?" For most of human history it has been the first of Montesquieu's questions that received the affirmative answer. Twentieth-century Americans have been blessed with extremely good fortune in this regard. Thanks to our Founding Fathers and the understanding of political economy they possessed, our Constitution placed severe limitations on the ability of government to enrich itself by impoverishing its subjects. Government was severely restricted in its use of taxation and regulation to insert wedges between the value generated by an individual's decisions and the return the individual received. The result was years of saving, investment, and productive effort that resulted in the accumulation of a capital base unparalleled in human history, a capital base from which each and every one of us benefits today.[2]

Unfortunately, over the last half-century the view that economic progress comes from government programs rather than private initiative became dominant. A constrained and limited government is hardly consistent with this view of progress; as a consequence, the constitutional barriers to political discretion have increasingly weakened. There is now little that the government cannot subsidize, regulate, or tax under the pretense of promoting the public interest. The result is that a growing percentage of the population has found that their private advantages are best served by using government to redistribute existing wealth rather than engaging in the production of new wealth. The tax and transfer function of government is now its reigning function, overshadowing, and often undermining, the limited role of protecting private property and maintaining an environment conducive to the *creation* of wealth.

2. For an extended discussion, see Dwight R. Lee, "Constitutional Reform: A Prerequisite for Supply-Side Economics," *The Cato Journal* 3 (Winter 1983/84): 793–810.

Having been fortunate enough to inherit an enormously productive capital base built up by the farsighted efforts of those who came before, we have, in effect, decided to realize the short-run benefits that come from consuming our capital. We can continue to do quite well for a time by squandering our inheritance, but the long-run effects of such a policy are obvious. And unless more attention is given to the capital formation consequences of our current tax and transfer policies, our descendants will surely have less reason to thank us for our economic stewardship than we have to thank our ancestors for theirs.

PART I

THE ECONOMIC EFFECTS OF TAXATION

1

TAXATION, CAPITAL ACCUMULATION, AND EQUITY

Edgar K. Browning

The performance of the U.S. economy over the past decade was unsatisfactory in a number of respects. From a long-run point of view, the most serious problem was a decline in the rate of productivity growth. During the 1960s, a relatively prosperous decade, real output per hour in the private sector grew at an annual rate of 3 percent. By contrast, during the 1970s it rose at an annual rate of only 1.4 percent. Since continued improvement in our standard of living depends on productivity growth, the slowdown would have disturbing implications if it were to continue into the future.

The cause of the productivity growth slowdown and ways in which it might be reversed have been major topics of study in the past several years. At present, it seems clear that there was no single cause; rather, several factors contributed to the slowdown, with the quantitative contribution of each factor not definitively known. All analysts agree, however, that capital accumulation plays an important role in generating productivity growth. Moreover, since the income from capital is heavily taxed in the United States, there is some suspicion that tax policy may have inadvertently contributed to the productivity slowdown.

Much of the impetus for reform of capital taxation has come from a concern over the slowdown in productivity. Capital taxes, however, have important consequences other than their effects on the general rate of capital accumulation. One such consequence is the impact of capital taxes on the *equity* of the tax system. Another is the impact of the tax system, especially provisions for depreciation allowances, investment tax credits, and the exclusion of some capital gains income from the tax base, on the *allocation* of capital among the different sectors of the economy. These topics—the effects of capital taxes on capital accumulation, equity, and capital allocation—are the focus of this chapter. Before turning to these questions, brief discussions of the process of capital accumulation and of the structure of the U.S. tax system may prove helpful.

CAPITAL ACCUMULATION AND ECONOMIC GROWTH

Most people do not adequately appreciate the extent to which our standard of living depends on capital accumulation. The capital stock of a society—its machinery, structures, vehicles, roads, and so on—makes it possible for a given labor force to produce more goods and services. The more capital there is per worker, the higher the output per worker will be and hence, other things equal, the higher the average real income will be. Human capital—people's acquired knowledge and productive abilities—is as important as physical capital, although in this chapter I will concentrate on the latter. People in the United States enjoy a higher standard of living than do those in Third World nations primarily because capital (both physical and human) per worker is much higher here.

Our current capital stock is the result of past decisions to consume less than the total output of the economy. It is convenient to think of total output as comprised of consumer goods and capital goods. In any period of time, our productive resources can be used to produce consumer goods, capital goods, or a combination of the two. Only by using some resources to produce capital goods, and therefore sacrificing the consumer goods these resources could have produced, is the capital stock augmented. A greater capital stock, in turn, makes it possible to produce more goods of both kinds in subsequent periods of time. Thus, the fundamental trade-off is between consumption now and consumption in the future: By consuming less in the present (adding to the capital stock), consumption in the future can be greater.

Capital accumulation makes it possible to increase future consumption by a dollar at a cost of less than a dollar of present consumption.

This is because capital investments—at least wisely chosen ones—have a positive real rate of return. The productivity of capital is, in fact, usually measured by its rate of return. Suppose a machine costs $100 to construct this year (which means we must sacrifice $100 in consumption to produce it) and its use next year will add $120 to output. If the machine wears out at the end of the year, we would say that its annual rate of return is 20 percent since it returns its initial cost plus 20 percent more. Of course, capital rarely wears out so quickly, but the same principle applies. A positive rate of return to capital investments means they make a positive contribution to output over their lifetime. It is this characteristic of capital accumulation that makes it a factor capable of raising standards of living over time.

In a free enterprise economy, the process of capital accumulation is accomplished through the workings of numerous interrelated capital markets. No single person or group or business decides what the rate of capital accumulation shall be. Instead, individuals and businesses make decisions to save and invest, lend and borrow, sell and purchase assets: The combined effect of all these decisions determines the nation's real net investment, that is, its capital accumulation. Some persons willingly choose to consume less than their income; their savings ultimately provide the funds necessary to finance investments in real capital. Savers are willing to forgo present consumption because they expect to receive a positive rate of return on the transaction and therefore increase future consumption by more than the present sacrifice. On the other side of the market, businesses and persons who have attractive investment projects are able to pay a positive rate of return to the providers of funds because of the productivity of capital.

Thus, the prerequisites exist for market transactions that result in real capital accumulation. In these markets, the independent decisions of savers and investors are coordinated through movements in interest rates and rates of return. If, at the current level of interest rates, savers should wish to save more than can be profitably invested, there would be downward pressure on interest rates. As rates fall, the amount of investment that is profitable increases, and the quantity of saving may consequently also change. The interest rate adjusts (as does the expected rate of return on investments that do not stipulate a specific return, such as stock market investments) until the desired quantities of saving and investment are equal.

The foregoing is a highly simplified description of a complex and dynamic process. It ignores, for example, how government deficits and international capital flows may affect the process, as well as many details concerning the institutions of capital markets. It is intended, however, to emphasize two important points: first, that savers, by consuming less than their current incomes, provide the funds that make capital accumulation possible; second, that capital accumulation is a primary source of improvements in living standards over time. These general points remain correct even in the more complicated real world.

Table 1–1 presents some interesting data relating to capital accumulation and productivity growth. It gives fixed investment as a percentage of gross domestic product for six developed economies over the 1970s, and the corresponding growth rates of output per hour in manufacturing industries. It is important to understand that it is net investment each year that adds to a nation's capital stock. A portion of gross investment each year is necessary to replace worn-out capital (to cover depreciation); this portion simply maintains the capital stock. Only investment in excess of depreciation, that is, net investment, represents an addition to the capital stock. In Table 1–1, note that the share of U.S. gross domestic product devoted to net fixed investment is much lower than for the other nations. Our net investment rate is only about a third as great as Japan's, and only a little over half as great as West Germany's and France's. In fact, no other major industrial nation has a net investment rate as low as that of the United States.

It is also instructive to note that there seems to be a strong rela-

Table 1–1.   Capital Accumulation in Six OECD Countries, 1971–1980.

| Country | Investment as % of Gross Domestic Product | | | Growth Rate Of Output Per Hour in Manufacturing |
	Gross Investment	Gross Fixed Investment	Net Fixed Investment	
	(%)	(%)	(%)	(%)
France	24.2	22.9	12.2	4.8
Germany	23.7	22.8	11.8	4.9
Italy	22.4	20.1	10.7	4.9
Japan	34.0	32.9	19.5	7.4
United Kingdom	19.2	18.7	8.1	2.9
United States	19.1	18.4	6.6	2.5

SOURCE: *Economic Report of the President, 1983* (Washington, D.C.: Government Printing Office, 1983), Table 4–2.

tionship between net investment rates and the rates of growth of productivity, at least as measured here by output per hour in manufacturing.
The United States has the lowest investment rate and the lowest productivity growth rate; Japan, by contrast, has the highest investment
rate and highest growth rate. While the net investment rate is by no
means the only factor that influences productivity growth rates, it is
difficult to avoid the conclusion that capital accumulation makes an
important contribution. That is in accord with our earlier analysis,
which suggested why such a relationship is to be expected.

On the basis of evidence like this, it is sometimes argued that increasing the productivity growth rate should be an objective of government policy. Increasing the economy's rate of growth is, however,
not always desirable. There is a definite benefit associated with a
higher growth rate; it means that output per person and living standards will be higher in future years. But there is also a cost associated
with a higher growth rate. One way to increase the growth rate, and
one of the few ways government policy can affect the growth rate,
is to increase the rate of real capital accumulation. As we have seen,
this can occur (with a given level of employment) only by reducing
present consumption, that is, by saving more. It is easy to see that
the cost of sacrificing present consumption could be greater than the
benefits people receive from greater future consumption. Thus, to argue that we should save and invest more requires more than pointing
out that the economy's growth rate will increase. Instead, it is necessary to compare explicitly the benefits from augmented future consumption with the costs of sacrificed present consumption. Only if
the benefits exceed the costs should we favor measures designed to
increase economic growth by fostering additional capital accumulation.

It should be clear that I am here suggesting the use of the economist's concept of efficiency as a guide to the appropriate rate of capital accumulation. The benefits of greater capital accumulation can be
measured by the rate of return that can be generated by new investments. The costs of greater capital accumulation can be measured by
the interest rate savers would require as compensation for sacrificing
additional present consumption. If the benefits exceed the costs, then
additional capital accumulation (and the higher growth rate it produces) is worthwhile. For example, if the return on new investments
is 10 percent and savers would be willing to provide funds if compensated with an interest rate of at least 5 percent, then increased
investment has benefits greater than its costs. As the rate of invest-

ment rises, of course, the rate of return on marginal investments will fall; as saving rises, savers may also require a higher return to sacrifice still more present consumption. When investment has been pushed to the point where the rate of return on investments exactly equals the return necessary to compensate savers, the efficient rate of capital accumulation has been achieved. Stimulating investment beyond this point will tend to make people worse off.

One of the major conclusions of modern economic analysis is that a competitive private economy generally leads to an efficient allocation of resources. This conclusion holds with regard to capital markets just as it does with regard to markets for shirts or televisions. When competitive capital markets determine the rate of return that savers can receive, that return reflects the real investment opportunities. Savers are then led to determine the volume of savings in light of the true benefit—the greater future output that saving makes possible—of sacrificing present consumption. Similarly, investors are led to undertake investments only if they promise a return at least high enough to compensate savers, that is, to yield a rate of return at least as high as the prevailing interest rate.

If competitive capital markets can be counted on to produce the efficient rate of capital accumulation, is there any reason to believe saving and investment are too low in the United States? There are in fact several reasons. Some have to do with imperfections in private capital markets themselves, but they are of debatable significance. More important are the number of government policies that lead private capital markets to produce results quite different from the competitive norm. Some of these, such as deficit financing of government expenditures and the Social Security system, are the subject of other essays in this volume. The remainder of this chapter deals with another policy that affects capital accumulation, the taxation of capital income.

CAPITAL TAXATION AND INCIDENCE

In the United States, federal, state, and local governments levy a variety of taxes on households and business firms. Table 1–2 identifies the major taxes and the revenues they generated in a recent year. Individual income and payroll (primarily Social Security) taxes are, by a wide margin, the largest sources of revenue. Together, these two taxes provide about 60 percent of all tax revenues and 80 percent of

Table 1–2. Governmental Revenue by Source and Level of Government, Fiscal 1980 (in billions of dollars).

Source	Total	Federal	State & Local
Taxes:			
Individual income	$286.1	$244.1	$42.1
Payroll[a]	190.0	146.4	43.7
Corporation	77.9	64.6	13.3
Property	68.5	—	68.5
Selective excises	53.2	24.6	28.6
General sales	51.3	—	51.3
Death and gift	8.4	6.4	2.0
Customs duties	7.4	7.4	—
Other	21.3	3.7	17.6
Total taxes	764.2	497.2	267.3
Charges and miscellaneous			
General revenue[b]	168.0	66.6	101.4
Total	$932.2	$563.8	$368.7

SOURCE: U.S. Department of Commerce, Bureau of the Census, *Governmental Finances in 1979–80*, Sept. 1981, Table 4.

Note: Detail may not add to total because of rounding.

[a]Includes all insurance trust revenues (including contributions to Social Security and unemployment compensation).

[b]Includes miscellaneous charges, assessments, interest earnings, and net revenues of public enterprises (e.g., school lunches, postal fees for parks and recreation, net revenues from utilities, liquor stores).

federal tax revenues. Trailing these two taxes are corporation income taxes and property taxes. All taxes together were about 35 percent of net national product in 1982.

In this section we will consider how taxes that fall on capital income place a burden on households. Of course, none of the taxes is designated as a capital income tax, but nonetheless part or all of several of the taxes are thought to fall on capital income. It will be convenient to begin by noting that in the absence of taxes, the total value of output of an economy is exactly equal to the total incomes received by owners of factors of production: Each dollar of sales ultimately is received as income by someone. Furthermore, total income can be represented as the sum of labor income and capital income. Labor income represents payments to workers for their contribution to production, while capital income represents payments to the owners of the capital stock for the contribution of capital to production.

Thus, considering total income as the sum of labor and capital income, any tax that reduces the income available for private use—and that is true of every tax—must do so by reducing either labor income or capital income or both. A tax that has the effect of reducing capital income is said to fall on, or place a burden on, the recipients of capital income. In the absence of any tax, current capital income reflects the rate of return to the capital stock. (The rate of return can differ among capital assets because of differences in risk and other factors, but this will be ignored here.) For instance, if the capital stock is valued at $7,000 billion and the common rate of return is 10 percent, current capital income would be $700 billion. This income would be received in many forms: dividends, interest income, a portion of rental payments, retained earnings of corporations, and so on. In all cases, however, it represents a return to past accumulated savings—the capital stock—a return that is made possible by the productivity of capital, as explained earlier.

Now let us examine the effects of a tax on capital income. To begin, consider a hypothetical tax that applies at a uniform rate to all types of capital income. We do not have such a tax in the United States, but this example brings out some important points. We will also initially assume that the rate of capital accumulation is not affected by the tax. In other words, the level of savings does not change in response to the tax, even though the tax will depress the rate of return received by savers. This assumption may be inappropriate, and we will consider the implications of modifying it later. But most economists, at least until quite recently, have thought this assumption to provide a reasonable first approximation.

Under these conditions, a tax on capital income will be borne fully by the owners of capital. This conclusion is also interesting because it implies that workers and consumers do not bear a burden from the tax. Since the capital stock is unaffected, its productivity is unchanged and so too will be the willingness and ability of users of capital to pay for its services. If the capital stock is $7,000 billion and the rate of return is 10 percent, $700 billion will continue to be the gross payment to capital owners. However, the tax must be paid out of this sum. If the tax rate is 40 percent, for example, $280 billion goes to the government and the remaining $420 billion is kept by the owners of capital.

Putting this somewhat differently, the tax on capital leaves the gross (before tax) rate of return on capital unchanged at 10 percent but reduces the net (after tax) rate of return received by owners of capital to 6 percent. The 40 percent tax enters as a "wedge" between the real rate of return generated by capital investments and the net rate of return received by savers. This way of looking at the effects of capital taxation is significant, because it emphasizes that savers will receive a lower rate of return on their savings as a result of the tax. Not only do owners of capital receive a lower income on their accumulated savings (the capital stock), but current and future savings will provide a lower net return, at least as long as the tax remains in effect. And this lower return to savings may lead people to save less, in which case the rate of capital accumulation will decline. Thus, our assumption that the tax does not affect capital accumulation really amounts to assuming that the volume of saving will not change when the tax leads to a lower rate of return. Whether or not this is a reasonable assumption will be discussed later.

As mentioned, the United States does not have a general tax that applies a uniform rate to all income from capital. Nonetheless, the combined effects of the several taxes that do fall on capital income have much in common with our hypothetical general tax on capital. To see this, let us begin by examining the corporation income tax. This tax is sometimes described as a tax on corporate profits, but it would be better described as a tax on the income from capital invested in the corporate sector of the economy. There is also a noncorporate sector that uses capital, but the capital income in the noncorporate sector—which employs about half of all physical capital—is not subject to the corporate income tax.

In analyzing the corporation income tax, the primary factor to keep in mind is the tendency for capital to be allocated so that its net returns in various uses are equal. Investors will channel capital to the uses where its rate of return is highest; if the return is higher in some uses, investors will shift capital to (increase investment in) those uses, thus driving down the rate of return until it is no higher than in alternative uses. Suppose that in the absence of the corporation income tax, the rate of return on capital investments is 8 percent in both the corporate and noncorporate sectors. Then assume that a tax of 50 percent is levied on net income (the return to capital) in the corporate sector. The immediate short-run effect is to lower the net return to corporate investors to 4 percent. That, however, will not be the final result, since investors in the noncorporate sector are still receiving a net (untaxed) return of 8 percent; thus investors in the corporate sector have incentives to shift their investments to where the returns are currently higher. As investors reduce the supply of capital to the corporate sector, its gross and net returns there rise, whereas increasing the supply of capital to the noncorporate sector drives down the return there. This process continues until the net return is equal in all uses; only then is there no further incentive to shift investments from one sector to the other.

Suppose that the final result is a net rate of return in both sectors equal to 6 percent, implying a gross (before tax) return of 12 percent in the corporate sector. Consider carefully what this implies: All persons receiving capital income now receive a lower rate of return, even if their capital is invested in untaxed uses. Before the tax, all investors received 8 percent; after the tax they receive 6 percent. Consequently, the corporate income tax places a burden on all owners of capital, regardless of whether their capital is employed in the taxed or untaxed sectors.

The significance of this general result extends beyond the corporation income tax itself; it shows how a tax that applies to only part of the capital stock comes to place a burden on all capital owners by depressing the common net rate of return to capital investments. In this sense the result is similar to a general tax on all capital income. There is one notable difference, however. Taxing only a part of the capital stock produces equality in the net rates of return but differences in the before-tax rates of return. In our corporate income tax example, the final before-tax return in the corporate sector was 12 percent, while it was 6 percent in the noncorporate sector. This difference in the before-tax, or real, rate of return to capital investments implies a misallocation of the capital stock. The corporation tax causes capital to shift from the corporate sector even when its real yield there is greater. This type of misallocation has received a great deal of attention in the tax literature, but I will postpone discussion of capital misallocation until the last section of this chapter. At present, I wish to emphasize the potential effect of capital taxes on general capital accumulation rather than on the allocation, among various uses, of a given stock of capital. As we will see, the effect on capital accumulation depends mainly on how taxes depress the net return received by savers, and not on differences in rates of return among various sectors of the economy.

In addition to the corporate income tax, the other major taxes that fall on capital income to some degree are personal income taxes (federal and state) and property taxes. Personal income taxes are interesting in that although in principle they are applied to all income from whatever source derived, they contain so many special provisions it is difficult to determine how heavily they fall on the income from capital. For instance, the income from capital invested by pension funds is exempt from personal income taxes, as is capital income earned by individual retirement accounts. However, to the extent that people have savings in excess of the amounts that can be sheltered in these ways, personal income taxes apply to the capital income received and thereby act to depress the net rate of return received. Property taxes, levied primarily by local governments, are also thought to fall largely on capital income. It is important to realize that taxing the value of property (that is, the value of physical capital subject to the tax) has the same effect as taxing the income generated by the property. A 2 percent tax on the market value of an asset that yields 8 percent takes one-fourth of the return, just as does a tax of 25 percent on the income from assets.

The preceding discussion suggests that several taxes fall on capital income, and it is the combined effect of these taxes that is most important in determining their economic effects. Overall, how heavily is capital income taxed in the United States? Unfortunately, it is not known exactly how heavily each tax falls on capital income. In particular, the question of how heavily personal income taxes, with all their special provisions, fall on capital income is hard to resolve.

Recognizing the difficulties that make precise estimates impossible, it is generally agreed that capital is taxed quite heavily, certainly more heavily than labor income. For example, William R. Johnson and I estimated that the average tax rate on capital income (capital taxes as a percentage of before-tax capital incomes) was 56.1 percent in 1976, while the rate on labor income was 26.6 percent. These rates represent an economy-wide average for all taxes together, apportioned to labor and capital income as best we could. Other scholars have obtained different estimates, but I think most would agree that capital income is taxed somewhere in the 45–65 percent range, on average.

The fact that taxes take perhaps half of all capital income is significant, but it is also important to take a less aggregate view of their burden. Of particular interest is how these taxes affect households at different income levels. A common view is that taxes on capital income fall disproportionately on the wealthy, that is, that capital taxes are highly progressive taxes. (A progressive tax is one where the average tax rate—the tax as a percentage of before-tax income—rises with income so that individuals with higher incomes pay a larger share of their incomes in taxes.) Indeed, it seems likely that the political appeal of these taxes derives in large part from the feeling that they fall on wealthy coupon-clippers and bloated business profits. Our earlier analysis has already indicated that this is only partly true: Recall how the corporation income tax burden tends to be spread to all capital owners, including those who own homes or have assets in pension funds.

Table 1–3 provides estimates of the distributional effects of capital taxes in 1976. In constructing this table, households were ranked on the basis of their before-tax incomes and classified into deciles, each containing 10 percent of all households. The first decile, for example, contains the 10 percent of households with the lowest incomes in 1976, while decile 10 contains the 10 percent of households with the highest incomes. The first column in Table 1–3 gives the burden from capital income taxed as a percentage of capital income in each decile. It shows that capital income is heavily taxed, as we have already emphasized. Note that even the capital income of low-income households is taxed at a high rate. This is because corporate and property taxes fall proportionately on capital income, regardless of how poor or wealthy the recipient of that income is. The average tax rate on capital income does rise with income, however, because of the con-

Table 1–3. Distributional Effects of Capital Taxes in 1976.

Income Decile	Average Tax Rate on Capital Income (%)	Average Tax Rate on Total Income (%)
1	45.9	6.6
2	48.3	5.3
3	49.3	5.7
4	50.3	5.8
5	52.1	5.6
6	53.5	5.5
7	54.7	5.3
8	56.0	5.9
9	57.6	7.9
10	58.5	23.4

SOURCE: Edgar K. Browning and William R. Johnson, *The Distribution of the Tax Burden* (Washington, D.C.: American Enterprise Institute, 1979). Tables 16 and 5.

tribution of personal income taxes, which apply at higher rates to those with higher incomes.

The second column in Table 1–3 is based on the same estimated tax burden, but these burdens are expressed here as a percentage of total before-tax incomes. It is this column that is relevant (with important qualifications noted below) in judging the progressivity of capital income taxes. Note first that these taxes are virtually proportionate to income through the first nine deciles. In fact, the tax rate is slightly higher for the poorest decile. This is not as surprising as it may seem once it is recognized that the lowest quintile is heavily populated with retired persons, many of whom own their own homes and receive capital income such as pensions. At the other extreme, the top decile is estimated to bear a substantially higher tax rate than any of the lower nine deciles. In large part this reflects the fact that capital income is a larger share of total income for the top decile than for any other.

Thus, Table 1–3 suggests that high-income households pay a substantially larger share of their total incomes as capital income taxes than do middle- and low-income households. However, two important qualifications to this conclusion must be mentioned. First, the estimates in Table 1–3 use data for a single year, 1976, as the basis for the calculations of tax incidence. A household's position in a single year, however, can give a misleading impression of its average income over a longer period of time. For this reason, most analysts acknowledge that estimating tax burdens relative to a longer-run (possibly even lifetime) measure of household income would be preferable.

An example will help show the potential significance of this point. Suppose all households have identical incomes at each age, and that they save part of their earnings during their working years to provide for retirement. As a household approaches retirement age, it will have accumulated substantial capital: Just before retirement, its total income will tend to be high, as will its capital income generated by prior savings. In this imaginary society, if we perform calculations such as those underlying Table 1–3, they would show a higher tax rate for the top decile than for others, even though all households are identical from a long-run, lifetime perspective. This is because looking at a single year's data, the top decile would contain mainly middle-aged persons in their peak earning years who have already accumulated substantial capital and for whom capital income was an unusually large share of total income. Putting this point more generally, capital income is more heavily concentrated in the top decile when one year's data is examined than when a more appropriate longer-run perspective is taken. When a longer-run point of view is adopted, capital income taxes are not as progressive at the top income class as Table 1–3 suggests; how much less progressive they would be is unknown.

A second qualification to the conclusion that capital income taxes place a large share of their burden on the wealthy derives from our assumption that the rate of capital accumulation is unaffected by the taxes on capital income. When the capital stock and its rate of growth are unaffected by taxes, the burden of capital income taxes falls fully on the owners of capital by reducing their rate of return, as we have seen. However, capital taxes may reduce the rate of savings and hence capital accumulation by reducing the net rate of return that savers receive. If capital taxes reduce the rate of capital accumulation, capital owners do not in the long run bear the entire burden, and that also makes the distribution of the tax burden less progressive than shown in Table 1–3.

Instead of falling completely on owners of capital, part of the burden of capital taxes is shifted to labor when saving falls in response to the taxes. If saving falls, the capital stock in later years will be lower than it would otherwise have been. A lower capital stock means less capital per worker, implying lower wage rates. One study has estimated that as much as one-fourth to one-half of the tax burden of capital income taxes may ultimately fall on labor under plausible conditions, but all such numerical estimates must be viewed as highly conjectural.[1] It should also be pointed out that the process by which some of the tax burden is shifted from capital owners to labor will take a long time to complete, probably on the order of twenty to forty years. The reason it takes so long is that a decline in saving has only a small effect on the capital stock in one year. For example, if annual net saving is $200 billion and the capital stock is $7,000 billion, a decline in saving to $100 billion implies that the capital stock one year later will be $7,100 billion rather than $7,200 billion, a small difference. Such a reduction in annual saving, however, continued over a period of twenty-five years or so would mean that the capital

1. Martin Feldstein, "Incidence of a Capital Income Tax in a Growing Economy with Variable Savings Rates," *Review of Economic Studies* 41 (1974):505–13.

stock would be 20 percent lower, and that would have a significant effect on wage rates.

Both of these qualifications imply that capital income taxes will have a less progressive effect on the tax burden in the long run than they seem to have when only the short-run effects are considered. This point takes on considerable significance if the political process is influenced primarily by short-run consequences. In the short run, capital income taxes appear to be useful devices to place a major part of the tax burden on the wealthy, but the longer-run effects suggest that the burden will be shared more widely across the population. Although I suspect that capital income taxes will ultimately be found to be progressively distributed over the long run, there is little doubt that Table 1–3 overstates the degree of progressivity.

CAPITAL TAXES AND EQUITY

Any tax can be judged by a variety of criteria, but certainly one of the most common is whether the tax apportions the tax burden in a fair or equitable manner. Probably one of the most important reasons the United States taxes capital income as heavily as it does is the view that equity is thereby served. As pointed out in the previous section, capital taxes probably absorb a larger share of the incomes of the wealthy than of the nonwealthy; while the exact degree of progressivity is not clear, especially when a long-run perspective is adopted, there is little doubt that most people believe capital taxes fall heavily on the well-off. Moreover, that is generally believed to be fair.

Despite the widely held view that capital taxes are fair, in recent years economists have become increasingly uneasy about accepting that proposition. To understand the issues involved, it may be useful to begin by outlining how economists think about equity. Traditionally, equity in taxation has been held to reflect two principles. The first, called horizontal equity, holds that two persons equally situated economically should bear the same tax burden, or that equals should be treated equally. The second, called vertical equity, holds that two persons unequally situated should bear different tax burdens, or that unequals should be treated unequally. These two principles do not by themselves resolve many questions (in particular, the definition of vertical equity does not tell us how unequally those who are unequal should be treated), but they do represent a useful point of departure.

To apply these principles, however, it is necessary to determine what conditions define equality and inequality for purpose of assigning tax burdens. In practice, most economists have held that a taxpayer's income is the appropriate basis to use. In other words, two persons with the same income are held to be equally situated economically; therefore, according to the principle of horizontal equity, they should bear equal tax burdens. And according to the usual interpretation of vertical equity, those with higher incomes should pay more in taxes.

Current income is widely and almost unquestioningly accepted as the appropriate criterion for assessing a person's or a family's tax liability. Critical to the credibility of income as the appropriate tax base is the way it is defined. Economists emphasize that a broad and comprehensive definition should be used. The definition most widely favored is that income is measured by the sum of consumption and the change in real net worth over a year. This defines income by how it is used: It either finances consumption or is saved (thereby affecting net worth). Equivalently, and more conventionally, income can be defined by its sources as the sum of labor earnings, the return to past investments, government transfers, and so on. Either of these definitions, applied carefully, should yield the same measure of a household's income.

Note that this definition of income is not the one embodied in the individual income tax law; instead, it is intended to provide a benchmark for purposes of making equity judgments about the tax system. Let us accept this definition provisionally and use it to evaluate the fairness of taxation of capital income. The first point to note is that total income, irrespective of its source, is conceived to be the appropriate criterion for assessing tax liabilities. Thus, two persons, one with $10,000 in wages and the other with $10,000 in income from investments, should bear the same tax burden. According to the argument thus far presented, capital income is a legitimate object of taxation, but only because it is part of total income.

However, capital income taxation as it is actually applied violates the standard of horizontal equity and, to some degree, of vertical equity because capital income is typically taxed at a higher rate than other types of income when the tax system as a whole is considered. As we have seen, capital income is taxed more heavily than labor income in the aggregate, and this is also true at each level of income. Thus, comparing two persons with equal total incomes, the individuals whose income comes from capital will bear a substantially heavier tax burden than the person whose income is exclusively wage earnings. Horizontal equity is therefore violated. Furthermore, vertical equity may also not be well served. For instance, it is likely that a retiree whose only income is $5,000 in capital income will bear a heavier tax burden than a worker whose only income is $10,000 in wages.

Equity would seem to call for equal taxation of capital and labor income at each level of total income. (Higher levels of total income could be subjected to higher tax rates if vertical equity is interpreted to call for this.) Since capital income is more heavily taxed at all income levels, does this imply that there is a good argument on equity grounds for reducing taxes on capital income? Before that conclusion is drawn, several counterarguments should be made. First, on average and in a crude way, capital taxes probably do add to the progressivity of the tax system, especially at the very top of the income distribution (see Table 1–3). This feature of capital taxes accords with the view of vertical equity held by many. Second, some believe that capital income should be taxed more heavily because it is "unearned income." Third, how heavily capital income is taxed is not a settled issue. Some economists believe that corporate and property taxes do not fall exclusively on capital income, in which case the estimates given earlier would overstate the rate on capital income and understate the rate on labor income. While I believe most tax specialists conclude that capital income is more heavily taxed, there is no consensus as to the exact degree.

The foregoing discussion suggests that there may be an equity argument for equalizing the tax rates applying to capital and labor income, presumably by reducing capital taxation. A number of economists, however, have recently taken the position that equitable taxation requires completely eliminating the taxation of income from capital—a position based on an analysis that concludes consumption rather than income is the appropriate criterion for assessing tax liabilities. Since income is so widely accepted as the appropriate criterion, the argument that income is inferior to consumption as a tax base from an equity standpoint deserves careful consideration.

Consider first horizontal equity, since the determination of what identifies equals logically precedes a determination of how unequals should be treated. Take a simple example: Two taxpayers, *A* and *B*, each have labor earnings of $20,000 in year 1 and no other type of income. Under an income tax, they would pay the same tax in year 1 since they have the same income. Under a consumption tax, if taxpayer B, for example, saves a larger share of his income (consumes less in year 1; recall that consumption plus saving equals income), he will pay less in taxes in that year. Which tax is fairer?

The first question is whether A and B should be considered as equals for tax purposes. A proponent of the income tax would argue that they are equally situated: Even though B consumes less than A, both have the same opportunity to consume $20,000, and the fact that B chooses to consume less is irrelevant. From this it is concluded that income is the best tax base since it means that A and B will pay the same tax. Proponents of consumption taxation agree that A and B are equals in one sense, but stress that we must examine how the taxes operate over a period of time longer than a single year. Under a consumption tax, the saver, taxpayer B, does not avoid paying taxes by saving; he merely postpones the tax until he ultimately consumes the funds accumulated through his savings.

Table 1–4 illustrates the alternatives. Here it is assumed that taxpayer A consumes his entire earnings in year 1, while taxpayer B consumes only $8,000 in year 1 and the proceeds of his savings (accumulated at a 10 percent rate of interest) are consumed later in year 2. Part I of the table shows the results for a 20 percent income tax. Both A and B pay an equal tax of $4,000 in year 1, but B pays an additional tax of $160 in year 2—20 percent of the $800 in interest

Table 1–4. Taxing Consumption or Income.

| | | Part I—Income Tax | | | |
Person	Earnings ($)	Year 1 Consumption (and tax) ($)		Year 2 Consumption (and tax) ($)	
A	20,000	16,000	(4,000)	0	(0)
B	20,000	8,000	(4,000)	8,640	(160)

| | | Part II—Consumption Tax | | | |
Person	Earnings ($)	Year 1 Consumption (and tax) ($)		Year 2 Consumption (and tax) ($)	
A	20,000	16,000	(4,000)	0	(0)
B	20,000	8,000	(2,000)	8,800	(2,200)

income earned on his $8,000 saving of the year before. Although both A and B have the same consumption opportunities over the two-year period, B pays a higher total tax solely because he chooses to save more. The income tax thus violates horizontal equity; equals are not treated equally. By contrast, a consumption tax places the same tax burdens on A and B, as shown in Part II of the table, with a 25 percent tax on consumption. B now pays $2,000 in tax in year 1, saves $10,000 which grows to $11,000 in year 2, and pays $2,200 in tax in year 2. In present value terms the tax burden on B is the same as on A: A $2,200 tax in year 2 when the interest rate is 10 percent is equivalent to a $2,000 tax in year 1.

An individual's lifetime tax liability under a consumption tax is the same (in present value) regardless of how much is saved. Savers do not avoid the tax, they just postpone paying it by saving. Under income taxation, those who save a large portion of their incomes pay more in lifetime taxes than do those equally situated who choose to save less. Thus, when a long-run, or lifetime, perspective is taken, this differential treatment of savers represents a strong argument favoring consumption, rather than income, as a tax base. Note that lifetime consumption could be taxed in two seemingly different ways. First, the amount of saving could be deducted from income, since consumption plus savings equals income. Second, the taxation of labor income but not capital income achieves the same results: in Table 1–4, part I, if B's $800 in interest income in year 2 is untaxed, he can consume $8,800 in that year—just as under the consumption tax shown in part II. From a lifetime perspective, a consumption tax and labor income tax have identical effects. Therefore, the equity argument for a consumption tax implies that capital income should not be taxed at all; either consumption or labor income should be the tax base.

Many people have trouble accepting this conclusion since it seems to favor the wealthy who save more and own large amounts of capital. This position, however, confuses vertical equity with horizontal equity. A tax on personal consumption (or labor earnings) levied on individuals can be as progressive as desired by using a graduated rate structure. For example, the first $5,000 in consumption could be exempt, the next $5,000 taxed at 20 percent, the next at 30 percent, and so on. Those with higher lifetime incomes would, if they consume their resources during their lifetimes, pay a larger share of their incomes to the government. To avoid the possibility of family fortunes passing from generation to generation untaxed, estates could be taxed at death as if they were consumption. In this way egalitarian goals, if deemed appropriate, could be achieved without taxing saving or capital income.

This analysis has not touched on many of the practical problems that would accompany the institution of a personal consumption tax. (These problems include administrative complexities and maintaining equity in a transition from income to consumption taxation.) Its main purpose is to indicate that there are serious questions about the equity of taxing capital income. The consumption tax argument emphasizes that a longer-run (longer than a single year) perspective on equity leads to the conclusion that capital income should not be taxed at all. Even if total annual income is considered the appropriate tax base, a case can be made to reduce the taxation of capital income, since it is currently more heavily taxed than labor income.

CAPITAL INCOME TAXATION AND EFFICIENCY

Aggregate Effects

As we have seen, there are a number of taxes that fall on capital income, and it is their combined weight that is relevant in ascertaining the effect they have on overall saving, capital accumulation, and efficiency. For example, suppose that a corporate investment yields $100 as a net return. Part of that return goes to pay property taxes and the remainder is subject to federal and state corporation income taxes. What is left is either reinvested by the corporation or paid out as dividends. If the remaining funds are reinvested, they lead to a capital gain on stock held by shareholders. When realized, this capital gain will be taxed under the individual income tax. If the remaining funds are paid as dividends, they will be immediately taxed under the individual income tax.

The combined effect of these (and possibly other) taxes determines how much of the real return to capital investment is retained by the individuals who ultimately provide the funds through their saving. Moreover, savers' decisions regarding how much to save will be guided by the final net-of-tax return they receive. Thus, it is important to know how much capital taxes depress the net rate of return. Table 1–5 presents some of the results of a recent study that examines this issue with regard to investments in the corporate sector. (Corporate

Table 1–5. Taxation of Corporate Capital Income.

| | | Contribution to Total Effective Tax Rate | | | | | | | | | |
| | | | | Individual Income Tax | | | | | | | |
Year	Federal Corporate Tax (1)	State and Local Corporate Tax (2)	State and Local Property Tax (3)	Tax on Dividends (4)	Tax on Real Capital Gains (5)	Tax on Nominal Capital Gains (6)	Tax on Interest (7)	Total Effective Tax Rate (8)	Before-Tax Rate of Return (9)	After-Tax Rate of Return (10)
1955	45.0%	2.1%	7.7%	7.7%	1.2%	0.8%	1.0%	65.4%	13.2%	4.6%
1960	40.1	2.3	11.6	8.6	1.0	0.7	2.1	66.5	10.4	3.5
1965	31.8	2.2	9.1	6.2	1.7	0.7	1.9	53.5	14.8	6.9
1970	30.8	3.6	15.4	7.7	1.8	3.5	6.6	69.5	9.8	3.0
1975	28.3	4.6	13.9	6.4	2.6	6.6	7.8	70.3	9.1	2.7
1979	31.7	5.5	10.5	6.9	2.6	4.2	8.0	69.4	9.0	2.7

SOURCE: Martin Feldstein, James Poterba, and Louis Dicks-Mireaux, "The Effective Tax Rate and the Pretax Rate of Return," Working Paper No. 740, (Cambridge, Mass.: National Bureau of Economic Research, Aug. 1981), Tables 2, 3, and 4.

sector investment is about 60 percent of total national investment.) Columns (1) to (7) show how much each of seven different features of the tax system contributes to the overall effective tax rate on capital income. Except for the federal corporation income tax, the separate rates are moderate, but together they produced a total effective tax rate of 69.4 percent in 1979. This is an average rate on all households; those in higher income brackets would confront a higher rate. (However, today the rate would probably be lower—but only slightly so— as a result of the tax changes in 1981 and 1982.)

The last two columns of Table 5 suggest how large is the "tax wedge" between before-tax and after-tax real rates of return. During the 1970s, the before-tax real rate of return to corporate investment (including years not shown in the table) averaged about 10 percent. With an effective tax rate of about 70 percent, the after-tax real rate of return was only 3 percent. These estimates pertain to investments in the corporate sector. Investments in the noncorporate sector are more lightly taxed. Nonetheless, the evidence suggests that capital income is, on average, taxed heavily in the United States, thus significantly reducing the net return received by savers.

How capital taxes affect the economy depends critically on how savers respond when the net rate of return they receive is reduced. If, for example, households save less when the reward for saving is smaller, then the rate of capital accumulation will be diminished and future living standards will suffer. Whether people do save less at lower net interest rates has been the subject of active debate, both on a theoretical and empirical level. As yet, there is no firm consensus on this issue, but recent research has tended to conclude that saving is adversely affected when the rate of return received by savers is reduced.[2]

In thinking about how the level of saving is affected by capital taxes, it is important that the question be properly posed. The net

2. Two major works demonstrating that capital taxation has a substantial negative effect on saving are Michael Boskin, "Taxation, Saving, and the Rate of Interest, *Journal of Political Economy* 86 (1978):3–27; and Lawrence Summers, "Capital Taxation and Capital Accumulation in a Life Cycle Growth Model," *American Economic Review* 71 (1981):533–44. However, in view of various criticisms of these studies, it seems premature to conclude that the effect of capital taxation on saving is necessarily large. See Owen Evans, "Tax Policy, the Interest Elasticity of Saving and Capital Accumulation: Numerical Analysis of Theoretical Models," *American Economic Review* 73 (1983):398–410; and Irving Friend and Joel Hasbrouck, "Saving and After-Tax Rates of Return," *Review of Economics and Statistics* 65 (1983):537–43.

return to savers could be increased by reducing tax rates on capital income. If such a reduction, however, would also reduce tax *revenues,* it would necessitate changes in other governmental programs, and these changes should be incorporated into the analysis of the effects of reducing capital taxes. The way this is generally done is by assuming that, in order to keep its revenues unchanged, the government increases other taxes when it reduces capital taxes. This assumption avoids complicating the analysis with considerations of whether it is desirable to change the level of government spending. For example, by assuming that reductions in taxes on capital income are accompanied by increases in taxes on labor income, we can focus on the merits of capital taxation relative to the main alternative way of raising revenue. When this comparison is made, it can be shown that taxes on capital income do adversely affect saving: Saving would be greater if capital taxation were not used and the revenue shortfall were made up with heavier taxation of labor income. Taxpayers on average would end up with the same current disposable incomes, but the higher rate of return they would receive on their savings would encourage greater savings.

Does this imply that saving (and thus real capital investment) is too low and should be encouraged by a shift from capital taxation to labor income taxation? Before explaining why many economists would answer these questions in the affirmative, let me briefly discuss two common arguments often given in support of government actions to stimulate saving and investment.

One frequently heard argument advocates increased capital accumulations as the cure for the relatively low rate of economic growth in recent years. As previously mentioned, increased capital accumulation can be expected to raise the growth rate, but the growth rate is determined by many factors (such as technological progress, labor force growth, and human capital investment) in addition to the rate of capital accumulation, and the independent contribution of more saving cannot be expected to raise the growth rate dramatically. Since the before-tax rate of return is what measures the contribution of saving and investment to output in subsequent years, let us use the 10 percent figure suggested by Table 1–5 to get an idea of the magnitude involved. Suppose a tax reform would increase investment by $100 billion annually; it is unlikely that the effect would be much larger at the present time, since this would represent an increase in net saving of about 30 percent. At a 10 percent return, $100 billion in additional capital invested would add $10 billion to annual output in subsequent years. If GNP is less than $4,000 billion, a $10 billion increment in annual output would add less than 0.25 percentage points to the growth rate—for example, raising it from 3 percent to 3.25 percent.

What this calculation indicates is that a reduction in, or even elimination of, capital income taxation is not likely to transform the United States into an economy growing at (or near) the 7 percent rate that Japan experienced for much of the post–World War II period. Physical capital investment is only one of a number of factors that interact to determine the rate of growth, and its independent contribution should not be exaggerated. On the other hand, neither should its contribution be minimized: A small increase in the rate of growth sustained for many years can, through the operation of compound interest, have a significant effect. As Michael Boskin has observed: "The United Kingdom, growing at about one percentage point less than did the United States, France, and Germany, managed to transform itself from the wealthiest society on earth toward the end of the nineteenth century to a relatively poor member of the Common Market today."[3]

Another argument for increased investment stresses that business requires more capital in order to increase employment as the labor force expands over time. Put differently, capital investment "creates jobs." This argument is almost totally fallacious. A given level of capital investment is consistent with any level of employment as long as wage rates can adjust. As evidence, it is worth noting that the number of jobs actually increased more rapidly in the 1970s than in any previous decade, despite an unusually low rate of investment. Increased investment can be expected to lead to better-paying jobs in the future—that is part of the benefit from consuming less in the present—but not necessarily more jobs.

In contrast to these two arguments, economists tend to evaluate the desirability of reducing taxes on capital income (along with increasing taxes on labor income) by considering whether people would be benefited by the change. I have argued that people would be encouraged to save more, but how does that benefit them? The benefit from increased saving is correctly measured by the before-tax rate of return on capital investment. If the before-tax return is 10 percent, giving

---

3. Michael J. Boskin, "Saving Incentives: The Role of Tax Policy," in Charles E. Walker and Mark A. Bloomfield, eds., *New Directions in Federal Tax Policy for the 1980s* (Cambridge, Mass.: Ballinger Publishing Co., 1983), p. 93.

up $1 in consumption today makes it possible to consume $1.10 one year later, or $2 after seven years.

The relevant question is whether people would be better off by sacrificing present consumption in return for future consumption on these terms. Since much saving is done to finance consumption in retirement, and since 20 years is the approximate average length of time during which a retiree accumulates his savings, the size of the trade-off can be illustrated in the following way. At a 10 percent rate of return, $1 saved now will grow to $6.37 in 20 years, so the present cost of $1 in retirement consumption is $0.15. Would people be better off saving more (consuming less in the present) in return for that pay-off? I believe the answer is yes, but that raises the further question of why they are not already saving more. The answer, as is perhaps obvious by now, is that households do not get to keep the before-tax return of 10 percent; they actually get to keep only a lower real after-tax return, which has sometimes been negative. Faced with a less favorable rate of exchange, it is understandable that saving would remain low, even though the real before-tax return to saving justifies the cost of reduced present consumption.

Capital income taxes thus lead people to save too little, in the sense that the benefits to greater saving (as measured by the real before-tax rate of return) are larger than the costs of giving up consumption in the present. The size of the net cost, or efficiency loss, of this distortion of individual choice is a matter of dispute, but several studies have suggested that it may be as large as $100 billion annually. If this research is correct, it constitutes a strong argument for reducing taxation of capital income.

Depreciation Allowances, Investment Tax Credits, the Exclusion of Capital Gains Income, and Capital Misallocation

Even if the overall rate of capital taxation were not reduced, there would be strong arguments for reforming the tax code with respect to capital. In our section on "Capital Taxation and Incidence," we noted the misallocation of resources that occurs when some portions of the capital stock are taxed at different rates than others. The corporate sector, for example, is taxed at a rate different from that of the noncorporate sector. And within the corporate sector itself, provisions for depreciation allowances, investment tax credits, and the exclusion of some capital gains income from the tax base distort the allocation of capital. The Tax Act of 1981 introduced "accelerated depreciation" and an expanded system of investment tax credits. Both have significantly contributed to the problems of capital misallocation. That is, taking the volume of investment funds and consumer preferences as given, the Tax Act of 1981 biased investment choices toward certain sectors of the economy and away from other sectors that, at the margin, consumers value more highly.

To see this, consider the concept of "neutral" or "economic" depreciation. Under such depreciation, firms can deduct the cost of a piece of capital as a business expense over the course of its life as an economic asset. The problem with respect to the law prior to 1981 was that the deductions to which firms were entitled were based on the nominal cost of the capital at the time of its purchase. As inflation occurred, the *real* value of depreciation allowances diminished.

To correct for the effects of inflation, one might simply have adjusted depreciation allowances for changes in the cost of living, but the Tax Act of 1981 bypassed such indexing in favor of "accelerated depreciation." Under the accelerated depreciation provisions of 1981, depreciation allowances were not indexed for inflation, but firms were permitted to take all their deductions over a period much shorter than the economic life of the capital in question. In other words, a building might last forty years, but a firm might be able to take all of its tax deductions over a fifteen-year period. Firms would generally prefer to take their deductions over a shorter period because of the time value of money and the greater likelihood of inflation over a longer period.

The effective or "true" rate of taxation here would thus reflect the nominal rate adjusted for the effects of inflation and the fact that the economic life of a piece of capital may differ from its "legal life" under depreciation law. The point here is that—depending on the above factors and others to be mentioned below—the effective rates of taxation on different types of capital have differed widely, being still very high in some cases and sometimes *negative* in other cases. In these latter cases, U.S. taxpayers are subsidizing the sectors in question at the expense of other sectors that are heavily taxed.

These disparities in effective tax rates were highlighted by the "leasing provisions" tacked on to the investment tax credit changes of 1981. Firms that, because of an absence of profits, had no tax liabilities against which to take tax credits were nevertheless permitted to collect credits by, in effect, selling them to other firms. In other words, given an investment tax credit rate of 10 percent, a firm investing $100,000 in new equipment would receive a credit of $10,000. Under previous law, if the firm had no profits, it would have no tax liability that could be offset by the tax credit, and no credit could be collected. Under the 1981 provisions, however, firms were permitted to make deals with other enterprises enabling them, in effect, to receive $10,000 from the U.S. Treasury. So again, the firm's tax rate could be effectively negative; consumers would be subsidizing the firm at the expense of more highly valued enterprises—an example of capital misallocation.

Table 1–6. Effective Tax Rates on Equity-financed Investments in Equipment and Structures, by Industry.

Industry	1985 law* Inflation rate 5%	10%
Agriculture	29	37
Mining	13	31
Logging	21	34
Wood products and furniture	28	38
Glass, cement, and clay	20	31
Primary metals	16	28
Fabricated metal	28	38
Machinery and instruments	26	36
Electrical equipment	26	38
Motor vehicles	8	26
Transportation equipment	25	36
Food	25	35
Tobacco	18	30
Textiles	19	32
Apparel	28	38
Pulp and paper	12	26
Printing and publishing	22	34
Chemicals	19	32
Petroleum refining	12	2
Rubber	18	30
Leather	30	40
Transport services	9	26
Utilities	28	38
Communications	19	33
Services and trade	31	40

SOURCE: Department of Treasury, Office of Tax Analysis, *Tax Reform for Fairness, Simplicity, and Economic Growth,* vol. 1 (Washington, D.C.: Government Printing Office, 1984), p. 108.
*Assumes a 46 percent corporate tax rate.

Finally, the exclusion of some capital gains income from the tax base has introduced distortions, in that some industries depend on the sale of securities to finance their operations more so than do others. On the other hand, the interest costs of *bank loans* to finance operations have, in most cases, been tax-deductible, and some "capital gains" on which taxes have had to be paid have simply reflected inflation rather than a real increase in the value of assets. The effective tax rate for the firm has thus depended on the complex interplay of the sources of corporate finance, the rate of inflation, and other factors.

As an example of the disparities in effective tax rates that can occur, Tables 1–6 and 1–7 show estimates across different industries and asset classes for 1985. As shown there, the effective rates differ tremendously, being highly positive in some cases and negative in others. The impact on the efficiency of capital allocation is obvious.

"Leasing provisions" and other distortions have by now been eliminated, but substantial disparities in effective tax rates remain. Meaningful reform of capital taxation thus requires not only a general lowering of effective rates of taxation, but assurances that there won't be capital misallocation, which can be just as harmful to economic efficiency as a general shortfall in capital accumulation. Effective tax reform thus requires (a) equalization of effective tax rates on capital

Table 1–7. Effective Tax Rates on Equity-financed Investments With Various Rates of Inflation for 46 Percent Taxpayer Under 1985 Law.

Asset class (years)		Inflation rate (percent)		
	:	0	5	10
3		−90	−8	22
5		−51	−3	19
10		−5	20	32
15		9	35	45
18		28	40	45

SOURCE: Department of Treasury, Office of Tax Analysis, *Tax Reform for Fairness, Simplicity, and Economic Growth*, vol. 1 (Washington, D.C.: Government Printing Office, 1984), p. 107.

Assumptions: Real rate of return after tax is 4 percent. The investment tax credit selected is the maximum allowable (6 percent on three-year equipment and 10 percent on five-, ten-, and fifteen-year equipment). Effective tax rates are the difference between the real before-tax rate of return and the real after-tax rate of return divided by the real before-tax rate of return.

across industries and types of plant and equipment, to be accomplished primarily by (b) a *decrease* of the effective rates that are relatively high rather than an *increase* of the effective rates that are relatively low, but (c) no firm or industry should have a rate that is effectively negative unless this is warranted by other considerations.

CONCLUSION

In this chapter, I have emphasized three broad issues related to the taxation of capital income: the equity implications of capital income as a tax base, the efficiency implications of reducing the net return to savers, and the implications of taxing different types of capital at different rates. In general, a case can be made that capital income is—despite the 1981 tax act—still too heavily taxed. It should be recognized, however, that the benefits from reforming capital taxation are primarily long-term in nature. The immediate, or short-run, effect may seem to be to benefit those who own large amounts of capital, typically the very well-off. There is a danger that the political process will focus on short-run considerations and forestall meaningful reforms that would benefit most people over the longer term.

2

TAXATION, SAVING, AND INVESTMENT: A LOOK AT THE EVIDENCE

Morgan O. Reynolds

Until the 1970s economists paid little attention to capital formation and productivity growth in the United States. This attitude reflected a general agreement that the American economy had worked reasonably well over the years to generate economic growth and capital formation. After the mid-1970s, however, we were inundated by literature on the sluggish growth of productivity and declining rates of real investment in this country.[1]

There was, at least until recently, a rare consensus among economists, businessmen, and politicians that the United States had the highest percentage of obsolete plant and equipment, the lowest rate of investment, and slowest growth in productivity of any industrial country. Further, many writers pointed to rapid increases in government spending, taxation, redistribution, and regulation as the primary villains in the problem. The association between growing government

---

1. Board of Governors of the Federal Reserve System, *Public Policy and Capital Formation* (Washington, D.C.: Federal Reserve System, 1981); James R. Wilburn, ed., *Productivity: A National Priority* (Malibu, Calif.: Pepperdine University Press, 1982); George M. von Furstenberg, ed., *The Government and Capital Formation* (Cambridge, Mass.: Ballinger Publishing Co., 1980); Herman I. Liebling, *U.S. Corporate Profitability and Capital Formation* (New York: Pergamon Press, 1980); Charles D. Kuehner, ed., *Capital and Job Formation* (Homewood, Ill.: Dow Jones-Irwin, 1978); Arnold W. Sametz, *Prospects for Capital Formation and Capital Markets* (Lexington, Mass.: Lexington Books, 1978).

and poor economic performance is consistent with the theory that a more interventionist system does not work as well to generate growth as does a less interventionist system.

While there is much to recommend prevailing opinion, we should not be too hasty to embrace the analysis or the policies based on it. Virtually all discussions of capital formation, including those in socialist countries, assume that the rate of capital accumulation must be raised. The *Economic Report of the President,* 1983, for example, began its chapter on "Increasing Capital Formation," with the sentence, "Attaining an adequate rate of capital formation in the United States is a crucial challenge for economic policy during the 1980s."[2] This approach is superficial. Too much is taken for granted. Who is to define an "adequate" rate of capital formation? A social engineering mentality dominates the modern mind; both the Reagan administration and businessmen who would commonly be labeled "free enterprisers" unthinkingly accept this approach, which implicitly leads to a search for fine-tuning, manipulative policies. A quite different view is to urge that government diminish and remove the impediments that distort and prevent the expression of private demands, including choices about present versus future consumption.

A more fundamental analysis of saving and investment is in order, especially for those interested in identifying policies that enhance both individual freedom and economic prosperity. A declining rate of net investment, as conventionally measured, is closer to being a symptom of the problem rather than the problem itself. Governmental attempts to manipulate saving and investment totals, or their patterns, are likely to prove disappointing, especially over the long run, if they are based on superficial analysis.

The purpose of this chapter is to review the evidence on the impact that taxation has had on private saving and investment. To do so intelligently requires that we consult the best available theory of saving, investment, capital formation, and interest rates. To do less dooms us to avoidable error. The first section, "Capital Theory," defines theoretical terms and brings the relevant parts of capital theory to bear on the problem. The second section, "Government Intervention," describes the five channels through which government can affect capital formation and economic growth. "Evidence," the following section,

---

2. *Economic Report of the President* (Washington, D.C.: U.S. Government Printing Office, 1983), p. 77.

demonstrates the extent to which government has discouraged saving and investment. The five categories of evidence discussed include anecdotal evidence for the United States, time series data, interstate data, and interindustry evidence, followed by international comparisons. Finally, the fourth section summarizes and concludes the analysis.

CAPITAL THEORY

Capital theory remains a controversial and complex area of economic theory. Much of the problem stems from the failure of economic writers to carefully define what they mean by terms like *capital, income, interest, saving,* and *investment.* This, in turn, leads many writers blindly to use statistics from the National Income and Product Accounts, which are faulty on conceptual and practical grounds—a topic taken up in our discussion on "Evidence." In accord with conventional usage, *saving* means the nonconsumption of income received during a given period of time, that is, an amount of commodities or money receipts set aside for future consumption. Saving is refraining from consumption rather than consuming goods within the same interval of time. The ultimate goal of people engaged in economic activity is consumption, the extermination of goods and services. Consumption is the opposite of production (though no moral connotation is intended) because consumption is the end of the economic process, the destruction of exchangeable goods for immediate gratification. *Production* is the use of resources to increase the social totals of economic goods, whether the goods be consumables or goods useful in the subsequent production of consumables. All valuable things of more than momentary duration can be described as *intermediate goods* or as *capital goods* because they are designed to satisfy future wants, including most of the expenditure classified as *consumption* in the National Income and Product Accounts.

Income is a troublesome concept. On a superficial level, income is the sum of saving and consumption during a given period of time. This definition is circular because saving is that part of income not consumed. The concept of income is unavoidably tied up with the concepts of *capital* and *interest.*[3] Business practice treats income, for the most part, as a consequence of the owners' capital, a logic econ-

---

3. Jack Hirshleifer, *Investment, Interest, and Capital* (Englewood Cliffs, N.J.: Prentice-Hall, 1970), p. 36.

omists will defend. Conversely, capital is anything that yields future incomes. The accepted definition of income is the Haig-Simons definition that income is the *maximum potential consumption* in a time period, or the highest amount that can be detached without impairing the prospects for future consumption—in other words, without decreasing the real value of capital (keeping capital intact). Income can be thought of as a per-period, sustainable flow from a productive endowment. Such an equalized flow is not independent of the interest rate because reductions in interest rates raise the value of capital and the maximum allowable consumption level without impinging on real capital value.

Irving Fisher, the great American economist, objected to this widely accepted notion of income.[4] He explicitly defined "real" income as actual consumption, thereby excluding savings from the definition of income. Fisher denied that additions to capital value (capital gains) were income, partly because he wanted them excluded from taxation, a view similar to that of today's advocates of abolishing the capital gains tax. As Frank Fetter pointed out, Fisher's definition flies in the face of conventional usage.[5] A thousand dollars in money received as a gift or as increment in capital value is "income," whether the thousand dollars is eaten up in immediate gratification or put aside ("saved") for later use. Fisher confused *sources* with *uses* of income. The crucial question is whether capital gains and losses in a given period are to be considered income, and the economics profession has answered with a resounding "yes."

Wealth is a collection of economic goods, including—but not limited to—physical goods. *Capital* is the market value of wealth: the capital value, present value, or sum of the market values of the individual goods. A subset of wealth is usually termed *"capital goods"* because these goods are not directly desired for themselves but because they aid in the production of other desired goods. Capital goods may be natural or produced by previous human labor and services of capital goods. Things that lose their market value are no longer counted as capital, no matter how large their original cost, including abandoned, rent-controlled buildings in New York City.

4. Irving Fisher, *The Theory of Interest* (New York: The Macmillan Company, 1930; reprinted [Kelley] 1955), pp. 11–12.

5. Frank A. Fetter, *Capital, Interest, and Rent,* edited with an Introduction by Murray N. Rothbard (Kansas City: Sheed Andrews and McMeel, 1977), pp. 114–18.

Investment is another source of confusion. Investing originated with the idea of an individual having a sum of money to spend on goods; this spending is called "investing" funds (a person's own or borrowed sums), consistent with the original meaning of "clothing" money in the form of material things ("investiture"). Today the investment may be in the form of research and development, increased human skills, business inventories, machines, buildings, natural resource development, and other forms of output-enhancing capacity. If an investment is wise or fortunate ("profitable"), the capital value exceeds the value of the resources expended; in other words, the income from the invested sum exceeds the amounts that would have been obtained from interest payments on the capital.

Interest is the price for borrowing money or the reward for lending money. It is the price of earlier availability. To put it another way, it is the "premium" or "agio" for getting goods earlier. Market interest rates are made up of four elements: an allowance for the administrative costs of the loan or debt transaction, an allowance for the anticipated depreciation in the value of the monetary unit, an allowance for the risk of default by the borrower, and finally the underlying time discount of the society. The last element is loosely called the "natural" or "real" interest rate, that is, the market rate of interest minus the contemporaneous rate of price inflation for a standardized debt.

The discount or interest rate basically reflects the positive rate of time preference in a society. Economic theory does not rule out individuals who subjectively value an amount of goods received ten or ten thousand years from today the same as the goods received today— nor a society that does the same—yet most individuals value goods for immediate use more highly than they value the same goods for later use. All known societies exhibit positive rates of interest, either openly observed in lending transactions or implicitly in the prices of goods of varying durability, despite the denunciations of positive time-discounts by religious and political dogma. A capital good is worth less than the simple sum of its net incomes over future dates because of subjective human preferences. An open market for loanable funds (time-dated consumption claims) clears or equilibrates at a positive time-premium (interest rate), and interest rates permeate all decisions about production, consumption, durability of goods, and intertemporal allocation. The essential mechanism can be described as follows: When consumers increase savings, interest rates fall, signaling producers to reallocate production toward *future* consumption, and thereby increase total investment in durable goods and toward longer-lived processes. When pure interest rates rise, it reflects an increase in time preference and directs producers toward more present-oriented production and smaller net investment.

While it is commonplace in textbooks to refer to the "productivity of capital" as a second determinant of the interest rate, it is a mistake to do so. The fact that capital goods are "productive" accounts for the positive rental rates they command in the market; this, in turn, explains why capital goods command a positive purchase price. But the productivity of capital cannot explain why the purchase price of capital goods is less than the simple sum of the stream of expected net rents (net marginal productivity) for the services of the capital goods. Interest rates are not the "price" of capital goods or the price of using capital goods. The explanation for positive interest rates basically lies in individuals' preferences for income today versus tomorrow. This conclusion is only slightly modified by the fact that the size of current income relative to the richness of productive opportunities also influences interest rates. For example, a community struck by a sudden disaster will tend to experience high rates of interest because such a disaster, if not too severe, reduces current income below what the community is capable of generating on a sustained, long-run basis. Members of the community are like "heirs with great expectations" and try to borrow from one another against future income.[6] As with all economic phenomena, individual choices, and hence social outcomes, are ultimately the products of two factors: subjective preferences and objective opportunities.

The interaction among individuals in perfectly competitive financial markets results in identical time-preferences for everyone at the margin. An individual's saving ("financial") can be greater or less than his or her investment ("real"), but in market equilibrium, across all individuals, total saving must equal total investment.

GOVERNMENT INTERVENTION

If capital and interest theory is a complex and unsettled corner of economics, the effects of unstable and expanding government on capital accumulation and economic growth are consensus principles among economists. As Mancur Olson says,

---

6. See Hirshleifer, *n*. 3, pp. 113–19 for a careful discussion.

Virtually all economists agree that events, or even expectations, that discourage investment or destroy productive capital will lower the level of income. Thus societies that are politically unstable or often subjected to foreign invasion are likely to have less productive investment and lower rates of growth than they would otherwise have had. There will be more flights of capital and fewer investments in plant or equipment that can pay off only in the long run.[7]

Increased taxation, including all explicit and implicit forms of taxation and regulation imposed by government, can decrease savings, investment, and productivity growth through five channels:

1. A higher tax burden lowers private income, and therefore savings.
2. A higher tax burden tends to redirect private decisions toward present consumption and away from future consumption.
3. Government consumes rather than invests most of the private savings that it borrows.
4. The savings invested by government tend to be in projects that yield less than do those in which the private sector invests.
5. Government regulations and taxes distort private investments toward an inefficient mix of projects.

The first three factors lower aggregate investment in society and the last two worsen the allocative efficiency of the available investment.

The first factor lowers saving because citizens have less income to allocate between current and future consumption—the "income effect." Total saving will fall even if people maintain the same fraction of income saved. The usual presumption is that as people's incomes rise over time, they are willing to increase the fraction of income saved. Cross-sectional evidence shows that wealthier people save a higher fraction of income, but this characterization is not supported by conventional time-series evidence.[8] Also, some low-income groups have been prodigious savers. There are only two ways that savings can be increased: (1) a restriction of current consumption, reflecting a greater subjective preference for future consumption, or (2) a higher income due to improved natural conditions, technical change, business innovation, or reductions in adverse conditions like war, strikes, crime, and taxation. To the extent that a given level of taxation

7. Mancur Olson, *The Rise and Decline of Nations* (New Haven: Yale University Press, 1982), p. 4.

8. Milton Friedman, *A Theory of the Consumption Function* (Princeton: Princeton University Press, 1957); Charles W. Baird, *Elements of Macroeconomics* (St. Paul: West Publishing, 1981), pp. 114–17.

falls especially hard on the thrifty, saving and investment decrease further.

The second factor is that not only do people have lower incomes with which to save, but private demands tend to be redirected toward present goods. People are likely to be more present-oriented because higher taxation tends to twist preferences toward the present and lower the opportunity cost of current consumption—a kind of substitution effect. The welfare state, by its very nature, tends to discourage individual responsibility for one's future and one's dependents. If confiscatory policies proceed, private capital formation approaches zero and then turns negative as real capital value is consumed and not replaced. As incomes fall and the state pretends to care for all, the future-orientation of the population decreases.

The third factor is that governmental policies (officials) tend to be present-oriented. As the citizens' power to spend and invest is curtailed by the amount the government spends, present-oriented spenders are substituted for future-oriented spenders. Government spending and unbalanced budgets are euphemisms for capital consumption. Government officials make *some* useful additions to future productive capacity in the form of public works, but the savings required are supplied by the citizens, not by government officials. Government, on its own, does absolutely no saving, and part of the citizens' savings is employed by government for current consumption. The fact that the federal government has no accounting for its capital and investment/disinvestment behavior, an intolerable situation in the private sector, shows that only weak restraints keep government officials from dissipating all the borrowed savings of the citizens. When government officials subsequently impose taxes to pay the interest on public debt, the taxes are not compensated by any service yielded by the officials' past investment. Taxpayers thus service debt on "capital" that has been consumed.[9]

The fourth factor is that government is a poor investor. Of all the investments that government officials make in structures, producers' equipment, research and development, and human skills, *some* almost certainly turn out to be profitable. Indeed, investments in stable, limited government; a reliable legal system; respect for property rights and their continuance—all yield extraordinary returns. Their value is at least partially measured in the prices of goods and services sold.

9. Ludwig von Mises, *Human Action*, 3d ed. (Chicago: Henry Regnery, 1966), pp. 226–27.

But many government investments are losers. Although losses occur in private markets too, private investors and entrepreneurs play with their own money and suffer the losses or enjoy the profits from their decisions. This concentrates minds wonderfully. The same profit-and-loss mechanism does not operate in government, with a consequent reduction in the efficiency of the sorting process. Politics directs these investments, not anticipated consumer spending in the marketplace. If politicians or bureaucratic investment decision-makers were as good or better than private investors, then government officials could out-perform the market and quickly become rich by managing market portfolios. There is no evidence that ex-bureaucrats have succeeded at this. Cost-benefit analysis, Planning Programming Budget System (PPBS), and sunset laws are attempts to mimic the discipline of the market, but no economist claims that they approach the efficiency of capital markets.

The fifth piece of damage that expansive government can wreak on capital formation is that government's tax and regulatory policies interfere with efficient deployment of private investment resources. The market process tends to equalize the private, post-tax rate of re-turn on investment options, adjusted for risk and transaction cost dif-ferentials, thereby maximizing the productive yield on capital assets—provided that government tax and regulatory policies are neutral. The problem is that government tax and regulatory policies are not neutral. Some investments receive privileged tax treatment (owner-occupied housing, tax shelters) while other investment returns are taxed heavily (interest rate ceilings, double taxation of corporate dividends). Trac-ing these impacts is complicated, perhaps impossible, in an interde-pendent economy. For example, pollution regulations disproportionately redirect capital out of certain industries, just as do safety regulations. Although economists encourage the government to intervene when "external effects" or social costs hinder the private expression of de-mands, few real life interventions demonstrably improve resource al-location under constantly changing conditions. The opposite seems to be more common. The Occupational Safety and Health Administra-tion, for example, has had no detectable effect on reducing accident rates at the workplace but has imposed costs on the production process.[10]

10. Robert S. Smith, "The Impact of OSHA Inspections on Manufacturing Injury Rates," *Journal of Human Resources* 14 (Spring 1979): 145-70; W. Kip Viscuisi, *Risk by Choice* (Cambridge: Harvard University Press, 1983); David P. McCaffrey, "An Assessment of OSHA's Recent Effects on Injury Rates," *Journal of Human Resources* 18 (Winter 1983): 131–46.

EVIDENCE

Economists take it as axiomatic that (1) investment increases productive capacity and is a major source of gains in productivity and
incomes, and (2) anything (including ordinary taxation, regulation,
and the inflation tax) that impedes capital accumulation diminishes
economic growth. The task of looking at the evidence is not so much
to "test" these propositions but to see how strongly the relationships
show up in the data.

No one would challenge the consequences of a 100 percent tax.
Capital is accumulated based on the expectation that government will
not expropriate it. If this expectation is absent, then people would
prefer to consume their capital instead of safeguarding it for the ex-
propriators. Rolls-Royce limousines on the streets of London illustrate
this phenomenon, a consequence of negligible after-tax returns from
investing in financial instruments under British tax policies. Periodic
cases of "capital flight" dramatically demonstrate what happens when
governments attempt to confiscate capital.

Anecdotal evidence also comes from a recent reduction in government's "capital punishment." In 1978 the federal tax on capital gains
was reduced from 49 to 28 percent. The tax revenue realized from
capital gains increased in 1979 and in 1980, and after a further rate
reduction to 20 percent, revenues were reportedly higher in 1982,
indicating that the tax rate was on the top side of the Laffer curve.[11]

There is a danger, not avoided by most economists, in being too
materialistic in analyzing capital and investment. Writers like Sowell,
Simon, Bauer, Gilder, and Brookes emphasize the intangibles such
as spiritual values, commercial attitudes, morale, and mental qualities
of the population.[12] Sowell, for example, says, "The long-run prosperity of any country depends not upon physical capital but upon the
ability to reproduce that capital."[13] Transferring capital goods from
one country to another, especially under government auspices, is not
nearly so important as transferring the ability and willingness to re-

---

11. *The Wall Street Journal,* 25 Feb. 1983, p. 22.

12. Julian Simon, *The Ultimate Resource* (Princeton: Princeton University Press, 1981);
P. T. Bauer, *Equality, the Third World, and Economic Delusion* (Cambridge: Harvard Uni-
versity Press, 1981); George Gilder, *Wealth and Poverty* (New York: Basic Books, 1980);
Warren T. Brookes, *The Economy in Mind* (New York: Universe Books, 1982).

13. Thomas Sowell, "The Economics and Politics of Race," *Policy Report* 6 (Jan. 1984): 7.

produce and maintain capital. The rusting machinery in poor countries around the world demonstrates that the problem was not a "capital shortage" but a shortage of human capital and appropriate institutional arrangements. Evidence from ancient Britain, Rome, and China reinforces the point.[14]

Thomas Sowell argues that immigrant groups like the Germans, Italians, Japanese, and West Indians were frugal and hard-working, lifting themselves above the median income and wealth in the United States, but "for generations, on into the twentieth century, black leaders themselves repeatedly complained about the wastefulness, extravagance, or improvidence of their own people."[15] Sowell attributes the "habits of carelessness, little foresight, and dependence on whites" to the slave system. It is not an exaggeration to say that such a system resembles today's welfare state. The welfare state's high implicit tax rates on effort promote dependence and a lack of thrift and foresight.

Human capital could be called 75 percent of U.S. wealth because labor receives 75 percent of national income, according to the National Income Accounts. Although formal education may be overrated as part of the development of productivity, fragmentary evidence suggests that human investment decelerated apace with physical investment. For example, the Scholastic Aptitude Test scores declined from a verbal achievement average of 466 in 1967 to 425 in 1983, and the math scores dropped from 492 to 468.[16]

The proportion of young people in school is greater than ever, dominated by dramatic increases in the proportion of women and minorities enrolled in higher education, yet some kinds of education add little to productivity. U.S. schools conferred 45,600 engineering degrees in 1960 and 100,500 in 1982, while the number of law degrees went from 9,200 to 36,000 in the same period—two law degrees for every five engineering degrees instead of one law degree for five engineers.[17] If engineers are skilled at expanding the pie and lawyers are skilled at dividing the pie, schools are graduating more "pie-cutters" today. A similar story holds for the rapid growth of accountants: U.S. schools conferred 26,000 accounting degrees in 1972 and 59,350 in 1984—a 130 percent increase. Another discouraging index of changes

14. Ibid.

15. Thomas Sowell, *Ethnic America* (New York: Basic Books, 1981), p. 199.

16. Bureau of Census, *Statistical Abstract of the United States* (Washington, D.C.: U.S. Government Printing Office, 1985), p. 147.

17. Ibid., p. 168.

in U.S. ingenuity is the "U.S. Balance of Patents" calculated by J. Peter Grace. Between 1966 and 1976 the number of foreign patents granted to U.S. inventors declined from 59,000 to 41,000 while the number of U.S. patents granted to foreign inventors rose from 13,700 to 25,500.[18]

U.S. History

What do the National Income and Product Accounts show over the course of U.S. history? Have saving and investment been low when taxation has been high and vice versa? What have econometric models shown on the issue?

Before examining the data, we should note two difficulties with the National Income and Product Accounts. First, the statistics are fraught with errors. Kuznets infers an average error for national income estimates of about 10 percent.[19] Although few users seem aware of the deficiencies, the statistics are in need of decisive improvement. One and 2 percent changes in these great aggregates convey no information. Although some progress probably has occurred since Morgenstern's critique (1963), a lack of critical appraisal of the data still undermines many alarmist conclusions about U.S. economic performance. Second, the definitions in the accounts are not in accord with the theoretical definitions in our section on "Capital Theory." Gross National Product, for example, excludes some relevant financial transactions, a notable example being transfer of title to existing assets, thereby excluding realized capital gains and losses from income. Also, imputations such as wages "in kind," food and fuel consumed on farms, and housing services consumed by homeowners increase GNP by nearly 10 percent, while the income from nonmarket household labor and the rental services yielded by consumers' durable goods (except housing) are excluded by the Accounts.

There is no explicit capital account (national balance sheet) to accompany the income accounts, though an integrated statement is in the works.[20] The U.S. Department of Commerce recently issued a

18. J. Peter Grace, "Removing the False Assumptions From Economic Policymaking," in James R. Wilburn, ed., *Productivity: A National Priority* (Malibu, Calif.: Pepperdine University Press, 1982), p. 10.

19. Oskar Morgenstern, *On the Accuracy of Economic Observations*, 2d ed. (Princeton: Princeton University Press, 1963), p. 255.

20. Douglas Greenwald, ed., *Encyclopedia of Economics* (New York: McGraw-Hill, 1982), p. 466.

wealth statement of $12.1 trillion for the capital value of all the land, structures, and equipment in the United States.[21] Raymond Goldsmith estimated the value of the United States at $21.65 trillion in 1980.[22] The Income Accounts define "Gross Private Domestic Investment" as purchases of nonresidential buildings, producers' durable equipment, and business inventory changes, plus additions to residential structures. This is a gross measure because it makes no allowance for depreciation in the value of existing physical assets. On the other hand, gross investment understates total investment because the conventional aggregate excludes changes in consumers' inventories of goods, especially consumer durables, additions to human capital, government investments, and research & development spending. R&D spending has varied between 2.2 and 3 percent of the U.S. GNP during the last twenty years.[23]

Net private domestic investment is conventionally derived by subtracting a capital consumption allowance, chiefly attributable to the business sector with only a minor portion attributable to owner-occupied houses. The capital depreciation series is notoriously unreliable, even though it is nominally based on replacement costs, the correct economic concept. Business reporting is guided by tax incentives and accounting conventions that may be out of step with reality, especially during a serious price inflation, and by other assumptions that sometimes bear little relation to a realistic appraisal of actual depreciation in the value of capital goods.

The accuracy problem also is severe for gross saving, because capital consumption is the biggest element of *gross* saving, as shown in Table 2–1. Gross saving, by definition, must equal gross private domestic investment. Americans usually save more than capital consumption through their businesses, but rates of personal saving also loom large in terms of funds for net investment.

The accounting convention of including government deficits as an offset to gross saving is a convention and nothing more. It does not mean that a dollar in deficit spending reduces gross saving available for investment by a dollar. Behavior is more complex than that.

21. *U.S. News & World Report,* 5 Sept. 1983, pp. 48–49.

22. Raymond W. Goldsmith, *The National Balance Sheet of the United States, 1953–1980* (Chicago: University of Chicago Press and NBER, 1982), p. 197.

23. U.S. Bureau of Labor Statistics, *Productivity and the Economy: A Chartbook,* Bulletin 2172 (Washington, D.C.: U.S. Government Printing Office, 1983), p. 59.

Table 2–1. Gross Saving and Investment in the United States, 1982.

Gross Saving	1982 ($ billions)	Percentage of GNP	Gross Investment	1982 ($ billions)	Percentage of GNP
Personal saving	141.1	4.6	Gross private domestic investment		
Retained corporate profits	32.1	1.0	Plant	141.7	4.6
			Equipment	205.8	6.7
Capital consumption allowances	356.8	11.7	Residential buildings	95.8	3.1
Government surplus or deficit	−116.1	−3.8	Business inventories	−22.4	−0.7
			Net foreign investment	−7.9	−0.2
Gross Saving	413.9	13.5 =	Gross Investment	414.0	13.5

SOURCE: *Economic Report of the President, 1983* (Washington, D.C.: Government Printing Office, 1983), pp. 180–81, 192–257.

Personal saving is a residual obtained by subtracting personal outlays from disposable personal income in the National Income Accounts, as calculated by the Commerce Department. The Federal Reserve System also publishes personal-saving figures based on its flow-of-funds accounts. The Fed calculates the change in personal holdings of financial assets such as bank accounts, bonds, and money market mutual funds, adds in new investment in houses and other fixed assets, and then subtracts the increase in personal debt. In the second quarter of 1983, the Fed put personal savings at $215 billion and the Commerce Department put them at $98 billion, a whopping difference of $117 billion.[24] Both figures are "residuals," and virtually every discrepancy in the aggregate statistics can fall into these savings numbers. Officials have no coherent explanation for the discrepancy. Any statement of how savings have reacted to the 1981 tax cuts based on these data is premature, at best. The Fed's data, however, were only $19.5 billion higher on an annual basis for *total savings,* a smaller difference in the context of over $400 billion in total saving.

With these limitations in mind, what do the data from the nineteenth and twentieth centuries show about growth in GNP, interest rates, and ratios of gross and net investment to real GNP? Table 2–2 groups the data in 20-year periods excluding the three major U.S. wars (1861–66, 1917–19, and 1941–46). The data show a pronounced decline in population growth from about 3 percent per year in the mid-1800s to 1 percent in recent years and a modest long-run decline in the growth of real GNP. There is no clear pattern, however, in the trend of the growth of real GNP per capita: The 2.3 percent per year gains for 1960–80 are exceeded only by the 3.5 percent per year for 1869–80 and the 2.6 percent for 1981–84. Most of the post-1970 gain, however, was due to increasing labor force participation rather than productivity gains per worker. From 1900 to 1940 the ratio of the total labor force to population aged 16–64 varied between 63 and 65 percent, rose to 66 percent in 1950, 68 percent in 1965, and 74 percent in 1980.

The striking feature about interest rates, measured as the interest rate on prime commercial paper (short-term notes issued by established companies), is the marked decline in the "real" interest rate over the long term, where the real rate is defined as the nominal rate

---

24. *The Wall Street Journal,* 11 Nov. 1983, p. 33.

Table 2–2. Average Annual Output Growth Rates, Interest Rates, and Investment for the United States, 1840–1984 (excluding war years 1861–66, 1917–19, and 1941–46).

	1840–1860	1867–1880	1880–1900	1900–1916	1920–1940	1940–1960	1960–1980	1981–1984
Growth in								
Real Output	4.9	5.8	3.0	3.3	2.4	3.5	3.5	3.6
Population	3.1	2.3	2.1	1.8	1.1	1.7	1.2	1.0
Output per								
Capita	1.8	3.5	0.9	1.5	1.3	1.8	2.3	2.6
Interest								
Rate	8.6	6.7	5.6	5.5	3.3	2.3	5.9	11.4
Price								
Inflation	−0.5	−2.4	−0.7	2.4	−1.6	2.5	4.7	5.8
Real Interest								
Rate	9.1	9.1	6.3	3.1	4.9	−0.2	1.2	5.6
Gross Invest.								
as % GNP	—	17.0	19.0	17.0	12.0	14.0	14.0	15.4
Net Invest.								
as % GNP	—	9.0	10.0	7.0	1.0	6.0	6.0	4.1

SOURCES: 1840 to 1980, Robert J. Barro, *Macroeconomics* (New York: John Wiley & Sons, 1984), p. 286; 1981 to 1984, *Economic Report of the President, 1985* (Washington, D.C.: Government Printing Office, 1985), pp. 237, 250, 310.

minus the change in the contemporaneous GNP price deflator since 1869. Data before 1869 use the consumer price index reported in *Historical Statistics.*[25] A long-run decline is consistent with a gradually reduced rate of time preference (as real incomes rise and human longevity increases), although the real rate remains high in the 1980s.

Gross private fixed investment, excluding inventories, shows a downward trend as a share of GNP, though it is not dramatic. Gross investment was as high as 19 percent of GNP from 1880 to 1900, and it has remained at about 15 percent in the post–World War II period. This is remarkable in view of the fact that government spends an increasing share of GNP, implying that people now save and invest a *larger* share of their after-tax incomes through personal and business saving. During the era of 19 percent gross investment, GNP growth rates per capita were only 0.9 percent per year, the lowest 20-year performance in the data.

Figure 2–1 shows the stock of private fixed capital measured in

25. Bureau of the Census, *Historical Statistics of the United States, Colonial Times to 1970* (Washington, D.C.: U.S. Government Printing Office, 1970), p. 211.

billions of constant 1972 dollars from 1925 to 1981. The stock grew during the 1920s, but declined (with only minor upturns) from 1931 to 1945, falling at an average annual rate of 1 percent from 1931 to the end of World War II. This is consistent with an expansive government consuming the nation's capital, but many economists would have a different interpretation of the data, arguing that the sick patient, the market system, simply did not respond properly to the ministrations of government during the Great Depression. The story after World War II is much different, with the stock of capital growing throughout at an annual average growth rate of 3.8 percent per year from 1945 until the end of 1981. During the post–World War II period, roughly half of total private fixed capital was in residential struc-

Figure 2–1.   Stock of Private Fixed Capital in the United States, 1925–1981.

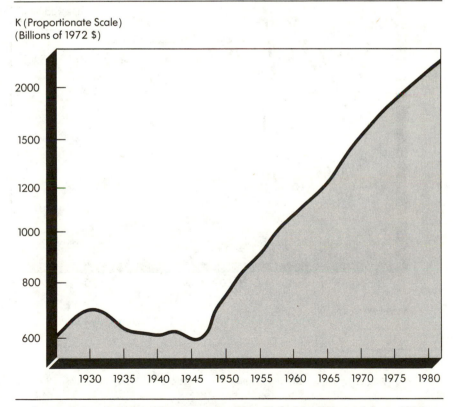

K (Proportionate Scale)
(Billions of 1972 $)

SOURCE: Robert J. Barro, *Macroeconomics* (New York: John Wiley and Sons, 1984), p. 234.

tures, about one-quarter in producer's structures, and about one-quarter in producers' durable equipment. Before World War II, about half was in residential structures, 35 percent in producers' structures, and only 15 percent in producers' equipment.

Figure 2–2 shows the behavior of gross investment, depreciation,

Figure 2–2.   Ratios of Investment and Depreciation to the Capital Stock, 1929–1982.

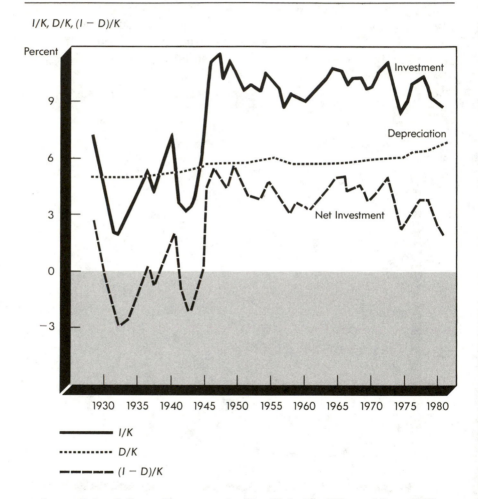

SOURCE: Robert J. Barro, *Macroeconomics* (New York: John Wiley and Sons, 1984), p. 242.

Note: The graph shows the ratios to the capital stock, K_{t-1}, of gross investment, I_t, depreciation, D_t, and net investment, $I_t - D_t$.

and net investment in the United States as a percentage of the capital stock at the end of the previous year, from 1929 to 1982. Changes in business inventories are excluded. The depreciation numbers are rough estimates that assume specified service lives for capital goods calculated on a "straight line" basis. For example, a building with a 50-year life is assumed to lose 2 percent of its initial real value each year. The ratio of measured depreciation to capital stock can change only when the average service life of capital goods shifts. The ratio of depreciation to capital stock is relatively stable, but with an upward trend. Between 1929 and 1945 the depreciation/capital stock ratio lies between 4.9 percent and 5.5 percent, rises to 5.8–6.2 percent from 1946 and 1977, and then to 7.1 percent by 1982. The movement away from structures and toward equipment accounts for the rising depreciation ratio.

Gross investment is more volatile than depreciation, as shown in Figure 2–2. During the 1930s the ratio of gross investment to capital stock averaged only 3 percent, less than the depreciation rate, resulting in an average annual loss of capital stock of 2 percent. World War II was also a period of disinvestment, consistent with government activism as a capital consumer. From 1946 to 1982 gross investment averaged more than 10 percent of the capital stock, with no strong trends. The cyclical pattern of investment is apparent, with the post-1978 decline especially clear. Given depreciation of 7.1 percent, net investment was only 1.7 percent of capital stock in 1982. This might be interpreted as "cyclical," but the late 1970s and early 1980s were so dismal that they triggered widespread concern about the long-run prospects of the U.S. economy.

Figure 2–3 shows the ratios of investment, depreciation, and net investment to GNP from 1929 to 1982. Gross investment fluctuates around 15 percent of GNP, except for the years 1930 to 1945 when investment averaged only 8.5 percent. From 1946 to 1982 the ratio of net investment to GNP averaged 5.6 percent, with the lowest ratios in recent recession years—2.7 percent in 1982, 3.3 percent in 1975, 3.6 percent in 1981, 4 percent in 1976, and 4.1 percent for 1980. The next lowest ratio of net investment to GNP since World War II was 4.3 percent in 1958.

The *Economic Report of the President, 1983* points out that the conventional investment figures understate the capital formation problem for two reasons. First, there has been a slump in growth of the *capital/labor ratio* because of the rapid growth in the labor force

Figure 2–3.   Ratios of Investment and Depreciation to GNP, 1929–1982.

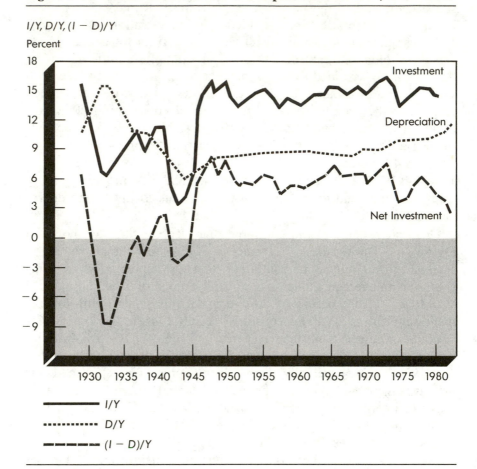

SOURCE: Robert J. Barro, *Macroeconomics* (New York: John Wiley and Sons, 1984), p. 243.

Note: The graphs show the ratios to real GNP, Y_t, of gross investment, I_t, depreciation, D_t, and net investment, $I_t - D_t$.

relative to growth of structures and equipment.[26] The amount of capital per hour of labor increased at a 3.5 percent annual rate from 1951 to 1975 but at only a 0.9 percent annual rate between 1976 and 1980. Kendrick also reports that capital per unit of labor grew by only 1.2 percent per year from 1973 to 1979, half the rate of 1948–1973.[27]

26. *Economic Report of the President, 1983*, p. 78.

27. John W. Kendrick, *Interindustry Differences in Productivity Growth* (Washington, D.C.: American Enterprise Institute, 1983), p. 14.

Second, the energy price shocks of 1973 and 1979 hastened the obsolescence of some of the capital stock, suggesting that actual depreciation may have been more rapid than official statistics indicate. One estimate placed premature obsolescence at an additional 0.5 percent of GNP per year, and another study placed it at a larger figure based on market prices of capital goods.[28] Further, a disproportionate share of new investment during the 1970s went to the energy-producing sector.

Since Robert Solow's 1957 article, most economists believe that technological change—human ingenuity in production techniques and product innovation—is the main determinant of economic growth.[29] Edward F. Denison, for example, attributes the adjusted growth rate of 2.6 percent per year in national income per employed person from 1948 to 1973 to an annual gain of 1.4 percent in advances in knowledge and "not elsewhere classified" (n.e.c.), a residual growth often called technical change.[30] Denison also assigns an annual gain of 0.5 percent to education and 0.4 percent to improved allocation of resources during the period. Changes in structures, equipment, inventories, and land are credited with only 0.4, with decreased labor hours and adverse age-sex composition of the labor force reducing growth per year by 0.4. From 1973 to 1976, Denison estimates that reductions in n.e.c. and advances in knowledge decreased the annual growth rate by 0.7. Changes in the legal and human environment decreased the annual growth rate by 0.4. These were major reasons why the annual growth rate during this period plummeted to −0.5.

Other growth-accounting models of the Denison type confirm conventional wisdom about the importance of investments, including R&D, education, training, and other factors such as changes in the composition of outputs and inputs, cyclical and scale factors, governmental regulation, changes in labor efficiency as such, and deterioration in the quality of natural resources.[31] Many of these factors are ulti-

28. *Economic Report of the President, 1983*, p. 79.

29. Robert M. Solow, "Technical Change and the Aggregate Production Function," *Review of Economics and Statistics* 39 (Aug. 1957): 312–20.

30. Edward F. Denison, *Accounting for Slower Economic Growth: The United States in the 1970s* (Washington, D.C.: The Brookings Institution, 1979).

31. John W. Kendrick, "Productivity Trends and the Recent Slowdown: Historical Perspective, Causal Factors, and Policy Options," in William Fellner, ed., *Contemporary Economic Problems, 1979* (Washington, D.C.: American Enterprise Institute, 1979); John W. Kendrick and Elliot S. Grossman, *Productivity in the United States: Trends and Cycles* (Baltimore: Johns Hopkins University Press, 1980).

mately embodied in capital goods because physical goods reflect ideas.

Few economists have investigated the link between government excesses and declining net investment, and with only modest empirical success so far. Martin Feldstein, for example, argues that from 1950 to 1979 the net savings of households, businesses, and state and local governments averaged 7.6 percent of GNP and since the federal government had deficits averaging less than 1 percent of GNP during these years, net national saving averaged 6.9 percent of GNP. After 1980, however, the net savings rate of households, businesses, and state-local governments slipped to 6.8 percent of GNP, while the federal deficit rose to 3.6 percent of GNP in fiscal 1982, 6.1 percent of GNP in fiscal 1983, and an estimated 6.0 percent in fiscal 1984, dropping net national saving to 1.5 percent of GNP in the first three quarters of 1983.[32] Much of this low, measured net investment is cyclical though, because projected spending on new plants and equipment was up a strong 9.4 percent in 1984 over 1983, the biggest one-year jump since 1977.[33]

Benjamin Friedman has found that the total volume of debt outstanding relative to GNP has remained at a remarkable ratio of $1.45 in debt for every $1.00 of GNP.[34] He argues that increases in government debt are offset by declines in household and business debt, thus displacing private capital formation.

Michael Boskin analyzed U.S. data for 1929 to 1969 and concluded that a 10 percent increase in the real after-tax rate of return on saving, other things being equal, increases net saving by 3–4 percent.[35] This is consistent with fundamental theory, because reductions in government obstacles to saving reduce the relative price of future consumption. Similarly, deregulation of the financial industry increases savings by raising the effective return to all savers, especially

32. Martin Feldstein, "Why the Dollar Is Strong," *Challenge* (Jan./Feb. 1984), p. 40. See also Feldstein's *Capital Taxation* (Cambridge: Harvard University Press, 1983).

33. *The Wall Street Journal*, 13 Jan. 1984, p. 3.

34. Benjamin M. Friedman, "Debt and Economic Activity in the United States," in Benjamin M. Friedman, ed., *The Changing Roles of Debt and Equity in Financing U.S. Capital Formation* (Chicago: University of Chicago Press, 1982), pp. 91–110; and "Debt Markets, Government Deficits, and Private Capital Formation," *NBER Reporter* (Fall 1983), pp. 6–8.

35. Michael J. Boskin, "Taxation, Saving, and the Rate of Interest," *Journal of Political Economy* 86 (April 1978, part 2): S3–S27; see also Boskin, "Some Issues in 'Supply-Side' Economics," in Karl Brunner and Allan Meltzer, eds., *Supply Shocks, Incentives and National Wealth* (Amsterdam: North-Holland, 1981), pp. 201–20.

small savers. An outpouring of recent work has estimated interest elasticities of savings as high at 2.5., though the empirical issue is disputed.[36]

Danziger, Haveman, and Plotnick reviewed work on the impact of government spending and redistribution, and they summarized their findings with the claim that transfer programs decrease savings by 0 to 20 percent.[37] The biggest imponderable is the impact of the Social Security program, now transferring 6 percent of GNP. Economists have become bogged down in a controversy—based on what is commonly called the Ricardian equivalence theorem—over the program's effects on capital formation. Ricardo argued that whether government financed its spending by borrowing or taxation, the present value of the tax liability would be identical and therefore the method of financing would make no difference on taxpayers' behavior. Only the present value of the tax liability would matter. Social Security is a form of debt finance because government taxes wage earners on a pay-as-you-go basis, which, in practice, is identical to servicing debt. Whether Social Security seriously harms capital formation depends partly on whether people see through the disincentives of Social Security on capital formation and therefore save more to offset the undesired consequences of Social Security on future generations; the division among economists is over whether people completely or only partially offset the capital-consuming impact of Social Security.

That the slowdown in capital formation played a role in the poor economic growth since 1973 is a noncontroversial statement among economists.[38] The controversy involves the exact role that government taxation, inflation, redistributive spending, and regulation have played in the stagnation, and forms the heart of the current research agenda.[39]

36. Robert E. Keleher, "Supply-Side Tax Policy: Reviewing the Evidence," in Bruce Bartlett and Timothy P. Roth, eds., *The Supply-Side Solution*, (Chatham, N.J.: Chatham House, 1983); for mixed evidence see Gerald A. Carlino, "Interest Rate Effects and Intertemporal Consumption," *Journal of Monetary Economics* 9 (March 1982): 223–34.

37. Sheldon Danziger, Robert Haveman, and Robert Plotnick, "How Income Transfers Affect Work, Savings and the Income Distribution," *Journal of Economic Literature* 19 (Sept. 1981): 1019.

38. J. R. Norsworthy, Michael J. Harper, and Kent Kunze, "The Slowdown in Productivity Growth: Analysis of Some Contributing Factors," *Brookings Papers on Economic Activity*, No. 2 (1979); reprinted in the *BLS Reader on Productivity*, Bulletin 2171 (Washington, D.C.: U.S. Government Printing Office, 1983).

39. Simulation methods are used in Martin Feldstein, ed., *Behavioral Simulation Methods in Tax Policy Analysis* (Chicago, University of Chicago Press and NBER, 1983).

Interstate Evidence

While most studies have concentrated on aggregate U.S. or international data to assess the effects of taxation on capital accumulation, a few have studied the effects of state governments on growth. Warren T. Brookes has been especially diligent in assembling evidence about the revival of growth in Massachusetts.[40] Between 1970 and 1978 the total tax burden in Massachusetts rose from less than 13 percent of income to 17.6 percent, from 3 percent less than the national average among the states to 11 percent above it, from twenty-second to the fifth highest taxing state in the nation. The primary reason for the fastest rise in a state's tax-burden was a 137 percent increase in real dollars of welfare costs, lifting the state to number one in that category. Exactly as supply-side economists would predict, the result of such disincentives in "Taxachusetts" was a corresponding decrease in the state's growth of output and personal income: Per capita pretax income fell from 10 percent above the nation's to 3 percent above in the eight years, and from one of the fastest growing incomes in the country to forty-seventh in 1977. The unemployment rate moved from 1–2 points below the national figure in 1965–72 and rose to 2–3 points above it during the middle 1970s.

Riding the winds of California's Proposition 13, the Massachusetts legislature passed a $340 million property-tax-relief program for fiscal 1979; the state's voters replaced free-spending Governor Michael Dukakis with conservative Edward J. King, who enacted a 4% spending cap in fiscal 1980; and voters overwhelmingly approved the Proposition 2 property-tax-limitation. Between 1979 and 1982 the state's tax burden dropped a full 3 percentage points, from 17.5 percent to 14.5 percent of total income, taking Massachusetts from fifth highest to below the national average for the first time in a decade. Personal income rose from 3 percent above the nation in 1979 to 8 percent above in 1982—the most dramatic upsurge in history for any state. The unemployment rate fell to the second lowest of the major industrial states. This turnaround was not performed with massive infusions of physical capital (its share actually continued to decline) but with the vigor of a high-growth, low-capital, high-technology economy.

40. Warren T. Brookes, *The Economy in Mind* (New York: Universe Books, 1982), pp. 180–202.

Knowledge, innovation, and human capital were the driving force of the expansion.

Brookes cites other studies showing the dramatic correlation between tax rates and economic progress. Perhaps the best known is the work of Colin and Rosemary Campbell comparing Vermont and New Hampshire.[41] While Vermont was the third most heavily taxed state in the nation, taking 19.2 percent of personal income, New Hampshire was forty-seventh, taking 13.4 percent. The Campbells could detect no measurable differences in the quality of public services. All measures of economic growth show New Hampshire far ahead of Vermont and Massachusetts. Other studies by David Wendell[42] and Robert Genetski[43] show that there is almost a perfect inverse correlation between the tax-burden growth and economic growth among the states. Ronald Grieson found that employment in Philadelphia and New York is sensitive to city taxation.[44] Specifically, he found that a 30 percent increase in the Philadelphia income tax rate reduced manufacturing employment by 11 percent and nonmanufacturing employment by 12–14 percent.

For the last two decades the South and Southwest have been the fastest growing regions in the United States, a major shift in the location of economic activity. Most of the early literature on industrial location found little evidence that tax differentials affected location decisions. Robert Newman, however, found that employment growth among the states was strongly related to corporate income tax rates, degrees of unionization of the labor force, and the presence of "pro-business" right-to-work (RTW) laws.[45] Newman's regression analysis showed that relatively capital-intensive firms were especially sensitive to changes in corporate tax differentials compared to labor-intensive firms, while capital-intensive firms were not as sensitive to interstate differentials in unionization as were labor-intensive industries. Tax rate differentials and RTW laws not only affected movement to the South, but also influenced movement within the South. The RTW

41. Cited in ibid., pp. 188–89.
42. Ibid., p. 187.
43. Ibid., p. 195.
44. Ronald E. Grieson, "Theoretical Analysis and Empirical Measurements of the Effects of the Philadelphia Income Tax," in Bruce Bartlett and Timothy P. Roth, eds., *The Supply-Side Solution* (Chatham, N.J.: Chatham House, 1983).
45. Robert J. Newman, "Industry Migration Growth in the South," *Review of Economics and Statistics* 65 (Feb. 1983): 76–86.

variable "carried its own weight" in both South and non-South regressions, and therefore the widely held notion that RTW laws are a uniquely southern phenomenon was rejected by the data. Newman found that the data supported the conventional assumption in regional science that external market forces cause an industry to grow at a common national rate in all states. Consequently, geographic shifts in economic activity are very sensitive to differentials in state tax and regulatory policies, as supply-siders and advocates of enterprise zones implicitly argue.

Interindustry Evidence

Although the evidence is sparse, cross-sectional analysis by industry tends to support the time series and geographical evidence. Between 1948 and 1979 output per unit of labor grew at an annual average rate of 2.5 percent and capital per unit of labor grew by 2.1 percent per year, according to Kendrick. Between 1973 and 1979, however, growth of output per unit of labor fell to 0.3 percent in the private sector at the same time that growth in capital per unit of labor fell to 1.2 percent per year.[46] Across industries, the rate of productivity growth is highly associated with the rate of growth of capital goods. Between 1973 and 1979, for example, the simple correlation between growth in capital per unit of labor and growth in output per unit of labor was 0.62 among industries.

During the 1970s two of the industries that performed most poorly in terms of productivity were mining and construction. Between 1973 and 1979 productivity in mining declined at an average annual rate of 5.2 percent while capital in the industry declined at an average rate of 3 percent per year. Some of the productivity decline can be attributed to a decline in the quality of active mines and some to strikes in bituminous coal, but health, safety, and environment regulations were also involved. Among the measures reducing output per miner-day were the 1969 Coal Mine Health and Safety Act, state reclamation laws, and the Federal Surface Mine Control and Reclamation Act of 1977.[47] The productivity declines in contract construction after

46. John W. Kendrick, *Interindustry Differences in Productivity Growth* (Washington, D.C.: American Enterprise Institute, 1983), pp. 12–15.

47. Rose N. Zeisel, "Productivity Challenge in Bituminous Coal Industry, 1950–79," *A BLS Reader on Productivity*, Bulletin 2171 (Washington, D.C.: U.S. Government Printing Office, 1983), pp. 56–57.

1966 reflected the vulnerability of the industry to the erratic and inflationary monetary policies that government visited on the private sector.

A series of in-depth studies is required to trace the specific impacts of government regulation and taxation on industries. Kendrick's interindustry regressions generally support macroeconomic growth accounting with respect to importance of the growth of capital per worker, research and development, education, economies of scale, and labor adjustment variables, but much more can be done.[48] We already know that hobbling an industry through union wages, strikes, work rules, taxation, and regulation imposes new costs and obstacles to success—just as common sense would suggest—but our empirical knowledge is meager at the industry level.

International Evidence

The common way to impress Americans with the urgency of the capital formation "problem" has been with post–World War II data comparing the United States with other major industrial nations. Figure 2–4 shows the positive association between shares of GNP devoted to gross investment and gains in labor productivity. Figure 2–5 shows the growth in output per labor hour in manufacturing in selected countries since 1950.

All is not gloom and doom in the relative U.S. performance, however. Figure 2–6 shows the convergence of output per person across countries between 1950 and 1979. Figure 2–7 shows the convergence in gross domestic product per employed person between 1960 and 1981 in a way that shows the flattening out in the other countries' convergence on the U.S. standard of living. Figure 2–8 shows the convergence in average growth rates of output per capita during the 1970s, a process that has continued into the 1980s. Herbert Stein put it dramatically in a *Fortune* magazine review: "Between 1960 and 1979 Japanese real per capita output rose from 31.5 percent of ours to 70.2 percent of ours. But the rate of gain on us fell sharply. If it continues to fall at the same pace, Japan's real per capita GNP would still be only 74 percent of ours in 2083."[49] Another instance of convergence is the gradual reduction in the average age of the capital

48. John W. Kendrick, *n.* 46, p. 54.
49. Cited by Melvyn Krauss, *The American Spectator*, September 1983, p. 17.

Figure 2–4.   Percentage Changes in Labor Productivity Versus Investment as a Percentage of GNP, 1963–1979.

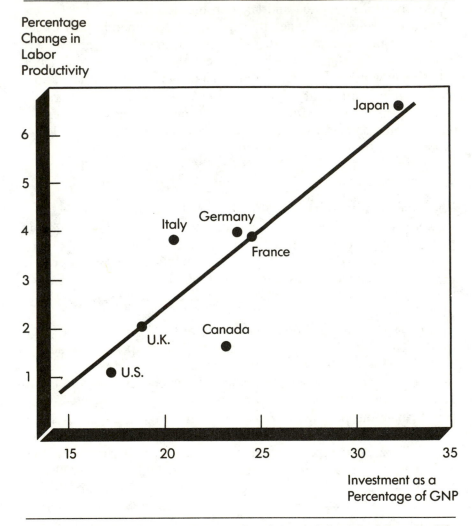

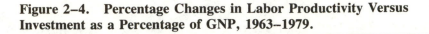

SOURCE: Robert M. Dunn, Jr., *Economic Growth Among Industrialized Countries: Why the United States Lags* (Washington, D.C.: National Planning Association, 1980), p. 15. Data sources: OECD and IMF.

Note: The following regression was used: percentage change in productivity = −4.0285 + 0.32397 (*I/GNP*); standard deviations of 1.78697 and 0.076735, respectively, and R^2 = 0.78.

Figure 2–5.   Output per Employee Hour in Manufacturing, Selected Countries, 1950–1983

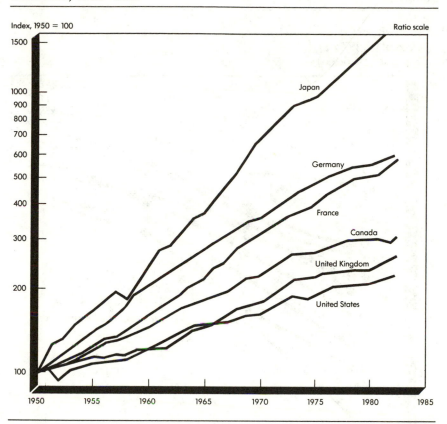

SOURCE: Bureau of Labor Statistics, Bulletin 2219, April 1985, p. 25.

stock in the United States and the gradual rise in Japan, shown in Figure 2–9.

The best explanation for these patterns is that the industrialized countries started with major differences in the amounts of capital goods and output per person at the end of World War II. The countries that began with low capital per person grew faster and invested larger fractions of their output. Output per capita converged over time, but there is a tendency for growth rates of output to fall over time, especially in countries that began with high growth rates.[50]

50. Irving Kravis, Alan Heston, and Robert Summers, *World Product and Income, International Comparisons of Real Gross Product* (Baltimore: Johns Hopkins University Press, 1982).

Figure 2–6.   Levels of Output per Capita for Nine Industrialized Countries.

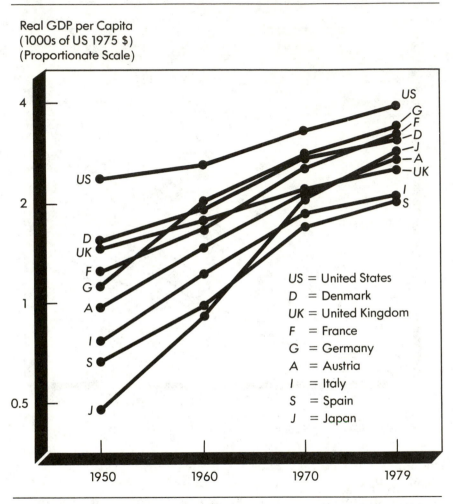

Real GDP per Capita
(1000s of US 1975 $)
(Proportionate Scale)

US = United States
D = Denmark
UK = United Kingdom
F = France
G = Germany
A = Austria
I = Italy
S = Spain
J = Japan

SOURCE: Robert J. Barro, *Macroeconomics* (New York: John Wiley and Sons, 1984), p. 291.

What role does government play in accounting for discrepancies in growth rates and investment across countries? Katsuro Sakoh, director of international trade policy at the Council for Competitive Economy, has most of the answer:

The Japanese government contributed to the enormous economic success of Japan . . . based not on how much it did for the economy, but on

Figure 2–7.   Relative Levels in Real Gross Domestic Product per Employed Person, Selected Countries and Years, 1960–1981.

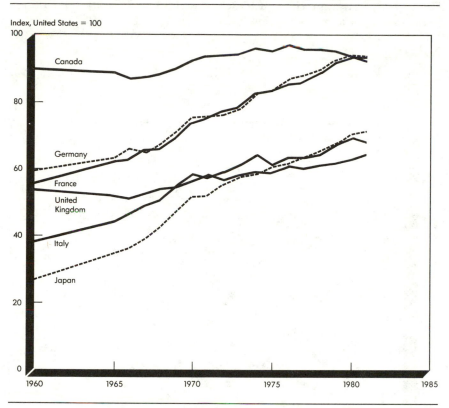

Index, United States = 100

SOURCE: Bureau of Labor Statistics, Bulletin 2712, June 1983, p. 23.

how much it restrained itself from doing. Its interference in the economy was only sporadic and slight, including efforts aimed at industrial development.

But the Japanese government helped provide an economic environment for private enterprise by maintaining a small and balanced budget, fairly low and stable interest rates, relatively low rates of taxation, stable prices, brief expenditures, and very few government-owned enterprises. Moreover, by maintaining the political stability necessary to promote private investment, the government contributed even further to a great increase in the growth of the economy.[51]

51. Katsuro Sakoh, "The Secret of Japan's Success," *Policy Report* 5 (Dec. 1983): 9.

Figure 2–8.   Average Growth Rates of Output per Capita for Nine Industrialized Countries During Three Decades—1950–1980.

Growth Rate
of Real GDP
Per Capita
(% per Year)

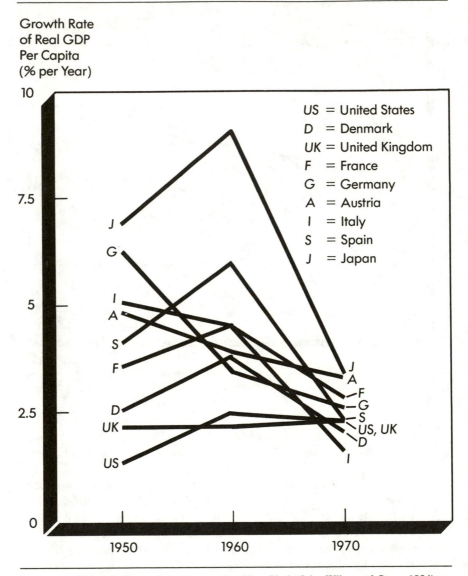

US = United States
D = Denmark
UK = United Kingdom
F = France
G = Germany
A = Austria
I = Italy
S = Spain
J = Japan

SOURCE: Robert J. Barro, *Macroeconomics* (New York: John Wiley and Sons, 1984), p. 292.

Figure 2–9.   Average Age of Capital Stock, United States and Japan, 1960–1978.

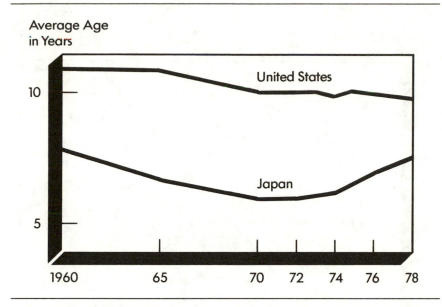

SOURCE: Ryuzo Sato and Gilbert S. Suzawa, *Research and Productivity* (Boston: Auburn House, 1983), p. 152.

This thesis is supported by many economists, though the argument is not universally accepted (few social propositions are).[52] Figure 2–10 lends statistical support to the hypothesis that expansive government reduces growth rates. The vertical axis plots the percentage decline in annual growth rates of gross domestic product during the 1970s compared with the 1960s, and the horizontal axis plots the percentage point increase between 1967 and 1980 in the ratio of government spending to GDP. The bigger the rise in government spending relative to GDP, the larger the reduction in economic growth. Japan and Sweden had the largest gains in government spending to GDP and experienced the largest declines in annual growth rates. The United States had the smallest increase in government spending relative to GDP gain, and suffered the smallest decline in economic growth. While this association does not "prove" that expanding government causes

52. See, for example, Chalmers Johnson, ed., *The Industrial Policy Debate* (San Francisco: Institute for Contemporary Studies, 1984) or Arnold C. Harberger, ed., *World Economic Growth* (San Francisco: Institute for Contemporary Studies, 1984).

82   *TAXATION AND THE DEFICIT ECONOMY*

Figure 2–10.   Percentage Declines in Annual GDP Growth Rates Versus Increases in Government Spending as a Share of GDP.

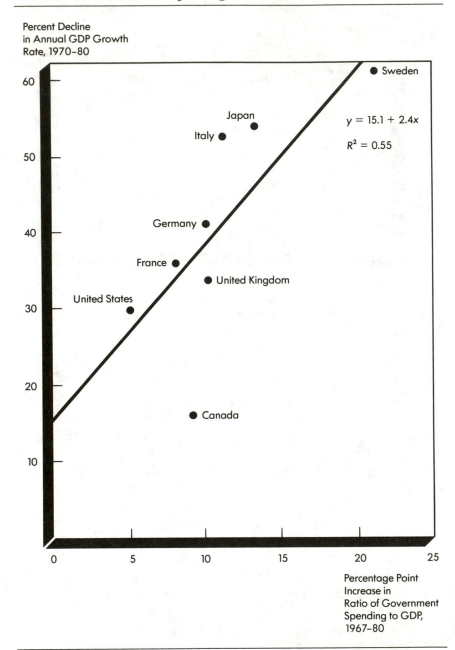

SOURCE: Data calculated from World Bank, *World Development Report*, 1982, and United Nations, *Supplement to World Economic Survey*, 1983.

declines in growth rate, the evidence offers no support for the idea that government spending "stimulates" higher growth rates.

A recent study of 104 countries for the years 1961–1976 found that government spending had a strong, negative impact on the growth rate of per capita gross domestic product. The negative relationship was shown to exist for the full sample of countries. It also was shown to exist within groups of countries with similar levels of development, whether weighted or unweighted by population, and excluding or including major oil exporters.[53]

During the period of rapidly growing government spending (mostly for transfer programs), gross private savings as a share of GDP have remained remarkably flat. In 1982, for example, the United States saved 18 percent of GDP, as conventionally measured, identical to the 18 percent of 1967; the United Kingdom saved 16 percent, up from 14 percent in 1967; Japan saved 27 percent, down from 29 percent in 1967; Germany saved 21 percent, the same as in 1967; and France saved 19 percent, down from 22 percent in 1967.[54] There is a modest suggestion, however, that the countries with the largest increases in personal transfer payments relative to GDP—Sweden, France, and Japan—experienced decreases in their private savings rates. Few detailed studies yet exist on the problem, and what exists is immersed in the confusion over the effects of social security.

Policy makers in other countries have been aware that savings and investment respond to changes in the real after-tax rate of return. This recognition, which was enhanced by the tendency of high inflation rates to reduce the real rate of return on financial assets, prompted changes in tax rules in some countries. Tax treatments affect not only aggregate savings but the allocation among investments. Differences in investment credits, tax deductions, and depreciation allowances differ across sectors and lead to capital misallocation, adversely affecting long-term growth. The classic example is the misallocation between the corporate and noncorporate sectors,[55] but King contends that there is no clear pattern in the effective average tax rates on savings and investment among countries.[56]

53. Daniel Landau, "Government Expenditure and Economic Growth: A Cross-Country Study," *Southern Economic Journal* 49 (Jan. 1983): 783–92.

54. United Nations, Department of International Economic and Social Affairs, *Supplement to World Economic Survey, 1983* (New York: United Nations, 1983), p. 26.

55. Martin Feldstein, "The Welfare Cost of Capital Income Taxation," *Journal of Political Economy* 86 (April 1978): S29–S51.

56. Mervyn A. King, "The Taxation of Income from Capital," *NBER Reporter*, Fall 1983, pp. 8–11.

There is enormous variance in tax rates within each country. Some returns are highly subsidized and others taxed at high rates. Among King's specific findings, the lowest tax rate on investment in the corporate sector is in the United Kingdom, with a rate close to zero; and the tax rate in the United States (37.2) has been slightly lower than in West Germany (46.1). Nakamura found that because of double taxation of income earned by corporate enterprises and the favorable taxation of owner-occupied housing, the productivity loss to the United States was more than 1 percent of GNP in 1976–77, while West Germany and Japan had negligible losses.[57]

CONCLUSION

As a result of dissatisfaction with the productivity and investment experience of the 1970s, an increased rate of capital formation became an important objective of U.S. policy in the 1980s. While there is theoretical and empirical support for this concern, economists know far less than most policy proponents would have the general public believe. Despite our knowledge of capital theory, economic growth, and the impact of taxation, we cannot say much more on the issue than common sense suggests.

The data fail to support alarmist conclusions about the American economy. By historical standards, total savings and investment held up remarkably well during the 1970s and early 1980s, especially given the growth of government. Many of the allegations about the laggard performance of the U.S. economy relative to other industrial countries have been true, but the convergence of other countries on the U.S. standard of living has tapered off, and the remaining gap seems unlikely to close in the near future.

Gross capital formation has not plummeted in the United States, despite plenty of government provocation. *Net* capital formation has fared less well, largely because of the rising depreciation share of GDP, but the unreliability of depreciation statistics makes it difficult to judge if something serious is going on or not. Alarmists emphasize the low rate of personal savings in the United States, but the numbers are questionable. *Total* savings count, not how much households save in personal savings versus through their business firms. Unmeasured

---

57. T. Nakamura, "Productivity Losses through Capital Misallocation in the U.S.A., Japan and West Germany," *Quarterly Review of Economics and Business* 21 (Autumn 1981)· 65–76.

factors like human investment, innovation, research and development spending, and other intangibles further complicate the question.

As a corollary, evidence concerning the potency of government obstacles to saving, investment, and productivity growth is less satisfactory than we might wish, despite theoretical confidence that government interventions reduce total investment and obstruct its allocation to activities where returns are the highest. Perhaps the interstate evidence most clearly shows that governmental policies affect investment. International and longitudinal data lend themselves to more controversy, although they also support the proposition that taxation reduces capital formation.

In terms of economic policy, the popular emphasis on government manipulation of the rate of capital formation seems misplaced on both pragmatic and normative grounds. Consumption taxation, for example, taxes both current and *future* consumption and therefore fails to make saving especially attractive *unless* the tax displaces a *less neutral* tax. If government would reduce its toll on private economic activity and substitute more neutral forms of exactions, there would be little for government decision-makers to "remedy" about savings, investment, and growth.

3

TAXATION, RELATIVE PRICES, AND CAPITAL FORMATION

Paul Craig Roberts

While the concept of relative prices is a foundation of microeconomic theory, it has been ignored by Keynesian macroeconomic policy.[1] As a result, capital formation has suffered. Capital formation requires that real resources be saved from current consumption and employed in investment. In the case of human capital, time is a resource that must be diverted from leisure and invested in improving skills. These decisions, which determine the rate of capital formation, are influenced by relative prices.

To begin with, consider the relative price that determines the allocation of income between consumption and saving. The cost to the individual of allocating a unit of income to current consumption is the future income stream given up by not saving and investing that unit of income. The value of that income stream is influenced by marginal tax rates. The higher the tax rate, the less the value of the income stream. High tax rates make consumption cheap in terms of forgone income; thus saving declines, and, with it, investment.

Consider a husband facing a 95 percent marginal tax rate on in-

Note: I would like to thank Peter Barlerin, my research assistant, for his help in preparing this chapter.

1. See Paul Craig Roberts, "The Breakdown of the Keynesian Model," *Public Interest* 52 (Summer 1978):20–23.

vestment income. He has, for example, the choice of investing $20,000 at 10 percent or buying his wife a diamond necklace. On a pretax basis the cost of giving his wife the necklace is to forgo an income stream of $2,000 a year—not an insignificant sum. After tax, however, the value of the additional income stream is only $100 a year (the 5 percent of $2,000 remaining after taxes). His tax bracket reduced the cost of the necklace to one-twentieth of its pretax cost.

While this may seem like an unrealistically high tax rate, until just a few years ago the top marginal income tax rate on investment income in Great Britain was 98 percent. This explains why there are so many Rolls Royces and other fine automobiles on the streets of London. The Rolls Royces have been mistaken as signs that the rich are prospering, when in fact they are warning signals that the tax rate on investment income is excessive. The effect was to reduce to almost zero the price of current consumption in terms of forgone income. As inflation and real economic growth pushed taxpayers into higher tax brackets, consumption became relatively cheaper—and saving more expensive—for large numbers of people.

The other important relative price governs people's decisions about how they allocate their time between work and leisure, or between leisure and improving their human capital by upgrading skills. The cost to the individual of allocating an additional hour to leisure is the current earnings sacrificed by not working (for example, overtime on Saturdays) or the future income given up by not improving human capital. The value of the forgone income is determined by the rate at which additional income is taxed. The higher the marginal tax rates, the cheaper the price of leisure. Work attitudes deteriorate, absenteeism rates go up, people are unwilling to accept overtime work, and they devote less effort to improving work skills. In other words, labor supply declines. With less labor to work with, the marginal productivity of capital falls. This reduces capital formation, and economic growth stalls.

High marginal tax rates shrink the tax base because they discourage people from earning additional taxable income. Professionals who reach the 50 percent tax bracket early in the tax year are faced with working the additional months of the year for only half of their pretax earnings. Such a low reward for effort encourages professionals to share practices in order to reduce their working hours and enjoy longer vacations. A tax rate reduction would raise the relative price of leisure to professionals and would give them the incentive to earn more taxable income and increase the supply of professional services.

The effect of tax rates on the decision to earn additional taxable income is not limited to professionals in the top bracket. Carpenters and bricklayers prefer some of their earnings to be paid "off the books" in order to avoid declaring the portion of their income that falls into their highest marginal tax bracket.

An alternative to taxable income is to use labor services to produce nontaxable household services. Consider a carpenter earning $100 a day whose take-home pay is $75. Suppose that his house needs painting and that he can hire a painter for $80 a day. Since the carpenter's take-home pay is only $75, he saves $5 by painting his own house. In this case the tax rate shrinks by $180—$100 that the carpenter chooses not to earn and $80 that he does not pay the painter. The higher the marginal tax rates, the more likely it is that people can increase their income by using their resources in nonmarket activities or in the underground economy.

The progressive income tax is perverse because it mismatches effort and reward. Each additional effort comes on top of existing effort, so the disutility to the individual of additional effort is high. But since the income from the additional effort goes on top of existing income, it is taxed at higher rates. As efforts rise, rewards fall. The tax system is not only perverse but self-defeating. By raising the price of activities that would otherwise expand the tax base, progressive tax rates reduce the tax base and frustrate the goal of raising revenues.

TAX BIAS AGAINST SAVING

Capital formation is subject to additional burdens when saving is taxed twice—once when it is earned and again when it yields an income stream. If there is no deduction either for the initial saving or for the income stream generated by the saving, the portion of income saved is taxed at a higher effective rate than is the portion of income used for current consumption.[2] The income tax bias against saving is illustrated in the following example. In the absence of taxes, the individual who earns an additional $1,000 must decide whether he wants to consume it now or save it at, for example, a 10 percent interest rate. The cost of current consumption in terms of forgone income is $100 a year. Now assume that the same individual is in a 50 percent

2. See Norman Ture, "Supply-Side Analysis and Public Policy," in David G. Raboy, ed., *Supply-Side Economics* (Washington, D.C.: Institute for Research on the Economics of Taxation, 1982); and Jack Kemp, "The Tax Bias Against Savings Shrinks Everyone's Pie," *Washington Star*, 21 Sept. 1975.

marginal income tax bracket; thus for every additional $1,000 he earns he is allowed to keep $500.

If the income stream from saving were not taxed, he would be faced with the same relative price: The cost of $500 in current consumption is a forgone income of $50 annually. But since the income from saving is also taxed, the cost of consumption in terms of forgone income drops by half to only $25 annually. For an individual in the 50 percent marginal income tax bracket, the inclusion of saving in the tax base cuts the relative price of current consumption in half.

Unless taxes are indexed to reflect changes in the cost of living, the disincentives in the progressive tax system are aggravated by inflation, which pushes people into higher marginal income tax brackets even though their real pretax income does not change. "Bracket creep" served as an undebated and hence ideal tax increase from the standpoint of big spenders in the government, but its effects have been devastating to the economy. In 1965 a median income family of four faced a 17 percent marginal income tax rate on personal income. By 1981, the rate had jumped to 24 percent—a 41 percent increase in the tax rate on additions to the family's income. If Social Security taxes and state income taxes are included, the median income family today is in the 40 percent marginal income tax bracket, or higher. A family with twice the median income saw its federal marginal tax rate nearly double, rising from 22 percent in 1965 to 43 percent in 1981. The steep increases in marginal tax rates hurt saving particularly, because income from saving and investment is added to wage and salary income and is automatically taxed at the taxpayer's top rate.

Tax law has interacted with inflation to erode saving in other ways as well. Inflation favors borrowers at the expense of lenders. A person who borrows $1,000 for one year at 10 percent pays back $1,100 next year. If the inflation rate is also 10 percent, the $1,100 paid back purchases no more merchandise than did the $1,000 the year before, so the real, or inflation-adjusted, interest rate is zero. It would seem like a reasonable goal for tax policy to offset the unfair advantage inflation presents to borrowers, but in fact tax policy has often worked in the opposite direction to reinforce the advantage of the borrowers.

Borrowing costs are lowered by the interest deduction, which rises with the marginal tax rate. As the marginal tax rate increases, the price of saving increases while the price of borrowing falls. An interest deduction for a 50 percent marginal tax bracket, for example, cuts the after-tax interest rate in half. When combined with inflation, interest deductibility frequently produces negative real after-tax interest rates—a form of reverse usury. The government has offered many carrots to borrowers, reserving the stick for savers. Government-imposed ceilings on interest rates, such as Regulation Q, forced a negative interest rate on savers when the inflation rate rose above the fixed interest rate. Many people found that the only way they could "save" at all was to go into debt. The many disincentives to save that have afflicted the economy, such as the double taxation of saving, bracket creep, interest deductibility, and interest rate ceilings, came on top of the bias against saving imposed by high marginal tax rates.

HOW TAXATION CROWDS OUT INVESTMENT

As the price of saving increased rapidly relative to consumption and borrowing, it is not surprising that the personal saving rate averaged only 6.1 percent between 1976 and 1980—one of the worst five-year periods in the postwar era and substantially below the 7.8 percent average rate from 1966 to 1975. The decline in the saving rate reduced funds available to the capital markets by $130 billion during 1976–80—a sum equal to half of the cumulative budget deficits for the period.

Business saving and investment fared equally poorly. Depreciation laws did not permit business to write off capital investments rapidly enough to recover replacement costs for worn-out plant and equipment. A large portion of business saving that should have gone toward the replacement of plant and equipment was instead taxed away by the government. In the nonfinancial corporate sector, the replacement values of inventories and fixed assets were understated by $262 billion during 1976–80—a sum equal to the cumulative budget deficits for the period. Note that the total preemption of private sector saving by the tax system was 50 percent greater than the preemption of private saving by the federal deficit.

Understating depreciation overstated corporate profits, thus raising the effective corporate tax rate above the statutory rate. When book depreciation allowances are adjusted to a replacement cost basis, corporate profits were taxed at a higher rate than the statutory rate for more than a decade, averaging 56 percent in the 1970s and reaching 77 percent in 1974 (see Table 3–1).

As in the case of individuals, the tax system encouraged businesses

Table 3–1.   Effective Corporate Tax Rates.

Year	%	Year	%
1960	54.1	1971	53.6
1961	53.4	1972	50.4
1962	47.0	1973	55.9
1963	46.2	1974	76.8
1964	43.4	1975	53.9
1965	42.0	1976	53.6
1966	43.3	1977	49.7
1967	43.3	1978	50.9
1968	49.3	1979	56.4
1969	53.8	1980	58.6
1970	58.4		

Note: The effective corporate tax rate is equal to nonfinancial corporate profits tax liabilities as a percentage of corporate profits. (Inventory valuation adjustments and depreciation of fixed assets were adjusted to replacement costs using a double-declining-balance method over 75 percent of Bulletin F service lives.)

to accumulate debt instead of equity. Because payments to equity are made from taxable income whereas debt service costs are tax deductible, businesses joined individuals in becoming "debt junkies."

When the term "crowding out" is used by conservative Republicans, it is intended to convey the image of private investment being pushed out of financial markets by Treasury borrowing forcing up interest rates. But government also crowds out by taxation. As noted above, during the Carter administration, the tax system crowded out private saving by an amount substantially greater than the budget deficit.[3] From an investor's standpoint, interest costs are deductible, but tax rates are not. A 50 percent tax rate doubles the rate of return necessary for an investment to pay out. If an investor in a 50 percent marginal tax bracket requires a 10 percent return, he will only undertake new projects that yield, before tax, a 20 percent return or higher. All investment projects that fall between the 10 and 20 percent rate of return are effectively crowded out by taxation.

The adverse change in relative prices, which made current consumption and leisure cheaper in terms of forgone income, followed from a demand management policy that saw taxation as a tool to raise

3. A March 1984 U.S. Treasury Department study, "The Effects of Deficits on Prices of Financial Assets: Theory and Evidence," suggests that, in general, taxes crowd out investment more effectively than do budget deficits.

or lower the level of aggregate demand or spending in the economy. In this view marginal tax rates do not carry any significance. They can be as high as egalitarians and politicians demand, as long as government spends the money. The effects of tax policy on the relative prices that influence capital formation were simply ignored.

The theory behind the Keynesian economic model is best reflected in the two alternative prescriptions for expansion—tax cuts or increases in government spending. Tax cuts are seen to have less impact or "bang for the buck" because people save a portion of their tax cuts while the government could be counted on to spend the full amount. Keynesians believe that demand creates its own supply and that if there is an adequate level of aggregate demand in the economy, supply moves to meet it. With a tax policy that concentrated on average tax rates and ignored the marginal rates, no notice was taken of the rising disincentive to produce. Consequently, demand pressures increasingly resulted in increases in prices instead of real output.

The Keynesians believed that too much saving in the economy was more of a danger than too little.[4] The Keynesian bias against saving led to declines in saving rates, capital formation, and productivity growth and to a deteriorating economic performance. The Keynesian Phillips curve postulated an inverse relationship between inflation and unemployment—if society wants less inflation it has to put up with more unemployment. Over time the Phillips curve began to change its slope so that eventually there arose a direct relationship—more inflation meant more unemployment and vice versa. The year 1979 capped a four-year period of expansion, but the unemployment rate in that year was nearly one full percentage point higher than the recession year of 1970. From 1979's inflation rate of 13.3 percent, one could not help but look back wistfully to 1970, when the inflation rate of 5.9 percent was regarded as so "intolerable" that the Congress passed legislation enabling the President to impose wage and price controls.

Neglect of the supply side of the economy caused productivity growth to decline. Starting in the late 1960s, the rate of growth of labor productivity fell off sharply. The annual growth of output per worker averaged 3.1 percent for the two decades 1948–68 but declined to 2.1 percent between 1968 and 1973. From 1973 to 1980, productivity

4. See, for example, Congressional Budget Office, *Closing the Fiscal Policy Loop: A Long-Run Analysis* (Washington, D.C.: U.S. Government Printing Office, 1977).

growth in the private business sector averaged only 0.6 percent per year—one-fifth of the rate over the 1948–68 period. Productivity actually declined in 1979 and 1980, when cyclical developments combined with a declining trend in productivity growth.

The rate of growth in the capital-labor ratio and the real net capital stock similarly declined. The capital/labor ratio is the amount of capital available to each worker in the labor force. The more capital a worker has access to, the higher the marginal productivity of his labor.

Between the years 1948 and 1968 the capital-labor ratio grew at an average annual rate of 3.2 percent. From 1968 to 1973 it slowed to 1.7 percent, and from 1973 to 1980 it grew, on average, only 0.7 percent a year. The standard explanation for the decline in the capital/labor ratio is a rapidly growing labor force due to the coming of age of the baby-boom generation and the influx of women and immigrants as job-seekers.

The growth of the work force may serve as a partial explanation, but it masks a slowdown in the rate of capital formation. The slowdown in the growth of capital formation occurred even though the ratio of gross business investment to GNP has been increasing over the years. The measure of gross investment is misleading, because an increasing share consists of capital replacement. The composition of capital spending has shifted over the years to shorter-lived assets, which depreciate at a faster rate.

The gross investment measure also reflects a larger volume of capital being depreciated. The share of *net* investment has trended downward, and a portion of that net investment has been directed toward meeting federally mandated regulations and environmental standards. Annual growth of the net capital stock averaged only 3.3 percent over the 1973–80 period, one percentage point less than earlier in the postwar period.

Many people blame the Arab oil embargo in 1973 and the subsequent energy price increases as the major cause of our productivity slide, but this fails to explain why our leading trading partners, almost all of whom are more dependent on energy imports than is the United States, outperformed us in productivity growth.

International productivity data for the manufacturing sectors prepared by the U.S. Department of Labor show a 1.7 percent rate of growth for the United States between 1973 and 1982 compared with 7.2 percent for Japan, 4.5 percent for France, 3.6 percent for the Federal Republic of Germany, 3.7 percent for Italy, and 1.8 percent for the United Kingdom. Only Canada, with a 1.6 percent growth rate, lagged behind the United States.

KENNEDY TAX CUTS AND SUPPLY-SIDE GROWTH

Theory provides a clear link between the relative price effects of taxation, the rate of capital formation, and the performance of the economy—and there is important empirical evidence to back it up. The 1964 Kennedy tax rate reductions have been thoroughly analyzed from a Keynesian perspective, which ignores the supply-side effects and the changes in relative prices that actually took place. The economic boom that resulted from the Kennedy tax rate reductions has been misinterpreted as a consumption-led expansion caused by higher spending from the tax cuts. In reality, the opposite occurred. As Figure 3–1 shows, after the marginal tax rate reduction went into effect, people spent a smaller percentage of their income. In 1964, actual consumer expenditures dipped below the trend rate predicted by a Keynesian consumption function. By 1967, consumption was at least $17.5 billion below the previous trend—a sum larger than the size of the personal tax cut (measured in constant dollars).

People were actually consuming a smaller percentage of their income and saving a larger percentage after the tax rate reduction than before. Following the tax reduction there was a significant increase in the real volume of personal saving, and the personal saving rate, reversing the decline begun in the early 1960s, rose sharply. The personal saving rate remained high for *nearly a decade* until rising marginal tax rates pushed it down.

In 1964 real personal saving rose $6.6 billion above the trend growth prior to the reduction in marginal tax rates. The gain in saving was 74 percent of the tax cut. In the next two years saving increased $10.2 billion and $10.8 billion above the previous trend, a gain equal to 72 percent of the tax cut. In 1967 saving was $19 billion above the previous trend—a gain equal to 121 percent of the size of the tax cut.[5]

The saving increase released real resources from consumption and allowed a rapid growth of business investment. In real terms, capital spending (for both the expansion of the capital stock and the replacement of worn-out capital stock) had grown at an annual rate of 3.5

5. See Paul Craig Roberts, *The Supply-Side Revolution: An Insider's Account of Policymaking in Washington* (Cambridge: Harvard University Press, 1984), p. 79.

Figure 3–1.   Real Consumer Expenditures, Actual Compared With Predicted Values from a "Keynesian" Consumption Function.

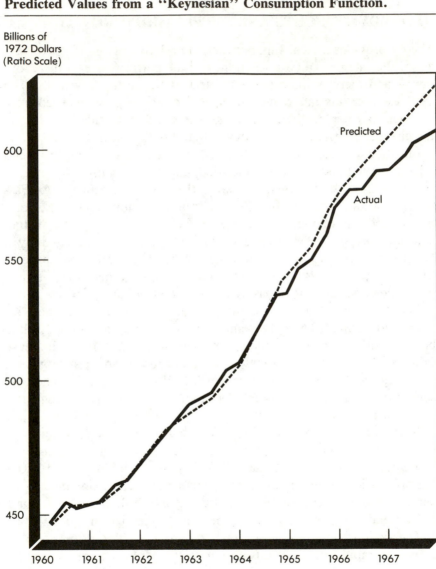

SOURCE: Paul Craig Roberts, *The Supply-Side Revolution: An Insider's Account of Policymaking in Washington* (Cambridge: Harvard University Press, 1984), p. 77.

percent during the 1950s and early 1960s through 1962. The remainder of the 1960s saw real capital spending rise over twice as fast, increasing 7.2 percent annually. The rate of growth from 1963 to 1966 was especially marked. While growth was high in the corporate sector, small business investment showed the greatest improvements.

The acceleration in investment greatly enhanced the economy's ability to produce. The net stock of capital had grown 3.8 percent annually between 1949 and 1963, but with the tax cuts it rose to a 5.5 percent growth rate for the remainder of the decade. Keynesian economists claim that the investment boom resulted from the investment tax credit, but the sharp rise in investment could not have taken place if consumers had not released resources from consumption by saving a larger share of their incomes.

Keynesians developed a relationship between actual GNP and what they call "potential" GNP. The relationship is based on their belief that economic growth is determined by the level of demand. The government can increase demand, either with a tax cut or a boost in government spending, and thereby push actual GNP closer to potential GNP. Once the ceiling of potential or full-employment GNP has been reached, the Keynesians believe that further attempts to stimulate the economy will result in production bottlenecks and inflation.

Keynesians credit the 1964 tax cut with raising GNP by $25 billion by mid-1965 and by $30 billion by the end of the year. But Edward Denison, who is known for his Keynesian models of the economy, estimated that the gap between actual and potential GNP was only $12 billion—the size of the Kennedy tax cut. How could a $12 billion gap accommodate a $30 billion expansion based on increased demand and unused capacity? If Denison's estimate is approximately correct, the substantial expansion that followed the Kennedy tax cut had to be based on a supply-side response to the higher after-tax rates of return earned by productive activities.

The Keynesian advisers to President Kennedy wanted to stimulate the economy to its full potential. They chose a policy that they thought would stimulate consumer spending, and the conventional wisdom today still holds that the resulting boom was consumption-led. The evidence shows, however, that what the policy makers really got was a burst of saving and investment activity that spurred the economy beyond fuller utilization of existing resources to faster growth of the ability to produce. Far from being a consumption-led expansion, real consumer spending actually declined as a percentage of income. Saving, investment, and tax revenues rose strongly.[6]

SOAKING THE RICH WITH TAX CUTS

An equal reduction in marginal tax rates reduces taxes by the same proportion for all income levels and initially leaves the shares of the tax burden falling on "rich" and "poor" unchanged. However, since the higher the bracket the greater the disincentives, a proportional reduction in marginal tax rates improves incentives the most for the "rich," encouraging them to earn and report more income. As they do, their share of the tax burden rises. The Internal Revenue Service's *Statistics of Income* show this to be the case whenever marginal tax rates are reduced.

For example, Gwartney and Stroup examine two cases of proportional marginal income tax rate reductions, the Mellon tax cut of the 1920s and the Kennedy tax cuts of the 1960s.[7] In the case of the Mellon tax cut, named after Treasury Secretary Andrew Mellon, marginal tax rates that reached 73 percent in 1921 were reduced to a top rate of 25 percent by 1926. The effect on the economy was positive: "The economy's performance during the 1921–26 period was quite impressive. Price stability accompanied a rapid growth in real output."

Gwartney and Stroup found the shift in the tax burden equally impressive. By 1926 personal income tax revenues from returns reporting $10,000 or less dropped to 4.6 percent of total collections, compared to 22.5 percent in 1921. In contrast, the percentage of total income tax revenues from returns by people with incomes of $100,000 or more rose to 50.9 percent in 1926 from 28.1 percent to 1921. The evidence supports the conclusion that "as a result of the strong response of high-income taxpayers, the tax cuts of the 1920s actually shifted the tax burden to the higher income brackets even though the rate reductions were greatest in this area."[8]

Their analysis of the Kennedy tax rate reductions (which reduced the top rate from 91 to 70 percent) yields similar results. In 1965, after the tax rate reductions, collections from the highest 5 percent of income earners rose to 38.5 percent of the total from 35.6 percent in

---

6. For a detailed discussion, see Roberts, *n.* 5, pp. 69–81.

7. James Gwartney and Richard Stroup, "Tax Cuts: Who Shoulders the Burden?" *Economic Review,* Federal Reserve Bank of Atlanta, March 1982, p. 20.

8. Ibid, p. 26.

1963. In contrast, the proportion of income tax revenues from the bottom 50 percent of tax returns fell from 10.9 percent in 1963 to 9.5 percent in 1965.

In testimony before the Joint Economic Committee of Congress in 1984, Gwartney noted that the Economic Recovery Tax Act of 1981 (ERTA) yielded similar results. The reduction of the top marginal tax rate from 70 to 50 percent cut the tax rates paid by high-income earners by as much as 28.6 percent, but tax revenues collected from the rich increased. Revenues from the top 1.36 percent of taxpayers, the group that most benefited from the rate reductions, rose from $58.0 billion in 1981 to $60.5 billion in 1982. The proportion of the total income tax collected from the top 1.36 percent of taxpayers rose to 21.8 percent in 1982 from 20.4 percent in 1981.

The tax liability of low-income taxpayers fell both in absolute terms and as a percentage of the total. Taxes paid by the bottom 50 percent of income earners fell from $21.7 billion in 1981 to $19.5 billion in 1982, and the share shrank from 7.6 percent in 1981 to 7.0 percent in 1982. Gwartney concludes that

> far from creating a windfall gain for the rich, as some have charged, ERTA actually shifted the burden of the income tax toward taxpayers in upper brackets, including those who received the largest rate reductions as the result of the 50 percent rate ceiling.[9]

This seems to be a general conclusion supported by the empirical results of all marginal income tax rate reductions in the United States. Far from "soaking the rich," high marginal income tax rates discourage people from making their best effort and serve as a barrier to upward mobility and financial independence.

ECONOMISTS MOVE TO THE SUPPLY SIDE

Despite the supply-side footprints left by previous tax rate reductions, some Keynesians still argue that there is no proof that people respond to marginal tax rate reductions by working or saving more. Some Keynesians have begun to acknowledge that society needs to save more,[10] but many still see tax cuts as an inefficient and ineffective

9. James Gwartney, "Tax Rates, Taxable Income and the Distributional Effects of the Economic Recovery Tax Act of 1981," testimony before the Joint Economic Committee, June 12, 1984, p. 19.

10. See Alice M. Rivlin, ed., *Economic Choices 1984* (Washington, D.C.: Brookings Institution, 1984).

tool. They argue that people have relatively constant levels of saving that are inelastic to changes in the after-tax rate of return. Similarly, they argue that people will work no more, and perhaps even less, after a tax cut because they experience an increase in after-tax income.[11] Several recent studies contradict this viewpoint, showing that people can and do respond to better incentives by increasing their saving and work efforts.

In "Taxation, Saving, and the Rate of Interest," Michael Boskin found that the total elasticity of saving (income and substitution effects combined) was positive and on the order of 0.3 to 0.4. While the size of this response has since been disputed by other studies, his findings are nevertheless interesting and valuable. On the basis of his research Boskin predicted that raising the after-tax rate of return to capital would "increase income substantially" and "remove an enormous dead-weight loss to society resulting from the distortion of the consumption-saving choice."[12]

Another interesting conclusion of his study is that not only will people respond positively to a change in the relative price of saving but that a larger share of total income will be transferred from capital to labor. Boskin confirms earlier studies indicating that the elasticity of substitution between capital and labor is less than one. If the elasticity of substitution between capital and labor is less than one, then an increase in the capital labor ratio (following an increase in saving) leads to a corresponding increase in labor's share of total income. Boskin wrote that

> the current tax treatment of income from capital induces an astounding loss in welfare due to the distortion of the consumption/saving choice. . . . Reducing taxes on interest income would in the long run raise the level of income and transfer a substantial portion of capital's share of gross income to labor.[13]

In a study for the National Bureau of Economic Research, Larry Summers modified three different theoretical models in order to better monitor changes in saving as a result of changes in the rate of return. Using the three alternative models, he then conducted empirical anal-

11. These arguments are logically inconsistent. If people in general respond to a tax cut by reducing their working hours, total income would fall. See Roberts, *n.* 1 and *n.* 5.

12. Michael J. Boskin, "Taxation, Saving, and the Rate of Interest," *Journal of Political Economy* 86 (April 1978, part 2):S 3.

13. Ibid, p. S 25.

ysis and found that "all three suggest a significant response of savings to changes in the rate of return."[14]

In a study of the effects of the 1981 tax reduction, Allen Sinai, Andrew Lin, and Russel Robins found that private saving is influenced by the after-tax rate of return and that the economy would have performed much more poorly in 1981–82 had it not been for the 1981 tax rate reduction.[15] They also found that the cash flow effects of the tax cuts reduce the burden of loan repayment and interest charges on debt, thereby strengthening home and business balance sheets.

Using an augmented Data Resources model of the U.S. economy incorporating previously neglected effects of after-tax interest rates on saving, investment, and consumption, Sinai and his associates found that the net tax reductions introduced by the Reagan administration raised business saving by $27 billion during 1981–82 and would add $181 billion over the 1981–85 period. The effect on personal saving is even more dramatic. Saving rose above the baseline trend by $48 billion in 1982 and would rise $136 billion in 1985, producing a projected cumulative increase in personal saving of $402 billion for the 1981–85 period.[16]

In a powerful vindication of the position taken by Treasury Department supply-siders, Sinai et al. conclude: "These results illustrate the sensitivity of saving to the changes in taxes and that ERTA is a program with major effects on personal saving." These economists found that in the absence of the tax cut, "the U.S. economy would have performed considerably worse in 1981 and 1982 than actually was the case," with an additional loss in real GNP of about 1.6 percentage points. They concluded that the "evidence indicates that ERTA has had a major impact on U.S. economic growth."

In 1983, despite highly publicized fears expressed by the chairman of the Council of Economic Advisers and the chairman of the Federal Reserve Board that high interest rates would produce a lopsided and weak recovery, the recovery was well balanced and the economy rebounded strongly. According to the 1984 *Economic Report of the President,* interest-sensitive categories such as consumer durables,

14. Larry Summers, "Tax Policy, the Rate of Return, and Savings," *Working Paper #995,* National Bureau of Economic Research, September 1982, p. 43.

15. Allen Sinai, Andrew Lin, and Russel Robins, "Taxes, Saving, and Investment: Some Empirical Evidence," *National Tax Journal* 36 (no. 3, Sept. 1983):5, 9, 22, 24.

16. Ibid, p. 23. The three quotations in the following paragraph appear on pp. 19, 24, and 27 respectively.

business fixed investment, residential investment, and inventories all contributed to GNP growth in proportions that either matched or bettered the average of postwar recoveries. One category of nonresidential fixed investment—investment in producer's durable equipment—performed particularly well, making three times its average postwar contribution to the first year of recovery.

The other component of nonresidential fixed investment—structures—contributed slightly less to the first year of recovery for the striking reason that it barely fell during the recession. Throughout most of the recession, investment in structures remained well above its prerecession level, instead of declining as it did in the seven previous cycles. Nonresidential construction showed little effects of recession because structures was the sector least affected by the 1982 tax increase.

As a result of improved cash flow from the 1981 tax cut, the credit crunch, which many predicted would result from the budget deficits, did not occur. According to the *Economic Report of the President:*

> The nonfinancial corporate sector did not place significant demands on the credit markets in 1983. As cash flow rose markedly due to the strength of the recovery, corporations obtained most of their funds from internal sources. Despite increases in business fixed investment outlays and a move from inventory liquidation to accumulation within the year, the nonfinancial corporate sector is estimated to have borrowed about $33 billion in the first three quarters of 1983, well below the amount borrowed over the same period in 1982.[17]

The source of the rise in interest rates was *not* Treasury borrowing crowding the private sector out of the financial markets, but the Federal Reserve Board's decision to tighten money supply growth. According to the economic report, "In the middle of 1983 the Federal Reserve became less accommodative in its provision of reserves. As a result, interest rates rose moderately."[18]

Other recent studies and experiments show that people's decisions about the allocation of time are affected by the relative prices of work and leisure. Jerry Hausman, for example, has devoted much time and energy to studying the effect of taxes on work decisions. In a Brookings Institution study, Hausman reports the following:

17. Council of Economic Advisers, *Economic Report of the President, 1984* (Washington, D.C.: U.S. Government Printing Office, 1984), p. 193.
18. Ibid, p. 195.

Although income and payroll taxes account for 75 percent of federal revenues, most economists have concluded that they cause little reduction in the supply of labor and do little harm to economic efficiency. The results of this study contradict that comforting view. Direct taxes on income and earnings significantly reduce labor supply and economic efficiency. Moreover, the replacement of the present tax structure by a rate structure that proportionally taxes income above an exempt amount would eliminate nearly all of the distortion of labor supply and more than half of the economic waste caused by tax-induced distortions.[19]

In another study Hausman finds that, using 1975 data, desired labor supply was 8.2 percent lower than it would have been without federal income taxes, FICA taxes, and state income taxes. He notes in particular that

> the effect of the progressiveness of the tax system is to cause high wage individuals to reduce their labor supply more from the no tax situation than do low tax individuals. . . . Of course, this pattern of labor supply has an adverse effect on tax revenues because of the higher tax rates that high income individuals pay tax at.[20]

Measuring the effects on labor supply of the tax system and of a 10 and 30 percent reduction in marginal income tax rates, Hausman reports that a person earning a nominal wage of $3.15 an hour worked 4.5 percent less than he would have in the absence of taxes. He would choose to work 0.4 and 1.3 percent more after 10 and 30 percent tax rate reductions, respectively. As income increases, the responses get larger. Taxes cause a person earning $10 an hour to reduce the number of hours worked by 12.8 percent. A 10 and 30 percent reduction would induce him to increase his work time by 1.47 and 4.6 percent, respectively.

Another interesting result of Hausman's work is his calculation of the "dead-weight loss" incurred by the imposition of the progressive income tax system. He defines dead-weight loss as the amount an individual would need to be given to be as well off after the tax less the amount of tax revenue raised. Hausman finds that there is an average dead-weight loss equivalent to 22.1 percent of tax revenue col-

19. Jerry Hausman, "Labor Supply," in Henry J. Aaron and Joseph A. Pechman, eds., *How Taxes Affect Economic Behavior* (Washington, D.C.: The Brookings Institution, 1981), p. 27.

20. Jerry Hausman, "Taxes and Labor Supply," *Working Paper #1102*, National Bureau of Economic Research, March 1983, p. 46.

lected, which is income that is "lost" because of the presence of taxes. As income increases, so does dead-weight loss. A person earning $10 an hour, according to Hausman, has a dead-weight loss of 39.5 percent of tax revenue.

The impact of income maintenance programs on the work effort of low-income earners also clearly demonstrates the relative price effects of taxation that supply-side economists have stressed. The Seattle/Denver Income Maintenance Experiments (SIME/DIME) was the fourth and most comprehensive of the experiments undertaken by the government in the 1960s and 1970s to examine the effects of a cash transfer program or negative income tax on low-income earners. People were given cash transfers of varying amounts, which guaranteed them incomes whether they worked or not. Their subsidies were taxed so that when they began earning income above a certain level, the subsidy would gradually be reduced to zero. The purpose of the study was to determine whether a cash transfer would be a more efficient way to transfer income to the poor than the variety of welfare programs already in existence.

The negative income tax lowers the relative price of leisure and, not surprisingly, the SIME/DIME results, published in May 1983, show "a significant negative effect on hours worked per year." Married males participating in the three-year cash transfer programs worked an average of 7.3 percent less than they would have in the absence of the negative income tax. Those who participated in the five-year program reduced their labor supply 13.6 percent, demonstrating that work disincentives rise with the permanence of income support programs. Wives and female heads of household showed a larger response to the cash transfer program. The report noted that

> by the end of the first post-treatment year, labor supply for NIT-eligible husbands had again returned essentially to the same level as that for controls, indicating strongly both that the observed response was indeed a result of the treatment and that husbands can adjust their labor supply fairly rapidly to changed incentives.[21]

Growth and Fairness Through a Flat-Rate Tax

The U.S. tax code of recent years has been counterproductive because of its adverse effects on relative prices. A broad-based flat-rate tax

21. Final Report of the Seattle-Denver Income Maintenance Experiment, SRI International, U.S. Department of Health and Human Services, May 1983, p. 13.

that exempts saving from the tax base removes the disincentives to earn additional income from work, saving, investment, and risk-taking. A broad-based flat-rate tax also eliminates the cost to the economy of the distortions caused by the differential treatment of income in the tax code.

Any tax system should meet a minimum of three goals: It should be simple and fair, it should minimize its own burden on the economic vitality of the tax base, and it should collect adequate revenues. The tax system of recent years has not been based on the principle of fairness but on the "ability to pay" argument. Fairness says that a person who earns twice the median income should pay twice as much in taxes. The ability-to-pay argument claims that the government should be able to extract, for example, five times as much in taxes from a person who makes twice the median income simply because he is better able to withstand the burden. The ability-to-pay argument introduces massive economic disincentives into the economy, because it increases the rate of penalty as additional effort is expended. (The tax system has even violated the ability-to-pay argument as bracket creep has pushed middle-income earners into marginal tax brackets that formerly pertained only to the rich.) As inflation and economic growth moved the people higher into the progressive tax system, the disincentives of progressivity spread into the population as a whole. The fairness principle was further breached because of discriminatory treatment of different sources of income and of marital status.

By discouraging work and investment, the tax system depressed the growth of the tax base. In addition, people were encouraged to make investments that minimize their taxes rather than maximize their income. In a 1984 publication the House Democratic Caucus echoed years of complaints by supply-side economists by declaring that "the whole system makes no economic sense."[22]

It is refreshing to see that at least some Democratic congressmen no longer think exclusively of redistribution when they call for tax reform. Perhaps they are beginning to realize that redistribution takes place through the expenditure, and not the revenue, side of the budget.

The third goal for tax policy, collecting adequate revenue, cannot be achieved independently of the other two goals. If taxpayers feel that the system is unfair, they are more likely to engage in tax avoid-

22. National House Democratic Caucus, "Renewing America's Promise: A Democratic Blueprint for Our Nation's Future," January 1984, p. 15.

ance. The large underground economy that developed in the United States is testimony to the fact that many Americans came to believe that the tax system was no longer worthy of support. Tax avoidance became a big business in which many participated, from the carpenter who willingly accepted a lower payment provided it was in cash, to the Wall Street entrepreneur who devised ingenious but hopelessly unproductive tax shelters.

The size and strength of the economy is the basis for the government's budget. The economy's strength determines how much the government must spend on such things as unemployment benefits, public housing, and income support programs and how much it can spend on defense, education, and public investment in roads and bridges. The size of the federal budget in relation to GNP depends not only on the budget, but also on the economy. Obviously, it is much easier for a government to "live within its means" if the economy is large, healthy and growing.

Discounting the effects of any remaining deductions or exemptions, marginal and average tax rates are equivalent in a broad-based, low flat-rate system, and the economic distortions that differential tax treatment causes are reduced to a minimum. A "revenue neutral" tax reform, in which the higher revenues from a broader base are fully offset by lowering the tax rate, could result in higher Treasury revenues because of the dynamic effect on the economy of better incentives and reduced distortions. This provides the potential for the budget to be balanced without raising the tax burden.

To ensure this result it is important that base-broadening measures do not increase the tax bias against saving. Neutral tax treatment of saving would add a bigger boost to investment, capital formation, and productivity than can be gained from eliminating distortions in the choice of investments. For too long and for too many people, the government's policies presented an ultimatum: Go into debt or go broke. Tax law that encourages consumption over saving and debt over equity is a source of low capital formation. Exempting saving from the tax base would treat income saved the same as income consumed.

Economic policy makers may be faced with an important opportunity. The healthy results of the initial supply-side reforms of 1981 are bound to add momentum to additional positive reforms. Now is the time to guarantee the future by further supply-side tax reform.

4

TAX RATES, TAX SHELTERS, AND THE EFFICIENCY OF CAPITAL FORMATION

James Gwartney and James Long

During the last two decades, the government emerged as a major redistributor of income from one group to another—from the working population to retirees, from the employed to the unemployed, and from current producers to various disadvantaged groups. In 1965, money income transfers were 5.9 percent of GNP. By the mid-1970s, the government was redistributing more than 10 percent of GNP. If, in addition, one counts transfers in kind (food, housing, and medical assistance, for example), transfers now account for nearly 20 percent of our national income.

As the transfers grew, so too did the tax revenues (and rates) to finance them. This chapter analyzes the impact of high tax rates on the decisions of taxpayers. Particular attention is focused on tax shelter activities—the actions of taxpayers designed to reduce their tax liability. The mechanics of tax shelters, their impact on capital formation and economic efficiency, and their growth in recent decades—each of these topics is investigated. Finally, we present estimates on the linkage between marginal tax rates and tax shelter activities (and therefore tax revenues). The chapter concludes with a brief discussion of the policy implications of our analysis.

TWO DECADES OF RISING MARGINAL TAX RATES

During the last two decades, the number of taxpayers confronting high marginal tax rates increased sharply. Table 4–1 presents the data for joint returns for the 1965–1979 period. In 1965, 1.13 million tax-payers (2.9 percent) filing joint returns confronted marginal federal income tax rates of 28 percent or more. As inflation pushed more and more taxpayers into higher tax brackets, the number of taxpayers facing high tax rates rose steadily throughout the 1970s. By 1979, 15.238 million taxpayers (35.3 percent) filing joint returns were paying marginal tax rates of 28 percent or more. Thus, there were more than thirteen times as many taxpayers confronting marginal tax rates of 28 percent or more in 1979 as was the case in 1965.

As Table 4–1 illustrates, the identical pattern was also present for still higher marginal tax rates. The number of joint-return taxpayers facing marginal rates of 32 percent or more rose from 722 thousand to 9.782 million between 1965 and 1979. Similarly the number of joint-return taxpayers paying marginal federal income tax rates of 37 percent or more rose from 376 thousand (1.0 percent) to 5.533 million (12.8 percent) during the 1965–1979 period.

As sobering as the figures of Table 4–1 are, they actually under-state the increase in the number of households facing high rates of

Table 4–1.   Rising Marginal Federal Income Tax Rates, 1965–1979.

	1965	*1970*	*1973*	*1977*	*1979*
No. of Joint Returns (in millions)	39.506	42.660	39.805	42.576	43.217
Joint Returns (in millions) Facing:					
Marginal Tax Rates of 28% or more	1.130	2.984	5.386	12.003	15.238
(percent)	2.9%	7.0%	13.5%	28.2%	35.3%
Marginal Tax Rates of 32% or more	.722	1.701	3.044	7.308	9.782
(percent)	1.8%	4.0%	7.6%	17.2%	22.6%
Marginal Tax Rates of 37% or more	.376	.797	1.321	2.965	5.533
(percent)	1.0%	1.9%	3.3%	7.0%	12.8%
Marginal Tax Rates of 43% or more	.219	.463	.756	1.584	3.306
(percent)	0.6%	1.1%	1.9%	3.7%	7.6%
Marginal Tax Rates of 49% or more	.136	.296	.481	1.032	1.541
(percent)	0.3%	0.7%	1.2%	2.4%	3.6%

SOURCE: Internal Revenue Service, *Statistics of Income: Individual Income Tax Returns* (annual).

taxation. They exclude Social Security and state income taxes. In 1965 persons facing marginal tax rates of 28 percent or more would generally have had earnings above the cutoff point of the Social Security payroll tax. This was not the case in 1979. Many taxpayers, particularly those in families with several income earners, continued to confront the 6.13 percent Social Security payroll tax (12.3 percent if we also consider the employer's share, the burden of which generally falls on the employee) in effect in 1979, even while facing marginal tax rates in the 30 percent range. Similarly, the marginal rates of taxation levied by state (and local) governments generally rose during this period. This factor would also contribute to the growth of taxpayers confronting high marginal rates. In addition, the marginal tax rates of Table 4–1 reflect the rates paid on taxable income *after* taxpayers have taken steps to shelter their income. Had they not purchased deductible items and engaged in various activities designed to reduce their current taxable income, they would have faced even higher rates.

The bottom line is that while only the top 2 or 3 percent of income recipients paid marginal tax rates of 28 percent or more in the mid-1960s, more than one-third of all persons filing joint returns were paying these high rates by the late 1970s. *Literally millions of middle-income Americans have been paying marginal tax rates that were previously reserved for only the very rich.*

Did not the Reagan tax cuts of the early 1980s roll back the high marginal tax rates of the late 1970s? Many lay observers adhere to this view. However, investigation of the evidence reveals that it is fallacious. Essentially what the Reagan tax cut did was offset the impact of "bracket creep" and higher Social Security taxes. In a nutshell, it kept tax rates from increasing. By 1984, marginal tax rates were modestly lower than they were for 1980, but they were about the same as for 1979 for taxpayers filing a joint return with an adjusted gross income of less than $75,000 (measured in 1979 dollars). Table 4–2 illustrates this point. A two-earner family of four earning $20,000, $40,000, $60,000, or $75,000 in 1979 faced almost the same marginal tax rate in 1984 if they earned the same amount of *real* income.[1] Since returns with an adjusted gross income of $75,000 or less (measured in 1979 dollars) constituted more than 99 percent of

---

1. For additional evidence on the magnitude of the changes in marginal tax rates during the early 1980s, see Richard McKenzie, "Supply-Side Economics and the Vanishing Tax Cut," *Economic Review—Federal Reserve Bank of Atlanta*, May 1982, pp. 20–24.

the total, it is clear that the Reagan tax cut failed to roll back the enormous increase in marginal rates that took place during the 1970s.

MARGINAL TAX RATES AND THE INCENTIVE TO SHELTER INCOME

There is a great deal of confusion about the impact of marginal tax rates because people fail to recognize three simple principles. These three principles are a reflection of the basic postulate of economics that incentives exert a predictable impact on human behavior. If economic policy reduces the personal gain derived from an activity, people will choose less of it. Alternatively, if policy makes something less costly, people will choose more of it.

Principle 1: *High marginal tax rates reduce the personal gain that taxpayers derive from generating additional taxable income. Predictably, taxpayers will generate less taxable income at higher marginal rates.* The marginal tax rate of an individual or family exerts an important influence on their incentive to earn additional income. The marginal tax rate determines the allocation of additional earnings between the income recipient and the tax collector. As the marginal tax rate goes up, the proportion of additional income that the earner gets to keep goes down. For example, when an individual confronts a marginal tax rate of 20 percent, he or she gets to keep $80 of each

Table 4–2. Marginal Tax Rates for a Two-Earner Family of Four, 1979–1984.

Adjusted Gross Income (1979 Dollars)	Marginal Tax Rate		
	1979	*1980*	*1984*
	%	%	%
20,000	24.13	27.13	24.7
40,000	38.13	43.13	39.7
60,000	49.13	55.13	48.7
75,000	49.00	54.00	48.7
100,000	54.00	54.00	45.0

Note: The data are for federal personal income and Social Security tax liabilities. The calculations are based on the following assumptions: The couple files a joint return and all income is earned income. The second wage earner earns one-half the amount of the first. Taxpayers take the zero-bracket amount or itemize deductions equal to 23 percent of income, whichever is greater.

additional $100 earned. The other $20 must be paid to the taxing authorities. In contrast, an individual confronting a 40 percent marginal tax rate would get to keep only $60 of an additional $100 of earnings. The tax collectors take the other $40. Of course, most of us work for after-tax income, since it can be used to increase our personal welfare. When high marginal tax rates prevent us from capturing the fruits of our labor, they reduce our incentive to work in the taxable-income garden. Predictably, we will generate less taxable income.

Contrary to traditional discussions of the topic, this does not necessarily imply that individuals will work fewer hours and consume more leisure. There are alternative ways of reducing one's tax liability. Some taxpayers will allocate more of their time and energy to projects designed to *reduce* their tax liability. Others will work more intensely in the underground economy, the vitality of which is heavily dependent upon high marginal tax rates. Still others will simply substitute untaxed household work and more pleasurable (but lower wage rate) work for the more heavily taxed market work. The key point is that as marginal tax rates rise, taxpayers will substitute activities that are untaxed (or taxed at lower rates) for heavily taxed activities.

Principle 2: *As marginal tax rates rise, taxpayers will increase their expenditure on items that reduce their taxable income*. Rising marginal tax rates make tax deductible purchases cheaper. For example, a $1,000 "business trip" to Hawaii will cost the taxpayer only $500 when he or she is in the 50 percent marginal tax bracket. In contrast, the personal cost of the same trip is $800 when the taxpayer confronts only a 20 percent marginal tax rate. Predictably, taxpayers will undertake more tax deductible expenditures when high marginal tax rates make the personal cost of deductible items cheap. In fact, as marginal tax rates rise, taxpayers can be expected to broaden their range of potential tax deductible expenditures. For example, more taxpayers will go into businesses that permit them to travel, drive a nice automobile, and enjoy the benefits of other "business related" purchases. Others will choose a bigger house with a larger mortgage because the home interest deductibility reduces the personal cost of this item for taxpayers in high marginal tax brackets. Of course, as taxpayers enlarge their tax deductible purchases, their taxable income (and tax liability) will decline.

Principle 3: *Taxable income is not invariant to the rate of taxation. As marginal tax rates rise, the taxable income base will shrink*. Invariably politicians and media commentators proceed as if taxable income is determined by the laws of nature. A 10 percent surtax on taxable income above $50,000 is perceived to raise 10 percent more revenue in the high-income tax brackets. Similarly, the impact of a tax increase (or decrease) is analyzed as if the level of taxable income is unaffected by the tax change. Purely and simply, this view is wrong.

Rising marginal tax rates encourage taxpayers to earn less taxable income, engage more heavily in tax shelter activities, and enlarge their tax deductible purchases. As a result, the tax base shrinks.[2] Many of these activities would be unprofitable at low marginal tax rates. We must not forget that tax shelter activities involve a cost. Most tax shelter projects increase the taxpayer's record keeping, accounting, and tax preparation costs. Sometimes tax shelters necessitate a new form of business organization, such as a limited partnership or corporation. Organizing, operating, and monitoring these organizations is costly. Specialized information services and management are often required. Again, the costs of these services must be covered. Tax shelters often involve loss of liquidity, exposure to additional risk, and dependency upon experts who may or may not be trustworthy. These and similar costs explain why the level of tax sheltering is responsive to changes in marginal tax rates. At low marginal tax rates, many tax shelter activities will simply not be worth the hassle and the additional costs. But rising marginal tax rates increase the tax savings derived from a reduction in one's taxable income. Some sheltering activities that are unprofitable at the low marginal tax rates become profitable at the higher rates. Thus, when marginal rates rise, taxpayers will engage in more sheltering activities, thereby reducing their taxable income.

Similarly, many potential tax deductible expenditures will be unprofitable at low marginal tax rates. When marginal rates are low, taxpayers will reduce their tax deductible expenditures since, under these circumstances, taxpayers bear a larger share of total cost of such expenditures.

HOW TAX SHELTERS WORK

There are many different types of tax shelters. Clearly, in some cases, Congress mandated favorable treatment of certain classes of activities because it wanted to channel additional funds into desired areas. For

---

2. As the backward bending Laffer curve indicates, in some cases the shrinkage in the tax base may mean a decline in the tax revenue collected at the higher rates. But Principle 3 is not dependent on this outcome.

example, income from municipal bonds is tax exempt because Congress wanted to reduce the cost of funds to municipalities. Similarly, the home mortgage interest deduction was instituted to encourage home ownership.

However, other tax shelters originate because of the nature of the activity. If a tax shelter is going to reduce one's tax liability, it must accomplish at least one of the following:

1. Generate a "paper loss" that will reduce one's current taxable income and thereby extend one's tax liability into the future.
2. Alter income in a manner that will move it to a lower marginal tax bracket.
3. Permit one to undertake personal consumption activities that generate business expenses.
4. Create a tax credit, which reduces directly one's tax liability. Let us consider how the major tax shelters accomplish these objectives.

Tax Savings through "Paper Losses"

Most tax shelter investments are designed to put off reported income into the future. Generally, tax shelter investments yield accounting ("paper") losses during the period immediately following the investment, with the expectation of generating future income from sale of either assets or services. Depreciation, set-up expenses, and interest costs usually play a central role in the generation of the initial accounting losses.

Real estate, oil and gas, cattle feeding (and breeding), equipment leasing, and farming investments have generally been used to shift income into the future. These investments can easily be structured to generate large interest, depreciation, set-up, and development costs that will result in substantial accounting losses in the early years of the projects, even while accumulating a valuable asset to be sold in the future. If the projects did nothing more than move taxable income into the future, they would reduce the present value cost of one's tax liability. However, they generally permit the taxpayer to derive additional tax savings from another source—the movement of income to a lower marginal tax bracket.

Moving Income Into a Lower Tax Rate Category

Under the tax code of recent years, there have been three major ways that taxpayers have moved income to a lower marginal tax rate category: (1) move income into a year for which their marginal tax rate is lower, (2) transform ordinary income into capital gain, and (3) move income into a closely held corporation, a pension fund, or a retirement fund for which income is taxed at a lower rate. We will consider each of these methods.

Shifting Income to a Low Tax Year.   If taxpayers can delay their taxable income into the future, they will not only be able to reduce the present value cost of a given tax liability, but they may be able to move the income to a lower marginal tax year. The likelihood that delaying income will reduce the marginal tax rate on the income is particularly high for income moved into one's retirement years. As individuals enter retirement, their taxable income generally declines sharply. Thus, they confront a lower tax rate. Investments that generate "tax losses" during one's prime earning years will reduce tax liability in proportion to the taxpayer's high marginal tax rate during these years. If these investments mature and generate positive income during retirement years or an otherwise low-income year, the income return will be taxed at a lower marginal rate.

Transforming Ordinary Income Into Capital Gains.   Taxpayers have also been able to gain from the transformation of ordinary income into capital gains income. Under the tax code of recent years, only 40 percent of the income derived from capital gains has been taxable. Thus, a person in a 50 percent tax bracket would pay only a 20 percent marginal rate on income derived from capital gains. Deductible expenditures that increase the value of an asset will, in effect, transform ordinary income into a capital gain. Since the deductible expenditures reduce the taxpayer's ordinary income, they generate a tax savings in proportion to the taxpayer's effective marginal tax rate. However, assuming the asset is held for more than a year, the appreciation in the value of the asset has been taxed at the lower capital gains rate.

The typical real estate tax shelter illustrates how income is both shifted into the future and transformed from ordinary to capital gain income. Investors, often using a limited partnership, put up the necessary funds to cover the down payment on an apartment complex, office building, or other physical structure. The project will usually be set up so that rental income from the structure will cover interest payments on outstanding debt, plus expected operating and maintenance expenses. Depreciation expenses against the physical structures leave investors with an accounting loss that reduces their current taxable income. However, if the investors follow wise maintenance and upkeep practices, the costs of which are fully deductible, the property will probably not decrease in value. In fact, with careful maintenance, the property will generally appreciate, particularly during a period of inflation.

With leverage and the use of accelerated depreciation methods, the accounting losses from real estate tax shelters will often sum to between two and four times the taxpayer's original investment within a five- or six-year period. These "losses" are fully deductible against the taxpayer's current income. For persons in a high marginal tax bracket, these accounting losses essentially mean that the taxpayer is undertaking an investment with dollars that would otherwise have gone to the IRS. Of course, when the asset is sold, the taxpayer will have to pay income tax on the capital gain. However, he will have moved income into the future and transformed ordinary income into a capital gain.[3] If sale of the property is timed to occur during retirement, a bad economic year, or a "year off," the tax saving will be further magnified.

Lower Tax Rates Through Corporations and Pensions. High-income taxpayers may be able to gain by conducting at least some of their business activities through a closely held corporation. In recent years, the first $50,000 of corporate income has been taxed at (effective) rates of less than 20 percent. Therefore, taxpayers at or near the maximum marginal rate have derived substantial tax savings from shifting income into a corporation. The asset value of the corporation improves the net worth of the taxpayer and thereby expands his or her ability to borrow to finance current consumption if so desired. The disadvantage of using a corporation to shelter current income is that once the income is paid out to the taxpayer, it will be taxed again, this time as ordinary income. However, investors can usually get around this limitation by using corporate income to accumulate highly marketable assets—stocks, bonds, and real estate, for example. Under these circumstances, the taxpayer has been able to sell the corporation and thereby pay the capital gains tax rate. Of course, timing of the sale can be arranged to minimize the tax liability.

3. When accelerated depreciation methods are used, depreciation allowance in excess of the straight-line method is not eligible for capital gains. If the asset is sold prior to expiration of the recovery period, excess depreciation above the straight-line method will be taxed as ordinary income.

In addition, the owner-manager-employee of the corporation can often gain by establishing corporate pension and profit-sharing plans. Regular corporation plans generally have more liberal limitations than those applicable to the self-employed. Of course, the contributions into such pension and profit-sharing plans will show up as accounting costs to the corporation without generating taxable income for the recipient. Once again, the effect is to delay taxable income and move it into a lower tax bracket.

Transforming Personal Consumption Into a Business Expense

Someone once remarked that the best tax shelter was a "business" that permits individuals to deduct the cost of doing what they like to do. In order to accomplish this feat, a taxpayer must be in a business where what he likes to do is a cost of doing business. The IRS also requires one to be in business with the intent of making money. While proof of intent to make money is sometimes a hassle, most people are capable of arranging their affairs so that what they like to do is "business related" if the payoff for doing so is large enough. After all, just about anything that you might enjoy can be conducted as a business. If you like to travel, start a business that provides you with ample opportunity to go to desired places to attend professional meetings, meet clients, or contact potential customers and suppliers. If you like to ski or play golf, open an instructional business. If you like to drive a nice automobile, start a business (e.g., Amway distributorship, insurance sales, part-time delivery service) that will necessitate the use of a car.

Some activities are much easier than others to indulge in as a business. Most professionals have almost unlimited opportunity to travel for business purposes. There are always professional meetings, seminars, and training sessions at exotic places. Almost any type of self-employment presents one with the opportunity to purchase furniture, automobiles, business-related equipment, and similar items that often provide personal consumption side-benefits. Farming is another area that provides the opportunity to enjoy "business related" activities that many find enjoyable. High-income households that enjoy horseback riding, hunting, cattle breeding, or fishing can purchase a plot of land, go into farming, and deduct the cost of these and similar activities from their ordinary income.

Of course, such tax shelter businesses may be secondary to one's main income-generating activity. The business may generate little income. In fact, it may often show an accounting loss. This is fine from the standpoint of the tax shelter investor. After all, the purpose of the business is to arrange one's affairs so that the activities one enjoys are tax deductible business expenses. Making money is strictly secondary.

TAX SHELTERS AND EFFICIENCY: WHY DO WE CARE IF THE TAX STRUCTURE ENCOURAGES TAX SHELTERS?

As Adam Smith pointed out long ago, the genius of a private-property-based market economy is its ability to bring private and social interests into harmony. Individuals gain by undertaking activities for which their *personal* benefits exceed their *personal* costs. If property rights are defined so that the decision makers bear the full costs and reap the full benefits, private and social interests harmonize. Individuals seeking to improve their own well-being simultaneously improve the welfare of the community at large.

However, problems arise when decision makers (a) cannot fully capture the benefits generated by their activities or (b) need not bear the full cost of their actions. When they are unable to capture the benefits fully, they have less incentive to undertake productive activity—to help others in exchange for income. Thus, they engage in fewer wealth-creating activities. Similarly, when the costs of an action are, at least partially, foisted onto nonconsenting parties, individuals may undertake actions that they value more than their personal costs, *but less than the total costs of the action,* including the costs imposed on secondary parties.[4] Such actions destroy, rather than create, wealth. The smaller the individual's private costs compared to the total costs of the action (including the costs imposed on secondary parties), the more likely is it that decision makers will choose a counterproductive alternative.

This is precisely the set of problems raised by taxation—particularly high marginal tax rates. When marginal rates are high, individ-

4. Economists refer to the costs imposed on secondary parties as external costs. See James Gwartney and Richard Stroup, *Economics: Private and Public Choice,* 3d ed. (New York: Academic Press, 1983), pp. 65–68 and 609–15, for additional details as to why external costs often lead to economic inefficiency.

uals have less incentive to engage in income-generating activities because the tax collector seizes a sizable portion of the income generated. Sometimes income-generating activities will be forgone because the *after-tax* income is insufficient to make the project worthwhile, even though it would have been profitable if the individual could have fully captured the income he or she earned. When taxpayers are permitted to keep only 40 or 50 percent of the fruits of their labor, they spend less time working for taxable income.[5] Lawyers, doctors, and other high-income professionals spend more time on the golf course and consulting with their accountants and less time serving their clients. Similarly, secondary workers decide that their job is not worth the hassle when they get to keep only a fraction of every dollar they earn. The harmony between private and social interests breaks down. Positive-sum activities are foresaken and wealth creation is retarded.

Simultaneously, high marginal tax rates encourage individuals to purchase business and personal deductible items because a sizable portion of the costs of these items is foisted onto others. Taxpayers in high marginal tax brackets can enjoy business-related vacations, luxury restaurants, nice automobiles, plush offices, and mortgage-financed homes at a fraction of their costs. These and other tax deductible items will often be chosen even though the individual would not choose them if it were not for the tax-savings the expenditures generate. Thus, we end up expending valuable resources on things that cost our economy, but not the individual taxpayer, more than they are valued. Wealth is destroyed by the process, and as a consequence, our standard of living suffers.

Perhaps a simple example will help illustrate the forces that are at

5. The incentive structure accompanying high marginal tax rates is similar to that confronted by workers on collective farms in the Soviet Union. Soviet farmworkers are able to capture only a small fraction of their productive efforts on the collective farm, since the income of the farm is shared equally with other members of the collective. Thus, each collective-farm worker confronts a very high marginal tax rate; he is able to capture only a small portion of the income generated by his efforts. However, collective-farm workers are also permitted to grow products on an assigned private plot, usually one acre in size. Products raised on the private plots may be consumed or sold in the marketplace. Thus, "income" generated on the private plots is fully captured by the worker. Unsurprisingly, the productive effort and efficiency of resource use is far superior on the private plots than on collective farms. In fact, even though the private plots accounted only for approximately 1 percent of the agricultural land under cultivation in the Soviet Union, products from these plots accounted for 25 percent of the total value of Soviet agricultural output in 1980. Clearly, Soviet workers labor much more intensely when they are able to capture the fruits of their labor more fully.

work. Rather than picking on others, at least initially, we will begin with an example close to home. Suppose an economist in a 40 percent marginal tax bracket was contemplating a business trip to Hawaii to attend the annual meeting of the Western Economic Association. Unambiguously, the trip qualifies as a professional development expense. The full cost of the meeting, including wining and dining in the nicest Hawaiian restaurants, staying in a luxury hotel, air and taxi fares, and other related expenses, is tax deductible. Suppose the total cost of the trip is $2,000. How much will the trip cost the economist? Since the trip generates an $800 tax saving for the economist, the personal cost of the trip is only $1,200. If the economist values the trip more than $1,200, it will be chosen. Since the economist does not bear the full cost of the trip, the alternative may be chosen even though it is counterproductive. For example, suppose the economist values the trip at $1,500—that is, he would be willing to give up only $1,500 of his own money in order to undertake the trip. Under these circumstances, the trip is inefficient because the full cost of the trip exceeds its benefits. Nonetheless, given the tax saving that the trip generates, it will be chosen. High marginal tax rates are a problem precisely because they induce each of us to undertake economically inefficient projects. They cause us to squander our resources by producing things we do not value very highly instead of undertaking projects—which we end up forgoing.

Perhaps the process exerts its most destructive impact in the area of capital formation. In recent years, high marginal tax rates have encouraged investors to undertake projects that reduce their taxable income and transform ordinary income into capital gains. The *private* cost of such projects has been low because of the accompanying tax saving. Thus, investors have been motivated to undertake such projects even when their yield, independent of tax considerations, has been extremely low.

The tax law of recent years has favored (a) projects that have yielded a small or even negative flow of taxable income and a large capital appreciation, over (b) investments that have yielded a large flow of taxable income and little capital appreciation. Projects like (a) yield substantial tax savings in the form of "deductible losses" against the taxpayer's ordinary income and have often been used to move income into a lower tax category (capital gains and/or a future lower tax rate year). In contrast, the after-tax yield of projects like (b) has been reduced by high marginal tax rates.

Table 4–3 illustrates how tax considerations can distort the after-tax rates of return and thereby induce investors to choose low (social) return projects. Here we consider a hypothetical investment of $100,000 ($90,000 of which is a fixed depreciable asset) undertaken by an investor in a 50 percent tax bracket. Several classes of real estate assets such as apartments, office buildings, or other rental properties have fit the general patterns outlined by Table 4–3.

If the investor expends $5,000 annually on maintenance and improvements, under the assumptions of A and B, the asset will actually appreciate at a 2 percent annual rate.[6] The asset yields a net cash flow of $5,000 per year ($10,000 in rents minus the $5,000 maintenance and improvements expense), a rate of return of 5 percent on the initial investment. Adding the 2 percent annual rate of appreciation, the project yields a social rate of return of 7 percent. Thus, from the viewpoint of efficiency, one would not want this project undertaken as long as projects yielding a rate of return of more than 7 percent were available.

Under assumptions of A, the investor is assumed to put up the full $100,000 to pay for the asset. Since $90,000 is a fixed depreciable asset, the annual depreciation cost will be $6,000 over the 15-year eligible life of the asset. (*Note:* For simplicity, we assume that the straight-line method of depreciation is utilized.) From an accounting standpoint, the investment yields an annual accounting loss of $1,000—gross revenue ($10,000) minus maintenance and improvement costs ($5,000) and depreciation ($6,000). Since the investor is in a 50 percent tax bracket, the $1,000 reported loss will reduce his tax liability by $500.

What accounting rate of return will the project yield, given that the investor holds the asset for five years and then sells it for $110,400, a sale price that reflects the 2 percent annual increase in the market value of the asset? Given the finance methods assumed for A, the project will yield a private rate of return of 7.5 percent. Since the taxable net revenues were approximately equal to the eligible depreciation, the private and social rates of return were quite similar under the assumptions of A.

The revenue and cost figures of B are exactly the same as A, except that the investor is assumed to purchase the asset with a $10,000 down-

---

6. In order to simplify the analysis, Table 4–3 assumes the absence of inflation. Thus, data are in "real" dollars.

Table 4–3. Private and Social Rates of Return on a $100,000 Investment Project for a Taxpayer in a 50 Percent Tax Bracket.

	Annual Accounting Revenues and Costs (Constant Dollars)		
	A. Annual Apprec. of 2 Percent	B. Annual Apprec. of 2 Percent	C. Annual Apprec. of 4 Percent
Cash Income (Rents)	$10,000	$10,000	$10,000
Less Cash Costs			
Maintenance & Improvements	5,000	5,000	5,000
Interest Costs	0	9,000	9,000
Cash Flow	$5,000	−$4,000	−$4,000
Less			
Depreciation (Accounting)	$6,000	$6,000	$6,000
Annual Accounting Profit or Loss	−1,000	−10,000	−10,000
Annual Tax Saving (50 percent bracket)	500	5,000	5,000
Annual Tax Saving plus Cash Flow	5,500	1,000	1,000
Sale Price After Five Years	110,400	110,400	121,665
Before-Tax Net Receipts (after five years)	110,400	20,400	31,665
Capital Gain	40,400[a]	40,400[a]	51,665[b]
Capital Gain Tax	8,080	8,080	10,333
After-Tax Net Receipts (after five years)	$102,320	$12,320	$21,332
Private After-Tax Rate of Return	7.5%	18%	32%
Social Rate of Return	7%	7%	9%

[a]$10,400 in appreciation plus $30,000 in prior depreciation during the five-year period.
[b]$21,665 in appreciation plus $30,000 in prior depreciation during the five-year period.

payment and a $90,000 loan at a 10 percent annual interest rate. Since the interest on the loan is tax deductible, the tax saving derived from the debt financing of B substantially alters the private rate of return on the project. As Table 4–3 illustrates, once the $9,000 interest cost (a 10 percent borrowing rate is assumed) is considered, the annual accounting losses jump to $10,000, up from $1,000 for A. These losses generate an annual tax saving of $5,000, more than enough to cover the negative cash flow of the project. Once the tax savings due to debt financing are considered, the private rate of return jumps to 18 percent, more than double the 7 percent social rate of return. Thus, an income-maximizing private investor in a 50 percent bracket will find projects like B advantageous, even though their social rate of return is quite low.

For project C, the accounting revenue and cost figures are the same as for B. However, an annual market appreciation rate of 4 percent is assumed. Thus, the investor derives a larger capital gain and therefore derives additional income if capital gains are more favorably treated. Even with the 4 percent annual appreciation, project C yields only a social rate of return of 9 percent. But look what happens to the private *after-tax* rate of return. It jumps all the way to 32 percent.

How would the options of Table 4–3 compare with simply supplying one's funds to the loanable funds market? Suppose the investor could earn a real rate of return of 12 percent in the bond market. This would leave the investor with only a 6 percent after-tax return. Despite the fact that their social rate of return is well below the 12 percent rate, the private, *after-tax* rate of return for each of the projects of Table 4–3 is greater than the after-tax rate of return derived in the loanable funds market.

As Table 4–3 illustrates, tax considerations have distorted the investment picture. They have encouraged investors to use loanable funds (which generate deductible interest expense) rather than equity financing. Tax considerations have favored projects that yield accounting losses coupled with capital appreciation rather than investments that yield a flow of taxable income. As a result, investors have been motivated to undertake tax shelter projects (like B and C) even when the social rate of return of such projects has been substantially less than projects (like savings accounts and bonds) that yield a flow of taxable income. In turn, this inefficient use of investment resources has retarded the growth rate of the economy.

THE GROWTH OF THE TAX SHELTER INDUSTRY

If our analysis is correct, we could have predicted that the rising marginal tax rates of the post-1965 period would lead to an expansion in the tax shelter industry and a reduced (relative to what it otherwise would have been) growth rate of the economy. The growth rate of real GNP prior to and subsequent to the mid-1960s is clearly consistent with the sluggish growth hypothesis. During the 1949–1966 period, real GNP grew at a 4.2 percent annual rate. By contrast, during the 1966–1983 period, the real growth of GNP declined to a 2.6 percent annual rate, a decline of almost 40 percent.[7]

What happened to the tax shelter industry after the mid-1960s? Given the broad range of strategies used to shelter income, there is no single indicator of tax shelter activity. However, as we have already discussed, the major tax shelter strategies generate investment and business losses designed to reduce taxable income. Real estate tax shelters generally show up as rental or partnership losses. Such popular tax shelters as oil and gas equipment leasing and movie syndication are usually organized as limited partnerships or sub-S small business corporations (corporations taxed as a personal business). Similarly, cattle feeding (and breeding) and various agriculture-related shelters tend to increase the likelihood of losses from either limited partnerships or farming. Consumption benefit tax shelters often lead to reported losses from business and professional practice, farming, or operation of a small business corporation. Thus, reported losses from rental, business, professional, farm, partnership and small business corporation activities provide insight on both the size and growth rate of tax shelter activities.

Table 4–4 provides data on the proportion of joint returns reporting losses in various categories from 1966, 1973, 1979, and 1981. Throughout this period there was a sharp increase in reported losses in each of the major categories where tax shelter activities influence the data. The *percentage* of joint returns reporting rental income losses rose from 4.48 percent in 1966 to 6.78 percent in 1981. The incidence of business and professional losses among joint returns jumped from 1.92 percent in 1966 to 5.20 percent in 1981. The percentage of returns showing losses from partnerships rose from 0.85 percent to 3.32 percent between 1966 and 1981. Substantial increases in the incidence of losses were also present for farming and small business corporations during the period. The data clearly indicate that more and more taxpayers reported losses—losses that reduced their taxable income—as marginal tax rates increased subsequent to the mid-1960s.

---

7. The number of persons employed grew more rapidly during the latter period. Therefore, the decline in the growth of real GNP *per employee* would show an even greater disparity.

Table 4–4. Proportion of Joint Returns Showing a Net Income Loss From Rents, Business or Professional Practice, Farming, Partnerships, or Small Business Corporations for 1966, 1973, 1979, and 1981.

	1966	1973	1979	1981
Number of joint returns (in thousands)	40,154.8	43,645.2	44,855.1	45,697.6
Number of joint returns with a net income loss (in thousands) from:				
Rents	$1,802.8	$2,095.0	$2,634.2	$3.097.7
Business and professional practice	770.1	1,289.8	1,770.6	2,376.3
Farming	877.2	1,067.0	1,164.7	1,407.4
Partnerships	343.3	669.5	951.3	1,518.4
Small business corporations	73.6	147.9	229.1	316.5
Percentage of joint tax returns showing a net income loss from:				
Rents	4.48%	4.80%	5.87%	6.78%
Business and professional practice	1.92	2.96	3.95	5.20
Farming	2.18	2.44	2.60	3.08
Partnerships	0.85	1.53	2.12	3.32
Small business corporations	0.18	0.34	0.51	0.69

SOURCE: Internal Revenue Service, *Statistics of Income Individual: Tax Returns* (Annual).

Table 4–5 presents data on the size of the reported losses, both in dollars and as a percentage of adjusted gross income. The size of the net income losses increased in each of the five categories throughout the 1966–1981 period. Whereas the net income losses for the five categories summed to only $6.39 billion in 1966, they rose to $67.19 billion in 1981. Measured in constant 1981 dollars, reported losses in these categories quadrupled from $16.1 billion to $67.19 billion. Perhaps what is more significant, the losses increased substantially relative to adjusted gross income (AGI). Rental losses rose from 0.39 percent of AGI to 1.12 percent. Losses from partnerships jumped from 0.31 percent to 1.77 percent of AGI. In 1966, reported losses in the five categories were only 1.74 percent of AGI. By 1973, the com-

Table 4–5. Size of Net Income Losses From Rents, Business or Professional Practice, Farming, Partnerships, and Small Business Corporations as a Proportion of Adjusted Gross Income for Joint Returns, 1966, 1973, 1979, and 1981.

	1966	*1973*	*1979*	*1981*
Number of joint returns (in thousands)	40,154.8	43,645.2	44,855.1	45,697.6
Adjusted gross income (in billions)	$367.63	$632.53	$1,048.17	$1,243.44
Net losses (in billions) on joint returns by source:				
Rents	$ 1.43	$ 2.76	$ 7.88	$ 13.94
Business and professional practice	1.65	3.34	7.66	12.52
Farming	1.72	3.67	7.90	14.40
Partnerships	1.15	4.94	10.09	22.00
Small business corporations	.44	1.09	2.54	4.33
TOTAL	6.39	15.80	36.07	67.19
Net losses as a percentage of adjusted gross income				
Rents	0.39%	0.44%	0.75%	1.12%
Business and professional practice	0.45	0.53	0.73	1.01
Farming	0.47	0.58	0.75	1.16
Partnerships	0.31	0.78	0.96	1.77
Small business corporations	0.12	0.17	0.24	0.35
TOTAL	1.74	2.50	3.44	5.40

SOURCE: Internal Revenue Service, *Statistics of Income: Individual Tax Returns* (Annual).

parable figure was 2.50 percent of AGI. In the latter half of the 1970s, reported losses continued to soar, reaching 3.44 percent of AGI in 1979 before jumping to 5.4 percent in 1981. Thus, in fifteen years losses from these five categories *as a percentage of AGI* more than tripled.

One might question whether the sharp increase in both the incidence and size of the reported losses merely reflects an expansion in certain forms of business organization during the period. Table 4–6

Table 4–6. Net Income Losses Compared With Net Income Gains for Selected Sources of Income, 1966 and 1981.

Source of Income Gain or Loss	1966 Returns			1981 Returns		
	Net Income Gain (in billions)	Net Income Loss (in billions)	Loss/Gain Ratio (percent)	Net Income Gain (in billions)	Net Income Loss (in billions)	Loss/Gain Ratio (percent)
Rents	$ 4.36	$1.75	40.1	$15.05	$17.82	118.4
Business and professional practice	28.14	1.95	6.9	68.53	15.46	22.6
Farming	5.99	1.92	32.0	8.53	16.34	191.6
Partnerships	12.08	1.35	11.2	25.91	26.05	100.5
Small business corporations	1.66	.46	27.7	4.26	5.07	119.0
Total	$52.23	$7.43	14.2	$122.28	$80.74	66.0

SOURCE: Internal Revenue Service, *Statistics of Income: Individual Income Tax Returns* (Annual).

126

helps us better isolate the nature of the losses. Here we present data on the size of the net income losses compared to income gains from these sources of income for 1966 and 1981. In each case the size of the net losses compared to income gains jumped sharply between 1966 and 1981. In 1966 rental income losses were only 40.1 percent as iarge as rental income gains. By 1981 net losses from rental property were actually greater than the net income gains. Whereas, the losses were modest compared to gains in 1966, the 1981 data indicate that taxpayers renting out properties were losing money hand over fist. The losses relative to the gains followed a similar pattern in other categories. In 1966, net income losses from farming were only 32 percent of the reported income gains. By 1981, farming losses were almost twice as great as gains. Losses from partnerships jumped from 11.2 percent of the income gains to 100.5 percent between 1966 and 1981. Small business corporation losses rose from 27.7 percent of the gains in 1966 to 119.0 percent in 1981.

In 1966, net income gains from these five categories were seven times the losses, $52.23 billion compared to $7.43 billion. By 1981, the gains ($122.3 billion) were only one and one-half times the losses ($80.74 billion). Yet, in spite of this enormous growth of reported losses relative to gains, more and more taxpayers continued to allocate funds to these areas. Perhaps more than anything else, this is telling evidence that the reported losses did not reflect a deterioration of *personal* after-tax returns in these areas.

THE LONG-RUN LAFFER CURVE—EMPIRICAL EVIDENCE

The findings of Tables 4–4, 4–5, and 4–6 are highly consistent with the view that the rising marginal tax rates of recent years have induced taxpayers to undertake business and investment tax shelter projects that they would not have undertaken at lower marginal tax rates. However, these data lack the precision necessary to estimate the impact of higher marginal tax rates on taxable income and tax liability. In order to add precision, we obtained detailed tax information from the *1979 Individual Tax Model File* available from the Internal Revenue Service. This data base provides information on deductions and sources of income (and losses). It also identifies the state of residence of the taxpayer, number of exemptions, and status of person(s) filing the return (e.g., married, filing joint return). Since the data base contains an oversampling of high income returns, analysis can be conducted for a full range of income categories. In order to reduce variability from factors outside the focus of our study, only taxpayers filing joint returns were included in our analysis.

Seeking to obtain an income measure that was not contaminated by tax sheltering, we developed a gross income variable. "Gross income" is defined as the positive components of income and thus is a measure of taxpayer income prior to engaging in tax shelter activities. In contrast, "adjusted gross income," as defined by the IRS, indicates the income of taxpayers *after* deduction of losses from many, if not most, tax shelter activities. Thus, gross income is a better indicator of the taxpayer's income level in the absence of tax shelter activity.

Initially, we disaggregated the data base into six gross income cells and investigated the incidence of losses in the major areas influenced by tax sheltering activities. As Table 4–7 illustrates, the incidence of losses from rents, business and professional practice, farming, partnerships, and small business corporations increased with gross income in 1979. For example, while only 3.7 percent of the joint returns with gross incomes in the 0–$25,000 class reported income losses from rents, more than 20 percent of the returns with a gross income of $75,000 or more reported rental losses. While less than 3 percent of the taxpayers with a gross income of less than $50,000 experienced losses from partnerships, 27.9 percent, 43.7 percent, and 79.8 percent reported losses in the three highest income groupings. A similar pattern was present for farm and small business corporation losses.

Table 4–7 also presents data on the mean dollar amount of losses for returns in each of the six income groupings. As expected, the data indicate that the dollar amount of the losses was largest in the three highest income categories where taxpayers confront the highest marginal tax rates. While the sum of the mean losses from the five sources reported in Table 4–7 was less than $1,000 for the two lowest income categories, the mean losses summed to $6,711, $17,575 and a whopping $150,345 respectively for taxpayers in the three highest income categories.

In order to isolate more fully the impact of tax rates on tax sheltering and, in turn, taxable income, we utilized the 1979 IRS sample data for joint returns to test a straightforward regression model. Our model hypothesizes the following relationship:

$$\text{Taxable Income} = f(MTR, GI, Age, PE, \text{ and } IA)$$

Table 4–7. Income Losses in Major Areas Influenced by Tax Shelter Activity According to Gross Income, Joint Return 1979.

	Gross Income (in thousands)					
	$0–25	$25–50	$50–75	$75–125	$125–200	Over $200
Number of joint returns	43,258	35,590	16,786	13,541	9,784	4,662
Percent of returns with losses from:						
Rents	3.7	7.9	16.9	19.9	21.8	29.8
Business and Professional practice	3.6	4.2	5.5	6.6	8.3	18.9
Farming	2.4	2.6	3.9	4.9	6.5	13.3
Partnerships	0.9	2.8	13.0	27.9	43.7	79.8
Small business Corp.	0.2	0.6	2.2	4.3	7.1	20.9
Mean dollar amount of losses[a] from:						
Rents	$60	$211	$795	$1,450	$2,189	$10,384
Business and Professional practice	116	138	364	699	1,736	16,706
Farming	120	153	440	928	1,927	12,927
Partnerships	28	88	779	3,042	10,312	96,061
Small business Corp.	14	40	176	592	1,411	14,267
TOTAL	$338	$630	$2,554	$6,711	$17,575	$150,345

SOURCE: Derived from *Internal Revenue Service: 1979 Individual Tax Model File and 1979 State Tax Model File.*

[a]The mean figure is for all returns in the class, not just those which reported losses from the source. Means and percentages are weighted.

129

where *MTR* is the combined marginal federal and state income tax rate the taxpayer would confront in the absence of deductible expenditures and deductions for losses, *GI* is the gross income of the tax return, *Age* is a dummy variable indicating the taxpayer is age 65 or over, *PE* is the number of personal exemptions, and *IA* is a dummy variable indicating taxpayers using the income averaging method to calculate their tax liability.

The state indicator allows us to integrate the state and federal tax structures. In fact, this is the major source of variation in marginal tax rates *within income categories*.[8] Taxpayers residing in states where the state marginal tax rate is higher will confront higher marginal tax rates than taxpayers in states with lower rates. State marginal tax rates range from zero in states without an income tax to maximum rates in the teens in several states.[9] Therefore, even after making allowance for the deductibility of state income tax payments on one's federal return, differences in state income tax rates lead to substantial differences in marginal rates among taxpayers with similar gross income and number of exemptions.

Within the framework of our model we are most interested in the impact of changes in marginal tax rates on taxable income. Since higher marginal rates increase the taxpayer's incentive to shelter income and thereby reduce taxable income,[10] we expect a negative relationship between taxable income and marginal tax rates. The regression equations for our model are presented in the Appendix to this chapter. Table 4–8 summarizes the results. As expected, higher marginal tax rates exerted a negative impact on taxable income for all income categories. Predictably, the largest negative impact was for the high income (and high marginal tax rate) categories. For the zero to $25,000 gross income cell, after adjusting for gross income, age, personal exemptions, and income averaging, taxable income de-

8. The marginal tax rates of taxpayers with the same gross income and number of personal exemptions will differ only because of differences in state income tax rates.

9. Florida, Nevada, South Dakota, Texas, Washington, and Wyoming did not levy a state income tax. In contrast, California, Delaware, Hawaii, Iowa, Minnesota, Montana, New York, and Wisconsin all levied maximum rates of 11 percent or more in 1979.

10. Since we are interested only in taxpayers' decision-making that influences their taxable income, our taxable income variable *adds* state and local tax deductions to the taxpayers' taxable income. Thus, the lower taxable income for taxpayers confronting high marginal tax rates reflects factors other than the deductibility of state and local tax liability from their gross income.

Table 4–8.   Estimated Elasticity of Taxable Income With Respect to Marginal Tax Rates for Various Income Categories, Joint Returns, 1979.

Gross Income	Impact of One-Unit Increase in Marginal Tax on Taxable Income	Estimated Elasticity of Taxable Income With Respect to MTR	Hypothetical Marginal Federal Income Tax Rate, Midpoint of Income Interval, 1979[a]
$	$		%
0– 25,000	−7	−.01	16
25– 50,000	−18	−.03	32
50– 75,000	−211	−.24	43
75–125,000	−1,593	−1.30	54
125–200,000	−4,043	−2.19	64
over 200,000	−5,708	−3.93	68+

SOURCE: Derived from Internal Revenue Service, *1979 Individual Tax Model File and 1979 State Tax Model File*. See Appendix for full equations.

[a]Assumes a family of four, with husband and wife filing a joint return. Deductions from gross income are assumed to be 22 percent of gross income.

clined by $7 for every one-unit increase in marginal tax rates. For the $25,000 to $50,000 gross income grouping, taxable income is estimated to decline by $18 for each one-unit increase in marginal tax rates. As one moves to income groupings above $50,000, the negative impact of marginal tax rates increases. For the $50,000 to $75,000 gross income cell, the negative impact of a unit tax rate change rose to $211. The parallel estimates for other income groupings were minus $1,593 for the $75,000–$125,000 grouping, minus $4,043 for the $125,000–$200,000 class, and minus $5,708 for tax returns with more than $200,000 of gross income.[11]

---

11. Our estimate for the open-ended $200,000 and above grouping should be interpreted with caution. Since the Internal Revenue Service does not provide information on state of residence for returns with an *adjusted gross income* of $200,000 and over, these returns had to be excluded from our analysis. Thus, we are left with persons who had an *adjusted gross income* of less than $200,000, but a gross income (positive components of income) of more than $200,000. The more tax sheltering undertaken by taxpayers with an adjusted gross income near the $200,000 cutoff, the more likely their gross income will place them in our $200,000 and over bracket. Therefore, taxpayers in our $200,000 and over gross income grouping may be a bias sample of all returns in this bracket.

These estimates can be easily converted to tax rate elasticities. The tax rate elasticity coefficient is equal to

$$\frac{\text{percent change in taxable income}}{\text{percent change in marginal tax rate}}$$

Since the tax base and tax rate generally change in opposite directions, a negative tax rate elasticity coefficient is expected. If the percentage change in the tax base (taxable income in our case) is less than the percentage change in the tax rate, the elasticity coefficient will be less than one. Under these circumstances, higher (lower) marginal tax rates would lead to an expansion (contraction) in tax revenues. In contrast, when a change in the tax rate leads to an even larger change in the tax base, the tax rate elasticity coefficient will be greater than one. When this is the case, higher (lower) tax rates would lead to a reduction (increase) in tax revenues. Tax rate elasticity coefficients in excess of unity indicate that taxpayers in the grouping are on the backward bending portion of their Laffer curve.

Table 4–8 (column 2) presents estimates for the tax rate elasticity coefficient for each of the six gross income groupings. For income cells below $75,000 (and federal tax rates of 43 percent or less), the tax elasticity coefficient is small—less than 0.24. However, beginning with the $75,000 to $125,000 gross income cell, the estimated elasticities rise sharply. For the three highest income (and marginal tax) groupings, the estimated tax elasticity coefficient is greater than one. This indicates that lower marginal rates in these cells would have raised more tax revenue.

Perhaps a little additional discussion is necessary to highlight the importance of these estimates. Consider the $50,000 to $75,000 gross income category. Our analysis indicates that taxpayers who have the same gross income (remember gross income is a control variable in the model) report $211 less taxable income for each one-unit increase in their effective marginal tax rate. Given the shrinkage in taxable income as tax rates rise in this grouping, it takes a substantial increase in tax rates in order to squeeze additional tax revenue from this tax bracket. In fact, the estimated tax elasticity of minus 0.24 indicates that a 10 percent increase in tax rates in this bracket will reduce taxable income by 2.4 percent. Thus, the 10 percent higher marginal rates will lead to, at most, only about an 8 percent increase in revenues from taxpayers in this bracket.

For higher incomes (and tax rates), the tax elasticity is still greater.

For example, the 1.30 estimated tax elasticity in the $75,000 to $125,000 grouping indicates that a 10 percent rate hike in this category would cause a 13.0 percent shrinkage in taxable income. Of course, since the decline in the tax base is larger than the increase in rates, higher rates for this bracket would lead to a reduction in revenue collected. As of 1979, our estimates indicate that taxpayers in this grouping were on the backward bending segment of the Laffer curve. As expected, the estimated elasticities are even larger for the two highest income categories.[12]

In interpreting our results, it is important to keep two points in mind. First, our estimates reflect long-run adjustments. As Buchanan and Lee have discussed, one would expect the short-run Laffer curve to be more inelastic than the long-run curve. Stated another way, one would expect a smaller shrinkage in the tax base in the year or two immediately following a rate increase than the shrinkage that will eventually take place as the result of a tax rate increase.[13] The major factor contributing to rate differences within income categories in our model is differences in state income tax rates. Since the general pattern of state rates has been in place for a considerable period of time, it is reasonable to assume that taxpayers have adjusted their tax sheltering activities accordingly. Thus, one should not apply our tax elasticity estimates to year-to-year changes in the rate structure. Time periods as short as a year or two may be too brief for taxpayers to fully adjust to a new rate structure.

Second, it is important to recognize that tax rate elasticities differ among income brackets. As our estimates indicate, the tax rate elasticities generally vary inversely with the marginal tax rate of an income bracket. In income brackets characterized by low marginal tax rates (say less than 20 percent), an increase in marginal tax rates will exert little negative impact on taxable income (see Table 4–8). Predictably, in low marginal rate categories, tax rate increases will lead to only a slightly less than proportional increase in tax revenues. In

12. Our model estimates the impact of a change in tax rates on taxable income, *holding gross income constant*. To the extent that higher marginal rates also induce taxpayers to consume more leisure, engage in the underground economy, shift income to closely held corporations, or take other steps (e.g., purchase municipal bonds) to reduce their reported gross income, our model will *under*estimate the negative impact of higher marginal tax rates on the taxable income base.

13. See James M. Buchanan and Dwight R. Lee, "Politics, Time, and the Laffer Curve," *Journal of Political Economy* 90 (no. 4, 1982): 816–19.

contrast, in income brackets characterized by high marginal rates (say composite federal and state rates of 40 percent or more), the same percentage increase in tax rates will exert a larger negative impact on taxable income.[14] For the higher rate brackets, tax revenues will increase considerably less than proportionally to the rate increases. At still higher rates, composite rates of approximately 50 percent according to our estimates, rate increases will eventually lead to a reduction in tax revenues collected from taxpayers confronting the higher rates, just as the backward bending Laffer curve implies.

Failing to recognize that tax elasticities vary across tax brackets, many commentators (economists among them) continue to discuss tax issues as if there is a single tax elasticity that applies to a nation. They pose questions like: "Is the United States on the backward bending segment of the Laffer curve?" or "Will the tax cut really increase tax revenues?" These are silly questions. There is no single tax elasticity that applies to a nation. Given the rate structure in the United States, most taxpayers are on the upward sloping segment of their Laffer curve. For these individuals higher marginal rates will increase tax revenues. However, at the same time, our analysis indicates that there have been other taxpayers in high marginal tax brackets characterized by the backward bending segment of the Laffer curve. In these brackets, higher tax rates do not expand tax revenues. In fact, at least in the long run, our evidence suggests that more revenue would have been collected if rates had been reduced in these high tax brackets.

Isn't this what the tax reductions of 1981–1984 accomplished? Of course, the lower rates increased the proportion of income the taxpayer was permitted to keep, thereby reducing the incentive to engage in tax sheltering. However, as Table 4–2 illustrates, the rate reduc-

14. Taxable income will fall by a larger amount because the same percentage increase in tax rates will cause a larger reduction in after-tax income (take-home pay) in the high tax brackets. For example, for a taxpayer initially in the 10 percent marginal tax bracket, a 20 percent increase in tax rates (from 10 percent to 12 percent) would reduce the take-home pay by only 2.2 percent (from 90 cents to 88 cents per dollar of additional earnings). In contrast, for a taxpayer confronting a 60 percent marginal rate, a 20 percent rate increase would reduce take-home pay by 30 percent (from 40 cents to 28 cents per dollar of additional earnings). From an incentive standpoint, the impact of a tax rate increase on the after-tax income of taxpayers as their earnings expand is what really matters. Therefore, predictably, the disincentive effects of a tax rate increase will be greatest in the highest tax brackets. See James Gwartney and Richard Stroup, "Tax Cuts: Who Shoulders the Burden?" *Economic Review— Federal Reserve Bank of Atlanta*, March 1982, for additional details on this issue.

tions were quite modest once the impact of "bracket creep" and higher Social Security taxes is factored into the analysis. In addition the 1981 legislation provided more rapid write-offs for depreciation. Fixed structures could be written off in 15 years (6.67 percent each year under the straight-line method) rather than the 25 to 30 year write-off period (3.3 to 4 percent per year) applicable prior to the legislation. The more rapid write-offs for depreciation made it easier (less costly) to move income into the future and transform it into capital gains. On balance, there is little reason to believe that the 1981 tax legislation significantly reduced the level of tax sheltering activity.

POLICY IMPLICATIONS

Our analysis indicates that existing marginal tax rates continue to induce taxpayers to engage in inefficient tax sheltering activities. Two reforms would substantially reduce the profitability of these activities.

1. *A True Flat-Rate Tax.* High marginal tax rates provide the major incentive for tax shelter activity. They distort economic choices and encourage people to purchase goods valued less highly than their production costs. Adoption of a low flat-rate tax would take much of the gain out of tax sheltering. Improved economic efficiency and more rapid growth of income would result. There are two major stumbling blocks to the adoption of a true flat-rate tax: (a) the perception that it would shift the tax burden away from the rich and (b) the opposition of persons and businesses who still benefit from tax sheltering. Briefly we will consider each.

Wouldn't a true flat-rate tax be a windfall for the rich? This question is confusing to many because they fail to recognize that taxable income is negatively related to tax rates. Thus, they incorrectly conclude that higher rates will mean a proportional increase in revenues. The old structure taxed the rich at a very high *rate,* but the high rates did not generate much additional *revenue.* In 1979, marginal tax rates above 28 percent generated only 10 percent of the total federal income tax revenue. Even this figure is an *overestimate* of the additional revenue generated by the higher marginal rates. If the rates had not been so high, tax sheltering would not have been as profitable for high-income taxpayers. The "rich" would have engaged in less tax sheltering, which would have left them with more taxable income. Our estimates indicate that a major portion of the revenue losses *from the rich* associated with a reduction in the highest marginal rates would be replaced with additional revenue collections *from the rich* because their taxable incomes will expand as the lower rates reduce the profitability of tax sheltering. Robert Hall and Alvin Rabushka have shown that a flat rate tax of 19 percent accompanied with larger personal exemption allowances and elimination of deductible personal expenditures would lead to approximately the same *average* tax liability across income groupings as does the current structure.[15] Our analysis indicates that, if anything, their projections were based on tax elasticities that were too low for the upper tax brackets.

The bottom line on the distributional issue is that it is clearly possible to devise a true flat-rate tax capable of generating an amount of *revenue* from high income taxpayers similar to that generated by the current structure. Remember, high marginal rates make tax deductible expenditures cheap for the rich. The move to a true flat-rate tax would bring a host of negative-sum activities to a halt.

Ideally, a flat rate tax should be accompanied by a substantial narrowing, if not a complete elimination, of personal deduction allowances. Of course, individuals and organizations that benefit from these allowances oppose their elimination. State and local policy-makers oppose eliminating the deductions for state and local taxes. Most politicians perceive that the home mortgage interest deduction is a sacred cow. Predictably, charitable organizations fight to preserve the deductibility of charitable contributions.

Without getting into a full-scale debate on the pros and cons of each individual deduction, we would like to note that the case for several of the deductible items is shaky at best. For example, why should the *after-tax* borrowing costs be lower for high-income taxpayers? The "other interest" (interest expense other than for home mortgage deductions) is primarily a subsidy to high-income taxpayers. In 1979, the mean "other interest expense" of taxpayers with a gross income of $200,000 and over was 62 times the mean deduction for returns with less than $25,000 of gross income![16] While the disparity across income groupings is less for the home mortgage interest deduction, it too provides disproportional tax savings to persons in upper income brackets.

15. See Robert E. Hall and Alvin Rabushka, *Low Tax, Simple Tax, Flat Tax* (New York: McGraw-Hill Book Company, 1983).

16. The mortgage interest and other interest deductions by gross income in 1979 were as follows:

2. *Integrate the Corporate and Personal Income Tax Structure.* It makes good rhetoric to talk about shifting the tax burden to business—implying a shift from individuals to nonpersons (business firms). But the truth is, all taxes are paid by people. Although corporations are sometimes the legal entity writing the check to the government, they do not pay taxes. They merely collect tax revenues from customers, employees, or stockholders and transfer them to the government. People pay all taxes.

Like other businesses, corporations generate profits or losses for their owners. But the way in which corporate income is taxed differs from that of other business income. Corporate income is taxed initially as corporate income. Then, it is taxed again as either (a) ordinary income if it is paid out as dividends or (b) capital gains (or losses) when the corporate ownership rights are sold to another after being held for more than one year.

There is no justification for using the tax system to discriminate among alternative forms of business organization. The conduct of business should be determined by business efficiency, not tax considerations. The discrimination imposed by the current tax system would be eliminated if the corporation and personal income taxes were integrated. Under this arrangement, corporate income (like other business income) would be taxed as it accrues to business owners. Like other business income, corporate income would be taxed only once. But all corporate income—regardless of whether paid out as dividends or maintained as retained earnings—would be taxed as ordinary income.

Integration of the corporate and personal tax structures would eliminate the incentive of individuals to play games in order to reduce their tax liability. Individuals would no longer expend unnecessary

Gross Income	Interest on Home Mortgages	Other Interest
($)	($)	($)
0–25,000	464	194
25–50,000	1,530	699
50–75,000	2,450	1,415
75–125,000	2,982	2,638
125–200,000	3,205	5,038
200,000 and over	4,258	12,673

legal and accounting fees to maintain the corporate form merely because of the tax advantages that it sometimes provides.

Simultaneously, distortions introduced by the double taxation of corporate income would be eliminated. If the corporate form is the least costly method of doing business, it will be chosen (rather than forsaken in order to avoid double taxation, as is sometimes the case under the current structure). Similarly, the bias against dividends and in favor of retained earnings would be eliminated, since the net earnings derived from the corporation would be taxable as personal income regardless of whether they are paid out to the stockholder. Predictably, corporate business expenses would be monitored more closely, since the stockholders would now be able to capture increases in net corporate income more fully. Managers would be able to turn their attention away from income-shifting schemes and toward the generation of real wealth, all of which would be fully taxable as personal income to the stockholders during the period in which it is generated.

In conclusion, we believe the evidence indicates that the system of recent years has involved an enormous amount of slippage—wealth-consuming activities motivated by the profitability of tax sheltering. The proposals we have suggested substantially reduce the profitability of such wasteful activities and improve the efficiency of our capital formation. As a result, a larger economic pie is made possible in the future.

Appendix.   Estimated Impact of a Change in Marginal Tax Rates on Taxable Income in 1979 for Various Gross Income Groupings, Joint Returns—Regression Model.

Independent Variables	Dependent Variable = Taxable Income[a] (T-ratios in parentheses)					
	Gross Income			Groupings (in thousands)		
	$0–25	$25–50	$50–75	$75–125	$125–200	Over $200
Marginal Tax Rate	−7 (−4.15)	−18 (−3.0)	−211 (−7.4)	−1593 (−35.4)	−4043 (−65.7)	−5708 (−55.4)
Gross Income	.923 (361.5)	.831 (143.1)	.768 (56.3)	.875 (59.2)	.708 (44.3)	−.050 (−6.1)
No. of Personal Exemptions	−23 (−3.8)	−241 (−15.8)	−511 (−8.8)	−1025 (−9.6)	−2665 (−11.6)	2199 (5.4)
Taxpayer over Age 65 (1 if yes)	−25 (−1.2)	218 (2.2)	2432 (8.9)	9711 (20.5)	22391 (23.0)	27501 (13.8)
Taxpayer Used Income Averaging	478 (8.1)	910 (16.22)	4020 (24.5)	8076 (25.7)	30487 (34.9)	43983 (28.0)
Constant	−2721 (−94.7)	612 (4.3)	11006 (8.6)	80669 (33.7)	247961 (57.1)	471078 (68.4)
R^2	.77	.39	.19	.39	.41	.59
Number of Returns	43,258	35,590	16,786	13,467	9,784	4,662
Mean Taxable Income (in dollars)	10,588	26,484	46,372	71,490	113,234	97,352

SOURCE: The data base was the IRS stratified sample of individual tax returns for 1979 contained in *1979 Individual Tax Model File* and *1979 State Tax Model File.*

[a]Taxable income is equal to adjusted gross income minus personal deductions. For persons who itemized, the state and local taxes were added to taxable income in order to avoid downward bias in the taxable income variable that merely reflected the deductibility of state and local taxes.

5

TITHING FOR LEVIATHAN: THE CASE FOR A TRUE FLAT-RATE TAX

Richard K. Vedder

In recent years, considerable interest, has developed in effecting a radical reform of our income tax system, with much of the attention focused on the "flat rate tax." A *true* flat-rate tax is an ad valorem levy on income, or some other basis of taxation (e.g., consumption spending), where the percentage tax rate applied is the same for all taxpayers. The most publicized pure flat-rate proposal, for example, that of Stanford University scholars Robert Hall and Alvin Rabushka, would levy a 19 percent charge on all income subject to taxation.[1]

Many so-called flat-rate tax proposals, including President Reagan's, involved significant changes in the tax system and a sharp reduction in the progressivity of marginal tax rates, but have not been truly "flat rate" in character. Another notable example was the proposal of Senator Bill Bradley and Congressman Richard Gephardt for an individual income tax with an expanded tax base and marginal rates of from 14 to 30 percent.

Some current flat-rate proposals, such as that of Hall and Rabushka, integrate business and individual taxation, taxing business income at the same rate as income that accrues directly to individuals. Other proposals involve substantially less integration or even ignore

---

1. For a discussion of that proposal, see Robert E. Hall and Alvin Rabushka, *Low Tax, Simple Tax, Flat Tax* (New York: McGraw-Hill, 1983).

the question of business taxation completely. Similarly, some proposals for a flat tax or a quasi-flat tax (e.g., the Bradley-Gephardt proposal) have maintained income as the basis for taxation, while others (e.g., Hall-Rabushka) use, explicitly or implicitly, a consumption or modified consumption basis for taxation.

THE EXPERIENCE WITH FLAT RATE TAXATION

The United States has never had a national, truly flat rate income tax, the closest approximation in modern times being the initial levy after the passage of the Sixteenth (income tax) Amendment, which had marginal tax rates ranging from 1 to 7 percent. The concept of flat rate taxation is not new, however. As the title of this paper suggests, in Biblical times the tithe (10 percent flat-rate levy) served as a basis of religious "taxation," and the faithful contributed at the same rate regardless of economic circumstance. In a sense, some of the current flat-rate proposals advocate "rendering unto Caesar" a double tithe of about 20 percent.

Victorian Britain introduced essentially flat rate income taxation as it phased out duties (e.g., the Corn Laws) and became a bastion of free trade. A combination of wars and changing political philosophy led to the breakdown of the flat rate concept, but one could argue that the golden age of Britain's economy was one in which income was taxed at a low (or zero) flat rate. Similarly, today flat rate or nearly flat rate taxes exist in a few locales, such as Hong Kong and the Isle of Man. Some scholars—Alvin Rabushka, for example— argue that Hong Kong's flat rate tax policies have contributed to that colony's extraordinary economic boom.[2]

The best example of flat rate taxation at work, however, is found within the United States itself, namely in a number of states that tax income at a low (or even zero) flat rate. While the overall income taxation in those states is obviously progressive in a marginal rate sense because of the federal income tax, these jurisdictions follow the flat rate principle in the tax laws they have created and administered. In addition to states that have flat rate taxation at some positive rate (e.g., Illinois and Michigan) or at zero rate (e.g., Texas and Florida), there are states that have nearly flat rate taxes (e.g., Mississippi), where there is very little marginal rate progressivity.

---

2. See, for example, Rabushka's book *Hong Kong: A Study in Economic Freedom* (Chicago: University of Chicago Graduate School of Business, 1979).

As the previous discussion implies, there are degrees of "flatness" or "progressivity" in the marginal rate structure. While a purist might insist that a tax is either truly flat rate or not, in fact a continuum exists between a truly flat rate tax at one extreme and a tax with exceedingly high levels of marginal rate progressivity (e.g., 1 percent to 99 percent) at the other.

There are a variety of ways of measuring the flatness of an income (or consumption) tax. One crude but straightforward way is simply to subtract the lowest marginal tax rate from the highest rate. The closer to zero that number is, the more truly flat rate the tax is. Figure 5–1 examines the flatness of the federal individual income tax since the passage of the Sixteenth Amendment. Note that while there has never been a true flat-rate tax, there have been short periods (before World War I, in the twenties) where the marginal rate progressivity was not too different from that proposed in some of the recent quasi-flat-rate proposals such as Bradley-Gephardt.

There are problems with this measure of flatness, one of which is that the proportion of the population impacted by the maximum and minimum rates has changed over time, in part because of changes in the income brackets subject to those rates and in part because of changes in deductions, exemptions, exclusions, and even in the definition of the taxpayer unit (e.g., the concept of a "joint return" has existed for only about half the history of the income tax). An alternative approach is to compare the marginal tax rate of a taxpayer with the effective or *average* rate. With a true flat rate with no income exclusions whatsoever (e.g., no allowance for dependents), the average and marginal rate would be identical. With a flat rate tax with only modest income deductions permitted, the ratio of the marginal to the average tax rate should be only modestly greater than one for most taxpayers. Let us illustrate. Suppose a family has $25,000 income and that a 20 percent flat-rate tax exists with a dependency allowance (income exclusion) of $5,000. The family would pay $4,000 in tax (20 percent of $20,000), which is 16 percent of total income of $25,000. The marginal tax rate of 20 percent is only 1.25 times the average tax rate of 16 percent. The ratio of the marginal to the average tax rate might be called the *flatness index;* the closer the index is to one, the more like a true flat-rate tax is the existing tax structure.

Thus an increase in the flatness index over time probably means that the tax system is becoming "less flat." The word "probably" is used because it is possible with a pure flat-rate tax to change the ratio of marginal to average taxation simply by changing the definition of

Figure 5–1.   Flatness of the U.S. Individual Income Tax, 1913–1984.

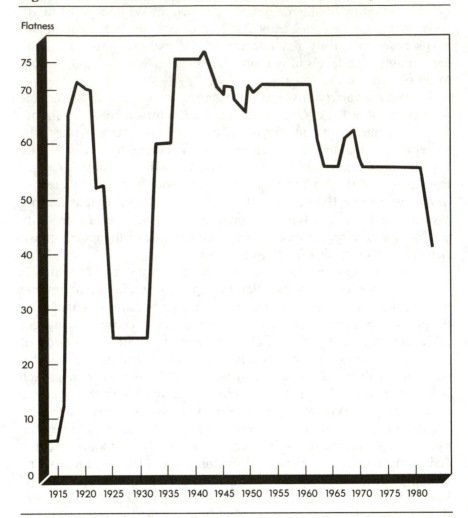

SOURCE: U.S. Department of Commerce.

Note: Flatness is measured by subtracting the minimal marginal rate from the maximum marginal rate.

the base subject to taxation. Accordingly there is some truth to the assertion that the issue of the flatness of the rate schedule can be logically separated from the issue of the size of the base subject to taxation. In a practical political sense, however, a moderately low rate flat tax with revenue-raising potential similar to that of a highly

Table 5–1.   Flatness Index, 1960–1982.

Year	$20,000	$35,000	$50,000
1960	1.80	1.61	1.58
1970	1.71	1.67	1.79
1975	1.81	1.74	1.90
1980	2.12	1.97	1.88
1982	1.91	2.12	1.84

SOURCE: U.S. Department of Commerce.

Note: The flatness index is the marginal tax rate divided by the effective (average) rate and is for a married couple with two dependents. Income figures are adjusted gross income in constant 1980 dollars, deflated by the personal consumption expenditure deflator.

progressive rate tax is possible only with a relatively broad tax base; thus the issue of "flatness" and the definition of the tax base are in fact logically related. All serious flat tax proposals introduced in Congress call for both increased flatness of the rate structure and a broadening of the tax base.

Aside from measuring the extent to which the tax system resembles a flat tax, the flatness index may say something about the efficiency effects of existing income taxation. Economists are generally agreed that economic activity is influenced by marginal rather than average tax rates and by disincentive effects and distortions in economic activity (to the degree that some activity is exempt from taxation).[3] A rise in the flatness index over time, then, would suggest that the disincentive effects of the system are growing.

Table 5–1 looks at the flatness index over recent years for various incomes, with the results suggesting that the federal income tax became less "flat" and that the potential economic problems associated with the deviation of average from marginal rates grew over time. This may explain why interest in flat rate taxation has grown sub-

3. On a nontechnical level, see Bruce Bartlett, *Reaganomics: Supply Side Economics in Action* (Westport, Conn: Arlington House, 1981). On a more technical level, see the essays in David G. Raboy, ed., *Essays in Supply Side Economics* (Washington, D.C.: Institute for Research in the Economics of Taxation, 1982). Other recent representative studies showing some of the distortion problems with the current tax system include Martin S. Feldstein, *Inflation, Tax Rates and Capital Formation* (Chicago: University of Chicago Press, 1983); Henry J. Aaron and Michael J. Boskin, eds., *Economics of Taxation* (Washington, D.C.: The Brookings Institution, 1980), and Aaron Wildavsky and Michael J. Boskin, eds., *Federal Budget: Economics and Politics* (San Francisco: Institute for Contemporary Studies, 1982).

stantially in recent years. Earlier, say in 1965, the tax system deviated far less from a flat rate structure than has recently been the case, so the need for a flat tax was not perceived by its potential proponents to be as strong as is the case now. To the extent that necessity is the mother of invention, the invention of flat rate tax proposals has reflected the growing deviation of the tax system from an earlier, more clearly "quasi-flat tax" form.

WHAT IS A "GOOD" TAX?

In evaluating the soundness of any tax, scholars of public finance and taxation conventionally look at three types of criteria: (1) the administrative costs of the tax, (2) the economic effects of the tax, and (3) the fairness or equity of the tax.

Administrative Costs

Other things being equal, a good tax will cost relatively little to collect. If it costs 90 cents to raise a dollar in revenues, the tax yields little net revenue for the government yet absorbs human resources that presumably could be used in a better fashion than in merely transferring income from individual taxpayers to the persons collecting taxes. Yet administrative costs should truly include not merely the explicit costs to the state of tax collection, but also the costs (which are usually implicit or hidden rather than involving a direct cash outlay) to the taxpayers of complying with the tax. A tax that takes one hour to complete and pay is more desirable than one that takes three hours, since the taxpayer presumably places some positive value on his or her leisure time and prefers other activities to computing taxes. The proliferation of tax services like H & R Block is ample evidence that many Americans want to reduce the time spent in tax preparation.

"Administrative costs" also relate to the question of tax compliance. If large numbers of people can evade a tax easily, the administrative costs of enforcing compliance rise. In addition, substantial noncompliance raises other problems. Is it fair for honest people to pay a tax and dishonest ones not to pay it? Does the disrespect for the rule of law cause by widespread tax evasion lead to an increase in other kinds of crime? What are the ethical and moral implications of having a large proportion of the population engaged in petty (or not so petty) thievery against the government?

Economic Effects

A tax that has the impact of reallocating resources from more valuable or productive activities to less productive activities will reduce output and cause a welfare loss, to the extent that the lost output would have provided utility or satisfaction to its recipients. While virtually every tax causes some changes in economic behavior, the extent to which taxes distort or alter economic activity varies.

A simple example is in order. Let us suppose that a high excise tax were levied on only, say, perfumes and deodorants. Such a tax would raise the relative price of these goods dramatically and lead to sharp reductions in the sale of these goods, whereas a very small sales tax raising the same revenue but levied on *all* goods and services would probably have a very small impact on deodorant and perfume sales, and a small impact on other goods as well. With the general sales tax there would be no large change in the price of any one good relative to other goods, and the tax would have comparatively "neutral" economic effects (i.e., it would not distort resources strongly toward or away from some use existing before the tax was imposed). The deodorant tax was decidedly nonneutral, leading to a sharp reduction in the resources that market forces would have otherwise allocated to deodorant protection. Unless it can somehow be demonstrated that market prices fail to reveal the true social costs of deodorant use, the nonneutral deodorant tax leads to a suboptimal use of deodorants and a reduction in human welfare.

Other things being equal, the more "neutral" a tax is, the better the tax. This applies to the supply as well as the demand side. As other chapters in this volume indicate, a major criticism levied against American income taxation has been that it is nonneutral with respect to savings and capital, favoring consumption. Savings have been reduced materially from the level a neutral tax system would provide.[4]

4. Studies abound. See, for example, Norman B. Ture and B. Kenneth Sanden, *The Effects of Tax Policy on Capital Formation* (New York: Financial Executives Research Foundation, 1977); Michael J. Boskin, "Taxation, Saving, and the Rate of Interest," *Journal of Political Economy* 86 (March–April 1978): 53–27; Arnold C. Harberger, *Taxation and Welfare* (Boston: Little, Brown, 1974); and Charles E. McLure, Jr., *Must Corporate Income Be Taxed Twice?* (Washington, D.C.: The Brookings Institution, 1979). Of course, there is also the whole question of the role played by Social Security payroll taxes and expenditures on savings. The most cited (and controversial) study is Martin S. Feldstein, "Social Security, Induced Retirement and Aggregate Capital Formation," *Journal of Political Economy* 82 (Sept.–Oct. 1974):905–26.

To cite but one example, the double taxation of profits at the corporate and individual level has served to raise rates of taxation on income from capital above taxes on income from labor; this in turn probably lowered the rate of capital formation and consequently the rate of economic growth. If a change in the form of taxation leads to a decline in the rate of economic growth, there is a very good possibility that the tax change can be criticized for leading to a less efficient use of economic resources, a point to which we will return shortly.

Fairness or Equity

Although a tax may be inexpensively collected and may have relatively few adverse economic effects, it can still be considered a bad tax on the grounds that it is unjust or unfair. Clearly the best tax on the grounds of both ease of administration and efficiency is a head tax: a levy of a fixed number of dollars on every citizen. Easy and cheap to collect, the tax involves no levy on additional or marginal work or on capital formation, and does not distort relative prices. It is as "neutral" a tax as possible. Yet head taxes are widely perceived to be most unfair, since they violate the "ability to pay" principle of taxation and are highly regressive, burdening the poor more than the rich.

While no one disputes the importance of equity as a consideration in taxation, it is nonetheless a rather subjective and even elusive concept. Scholars have written reams of material on tax fairness, yet no amount of expertise can determine the "optimal" tax from an equity perspective, since determining fairness essentially involves making value judgments, and values differ widely. What is perceived as "fair" by one person may be viewed as terribly unfair by another. Most people believe that equity dictates at least a modest amount of progressivity in the tax system, since the relatively rich can "better afford" to pay a higher proportion of their income in taxes. Even on that point, however, there is a minority that disagrees, and increasingly the public at large seems less enamored of the notion that a fair tax must be progressive. In the final analysis in a democratic society, the fairness of a tax is probably best measured by general public perceptions of the equity of the levy, not by the opinions of the so-called experts.

ADMINISTRATIVE COSTS AND THE FLAT TAX

The costs of administering the federal tax system rose sharply in recent years with the increased complexity of tax laws and heightened incentives for tax evasion associated with higher effective tax rates. While authoritative estimates of the costs of the tax system are not available, Tables 5–2 and 5–3 show that tax administration absorbed an increasing proportion of the nation's human and financial resources. The "guesstimate" of the size and growth of the tax industry

Table 5–2.   Professional Employment in the Tax Industry, 1950–1981 (in thousands).

Year	Accountants	Lawyers	IRS Employees	Total
1950	192.5	45.5	59.2	297.2
1960	248.0	57.0	67.8	372.8
1970	356.0	68.2	79.8	504.0
1980	523.5	136.8	97.3	757.6
1981	563.0	145.2	100.4	808.6

SOURCE: Author's calculations from U.S. Department of Labor and U.S. Department of Commerce data.

Note: The figures for accountants and lawyers exclude nonprofessional (e.g., clerical) ancillary staff, while the figures for IRS employees include both professional and nonprofessional staff. It is assumed that accountants spend 50 percent and lawyers spend 25 percent of their time respectively on tax work.

Table 5–3.   Internal Revenue Service Outlays, 1960–1985.

Year	Outlays[a]
1960	$ 463,386
1965	706,806
1970	1,067,855
1975	1,959,041
1980	4,331,943
1985	6,384,422[b]

SOURCE: *Budget of the United States,* for fiscal years 1962, 1967, 1972, 1977, 1982 and 1985.

[a]In thousands of dollars.
[b]Proposed.

in Table 5–2 is probably conservative, as it implicitly assumes that the proportion of time that accountants and lawyers spent on tax work remained constant over time, while in fact it probably increased. In any case as Figure 5–2 suggests, the army of tax collectors, tax preparers, tax advisers, etc., has been estimated to be larger in numbers than the U.S. Army. Similarly, the budget of the Internal Revenue Service grew rapidly over time.

The estimates above ignore, of course, the considerable amount of time and money spent by individuals and corporations in tax planning and preparation. If individual taxpayers spent just ten hours a year on tax matters (saving receipts, calculating tax liabilities, reading about legislative changes and tax shelters) and valued their time at just $5 per hour, the cost of this activity would approximate $5 billion a year, or nearly as much as the explicit cost of the Internal Revenue Service to the taxpayer.

With the rise in tax liabilities in recent years, the incentive to evade taxes rose. Official IRS guesses are that roughly $300 billion in income is not reported annually, at a cost of nearly $100 billion in revenue loss a year. The latter figure is roughly quadruple what it was in 1970.[5]

When people want to evade taxes, they often disguise activity by paying for transactions in cash instead of by check. This lowers the ratio of bank deposits to currency. The incentive to do this, of course, varies directly with tax rates. Therefore, one would expect a statistical relationship between effective rates of taxation and the deposit-currency ratio. Using regression analysis, the evidence is that this is precisely the case over the entire period since the introduction of the federal income tax.[6] There is a strong statistically significant negative relationship between effective federal income taxes and the deposit-currency ratio, the proxy measure for tax evasion activity. The results are reported in greater detail in the statistical appendix to this chapter.

What does all of this have to do with the flat rate tax? The flat rate or quasi-flat-rate proposals have all involved a vast simplification of the tax system by eliminating many (or even all) of the deductions, exclusions, and credits that have complicated the tax code. The ability

---

5. For an analysis of the growth of the underground economy generally, see Vito Tanzi, *The Underground Economy in the U.S. and Abroad* (Boston: D. C. Heath and Co., 1982).

6. The legitimacy of the deposit-currency ratio as a proxy for underground activity is subject to debate. See Tanzi, *n.* 5 above.

Figure 5–2. Tax Army vs. U.S. Army, 1950–1981.

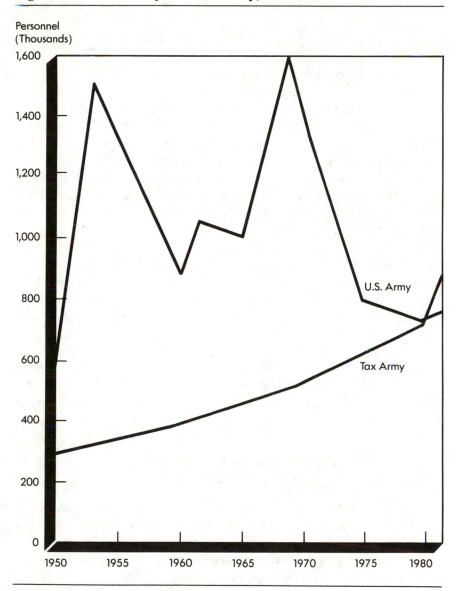

Personnel
(Thousands)

Source: U.S. Department of Commerce, author's calculations.

Note: Both armies include only uniformed personnel; civilians are excluded from U.S. Army totals and clerical, nonprofessional workers from tax army totals.

to engage in tax avoidance activities may be very severely limited, reducing the need for "expert" advice. There may be a dramatic decrease in the demand for the services of tax professionals, and the tax army could shrink in size. The precise magnitude of the administrative savings is impossible to state with any accuracy; it certainly varies with the form of flat rate tax.

It should be pointed out in this connection that the flatness of the tax rate by itself only very modestly lowers administrative costs by making calculation of tax liabilities easier; the real administrative savings come from an end to innumerable tax preferences and loopholes, a feature of virtually every flat and quasi-flat tax proposal. The savings to the taxpayer in time and effort in preparing tax returns are potentially dramatic. For example, the Hall-Rabushka proposal would make possible a tax form the size of a postcard that would take only a few minutes to complete. Other proposals are more complex, but generally vastly simpler than the tax system of recent years.

Most flat rate or quasi-flat-rate schemes have set the top marginal rate of taxation to somewhere between 15 and 30 percent, with the higher rate schemes being found in pseudo-flat-rate proposals, like Bradley-Gephardt, which in fact retain some progressivity. The much lower marginal rates for most taxpayers should lead to a reduction in underground tax evasion activity, with its associated inefficiencies and social problems. After all, for most tax evaders the tax rate of extra or additional income determines the "cost of being honest," and a sharp reduction in that rate associated with a broadening of the definition of taxable income should reduce illicit activity by making it less costly to comply with the law.

FLAT RATE TAXATION AND ECONOMIC EFFICIENCY: EMPIRICAL FINDINGS

Earlier discussion of the efficiency arguments of flat rate taxation suggested that a broad-base flat-rate tax avoids the nonneutral aspects of a highly progressive (in a marginal rate sense) system with its myriad tax preferences, and that the lowering of marginal rates with flat rate taxation should reduce disincentive effects, since marginal rates are the relevant ones with regard to the determination of the growth of resources that will occur in a given period. The best "bottom line" measure of economic incentives and efficiency is the rate of economic growth, that is, the real growth in income or output per capita. If in any given time period a flat rate system were associated with economic growth higher than that seen under a system of nonflat taxes, we would conclude that the evidence supports the view that flat rate taxation is superior on grounds of efficiency.

An excellent laboratory in which to test the relative economic growth effects of alternative tax systems is the 50 states of the United States, with their widely varying approaches to taxation. Also, U.S. income statistics are among the best in the world, reducing data problems. With this in mind, an examination was undertaken of the growth experience of the states in recent years, classifying the states into two categories, "flat rate states" and "nonflat rate states." The period examined is 1970 to 1982. States were judged to be "flat rate" in character only if they had a flat rate tax both at the beginning and near the end (1981) of the period in question. Four states (Illinois, Indiana, Michigan, and Pennsylvania) had flat rate income taxes at positive rates, while Mississippi's tax was so nearly flat rate (the top rate was 1 percent higher than the bottom rate) that it was appropriately included in this category. Eight other states (Florida, Nevada, New Hampshire, South Dakota, Texas, Washington, Connecticut, and Wyoming) had no general income tax, meaning that they had a "zero rate flat tax," and are most appropriately considered with the flat rate tax states rather than with states with considerable marginal progression in income taxes.

Table 5–4 compares the growth experience of the flat rate states with that of 14 states that had high marginal rate progressivity throughout the period, and with all 50 states. Using the median as a measure of central tendency, the results suggest that the flat rate states grew more than 50 percent faster than states with high progressivity,

---

Table 5–4. Growth in Real Per Capita Median Income, 1970–1982.

Category	1970	1980	Percent Growth
13 Flat Rate Tax States	$4,132	$5,511	33.4%
14 Highly Progressive Marginal Tax Rate States	4,134	5,020	21.4
All 50 States	4,311	5,361	24.3

SOURCE: Author's calculations, derived from U.S. Department of Commerce data.

Note: Numbers are expressed in 1970 dollars.

and one-third more than the median growth rate for all states. The same pattern holds with somewhat less substantial differentials if the arithmetic mean is used.

Interestingly, the median flat-rate-tax state in 1970 had almost precisely the same income as the median progressive-tax state. By 1982, however, the typical flat-rate state had a per capita income almost 10 percent higher than its progressive tax counterpart. Similarly, the flat rate states were below the national median in 1970 but above it in 1982.

Examining simple tabular evidence is useful, but that approach can be criticized on the grounds that it does not control for other factors that influence growth. Moreover, it does not provide a precise estimate of the impact that, say, adding 1 percent more progressivity to the income tax will have on economic growth. Accordingly, some multivariate statistical analysis was performed, specifically, ordinary least squares regression analysis. A variety of different growth models were constructed in an attempt to explain variations in real output growth per capita from 1970 to 1980, some emphasizing pure fiscal policy variables, while others included up to four other possible influences on growth rates. The fiscal policy variables introduced included the degree of progressivity in the individual personal income tax at the beginning of the period, as determined by subtracting the lowest marginal rate from the highest rate. A second fiscal variable was the overall level of taxes in 1970, as measured by state and local tax payments per $1,000 in personal income. The third fiscal variable was the amount of federal grants-in-aid per capita disbursed to the states in 1970. It is hypothesized that economic growth, other things being equal, would be greater the lower *both* the progressivity in the tax structure and the overall tax burden, and would be greater the greater the amount of federal aid disbursed.

A variety of nonfiscal factors can be introduced into the analysis for control purposes. The celebrated rise in energy prices in the seventies suggests, other things being equal, that energy-rich states in 1970 probably fared better during the ensuing decade; thus an energy production variable was included in two models. Farming states typically have wide income fluctuations, so agriculture-intensive states are likely to have a different growth experience because of fluctuations in agricultural terms of trade. Accordingly, a variable measuring the proportion of the total population in farming at the beginning of the period was introduced, with no apriori expectation regarding the direction of the relationship. More generally, the rise in prices of goods exported by states relative to goods imported should lead to a rise in income. Using detailed data on industrial structure and producers prices for 1970 and 1980, it was possible to quantify (somewhat crudely) the change in manufacturing and mining terms of trade (including energy production) over the period.[7] States concentrating on producing goods whose prices rose relatively fast, other things being equal, should have grown more than other states. Lastly, states with a high proportion of unionized labor in 1970 were expected (again, other things being equal) to have lower growth, since unions raise labor costs and potentially reduce profitability.

Table 5–5 reports the regression results. The progressivity variable measuring the degree of flatness in the individual income tax has the expected negative sign in all five regressions, is statistically significant at the 5 percent level in three of them, and is modestly robust statistically in a fourth model. The decline in the statistical quality of the results as variables were added to the model may well reflect an increasing problem of multicolinearity. For example, in the model with seven explanatory variables there was a moderately high simple correlation (.30 or higher) between tax progressivity and three of the other variables.

The expected negative relationship between the overall level of tax burden and economic growth is observed in all five models, being more significant in the more elaborate models. Low tax states, other things being equal, grew faster than high tax ones, independent of the issue of the flatness of the tax base.

The two simple models incorporating only fiscal variables can explain roughly one-third of the total variation in economic growth, suggesting that tax variables are important but not dominant determinants of the variation in the rate of economic growth between the states. It should be noted that these fiscal variables are easily manipulated by policy makers in state capitals or in Washington, whereas the other variables are not so controllable by governmental action. The explanatory power in the most expanded version of the model is only 20 percent more than in the three-variable fiscal model, suggesting that fiscal policy variables were indeed as important or more so than

7. The underlying data were collected for each Standard Industrial Classification category by the U.S. Bureau of the Census (for state-specific levels of industrial activity) and the Bureau of Labor Statistics (for producer prices by SIC code.)

Table 5–5. Determinants of Interstate Variations in Economic Growth, 1970–1980 (between states, as measured by personal income per capita).

Eq. No.	Constant	1970 Tax Burden	Progressivity Index 1970	Federal Aid per Capita	Energy Output	Terms of Trade	% of Workers in Unions	% of Output Farming	R^2
(1)	121.164		−.679 (2.58)	.252 (4.36)					.30
(2)	132.624	−.103 (1.54)	−.565 (2.10)	.256 (4.49)					.34
(3)	134.167	−.095 (1.70)	−.263 (1.12)	.073 (1.17)	.044 (4.58)				.55
(4)	134.689	−.137 (2.13)	−.495 (1.95)	.234 (4.32)		.423 (2.68)			.43
(5)	145.045	−.155 (2.73)	−.043 (0.16)	.114 (2.06)	−.014 (0.72)	.317 (4.52)	−.144 (1.61)	.404 (2.91)	.60

SOURCE: Regression equations; see text for explanation of variables.

Note: Numbers in parentheses are t-values.

several nonfiscal factors combined. The nonfiscal variables behaved as expected. It is interesting to note that in the most elaborate model the coefficient for the energy variable is statistically insignificant and indeed has the wrong sign. This suggests that the reason that energy-oriented states grew faster was not that they had energy supplies, but that the relative prices of energy-related goods rose. Interestingly, the union variable is significant at the 10 percent level, providing some modest confirmation for the view that unionization is inimical to growth.

The coefficients on the tax variables suggest that alterations in tax levels and structure can have a big impact on growth. The coefficients on the variable measuring tax flatness varied considerably. Using the median value, in the fourth equation, the results suggest that a state with a range in its income tax rates from 1 to 11 percent would have had nearly 5 percent less income per capita in 1980 as a consequence of that progressivity compared to a state with a flat rate of, say, 3 percent. Using the much lower coefficient found in the third equation, the results for the same situation suggest that the flat rate state would have had about 2.6 percent greater income growth than the state with high tax progressivity, still a considerable magnitude. Only with the fifth equation does one find results suggesting that the impact of progressivity is rather small.

The results generally convey the impression that both the level of taxation and the progressivity of marginal income tax rates are relevant to growth, and that an optimal state fiscal strategy would be to lower the tax burden generally by reducing the progressivity in marginal income tax rates. Precisely this strategy was used in New York after 1978, when a state income tax cut reduced top rates dramatically. Thereafter, economic growth in New York escalated relative to the rest of the country, in marked contrast to the extremely sluggish growth earlier. During the depths of the 1982 recession, unemployment and growth indicators were far more favorable in New York than in almost all other major industrial states.[8]

---

8. For example, in July 1982 when the national unemployment rate was 9.8 percent, the New York rate was but 8.2 percent, well below that in such other Snow Belt industrial states as Illinois, Michigan, Ohio, Pennsylvania, and Massachusetts, and even below that of some major Sun Belt states (e.g., California). See U.S. Department of Labor, Bureau of Labor Statistics, "The Unemployment Situation: July 1982," Table A-11. By contrast, in the 1975 recession, unemployment in New York (9.5 percent in 1975) was sharply *higher* than in the nation as a whole (8.5 percent) and higher than in most other major industrial states (e.g., Pennsylvania, Ohio, Illinois). See U.S. Department of Commerce, *Statistical Abstract of the United States, 1977* (Washington, D.C.: Government Printing Office, 1977), p. 396. In 1975, marginal tax rates in New York were sharply higher than they were in the 1982 recession.

At the same time, however, it is possible to overstate the argument. Much of the variation in economic growth cannot, it would appear, be readily controlled by government policy. For example, some variation in growth is explained by such factors as changing relative prices, something that cannot be effectively controlled by political action, particularly at the state and local level. Moving to lower, more flat-rate taxation will aid the process of economic growth, but at the same time it will not guarantee that a lower growth state will instantly become a high growth state. Still, on balance, such a tax strategy has been demonstrated to have positive effects on growth.

It is interesting that the empirical findings are highly consistent with public perceptions. A *USA Today*/Gordon Black poll, reported on March 13, 1984, asked respondents to comment on the statement: "I would work harder if my added income were taxed at a lower rate."[9] Some 61 percent agreed with the statement, with some 80 percent of those from 18 to 25 years of age saying they would work more if marginal rates were reduced. As one prominent supply-sider, Jude Wanniski, noted: "The public at large is much smarter than many officials think."[10]

THE FLAT RATE TAX AND CAPITAL FORMATION

The demonstrated relation between flatness of tax rates and economic growth is consistent with the view that progressivity retards savings and reduces funds available for capital formation. The mechanism by which lower progressivity in the tax rate structure raises growth is not clear from the results, but probably reflects increases in both capital formation and work effort associated with lower tax rates at the margin.

The implementation of a flat rate tax could have even more beneficial results if the move to flatness in marginal rates is accompanied by a shift to a purely consumption basis for taxation. A good argument can be made that consumption, not income, is the more appropriate basis for taxation on both equity and efficiency grounds.

Enjoyment or utility derives more from the act of consuming income than the act of earning it. Accordingly, is it fair to tax a person making $40,000 a year who consumes $20,000 and saves a large amount for his children's college education more than someone making $35,000 a year who consumes $28,000, living more luxuriously than the person who is saving a great deal? Most persons would probably say no.

9. As reported in *USA Today*, 13 March, 1984.
10. Ibid.

Yet under the law as it has existed in the past, the probability is high that the higher income person would pay more, as relatively little of his or her saving is likely to escape taxation.

On efficiency grounds, moving to a purely consumption basis for taxation would (1) make the tax system more neutral and (2) help remove high and arbitrary taxation of returns to capital, which retards capital formation and growth. A host of inefficient gimmicks to shelter savings (e.g., Individual Retirement Accounts, Keogh plans, special treatment of municipal bonds) could be eliminated since income, per se, would not be taxed. In the past, many Americans have had to earn about two dollars to save one dollar in most forms because saved income has been taxed. Exempting savings from taxation lowers the opportunity cost of savings and should raise the percentage of disposable income saved closer to the double-digit levels observed in most other countries (including neighboring Canada). This would, other factors being equal, lower interest rates and stimulate capital formation.

Also, a purely consumption basis for taxation would remove the distortions in the form that savings take owing to the fact that some forms of savings are tax-exempt. While the issue of the nature of the tax *base* and the size of the tax rate can be separated, practically speaking any major reform in rates requires a redefinition of the tax base, thus affording an opportunity to move to a consumption basis for taxation. A radical tax reform in the taxation of individuals makes it perhaps politically easier to gain—via a whole new tax package rather than through piecemeal patching of the existing tax structure—the changes needed to stimulate capital formation.

Of course, any move to a purely consumption base for taxation would remove personal savings from the tax base, necessitating higher rates to raise any given amount of revenue. The direct savings-enhancing impact of not taxing savings could conceivably be offset by the disincentive effects (on savings) associated with a somewhat higher marginal tax rate on consumption. That is not likely to be the case, however, given the comparative paucity of personal savings in the United States. A 22 percent flat rate of taxation on consumption would currently raise *more* than a 20 percent flat rate on all personal income.[11] Thus any increased disincentives on savings associated with

---

11. This is so because savings in recent years has been only roughly 5 percent of disposable income and even a smaller proportion of personal income. Even if the savings rate almost doubled as a consequence of exempting it from taxation (a real possibility), the 22 percent consumption tax would raise as much as 20 percent income tax, other things being equal.

higher marginal rates on consumption would probably not be very large.

Attention has focused on the taxation of individuals. Movement to a purely consumption basis for taxation would remove many of the problems associated with a lack of integration of individual and corporate taxation, and a far-reaching reform might allow for changes in business taxation, possibly including the elimination of the corporate income tax, a levy that makes little sense on either efficiency or equity grounds. For fiscal year 1985, corporate income tax revenue is estimated at $76.5 billion, about 10 percent of total tax revenues and about 23 percent of the revenues raised from the individual income tax.[12] Revenues lost from abolishing the corporate income tax could be replaced by a 26 percent instead of a 22 percent rate in a flat rate levy on all consumption, even allowing for rather generous dependency allowances. Thus a 26 percent flat rate consumption tax and *no* corporate income tax would raise as much revenue as the existing system or a 20 percent flat rate income tax that retained corporate taxation.[13] In the long run, of course, the stimulus to capital formation and real output (and consumption) growth would in all likelihood lead the 26 percent flat-rate consumption tax to raise a greater amount of revenue than the existing system or a truly flat rate income tax alternative that retained existing corporate taxation. It is noted that several popular congressional tax reform proposals, such as the Bradley-Gephardt bill or the bill sponsored by Congressman Jack Kemp and Senator Robert Kasten, have had top rates that about equal (Kemp-Kasten) or exceed (Bradley-Gephardt) this 26 percent rate. The bill approved by the House of Representatives in late 1985 had a top rate of 38 percent, *double* that of the Hall-Rabushka true flat-rate proposal.

EQUITY AND THE FLAT RATE TAX: SOME EVIDENCE

The major single argument used against the flat rate tax concept is that it is unfair. It is argued that the flat rate tax violates the ability-to-pay principle by taxing lower income persons proportionally the same as richer persons with a greater ability to absorb the tax burden.

12. 98th Congress, 2nd Session, House Document No. 98–138, *Budget of the United States Government, 1985* (Washington, D.C.: Government Printing Office, 1984), p. 4-3.

13. This assumes, of course, that the flat rate tax is a broad-based one with almost no income exclusions except for a dependency allowance.

This argument suggests that a dollar of lost income to a rich person brings about less loss of personal satisfaction than a dollar of income taxed away from a poor person; this is what economists call "diminishing marginal utility of income." While this argument is accepted by many economists, there is no demonstrable empirical basis for the belief, since "utility" or "satisfaction" cannot be measured with any precision, and interpersonal utility comparisons are particularly difficult to make.

Consider Figure 5–3, presenting two possible relationships between income and satisfaction. In the first graph, the additional satisfaction derived from one more dollar of income falls continuously as one moves to a higher income; in the second graph, the additional satisfaction from one more dollar of income declines as one moves from a low to a near-middle income, but then levels off, so the person with $150,000 annual income derives about as much additional satisfaction from a dollar more income as someone making $30,000 a year. If the first graph depicts the real world, a case can be made to use the tax system to redistribute income from the rich to the poor and the middle class, and a steadily more progressive tax system might well permit total social utility to be greater than would a truly proportional tax. If the second graph more accurately depicts the real world, however, some progressivity in rates would seem desirable as one moves from low to middle income ranges, but beyond that point progressivity is undesirable on equity grounds, as the loss of utility to the relatively high income groups from taxation is as great as it is to middle income ones. Some economists, notably John Stuart Mill, have suggested that the second graph may more accurately depict reality than the first, but no one really knows.[14]

Since utility is essentially unmeasurable, economists and other professionals have no particular authority to declare what form of income progressivity is optimal. Essentially, it is a matter of opinion, not fact. In a democratic society, the appropriate public policy would seem to be the one that is preferred by a majority of the citizenry. "Equity" is an elusive concept, but a "fair" tax is probably one that most people *think* is fair, and an unfair tax is one that most people regard as inequitable.

14. John Stuart Mill, *Principles of Political Economy* (London: Longmans, Green and Co., 1921), pp. 806–7. See also Richard A. Musgrave, *The Theory of Public Finance* (New York: McGraw-Hill, 1959), chap. 5.

162

Figure 5–3. Marginal Utility and Income: Two Possibilities.

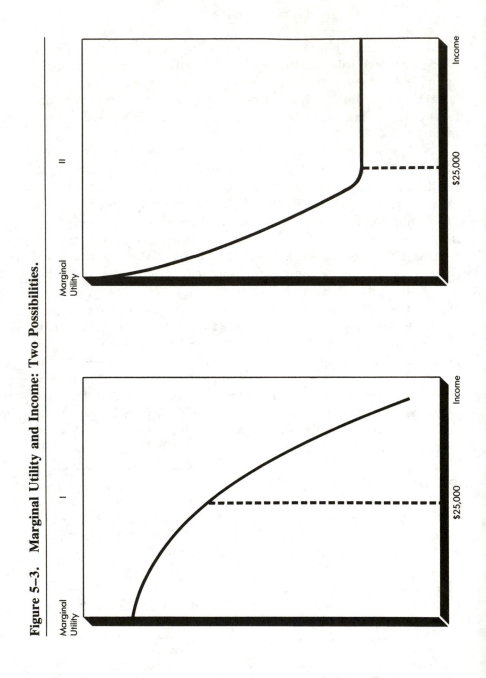

An absolutely pure flat-rate tax with no deductions would be proportional; that is, tax payments would be the same percentage of income for all income groups. Most flat rate proposals have had generous dependency allowances and have in fact been somewhat progressive, but have shown little progressivity as one moves from a fairly typical middle class income (say $25,000) to higher incomes (say $100,000).

Table 5–6 shows that degree of progressivity for a flat rate tax of 20 percent imposed on income, where $7,500 dependency allowance is provided (this is similar to the Hall-Rabushka and some other proposals). Very low income households would pay no tax. As one moves up to about the median income ($20,000–$25,000 a year), the tax is steeply progressive; from that income upwards, however, there is only modest, and diminishing, additional progressivity. This structure is consistent with the view that most of the decline in marginal utility of income occurs between the low and middle income ranges, and that fairness dictates relieving truly poor or near-poor families from a significant tax burden, but that the upper middle and upper income classes do not require significant differentiation of tax treatment on equity grounds.

A sharp rise in the progressivity of the tax system in the last two decades has been to a considerable extent *unlegislated,* a byproduct of the impact of inflation-caused bracket creep on tax liabilities. An examination of tax burdens in, say, 1960, or even in 1965, just before and just after the Kennedy administration, shows that the progressivity of the tax system was *little different* from that suggested by a flat rate tax with a large dependency allowance, similar to that outlined

Table 5–6. Flat Rate Taxation and Progressivity.

Taxable Income	Tax	Tax as Percent of Income
$ 5,000	$ 0	0.0%
10,000	500	5.0
25,000	3,500	14.0
50,000	8,500	17.0
100,000	18,500	18.5

SOURCE: Author's calculations.

Note: Assumes a 20 percent pure flat-rate tax with no deductions except a $7,500 allowance for dependents.

in Table 5–6.[15] Most flat rate proposals, then, have not involved adoption of a tax system that differs much in progressivity from what the tax system was like before unlegislated bracket creep had a profound impact. To give just one illustration of that impact, in 1980 a family of four with $75,000 income paid more than eight times the proportion of income in taxes as the $10,000 income family; in 1970, the higher income family paid only four times the proportion.[16]

People increasingly regarded the highly progressive income tax as unfair, despite the fact that the progressivity of the tax increased markedly over time. Table 5–7 shows that the total public, as well as many important groups within it, became increasingly disenchanted with the federal income tax at a time when its progressivity had grown. Louis Harris in 1982 found that *less than half* the American population considered the principle of progressive taxation to be fair and equitable.[17]

A 1984 poll conducted by Gordon Black for *USA Today* showed that a minority of respondents affirmatively answered the question: "Do you think you're treated fairly by the tax system?" Some 72 percent agreed that "tax laws are written to give special advantages to the rich."[18] Thus the growing underground economy in part may have reflected not only the impact of higher tax rates, but also a growing perception of an unjust tax system. The feeling that the tax system was unfair was rather uniform over most income groups, but was most pronounced in middle income families ($25,000 to $40,000 a year in income).[19]

These results suggest that a reduction in progressivity under a flat rate system is not necessarily to be viewed as increasing the inequities; in fact, it is more likely to be viewed by the public as a move

15. In 1960, a married couple with two dependents making $50,000 in 1980 dollars typically paid an average tax rate of 19 percent, slightly over three times that paid by a similar family with $10,000 income. In 1983 if a flat tax such as that outlined in Table 5–6 were used, a similar $50,000 income (in 1980 dollars) family would have paid 17.5 percent in taxes, about two-and-one-half times the proportion paid by the $10,000 income family. With a larger family dependency allowance of $9,000 with the flat tax, the progressivity, so measured, would have been slightly greater with the flat tax than with the 1960 federal income tax. In very high income ranges, the flat tax is less progressive than the tax system in 1960.

16. United States Department of Commerce, *Statistical Abstract of the United States, 1982–83* (Washington, D.C.: Government Printing Office, 1982), p. 258.

17. Testimony before the Senate Finance Committee, September 29, 1982.

18. *USA Today,* 13 March 1984.

19. Ibid.

Table 5–7. Percentage Viewing Income Tax as Most Unfair, 1972–1981.

Group	1972	1977	1981
Total public	19%	28%	36%
White	20	28	36
Nonwhite	12	27	33
Managerial, professional[a]	19	29	38
Homeowners	19	27	36
Renters	19	30	36

SOURCE: Advisory Commission on Intergovernmental Relations.

[a]1972 figure is partly estimated owing to change in groupings over time.

in the direction of *greater* fairness, especially when accompanied by the elimination of many tax shelters.

This brings us to an important distinction: There are two types of equity, vertical (fairness between different income groups) and horizontal (fairness among taxpayers of similar incomes). Much of the rising concern in recent years about the income tax on equity grounds probably reflected a growing perception that there are large horizontal inequities. Two persons with any given income could pay widely varying taxes, since one will take advantage of numerous tax shelters or, increasingly, simply illegally evade taxes, while the other pays a substantial tax bill. A flat rate tax eliminates tax shelters and, by cutting marginal rates significantly, reduces incentives for tax evasion. The tax is almost certainly superior to the tax system of the recent past on horizontal equity grounds, and is possibly superior on vertical equity grounds as well.

FLAT RATE TAXATION: POLITICAL POSSIBILITIES AND REALITIES

This chapter has demonstrated that a flat tax is superior to our present federal income tax on administrative and efficiency grounds—and probably on equity grounds as well, although equity is difficult to assess. Nonetheless, the conventional wisdom in Washington for years was that a flat rate tax, or even a moderately close approximation thereto (e.g., the Bradley-Gephardt or Kemp-Kasten proposals), was not politically feasible.

The conventional wisdom may well have had strong justification.

Why? The public-choice literature suggests some of the difficulties in passing legislation that is on balance beneficial to society but that on balance might place costs on some groups within the society.[20] Briefly summarizing some of that literature, the social benefits of the legislation are often widely dispersed, while the social costs of the new laws are often very concentrated. For a very simple example, let us suppose that a given tariff reduction will confer $5 billion in benefits on 230,000,000 Americans, but will also place $3 billion in costs on another 100,000 Americans involved in the industry currently enjoying tariff protection. The net benefits to society as a whole from removing trade restrictions is $2 billion ($5 billion minus $3 billion). The average benefit to the 230,000,000 who gain from the legislation is $22, while the average cost to the losers from the legislation is $30,000. The typical potential beneficiary will not lobby Congress for passage of a bill, since the possible gains from lobbying are not worth the time and effort involved. The losers, though, are hard hit and will thus spend lots of money and time on defeating the bill. The "special interests" will raise more money and lobby harder for defeat of the bill than those who would gain from the legislation.

Any move to flat rate taxation at relatively low marginal rates involves ending many exemptions, shelters, and exclusions, since a broadening of the tax base means that marginal rate reductions must occur without revenue loss. The removal of tax preferences is infuriating to several powerful special interests: homebuilders, state and local governments, municipal bond dealers (because of the tax-exempt nature of state and local bonds), charities, universities, churches, realtors and real estate speculators, etc. In addition, the army of tax professionals mobilizes for all-out political warfare.

Following the argument developed earlier, these groups pour literally millions of dollars into defeating the legislation. They can, for example, threaten to support the opponents of uncooperative congressmen with massive "Political Action Committee" contributions. Conventional wisdom had it that such threats would lead to the defeat or severe dilution of legislation providing for a flat rate, simplified tax with a broadened base.

20. Much of the research in this area has been done by James M. Buchanan, Gordon Tullock, and associates. Representative studies include Buchanan and Tullock's *The Calculus of Consent* (Ann Arbor: University of Michigan Press, 1962); Buchanan's *Demand and Supply of Public Goods* (Chicago: Rand McNally, 1968); and Buchanan, Robert D. Tollison and Tullock, eds., *Toward A Theory of the Rent-Seeking Society* (College Station: Texas A and M Press, 1980).

At the same time, however, a flat rate tax system radically different from the system that has existed in the past may in fact prevail, for two reasons. First, by engaging in radical rather than piecemeal reform, the normally dispersed benefits for the general public are of such a magnitude that they exceed the threshold level necessary to generate significant grass roots political action; the expected future benefits from reform exceed the expected costs of responding politically. Second, some special interests that would fight piecemeal reform find the benefits of radical reform of a magnitude to exceed the costs of tax preferences that are given up.

The income tax as it has existed in the past is regarded as unfair and burdensome. A radical proposal that in effect gets rid of the tax as we have known it can be viewed by the average citizen as having enormously valuable benefits, perhaps a present value of perceived future benefits amounting to thousands of dollars. These benefits reflect not only perceptions of a lower tax burden, but also the value associated with the sense of well-being that comes from ending inequities in the tax code, not to mention the benefits from the end of spending dozens or hundreds of hours of time on agonizing and frustrating tax calculations.

The expected benefits to the individual from an extremely simple flat-rate tax may be great enough so that even though most individuals feel that their political action has little chance of altering the course of legislation, the net expected benefits may still exceed the costs of the action, be those costs in the form of writing letters, calling congressmen, contributing money to candidates who endorse that flat rate tax, etc. The point at which the gains of action exceed the costs for the average voter probably cannot be reached with tax legislation that merely tinkers with the system but perhaps can be reached with a radical measure. Vote-maximizing political entrepreneurs who discover that fact (if it is indeed true) can exploit it for their own (and society's) advantage.

Likewise, some special interest groups that ordinarily fight such legislation, on the ground that widening the tax base costs them some valuable tax preferences, may favor it instead, since the gains to their special interest from general marginal rate reductions permitted by getting rid of *all* (or almost all) tax preferences exceed the cost of losing a specific preference of value at that special interest.

For example, many in the financial community vehemently oppose the idea that, say, municipal bonds should be taxed, or that the exemption on interest deductions for home purchases should be ended.

Yet a flat rate tax that lowers effective marginal rates on capital gains for most Americans and that favors investment (by exempting savings from taxation) is received extremely favorably by most of the investment community, and the protests of a few municipal bond houses and savings and loan associations can be more than offset by support from other parts of the investment community. Indeed, with a tax based on consumption, the investment community could probably be correctly perceived as "special interest" *supporters* of the legislation.

The failure of the Reagan administration and its Treasury Department to come forth with a truly flat rate tax in early 1985 probably explains why the grassroots support for tax reform failed to develop during the 1985–86 tax debate, and why the special interest groups were largely (although not completely) able to defend existing tax preferences. The initial administration proposal, now called Treasury I, was not sufficiently radical or simple enough to excite the general populace to political action. It is thus a miracle that any significant tax bill incorporating lower rates and a broader tax base made it through the House of Representatives. By anticipating objections from special interest groups and meeting some of them in its initial proposal, the Reagan administration neither placated those interests nor achieved the countervailing political force it desired to deal with the lobbies. The bill drafted by the Senate Finance Committee in 1986 was, on the other hand, radical enough to overcome special-interest pressures within the committee, and won its approval.

CONCLUSIONS

The evidence is strong that a flat rate tax holds considerable promise as an improvement over the system we have known. Such a tax permits a sharp reduction in human capital resources devoted to tax preparation, administration, and avoidance, and reduces the size of the morally debilitating underground economy. More important, such a tax ends distortions in resource allocation in the tax code, especially distortions reducing the quantity and quality of capital investment. Empirical evidence from the states suggests that flat rate taxation is conducive to greater economic growth. Also, the old system is considered unfair by increasing numbers of people, and polling information is consistent with the view that the flat rate concept is considered fairer by most of the public, partly because it reduces horizontal inequities. There are severe political problems facing a flat rate tax, but the perceived benefits may well be so great as to mobilize general taxpayer support and weaken and split the opposition of special interest groups. This was the experience of the Senate Finance Committee in 1986. Whether the federal government will some day take the even more radical steps of eliminating the corporate income tax and instituting a true flat-rate tax on consumption, only time will tell.

APPENDIX

The deposit-currency ratio (*D-C*) was regressed against the effective rate of federal individual income taxation (*T*), a dummy variable (*W*) for World War II years 1942–45 (reflecting a period when wartime controls may have changed normal relationships), and a dummy variable (*B*) for the banking crisis of the Great Depression and immediate aftermath (years 1931–34).

The results, using annual data for the period 1914 to 1970, follow:

$$D\text{-}C = \underset{(53.34)}{5.45} - \underset{(13.60)}{.083\,T} - \underset{(6.90)}{1.36\,B} + \underset{(1.72)}{0.38\,W}, R^2 = .81, D\text{-}W\ 0.95,$$

where the numbers in parentheses are *t*-values. The negative relationship between the deposit-currency ratio, a proxy for underground activity, and the tax rate is highly significant in a statistical sense. However, the Durbin-Watson statistic indicates the existence of serial correlation. To correct for that, an alternative model expressing the variables in "first difference" form (e.g., the change in the tax rate, the change in the deposit-currency ratio) was used; in this model, the tax-deposit-currency ratio relationship was still statistically significantly negative at the 5 percent level, and the hypothesis that serial correlation existed could not be accepted at the 5 percent level. Thus the results suggest that a negative relationship between tax rates and the deposit-currency ratio has in fact existed. To the extent that the deposit-currency ratio reflects the magnitude of underground activity (tax evasion), one can conclude that tax rates have influenced the size of the underground economy even before the last decade or so, when the problem was explicitly recognized.

SELECTED BIBLIOGRAPHY
PART I

Aaron, Henry J., and Joseph A. Pechman, eds. *How Taxes Affect Economic Behavior*. Washington, D.C.: Brookings Institution, 1981.

Advisory Commission on Intergovernmental Relations. *Significant Features of Fiscal Federalism: 1979–1980*. Washington, D.C.: Government Printing Office, 1980.

Bailey, Martin J. "Progressivity and Investment Yields Under U.S. Income Taxation." *Journal of Political Economy* 82 (November/December 1974): 1157–75.

Ballentine, J. Gregory. *Equity, Efficiency, and the U.S. Corporation Income Tax*. Washington, D.C.: American Enterprise Institute, 1980.

Barro, Robert J. *Macroeconomics*. New York: John Wiley & Sons, 1984.

Barro, Robert J., and Chaipat Sahasakul. "Measuring the Average Marginal Tax from the Income Tax." *Journal of Business* 56 (1983): 419–52.

Boskin, Michael J. "Taxation, Saving, and the Rate of Interest." *Journal of Political Economy* 86, no. 2, part 2 (April 1978): S3–27.

———, ed. *Federal Tax Reform: Myths and Realities*. San Francisco: Institute for Contemporary Studies, 1978.

Browning, Edgar K., and Jacquelene M. Browning. *Public Finance and the Price System*. 2d ed. New York: Macmillan, 1983.

Browning, Edgar K., and William R. Johnson. *The Distribution of the Tax Burden*. Washington, D.C.: American Enterprise Institute, 1979.

———. "The Trade-off between Equality and Efficiency." *Journal of Political Economy* 92 (April 1984): 175–203.

Buchanan, James M., and Dwight R. Lee. "Politics, Time, and the Laffer Curve." *Journal of Political Economy* 90 (August 1982): 816–19.

Carlino, Gerald A. "Interest Rate Effects and Intertemporal Consumption." *Journal of Monetary Economics* 9 (March 1982): 223–34.

Clotfelter, Charles T. "Tax-Induced Distortions and the Business-Pleasure Borderline." *American Economic Review* 91 (December 1983): 1053–65.

————. "Tax Evasion and Tax Rates: An Analysis of Individual Returns." *Review of Economics and Statistics* 65 (August 1983): 363–73.

Clotfelter, Charles T., and Eugene Steuerle. "Charitable Contributions." In H. Aaron and J. Pechman, eds., *How Taxes Affect Economic Behavior*. Washington, D.C.: Brookings Institution, 1981.

Council of Economic Advisers. *Economic Report of the President, 1983*. Washington, D.C.: Government Printing Office, 1983.

Darby, Michael R. "The U.S. Productivity Slowdown." *American Economic Review* 74 (June 1984): 301–22.

Dennison, Edward F. *Accounting for Slower Economic Growth: The United States in the 1970s*. Washington, D.C.: Brookings Institution, 1979.

Dunn, Robert M., Jr. *Economic Growth Among Industrialized Countries: Why the United States Lags*. Washington, D.C.: National Planning Association, 1980.

Feldstein, Martin S. "The Income Tax and Charitable Contributions: Part I—Aggregate and Distributional Effects." *National Tax Journal* 28 (March 1975): 80–100.

————. *Capital Taxation*. Cambridge: Harvard University Press, 1983.

Feldstein, Martin S.; Joel Slemrod; Shlomo Yitzhaki. "The Effects of Taxation on the Selling of Corporate Stock and the Realization of Capital Gains: Reply." *Quarterly Journal of Economics* 99 (February 1984): 111–19.

Fetter, Frank A. *Capital, Interest, and Rent*. Kansas City: Sheed, Andrews and McMeel, 1977.

Fullerton, Don. "On the Possibility of an Inverse Relationship Between Tax Rates and Government Revenues." *Journal of Public Economics* 19 (October 1982): 3–12.

Galper, Harvey, and Dennis Zimmerman. "Preferential Taxation and Portfolio Choice: Some Empirical Evidence." *National Tax Journal* 30 (December 1977): 387–97.

Gwartney, James, and Richard Stroup. "Tax Cuts: Who Shoulders the Burden?" *Economic Review: Federal Reserve Bank of Atlanta* 67, no. 3 (March 1982): 19–27.

————. "Cooperation or Conniving: How Public Sector Rules Shape the Decision." *Journal of Labor Research* 3 (Summer 1982): 247–57.

Harberger, Arnold C. *World Economic Growth*. San Francisco: Institute for Contemporary Studies, 1984.

Higgs, Robert. "Crisis, Bigger Government, and Ideological Change: Two Hypotheses on the Ratchet Phenomenon." *Explorations in Economic History* 22 (January 1985): 1–28.

Hirshleifer, Jack. *Investment, Interest, and Capital*. Englewood Cliffs, N.J.: Prentice-Hall, 1970.

Holzer, Mare, and Stuart S. Nagel, eds. *Productivity and Public Policy*. Beverly Hills, Calif.: Sage Publications, 1984.

Hulten, Charles R., and Isabell V. Sawhill, eds. *The Legacy of Reaganomics: Prospects for Long-Term Growth*. Washington, D.C.: Urban Institute Press, 1984.

Kendrick, John W. *Interindustry Differences in Productivity Growth*. Washington, D.C.: American Enterprise Institute, 1983.

———. *Improving Company Productivity*. Baltimore: Johns Hopkins University Press, 1984.

Landau, Daniel. "Government Expenditure and Economic Growth: A Cross-Country Study." *Southern Economic Journal* 49 (January 1983): 783–92.

Lindsey, Lawrence. "Is the Maximum Tax on Earned Income Effective?" *National Tax Journal* 34 (June 1981): 249–55.

———. "Alternatives to the Current Maximum Tax on Earned Income." In M. Feldstein, ed., *Behavioral Simulation Methods in Tax Policy Analysis*. Chicago: University of Chicago Press, 1983.

Long, James E. "Tax Rates and Tax Losses: A Preliminary Analysis Using Aggregate Data." *Public Finance Quarterly* 12 (October 1984): 457–72.

Long, James E., and Frank A. Scott. "The Income Tax and Nonwage Compensation." *Review of Economics and Statistics* 64 (May 1982): 211–19.

Meiselman, David I., and Paul Craig Roberts. "The Political Economy of the Congressional Budget Office." In K. Brunner and A. Meltzer, eds., *Three Aspects of Policy and Policymaking: Knowledge, Data and Institutions*. New York: North-Holland, 1979.

Minarik, Joseph J. "Alternatives to the Current Maximum Tax on Earned Income: Comment." In M. Feldstein, ed., *Behavioral Simulation Methods in Tax Policy Analysis*. Chicago: University of Chicago Press, 1983.

———. "The Effects of Taxation on the Selling of Corporate Stock and the Realization of Capital Gains: Comment." *Quarterly Journal of Economics* 99 (February 1984): 93–110.

Newman, Robert J. "Industry, Migration, and Growth in the South." *Review of Economics and Statistics* 65 (February 1983): 76–86.

Olson, Mancur. *The Rise and Decline of Nations*. New Haven, Conn.: Yale University Press, 1982.

Roberts, Paul Craig. "Idealism in Public Choice Theory." *Journal of Monetary Economics* 4 (1978): 603–615.

———. *The Supply-Side Revolution: An Insider's Account of Policymaking in Washington*. Cambridge: Harvard University Press, 1984.

Sametz, Arnold W. *Prospects for Capital Formation and Capital Markets.* Lexington, Mass.: Lexington Books, 1978.

Simon, Julian. *The Ultimate Resource.* Princeton, N.J.: Princeton University Press, 1981.

Stuart, Charles E. "Swedish Tax Rates, Labor Supply, and Tax Revenues." *Journal of Political Economy* 89 (October 1981): 1020–38.

————. "Welfare Cost per Dollar of Additional Tax Revenue in the United States." *American Economic Review* 74 (June 1984): 352–62.

United Nations. Department of International Economic and Social Affairs. *Supplement to World Economic Survey.* New York: United Nations, 1983.

U.S. Bureau of Labor Statistics. *A BLS Reader on Productivity.* Bulletin 2171. Washington, D.C.: Government Printing Office, 1983.

————. *Productivity and the Economy: A Chartbook.* Bulletin 2171. Washington, D.C.: Government Printing Office, 1983.

————. *Trends in Multifactor Productivity, 1948–81.* Bulletin 2178. Washington, D.C.: Government Printing Office, September 1983.

————. *Productivity Measures for Selected Industries, 1954–1983.* Bulletin 2224. Washington, D.C.: Government Printing Office, February 1985.

————. *Trends in Manufacturing: A Chartbook.* Bulletin 2219. Washington, D.C.: Government Printing Office, April 1985.

U.S. Treasury. Office of Tax Analysis. *Blueprints for Basic Tax Reform.* Washington, D.C.: Government Printing Office, 17 Jan. 1977.

U.S. Treasury. Internal Revenue Service, Statistics of Income Division. *General Description Booklet for the 1979 Individual and State Tax Model File.* Publication 1023. Washington, D.C.: Government Printing Office, 1982.

Von Furstenberg, George M., ed. *The Government and Capital Formation.* New York: Pergamon, 1980.

Woodbury, Stephen A. "Substitution Between Wage and Nonwage Benefits." *American Economic Review* 73 (March 1983): 166–82.

PART II

SPENDING, DEFICITS, AND OTHER FORMS OF HIDDEN TAXATION

6

PUBLIC DEBT AND CAPITAL FORMATION

James M. Buchanan

> *"The practice of contracting debt will almost infallibly be abused in every government. It would scarcely be more imprudent to give a prodigal son a credit in every banker's shop in London, than to empower a statesman to draw bills, in this manner, upon posterity."*
>
> *David Hume*

A SUMMARY HISTORY OF SOME IDEAS AND THEIR CONSEQUENCES

To the Victorians, the consumption of capital was venality itself, and even full consumption of income was prodigal in the extreme. Ordinary prudence demanded that some share of income be put aside for adding to the capital stock. In their world, capital, once created, was indeed permanent, whether it was measured separately in each family's portfolio or jointly in the national aggregates. Further, there were no essential differences between the precepts for fiscal prudence applicable to the family and those applicable to the nation. Basically these same attitudes carried over into the Victorians' approach to the institutions of law, politics, and the economy. The Gladstonians did

Note: I am indebted to Geoffrey Brennan, Australian National University, for helpful comments.

not really expect to live forever, but they acted as if they did, and their moral precepts matched their behavior. (The Ricardian theorem on the equivalence of public debt and taxation may, indeed, have been descriptive of at least some of the Victorians.)

We are a century away from "capitalism's finest hour," if we restrict our definition of "capitalism" to refer to prevailing public attitudes on the accumulation and maintenance of "the capacity to satisfy wants stored up in things."

How distant these Victorians seem to us now!

We have passed through several shifts in ideas and attitudes. Even before Keynes, economists had challenged the classical (and Victorian) equivalence of public and private debt. Fallacies of aggregation antedate the Keynesians, and the argument that "we owe it to ourselves" was ushered in early in this century. This aggregation fallacy, to the extent that it gained acceptance, served to loosen somewhat the precepts of fiscal prudence for governments, although the principle of budget balance kept public debt creation within bounds of reason. Norms for private capital accumulation and preservation remained pervasive, however, until Keynes and the Keynesians promulgated the "paradox of thrift." With this step, even the norms for private, personal prudence came to be undermined. Spending, not saving, spilled over to benefit society. Alongside this inversion of private norms, the Keynesian theory of public policy directly undermined any intellectual basis for the maintenance of balance in governmental budgets. The modern era of profligacy, public and private, was born.[1]

Through their effects on public and political attitudes, ideas do have consequences. But these consequences emerge slowly and with significant time lags. After Keynes, the anticlassical, anti-Victorian ideas were firmly in place in the academies and in the dialogues of the intellectuals. Politics, however, reflects the behavior of politicians, whose ideas change but slowly. Hence, during the years immediately after World War II, many politicians adhered to the old-fashioned precepts for fiscal prudence, only to be treated condescendingly and with scorn by academics and intellectuals. Some of us now recall with

---

1. For more extended treatment of the divergent classical and Keynesian attitudes toward public debt, see James M. Buchanan, *Public Principles of Public Debt* (Homewood, Ill.: Richard D. Irwin, 1958); for extended treatment of the impact of the Keynesian theory of policy on governmental creation of deficits, see James M. Buchanan and Richard E. Wagner, *Democracy in Deficit* (New York: Academic Press, 1977).

both amusement and sadness, the derision that greeted President Eisenhower's reference to public debt as a burden on our grandchildren.

By the late 1950s, there was a marked shift in the thinking of economists, characterized by a revival of essentially classical ideas on the incidence and effects of public debt. These then-novel notions were by no means universally accepted by academic economists, but the challenge to the aggregation fallacies was not refuted. Among academic economists, the discussion of public debt changed, slowly but surely, toward the earlier verities, a change that took place over the 1960s and 1970s.

As with the onset of the Keynesian ideas three decades earlier, however, public and political attitudes lagged behind those emerging in academia. And the politicians who made the policy decisions of the 1960s and 1970s had fully absorbed the Keynesian lessons on both macroeconomic policy and public debt. They were ready and quite willing to apply the policy messages appropriate for the 1930s to the policy environment of the 1960s and 1970s, because these messages offered apparent intellectual support for their natural proclivities to spend and not to tax. The era of seemingly permanent and increasing governmental deficits was upon us, an era from which we have not yet escaped.

In 1986, we can only hope that the political decision-makers of the 1980s and 1990s will have become familiar with the post-Keynesian challenges to the aggregation fallacies and that something akin to the classical Victorian precepts for private and public prudence will come to inform the observed politics of these decades. The restoration of old ideas that have been for a long time displaced by fallacies is, at best, more difficult than acceptance of ideas that have been carried forward in an unblemished tradition. We can hope that such restoration goes forward. As of 1986, there are both encouraging and discouraging signals to be observed. The financial politics for the remaining years of this century remain unpredictable.

THE ELEMENTARY LOGIC

A debt instrument (bill, note, or bond) is a contractual obligation, on the part of a person or entity, that promises payment of stipulated amounts of things (or claims on things) over a sequence of designated periods subsequent to the period in which the instrument is signed.

That is to say, debt is an obligation to pay *later*. Taken separately, therefore, the contracting of debt by an owner of a portfolio of assets amounts to a claim against the anticipated stream of net returns from those owned assets. This claim must reduce the present value of the assets, which is determined by discounting the anticipated stream of net returns. At this level of very elementary logic, the issue of debt is identical to the destruction of capital value.

This basic relationship between debt issue and the destruction of capital value tends to be obscured or overlooked because of the mindset imposed upon us by double-entry bookkeeping or balance-sheet accounting. The issue of debt, the incurrence of the obligation to make payments in future periods, is more or less automatically treated as only one side of a two-sided transaction. The issuer of debt is a borrower, who receives a transfer of payment during the period of the contract itself. This payment *now* is that which is received in exchange for the promise to make payments *later*. In this two-sided treatment, the balance sheet of the borrower is adjusted by adding the present value of the debt instrument to the liability side of the account and the present value of the current payment received to the asset side. There is no change in net worth. There seems to be no destruction of the capital value of the whole portfolio or enterprise.

The legitimacy of this double-entry procedure is based on the implicit presumption that the funds secured currently in exchange for the debt instrument will be used productively, at least in some prospective or anticipated sense. Such a presumption is invalid when the borrower simply uses up or consumes the funds that are currently received in exchange for the promise of future period payments. In this case, the separated or one-sided model of debt issue is more helpful than the double-sided model. Debt issue becomes equivalent to the "eating up" of capital value, pure and simple.

This elementary logic of debt applies, of course, to any intertemporal contract. There is no difference between individual, firm, agency, or public borrowing. In all cases, the issue of debt for the purpose of financing current-period use or consumption is equivalent to the destruction of the capital value of the asset stream that is anticipated. This basic proposition holds independently of the value of the portfolio. If there is no capital value, the creation of debt will, in this case, produce negative capital. If the capital value is initially negative, debt will merely increase the negative total.

PUBLIC DEBT AND PUBLIC CONSUMPTION

What connection has the elementary logic of the above discussion with the summary history of ideas sketched out at the very beginning of this chapter? And, indeed, with the title and purpose of the chapter? The connection and relevance should be clear enough. The public debt incurred by the U.S. government during the regime of ever increasing, and apparently permanent, budgetary deficits has financed public or government *consumption* rather than public or government investment. The classical rules for fiscal prudence have been doubly violated. Not only has government failed to "pay as it goes"; government has also failed to utilize productively the funds that have been borrowed. There has been no offsetting item on the asset side to match the increase in net liability that the debt represents. The capital value of the income stream of the national economy has been reduced, dollar for dollar, with each increase in present value of liabilities represented by the debt instruments issued.[2]

Proper accounting would, therefore, require that any estimate of "national capital stock" derived by discounting the net national income be written down or reduced by the present value of the outstanding national debt instruments. A somewhat different way of putting this point is to say that a share of the anticipated national income over future periods has already been precommitted for the payments of amortizaton and interest charges on the debt. This share is simply not available for free disposition, either privately or publicly, in accordance with the preferences of persons who nominally "earn" the income in the periods to come. The national debt obligation is an overload, a burden, that carries forward with it no compensating asset or claim. For U.S. citizens, the national debt is fully analogous to a private debt that has been incurred to finance a consumption spree in some past period.

Objections may be raised to my simplistic approach to such weighty

---

2. The present value of the liabilities presented by the debt instruments may not be so high as the maturity values of the debt. There will be a difference here to the extent that government borrows at rates of interest lower than the rate appropriate for discounting future tax liabilities, which would normally be the market rate of return. To the extent of this difference in present values, the government has not issued what we may call "real debt" but has, instead, imposed a tax on persons living during the period of the public consumption. The extreme case is, of course, that in which the government "sells" bonds to the central bank at zero or very low nominal rates.

issues of national fiscal policy. An initial, if unsophisticated, argument might suggest that federal government outlays (that have, admittedly, been partially financed by debt) have not been "wasteful" and that any analogy to a private consumption spree is misleading. After all, or so such an argument might run, these outlays financed spending on the provision of goods and services that were deemed to be collectively beneficial, including transfers to the needy and to those who hold legitimate entitlement claims.

My analysis does not, however, imply that the outlays made by the government were "wasteful" in any such sense of the term. The spending that was debt- or deficit-financed during the 1970s and 1980s may well have provided benefits of a higher value than the then-present value of the debt instruments required to finance such spending. But precisely the same point may be made about the spending made by an individual during a private consumption spree. The pitiable character who, after having blown his whole week's wages, borrowed still more funds to finance last Saturday's spending at the local pub, may well have enjoyed Saturday-night benefits that he estimated, *then,* to be higher than the opportunity costs of the debt obligation that he assumed. The rationality or irrationality of the choices made last Saturday night cannot, however, affect the burden of the debt obligation at next week's payday. The improvident one may, of course, have warm memories regarding last Saturday's pleasures, and he may sigh that "it was worth it all," but, come Friday, he will have fewer dollars of net income available for current spending than he would have had if last Saturday's binge had not taken place at all. The fact that the benefits or pleasures then enjoyed may have been more than, equal to, or less than the properly estimated choice-influencing opportunity cost becomes irrelevant to the temporal location of the postchoice costs. The benefits, no matter how great or small they might have been, *have been enjoyed.* The postchoice consequences must be suffered *now.*[3]

PUBLIC DEBT AND PUBLIC INVESTMENT

A more sophisticated argument may commence with an explicit denial that federal outlays financed by debt have, in fact, been exclusively

3. For a generalized discussion of costs that makes the distinctions between prechoice and postchoice costs, see James M. Buchanan, *Cost and Choice* (Chicago: University of Chicago Press, Midway Reprint, 1975).

devoted to current public consumption. It may be suggested that some share in federal government outlays represents investment spending on long-lived capital assets. To the extent that federal outlays are investmentlike, it is appropriate that these be financed with debt issue. Government practice in this respect is no different from ordinary business procedures, and responsible financial planning must allow for borrowing to finance the purchase of genuine asset items. A practical suggestion that often emerges from this argument is that the government's fiscal account should be improved by the introduction of a categorical separation between consumption and investment items, between the current consumption and the capital budget, sometimes referred to as above-the-line and below-the-line items. This distinction does characterize public accounting procedures in several countries.

Cursory examination suggests that this argument warrants close consideration. If, in fact, the share of federal government outlay financed by debt should be roughly similar to the share that might appropriately be classified to be investment in public capital, there would be an offsetting item on the asset side of the nation's balance sheet that would match the liability that the present value of debt represents. In this setting, when *both* sides of the transaction are recorded, both the issue of debt and the purchase of the assets, there need be no net change in the present value of the national capital stock. And, indeed, if the investment outlay should prove productive in some net sense, a properly measured present value should record some increase.

The question would seem to be empirical. How much federal spending during the observed era of deficits can properly be classified as public capital investment? And does this estimated share in total outlay come close to that share that has, in fact, been financed by debt?

Care must be taken, however, to specify precisely what is required for an item of budgetary outlay to be classified as a public capital investment. The durability of an asset alone is not sufficient to make its purchase qualify as capital investment for purposes of the exercise here. In order that an item of governmental outlay be labeled a net asset, with a positive present value to be entered on the balance sheet as offsetting the debt liability, there must be an increment to the net income stream directly attributable to that asset.

As an example of a long-lived asset that cannot qualify as public capital for our purposes, consider a monument that is designed to last forever. There is no measured income flow associated with the monument. While there may be benefits anticipated from the monument over the whole sequence of future time periods, these anticipated benefits cannot be appropriated as a source for the tax payments that may be required to service the debt if the initial outlay is debt-financed.

In terms of criteria for tax equity, the anticipated flow of benefits over time may seem to suggest the appropriateness of debt- rather than direct-tax financing. In this sense, the outlay on public "capital" like monuments is quite different from that on current public consumption, the benefits from which accrue during the period when the public goods are actually consumed. The anticipated benefits from the monument add to the stream of psychic income or utility. And a measure of utility levels in any future period should, ideally, include some imputed value for these particularized benefits. Note, however, that persons receiving these benefits have no choice as to the form that these take, and there is no prospect of converting income benefit flows into other channels that might be helpful in covering amortization and interest charges on the debt.

Public "capital" like monuments, which does seem to include much durable investment of government (public buildings, defense hardware), may be likened to personal, private investment in specific human capital designed to yield consumption benefits over time. Consider, as an example, outlays for a course in music or art appreciation. The anticipated benefits extend over a lengthy sequence of periods, and utility streams over these periods are higher than they would otherwise be without the initial investment outlay. But once the initial outlay is made, these benefits are "locked in," so to speak; they are inalienable in the sense that there is no prospect of converting them into realizable monetary equivalents. The person who has incurred a debt obligation to take the course on art appreciation may enjoy knowing all about art, but the enhancement in his utility in this respect will not reduce the burden of the debt overload during the relevant payout or debt retirement periods. If double-entry books were kept in utility dimensions, the inclusion of an offsetting asset value to the debt liability might seem appropriate. Double entries in accounts normally, however, refer only to realizable values and enforceable obligations. Unless this elementary precautionary precept for prudence is followed, persons who might indeed be wealthy in the utility dimension will find themselves in the bankruptcy courts.

For governments, this precept for fiscal prudence would suggest that assets be classified as "public capital," and hence introduced as offsetting items on the balance sheet, only if measurable and realizable money income flows are anticipated. For example, if government constructs a toll highway or an urban transport network, it is appropriate to discount the expected stream of anticipated facility revenues or fees to produce a capital value of asset that the facility represents. This asset value should, however, be limited to the discounted value of the fees that are actually expected to be collected. It should not include the full cost outlay on the facility if fees are not expected to cover these costs. Government's announced or expressed unwillingness to collect fees from a debt-financed facility's users sufficient to cover full costs becomes equivalent to precommitment of a share of nonfacility income. The result is precisely the same as if the funds secured in exchange for the debt instruments are used for current public consumption.

Since we know that a relatively small share of governmental outlays reflect "public capital investment," even in the broadest definition, and since even within this share there are precious few facilities or projects that carry an associated direct income stream, the analytical treatment of all public outlays as current public consumption does not seem far off the mark, and surely not far enough off to yield wildly misleading conclusions. This result should not be surprising in itself, since federal fiscal accounts are not arranged or discussed in terms of the distinction between current and capital outlays, and decisions on the sizes of the deficit are never related to the composition of the budget.

BUT, AFTER ALL, WE DO OWE IT TO OURSELVES

The elementary logic carries through. The issue of public debt to finance the great and continuing fiscal spree of the 1960s, 1970s, and 1980s, has been equivalent, in all relevant respects, to the destruction of capital value. A substantial and ever increasing share of our future income has been precommitted. There are no offsetting asset items in the national balance sheet.

As I suggested in the first section of the chapter, this spree is at least partially the result of the widespread acceptance of aggregation fallacies, a set of ideas that were in the air long before Keynes, but which were putatively legitimized intellectually by the Keynesian macroeconomic methodology. It seems useful at this point to see precisely how this methodology served to undermine the classical Victorian theory of public debt.

To do this, let us return to the elementary logic of the personal consumption loan. An individual, let us call him *B* for borrower, desires funds in excess of those available to him during time period, t_o. To secure these required funds, he contracts a loan; he issues debt and proceeds to finance current spending for consumption in t_o. Having consumed the funds, but with the contractual promise to pay later still before him, *B* has suffered a reduction in his net wealth position. He has, in effect, eaten into his capital; he has precommitted some share of his anticipated future income.

The funds that *B* used in t_o were obtained from *L*, whom we shall call the lender. She gives up funds in t_o in exchange for *B*'s debt instrument, *B*'s promise to pay later. Let us now look at the balance sheet adjustment for *L*. At the time of the contract, in t_o, she writes down the *Cash* item and writes up the *Notes Receivable* item, both on the asset side of the ledger. There is *no* change in *L*'s net worth in the transaction.

Let us now make *B* and *L* man and wife, and combine their two separate balance sheets to create a single family account. The combined balance sheet will record the debt liability item of *B* and the notes receivable item for *L*, which seem to offset each other. But the balance sheet, struck as of t_1 after the marriage, will not directly reflect the history of the transaction. By comparison with the family balance sheet that might have been had *B* not engaged in the consumption spending spree, the net wealth of the family is lower by the size of the debt liability.

Straightforward, simplistic, elementary. Indeed so. But it is the failure to go through these very simple steps that has led many fine intellects to go wildly wrong in their analyses of public debt. The central failure was that of comparing irrelevant rather than relevant alternatives. In our highly simplified two-person example, the macroeconomic methodology would have involved taking a balance sheet snapshot of the combined account of *B* and *L*, whether or not the conjectural marriage had taken place. Such a snap would have revealed the debt liability of *B* and the offsetting claim of *L*. From this simple offsetting balance, the conclusion emerges that there is no net debt for the community as a unit. To be sure, or so the argument would have proceeded, *B* holds a present-value liability, and *L* a present-value claim. But these are precisely canceling in the net. There can, then, be no community "burden" of debt. The conclusion appears totally absurd in his two-person model. It is not the two-person "community" that has incurred the debt; B has, and B must pay L. And it is not the "community" that has enjoyed the consumption spree; B has done so. Indeed, L has financed the spree by voluntarily giving up command over resources in t_o, but only in explicit exchange for the debt commitment.

The aggregation fallacy surfaces when the "community" in the form of a government that acts for all citizens assumes the role here of B, the borrower in the two-person example. Here it is the government, acting on behalf of the whole "community," that spends beyond its means in t_o, and, in so doing, incurs the debt obligation. The fact that the lenders, the Ls, may also be members of the community is totally irrelevant to the calculus. These persons, the lenders, sacrifice or give up purchasing power over goods or other assets in exchange for the promises of future payment written into the debt contract. In this latter capacity, these Ls act privately, and not at all for the "community." A proper combination of private and public accounts can only record a net decrement to the community's net wealth as a result of the consumption spending–debt issue transaction. Analytical clarity requires that the macroeconomic aggregates be broken down into relevant components attributable to private and to public or governmental accounting records.

IS PUBLIC DEBT EQUIVALENT TO A TAX ON CAPITAL?

The elementary logic of our second section cannot be challenged. The financing of public consumption outlay by government borrowing is equivalent to reducing the income stream available for private and/or public disposition in all periods of time subsequent to that period in which the funds are initially transferred from lenders and the revenues utilized. If the national capital stock is measured as the present discounted value of the anticipated future income stream, debt-financed spending of this sort amounts to a destruction of this stock.

This simple result must stand. But this result is not identical to the related, but different, proposition to the effect that public-debt financing and capital taxation are equivalent. These two revenue-raising instruments become equivalent in all respects only under a particular set of circumstances. And these circumstances are not the ones usually associated with the two alternatives in practical fiscal operation.

In the first place, capital taxation, as this fiscal instrument is nor-

mally discussed, does not often include the present value of anticipated income from labor in the tax base. In other words, human capital,
or the value thereof, is often not subject to the capital levy. Unless
it is so subjected, however, the so-called capital tax is only partial.
Such a tax is in no sense identical in effect to the issue of debt if the
interest and amortization charges on the latter are to be financed by
general taxes on income flows. The important difference is suggested
in the above statement. This difference lies in the fixing of the pattern
of incidence in the one case and the effective postponement in the
other. With a tax on capital, whether this be entirely general or limited to particular forms of capital, the imposition of the tax defines,
once and for all, the distribution of the burden. With public-debt issue, by contrast, there is no immediate or first-period definition of
the ultimate pattern of incidence. To make the debt equivalent to the
tax, it would be necessary to assign to each current asset-holder a
specific share in the liability that the public debt represents. Through
such a procedure, any public debt could be converted into an instrument that is fully equivalent to any tax on capital, whether this be
general or specific. Unless such first-period assignment of liability is
made, however, the actual incidence of debt would seem to be highly
unlikely to be equivalent to that resulting from the levy of the equal-
revenue capital tax that might have been imposed in lieu of debt issue.

DEBT RETIREMENT AND CAPITAL CREATION

The elementary logic is fully symmetrical. If an issue of debt to finance current consumption is equivalent to a destruction of capital
value, then the retirement of existing debt that is financed by the drawing
down of current consumption must be equivalent to the creation or
restoration of capital value. This simple result holds for either private
or public debt. To retire outstanding debt from current consumption
is identical to the financing of new income-yielding investment. In
balance-sheet terms, the value of the liability item measured by the
debt is reduced; there is no explicit change on the asset side of the
account. New worth, or capital value of the enterprise, be this of a
person, firm, or nation, is increased, dollar for dollar, by the net payoff of debt.

The symmetry carries through, however, only if both sides of the
account are analogous. Debt creation to finance current consumption
destroys capital value; debt retirement financed from current con-

sumption creates capital value. But debt retirement out of current investment does no such thing. If a debt-amortization program is financed from funds that would otherwise be destined for investment, the effect is neutral with reference to the value of capital. From this result it follows that the explicit retirement of outstanding national debt by the imposition of a once-and-for-all capital levy will not affect the properly measured value of the national capital stock.

The analogy with capital taxation to finance outlay in lieu of debt applies in reverse here. There will normally be significant differences between the effective distributional incidence of any capital levy aimed at debt retirement and the distributional incidence of the continuing liability that an existing debt embodies. The explicit imposition of a capital tax will fix, once and for all, the final incidence of the aggregate charges for the outlays that were initially debt financed. On the other hand, and by contrast, the carry-forward of the debt allows such final incidence to be in part postponed. *Someone* in the polity, now or in some future period, owes the full liability value of the debt that is on the books. But *no one* has an *assigned* share in this liability. A person may behave under the expectation that successful political strategy can remove, from himself, all or most of the debt-measured liability. The debt liability is a continuing zero-sum game.

There is a direct public-choice implication in this comparative incidence of the two institutions. Precisely because any tax levy, whether on consumption or investment, fixes the distribution of the ultimate charges, there will be directed political opposition by those persons and groups on whom the tax incidence falls. Politically, therefore, the choice is far from neutral. There will be a natural bias against any proposal to retire debt from tax-financed revenues. Those who are to be taxed will oppose; those who may be the net beneficiaries may not exist (future generations) or, if they do, may not treat the aggregate reduction in liability as personally experienced increases in their own net wealth. For the same reasons that politicians find it much easier to finance outlays with debt rather than with taxes, they also find it much easier to carry forward debt, once issued, than to retire debt from tax sources. In a very real sense, the Victorian model has been reversed. National capital, once destroyed by debt creation, will not be restored. Or, to put this point differently, public debt, once created, is *permanent,* regardless of the initial usage to which the funds might have been devoted.

DEFAULT, INFLATION, AND CAPITAL VALUE

The only means through which public or national debt is likely to be "retired" is via default, whether this be explicitly or implicity carried out. But default does absolutely nothing toward restoring the capital value destroyed when the debt was created and the resources used up. Default is equivalent to the levy of a discriminatory tax on those persons and entities, internal and external, who hold debt instruments in their investment portfolios. Consider, first, a model in which all holders of debt are citizens of the issuing jurisdiction. Repudiation of the government's debt obligation will reduce to zero the liability item in the imagined balance sheets of all future taxpayers. It will also reduce to zero the capital value of the debt instruments carried in the balance sheets of all holders of the relevant securities. Since these two items, aggregated over the whole community, are precisely offsetting, there is no net effect on capital value. Some persons are made better off; others are harmed. There is no increase in the expected value of the national income stream over future periods, and, hence, no increase in the value of the national capital stock.

The crudest of aggregation fallacies must be avoided here. Because default does not, in itself, affect capital value in the aggregate, it should not be concluded that the debt itself had no effect. Again, the relevant alternatives must be examined. If the debt had not been issued and the funds used up, those who invested in government debt instruments could have invested in income-yielding assets. The net income stream, and therefore the capital value, would have been greater in the absence of the debt. The fact that explicit default neither increases nor decreases the value of the national capital stock, in the aggregate, suggests only that there is no miracle of fiscal process that will remove the burden of error once made. Indirectly, of course, explicit default may reduce the effective value of the government's exploitable capital value. If, because of a past default on debt, government cannot borrow at or near market rates, government's own net worth is reduced. But in such case, government, as an entity, becomes distinguishable from the community.

If some holders of government debt instruments are foreigners, default can, by repudiating the capital values of these external holders of claims, increase somewhat the net wealth of the members of the internal community. This international redistribution of burden is fully analogous to the internal redistribution of burden in the previous model. It becomes somewhat arbitrary to aggregate only within national boundaries. And, in this model of externally held debt, the indirect effects of repudiation are likely to be more severe than with internally held debt. Default is likely to make it difficult for governments to borrow in international markets except on unfavorable terms. If the potential for foreign borrowing is included as an asset item in a national balance sheet, default on debt will reduce the capital stock.

Implicit rather than explicit default is the much more likely consequence of goverment debt. History provides more than sufficient evidence to suggest that governments find it relatively easy to default on their real-valued debt obligations through inflation. With access to money-creation powers, governments find it almost irresistible to destroy capital values of debt holders. Nominal obligations are honored; real-valued obligations are ignored and capital values confiscated. The basic analysis is almost identical to that for explicit default sketched out above.

But there are important differences. As public debt continues to increase in a deficit-financing regime, interest charges on this debt increase. The share of total budgetary outlay devoted to the service of previously issued debt increases. At some point, political pressures will ensure resort to inflationary financing, if this avenue of revenue creation is possible. Through inflation, the real value of current government outlays may be maintained, and possibly even expanded, in the face of ever mounting interest charges on the debt, charges that are denominated in nominal monetary units rather than in real values.[4] This result would be impossible in a regime that honored the real value of the debt claims.

So long as the inflation is unanticipated, in whole or in part, government can continue to be responsive to demand pressures for expanded outlay on goods, services, and transfers, and to counter pressures against tax increases, while appearing to remain "responsible" in meeting its interest charges on the debt that is outstanding. Through the inflationary process, the government may, over a considerable period of time, succeed in confiscating the real values of previously issued debt claims, while, at the same time, it may continue to issue new debt to finance flows of current outlays. Open and explicit re-

---

4. For an analysis of such a sequence, see my paper "Debt, Demos, and the Welfare State (Presented at the CIVITAS Conference, Munich, Germany, October 1982).

pudiation of public debt would confiscate values at one moment, but because of the explicit signal such repudiation would provide, the potential for exploitation would be much more limited than with the implicit repudiation through inflationary financing. As the inflationary process continues, default risk will, of course, come to be incorporated in borrowing rates. As such rates increase, the weight of interest charges in the budget grows, generating, in turn, political pressure for still further inflationary financing of outlay, including debt service. An equilibrium of sorts is attained only when government becomes unable to borrow at any rate, a position that is then identical to that reached immediately with open and explicit default.

As the basic analysis suggests, default on public debt as such neither destroys nor creates capital value in the aggregate, except through the indirect effect on government's potential borrowing capacity. Other indirect effects may emerge, however, through incentives on private decisions to create capital. If the government defaults, explicitly or implicitly, if it levies what amounts to a discriminatory tax on the holders of its own debt instruments, individuals who might be potential investors may become concerned about potential government seizure of other forms of capital, through the fiscal structure or otherwise. The direction of effect on capital creation seems clear; individuals will tend to put aside relatively fewer resources for investment than they would in a regime characterized by government dedication to honor its own debt obligations.

Default through inflationary financing has, in this respect, even more severe incentive effects than open default. With inflation, the discriminatory tax cannot be levied exclusively on holders of public debt claims. Inflation tends to destroy the value of all assets and claims that are denominated in monetary units, including the holders and users of cash balances. In this setting, therefore, individuals who might be potential creators of capital will predict that government will, indeed, destroy such values once they are created. That which remains only a fear with open default becomes a predictable consequence of continued inflationary financing. In terms of criteria for capital accumulation and preservation, therefore, explicit repudiation of public debt seems clearly preferable to default by means of inflation.

CONSTITUTIONAL CONCLUSIONS

In 1986, we live with a large and ever increasing national debt. Funds secured in exchange for the government securities that make up this debt have been used, largely if not exclusively, to finance public consumption. The resources so commanded by government have already been used up. Whether or not these resources were "worth" the value that the debt liability now embodies is an irrelevant question. Capital value that cannot be restored has been destroyed. We live with a capital stock that is permanently lower than that stock might have been had the government not embarked on the great fiscal spree of the 1960s, 1970s, and 1980s.

If we look at political reality, it seems unlikely that we shall act to restore the national capital stock by retiring debt out of funds drawn from current consumption. We shall not deliberately reduce the flows of goods and services, public or private, that we enjoy. We may, and presumably will, continue to default on real debt obligations through inflation, but this behavior will in no way restore capital value already lost.

Realistically, we can at least hope to "stop the bleeding." We can stop the continuing destruction of capital value through deficit-debt financing. As our institutions are now organized, however, we cannot hope to accomplish even this minimally desired result. The temptations of ordinary pressure or interest group politics are simply too overwhelming for those who hold elective office, whether in the executive or legislative branch of government, to resist. The response behavior exhibited in ordinary politics cannot be behavior that would satisfy the demands of reasonable fiscal prudence.

What to do? Our politicians will not be reconverted easily to the Victorian fiscal religion, especially since the Keynesian alternative fits so closely with their natural proclivities to spend without taxing. But we can, as politicians, as academicians, and as laymen, recognize what is happening. And diagnosis is the first step toward cure. Once sufficiently recognized, fiscal profligacy can be contained by appropriate *constitutional* remedies. Ordinary politics will simply not allow fiscally responsible outcomes to emerge from modern democratic institutions. But ordinary politics operates within a set of *constitutional rules,* and these rules have been and may be changed so that more desired patterns of outcomes will emerge.

In this respect, the proposed constitutional amendment that would require budget balance on the part of the national government becomes the most important fiscal reform that has been discussed in the century. Such an amendment, considered as a *general rule* of fiscal prudence, can be discussed, evaluated, and possibly approved largely in independence from the demand-side pressures of day-to-day politics. The fiscal outcomes of ordinary politics now resemble the behavior of the compulsive gambler who finds himself in Las Vegas or Atlantic City. Who can expect the gambler to refrain from "irresponsible" behavior, given the temptations that he faces? But just as the compulsive gambler can know his own proclivities and stay home, so can those who ultimately make political decisions, the citizens, know the proclivities of our ordinary politicians and keep their fiscal activities within bounds of prudence by the enactment and enforcement of constitutionally restraining rules.

No such rule can be expected to work miracles. But an effective balanced-budget constraint, along with some accompanying rule that limits access to money creation as a financing device, could make the U.S. economy the genuine "fiscal wonder" of the late 1980s and 1990s. We cannot undo the damage that has been done. But we can move to levels of economic activity undreamt of in our philosophy.

Do we possess the requisite political understanding, along with the courage, to implement a new fiscal regime? I shall wait upon the answer.

7

SOCIAL SECURITY, SAVING, AND OUR LEGACY TO THE FUTURE

Marilyn R. Flowers

INTRODUCTION

Do the citizens of the United States save too little? If so, is the Social Security retirement program a significant cause of the problem? These two questions became the subject of heated debate during the decade of the 1970s. The major issues in the debate have not been resolved as we pass the midpoint of the 1980s. In this chapter we will survey and attempt to clarify these issues. The primary focus of the discussion is the second question relating to the effect of Social Security on private saving. However, this question is interesting from a policy perspective only if we have some criterion that makes it possible to evaluate any policy-induced change in the savings rate. As we shall see, developing such a criterion is not an easy task.

A general outline of the chapter is as follows. We begin with a simple description of a pay-as-you-go government pension program. Although the description is grossly simplified relative to the actual Social Security retirement program, it still captures the essential features of that program with respect to its potential effect both on individual private saving decisions and on total saving in the economy. We then turn to a discussion of the effects of the Social Security program on private saving decisions. The direction and magnitude of this effect is subject to vigorous dispute among economists. The potential effect is theoretically ambiguous, and the empirical evidence to date is inconclusive.

Finally we turn to the policy implications of the debate. A conclusion that Social Security has significantly depressed private savings does not necessarily justify changes in the program. At any point in time, the welfare of those currently living is related to the saving decisions of past generations. Generally speaking, the higher the savings rate in the past, the higher is current income and consumption; correspondingly, the higher the current savings rate, the higher will be future income and consumption. However, it is also the case that in making the transition from a lower savings rate to a higher one, many individuals who are alive at the time the transition begins will, as a consequence, experience a permanent reduction in their own lifetime consumption. Is this sacrifice of current consumption justified by the improved consumption opportunities of future generations? This is a seemingly unavoidable policy dilemma.

SOCIAL SECURITY AS AN INTERGENERATIONAL TRANSFER

The Social Security retirement program in the United States is often described as an ongoing program of intergenerational transfers. Individuals are taxed during their working years in order to provide benefits to the elderly. There is an implicit promise to current workers that when they retire, benefits—financed by taxes levied against the next generation of workers—will be paid to them.

Three features of the program are especially important with respect to a potential effect on saving and capital formation in the economy. First, the Social Security program is unfunded. No effort is made to accumulate an actuarially sound trust fund by investing the taxes of current workers in income-producing assets that could finance their future retirement benefits. Instead the program is run on a pay-as-you-go basis with current tax receipts used to finance current retirement benefits. Current and future beneficiaries must rely on the continuing economic and political feasibility of taxing workers.

The other features relate to the implicit rate of return provided by participation in a pay-as-you-go public retirement program. Two categories of participants can be identified. Individuals who are at or near retirement age when the program begins receive extremely high implicit rates of return because the number of years spent as taxpayers is short relative to the number of years during which benefits are received. Individuals who spend their entire working lives in the program will receive a lower implicit return on their tax payments. Assuming a constant tax rate, a mature program will pay retirees a return equal to the rate of growth in the tax base, which in turn will reflect the rate of growth in the economy. This rate of return will generally be lower than the rate of return on private investment.

These factors are important for the following reasons. First, the unfunded nature of Social Security lends special importance to the question of what effect, if any, the program has on private saving. Any depressing effects on private saving will not be offset by increased public saving. Second, differences in the implicit return offered by Social Security and the return that could be received on private saving and investment have potential effects on perceived wealth that could affect private saving decisions. The third reason relates to the possible interaction between the intergenerational transfer offered by Social Security and privately planned transfers between generations. It is possible that Social Security will not have any effect on private saving if individuals, correctly perceiving the nature and magnitude of the intergenerational transfer it offers, respond privately to prevent the public transfer from altering either the direction or the magnitude of privately planned transfers. We now turn to a detailed discussion of these issues.

SOCIAL SECURITY AND PRIVATE SAVING: THEORY AND EVIDENCE

Does the existence of Social Security have any effect on the private saving decisions of individual Americans? If so, what is the direction of that effect, and is it substantial or trivial in magnitude? Economists who have carefully examined these questions have yet to reach a consensus on the answers. This lack of agreement, which fuels ongoing and heated debate, stems from competing theoretical models and inconclusive empirical evidence. In this section we will examine the alternative models in order to clarify the theoretical ambiguity of the relationship between Social Security and private saving and capital formation.

Although numerous scholars have made important contributions, models developed by Martin Feldstein and Alicia Munnell, on the one hand, and Robert Barro, on the other, have provided the primary analytical focus of the debate. Both models take as a starting point an assumption that individuals plan their consumption and saving from a lifetime perspective. In the absence of a government pension program, individuals would save during their working lives in order to accumulate assets to support consumption during retirement. At issue is whether introduction of a government pension program will be viewed by individuals as an effective substitute for the retirement component of their private saving program. More specifically, will individuals substitute payroll tax payments for private saving during their working lives with a corresponding intention of substituting Social Security benefits for dissaving as a source of retirement consumption? This can depend critically on whether and how the Social Security program affects individual choices with respect to retirement age and also on the role played by intergenerational transfers in motivating private saving behavior. The latter is the primary issue that distinguishes the Feldstein-Munnell model from that of Barro.

The Feldstein-Munnell Model

The model of individual saving and consumption behavior used by Feldstein and Munnell in their respective 1974 studies[1] is a straightforward application of the "life cycle" model first developed by Modigliani and Brumberg in 1954 and by Ando and Modigliani in 1963.[2] The basic premise of the life cycle model is that individuals plan their consumption from a lifetime perspective and will seek means to smooth their consumption pattern relative to their income pattern. Two features of the model are of particular importance in analyzing the relationship between Social Security and saving. First, because most individuals can reasonably anticipate much higher earnings during their middle years than during the last years of their lives, the smoothing hypothesis implies that they will save during the high-earning middle years in order to be able to maintain a stable level of consumption later. Second, the life cycle model assumes that individuals plan to

---

1. Martin Feldstein, "Social Security, Induced Retirement and Aggregate Capital Accumulation," *Journal of Political Economy* 82 (no. 5, 1974):905–26; Alicia Munnell, *The Effect of Social Security on Personal Saving* (Cambridge, Mass.: Ballinger Publishing Co., 1974).

2. Franco Modigliani and R. Brumberg, "Utility Analysis and the Consumption Function: An Interpretation of Cross Section Data," in K. Kurihara, ed., *Post-Keynesian Economics* (New Brunswick, N.J.: Rutgers University Press, 1954); Albert Ando and Franco Modigliani, "The 'Life Cycle' Hypothesis of Saving: Aggregate Implications and Tests," *American Economic Review* 53 (no. 1, 1963): 55–84.

consume their entire income during their lifetime and correspondingly do not plan to leave any bequests.

Some simple numerical examples can clarify this model and its implications. Suppose we have an individual who anticipates working for 30 years and then spending another 10 years in retirement. Annual earnings while working are $400. Assume that this individual wants to maintain a smooth stable level of annual consumption over his or her lifetime. In the absence of any government pension program, this implies saving during the working years and dissaving during retirement. Assuming, for simplicity, that the market interest rate is zero, the individual's $12,000 of total lifetime earnings can sustain annual consumption of $300. The individual must save $100 per year for 30 years, accumulating $3,000 which is then drawn down by $300 per year for each of the 10 retirement years.

Now suppose that the government imposes a pension program in which the individual is taxed $20 per year during his or her working life and is paid an annual retirement benefit of $60. The government program, in other words, implicitly pays the individual a return on taxes paid which is equal to the return that could have been earned had the money been privately saved and invested. It seems entirely plausible, in this example, that the new tax will be paid by individuals reducing saving rather than consumption during their working years. By so doing, the same level of annual consumption can be maintained as before. Feldstein and Munnell refer to this as an asset substitution effect.

The asset substitution effect suggests that there should be a strong negative correlation between Social Security and private savings. However, Feldstein and Munnell also recognize an offsetting factor that, when properly taken into account, could reduce the negative impact on saving and might even reverse the direction of the effect. This is the induced retirement effect. In the previous example, the relative lengths of the working and retirement periods were arbitrarily fixed. However, suppose that this were actually subject to individual choice. Consider the implications of the individual choosing a somewhat shorter work period, 28 years, for example, and a correspondingly lengthened retirement period of 12 years. Although total lifetime earnings would be smaller by $800, total saving during the working period would actually increase. In order to sustain annual consumption of $280 over the 12-year retirement period, the individual must save $3,360 during his or her working life instead of the $3,000 previously required.

There are features of the Social Security benefit structure that encourage individuals to retire earlier than they otherwise would. For example, individuals can only increase their annual retirement annuity by continued labor force participation up until age 65. In addition, once individuals qualify for a Social Security retirement benefit, any labor earnings above a minimum amount[3] result in that benefit being reduced by $1 for every $2 earned.[4] If one effect of the Social Security program is to encourage early retirement, the stimulus to saving as a consequence of individuals planning to finance a longer retirement period may partially or totally offset the asset substitution effect noted earlier. An extension of our earlier numerical example can clarify this point. Recall that the asset substitution effect reduced private saving during the individual's 30-year working life by $600. Suppose, however, that as a consequence of the Social Security benefit structure, the individual reduced the length of his or her working life to 28 years. With the shorter working period the individual will qualify for an annual pension of $46.50. The remainder of desired annual retirement consumption of $280 will have to be financed by private saving of $2,802. The early retirement effect has resulted in a net reduction in private saving of $198 instead of the $600 predicted by the asset substitution effect alone. In this example, there was still a net reduction in saving as a consequence of Social Security. However, had the early retirement effect been stronger or the asset substitution effect weaker, it is actually possible for private saving to have increased rather than decreased. Because the asset substitution effect and the induced retirement effect work in offsetting ways, both the direction and magnitude of the effect of Social Security on private savings are theoretically ambiguous in the Feldstein-Munnell model.

Implications of Differing Rates of Return

The previous discussion assumed that the rate of return available to individuals in an unfunded government pension program was comparable to that offered by a private, funded program. This assumption is empirically false. Current retirees and those nearing retirement have received a fairly high rate of return relative to that which could have

3. $7,320 in 1985.
4. Individuals are not subject to this penalty after age 70. Therefore the induced retirement effect is relevant for individuals who, in the absence of Social Security, would have chosen to retire between the ages of 65 and 70.

been earned through private saving. For young workers, on the other hand, Social Security is probably a bad deal. A higher return would be available if their payroll tax contribution could be invested privately. These differences between the return offered by Social Security and that available from private saving can have significant implications, in the context of the Feldstein-Munnell analysis, for the size of the asset substitution effect. If the public return is higher than the private return, this effect is strengthened, and vice versa.[5]

A simple diagrammatic example can clarify these points. Consider an individual whose lifetime can be effectively divided into two periods, working and retirement.[6] In Figure 7–1, the individual's earnings (E) and consumption during her working life (C_w) are measured on the horizontal axis. Retirement consumption (C_r) is measured on the vertical axis. Suppose that earnings during the individual's working life total OE. The budget constraint EF represents feasible consumption opportunities in the absence of a compulsory government pension program. The slope of EF is $-(1 + r)$ with r being the market interest rate. Thus if this individual were to save BE during her working life, she could consume $Bf = BE (1 + r)$ in retirement.

Suppose that the individual would in fact choose to save BE during her working life. The preferred lifetime consumption pattern, in other words, would be that combination of C_w and C_r corresponding to point f in the diagram. What would be the implication of introducing a government pension program that taxes the individual during her working life and pays a benefit during retirement? There are three cases to be examined. In one, the government program offers a rate of return, g, which is equivalent to the market interest rate. In the other two cases, g is, respectively, greater than and less than r.

If $g = r$, the budget constraint EF is unchanged and, from the individual's perspective, any tax paid during the working period is a perfect substitute for private saving. If the tax is less than BE, private saving will remain positive but will decline by the amount of the tax. Suppose, for example, that the tax is equal to DE. The individual can still obtain the preferred lifetime consumption pattern at f by saving BD. If the tax should equal or exceed BE, private retirement saving will fall to zero.

---

5. This effect is discussed in Michael R. Darby, *The Effects of Social Security on Income and the Capital Stock* (Washington, D.C.: The American Enterprise Institute, 1979).

6. Because we are concerned only with the size of the asset substitution effect, the possibility of altering the relative lengths of these two periods is ignored.

Figure 7–1.   Life Cycle Consumption and Saving Under Alternative Rate of Return Assumptions.

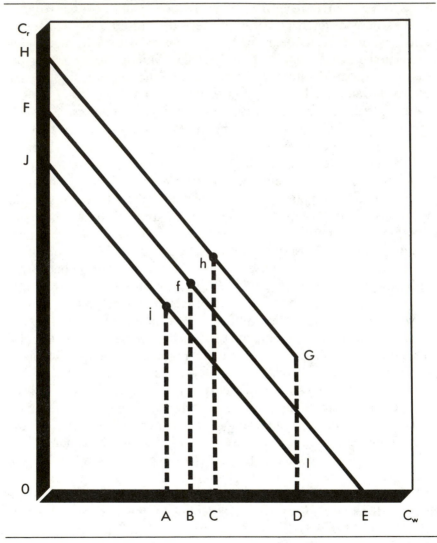

Suppose that the implicit return offered by the government program exceeds the market interest rate. If a tax of DE is levied during the individual's working life, the effective budget constraint will shift out to a position similar to the one indicated by GH in the diagram. The vertical distance DG measures the increment in C_r offered by the government retirement benefit and is equal to $DE (1 + g)$. The effect on private saving depends on how the individual reacts to the wealth increment made possible by the government program. If, as seems plausible, the individual seeks to increase both working and retirement consumption, private saving will decline by even more than was the case when the budget constraint was unchanged by the government program. Suppose, for example, that point h on GH is the new preferred combination of C_w and C_r. Private saving to supplement the government pension would be $CD < BD$. The asset substitution effect has been strengthened by the higher rate of return.

Opposite results emerge if the government program offers a lower return than private saving. Again suppose that a tax of DE is levied during the individual's working life, but the accompanying promised retirement benefit is only DI ($=DE(1 + g')$; $g' < r$). The new budget constraint IJ lies below EF. If, as again seems plausible, the individual responds to this reduction in wealth by lowering both C_r and C_w, private saving will decline by less than was the case when the budget constraint was unchanged by the government program. Suppose, for example, that the individual chooses the consumption combination at point j. Private saving would then be $AD > BD$. The low rate of return on the government program weakens the asset substitution effect.

A mature, pay-as-you-go intergenerational transfer with a stable tax rate can offer its participants a rate of return equal to the growth rate in the economy. Private saving offers a return equal to the market rate of interest which, in turn, will tend to reflect the marginal productivity of investment in the economy. In theory, these two rates of return can be equal but do not have to be. In point of fact, the growth rate in the American economy has been lower than estimates of the rate of return on private investment. Average annual growth in national income between 1948 and 1973 was 3.65 percent.[7] Professors Martin Feldstein and Lawrence Summers estimated that during the comparable period 1946–75, the average net rate of return on investment was 12.4 percent.[8]

As we shall see in later discussion, this difference is critically important for the normative evaluation of an unfunded Social Security

---

7. Edward F. Denison, *Accounting for Slower Economic Growth in the 1970's* (Washington, D.C.: The Brookings Institution, 1979), p. 104.

8. Martin Feldstein, "Does the United States Save Too Little?" *American Economic Review* 67 (no. 1, 1977): 116–21.

system. Some care must be used, however, in drawing inferences about the positive effect of this difference on the saving behavior of individuals. In analyzing the asset substitution effect, it is important to know what rate of return individuals anticipate and whether (at the time saving choices are made) they expect that their Social Security taxes will provide a return different from that available through private saving and investment. As noted earlier, individuals who are currently retired or nearing retirement have done very well under the Social Security program. Parsons and Munro estimated that the average retirement annuity of males who retired in 1970 at age 65 was almost 70 percent higher than that which could have been earned by private investment of the payroll taxes levied against their earnings during their working years.[9] However, it is not clear that this high return could have been anticipated by individuals during their working years. Especially in view of the significant expansion of Social Security benefits that began in the latter half of the 1960s, it seems entirely possible that the high ex post return on payroll tax payments was an unanticipated windfall that had no effect on earlier saving decisions.

In the absence of offsetting private intergenerational transfers, an issue to be discussed in the next section, today's young workers are almost certainly in a position comparable to that described by budget constraint *IJ* in Figure 7–1. The very high return current retirees have enjoyed from Social Security was generated from several sources that will probably not be available in the future. Today's retirees are benefiting in large part from the fact that they retired before the Social Security program reached full maturity. They spent fewer years in employment subject to payroll taxation and were taxed at much lower rates than will be the case for future retirees. In addition, each current retiree supported fewer retirees during his or her working life than will be the case for workers in the future.[10] Finally, it is inescapable that the return offered by a pay-as-you-go retirement program must ultimately be constrained by the growth rate in the economy. Historical experience suggests that it is unlikely that this growth rate will ever equal or exceed the return on investment.

Do current workers accurately perceive the lower return implicit in

9. Donald O. Parsons and Douglas R. Munro, "Intergenerational Transfers in Social Security," in M. Boskin, ed., *The Crisis in Social Security: Problems and Prospects* (San Francisco: Institute for Contemporary Studies, 1978).

10. For a more complete discussion of these points, see Parsons and Munro, n. 9 above.

their continued forced participation in the Social Security program? This is the relevant issue with respect to the effect of the Social Security program on current private saving decisions. Several factors make it difficult for individuals to accurately anticipate how well or poorly they will do under Social Security. For example, the American tax system taxes capital income rather heavily. This drives a wedge between the gross return on investment (r) and the net return received by savers. (r_N). This makes it possible for $r > g > r_N$. Individuals may perceive that they can do better under Social Security than by saving and investing privately because of preferential tax treatment of Social Security retirement benefits relative to private investment income.[11]

Finally, it is generally difficult for individuals to predict the future level of payroll taxation and benefits. Social Security does not offer a guaranteed return but rather is ultimately dependent on future growth in the payroll tax base and the economy. Future growth is notoriously difficult to predict. For example, growth in the wage base is heavily dependent on growth in labor productivity and wages, and also on expansion in the size of the work force. Forecasters have been surprised in the past by unexpected changes in these factors and undoubtedly will be surprised in the future. How does this uncertainty affect individual retirement planning? Many individuals may base their expectations of the future on past experience. Having observed that their parents and grandparents received a very good deal from Social Security, they may anticipate a similar good deal for themselves. On the other hand, the current concern with long-term financing for Social Security may lead many young workers to anticipate the demise of the program before they reach retirement age. Different individuals may have different expectations with correspondingly different effects on private saving decisions. The net effect is an empirical rather than a theoretical issue.

Implications of Private Intergenerational Transfers

The major theoretical competitor to the Feldstein-Munnell analytical framework is that advanced by Professor Robert Barro.[12] Barro also

---

11. For a discussion of this issue, see Martin Feldstein, "Perceived Wealth in Bonds and Social Security: A Comment," *Journal of Political Economy* 84 (no. 2, 1976): 331–36.

12. Robert J. Barro, "Are Government Bonds Net Wealth?" *Journal of Political Economy* 82 (no. 6, 1974): 1095–1118; "Reply to Feldstein and Buchanan," *Journal of Political Economy* (no. 2, 1976): 343–50.

works with a version of the life cycle model in which individuals plan their saving and consumption from a lifetime perspective. However, he is concerned with the interaction between Social Security and private intergenerational transfers. Although the analysis is quite complex, the major implication can be summarized quite simply. Suppose that in the absence of a Social Security program, individuals would make private intergenerational transfers. These transfers might either be from children to their parents or from parents to their children. Now suppose that the government imposes a pay-as-you-go retirement program that, taken by itself, involves a collective transfer from young to old. Barro argues that rational individuals would adjust their private transfers to prevent the government program from altering either the direction or magnitude of the net transfer between generations. If this occurs, private saving will be unaffected by introduction of the Social Security program.

The Barro model and its implications can be clarified by using the model developed in the preceding two sections. As before, we assume that an individual's lifetime can be effectively divided into two periods, working and retirement. For the sake of simplicity, we also assume that these periods are of equal length. This does not affect any of the model's implications, but it does simplify present value computations and illustrations. The market interest rate is assumed to be 10 percent.

Consider first a situation in which the representative individual saves not only to provide for retirement, but also to leave a positive bequest to his or her heirs. Suppose that in the absence of a program like Social Security, the individual would arrive at retirement with assets valued at $100. In contrast to our earlier discussion, however, suppose the individual plans to consume only $90 during retirement and to transfer the remaining $10 to his or her children.[13] In other words, the parent is voluntarily giving up $10 of potential retirement consumption in order to increase the wealth of his or her children by a like amount.

Now suppose that the government imposes a pay-as-you-go retirement program in which the children of the individual in our example are taxed $10. The proceeds of this tax are transferred to the parent.

---

13. For simplicity in our numerical illustration, we will assume that the transfer is made at the beginning of the individual's retirement period. This is, of course, the same in present value terms as a bequest of $11 to the children at the end of the parent's life.

Two questions are important. Will the older generation perceive that the government program effectively reduces the wealth of their children? If so, will they respond privately to nullify this collective reversal of their privately planned transfers? If the answer to both questions is yes, the government program will have no effect on private saving.

The analysis is straightforward if the collective transfer from young to old is made on a one-time basis without the children receiving any promise, implicit or otherwise, that their own retirement consumption will be supported by taxes on the next generation of workers. Under these circumstances, it seems obvious that the older generation would effectively refuse to accept the government-imposed transfer to them from their children. The reason is as follows. Prior to the government program, parents had the option of increasing their own retirement consumption at the expense of reducing the wealth of their children by a like amount. This could have been accomplished by simply eliminating planned bequests. Because parents did not find this a desirable option before the government program, there is no reason to expect that they would find it desirable afterward. The transfer implicit in the government program can be effectively nullified if parents simply increase the transfer they make privately to their children. The wealth of neither generation is changed, nor is net consumption and saving in the economy.

The analysis is considerably more complex if the government pension program is expected to continue indefinitely. The added complexity arises because although each generation makes a transfer to its parents, it also receives a transfer from its children. In the preceding example, recipients of government benefits transferred those benefits back to their children to avoid any reduction in the lifetime consumption of the children. However, if the intergenerational transfer is perpetual, will immediate descendants of retirees or, in fact, any future generations be forced to suffer a reduction in lifetime consumption?

If the rate of growth in the economy should equal or exceed the market interest rate, no generation must lower consumption as a consequence of the government pension program. This will be true even if parents do not make compensating bequests to their children. Correspondingly, the motivation for such bequests will be absent. However, although this proposition has theoretical validity—a point that will be clarified in later discussion—it is not empirically relevant. As has already been noted, evidence suggests that the marginal productivity of investment is higher than the long-term growth rate for the economy.

If $g < r$, future generations will suffer a reduction in lifetime consumption by being forced to participate in a collective intergenerational transfer from children to parents. This loss has already been illustrated in Figure 7–1 by the shift in the budget constraint of a young worker from *EF* to *IJ*. Barro argues that if, at any point in time, the elderly realize this effect, they will act to offset it by increasing private gifts and bequests to their children.

The Barro model also predicts that Social Security will not affect private saving if planned private intergenerational transfers are from young to old. Suppose that, in the absence of Social Security, consumption of the elderly would be financed at least in part by gifts from their children. If a Social Security program that taxes children and pays benefits to parents is then imposed, it seems plausible that children will pay the new taxes by reducing private gifts to their parents rather than reducing their own consumption or saving. By so doing the consumption of both groups is unchanged relative to the previous private equilibrium.

Social Security and Investment in Human Capital

The Barro model hypothesizes that in the empirically relevant case of $g < r$, a program like Social Security will have no effect on private saving, capital formation, or the welfare of current or future generations. Professor Allan Drazen has extended Barro's analysis to examine the interaction between Social Security and investments in human as well as physical capital.[14] He hypothesizes that Social Security could result in higher welfare for all generations even if investment in the physical capital stock is reduced. This is because a government enforced intergenerational transfer from young to old stimulates investment in human capital, which may have higher return than investment in physical capital.

Drazen notes that all parents transfer some resources to their children in the form of expenditures on education. This investment in human capital pays a return in the form of higher productivity and earnings when the children enter the labor force. As long as invest-

14. Allan Drazen, "Government Debt, Human Capital and Bequests in a Life-Cycle Model," *Journal of Political Economy* 86 (no. 3, 1978): 505–16.

ment in human capital pays a higher return than investment in physical capital, parental gifts to their children will take the latter form. Parents who are saving for retirement would prefer to invest that saving where the rate of return is highest. However, unlike gifts or bequests to children that can take the form of either human or physical capital, Drazen argues that in the absence of a program like Social Security, individuals are constrained in their retirement planning to invest only in physical capital. Even though the return on human capital may exceed that on physical capital, individuals cannot rely, with complete confidence, on the latter as a means of financing their retirement. This is because they have no legal claim to the higher earnings that children receive as a result of increased parental investment in their human capital.

If parents are unable to finance their retirement privately by investing in the human capital of their children, a private market equilibrium may be characterized by the marginal return on human capital investment exceeding that on physical capital. In this case, a government-enforced transfer from young to old can increase the welfare of all generations, even if the older generation reacts to the program by increasing its private bequest to the young. The reason is that the tax payments of the young can be returned to them in the form of human capital investments. Owing to the higher return on such investments, the elderly will not need to return all of the government transfer in order to prevent their children from being harmed by the program. Even if total saving and investment is unchanged, the efficiency gain from a more profitable mix of human and physical capital investment can enable all generations to enjoy greater lifetime consumption.

Drazen's analysis is dependent on his assumption that the absence of legally enforceable claims on human capital prevents individuals from receiving any return from such investment in their children. He also implicitly assumes that gifts and bequests from parents to children are the dominant form of private intergenerational transfer. If these assumptions are relaxed, there is a potential for Social Security to discourage rather than encourage efficient investment in human capital.

Suppose that in the absence of a public pension program, elderly parents would receive at least a portion of their retirement support from their children. This support is not a legal right of the elderly, but rather derives from traditional societal mores. In such a situation, individuals could invest in the human capital of their children in anticipation that wealthier children would provide greater support to their aged parents. Collectivization of this private intrafamily transfer would weaken the incentive for parents to make such investments. Although the ability of children *as a group* to support their parents would still be directly related to their human capital, the investment that individual parents make in their own children would have no significant effect on the level of retirement support that those parents receive from the public pension program. Rather than stimulating private parental investment in the human capital of their children, such investment would be reduced.[15]

Social Security and Individual Myopia

The life cycle models discussed in the preceding sections assume that well-informed individuals carefully plan their consumption and saving from a lifetime perspective. An alternative model assumes, to the contrary, that many individuals are shortsighted and will not engage in any long-term retirement planning. As a result, if left to their own devices, they will not save enough during their working lives to ensure adequate retirement consumption.[16]

This model is often used to justify a government program like Social Security on the paternalistic presumption that government intervention can provide individuals with more desirable lifetime consumption patterns than they could achieve independently. A careful examination of the normative attractiveness of this argument is beyond the scope of this paper. However, even if the model of individual behavior upon which it is based has empirical validity,[17] some care must be exercised in interpreting the implications of that result with respect to the interactions among Social Security, saving, and capital formation. A pay-as-you-go government pension program cannot displace nonexistent private retirement saving. However, the relevant choice with respect to the Social Security program is between the unfunded program that we actually have and either a funded program with government saving or a program of forced private saving.

15. For a discussion of this point, see Marilyn R. Flowers, "The Political Feasibility of Privatizing Social Security: Comment on Butler and Germanis," *The Cato Journal* 3 (no. 2, 1983): 557–62.

16. For a more thorough discussion of this issue, see Peter Diamond, "A Framework for Social Security Analysis," *Journal of Public Economics* 8 (no. 3, 1977): 275–98.

17. Ibid.

Even if the Social Security program has not depressed private saving relative to the level that would have prevailed in its absence, it remains plausible that the program has depressed saving relative to that which would have prevailed with a funded program.

Social Security and Saving: Empirical Evidence

The various models described in the preceding sections yield conflicting hypotheses about the effect of Social Security on private saving. The zero-bequest life-cycle model employed by Feldstein and Munnell has ambiguous effects on saving because of the offsetting effects of asset substitution and induced retirement. The Barro model predicts no effect on saving and capital formation as long as individuals would, in the absence of Social Security, make private intergenerational transfers. Drazen's extension of the Barro model suggests the possibility that Social Security could cause an efficiency improving marginal substitution of investment in human capital for investment in physical capital. Finally, the hypothesis generated by the extreme myopia model is that an unfunded Social Security program will not displace private retirement saving.

What is the truth of the matter? Is the average American today suffering lower income and consumption because the unfunded Social Security program systematically reduced private saving and capital formation over the past forty years? Will continuation of the program extend this burden to future generations? Or, alternatively, is the flurry of concern over a possible adverse impact on the capital stock much ado about not much? Given the theoretical ambiguity about the relationship between Social Security and capital formation, empirical analysis and evidence is obviously of critical importance. Unfortunately, conclusive evidence has yet to appear.

Without question, the most startling empirical results were those reported by Feldstein in his 1974 paper.[18] He estimated that Social Security had reduced private saving and capital formation by almost 40 percent. However, his results have been subject to serious challenge. One of the key variables in his empirical model was miscalculated as a result of a computer programming error.[19] After correcting

18. Martin Feldstein, "Social Security, Induced Retirement and Aggregate Capital Accumulation," *Journal of Political Economy* 82 (no. 5, 1974): 904–26.

19. Dean R. Leimer and Selig Lesnoy, "Social Security and Private Saving: New Time Series Evidence," *Journal of Political Economy* 90 (no. 3, 1982): 606–29.

this purely technical problem, Feldstein still found that Social Security had a large negative impact on private saving and capital formation.[20] However, other questions have been raised about his choice of independent variables; specifically about the way he modeled individuals' perceptions of their Social Security wealth. Questions have also been raised about the sensitivity of his results to the time period used and the inclusion or exclusion of other potentially relevant variables.[21] Other studies have found much weaker effects of Social Security on private saving. Munnell found that the asset substitution effect and the induced retirement effect had been almost precisely offsetting in the past. However, she did express concern that a slowing down of the decline in labor force participation of the aged combined with benefit increases might mean that the asset substitution effect would become dominant in the future.[22] Darby concluded that "the effect of social security on saving is still an open issue. The reduction in the saving-income ratio is certainly not much larger than 25 percent . . . and is probably closer to or less than 10 percent."[23]

THE EFFECT OF SAVING ON LIVING STANDARDS

There is some irony in the history of the debate over the effect of Social Security on private saving. When the program was begun, many economists uncritically accepted the proposition that an unfunded government program would reduce private saving. Haunted by the specter of the Great Depression and converted to the simple Keynesian explanation that the catastrophe might be due to a surfeit of saving, many economists viewed as desirable government policy that reduced saving.

The perspective of modern economists is dramatically different. As we have seen, the empirical issue of what, if any, effect Social Security has had on private saving is the subject of a lively and unresolved debate. In addition, the normative context within which the savings rate is considered has shifted from short-term stabilization policy to capital formation and long-term economic growth. Within this context, the issue of concern is whether the savings rate is too

20. Martin Feldstein, "Social Security and Private Saving: Reply," *Journal of Political Economy* 90 (no. 3, 1982): 630–42.

21. See Leimer and Lesnoy, *n.* 19 above, and Darby, *n.* 5 above.

22. Alicia Munnell, *The Effect of Social Security on Personal Saving* (Cambridge, Mass.: Ballinger Publishing Co., 1974).

23. Darby (p. 54), *n.* 5 above.

low rather than too high. A framework for examining the interaction among Social Security, saving, and growth will be presented in this section.

At any point in time, the productive capacity of the economy is critically dependent upon three factors: (1) the size and quality of the labor force, (2) the state of technology, and (3) the stock of physical capital. This capacity can be devoted to producing goods and services for current consumption or to investment in maintaining and expanding the capital stock. It is this necessary trade-off between consumption and investment that makes the savings rate such an important element in the theory of economic growth. The share of GNP that is saved reflects the share of the productive capacity of the economy that is devoted to capital formation.

The economic performance of a country is generally measured in terms of the standard of living its residents enjoy. This suggests that the variables of primary concern are per capita income and consumption. The rate of saving and capital formation is important in this context because of its effect on long-run sustainable levels of income and consumption. An increase in the savings rate will generally, though not always, make possible a permanent increase in future consumption. However, this increase cannot be achieved without cost in the form of lower current consumption. If this potential trade-off between current and future consumption extends across generations, the normative evaluation of government policies to increase saving becomes especially complex.

Some simple diagrammatic analysis common to modern growth theory can clarify these issues. In Figure 7–2, output per worker, y, is measured in the vertical axis and capital per worker, k, on the horizontal axis. OA depicts a hypothesized relationship between these two variables. Two characteristics of this relationship are especially important. First, labor productivity is positively related to the capital-labor ratio. The second is that output per worker increases less rapidly than capital per worker.

If a given capital-labor ratio is to be maintained over time, some portion of total output must be invested both to replace worn-out capital and, if the labor force is growing, to increase the total capital stock at the same rate. The ray OB in the diagram measures the amount of y that must be invested to maintain any given k. Its slope reflects both the depreciation rate and the rate of growth in the labor force. An increase in either of those variables would cause OB to rotate counterclockwise through the origin.

Figure 7–2.   Equilibrium Income and Consumption per Capita in the Neoclassical Growth Model.

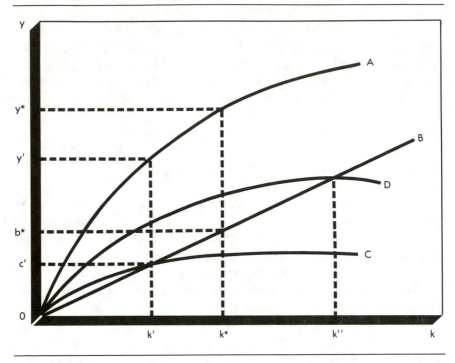

The relationship among OA, OB, the savings rate, and sustainable consumption can be interpreted in the following way. Suppose that at a particular point in time the capital-labor ration is k^* as indicated in the diagram. If saving per worker is Ob^* as measured on the vertical axis, the capital-labor ratio and output per worker will be sustained indefinitely—barring changes in such factors as technology, labor force growth, and depreciation rates. In this steady state equilibrium, consumption per worker of $Oy^* - Ob^*$ can also be sustained indefinitely. Given that the labor force in steady state is a fixed fraction of the population, this latter variable can be easily transformed into a more relevant variable: consumption per capita.

There is no unique steady state equilibrium. Instead, the equilibrium levels of k and y are determined by the savings rate. Suppose, for example, that the savings rate, expressed in terms of saving per worker, were as depicted by OC in Figure 7–1. In other words, saving per worker would be a constant fraction Oc'/Oy' of output per worker. Steady state equilibrium would then be attained with output per worker of y' and a capital-labor ratio of k'. If actual k at any point in time were less than (greater than) k', saving would exceed (fall below) that required to maintain that capital-labor ratio and, correspondingly, k would increase (decrease) over time. A higher saving rate as depicted by OD would yield a steady state capital-labor ratio k''.

Several features of this model are useful in evaluating the interaction among Social Security, saving, and capital formation. First, the steady state equilibrium described in Figure 7–2 is not a zero-growth equilibrium. If the population is growing, both the labor force and the capital stock are growing at the same rate. These factors obviously contribute to expansion in the productive capacity of the economy. Ignoring temporarily the role of technological advance, steady state growth in an economy will be equal to the growth in population. This growth rate will determine the rate of return offered by a mature pay-as-you-go government pension program. The savings rate does not affect this steady state growth rate but instead determines the level of per capita income and consumption, which remain constant. Changes in the savings rate can have only temporary effects on the growth rate as the economy makes the transition from one steady state equilibrium to another.

Technological advance has traditionally played a large role in economic growth and improved living standards. If we were to allow a steady rate of technological improvement in our model, the steady state growth in the economy would reflect both population and technology growth. In addition, per capita income would not remain stable over time, but rather would grow at the same rate as technology. However, despite the obvious importance of technological advance, it will be ignored in the analysis here. None of the major implications of the analysis are altered by this omission because the issue of concern is the relative effect of different savings rates on per capita income and consumption.

The model described in Figure 7–2 implies the existence of a unique savings rate that maximizes steady state consumption per capita. In Figure 7–2, this is the savings rate that produces k^* in steady state equilibrium. If the savings rate is lower than Ob^*/Oy^*, steady state consumption will be less than the maximum attainable. Interestingly, it is also possible for the savings rate to exceed that required for maximum steady state consumption, as, for example, that depicted by OD in the diagram. The intuitive explanation of this result is that when the steady state capital-labor ratio is increased from $k*$ to k'', the increase in saving per worker required to maintain the higher capital-labor ratio exceeds the increase in output per worker.

The savings rate that might emerge in a pure laissez-fare economy will not necessarily be the one that maximizes steady state consumption. In theory, nothing prevents it from being higher or lower than that rate. This has provided a basis for some arguments that government policy might be desirable to stimulate or depress saving depending on the circumstances.[24] If, for example, the laissez-faire savings rate were in excess of the desired level, an unfunded Social Security program that reduced private saving would be desirable and essentially costless. This corresponds to the case discussed earlier in which the growth rate in the economy exceeds the return on investment. However, as noted earlier, this case is not an empirically realistic one, despite its theoretical possibility. The more relevant case in which an increase in the savings rate is required to achieve higher long-run steady-state consumption presents a much more difficult problem, from the perspective of both normative evaluation and political feasibility.

These problems can be clarified if we consider the time path that consumption must follow during the transition from a lower to a higher saving steady state equilibrium. A higher savings rate means that a lower share of the output per worker is consumed. Thus, although output per worker will begin to increase immediately as k is increased, consumption declines initially and will attain its previous level only after some time has elapsed. This is illustrated in Figure 7–3. Output and consumption per worker are measured on the vertical axis, and time on the horizontal axis. Suppose an initial steady state equilibrium is characterized by output and consumption per worker of y_o and c_o respectively. The savings rate is $(y_o - c_o')/y_o$. Now suppose at time t_o the savings rate increases to $(y_o - c_o)/y_o$. If this savings rate is maintained, y increases over time until the new steady state equilibrium is attained at time t_2 with equilibrium output and consumption per worker at y_2 and c_2 respectively. However, note that there is an initial

24. For a direct application of this argument to the issue of having a funded or unfunded Social Security program, see Paul A. Samuelson, "Optimum Social Security in a Life-Cycle Growth Model," *International Economic Review* 16 (no. 3, 1975): 539–44.

Figure 7–3. Effect on Consumption of Changing the Savings Rate.

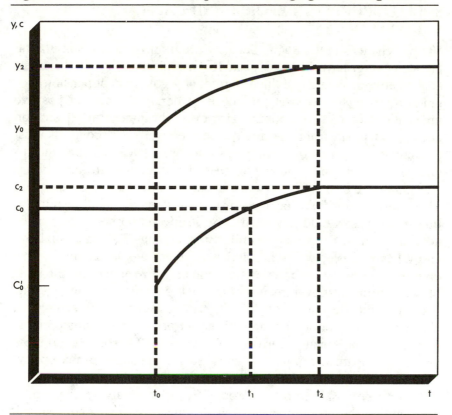

portion of the transition period extending from t_o to t_1 when consumption per worker is actually less than during the original steady state.

Generally, this transition from lower to higher consumption can be expected to extend across generations. Future generations enjoy higher consumption only if a current generation lowers its lifetime consumption. Unless those currently alive are willing to make this transfer to their descendants, there is no obvious argument that such a transfer is normatively justified. The case becomes especially ambiguous if, owing to technological advance, future generations can be expected to enjoy higher living standards even without an increase in the savings rate.

SOCIAL SECURITY REFORM AND CAPITAL FORMATION

Various changes in the Social Security program, aimed at stimulating private saving, have been suggested. An understanding of the interaction between saving and the design of any government pension program is obviously necessary if one is to derive the correct positive implications of these proposals. However, the preceding discussion also suggests that, from a normative perspective, such proposals must be evaluated in terms of the implied transfer between current and future generations. In this context, past effects of Social Security are essentially irrelevant. Changes in current policy cannot undo the past. Thus, verification that Social Security has slowed capital accumulation in the past would not justify, by itself, support for more rapid accumulation in the future. Similarly, a conclusion that Social Security has not affected saving and investment would not imply that current levels of those variables are optimal. More generally, the issue of whether or not government policy should change the savings rate is essentially independent of Social Security except to the extent that changes in that program are among the set of feasible policy options. Can changes in Social Security stimulate saving? If so, how do these changes compare with other policies, such as changes in tax policy, in terms of the fairness of distributing costs?

Various proposals to reform Social Security involve either gradually funding the program by increasing the trust fund or phasing it out with replacement by private retirement saving on either a voluntary or a mandatory basis.[25] The objective of both types of proposals is to increase the extent to which the benefits of future retirees are financed by saving done by those generations during their working years rather than transfers from their children. Whether this objective can be achieved depends on the response of aggregate saving to changes in Social Security. This, in turn, depends not only on how individuals would like to respond to such changes but also on whether or not they are allowed to make the desired adjustments. Either a funded Social Security program or a mandatory private saving requirement would

25. A detailed proposal for allowing individuals to opt out of Social Security may be found in Peter J. Ferrara, *Social Security: The Inherent Contradiction* (Washington, D.C.: The Cato Institute, 1980). See also Ferrara, "The Prospect of Real Reform," *The Cato Journal* 3 (no. 2, 1983): 609–21; and Martin Feldstein, "Toward a Reform of Social Security," *Public Interest* 40 (1975): 75–95.

introduce the possibility that individuals would be forced to save more than they would privately prefer to do.

If the Barro model explains a substantial share of the reaction of workers and retirees to Social Security and if individuals are free to adjust their saving to privately desired levels, attempts to fund, either privately or publicly, the retirement benefits of future generations are unlikely to have any significant effect on total saving in the economy. If operative private transfers are from old to young, government-mandated increases in retirement saving by current workers will be accompanied by reductions in private saving for bequests. Current workers will eliminate that portion of planned bequests previously needed to compensate for the loss in wealth their heirs would experience as a result of forced participation in an unfunded government pension program.

If, in the context of the Barro model, planned private transfers are from young to old, elimination of Social Security would not affect private retirement saving except to the extent that the existence or nonexistence of Social Security affects relative levels of investment in human and physical capital. The possibility that Social Security reform might include mandatory saving requirements is especially interesting in this case because the generation upon which the requirements are imposed does not have the option of reducing bequest saving. Forcing individuals to save for their retirement could result in the retirement of future generations being financed to a greater extent by saving and to a lesser extent by gifts from their children than would be the case if individuals were freely allowed to make their own retirement plans.

Within the context of the Feldstein-Munnell zero-bequest model, there are potentially significant differences between proposals to reform Social Security by retaining it as a government pension program—but with a larger trust fund—and proposals that would involve the eventual termination of the program. Because the induced retirement effect is purely a consequence of the Social Security benefit structure, it would obviously disappear if retirement planning were privatized. However, it is also relevant to note that recent changes in the existing Social Security program have probably significantly weakened that effect. These include increases in the base amount beneficiaries can earn before having their benefits reduced, a lowering of the age at which the earnings test is eliminated, and most recently, provisions to increase the retirement age gradually from 65 to 68.

This suggests that the primary effect of future Social Security reform will be concentrated on the asset substitution effect. Proposals to fund Social Security or to phase it out differ with respect to this effect if there are significant differences in the efficiency of increased private as opposed to public saving. These differences plus the nature of the intergenerational transfer involved in Social Security reform will be discussed below.

A common element in most proposals either to increase the degree of funding in Social Security or to phase it out is a requirement that current retirees not suffer any reduction in benefits. Proposals to phase out the program would essentially freeze benefits of all individuals, including current workers, at some level earned by previous participation in the program, but would stop the accrual of any new entitlements. These proposals have intuitive appeal, especially if privately accumulated retirement resources have been reduced in anticipation of a Social Security pension. However, they also have the effect of concentrating the cost in increased capital accumulation on workers rather than on the population at large.

This point can be illustrated quite simply by extending the simple example from Figure 7–1. In Figure 7–4, the position of a representative member of the working generation is again depicted with working and retirement consumption measured on the horizontal and vertical axes respectively. As before, budget constraints IJ and EF reflect lifetime consumption opportunities available to the individual with and without a requirement to participate in a pay-as-you-go government pension program that offers a lower return than private saving.

Although the worker would clearly benefit if allowed to plan lifetime consumption along constraint EF as opposed to IJ, it does not follow that termination of the program would be beneficial. If termination applies only to the benefits of future retirees, with unchanged payments to those currently retired, the tax burden on current workers cannot be lowered. This tax payment is measured by DE on the horizontal axis. Unchanged current taxes accompanied by the elimination of promised future benefits shifts the effective budget constraint for the current worker from IJ to the even less favorable constraint $I'J'$. Assuming that both private and future consumption will be reduced in response to lower wealth, private saving will increase. However, this increase in saving cannot replace the loss in lifetime consumption brought about by elimination of Social Security benefits.

Figure 7–4.   Transitional Wealth Implications of Privatizing Social Security.

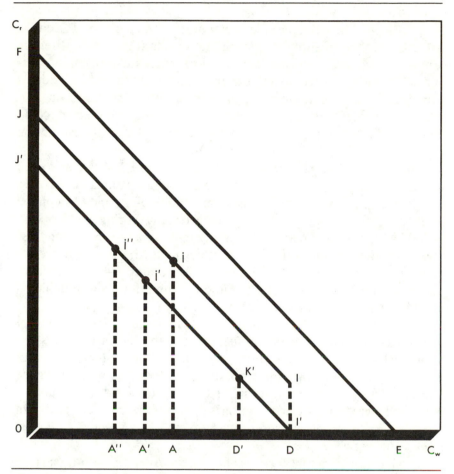

Alternative approaches to terminating Social Security could reduce the burden imposed on current workers, but only by increasing that on retirees. If, for example, benefits to current retirees were reduced, the budget constraint *I'J'* would shift out correspondingly. Alternatively, benefits could be maintained, but the source of revenue for those benefits could be changed from a tax on workers to a more general tax consumption, some of the burden of which would be borne by the currently retired. However, although the relative burden between current workers and current retirees is subject to manipulation, the requirement that those currently living reduce consumption in order to bequeath a larger stock of capital to the next generation seems inescapable.

In the preceding example, the decision to terminate Social Security affected only the position of the budget constraint defining lifetime consumption opportunities for current workers. Some proposals to terminate the program would require mandatory saving by individuals to replace Social Security benefits. For members of the transition generation, and indeed for all future generations, such a requirement could limit the ability to choose the most preferred lifetime consumption pattern on the relevant budget constraint.

Suppose, for example, that the worker in Figure 7–4 is confronted with budget constraint $I'J'$ after Social Security is terminated. Assume that the individual would prefer the combination of C_w and C_r depicted at point j'. This requires private saving of $A'D$ during the working period. As long as the mandatory saving requirement is less than this, it has no relevant effect. If, on the other hand, the worker were required to save a greater amount–$A''D$, for example—an additional burden is imposed because the lifetime consumption pattern depicted at j'' is not as satisfactory as that depicted at j'.

The primary difference between proposals to fund Social Security as opposed to phasing it out is that, in the former case, assets are accumulated in the Social Security trust fund while, in the latter case, increased private asset accumulation is generated. Any real difference between the two policies in terms of the direction and magnitude of the intergenerational transfer can arise only if there is a significant difference between public and private saving. This point can be clarified using Figure 7–4.

Funding requires an increase in Social Security taxes with no change in the benefit structure. The resulting surplus is invested in the Social Security trust fund with the objective of paying future benefits out of the income from the fund. For the current worker, this is equivalent to shifting the budget constraint from IJ to $I'K$. Taxes are increased from DE to $D'E$. The retirement benefit is the same as before ($D'K' = DI$). However, this benefit is now financed by investing the worker's additional taxes in the trust fund. Future workers will continue to pay taxes, but these taxes are invested and not used to pay retirement benefits to the older generation.

The preferred consumption pattern remains at j' as was the case with our earlier analysis of phasing out the program. Private saving is less than before ($A'D'$) but this reduction in private saving has been replaced by increased public saving ($D'D$). The surplus in the Social Security trust fund could be invested directly in the financial assets of private enterprises or, alternatively, in government bonds. Both have uncertain implications for capital formation.

Direct government investment in the private sector is a dubious prospect at best. Investment decisions guided by a desire to secure votes are likely to differ sharply and in an adverse way from decisions motivated by a desire to secure profit. Democratic political process is, in large part, the servant of the status quo. Investments that preserve existing jobs and incomes tend to be relatively more attractive because of the existence of a well-defined constituency that gains from such investments. Even though alternative investments may channel resources into new and more productive employment, the gainers are less clearly identified; accordingly, they are less able to organize and lobby effectively for access to government funds. In addition, substantial government interest in particular private enterprises presents the obvious threat that governmental power will be used to protect that investment by suppressing competition.[26]

The implications for saving and capital formation of investing Social Security taxes in government bonds depends on the political response to the influx of new revenue. If federal government spending is held constant—leading to a net reduction in the size of the overall federal deficit—private saving and capital accumulation could be favorably affected to the extent that government borrowing tends to crowd out private investment. If, on the other hand, the added revenue stimulates government spending with little effect on the deficit, higher Social Security taxes are effectively channeled into increased public consumption, with none of the desired effects on capital accumulation. Both the relationship between government deficits and private investment and the political determinants of the size of both the deficit and the expenditure side of the public budget are currently topics of considerable controversy. Without going into the details of these debates, it is sufficient to note that one of the ideas currently receiving consideration is highly controversial, namely, that private

26. For a particularly devastating critique of both public and private funding for Social Security, see Richard Wagner, "Funded Social Security: Collective and Private Options," *The Cato Journal* 3 (no. 2, 1983): 581–602.

capital formation could be stimulated by using higher Social Security taxes to purchase government bonds.

CONCLUSION

Social Security reform is one of the most complex issues confronting current policy-makers. The issue is obviously complicated by uncertainty about the positive implications of various reform proposals. However, a better understanding of how Social Security affects the saving and investment decisions of individuals would not necessarily resolve the dilemma of deciding what, if any, changes should be made in the program. In particular, if unfunded Social Security does significantly retard saving and capital formation, the question of whether and how to reverse that process has no easy answer from either a perspective of fairness or political feasibility.

Suppose, for example, that increased reliance on funded (private or public) retirement programs would increase the savings rate and capital stock. Future generations would undoubtedly benefit from any changes in public policy that achieved such an objective. However, the transition from an unfunded to a funded retirement program unavoidably requires one generation of workers to essentially pay twice for their retirement. They pay once by reducing consumption during their working years in order to accumulate the assets to finance their own retirement. They pay again when required to finance the benefits promised their elders under the old, unfunded program. It is this inescapable double burden that makes social security reform such a thorny issue.

8

BISMARCKISM

Gordon Tullock

INTRODUCTION

The largest tax paid in a direct sense by the average American is the Social Security tax. When we add on (1) the money he pays for what amounts to a state medical insurance program (medicare), which will benefit him only if he is under certain income levels or old enough to be pensionable, and (2) the money paid by his employer for unemployment insurance, the total is probably half or more of the total taxes he pays. Further, all of these taxes are used to provide him with a substitute for what traditionally would have been a strong motive for saving. As a result of paying these taxes, he is guaranteed an income when he is old; he is guaranteed his medical expenses now if he is in the lower income brackets, and in any event, when he becomes older; and lastly, he is provided with income for any period of unemployment. Thus he no longer has nearly as much need of savings as the traditional citizen had before these programs were introduced.

Consider that a citizen of the United States in the 1920s would be motivated to save money to provide for his old age, to take care of medical emergencies, and to act as a cushion in the event that he lost his job. He might do some of his savings by way of a private insurance company, but that insurance company would, of necessity, invest a large part of any premium he paid in order to have the funds available when he became pensionable or unemployed, as the case might be.

Thus, the general program of the welfare state directly reduces an individual's after-tax income, thus lowering the amount that he is likely to save, and eliminates or greatly reduces a number of the motives for saving. It does not of course *cancel out* the motives for saving, but it certainly makes them weaker than they would be without the welfare state.

Any economist looking at this would predict that in a society with this kind of welfare state, there would be a lower level of saving, leading to a lower level of capital investment and hence a lower level of growth and productivity than otherwise. This does not of course, prove that it is a bad thing. If values are appropriate, one could prefer a slower rate of growth with "security" to a higher rate of growth without it.

It is frequently argued that the welfare state is necessary in order to help the poor. Prince Otto von Bismarck, the Prussian statesman, invented the welfare state, and there is no reason to believe that he was overly concerned about the well-being of the poor. To digress briefly into German history, Bismarck was concerned about winning elections and centralizing the newly founded German Empire. Iron- ically, he lost the election immediately after introducing the welfare state, but the centralization worked. A large centralized bureaucracy was set up at a time when the new German Empire was basically a federation of kingdoms.

But to return to our main theme: the development of the welfare state, first in Germany and then in the rest of the world. I suppose that politicians other than Bismarck found it politically attractive, be- cause it was copied by nation after nation. The order in which nations adopted it tended to follow their proximity to Germany, both physi- cally and culturally. Today the welfare state is more or less universal. It can, however, be studied by examining it on a country-by-country basis. I propose to discuss primarily the American system, mainly because that is the one that I know best. The discussion, although not completely applicable to other countries, would nevertheless fit most of them quite well. The reason is simply that Prince Bismarck's in- vention has been adopted in pretty much the same form almost every- where. Prince Bismarck was a consummate politician, and other politicians found that his work met their needs almost perfectly.

SOCIAL SECURITY

In talking about the American welfare system—or its impact on saving and capital formation—I propose to confine myself to its old age pension provisions. Although there is much to learn from consideration of the medical and unemployment insurance portions of this Bismarckian program, in view of space constraints I have selected for discussion the old age pension, since it is the largest segment of the system.

The Social Security system is set up as an independent fiscal entity. Instead of being part of the general budget, it is supported by a special tax on employees—one of the rare taxes that is genuinely regressive. The benefits come solely out of that tax arrangement.[1] In other words, it is our largest example of a rigorously earmarked tax system.

Economists have frequently argued for *use* taxes, that is, to have people taxed for the cost of some service more or less in proportion to the degree to which they take advantage of the service. The economic advantages of a use tax are obvious, but of course it cannot be used to redistribute money to the poor. The Social Security system to some extent is a use tax, in that if it ever reached its stable state (and one of the points of this chapter is that it will probably never do so), the individual would pay into it much the same amount that he got out, although the payment and receipt would be in different parts of his life. Note that I said "much the same." The system does permit transfers of funds from the well-off to the poor, and in fact there are some gestures in that direction albeit little real substance in the current act.[2] An earmarked tax has political advantages (first brought to public attention by James Buchanan[3]), in that it automatically creates two groups of people who are especially interested in this government action: those who pay the tax and those who receive the benefits. If the two groups are of about equal size, we can anticipate that since it will be equally easy for them to mobilize politically, the resulting

1. I am ignoring here the arrangement under which some of the benefits are subject to income tax, with this tax then rebated to the Social Security Administration.

2. As will be shown below, there is a substantial transfer from the upper income groups to the middle classes.

3. James M. Buchanan and Gordon Tullock, *Calculus of Consent* (Charlottesville: University Press of Virginia, 1965), p. 293. Although the book is jointly authored, this particular idea was Buchanan's.

pressure groups will tend to cancel each other out. We will see that the Social Security system is an example of this sort.

For the novice let us simply analyze the way this joint system of tax and payment works. Let us begin by considering a state in which there is no rate of interest, no growth, and no change. Individuals live 80 years, the first 20 of which are spent going to school. They work from the age of 20 to the age of 65, then retire and live on their savings during their last 15 years. Each of them, we will assume, saves 20 percent of his income each year with a result that for the last 15 years they can live on 60 percent of their original income. It is not too much of a drop from the 80 percent of income that they had spent in the earlier part of their life.

Now, suppose that a Prince Bismarck arrives and suggests changing this system. He suggests that all employed persons be taxed 20 percent and that the money derived be paid in the form of a pension of 60 percent of lifetime income to all people over the age of 65. The taxes and expenditures will be exactly balanced. At first it looks as if there is no change—and eventually that will be true. But consider the generation in existence at the time of the proposal. All of them except those just entering the labor market have existing savings. They are now free to spend those existing savings without affecting their eventual pension. They can, of course, if they wish, retain the savings and spend them when they are old. Clearly, they all benefit. The ones at the age of 65 benefit more than the ones at the age of 21, but all of them benefit.

This looks like magic. Nobody is injured and everybody benefits. Note that new people entering the system—18-year-olds, let us say, who are shortly going to become 20—will pay in taxes the same amount they would previously have saved and will upon retirement receive the same payment they would have obtained out of their savings, had this new system not come into existence. The problem, however, is that under this system the present generation of voters makes a promise that the next generation of voters will have to fulfill. If the pensions and tax were simultaneously canceled, by revolution, by foreign conquest, or perhaps by some kind of natural disaster, everybody over the age of 20 would lose because they would have no savings and they would lose their pension rights. Once again people under the age of 20 would not be injured because they could simply switch back to the savings mode. Thus we have a system that is beneficial to all voters when it is installed. When it is in a stable state, it neither benefits nor injures anyone. Terminating the system, however, would be injurious to everybody old enough to vote. Clearly, there would be suitable voting power to defend such a system. We would never need to worry about its termination.

Unfortunately, in the real world the credibility of the system is not that good, and indeed one can readily imagine the system gradually disappearing. To further explain this, however, we must complicate our model a bit. For this purpose we must introduce the rate of interest and a rate of growth of the economy. Suppose merely that the rate of interest is higher than the rate of growth of the economy, a situation that is more or less the world norm, although there have been, of course, periods when the reverse condition obtained. For these circumstances the system that I have described would have to have built into it some procedure for increasing the total pensions people received. The easiest way is to simply arrange that whatever is collected by the 20 percent tax on all income is then disbursed to older people. Under these circumstances the pensions granted to older people will increase at the same rate at which the economy grows.

Now compare this with savings as the alternative. It is immediately clear that even at the point at which the system is in a stable state, younger people lose because they would be better off if they invested their money at the rate of interest—which is higher than the rate of growth of the economy—than if they paid the tax. Thus it is no longer true that, looked at as a lifetime investment, the system is essentially neutral. It now injures all the people who come into the system. It is still true, however, that if we start with a situation where people are investing to support themselves in their old age and a Prince Bismarck comes along and suggests this system, many people could be made better off. It depends on the rate of interest as opposed to the rate of growth of the economy. Before the most recent changes in the Social Security program, it was generally thought that the break-even point was about 43—that is, that people under the age of 43 were losing on the deal and people over the age of 43 were gaining.[4] These calculations assume that the individual is concerned only with his own well-being—they ignore the prospect that he might find himself supporting his elderly parents. This rather complicated issue, however, will be deferred until later. For the time being I will use the number 43 as the break-even point and will make adjustments later in the chapter.

This situation is a little complicated. A new entrant into the labor

---

4. The calculations are extremely difficult and uncertain.

force can look forward to a pension very materially smaller than the pension he could receive if he simply invested the tax money. As we take older and older people this disadvantage shrinks. Someone at the age of 35, for example, assuming that he regards his previous tax payments as a sunk cost, could look forward to a pension that would be less—but not very much less—than he would receive if he saved the money he is paying into the fund as taxes. At the age of 43 the two alternatives would be valued equally, and at the age of 50 he would prefer the Bismarck-state program. Once again, this assumes that these older citizens regarded their previous taxes as a sunk cost. This is, of course, the correct way of thinking about the matter if you are contemplating a change of policy in the future.

In a famous article Browning argued that this situation would lead to the Social Security payments always being higher than they should be.[5] He defined the desirable level of Social Security as that which would be chosen by a voter who was contemplating his whole lifetime of payments and receipts. Except for a small minority who are just entering the system, that is not the situation of any voters. For most voters the taxes that they have already paid in are, in fact, a sunk cost in considering changes for the future. They therefore underestimate the total cost of the system. One would, however, expect people under the age of 43 to be in favor of cutting back the system, and those over the age of 43 to be in favor of enlarging it. The two groups are not radically different in size. Thus a functioning system of this sort might have much the same political support for an increase as for decrease in program expenditures and hence remain stable. Obviously, however, the equilibrium would be an unstable one.

It seems likely that the observed tendency of these programs to expand depends more on another bit of Prince Bismarck–type genius than on the Browning effect. Prince Bismarck financed his program by a tax that, of course, fell on the laborers. Although our tax is nominally half on the laborer's salary and half on his employer, the employer in fact pays it and uses a single check for both halves of it. The wages of the laborer are reduced proportionately.[6] This par-

---

5. Edgar K. Browning, "Why the Social Insurance Budget Is Too Large in a Democracy," *Economic Inquiry* 13 (Sept. 1975):373–88.

6. It is sometimes argued that part of the cost, instead of being paid by the employee, is added to the price of the product. Since employees buy products, roughly in proportion to their income, this also means that the employee pays it—but by a different mechanism.

ticular bit of deception has had a long and very successful history. The Social Security Administration has never been willing to admit that employees pay the full cost of the system, and I think we can assume that they know their business. Economists, who do not have such a large material motive to mislead the workers, are unanimous in believing that the employer does not actually pay the "employer contribution."

It can be seen that every time the system is expanded, you have a small-scale version of the situation that has arisen for the system as a whole. Suppose, for example, the legislature raises the tax and the pension, or imposes the tax on a new group and gives them a pension. There is here a gain for all members who are over 43 and a loss for those under 43.

Continued success of the system requires that people now in the system believe that when they retire it will be retained intact. They are in essence "betting" that people will keep the bargain made by their parents. Consider, once again, our 43-year-old man. By the time he becomes 65, a little less than half of all voters will be people who were too young to vote at the time he was 43. Indeed there will be a substantial group of voters who were not even born at the time he passed his 43rd year. His prospects of a pension depend on these voters keeping, in essence, a promise made by their predecessors. And, of course, the situation is much more severe if we think of the pension he will receive when he is 75, at a time when a clear majority of the voters will be people who were too young to have voted when he was 43. His confidence that he will continue to receive the pension has to be based, not on the faith that people will keep their promises, but on the faith that certain voters will keep promises made by other voters.

IS IT TRUE?

This is the basic problem of credibility for the Social Security system. Suppose, theoretically, that an individual feels—when he decides to retire—that there is only a fifty/fifty chance the voters will decide to keep their "promises." Under these circumstances he would discount the future pensions by a very large risk premium. As a result the turnover rate, the point at which he would begin regarding the net benefit to him from the system to be greater than the net cost, would be moved forward to somewhere around 56 or so. If the voters reach that conclusion, an overwhelming majority of them would have a selfish motive for terminating the system.

In the traditional literature on this point, the matter has hardly been discussed at all; when it has been discussed, it has simply been stated—very, very, firmly—that there is no prospect of the scheme being canceled. Of course, if everyone believes that, the scheme is highly credible, and voters over the age of 43 have a selfish motive for favoring it. If the credibility of the system falls, the turnover point is moved, thus changing the probable vote in the future. This, in turn, affects the credibility still further. One can easily imagine a step process like the following:

1. Something happens that leads the voters to feel that everyone under the age of 45 will lose on the system.
2. The system is thus rendered politically less credible.
3. As a result, everyone under the age of 47 is led to believe that he will lose on the system.
4. The system is thus rendered still less credible.
5. As a result, and so forth . . .

Such an ongoing sequence of events will ultimately make the system literally vanish.

Here we have, simply, two theories. The implicit, unstated one of the conventional literature is that the system is completely credible and, hence, people can depend on it; the other hypothesis, which I have been outlining here, is that if it is at all suspect, the loss of faith may gradually weaken the political support, thus making it more and more likely that the system will fail. So far we have generated no evidence against either hypothesis.

If we look at the history of these systems, we observe that until quite recently they steadily expanded. You could find examples in almost all of the systems, and certainly in the American system, in which some technical change made by Congress did in fact lower the pension receipts of some particular, usually narrowly defined, group. This was, however, quite exceptional. Further, most of the advocates of the system (and after all, at the moment, they are most of the people who have written about the system) concealed the existence of these minor downward adjustments and simply said that the system never was cut.

Recently, however, all over the world countries have been cutting back on the system. I will be talking about the American adjustments in the most recent reform act, but similar steps were taken by such strong welfare states as West Germany, Denmark, and Sweden. The apparent reason for these cuts was simply that the system was becoming expensive enough to make younger voters object and threaten to "throw the rascals out."

SOCIAL SECURITY CUTS

Cuts have taken two different forms. First, they have literally reduced the pensions, one way or another. And second, they have deferred eligibility for them. We will discuss these one at a time.

In the United States the most recent reforms cut pensions in two ways. First, pensions above a certain level were made subject to regular income tax; this meant that upper income people would, in fact, receive markedly smaller after-tax pensions than they had expected. Since the special tax on these particular pensions was not put into general receipts but rebated to the Social Security Administration, this involved a cutting of the benefits of these groups. However, the number of people counted as upper income for this purpose was by no means small and, further, they were probably the most politically influential of the pensioners. And the people who are currently receiving pensions were cut quite significantly in real terms by deferring their cost of living adjustment. This was in fact the second such adjustment. The Congress had originally calculated the cost of living index in such a way that the pensions rose markedly faster than the cost of living. It then adjusted back to a new procedure in which they rose, as it turned out, somewhat faster than the growth of the wages of people who were paying the tax, but not faster than the cost of living index. The lowered expectations from the first cut were probably greater than those for the most recent cut, but in both cases they were sizable.

These cuts represented about half of the dollar value of the measures taken to bring the system back into potential solvency. The other half were accounted for by tax increases, and one of the tax increases clearly lowers the political credibility of the system. The payroll tax for Social Security has always been regressive in that it is a tax only on some segment of income, let us say the first $X of income a person earns. The value of X to be taxed was raised, while, as we have pointed out, the return received by upper income people was cut back quite sharply. If we assume that upper income people (and remember here we are talking of people with incomes above about $25,000) tend to be politically influential and that it is dangerous to cross them, this group probably now faces a situation where any of them under the age of 60 or so will actually lose from the continuation of this system.

There was in addition, a general raising of taxes on everyone; in particular, arrangements were made to compel various people who had been opting out the system—federal employees, employees of state and local governments, etc.—to come back in. The federal employees, a politically powerful group, were pretty much protected from the change, but the very junior members of the federal civil service and new employees, groups without much political power, were not protected.

The net effect of all of this has been to move the turnover point up. You now pay more for your pension, and the pension is worth less than it was before. The difference in pension value between upper income people and lower income people has been increased. It should be pointed out here, although we will elaborate on it later, that the poor did not gain from the change. The gainers were what we might call the lower middle class. The end result of this is that the turnover point is different for different income classes, with somebody who is paying the maximum or near the maximum amount of "contribution" probably having his turnover point somewhere around the age of 55 to 60; and someone in the $15,000 income bracket probably having the turnover point somewhere around 45. All of this assumes that the new arrangements are permanent and *thought* by the voters to be permanent, i.e., not likely to change.

The second change that was made was to move back the point for eligibility for a full pension. This was done in such a way that people over the age of 43 were unaffected, those below or at the age of 43, roughly speaking, got a one-year deferment of their eligibility.[7] Another category, those people under 25, got a two-year deferment. The fact that the break point was the age of 43 indicates, I think, that the Social Security actuaries had *calculated* that 43 was the turnover point, and I regard it as confirmation of my use of that number. They saw to it that the deferment applied only to people who are already provided with a material motive for being opposed to the system.

The cost of this kind of deferment is very great in present dis-

---

7. It was actually phased in over five years, but the details are unimportant.

counted terms. Roughly speaking, taken all by itself, it moves the turnover point back about eighteen months for people who have only the one-year deferment and about three years for people who have the two-year deferment. Note, however, that at the time the bill was passed even the people who had the one-year deferment were already young enough so that the payment they would receive on the Social Security was less than the amount they put in. Looked at from the standpoint of the Social Security Administration, however, this last figure is not all that consoling. It is fairly obvious that further "reforms" will be necessary in the Social Security system in the near future. By the time these reforms get discussed in Congress, it will already be true that this deferment has moved the turnover point for voters in their forties back about eighteen months. Thus, the Social Security system will enter into the next reform drive in a worse condition than it is now politically. Further, the credibility of the view that no cuts will ever be made clearly is no longer high. Cuts have been made, not only here but in many other places in the world. The combination of the weakening political support and lowering credibility may mean that the cuts could be very severe indeed.

Obviously I am not here making a prediction. The Gray Panthers are well organized and have a lot to fight for. Further, they have the bulk of the civil servants on their side, although with every year the number of civil servants ready to fight and die for their special pension rights under the Social Security Act declines.

Further, as we all know, the voters are not very well informed and the rather abstract calculations I have been going through so far may be above them. Nevertheless, if they make random errors, the average would come out more or less where we have come out. This would be true no matter how large the random errors were.

OTHER ISSUES

I have deferred to this point two important issues. The first concerns the Social Security system as a way of transferring funds from upper income people to lower income people. The second concerns the role of Social Security in replacing other methods families would normally use to take care of their older members. These two matters must now be dealt with.

Let us begin with the issue of general income transfers. The first thing to note here is that it has little or nothing to do with the genuine poverty population. If we go back to the 1920s, before the Social Security Administration was inaugurated and before the Great Depression (which, after all, was a highly abnormal circumstance), we find that only about 10 percent of all the people over 65 were thought to need state support.[8] These people were taken care of by various local programs, but not by social security.

Today if we look at the bottom of the income pyramid, particularly among older people, we find that a good many of them are indeed drawing Social Security pensions but these pensions are too small to be thought adequate for their support. Our elderly citizens, therefore, receive a *supplementary* security payment that brings their income to the socially desired minimum. Those elderly who for one reason or another have not gotten into the Social Security system, and hence have not paid taxes, receive the same payment in their old age. Thus, the true poverty population depends not on Social Security, but on Supplemental Security Income (SSI), essentially a relief program, just as they depended on relief in 1929. Further, as far as we can tell, in relative terms, the present scheme is not any more generous than its 1929 counterpart.[9]

There is, however, a difference between the treatment of the poor under Social Security and under the previous system. They now have to pay Social Security taxes. The average poor person is currently taxed on 12 percent of his earned income all of his life, and when he finally retires, he receives the same amount, roughly speaking, as he would if the Social Security system did not exist. Clearly, this makes the poor worse off.

Indeed, this is one of the arguments normally offered for the Social Security system. Again and again one can hear, "Lots of people wouldn't voluntarily save for their old age; if they weren't compelled to save for their old age by Social Security, we would have to support them." Regardless of whether this argument is true or false, it should be pointed out that, in any event, if we would have to support them *without* Social Security and now *tax* them significantly, clearly they are worse off. The nonpoor may be better off, but the poor are not.

There is, however, a substantial transfer away from upper income

8. Carolyn Weaver, *Crisis in Social Security* (Durham, N.C.: Duke University Press, 1982), pp. 41–44.

9. Here I must concede that the research is not very good. It seems to me that there is room for a good many doctoral dissertations looking into the question of whether the welfare state does or does not treat the poor better, in relative terms, than did the older, pre-Bismarckian system.

groups, not as much as via the income tax (because of the regressive nature of the upper end of the Social Security tax), but there is nonetheless a substantial transfer. This transfer does not, however, go to the poor, defined as let us say, the bottom 20 percent of the population. These people would be better off without the Social Security system (if we use as a basis their total lifetime income) because they would be saved the tax and would receive either the same income they now do—if their Social Security pension is smaller than the security minimum—or not very much less than they now do—if their Social Security payment was large enough to bar them from receiving SSI. Most of these people have their lifetime incomes reduced as a result of the existence of Social Security.

It does not, of course, follow that the elderly among them would positively gain from the abolition of the Social Security program. Some of them, indeed, might be hurt, but the difference would be small, and if we look not at the situation they face at present but at their lifetime earnings, they would have been better off had the system never existed. Further, people who are now poor and young are paying taxes; they too would be better off if the system were abolished. The gainers from Social Security are also not the well-off who suffer considerable transfers away from themselves as a result of (1) the progressive nature of the repayment schedule, and (2) the new provisions requiring them to pay income tax on one-half of their Social Security receipts. Roughly speaking, the bottom 20 percent and the top 30 percent of the population lose and the 50 percent lying between them gain. The gain is probably largest at about the median of the population.

What all of this means is that the turnover point for the decision as to whether you are better off under the Social Security system varies a good deal according to your income. For the poor, abolishing it immediately would probably be a good deal, almost irrespective of their age. For the wealthy, unless they are very close to receiving their pension, abolishing it would probably be desirable. On the other hand, there surely are at least some people who are going to receive exceptionally large transfers and for whom the turnover point may be below 40.

OLDER POOR PEOPLE

Let us now turn to the problem of taking care of older members of society without the Social Security system. Here I am not talking specifically about those who are poor and are taken care of by the state, but those who are better off and traditionally were taken care of by their families. I am old enough to remember the pre–Social Security situation. At different times we had two grandmothers living in our house. Indeed, both of them died there. Obviously, taking care of one's elderly parents puts some cost on the working generation.

In addition to the elderly people tending to live with their children—if they had them, of course—they normally made at least some contribution to the well-being of the family. Once again in 1929, 95 percent of people over 65 were working one way or another.[10] Generally, however, they were working at jobs where their productivity was low. After all, they tended not to be in the best of health; moreover, their pay was low. They were, however, making some contribution to the family income and, of course, since they were living in an established household, the total cost of supporting them was not great. Contrast this with the present situation. Most elderly people are now living independently, either because the minimum income provided by the state is itself high enough so they can do it, or because they have Social Security and/or other income. Furthermore, not very many of them are working.

Here we must pause briefly to point out one rather peculiar characteristic of the Social Security payment. Those elderly people whose own income is good are nevertheless receiving transfers from the younger generation, rather indirectly from their children. This is something that would not have happened before. Moreover, because of the nature of the Social Security system, they normally actually receive larger absolute payments than do other elderly people without good private incomes. There seems to be no reason—other than the votes it affords aspiring politicians—for this particular feature to be considered desirable.

Let us return to the situation of those people who, in the absence of the Social Security system, would be living with their children and working at various low productivity jobs to contribute to the family income but who are, instead, living on their own in Winter Park or Miami, Florida. The first thing to be said is that (since there is no law prohibiting them from continuing to work and living with their children) it is obvious that these seniors and their children prefer the present arrangement. It is true, of course, that the kinds of jobs for-

10. Weaver, *n*. 8.

merly filled by this rather poor quality of labor[11] are no longer there, and elderly people might have some difficulty in finding jobs. Note that there is a separate labor market of this general sort in and around Winter Park, where a great many retired people live. It is organized in such a way that it does not cut very heavily into their Social Security pension, since work is done on a part-time basis. Of course, the minimum wage act might eliminate some of these specially contrived jobs. To repeat, such labor is not very productive.

If the elderly do prefer the present situation, the cost of the present pensions is not a good measure of the benefit they receive. The benefit received is the difference between the previous arrangement in which they normally lived with their children and had various low productivity jobs, and the present situation where they normally live in some place like Winter Park and do not have any employment at all. Clearly, the real improvement in welfare is considerably less than the full value of their pensions. Indeed, I would doubt in most cases that it is more than one-third of their pensions. I have included in this one-third the benefit their children receive from not having their parents live with them. As a matter of fact, however, if my recollection is correct, neither of my grandmothers was regarded as a significant cost to the family. They baby-sat, did odds and ends around the house, and participated in most household activities. This was generally thought to more or less compensate for their food and room.

In any event the present scheme does have certain benefits, which would be lost if it were canceled. However, to repeat, the benefits are clearly much smaller than the monetary value of the system.

CONCLUSION

All of this means, once again, that for different people the actual turnover point will be different. It is still true, however, that raising the tax, lowering the benefit, deferring the time when it will come into effect, and making the credibility of the promise of future pensions somewhat weak—have all weakened the political support for the system. Whether the Gray Panthers will be able to mobilize well enough to more than compensate for that I cannot say. I can imagine a return to the previous situation in which Social Security programs increase steadily because of political pressure. However, I can also

11. Retirees are frequently skilled, but rarely very strong.

imagine a system in which, over time, the program will shrink because each time it is cut, its credibility goes down, making the voters who pay the tax less and less sure of repayment in their old age. Altogether, it seems to be likely that the Bismarckian system has no steady state. It is either expanding or contracting.

So much for a survey of how the Social Security system actually works. I very much fear that many people who are now depending on the Social Security system will find that their confidence was misplaced. Note that I do not feel happy about this. I would prefer that the system had never been introduced to begin with. Once it is in, and once many people have planned their lives on the assumption that it will work, its cancellation or gradual shrinkage would be a true tragedy.

There is, of course, another tragic aspect of this program. As I had mentioned in the beginning, it reduces people's incomes, giving them less money to save, and it weakens their incentives for saving. The result surely is a fall in real savings, in real capital investment, and hence in income levels. If economic theory means anything, it means we have not been growing as fast as we would have grown had the Social Security system not existed. It may well be that without the Social Security system, our per capita incomes would be high enough to make the elderly, on the whole, markedly better off than they are now. Of course, that is mere speculation. What we *can* say is that the system certainly has not contributed to productivity but in all probability has sharply lowered it.

9

THE WELFARE STATE, CAPITAL FORMATION, AND TAX–TRANSFER POLITICS

Richard E. Wagner

This chapter examines some aspects of the disparity between the rationalizations or justifications that have been advanced for what has come to be called the welfare state and what in many cases appears to be a quite different reality. In making this examination, particular attention is paid to the insights offered by the contemporary literature on rent seeking and public choice. Some ambiguity is, of course, necessarily present in defining the welfare state, as well as measuring its size, because this term refers to a congeries of programs that are administered by many different agencies. Different people could reasonably enumerate differently the programs that constitute the welfare state and thus arrive at different budgetary magnitudes. For Thomas Wilson, the welfare state is characterized by a situation "in which benefits in cash or kind are provided by the state and do not correspond to any contribution to production over the same period of time on the part of the beneficiaries."[1] In a related vein, such authors as Charles Hobbs and Jonathan Hobbs refer to the welfare state as that mélange of programs in which earned incomes are taxed to provide unearned incomes.[2]

1. Thomas Wilson, "The Finance of the Welfare State," in Alan Peacock and Francesco Forte, eds., *The Political Economy of Taxation* (New York: St. Martin's Press, 1981), p. 98.
2. Jonathan R. Hobbs, *Welfare Need and Welfare Spending*, Heritage Foundation Backgrounder no. 219 (Washington, D.C., 1982); Charles D. Hobbs, *The Welfare Industry* (Washington, D.C., Heritage Foundation, 1978).

In any event, the general idea seems clear, even if the specific content is not. There are hundreds of such programs, including Aid to Families with Dependent Children (AFDC), Supplemental Security Income (SSI), food stamps, Medicaid, unemployment compensation, rent and mortgage interest subsidies, school lunches and breakfasts, low-income energy assistance, earned-income tax credits, and the package of programs that constitute the Social Security program— Old Age, Survivors, Disability, and Health Insurance (OASDHI). Moreover, regulation is a substitute for taxation, and any regulation can be stated as an equivalent budgetary transaction, as I shall explain more fully below. Accordingly, there are many acts of legislation and regulation that are also elements of the welfare state, even if they have little explicit budgetary outlay. Minimum wage legislation, the Wagner Act, and Davis-Bacon provisions are three such acts.

Granted, many of these programs are not properly envisioned simply or solely as transfer programs. For instance, the Old Age and Survivors Insurance (OASI) component of Social Security serves to some extent as a substitute for a market purchase of retirement annuities. However, it is generally recognized that OASI is predominantly a welfare and not an insurance program.[3] The payments people receive during their retirement years are only remotely related to the payments they make during their working years; conversely, the taxes that people pay while they work bear little relation to the payments they can anticipate receiving after they retire. Indeed, a basic ingredient in the rationalizations advanced in support of such programs as OASI is that they are important for enhancing the standard of living of people who would otherwise be poor, i.e., that they are essentially transfer and not insurance programs.

It was during the middle 1960s that the programs of the welfare state began making significant payments to people who were working. Since then, those programs have come increasingly to be seen as a means of enhancing the standards of living of people who are thought, or declared by program supporters, to be unjustifiably poor. And since the mid-1960s, expenditures on the welfare state have grown about 150 percent as fast as GNP; in the process they have more than doubled their share in GNP—going from below 5 percent to above 10 percent. For fiscal 1982, Jonathan Hobbs estimated spending by

3. This point is developed particularly clearly in Peter J. Ferrara, *Social Security: The Inherent Contradiction* (Washington, D.C.: Cato Institute, 1980).

the welfare state to be \$404 billion.[4] Yet it would have required only \$103 billion in 1982 to raise to the official poverty level the income of everyone below it. Hence, through a simple process of division it can be said that only about 25 percent of the spending of the welfare state is required to overcome the existence of income levels below the poverty line—assuming that the amount of income earned is not affected by the presence of the welfare state in the first place. Much of the remaining expenditure goes to beneficiaries whose incomes are above the poverty level. Moreover, even narrower construals of what programs constitute the welfare state portray a similar pattern of growth. Daniel Hamermesh, for instance, limited his definition of those programs to OASDHI, AFDC, SSI, unemployment insurance, workman's compensation, and food stamps.[5] He found that between 1966 and 1978 the growth rate for those programs was 13.4 percent. This compares with an 8.7 percent rate of growth in disposable income, which indicates that the welfare state grew about 75 percent faster than did disposable income.

Stated in different fashion, the expenditures by the welfare state could provide nearly \$2,000 to each person in the United States. Alternatively, that amount would have been sufficient *by itself* to support 60 percent of the family units in the United States at the poverty-escape level. Moreover, the number of people whose money income would place them below the poverty line has increased by about 50 percent over the past decade, although the in-kind benefits from the programs of the welfare state have become quite substantial over this period.[6] Taking account of these in-kind benefits, Charles Hobbs estimated for 1976 that a family of four living on the welfare state received about \$15,000, which compares quite favorably with a median family income of \$14,500 in 1976.[7]

Doubtlessly inspired to some extent by such observations as these, a growing number of people have come to question whether there might be a conflict between what the welfare state is rationalized as

4. Jonathan R. Hobbs, *n.* 2.

5. Daniel S. Hamermesh, "Transfer Policy, Unemployment, and Labor Supply," in Robert H. Haveman and Julius, Margolis, eds., *Public Expenditure and Policy Analysis,* 3rd ed. (Boston: Houghton Mifflin, 1983), pp. 353–68.

6. On the distinction between income measures based only on money income and those that include the in-kind benefits of government programs, and the substantially different interpretations of recent trends that results, see Edgar K. Browning, "The Trend Toward Equality in the Distribution of Net Income," *Southern Economic Journal* 43 (July 1976): 912–23.

7. See Charles D. Hobbs, *n.* 2, pp. 83–84.

setting out to accomplish and the reality of what it actually accomplishes. There are several particular approaches to rationalization or justification, all of which see the welfare state as something that corrects defects thought to be inherent in an enterprise economy. There is a presumption that the natural outcome of a market economy entails substantial poverty, and that the welfare state is a means of softening those harsh features while still retaining the central features of an enterprise economy. Moreover, in modern, complex societies characterized both by an extensive division of labor and by rapid technological change, the riskiness of particular investments in human and physical capital perhaps increases; obsolescence of particular capital investments, human as well as physical, perhaps becomes an increasingly difficult problem for people to deal with, and so providing social arrangements for creating some semblance of security takes on increasing importance.

However, and pointing toward a possible conflict between the rationalizations advanced for the welfare state and what would seem to be some of its actual realities, there seem to be increasingly strong grounds for suggesting that a significant aspect of the welfare state is its promotion of the expansionary interests of what can be called the welfare industry. This interest is not so much promoted by the genuine elimination of poverty as by an expansion of welfare spending through such things as liberalization of benefits, development of new programs, and centralization of programs. This possible conflict between rationalization and reality is, in turn, apprehensible in terms of some basic principles of public choice, principles that take as their point of departure the presumption that the creation and operation of public programs of all types is guided not merely by idealistic wishes and altruism, but also by special interests and considerations of self-interest. This chapter aims to explore some facets of this possible conflict between the rationalizations that are commonly advanced for the welfare state and what might be a quite different reality as to its actual conduct.

RATIONALIZING THE WELFARE STATE

Numerous particular arguments have been advanced to rationalize the various programs of the welfare state. The common theme that unites these varied efforts is the proposition that the "natural" outcome of an enterprise economy is one of "excessive" inequality. Although it might be accepted that an enterprise economy promotes the wealth of a nation, it would also be argued that it tends at the same time to generate a highly unequal distribution of income and wealth. As for what constitutes "excessive" inequality, a number of different approaches have been taken, some within a Paretian or consensual framework and some outside of it. Outside the Paretian framework, injunctions are commonly invoked to the effect that certain distributive outcomes are simply improper. This approach is exemplified by Henry Simons's noted declaration that he found inequality beyond a certain degree to be "distinctly evil or unlovely."[8]

For the most part, however, effort has proceeded within the Paretian framework, and here there have been two main lines of argument, one that is ex post in its orientation and one that is ex ante. The ex post line of argument sees the welfare state as a collective response to individual desires to equalize the outcomes of an enterprise economy. A considerable literature on the idea of Pareto-optimal redistribution has been spawned since Harold Hochman and James Rodgers first explored the idea.[9] In their initial article and in the subsequent literature, redistribution was conceptualized as resulting from voluntary transfers from donors to donees. Redistribution was seen essentially as an act of charity, in which people react to what they regard as excessive inequality by trying to mitigate it. What was used to rationalize state participation in the redistribution of income, in place of an exclusive reliance upon private charity, was the presumption that free-rider problems would plague private efforts at redistribution. Although each person might like to see inequality reduced, no one person acting alone could make a significant contribution toward the reduction of inequality, and so without some guarantee that everyone would contribute, few or none would do so. In this event, the use of government to redistribute income was rationalized as a vehicle for overcoming the free-rider dilemma, thereby promoting Pareto optimality in the allocation of resources.

The alternative, ex ante approach, though still within the Paretian framework, casts the tax-and-transfer operations of the welfare state

---

8. Henry C. Simons, *Personal Income Taxation* (Chicago: University of Chicago Press, 1938), p. 19.

9. Harold M. Hochman and James D. Rodgers, "Pareto Optimal Redistribution," *American Economic Review* 59 (Sept. 1969): 542–57. For a critical treatment of this perspective, see E. C. Pasour, Jr., "Pareto Optimality as a Guide to Income Redistribution," *Public Choice* 36 (no. 1, 1981): 75–87.

as arising out of a general interest of people in acquiring protection against unforeseen contingencies. As formulated by James Buchanan and Gordon Tullock, this was seen as a possible rationalization for progressive rather than proportional income taxation.[10] People can never be certain as to their future incomes. And when they confront this uncertainty, people may prefer progressive over proportional income taxation, because progressive taxation allows them to attain smoother time-paths of consumption than they otherwise would be able to attain. Moreover, this uncertainty about future income surely looms larger when future prospects are projected forward from youth than when they are seen from the perspective of middle age, let alone when seen from the hindsight of old age. Therefore, the younger that people are, the greater is the scope for their reaching some agreement about the type of tax system they will live under.

John Rawls's formulation of the problem of justice is cast within this same ex ante perspective, only he chose a broader setting than the selection of different forms of taxation.[11] At base, Rawls conceptualized people as making basic institutional choices not after they had some good idea of their comparative income prospects, but before they had any such idea, and this conceptualization was reflected by his hypothetical construct of the veil of ignorance. When viewed from behind a veil of ignorance, much variation in distributional outcomes doubtlessly reflects the operation of risk that people might wish to insure against, and many activities of the welfare state might be rationalized in this light. Many of the things such people might wish to insure against, for instance, are commonly referred to in various ways as accidents of birth. A person who contracts multiple sclerosis will face a more constrained set of options than someone who does not. Some type of transfer program from those who are free from multiple sclerosis to those who are not might be conceptualized alternatively as the outcome of an insurance contract that everyone would have agreed to from behind a veil of ignorance.

Beyond these accidents of birth, a market economy is characterized by an inherent uncertainty that people might nonetheless wish to protect themselves against. G. L. S. Shackle advanced the notion of a

10. James M. Buchanan and Gordon Tullock, *The Calculus of Consent* (Ann Arbor: University of Michigan Press, 1962), pp. 189–99. Relatedly, see James M. Buchanan, *Public Finance in Democratic Process* (Chapel Hill: University of North Carolina Press, 1967), pp. 225–40.

11. John Rawls, *A Theory of Justice* (Cambridge: Harvard University Press, 1971).

"kaleidic society" to portray the idea that societies are confronted continually with various disruptions and new opportunities, which result from such things as inventions, the introduction of new products, and changes in people's desires.[12] The realized value of any investment in physical or human capital will depend upon numerous future circumstances. Moreover, we seem to live increasingly in an age of change, which suggests that the useful life of particular capital goods, including investment in human capital, is perhaps shorter than in the past. Skills acquired in youth are perhaps less likely to be serviceable throughout one's lifetime than in former times. Enterprises established may be left behind by new technologies, changing consumer preferences, or population relocations. For example, someone who invests in equipment for washing cars may subsequently find his equipment rendered obsolete by the development of a new finish for cars, one to which dirt cannot adhere. This line of reasoning suggests that some of the apparent transfers that constitute the welfare state might be seen more appropriately as a method by which the members of a society seek to protect themselves against the inherent uncertainty that characterizes a progressive market economy. Such progressiveness is wealth-enhancing overall, and some type of insurance against being in the losing subset in such a progressive economy might potentially be agreeable to all participants, thus serving as a rationale for various of the activities that constitute the welfare state.

DISSONANCE BETWEEN RATIONALE AND REALITY?

It is one thing to develop a rationalization for the activities of the welfare state; it is quite a different thing to develop an explanation for those activities. The redistributive activities of the welfare state may well be rationalized by some sort of argument based on utility interdependence, but such an act of rationalization cannot be equated automatically and necessarily with an act of explanation. There may be other, more satisfactory explanations as to why such transfers are actually made. Pareto-optimal redistribution treats redistribution as a type of agreement among donors that allows them to escape the free-rider dilemma they would confront if charity were a purely private

12. G. L. S. Shackle, *Epistemics and Economics* (Cambridge: Cambridge University Press, 1972).

activity. Since, in this analytical framework, the size of the transfer is chosen by the donors, the presence, or the extent, of Pareto-optimal redistribution can be gauged only if the recipients of those transfers are disfranchised. But when recipients are enfranchised, transfers may result even if donors are opposed to them. The presence of transfers, therefore, cannot be used to validate the presumptions of Pareto-optimal redistribution. This is not to say that notions of utility interdependence have nothing to do in explaining transfers of income, but only to note that they can at most provide only a partial explanation.[13]

Arguments about income insurance would similarly seem surely to have some value in explaining the development and support of various programs of the welfare state. However, those arguments would also seem at most to be only partial explanations, because actual programs are not chosen in the absence of knowledge of particular circumstances, as behind some veil of ignorance, but are chosen in light of a good deal of knowledge about relevant circumstances. The approach based on the construct of a veil of ignorance is one that attempts to envision the choices that people would make if they had equally likely chances of occupying any particular place in the resulting distribution of income. However, choices regarding the various activities of the welfare state are made by people who know their present positions and who generally have good information about their future prospects. This particular knowledge could be avoided, or at least mitigated, only if in some way collective choices, or at least some general rules pertaining to the making of those choices, were made in advance, as when one generation chooses rules that are to apply for a subsequent generation—a possibility that has been explored in different ways but in the same spirit by James Buchanan and Friedrich Hayek.[14]

When people know their present positions in the distribution of income, it is possible for excessive transfers, as compared with a veil-of-ignorance standard, to emerge from democratic processes, especially if the median income is below the mean income. The veil-

13. For an examination of how government transfers have crowded out private charity and have become excessive in comparison with the Paretian criterion because of the political power of recipients, see Russell D. Roberts, "A Positive Model of Private Charity and Public Transfers," *Journal of Political Economy* 92 (Feb. 1984): 136–48.

14. Buchanan, *Public Finance in Democratic Process,* n. 10, pp. 280–300; F. A. Hayek, *The Political Order of a Free People,* vol. 3 of *Law, Legislation, and Liberty* (Chicago: University of Chicago Press, 1979).

of-ignorance construct envisions people assessing different distributions of income by assuming they are equally likely to occupy each position in that distribution. But once people know their distributional positions, their evaluation of those distributions will change. The majority of people who have below-average incomes will evaluate more equal distributions more highly than the veil-of-ignorance construct would suggest, because their evaluations will be less tempered by the possibility of their having an above-average income. Therefore, people may choose more equalization than is consistent with the veil-of-ignorance framework, even though that framework may well explain some aspects of the support for various activities of the welfare state.

Gordon Tullock has argued that the main explanation for transfers is surely neither utility interdependence nor income insurance, but rather is simply the interest of recipients in receiving transfers.[15] But even if redistribution is explained to an important extent by the desire for transfers by recipients, a question still exists as to why there is such a demand in the first place. The demand for transfers could be interpreted as a sign of the poverty-spreading character of an enterprise economy. Suppose those critics of enterprise economies who argue that the affluent rise at the expense of the poor are correct. If so, the demand for the transfers of the welfare state might represent a cry for justice, and might even be interpreted as consistent with a veil-of-ignorance framework, in a context in which the affluent dominate political outcomes and are reluctant to support the degree of equality they would have agreed to from behind the veil in the first place. If so, the very presence of a significant demand for transfers might itself be construed as an indictment of an enterprise economy. Alternatively, the demand for transfers might represent a desire for rents by recipients, and the supply of transfers might likewise represent a desire for market restrictions by nonrecipients. Rather than the poor being the victims of a poverty-spreading enterprise system, they may rationally be pursuing their interest in response to opportunities offered by a democratic polity, and might well have different incomes under some alternative institutional regime. In other words, transfers might substitute for income that would otherwise have been earned, rather than providing income that could not have been earned.

There are, in other words, questions of knowledge and incentive

15. Gordon Tullock, "The Rhetoric and Reality of Redistribution," *Southern Economic Journal* 47 (April 1981): 895–907.

that must be addressed in any effort to distinguish between rationale and reality. The question of knowledge concerns the sources of poverty, or of wealth. The rationales for the welfare state see it as acting to overcome "natural" and inescapable defects of an enterprise economy. That form of economy, it is argued, may promote the wealth of a nation, but it also leaves behind many people in the wake of progress. But alternatively, poverty might result not so much through the operation of a genuine market economy as through the innumerable restrictions on its very operation, restrictions that tend to insulate people in established wealth positions from competition from outsiders, on the one hand, and to enfeeble the ability of others to cultivate and employ their talents, on the other. The question of incentive concerns the properties of different political or institutional regimes. In recent years economists have begun to recognize that the production of public policy can itself be usefully conceptualized as a type of economic activity.[16] The types of policies that are produced, however, may have little to do with common rationalizations or justifications, and may instead reflect outcomes that differ greatly from those rationalizations or justifications. For instance, the interests of the people who are decisive in policy outcomes might be better advanced through policies that create rather than avoid poverty. These considerations of knowledge and incentive will be addressed in the following two sections, after which I shall contrast two approaches to the generic idea of the welfare state construed as a state that seeks to enhance the common welfare.

WEALTH, POVERTY, AND THE GUARANTEE STATE

The primary question of knowledge in relation to the welfare state is whether the activities of the welfare state represent a response to "natural" conditions or whether those activities themselves represent the "man-made" creation of those conditions: Is poverty a natural or a self-inflicted affliction? In other words, does the welfare state provide income that could not have been earned within an enterprise economy? Or does it substitute for income that could have been earned within such an economy, even if perhaps it could not have been earned within the strongly restricted economy of the United States. More-

16. The literature on this topic has been growing rapidly. A nice statement is presented in Robert E. McCormick and Robert D. Tollison, *Politicians, Legislation, and the Economy* (Boston: Martinus Nijhoff, 1981).

over, poverty can be man-made or self-inflicted for two quite different reasons: because of (1) choices that are exercised by those who are impoverished and (2) constraints that are imposed on those people by others. The various efforts to formulate canons of distributive justice typically assume that the "natural" order of things will necessarily violate such canons. Those efforts take it for granted that what Robert Nozick calls the minimal state, in which government enforces contracts and protects against force and fraud, would violate those canons, and so some supplementary distributive activity of the state is required.[17] Yet this central presupposition may be wrong. As I shall discuss below, there is much evidence to show that many public policies promote inequality rather than equality. At the very least, it is quite clear that public policies relating to the distribution of income do not generally have the character of policies designed to offset the maldistributive consequences of a market economy. To a substantial degree, poverty may result from the restrictions on freedom of contract that are part of a rent-seeking society, rather than being an inherent attribute of an enterprise economy.

The poor may be victims or they may be responsible for their own fate, and in either case they may be so for two different reasons. They may be victims by virtue of the very nature of a well-working enterprise economy, or they may be victims precisely because the operation of that enterprise economy is constrained, shaped, and distorted by a variety of laws and regulations that in turn have been "purchased" by others in an effort to insulate their own positions of wealth. People may be poor because they have been left behind by a well-working enterprise economy, or they may be poor because other people were able politically to secure restrictions on their ability to employ their talents. Someone may have been born blind or without arms. But someone else may have been fully able and willing to show people to their seats in theaters for $3 per hour, but was prevented from doing so by the requirements of minimum wage legislation. And insofar as the poor might be regarded as responsible for their own fate, this may be because they have actively sought the activities of the welfare state, or it may be because they have responded rationally to the options they have faced, but which they had little hand in creating. Some recipients of AFDC may have actively sought transfers in that form in their capacity as demanders of transfers, because of

17. Robert Nozick, *Anarchy, State, and Utopia* (New York, Basic Books, 1974).

its offer of support without work. But others may simply have responded to what was made available, and as a result of the incentives
contained within that offer, found themselves saddled with transgenerational rates of welfare dependency in the vicinity of 40 percent.[18]

Experience since the mid-1960s certainly confirms the elementary
principle that people's incomes are not independent of their choices.
People do not make choices regarding the formation and use of their
human capital, and then take the activities of the welfare state into
account without revising those initial plans. Rather, the offer of welfare payments will bring about some substitution of those payments
for the earning of income.[19] There are too many observations on this
point to think otherwise. For instance Victor Fuchs, among others,
has noted that the AFDC program encourages unmarried women to
have children and to refrain from working. AFDC, along with food
stamps, day care, subsidized housing and health care, among other
programs, has clearly played a part in encouraging the growth of one-
parent households since 1960.[20] Indeed, births to unmarried women
have roughly tripled over the past two decades—despite the diffusion
of the technological revolution in birth control that has taken place.
Moreover, there are substantial differences in the labor force participation rates of women with children that are surely due in some measure to the incentives contained in such programs of the welfare state
as AFDC. About 14 percent of AFDC mothers work, and this percentage has remained approximately constant over the past two decades. But among the population as a whole, the percentage of women
whose youngest child is at least six and who work is 62 percent. And
even the percentage of mothers whose youngest child is less than six
and who hold a job is 45 percent.[21] It certainly seems reasonable that
the guarantees offered by AFDC and related programs have something to do with the lower rates of labor force participation by recip-

18. This means that about 40 percent of the adult recipients had been recipients as children. On this, see Morley D. Glicken, "Transgenerational Welfare Dependency," *Journal of
Contemporary Studies* 4 (Summer 1981): 31–41.

19. This is referred to as the "samaritan's dilemma." See James M. Buchanan, "The
Samaritan's Dilemma," in Edmund Phelps, ed., *Altruism, Morality, and Economic Theory*
(New York: Russell Sage, 1975), pp. 71–85. More generally, this is the problem of moral
hazard associated with the welfare state.

20. Victor R. Fuchs, *How We Live* (Cambridge: Harvard University Press, 1983), pp.
104–6.

21. Peter G. Germanis, *Workfare: Breaking the Poverty Cycle*, Heritage Foundation Backgrounder no. 195 (Washington, D.C., 1982).

ients. More generally, since the late 1960s, when the working poor became increasingly eligible for recipient status while working, there has been about a 50 percent increase in the number of people whose earnings lead to their being classified as poor.

What would seem to result is what Morley Glicken refers to as "learned helplessness."[22] This is the contrary of the common presumption that significant numbers of people will be characterized by such things as shortsightedness, so that they fail to make sufficient investment in their own capacities. As to whether or not people can be trusted to choose their own strategies for the conduct of their lives, it is often asserted that substantial numbers will fail to do so effectively, and so some form of compulsion is required to overcome such failures. Basic economic principle, however, suggests that what might appear to be shortsightedness is really a rational response to existing opportunities that reward people for failing to provide for their future, or at least reduce the price of failing to do so.[23] On this point, evidence presented by Carolyn Weaver suggests that in the period before Social Security, there was little dependency among the aged.[24] In New York State in 1929, for instance, nearly 95 percent of people over age 65 were self-supporting. Moreover, in a number of surveys of the elderly in different cities over the 1925–29 period, less than 10 percent were regarded, by government commissions, as in need of assistance. Moreover, most of the source of low standards of living among the elderly was attributed not to failures to exercise foresight, but to low incomes throughout their working lives.

It is costly to provide for one's future, and the less costly a failure to do so becomes, the less people will make such provisions. Therefore, the transfer programs of the welfare state can evoke a rational response that might, erroneously, be characterized as shortsightedness. Thomas Szasz's work on *The Myth of Mental Illness* is quite pertinent here, especially his chapter on "The Ethics of Helplessness and Helpfulness," where he notes the following: "Not only do some Biblical rules foster dependency; they also lay the groundwork for

22. Morley D. Glicken, *n.* 18, p. 40. For further elaboration see Richard E. Wagner, "Funded Social Security: Collective and Private Options," *Cato Journal* 3 (Fall 1983): 581–602.

23. See, for instance, George J. Stigler and Gary S. Becker, "De Gustibus Non Est Disputandum," *American Economic Review* 67 (March 1977): 76–90.

24. Carolyn L. Weaver, *The Crisis in Social Security* (Durham, N.C.: Duke University Press, 1982), pp. 41–44.

using lack of foresight and incompetence as weapons to coerce others to provide for one's needs."[25] In other words, it is not so much that people are inherently shortsighted as that they will act in this manner if it pays to do so. If disability and shortsightedness are rewarded while self-reliance and farsightedness are taxed, appearances of disability and incompetence will rise within the population relative to appearances of effectiveness and self-reliance. Hence, to some extent it is the paternal or welfare state that corrodes self-reliance and the supporting institutions that would otherwise develop in response, and not self-reliance that somehow weakens, with the paternal state then arising in response.[26] And to the extent this is so, the rationalization for the welfare state will contradict its reality.

ASSESSING THE DISTRIBUTIONAL IMPACT OF PUBLIC POLICIES

It is almost universally presumed in discussions about the welfare state that the distributive outcomes of what Robert Nozick called a minimal state would violate any reasonable canon of distributive justice. For this reason, if for no other, it is commonly presumed that the welfare state is necessary to soften some of the distributive harshness of a market economy. Most discussions concerning the welfare state operate from within this presumption and differ only as a matter of degree, with some people advocating a more active welfare state than others, because they think the distributive outcomes of the market economy are significantly harsher than those who would advocate a less active welfare state.

This presumption about how the welfare state relates to the distributive outcomes of the minimal state pervades discussions about the impact of government on the distribution of income and wealth. This can be seen very clearly, for instance, by comparing the well-known studies of Joseph Pechman and Benjamin Okner on the one

---

25. Thomas S. Szasz, *The Myth of Mental Illness* (New York: Harper and Row, 1961), p. 197. A particularly clear statement of Szasz's central theme appears on p. 225: "Mental illnesses thus differ fundamentally from ordinary diseases and are similar, rather, to certain moves or techniques in playing games. Suffering from hysteria is thus far from being sick and could more accurately be thought of as playing a game, correctly or incorrectly, skillfully or clumsily, successfully or unsuccessfully, as the case might be."

26. For supporting reason and evidence, see Russell D. Roberts, *n.* 13.

hand and Edgar Browning and William Johnson on the other.[27] Both of these studies attempt to assess the extent to which taxes at all levels of government reduce the degree of inequality in the distribution of income. These studies differ substantially in their conclusions, but they share the same central approach. Pechman and Okner conclude that tax policies have little effect in equalizing the distribution of income, with their prime evidence being their judgment that the average rate of tax paid by people in different income categories is approximately constant at all income levels. By contrast, Browning and Johnson conclude that tax policies have a substantial equalizing effect, with their prime evidence being their judgment that the average rate of tax rose from a little over 10 percent for people in the lowest income decile to nearly 40 percent for people in the highest decile.

The reason for these different judgments is that the authors differed in the assumptions they made about the burdens of different taxes. For instance, Pechman and Okner assumed that sales and excise taxes led to higher prices paid by consumers, whereas Browning and Johnson assumed that they led to lower prices (i.e., incomes) received by producers. This was the main source of difference, but the two pairs of authors also differed in the assumptions they made about who bore the burdens of the taxation of property and of corporate income. Pechman and Okner assumed that at least part of those taxes was paid by consumers through higher prices of corporate products and of housing. By contrast, Browning and Johnson assumed that those taxes were paid by various suppliers of capital (savers), who suffered a decline in their net income.

That such differences in assumptions about tax incidence could make such differences in conclusions about the distributive impact of tax policies is not surprising. It is important to note, however, that this entire approach is biased in the direction of finding that the welfare state softens the distributive outcome of a market economy. The approach is one in which some market-produced distribution of income is compared with some alternative distribution, a distribution in which that market outcome has been modified by various governmental policies and programs. This method of approach is illustrated by Figure 9–1. There, the Lorenz curve labeled L_1 describes the distribution of

27. Edgar K. Browning and William R. Johnson, *The Distribution of the Tax Burden* (Washington, D.C.: American Enterprise Institute, 1979); Joseph A. Pechman and Benjamin A. Okner, *Who Bears the Tax Burden?* (Washington, D.C.: The Brookings Institution, 1974).

Figure 9–1.   Common Approach to Estimating Distributive Impact of Government.

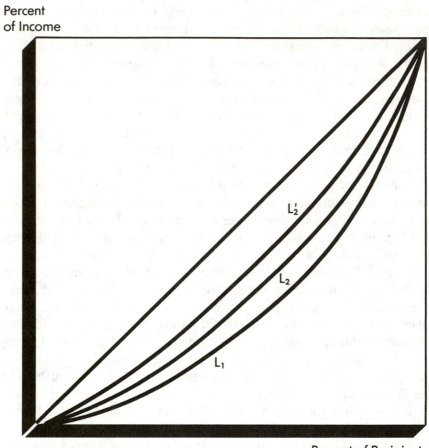

Percent
of Income

L_2'

L_2

L_1

Percent of Recipients

income that is observed to result from market activity, whereas the Lorenz curve labeled L_2 describes the distribution that results after various government programs have been taken into consideration. The stronger the equalizing effect of governmental programs, the more the post-fisc Lorenz curve L_2 will move away from the pre-fisc curve L_1, toward the diagonal line of full equality. For instance, the post-fisc Lorenz curve L_2 describes a government that has reduced inequality by less than that government where the post-fisc Lorenz curve is L_2'.

In comparing the two sets of authors, Pechman and Okner would say that L_2 lies comparatively close to L_1, whereas Browning and Johnson would say that L_2 has moved some substantial distance away from L_1 toward the diagonal line of full equality. Both, however, would concur in the central method of approach: comparing a pre-fisc distribution of income, as indicative of the central properties of a market economy, with a post-fisc distribution, which then indicates the extent to which such governmental activities as those represented by the welfare state modify that initial, essentially free-market distribution.

But this entire approach of comparing pre- and post-fisc distributions of income as a way of determining the impact of government upon the distribution of income is grounded on the presumption that the pre-fisc distribution of income represents the "natural" and inescapable outcome of an enterprise economy.[28] However, a central principle of public finance is that any law or regulation can be translated into a budgetary equivalent. Minimum wage legislation, for instance, is equivalent to a program that taxes the earnings of members of the low-wage labor force and uses those revenues to subsidize higher-wage workers. Relatedly, consider the prohibition on various types of garment manufacture at home, which has recently come under some discussion.[29] By preventing such manufacture at home, the supply of lower-priced alternatives to garments manufactured in factories is reduced. This increases the demand for factory-produced garments, as illustrated by the shift from D_1 to D_2 in Figure 9–2. To the extent the supply of labor to the manufacture of garments is less than fully elastic, as is illustrated by S, the prohibition of homework will increase wage rates, from W_1 to W_2 in Figure 9–2. This program is equivalent to placing a tax on homeworkers and using the revenues to subsidize factory workers. So long as those who would work at home if they were able would generally have lower incomes than those who work in the unionized factories, the effect of such a regulation would be to increase the degree of inequality in the "market" distribution of income.

Indeed, various legislative acts that give unions and professional associations an ability to restrict the supply of labor provide some of the most fully studied illustrations of how legislation can alter what

28. The problematical character of pre- and post-fisc comparisons is explained lucidly in A. R. Prest, "The Statistical Calculation of Tax Burdens," *Economica* 22 (Aug. 1955): 234–45.

29. See the discussion on this point in Peter Germanis, *Why Not Let Americans Work at Home?* Heritage Foundation Backgrounder no. 325 (Washington, D.C., 1984).

Figure 9–2.   Distributive Impact of Restrictions on Home-Produced Garments.

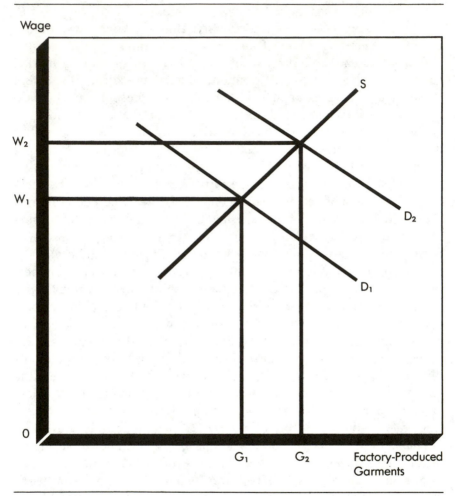

Wage

W_2

W_1

O

G_1 G_2 Factory-Produced Garments

S

D_2

D_1

is commonly, though erroneously, called the "market" distribution of income. This alteration is illustrated by Figure 9–3, where Panel A refers to union labor and Panel B refers to nonunion labor. Unions reduce the supply of labor in activities subject to their control from U_1 to U_2, which increases wage rates from W_1^U to W_2^U. The disemployed labor finds employment in nonunionized pursuits, as illustrated by the increased employment from N_1 to N_2, which reduces nonunionized wages from W_1^N to W_2^N. Since unionized workers gen-

Figure 9–3.   Effect of Unionization on Relative Wages and Labor Supplies.

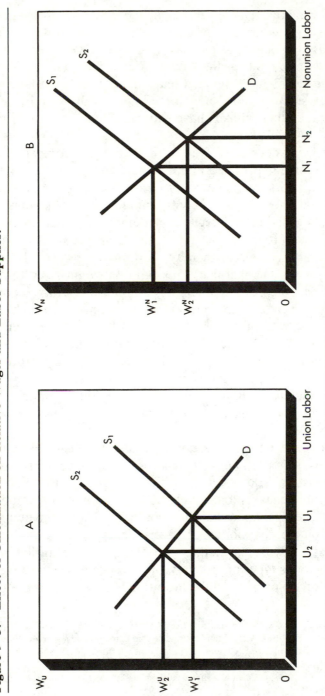

erally have above average earnings, the effect of such legislative restrictions on freedom of contract is, as compared with a minimal state,
to increase the degree of inequality in what is commonly, though erroneously, referred to as the "market" distribution of income. Indeed,
H. Gregg Lewis has estimated that unions have increased the differential between union and nonunion wages in the vicinity of 10 to 15
percent, and other scholars have estimated that differential to be even
larger.[30]

There is, of course, no way to make a direct comparison between
the distributive impact of a minimal state and that of the existing economic order, for we have no present observation of life under the
former. However, results of a substantial number of studies of various
types of legislation and regulation demonstrate that in many cases
governmental programs transfer wealth from people who have less to
people who have more, thereby shifting the pre-fisc Lorenz curve
away from the diagonal line. This point is summarized by Figure 9–
4, in which Y represents a person with below-average income and X
represents a person with above-average income. Point A corresponds
to such a Lorenz curve as L_1 in Figure 9–1, and represents what is
commonly called the pre-fisc distribution, whereas point B corresponds to such a Lorenz curve as L_2, representing the post-fisc distribution. However, the observed distribution of income does not
represent the distribution that would result within a minimal state, and
such an alternative distribution might be represented by some such
outcome as C.

Moreover, the greater freedom of trade within such a minimal state
will surely increase total income in the first place. If so, some such
outcome as D could result, in which the distribution of income has
become more equal and in which the total amount of income has risen
as well. The likelihood that this would happen is a matter for future
studies, but the possibility of its happening has certainly not been
made less likely by the results of contemporary inquiries into the effects of various types of protective and restrictive legislation upon the
distribution of income and the incentive to produce. At the very least,

---

30. H. G. Lewis, *Unionism and Relative Wages in the United States* (Chicago: University
of Chicago Press, 1963). A maximum estimate of 60 percent is developed in Gordon Tullock,
The Sources of Union Gains (Charlottesville: Thomas Jefferson Center for Studies in Political
Economy, University of Virginia, 1959). Lewis suggests that Tullock's estimate is on the high
side, but if the changes that Lewis suggests were made, there would still be a differential in
the vicinity of 30 percent.

Figure 9–4.   Alternative Perspectives on Government's Distributive Impact.

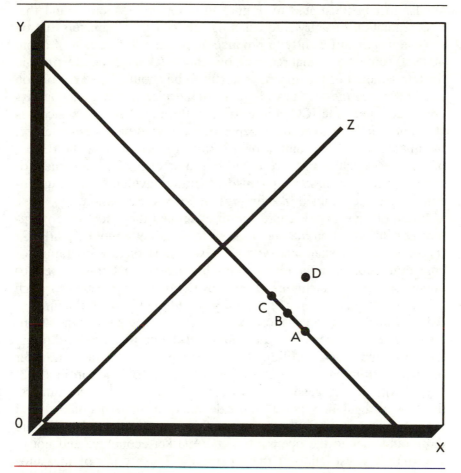

however, it is improper to make any inferences about the character of a minimal or liberal state from observing the distributive properties of present institutions, for those institutions are vastly removed from those of such a state. Moreover, the impact of that removal may be one that *both* reduces the overall level of income and, by reducing the competition that people with established wealth positions face, increases the degree of income inequality.

Consider, for instance, the findings of two quite typical and pertinent studies, both of which treat, among other things, the distributive consequences of regulatory policies. In one, Thomas Moore estimated the effect of the Interstate Commerce Commission's regulation of entry into trucking, and did so within a frame of reference similar to that illustrated by Figure 9–3 above.[31] Moore found that ICC regulation of entry into trucking allowed the Teamsters' union to raise wages sufficiently to produce an income differential of about 40 to 50 percent over that received by other truckers. Moore estimated the total amount of this income transfer to be about $1 to $1.3 billion in 1972. Since the incomes of such truck drivers are higher than average, and since the ICC control over entry increased those incomes still more, and did so at the expense of those who were denied entry, the impact of ICC regulation of trucking was to increase the degree of income inequality. Moore found the same effect on the owners of trucking licenses; these people also generally have above-average incomes, and they gained in the range of $1.5 to $2 billion.

In the other study, Richard Smith examined the effect of governmental restrictions on the operation of the retail automobile market.[32] In particular, he examined various restrictions on the operation of competitive forces in the retail automobile market that gave more monopoly power to franchisees. These restrictions were created through governmental regulation of the ability of automobile manufactures to induce franchisees to act more competitively. The result was an increase in the price of new automobiles of about 10 percent, through the restriction of competition. In consequence, there was a transfer of income from consumers to dealers of about $6.7 billion in 1972. Again, with dealers generally having higher incomes than consumers, this type of regulation increased the degree of income inequality. And yet, observed pre-fisc distributions of income erroneously attribute those outcomes to the operation of the market economy, and not to government's restriction of that operation. These types of measures could be treated alternatively as an equivalent tax-and-transfer program. Moreover, a large number of similar studies could be discussed, all of which would show a wide variety of regulations that, if they were given a budgetary translation, would show people with lower incomes being taxed to subsidize people with higher incomes.

31. Thomas Gale Moore, "The Beneficiaries of Trucking Regulation," *Journal of Law and Economics* 21 (Oct. 1978): 327–43.

32. Richard L. Smith II, "Franchise Regulation: An Economic Analysis of State Restrictions on Automobile Distribution," *Journal of Law and Economics* 25 (April 1982): 125–57.

THE WELFARE STATE AND THE MARKET FOR PUBLIC POLICY

The activities of the welfare state can be examined from within the purview of the economic theory of legislation and rent seeking.[33] This theory treats public policy outcomes as resulting from the rational pursuit by legislators and bureaucrats of their self-interest, as this interest is channeled through a particular set of institutional constraints. And, as this literature has explored, the institutional constraints that constitute what can be called a system of majoritarian democracy seem to have no inherent tendency to yield efficient or equitable policy outcomes. Indeed, this contemporary literature has been exploring with contemporary modes of analysis what have long been recognized as some of the main problematical features of democratic forms of government. Students of political theory and history have long noted that while democracy may support the liberty and prosperity of those who live within its boundaries, it also contains a latent tendency to replace the promotion of the common interest in liberty and prosperity with the promotion of particularized interests, and with the common interest ultimately suffering in the process. As one example of the ability of unlimited democracy to erode liberty and wealth, Alexander Tytler, an eighteenth century Scottish historian, summarized and generalized as follows from his study of democracy in ancient Greece:

> A democracy cannot exist as a permanent form of government. It can only exist until a majority of voters discover that they can vote themselves largesse out of the public treasury. From that moment on, the majority always votes for the candidate who promises them the most benefits from the public treasury, with the result that democracy always collapses over a loose fiscal policy. . . .[34]

The danger to prosperity and liberty that results from the tax-transfer politics that Tytler, among others, saw as inherent in majoritarian democracy, and which has surely proliferated in contemporary America, is what James Madison described as the "violence of faction" in

---

33. For a thorough survey of the literature on rent seeking, see Robert D. Tollison, "Rent-Seeking: A Survey," *Kyklos* 35 (no. 4, 1982): 575–602.

34. As quoted in William A. Niskanen, "The Prospect for Liberal Democracy," in James M. Buchanan and Richard E. Wagner, eds., *Fiscal Responsibility in Constitutional Democracy* (Leiden: Martinus Nijhoff, 1978), p. 159.

his famous essay, *Federalist* No. 10. As Madison noted there: "By a faction I understand a number of citizens, whether amounting to a majority of minority of the whole, who are united and actuated by some common impulse of passion, or of interest, adverse to the rights of other citizens, or to the permanent and aggregate interests of the community." Recent scholarship in public choice, stemming from the seminal work of James Buchanan and Gordon Tullock, has extended and deepened our knowledge of the operation of majority rule, reaffirming in the process such insights as those articulated by Tytler and Madison.[35]

As seen from the perspective of this literature, such governmental programs as those represented by the welfare state grow, at least in part, because this growth facilitates a transfer of wealth to the members of a winning coalition, with those transfers being accompanied by the imposition of even larger costs on the remainder of the population.[36] There is a net destruction of wealth because those transfers of wealth reduce the gains, both to the winners and to the losers, from the productive employment of labor and capital. For one thing, productive activity becomes rewarded less heavily as working and saving become taxed more heavily. Furthermore, the pursuit of wealth through seeking transfers becomes more rewarding to people relative to the pursuit of wealth through productive activity. The resulting redirection of economic activity is a cost of a type of civil warfare; it represents the employment of resources that could otherwise be turned to productive use, were it not for the individually productive though socially wasteful incentive to engage in transfer activity under a system of factional or majoritarian democracy.[37]

A century ago, such morality tales as that expressed by the adage, "Build a better mousetrap, and the world will beat a path to your

35. James M. Buchanan and Gordon Tullock, *n.* 10.

36. For a fuller examination of many questions concerning the growth of government than that offered here, see Richard E. Wagner, "Tax Reform through Constitutional Limitation: A Sympathetic Critique," *Cumberland Law Review* 15 (no. 2, 1984–85): 475–97.

37. This point was originally developed in Gordon Tullock, "The Welfare Costs of Tariffs, Monopolies, and Theft," *Western Economic Journal* 5 (June 1967): 224–32. For further discussion on this theme, see the various essays in James M. Buchanan, Robert D. Tollison, and Gordon Tullock, eds., *Toward a Theory of the Rent-Seeking Society* (College Station: Texas A & M Press, 1980), as well as Tollison's survey article, "Rent-Seeking" (*n.* 33). For a careful study of the shift of incentives away from productive activity toward transfer activity in the United States, see Terry L. Anderson and Peter J. Hill, *The Birth of a Transfer Society* (Stanford, Calif.: Hoover Institution Press, 1980).

door," were commonplace. It is perhaps not surprising that such tales of industry and thrift have decreased in importance in recent school curricula, for this type of activity is surely less effective than it once was. These days you might be better advised to stay with your inferior mousetrap, to contribute to the campaigns of your congressman and senator, and then to hire someone to lobby for tariff or other restrictions on the importation of foreign-made mousetraps. You might even direct some effort to getting a safety commission to set standards of durability and strength for mousetraps, which would reduce the ability of competitors to offer lower-priced mousetraps. It might even be worthwhile to try to secure restrictions on the over-the-counter sale of rodent poisons, because those restrictions would increase the demand for mousetraps. Any such shift of resources from pursuing the creation of wealth through building better mousetraps to securing— as well as to guarding against—the transfer of wealth is actually a destruction of wealth. It is also, of course, a destruction of liberty.

Madison's concern over factions within a system of majoritarian democracy reflected a concern with what Alexis de Tocqueville, in *Democracy in America,* subsequently labeled the "tyranny of the majority." Madison was not concerned about a possible tyranny of the minority because he assumed that majority voting would prevent this. The problem he wrestled with was how to prevent majority tyranny. However, one of the major contributions of the recent literature on public choice has been a heightened understanding of how it is possible for successful minority factions, a tyranny of the minority, to arise within a system of majoritarian democracy.

Within a system of representative democracy, how much support is required to enact legislation? It is easy to show that the support of a majority within a legislature does not imply the support of a majority within the population at large. Indeed, it is possible for the support of as little as one-quarter of the citizenry to translate into a legislative majority. To illustrate this point, suppose the population of the nation falls into two categories. A little over one-quarter of the population is employed by producers of products for which prices and wages are relatively high. A little less than three-quarters of the population is employed by producers of products for which prices and wages are relatively low. Suppose the high-priced producers and their associated labor are located in such a way that they comprise a slim majority in 218 of the 435 congressional districts, as well as in 26 of the 50 states, and are found hardly at all in the other congressional districts and states. A legislative proposal to establish a minimum wage somewhat higher than the wage presently paid by the low-cost producers would be able to secure majority support. Such legislation would increase the prices of the products produced by the low-cost producers and would reduce employment among those producers. The legislation would not affect the cost of labor to the high-cost producers. By narrowing the differential in price between the high-cost and the low-cost producers, that legislation would bring about some shift in business from the low-cost to the high-cost producers. Wealth would be transferred from low-priced producers and labor, who comprise nearly three-quarters of the population, to high-priced producers and labor, who comprise little more than one-quarter. Numerous other illustrations could be developed to show how minority positions within the population at large can nonetheless secure dominance within a legislature.

The conjunction of minimum wage legislation and AFDC, as examined by Keith Leffler, is a particularly instructive illustration of the political economy of the welfare state, although other illustrations of the same central theme could also be developed.[38] The effects of minimum wages have by now been widely studied, and the central feature of this body of literature is that such legislation aids some people and harms others in a way consonant with the emerging economic theory of legislation, notwithstanding harmful effects on the supposed beneficiaries of minimum wages, i.e., the poor. Numerous analysts have pointed to the negative effect of minimum wages on teenage unemployment. Minimum wages also have significant differential effects among adults, as can be seen especially clearly from Peter Linneman's work on this topic.[39] In his analysis, Linneman found a variety of significant differences in the impact of minimum wage legislation among different categories of adults. Men gained and women lost: 76 percent of white men gained and 62 percent of black men gained, while 72 percent of black women lost and 73 percent of white women lost. As between members and nonmembers of unions, 85 percent of union members gained while 56 percent of nonmembers

38. Keith B. Leffler, "Minimum Wages, Welfare, and Wealth Transfers to the Poor," *Journal of Law and Economics* 21 (Oct. 1978): 345–58.

39. Peter Linneman, "The Economic Impacts of Minimum Wage Laws: A New Look at an Old Question," *Journal of Political Economy* 90 (June 1982): 443–69.

lost. For the 10 percent of the population that Linneman estimated to comprise the subminimum population, 69 percent lost from the minimum wage, but 52 percent of the remainder of the population gained.

By itself then, minimum wage legislation would seem to harm the poor. But legislators from low-income districts generally support minimum wage legisltion. This might seem anomalous, except that, as Leffler has shown, those who are rendered unemployed by minimum wage legislation do not lose income. They lose wage income, but that loss is replaced by transfers from such programs as AFDC. The welfare state, at least in this instance, would seem to demonstrate certain features that seem apprehensible within the framework of the economic theory of legislation. Minimum wage legislation in conjunction with AFDC, for instance, would seem to represent a coalition of high cost industries and labor along with certain segments of the low wage population. By reducing the rate of accumulation of human capital through diminishing the ability of people to acquire initial job experience, minimum wage legislation surely reduces the lifetime earnings of the recipients of the offsetting transfers, though it may not reduce their lifetime consumption. It does, however, clearly promote transgenerational welfare dependency.

A welfare state that discourages work and capital accumulation, and encourages instead the reliance on transfer payments for support would seem to be complementary to rent-seeking legislation that also tries to maintain the value of particular investments in human and physical capital by seeking to curtail sources of competition. Any creation of an entitlement or sheltered status concomitantly entails either a limitation on the ability of someone else to earn a livelihood or a taking of some of the results of previous effort. If the position of high-cost garment manufacturers is to be sheltered, as it is by (among other things) preventing people from manufacturing garments in their homes for subsequent sale, the ability of other people to earn a livelihood, in this case by sewing, must be impaired. Alternatively, by sheltering existing owners of taxis, others who might be willing to support themselves by driving people around town are prevented from doing so.

Similarly, minimum wage legislation in conjunction with child labor laws and restrictions on apprenticeships serve to reduce the options available to people who lack the interest or ability to prepare for various professional and white collar careers, as also does the presence of more than a thousand occupations that are licensed.[40] Moreover, if some people are to be entitled to food, shelter, and medical care without payment, others must work to provide those services. And the substantial growth of entitlements indicates that what Hilaire Belloc called the servile state—"that arrangement of society in which so considerable a number of the families and individuals are constrained by positive law to labor for the advantage of other families and individuals as to stamp the whole community with the mark of such labor"—has arrived.[41] The factor market equivalent of the awarding of entitlements in the product market is, after all, forced labor, regardless of what it may actually be called.

STATUS-EXTENDING VS. CONTRACT-EXTENDING APPROACHES TO SECURITY

People clearly have substantial interest in bringing some measure of security to their futures. And even though the proliferation of such activities as the awarding of entitlements and the conferral of sheltered statuses can be examined from within a rent-seeking perspective, I do think, nonetheless, that much of the underlying interest that produces the welfare state represents the insurance motive discussed above. One way by which people can reduce the uncertainty they necessarily must face is by trying to gain control of sources of uncertainty that might arise from the actions of competitors in introducing new products, new techniques of production, new approaches to business conduct, and the like, as Jack Wiseman has noted.[42] The creation of sheltered or protected wealth positions and the rewarding of entitlements or transfers are complementary facets of the existing welfare state.

Borrowing a term from Sir Henry Maine's famous statement to the effect that the history "of the progressive societies has hitherto been a movement from status to contract" as the basis of social relations, I should like briefly to contrast status-extending and contract-extend-

40. On the proliferation of occupational licensing, see Janet Kiholm Smith, "Production of Licensing Legislation: An Economic Analysis of Interstate Differences," *Journal of Legal Studies* 11 (Jan. 1982): 117–37.

41. Hilaire Belloc, *The Servile State* (1913; reprint, Indianapolis: Liberty Press, 1977), p. 50.

42. Jack Wiseman, "Uncertainty, Costs, and Collectivist Economic Planning," *Economica* 20 (May 1953): 118–28.

ing approaches to the welfare state.[43] The present welfare state represents a status-extending approach to the provision of personal security. It operates by awarding subsidies and entitlements and by imposing taxes and limiting options. Security is dispensed through the taxing-and-transferring apparatus of the state and its bureaucracy. The status-extending welfare state is an aspect of the servile state. It operates by trying to prevent the erosion of wealth positions through retarding the operation of forces for change within a society, such as entrepreneurial activity outside of established channels. It is, in other words, atavistic.

Yet the only way that security can truly be provided, to the extent it can be provided at all, is through capital accumulation within a well-integrated capital structure.[44] But the status-extending welfare state actually impedes the accumulation of capital, and so undermines its own justification. Nonetheless, prevailing political processes seem biased toward the programs of the status-extending welfare state, perhaps in part because the very shortsightedness that is sometimes used as justification for the welfare state actually operates more fully in the polity than in the economy. The benefits of the welfare state are concentrated in the present, whereas an important part of the costs accrue only in the future, a future that lies beyond the electorally truncated time horizons that seem to epitomize democratic political processes.

When viewed from a short-run perspective, the programs of the welfare state seem primarily to concern the distribution of income and wealth. Any proposal to expand the welfare state appears centrally to revolve around questions of whether or not some people should be taxed more heavily so that other people can be given higher benefits. And the outcome depends on the political strengths of the various affected parties of what appears essentially to be a zero-sum, purely distributional choice. But when viewed from a longer-term perspective, those tax-and-transfer programs, and possible alternatives to them, primarily concern the production—and the destruction—of wealth. Both the tax and the expenditure sides of the status-extending welfare state promote the consumption of capital: The taxation of productive

43. Henry Sumner Maine, *Ancient Law*, 5th ed. (New York: Henry Holt, 1864), p. 165.
44. The significance of the "well-integrated" attribute of a capital structure is noted especially clearly in Ludwig M. Lachmann, *Capital and Its Structure* (1956; reprint, Kansas City: Sheed Andrews and McMeel, 1978).

activity to finance the transfers of the welfare state reduces the incentive of producers to accumulate capital, and the subsidization of various consumption activities by the welfare state likewise reduces that incentive for recipients. As a result, people generally will be less wealthy in the future than they would have been had the tax-and-transfer programs of the welfare state not been extended. Although the outcome is negative-sum and not merely zero-sum, the negative consequences on wealth and security lie in the future and are not realized in the present; thus its political impact would seem to be weak relative to what its magnitude would seem to warrant.

This point can be illustrated quite simply by adapting a model developed by Irving and Herbert Fisher.[45] Suppose capital yields an annual return of 20 percent, with that yield being taxed at 50 percent to finance transfer payments. (The implicit policy alternative in this illustration is one of simultaneously reducing taxes and transfer payments.) Further suppose that the after-tax yield on investment is reinvested. If $10,000 is invested at the start of year one, $2,000 is earned at the end of the year, $1,000 of which is taxed away and $1,000 of which is reinvested. The capital stock at the start of year two, $11,000, yields $2,200 at the end of the year, $1,100 of which is taxed away and $1,100 of which is reinvested. In like manner, the capital stock at the start of year three will be $12,100, which will yield $2,420 at the end of the year, $1,210 of which is taken by the government and $1,210 of which is reinvested. Consequently, the capital base at the start of year four is $13,310.

Each year the budgetary process seems essentially to concern the transfer of wealth from savers and investors to the recipients of transfer payments. In year one, the central budgetary question appears to be whether or not to impose a tax of $1,000 on investment income, with the revenues used to expand various transfer programs. It is the same in years two and three, only with the amounts in question being $1,100 and $1,210 respectively. In any event, the essential nature of the budgetary process appears to be whether or not to raise taxes on investment income so as to raise the level at which transfer or entitlement programs are supported.

This simple zero-sum appearance vanishes, however, once the entire process is examined over a sequence of years. If investment in-

45. Irving Fisher and Herbert W. Fisher, *Constructive Income Taxation* (New York: Harper, 1942).

come were not taxed, $2,000 would have been reinvested at the end of year one. The resulting capital base of $12,000 would, in turn, have yielded $2,400, which would have made possible a capital base of $14,400 at the start of year three. And continuing the illustration one more year, this base would have yielded $2,880, which would have left a capital stock of $17,280 at the start of year four. When seen from this longer-term perspective, the tax-and-transfer programs of the status-extending welfare state have been responsible for the destruction of capital and thereby have weakened the very means of achieving security. Moreover, the value of the capital destroyed exceeds the amount of taxes collected and revenues spent. Only $3,310 of capital is accumulated in the presence of the welfare state, whereas $7,820 would have been accumulated otherwise. Hence, $3,970 of capital has been destroyed through the resulting nonaccumulation. Furthermore, the size of this capital destruction relative to the size of the taxes and expenditures increases sharply with the passage of time. Continuing with the same assumptions about yield, accumulation, and taxation, for instance, wealth will be $453,000 at the end of year 40, and total tax collections over the 40 years will have been $442,000. But in the absence of tax, wealth would have been $14,800,000 at the end of year 40. Therefore, the collection of $442,000 in taxes to finance transfer programs was responsible for the destruction of $14,347,000 of capital. However, this strongly negative-sum character of the status-extending welfare state asserts itself only with the passing of time, time that would seem at best to have minuscule impact upon the conduct of electorally dominated democratic politics.

In contrast to a status-extending approach to the provision of security, with its inherent, inescapable contradictions between the requirements for security and the incentives it contains, a contract-extending approach to the provision of security might offer the possibility of encouraging the personal accumulation of capital within a well-integrated capital structure. There are many particular forms such an approach might take. For instance, what Belloc, along with G. K. Chesterton, called the distributive state, in which the ownership of property is widespread and is held severally and not collectively, would seem to be one illustration of the contract-extending approach to security, for security is sought in the extension of the domain over which property and contract operate. All such contract-extending approaches, which may perhaps be thought of, in current parlance, as representing a privatization of welfare, are grounded in personal responsibility and the ownership of assets. If such characteristics as self-reliance and personal responsibility may be nurtured or starved, depending on, among other things, whether the approach to security in society is contract- or status-extending, the ownership of property and the responsibility for it may be important in supporting social relations grounded in reciprocity and contract—just as the absence of such ownership and responsibility may reinforce social relations grounded in status and orders. If so, the particular approach to the provision of security, by influencing knowledge and incentives and their political expression, might exert some influence over whether society will be more or less servile in the future, as well as more or less secure.

CONCLUSION

My purpose in this chapter has not been to challenge what I regard as the central premise of the welfare state, namely, that the provision of security is a common and legitimate interest of all people within a society. Yet at the same time, there is a growing body of literature that documents a variety of consequences of the welfare state—ranging from increases in teenage pregnancies to reductions in saving and labor force participation—that few people would defend as desirable. In this regard I would certainly echo Morley Glicken's concluding statement about the "paradox of welfare: not to help the needy would be simply inhumane; yet the help we provide, it now becomes clear, has proved in the long run likewise inhumane."[46] Furthermore, the policies that have brought about these consequences seem to be apprehensible within the framework of majoritarian democracy, as this has been elucidated by recent scholarship on rent seeking and public choice. The present, status-extending approach to the welfare state entails an inescapable contradiction. Security can be provided only through capital accumulation within a well-integrated capital structure, but the status-extending welfare state—which operates by awarding entitlements, conferring sheltered wealth positions, and generally attenuating and otherwise abridging ownership rights—both discourages people from accumulating capital and encourages them to be less responsible in the conduct of their lives. By contrast, contract-ex-

---

46. Morley D. Glicken, *n.* 18, p. 40. Relatedly, see Michael J. Boskin, "Reaganomics and Income Distribution: A Longer-Term Perspective," *Journal of Contemporary Studies* 5 (Summer 1982): 31–44.

tending approaches, which look to the encouragement of the widespread accumulation of capital and which might be thought of as representing a privatization of welfare and security, might offer a different and more effective approach to the provision of security in a society. However, the specifics of such an approach, as opposed to the articulation of the existence of such an alternative, must be the subject of a different, and lengthier, essay.[47]

47. As, for example, in my book, *Myth, Reality, and the Welfare State: A Study in Political Economy* (San Francisco: Pacific Research Institute for Public Policy, forthcoming). Note also, Charles Murray, *Losing Ground: American Social Policy, 1950–1980* (New York: Basic Books, 1984).

10

CREDIT ALLOCATION AND CAPITAL FORMATION: THE POLITICAL ECONOMY OF INDIRECT TAXATION

James T. Bennett and Thomas J. DiLorenzo

INTRODUCTION

The concern over the unprecedented size of federal budget deficits has intensified because of fears that deficit spending contributes to higher real interest rates, economic stagnation, and, eventually, inflation. Historically, it has been popular to "solve" the deficit problem by raising taxes. Current discussions focus on proposals to increase taxes even further and possibly, at the same time, to reduce spending. But higher taxes generally result in larger, not smaller, deficits. During the past decade, tax revenues steadily increased while deficits continued to grow, and higher taxes only encourage elected officials to spend even more on their constituents. Furthermore, it is not so much the deficit that causes economic instability but the total amount of government spending.[1] Since the economic cost of government spending is private sector spending forgone, increased spending contributes to economic stagnation in the private sector. Thus, the true measure of taxation or the cost of government is not explicit taxes— it is *spending*.

This is not to imply that deficits are unimportant. The main reason they are important, however, is that by concealing the true cost of

1. See Milton Friedman, "The Limitations of Tax Limitation," *Policy Review 5* (Summer 1978): 1–10.

government spending, the process of deficit spending encourages a more rapid growth of the public sector than would occur if taxpayers were better informed of the costs of government. As government grows, private sector economic activity is increasingly displaced. Moreover, no matter how government spending is financed, private sector economic activity is crowded out. If taxes are raised, there will be less consumer (or other private) spending; if government borrows, private borrowing is curtailed; and if money creation is the financing vehicle, there is an even more hidden tax on private wealth in the form of the inflation tax.

Another important but largely neglected form of hidden taxation is the resource cost of federal credit activity. In addition to borrowing to finance deficits, the federal government plays a major role in allocating credit through direct loans, loan guarantees, and government-sponsored enterprises such as the Federal National Mortgage Association. In 1983, for example, there were $41.4 billion in direct loans, $12 billion in off-budget credit activity, $125.5 billion in loan guarantees, and $167 billion in government-sponsored enterprise lending.[2] These amounts clearly overshadow the federal budget deficit, and they constitute indirect taxation that falls most heavily on private sector capital markets. In short, by indirectly financing governmental activities through federal credit activity, the federal government is a much greater hindrance to private capital formation and economic growth than is generally believed. Even though borrowing to finance federal deficits may crowd out some private borrowing, such amounts pale in comparison to other forms of federal credit activity.

This chapter examines the economic consequences of the major forms of federal credit activity: direct lending, off-budget federal credit activity, loan guarantees, and government-sponsored enterprises.

DIRECT LOANS

In 1983 the federal government extended $41.4 billion in direct loans financed from a variety of sources, including taxation, borrowing, and repayment of previous loans. The economic distortions caused by federal loan activity are clearly acknowledged in the *Budget of the*

2. Executive Office of the President, *Budget of the United States Government, FY 1985* (Washington, D.C.: U.S. Government Printing Office, 1984). As this was written, the Reagan administration was estimating that direct loans would be $41.6 billion in 1986, only a small nominal change from 1983. Since we have complete data for 1983, we will use the 1983 figures to highlight the points we wish to make.

United States Government, which states: "Direct loan programs are designed to redirect economic resources to particular uses by providing credit on more favorable terms than would otherwise be available from private sources. A direct loan is justified when the Federal objective could not be met with financing from private sources, even with a Government guarantee." [3] Moreover, the budget document states that "since Federal credit is subsidized, it can alter resource allocation relative to the market and, therefore, may result in a loss of economic efficiency." [4] In short, granting direct loans provides well-disguised (to the taxpayer) benefits to various special interests at a cost of hampering economic growth (See Table 10–1). To the extent that federal credit is channeled to inefficiently run business enterprises that the private capital markets deem uncreditworthy, it subsidizes inefficiency and waste and diverts resources from more highly valued uses. Furthermore, federal credit also reduces consumer sovereignty to the extent that private credit is unavailable for other activities.

Some of the inefficiencies generated are exemplified by the actions of the largest lender, the Commodity Credit Corporation (CCC), which lent $13.9 billion in 1983 for its "price support loans." This amount represented a $2.4 billion, or 20 precent increase over 1982. In essence, the subsidized loans granted to farmers by the CCC help contribute to the oversupply of many agricultural commodities, which in turn leads these same farmers to lobby for output *restricting* programs, whereby they are paid for producing less. A recent example is the Payment-in-Kind (PIK) program, which withdrew from production thousands of acres of farmland.

The second largest lender, the Farmers Home Administration, grants special preferences to farmers who purchase homes; and the Rural Electrification Administration subsidizes the owners and customers of power plants.

The $5.1 billion of foreign military sales represented a way of using taxpayers' funds to subsidize the military purchases of foreign governments (Israel and Egypt have been the largest recipients of such subsidies). The Export-Import Bank continues to prop up certain politically favored business firms that do business overseas. In this instance, American taxpayers are indirectly subsidizing the citizens of foreign countries by permitting exporting firms to reduce the prices

3. Executive Office of the President, *Budget of the United States Government, FY 1985, Special Analyses* (Washington, D.C.: U.S. Government Printing Office, 1984), p. F13.
   4. Ibid., p. F1.

Table 10–1.   Direct Federal Loans, 1983 ($ billions).

Agency	Amount of Loans
Commodity Credit Corporation	$13.9
Farmers Home Administration	6.7
Rural Electrification Administration	4.5
Foreign Military Sales	5.1
Export-Import Bank	.8
Other	10.4
Total	$41.4

SOURCE: Executive Office of the President, *Budget of the United States Government, FY 1985* (Washington, D.C.: U.S. Government Printing Office, 1984).

charged in foreign countries. This practice also discourages American firms from cutting costs through greater efficiency, since they can increase profits just as easily by lobbying for continued Export-Import Bank support.

In summary, the federal government uses direct loans to subsidize economically inefficient but politically popular investments. The argument that such activity is justified by what economists call "external effects" is weak. The major beneficiaries are farmers, foreign governments, and politically influential businesses. The losers are the American taxpayers who must foot the bill and suffer the effects of greater economic instability and stagnation.

OFF-BUDGET CREDIT ACTIVITY

The Congressional Budget and Impoundment Control Act of 1974 has been praised by *U.S. News and World Report* as a "revolutionary budget reform intended to give Congress a tighter grip on the nation's purse strings."[5] The so-called Budget Reform Act emerged from a recognition that existing budgetary procedures generated a bias toward overspending and budget deficits. Prior to 1974, the total amount of federal spending was the product of many individual appropriations decisions, with no explicit limit placed on the total amount of public expenditure. Each congressman had a very strong incentive to maximize spending on his own voting constituency, while limiting the

5. See James T. Bennett and Thomas J. DiLorenzo, *Underground Government: The Off-Budget Public Sector* (Washington, D.C.: Cato Institute, 1983), chap. 7.

extent to which he must pay for that spending. No congressman, how-ever, was required to take responsibility for the total amount of fed-eral spending that resulted from the appropriations process. The Budget Reform Act created for each house of Congress a budget committee responsible for setting overall targets for revenues, expenditures, and the resultant deficit or surplus. The Congressional Budget Office was created to assist in this process.

The main impact of the Budget Reform Act is to make taxing, spending, and deficit levels explicit and to hold Congress accountable for them, but the Act itself does nothing to curb spending. However, the relatively mild budgetary discipline set forth in the Act elicited a great deal of "backdoor spending" at the federal level. In the wake of the Act, numerous agencies have been placed off-budget and be-yond the purview of any appropriations process. Thus, while the Con-gress was publicly proclaiming a need for fiscal discipline in federal budget matters and enacting legislation to deal with "uncontrollable" spending, it was establishing mechanisms through which spending could be placed off-budget.

The Federal Financing Bank (FFB) is by far the most active off-budget agency. The FFB, a part of the Treasury Department, does business with both on- and off-budget agencies. The predominant ac-tivity of the FFB is the purchase of agency debt from funds obtained by borrowing directly from the Treasury. FFB borrowing is not, how-ever, included as part of the Treasury's budget outlays; yet interest payments from the FFB to the Treasury are counted as *deductions* from Treasury outlays. Consequently, FFB borrowing actually results in a reduction in outlays reported by the Treasury Department. In essence, the FFB serves as an intermediary that permits the spending of federal agencies to be placed off-budget.

A second type of FFB activity is the purchase of agency loans or loan assets. When a federal agency sells a loan to a private entity, the loan is considered repaid for budgetary purposes. Loans made by federal agencies are afforded the same treatment when the FFB is the purchaser. Proceeds from the sale are counted as loan repayments rather than as a means of financing and are thus an offset to the agen-cy's gross expenditures. An agency's on-budget loan can therefore be converted to an off-budget loan by selling it to the FFB.

Rather than selling individual loans, an agency can sometimes pool its loans and issue securities backed by the pooled loans. These se-curities, known as *Certificates of Beneficial Ownership,* are then turned over to the FFB for cash, placing them off-budget. The agency has cash to loan again and can repeat the process as many times as it chooses. This procedure allows federal agencies to make loans—with virtually no budgetary limit—to privileged customers.

Another type of FFB activity is the granting of off-budget loans to guaranteed borrowers. Typically, a loan guarantee occurs when a federal agency sanctions a loan between a private lender and a private borrower. The result is an interest subsidy to the borrower at no *explicit* cost to the Treasury unless the borrower defaults. Frequently, however, an agency will ask the FFB to act as the private lender and purchase the borrower's note. In this case the loan guarantee be-

Table 10–2.   FFB Outstanding Holdings, 1983 ($ millions).

Activity	Debt Outstanding
Loan Assets	
Overseas Private Investment Corp.	$ 18
Farmers Home Administration	24,107
Rural Housing Insurance Fund	25,676
Rural Development Insurance Fund	6,908
Rural Electrification Administration	3,468
Other	330
Direct Loans	
Foreign Military Sales	14,293
Rural Electrification Administration	18,939
Student Loan Marketing Association	5,000
Public Housing (HUD)	2,067
Railroad Programs (DOT)	1,064
Seven States Energy Corp. (TVA)	1,418
Other	4,602
Agency Debt	
Export-Import Bank	14,676
Tennessee Valley Authority	13,115
U.S. Postal Service	1,154
Other	169
Total FFB Outstanding Holdings	**$135,923**

SOURCE: Executive Office of the President, *Budget of the United States Government, FY 1985, Special Analyses* (Washington, D.C.: U.S. Government Printing Office, 1983), pp. F69–72.

comes, in effect, a direct loan from the government, a loan that is not reflected in the budget.

As seen in Table 10–2 the total outstanding holdings of the FFB as of 1983 exceeded $135 billion. The primary beneficiaries have been the Farmers Home Administration (FmHA) and, to a lesser extent, other agencies that can transfer enormous sums off-budget. The FmHA increased its loans by over 500 percent in the first five years after the FFB was established.

In sum, the activities of the FFB give federal politicians and bureaucrats a virtual blank check, with no *direct* budgetary consequences, which allows them to dispense rapidly growing amounts of loans and subsidies to their constituent interest groups. The political costs of federal largesse are effectively reduced by the FFB. As an indication of the political bonanza being enjoyed by various federal politicians and their supporting federal agencies, Table 10–3 lists outstanding FFB loans to guaranteed borrowers during the 1980–81 period.

In essence, the loan guarantees administered by the FFB constitute the "backdoor financing" of additional governmental control and regulation of the economy's resources. Government agencies can grant special privileges to select groups of individuals, business firms, foreign governments, or even other government-sponsored enterprises (e.g., the Tennessee Valley Authority) without being subjected to congressional scrutiny and, theoretically, without budgetary limit. The FFB, therefore, provides federal agencies with a powerful potential for wide-scale intrusion into credit market decision-making.

Table 10–3. Outstanding FFB Loans to Guaranteed Borrowers, Fiscal Years 1980, 1981 ($ billions).

Agency and Borrower	1980	1981
REA guaranteed loans to rural electric cooperatives	$ 8.4	$12.3
DOD guaranteed loans for foreign military sales	7.2	9.1
HUD guaranteed loans to low-rent public housing	.1	.9
TVA guaranteed loans to Seven States Energy Corporation	.7	.9
Other	2.8	3.1
Total Loans Outstanding	$19.2	$26.3

SOURCE: U.S. Congress Joint Economic Committee, *The Underground Federal Government* (Washington, D.C.: U.S. Government Printing Office, April 20, 1982), p. 12.

ECONOMIC IMPLICATIONS OF FFB LOAN GUARANTEES

Many advocates of free enterprise have objected to congressional action that granted New York City and the Chrysler Corporation several billion dollars in highly publicized loan guarantees. The New York City loan guarantee did little to address the city's fiscal problem—deficit spending—and encourages other cities to follow the same route to bankruptcy, hoping to be "rescued" by the taxpaying public. The Chrysler loan guarantee, its critics have observed, simply bailed out an inefficient business enterprise by siphoning to it over a billion dollars in credit that would have been put to more highly valued uses by more credit-worthy borrowers. The general consequences of subsidizing failing businesses are well known and are diagnosed as the "British disease." Great Britain's anemic industrial performance during the past several decades is due in large part to the fact that the British government forces taxpayers to subsidize failing or grossly inefficient business enterprises. The Chrysler loan guarantee is a step in this direction and has been denounced both by conservatives who favor free enterprise and oppose subsidies to business, and by liberals who proclaim a fear of the powers of "big business." Nevertheless, the Chrysler and New York City loans pale in comparison with the off-budget guaranteed loans administered by the FFB. Whereas these two loan guarantees were subjected to congressional oversight and subsequently received much media exposure, FFB loan guarantee decisions are made by a few nonelected bureaucrats in a small office located at the Department of Treasury.

That this system provides for more opportunities for "social engineering" by nonelected bureaucrats than does the Chrysler loan can be seen from the $2 billion in off-budget loans recently extended to the Tennessee Valley Authority (TVA), a federally sponsored off-budget enterprise.[6] In 1979 the TVA decided that its nuclear fuel inventory had become excessive owing to delays in construction of nuclear power plants. To remove the burden of excessive inventories from its books, the TVA created a wholly owned subsidiary—the Seven States Energy Corporation—with which TVA could enter into

6. See Cliff Hardin and Arthur Denzau, *The Unrestrained Growth of Federal Credit Programs* (St. Louis: Washington University Center for the Study of American Business, December 1981).

a leaseback arrangement. Seven States would purchase TVA's nuclear fuel inventory and then lease it back as needed. To finance the arrangement, TVA originally approached a private investment banking firm, which suggested a $1 billion line of credit. Before the agreement was completed, however, the Department of Treasury suggested that the FFB could provide the credit and would increase the amount of the loan to $2 billion. The TVA, in effect, extended a $2 billion line of credit to itself—more than either the Chrysler or New York City loan guarantees—and Congress was not involved at all. There are far-reaching implications of this with respect to the future role of the federal government in allocating credit—a role that in the past has been played with most unfortunate consequences in terms of both equity and efficiency. According to the FFB Act, *any* entity wholly owned by the federal government has this access to off-budget federal financing. Several such entities do exist and have the legal authority to order the FFB to lend money to anyone, provided that they guarantee the loan.[7]

In addition to substituting inefficient and inequitable political resource allocation for the more efficient market allocation of capital, the existence of the FFB also *increases* the borrowing costs to the federal government, despite the argument that by pooling agency borrowing the costs of financing are reduced. The reason for this is that the increased interest rate on federal debt resulting from FFB borrowing from the Treasury is far more expensive than the minimal savings to federal agencies. Agency debt appeals to a market different from that for Treasury debt, as the difference in interest rates attests. When the Treasury issues more debt (to finance the FFB), it crowds the market segment to which its issues appeal, and that forces rates up on Treasury debt. One would think that this invalidates the entire economic (but not the political) rationale for the FFB.

Loan Guarantees and the Allocation of Credit

In addition to the loan guarantee and other functions of the FFB, federal agencies administer over 150 federal loan guarantee programs that comprise yet another category of off-budget operations. Loan

---

7. There are several such agencies, including the Commodity Credit Corporation, Export-Import Bank, Corporation for Public Broadcasting, Government National Mortgage Association, Community Development Corporation, U.S. Railway Association, Pension Benefit Guarantee Corporation, and Legal Services Corporation.

guarantees to individuals, businesses, state and local governments, and foreign governments are reflected in the budget only if the borrower, dealing through a private bank, defaults. In that case, the federal government is liable for part or all of the principal and interest on the loan. Although they are not reflected in the budget document, loan guarantees serve the same purpose as direct, tax-financed appropriations: They provide transfer payments to select groups at the expense of the general public. The major difference between tax-financed subsidies and loan guarantees is that the latter are far less visible and do not arouse as much taxpayer resistance as would the former. For example, a tax-financed subsidy to a college student whose parents earn $100,000 per year will surely meet more resistance, especially from the less wealthy, than will a guaranteed loan that is often (mistakenly) not considered to entail a subsidy. The partial or full guarantee of such loans, however, does permit the favored borrowers to borrow at reduced interest rates. Because of the hidden nature of these "interest subsidies," loan guarantees have become the largest components of federal credit activity. In 1983 the $97.2 billion in new loan guarantees was more than twice the $41.3 billion level of direct loans (see Table 10–4).

Both the costs and benefits of federal loan guarantee programs are indirect. A major difference, however, is that the benefits of loan guarantees accrue to well-organized interest groups, whereas the costs are widely dispersed among the general public. The predominant indirect cost of federal loan guarantees is borne by less-favored borrowers, who are crowded out of the credit market or who must pay higher interest rates on the loans they obtain. Loan guarantees tend to increase the overall demand for credit and at the same time reduce the supply of credit available to nonguaranteed borrowers. The effect is to increase the rates charged to nonguaranteed borrowers to levels higher than they would be otherwise, thus crowding out much borrowing by business, individuals, and state and local governments. This process seriously distorts the market process whereby, given well-defined property rights, unregulated markets allocate credit to its most highly valued uses—enhancing economic growth.

Credit markets serve to evaluate the riskiness of alternative projects, and those with higher probabilities of failure (to meet consumer demands) are charged higher borrowing costs. In this way, the credit markets provide consumers and producers with invaluable information regarding the most productive uses of resources. By socializing

Table 10–4. New Guaranteed Loan Transactions of the Federal Government, 1983 ($ millions).

Agency or Program	Guaranteed Loans
PRESIDENTIAL APPROPRIATIONS	
Overseas Private Investment Corp.	$ 33
Housing	142
AGRICULTURE	
Farmers Home Administration	141
Rural Housing Insurance Fund	2
Rural Development Insurance Fund	82
Commodity Credit Corporation	2,643
Rural Electrification Administration	120
COMMERCE	
International Trade Administration	12
Nat'l. Oceanic and Atmospheric Admin.	12
EDUCATION ACTIVITIES	
ENERGY	6,784
Geothermal Resources Development Fund	9
HEALTH AND HUMAN SERVICES	
Health Maintenance Organization Fund	5
Health Professions Graduate Student Fund	225
HOUSING AND URBAN DEVELOPMENT	
Public Housing	22,632
Federal Housing Administration	27,564
Government Nat'l Mortgage Assoc.	45,624
Indian Loan Fund	14
TRANSPORTATION	
Maritime Administration	575
Rail Service Assistance	14
Aircraft Purchase Loans	9
TREASURY	
Biomass Energy Development	45
VETERANS ADMINISTRATION	
Loan Guarantee Revolving Fund	13,643
EXPORT-IMPORT BANK	2,714
NATIONAL CREDIT UNION ADMIN.	34
SMALL BUSINESS ADMINISTRATION	
Business Loan Guarantees	2,088
Pollution Control Bond Guarantee	8
SYNTHETIC FUELS CORPORATION	247
OTHER AGENCIES	25
TOTAL NEW GUARANTEED LOANS	$125,500

SOURCE: Executive Office of the President, *Budget of the United States Government, FY 1985, Special Analyses* (Washington, D.C.: U.S. Government Printing Office, 1984), pp. F58–63.

risk, loan guarantees make it impossible for consumers and producers to make accurate benefit-cost calculations, and resources are put to lower-valued uses once politics rather than the market is used to allocate credit. While high interest rates force private firms to invest in only the most productive projects that promise very high yields, federally assisted borrowers may continue to invest in projects that yield only a fraction of the nonguaranteed investments. Thus, the federal government is actively subsidizing inefficient investments, reducing the productivity of the nation's capital stock and, consequently, lowering the rate of economic growth. The slower rate of economic growth is often accompanied by higher inflation and higher unemployment.

As an example of how private sector investments are crowded out in favor of governmentally sponsored investments, consider the following: In 1980 when a 20 percent prime rate and 16 percent consumer loan rate contributed to the bankruptcy of thousands of small businesses (such as auto dealerships and grocery stores), the Rural Electrification Administration began a new program to provide 35-year loans at 5 percent interest to finance rural cable television systems; rural home mortgages were available at 3.3 percent; and insured student loans were granted at 7 percent. Also during that year, while many private utilities were paying 16 percent on their long-term bonds, the TVA was borrowing at a rate several percentage points lower. As a result of this and other subsidies, the cost of electricity supplied by the TVA is lower than it is in many areas served by less favored private companies. In 1979, for example, TVA rates were about 50 percent lower than they were in such states as New York and Massachusetts, and about 38 percent lower than the national average.[8]

It is difficult, if not impossible, to gauge the extent of crowding out caused by federal loan guarantees, but some preliminary estimates have been made. Economist Herbert M. Kaufman of the University of Arizona conducted an empirical study of federal loan guarantees in which he estimated that for every $1 billion in loan guarantees, between $736 million and $1.32 billion in private investment is crowded out.[9] These are rough estimates, but they nevertheless indicate that loan guarantees, which are being extended at a rate of over $100 bil-

8. As cited in R. Utt, "Federal Lending Programs," Testimony before the U.S. Senate Committee on Banking, Housing, and Urban Affairs, October 7, 1981.

9. Herbert M. Kaufman, "Loan Guarantees and Crowding Out," in Congressional Budget Office, *Economics and Federal Credit Activity* (Washington, D.C.: U.S. Congressional Budget Office, April 1980), pp. 35–39.

lion per year, are sure to have a profound negative impact on economic growth, employment, and inflation. The immediate effect on inflation is not likely to be very significant, since changes in aggregate output occur relatively slowly as a result of reductions in private investment spending. However, there is the potential that the upward pressure on interest rates caused by federal intrusion into the credit markets via loan guarantees may bring pressure on the Federal Reserve to "accommodate" the Treasury by expanding the money supply, thereby "reinflating" the economy.

A more subtle way in which federal loan guarantees are used to exert governmental control over the allocation of resources without explicit budgetary entries is the exercise of influence over the recipients of the subsidies. For example, the Federal Housing Administration (FHA), which administers the largest loan guarantee program, attempts to implement social policies by vetoing a loan application if a builder does not comply with FHA's regulations regarding marketing to minority groups, environmental impact statements, architectural review, underwriting minimum wages, and so on. The division of responsibility for all these objectives causes considerable confusion and delay, all of which increase construction costs. Further, once a firm or an industry is dependent upon financial assistance from the government, its dependence is often used by the government as a lever to impose additional regulatory controls that may be totally unrelated to the government's contingent liability. Current efforts by some members of the executive and legislative branches of the federal government to deregulate the private sector in order to foster more rapid economic growth are sure to be confounded somewhat by the regulatory requirements that accompany the rapidly growing volume of loan guarantees.

A closer look at the pervasive influence of the federal government through its loan guarantee programs is provided by the data in Table 10–4, which show the guaranteed loan transactions of the federal government in 1983 by agency or program. Housing and agriculture, two of the strongest political constituencies in the nation, dominate the field, accounting for over 80 percent of all loan guarantees. The use of guaranteed loans for housing exceeded the direct loan program by a multiple of nine in 1980 and contained forty-three separate programs. The Export-Import Bank, student loan programs, and the Small Business Administration also administer a large volume of guaranteed lending, which in 1983 amounted to approximately $12 billion.

Equity Aspects of Federal Loan Guarantees

In addition to fostering a less efficient allocation of resources and hindering economic growth, many would consider the loan guarantee programs listed in Table10–4 to be inequitable. An extreme case in point is the student loan program, which, with few eligibility requirements, creates generous subsidies for higher-income households. With such loans available to students and their parents at 7 percent interest regardless of financial need, the high market interest rates of the late 1970s and early 1980s have provided many lucrative investment opportunities for wealthy families. As the spread between interest rates on student loans and market rates widened, new student loans rose from $2.7 billion in 1979 to $7.2 billion in 1981, reflecting a widespread recognition of the opportunities to borrow thousands of dollars at 7 percent and invest the proceeds in long-term bonds or money market funds paying 14 to 16 percent. Furthermore, hundreds of millions of dollars in student loans are now in default, rendering these loans outright gifts to the students and their parents.

The vast majority of federal loan guarantee programs provide subsidies to individuals who are not generally considered to be financially disadvantaged, regardless of the rhetoric associated with such programs. There is a strong incentive for the administrators of loan guarantee programs to subsidize politically powerful groups, regardless of income, who will then provide support for the agency at appropriations time. As an illustration, even though the major goals of the Department of Housing and Urban Development (HUD) are supposedly "the elimination of substandard and inadequate housing through the clearance of slums and blighted areas," it has established hundreds of programs that have nothing to do with slum clearance. For example, HUD's housing rehabilitation loan program has extended 3 percent guaranteed loans to individuals earning over $50,000 per year to finance skylights and greenhouses.[10]

In sum, if there is a pattern of behavior guiding the granting of loan guarantees by the federal government, it is based on the ability of the subsidized group to provide political support for the agency, certainly not on either efficiency or equity. Eliminating many, if not all, loan guarantees would inflict short-term losses on specially priv-

10. As reported in Donald Lambro, *Fat City: How Washington Wastes Your Taxes* (South Bend, Ind.: Regnery, 1980), p. 213.

ileged groups, but it would increase the productivity of the nation's capital stock and limit the negative-sum transfers of wealth to higher-income groups, all of which transfers come at the expense of the general public.

Debt Collection, Default, and Debudgeting the Budget

The indirect costs of federal loan guarantees and off-budget lending are accompanied by billions of dollars of direct costs in the form of loan defaults. When a borrower defaults, the loan or loan guarantee becomes a gift to the borrower and also a way in which the federal largesse can be distributed without undergoing the scrutiny of the appropriations process. Many federal credit programs appear to be designed to do exactly that.

It is difficult, if not impossible, to obtain an accurate account of the volume of loan defaults, for federal agencies are reluctant to make such data available. The General Accounting Office (GAO) conducted a limited survey of debts owed the federal government in 1979 and found that by the end of 1978 over $140 billion in overdue loans were outstanding, a $22 billion increase over the previous year.[11] One GAO auditor stated, "I'd say we're losing about a half-billion dollars a year in bad debts that go uncollected."

GAO surveyed twelve federal agencies and found that most do not even attempt to collect many of their debts. Nine major agencies simply wrote off $428 million in uncollected debts in 1978, and many agencies do not even report their "uncollectibles" at all. When federal agencies do attempt to collect their debts, they are notoriously inefficient and slow in doing so. For example, GAO found that one federal agency that kept data on debt collection costs spent $8.72 per account in 1976 compared to a large commercial agency that averaged $3.50 per account for the same function. Private firms surveyed by GAO stated that it is profitable to attempt to collect debts as small as $25 to the point in the collection process where a decision is made on whether to seek a court judgment. By contrast, in 1977 most federal agencies simply wrote off debts of up to $600. In one instance, an individual could afford a $170,000 mortgage, but the Veterans

11. U.S. General Accounting Office, *The Government Can Be More Productive in Collecting Its Debts by Following Commercial Practices* (Washington, D.C.: U.S. Government Printing Office, Feb. 23, 1979).

Administration wrote off his $638 debt as "uncollectible." Whenever the federal government does seek a court judgment, it takes a minimum of one year to reach the court stage, compared to about five months for private firms surveyed by GAO. Among the agencies failing to collect debts are the Small Business Administration, the Veterans Administration, and the Farmers Home Administration, which wrote off $274 million in bad debts in 1978, a 66 percent increase from 1976 figures. The Small Business Administration has a particularly high default rate, and for good reason—a loan applicant must prove that he is *not* credit worthy in order to qualify! That is, a borrower is eligible for a direct SBA loan only if he can prove that he was turned down by at least two banks *and* that his loan is too risky for even SBA's loan guarantee program. The SBA direct loan program wrote off $166 million in loans in 1980, which was topped by the SBA's $368 million in guaranteed loan defaults during that year.[12]

The Office of Education (which was part of the former Department of Health, Education, and Welfare and which is now a separate Department of Education) was another GAO-surveyed agency that had severe debt-collection problems. Defaulted guaranteed student loans soared from $52 million in 1974 to $1.7 billion in 1982, a 3,300 percent increase in just eight years. The Office of Education also has a collection problem with direct loans. As of July 1982, an estimated 1.2 million students had defaulted on direct loans amounting to about $600 million. Several state and local governments have actively encouraged students to believe in the student loan Santa Claus by passing legislation making it illegal for personal credit checks to make any mention of student loan defaults.

In sum, billions of dollars in loans and loan guarantees that distribute indirect, off-budget subsidies are being turned into direct gifts by simply not enforcing the terms of the loan. Furthermore, it is difficult to believe that members of Congress did not intend for the system to work that way, for it is in their self-interest that it do so.

FEDERALLY SPONSORED OFF-BUDGET ENTERPRISES

Another category of federal off-budget operations consists of "government-sponsored enterprises," of which there are many. The major

12. Hardin and Denzau, *n.* 6, p. 25.

types of federally sponsored off-budget enterprises (OBEs) are those which engage in credit activity. Included among them are the Federal National Mortgage Association (FNMA), the Farm Credit Administration (FCA), the Federal Home Loan Bank (FHLB), the Federal Home Loan Mortgage Corporation (FHLMC), and the Student Loan Marketing Association (SLMA). At one time these agencies were on-budget, but their large and rapidly expanded borrowings became an embarrassment to some members of Congress and were, therefore, omitted from the budget in 1968. For example, in 1968 when federal officials were debating whether the FNMA should become investor-owned but still government controlled, Senator John Sparkman, chairman of the Senate Banking Committee, asked, "Why not . . . postpone specific details of the new corporation until 1969 after a year's time to study its full implications?" [13] The secretary of Housing and Urban Development, Robert C. Weaver, replied that this would not be acceptable since it would not immediately "exclude mortgage purchases under the Secondary Market Operations from the 'net lending' in the Federal budget." [14] Including these expenditures in the federal budget was a recent development, following recommendations by the President's Commission on Budget Concepts in 1967.[15] Since 1968 was an election year, it is clear why there was a rush to delete the FNMA from the rapidly escalating federal budget.

Government-sponsored enterprises were originally chartered by the federal government, but are now privately owned. They are, however, subjected to governmental supervision. For example, the federal budget document states: "These enterprises are privately owned and are included neither in the Federal budget nor in the credit budget. However, . . . they are established by the government to carry out federally designed programs and benefit from substantial forms of government assistance." [16] Moreover, the budget document also explicitly states the role of government-sponsored enterprises (GSEs) in allocating credit: "Government-sponsored enterprises redirect credit by acting as financial intermediaries to stimulate greater amounts of lending to certain sectors. This is accomplished in two ways: by in-

---

13. Hearings before the U.S. Senate Subcommittee on Housing and Urban Affairs, 1968, pp. 1416–17, as cited in Lloyd Musolf, *Uncle Sam's Private, Profitseeking Corporations* (Lexington, Mass.: Lexington Books, 1983), p. 45.

14. Ibid.

15. Ibid.

16. Executive Office of the President, *Budget of the United States Government, FY 1985, Special Analyses*, p. F21.

creasing the liquidity of other direct lenders in the housing and education sectors and by direct lending in the agricultural sector. In both cases, GSEs make more capital available to politically favored borrowers in these sectors. Sectors that do not benefit from the presence of a GSE will have less capital available to them; capital that is available will be more expensive."[17] Thus, government-sponsored enterprises also redirect capital to many economically inefficient but politically popular uses. Economic growth is thereby stifled in the unfavored sectors.

It is clear that government-sponsored enterprises are privately owned in name only, for they are tightly controlled by federal politicians. Many of the board members of these enterprises are presidential appointees, and various decisions must be cleared by other government agencies and the Treasury. For example, many of the FNMA's decisions must be approved by the secretary of HUD. These agencies are also granted special preferences and certain tax exemptions, which permit federally sponsored OBEs to borrow funds for governmentally authorized purposes at rates only slightly above the Treasury's own rates and to lend the money to specified groups. In 1977 Secretary of Housing and Urban Development Patricia Harris noted the mythical nature of "private" corporations such as the FNMA (or "Fannie Mae"). She cited the following differences between the FNMA and private firms:

1. "A large, ongoing and profitable business was turned over to the management and the holders of the equity interest in FNMA. By inheriting the assets and liabilities of the predecessor corporation, FNMA was assured that it would face no effective competition."
2. "Fannie Mae has the benefits of federal economic support through: authority to borrow up to 2-1/2 billion dollars from the U.S. Treasury; receiving the same preferential treatment for its securities as is accorded to the government-owned Ginnie Mae; and use of federal reserve banks as fiscal agents."
3. "Fannie Mae is exempt from state taxes . . . as well as from Securities and Exchange Commission requirements, just as government entities are."[18]

17. Ibid., p. F21.
18. Lloyd Musolf, *n.* 13, p. 47.

The idea that government-sponsored enterprises are "businesslike" is a myth, for actual businesses do not often enjoy such privileges. In fact, private mortgage lenders have protested the unfair competition from a government agency that "raised its investable funds under the protection of the Treasury at rates below the rates private investors paid for their funds." [19] The FNMA obviously crowds out more efficient private firms. For instance, in 1980 the FNMA owned $56 billion of mortgages with an average life of over 14 years and an average yield of about 9.5 percent. [20] While betting on long-term rates to drop, "Fannie Mae" relied heavily on short-term financing, accumulating $17 billion in short-term debt that must be rolled over within a year. About half of that $17 billion was costing the agency 17 percent, with the rest at around 9.7 percent, which would have to be refinanced at about 17 percent. Consequently, Fannie Mae lost $146 million in the first half of 1981. Despite these huge losses, Fannie Mae has had no trouble in rolling over its debt, which has been trading at less than a percentage point above short-term Treasury bills. The reason for this is the implicit guarantee of the federal government. Unlike a private firm, Fannie Mae has the legal right to ask the Treasury to purchase up to $2.5 billion of its debt to give it liquidity. Unlike a typical private firm, which bears the brunt of hundreds of millions of dollars in losses, Fannie Mae and other federally sponsored OBEs are legally protected from such losses and, therefore, have weak incentives to do anything about them.

The total estimated volume of lending and borrowing by federally sponsored enterprises during 1983 is shown in Table 10–5. Lending was approximately $168 billion, while borrowing amounted to about $41 billion. There has recently been a rapid expansion in borrowing by federally sponsored enterprises, which until 1974 had never borrowed more than $14.9 billion annually. This amount increased sharply to $24.1 billion by 1978, to $27.5 billion in 1980, and to more than $38 billion in 1981. Thus, during periods of high and rising interest rates that crowded out many private sector borrowers, federally sponsored and controlled borrowing expanded rapidly. Nearly three-fourths of all federally sponsored borrowing is used to support the mortgage market, while other credit goes largely to student loans and agriculture. As one senator recently said, it seems as though the federal gov-

19. Ibid., p. 32.
20. A. Sloan, "Saving Fannie," *Forbes,* 26 Oct., 1981, pp. 54–55.

Table 10–5.   Lending and Borrowing by Government-sponsored Enterprises, 1983 ($ millions).

Enterprise	Lending	Borrowing
Student Loan Marketing Assoc.	$ 2,463	$ 1,332
Federal National Mortgage Assoc.	35,698	19,105
Farm Credit Administration	50,299	1,172
Federal Home Loan Banks	53,817	—
Federal Home Loan Mortgage Corp.	24,998	20,193
Totals (gross)	$167,275	$41,802

SOURCE: Executive Office of the President, *Budget of the United States Government, Special Analyses, FY 1985* (Washington, D.C.: U.S. Government Printing Office, 1984), pp. F66–68.

ernment is trying to make *everyone* a "preferred borrower" of some sort these days.

It should also be noted that there are numerous other federally sponsored enterprises throughout the country that provide various services to specific constituent groups but that bypass the federal appropriations process. Two well-known examples are the TVA and the Bonneville Power Administration, both federally chartered OBEs, which obtain most of their funds by issuing revenue bonds but which are also recipients of federal revenues and subject to federal mandates.

SUMMARY AND CONCLUSIONS

The key to economic growth is capital formation, for it is capital investment that largely determines the productivity and health of all industries. Discussions of government policy toward capital formation and economic growth generally focus on two areas: the deficit problem and the effects of the tax system on investment and productivity growth. It is well known that the tax system of recent years has diminished the attractiveness of business investment and of individual work effort, thereby hindering economic growth. Federal deficits are of perennial concern because of the crowding-out effects of federal borrowing. This chapter has focused on a third type of government policy that is inimical to capital formation and economic growth, federal credit allocation.

Federal credit allocation is a severe hindrance to capital investment in "unfavored" sectors of the economy, for hundreds of billions of dollars of credit are allocated to economically inefficient but politically popular uses, particularly housing and agriculture. Homeowners and farmers are among the most heavily subsidized interest groups in the nation, although the subsidies received are not for the most part in the form of direct cash transfers. In the case of federal loans, loan guarantees, and government-sponsored enterprises, special interest groups receive preferential treatment in the credit markets, while unfavored groups (i.e., much of manufacturing industry) are *indirectly* taxed through the unavailability or the increased cost of credit. The benefits of these transfers are clearly defined, whereas the costs are hidden and widely dispersed. This explains why they are so popular politically. They appear to be a means of providing a political free lunch, even though the bill always comes due in the form of slower economic growth and inflation.

One consequence of this and other ill-conceived government policies toward capital formation is that the sluggish productivity growth brought about by these policies has given rise to proposals among some businessmen, unions, and government officials to "take charge" of the situation with even more interventionist policies, especially in the area of government credit allocation. The resurrection of Herbert Hoover's Reconstruction Finance Corporation (RFC), for example, is now being considered by some members of Congress.[21] The RFC was the origin of federal credit activities, such as loan guarantees and government-sponsored enterprises. By diverting capital from its more productive uses, the RFC may have even *intensified* the Great Depression. Its resurrection would have similar effects today.

Private capital markets can best channel capital into its most productive uses, for it is only through the price system that we can learn what the most efficient uses of resources are and where capital should be "targeted." Moreover, political rather than market allocation of capital leads to even further inefficiencies as potential recipients of the federal largesse engage in rent-seeking behavior to attain "their share" of the largesse. The opportunity cost of the time and resources

---

21. See, for example, James T. Bennett and Thomas J. DiLorenzo, *Labor Unions and the State: The Political Economy of Pushbutton Unionism* (Dallas: The Fisher Institute, forthcoming).

spent lobbying for political favors represents a further hindrance to economic growth caused by federal credit allocation.[22] Despite its conservative rhetoric, the Reagan administration has to date shown just as much impotence in curtailing this process during its second term as it did during its first.

22. On the topic of rent-seeking behavior, see James Buchanan, Robert Tollison, and Gordon Tullock, eds., *Toward a Theory of the Rent-Seeking Society* (College Station: Texas A & M Press, 1980). On rent-seeking behavior as a cause of economic stagnation, see Mancur Olson, *The Rise and Decline of Nations* (New Haven: Yale University Press, 1982).

11

UNION MYOPIA AND THE TAXATION OF CAPITAL

Dwight R. Lee

INTRODUCTION

It is widely believed that entrusting economic decisions to the private market is a prescription for shortchanging the future. The argument seems to be that since market decisions are made in response to narrow self-interest and a lust for profit, they will reflect little concern for future consequences. Businessmen are viewed as concerned primarily with increasing sales now, with cutting costs now, and with investment projects that pay off now. The profits made today are theirs, while the resulting problems that materialize in the future represent costs others will bear. It is this market myopia that supposedly explains both the eroding productivity of many of our major industries and their increasingly precarious position in the face of global competition.

Although seen as a problem inherent in the market mechanism generally, myopia is considered to be a particularly troublesome problem in the case of corporations, where decisions are made not by owners but by professional managers whose tenure with the corporation is often short.

This view is epitomized by national industrial policy advocate Robert Reich: "Managers who anticipate a short tenure with their firm unsurprisingly have little interest in long-run solutions to its basic problems. Their goal is to make the firm (and themselves) look as good as possible in the immediate future."[1] Certainly at a superficial level, this appears to be a plausible line of argument. Corporate managers do, on average, have relatively short tenures in their jobs. According to data compiled by Crain, the average tenure of chief executive officers in major corporations is less than that of the average member of the U.S. House of Representatives.[2]

Those who assert that people in business are excessively short-sighted are never at a loss for a solution to the problem. A common argument is that workers should have more say in management decisions. After all, the stake that workers have in their jobs is equal to (if not greater than) that of corporate managers who are "here today and gone tomorrow." If the decision-making environment were restructured to give all workers some managerial control, business would supposedly be forced to shift its myopic vision more toward the future. Reich, for example, suggests "labor-management councils . . . comprised of worker representatives [in which] workers will participate in company decisions about physical capital, helping choose the direction and magnitude of new investment in research, plant, and machinery."[3]

The question that comes immediately to mind is, If "worker participation" management arrangements are a more farsighted and efficient way to run a business, why have not more such arrangements emerged from market competition? There are no legal restrictions against workers purchasing a business and running it any way they choose; this has indeed been done and, on occasion, it has succeeded.[4] Yet worker-managed plants are rare, a fact that fails to raise doubt in the minds of those who see more worker control as the answer to the "failure" of private business. Their response is for government to "promote" worker-management schemes. For this purpose

1. Robert B. Reich, *The Next American Frontier* (New York: Times Books, 1983), p. 164. This book has been hailed as the blueprint for economic survival by those who tend to see the market as a flawed vehicle for economic progress. The 1984 nominee of the Democratic Party, Walter Mondale, described Reich's book as "one of the most important works of the decade."

2. See W. Mark Crain, "Can Corporate Executives Set Their Own Salaries?" in M. Bruce Johnson, ed., *The Attack on Corporate America* (New York: McGraw Hill, 1978), pp. 272–75.

3. Reich, *n.* 1, p. 248.

4. See, for example, Staughton Lynd and Peter Pitegoff, "Workers Can Be Choosers," *New York Times,* 27 Oct. 1982.

Reich, for example, favors having government make grants available to firms, with the size of these grants determined by the firm's co-operation in implementing appropriate policies and with the firm's employees collectively managing the use of the funds.[5]

The reason, of course, that such proposals are seldom the result of voluntary contract is that worker-management arrangements are, in general, less efficient and less farsighted than traditional management arrangements. This does not mean that worker-management proposals can be dismissed as far-fetched. They combine romantic appeal with the promise to redistribute wealth, and on that basis will generate political support. It is well to recall the Chrysler bailout, which not only provided government assistance (in the form of loan guarantees) to the Chrysler Corporation, but did so in an agreement that put the head of the United Auto Workers on the corporate board of directors. Such an arrangement is not the full-fledged worker control that many would like to see, but it is clearly a step in that direction.[6]

As insidiously appealing as worker-management schemes are to those who covet corporate wealth and to their well-meaning but analytically innocent supporters, this is not the source of the most immediate worker-related threat to efficient business decision-making. Labor unions, with the assistance of government legislation, have already given worker representatives more control over business decisions than most people realize. And, contrary to the widespread view, this control has ham-pered the ability of business to pursue long-run goals through far-sighted and productive investment commitments. Private business concerns may not give the future the weight that, in some ideal world, would be considered appropriate. But a realistic assessment of the motivations driving labor union activity and of the institutional setting within which this activity takes place leads to the unmistakable con-

5. Reich, *n.* 1, p. 247–48. It is convenient to cite Reich's book for the simple reason that it has received wide attention. Also, his views are moderate in comparison to many advocates of worker-management arrangements. For more radical proposals to restructure American business, see Richard Barnett, *The Crisis of the Corporation* (Washington, D.C.: Institute for Policy Studies, 1975); and Martin Carnoy and Derek Shearer, *Economic Democracy: The Challenge of the 1980s* (White Plains, N.Y.: M. E. Sharpe, Inc., 1980).

6. Chrysler claimed from the very beginning that the election of Douglas Frazer was a personal recognition, while the UAW declared that the seat belonged henceforth to the union. This significant difference of opinion became a public issue when Frazer retired as UAW president and his successor, Owen Bieber, sought to replace Frazer as a Chrysler director. See John Holusha, "UAW's Departing Chief to Stay in Board," *New York Times,* 6 March 1983.

clusion that giving more control over business decisions to labor unions will shorten the planning horizon of business firms.

Unfortunately, government regulation of labor relations has increasingly diminished business control over decisions relevant to capital investment and has passed that control to union officials. As a consequence, government has shortened the planning horizon of business decisions, allowed excessive wages to be substituted for capital formation, and reduced the long-run competitive vitality of major sectors of the U.S. economy. In other words, government, through its regulation of labor relations, is imposing a tax on capital just as surely and perniciously as if it were confiscating capital directly. It is the myopia of labor unions—and the tax this myopia imposes on capital and long-run economic productivity—that serves as the focus of this paper.

THE FUTURE VERSUS THE PRESENT

All economic decisions embody a consideration of time. If they are to generate the greatest value possible, decisions on consumption, just like decisions on investment, require comparisons between current values and future values. Since people do not place as much value on a postponed benefit, or cost, as they do on one of the same magnitude that is immediate, future values have to be discounted if they are to be usefully compared with current values. This, of course, raises the question, What is the appropriate discount rate? At a theoretical level the answer is not difficult. The appropriate discount rate is that which reflects the willingness of individuals to exchange current benefits for future benefits after all mutually advantageous exchanges between borrowers and savers have been made. Needless to say, real-world applications of this formulation are more complicated.

Complicated or not, applying something close to the appropriate rate of discount to business decisions is important, and the charge that business firms are myopic is a serious one. The future prosperity of ourselves and our descendants depends on economic decision-makers being willing to sacrifice opportunities for current consumption by directing output and resources into the maintenance and expansion of our capital stock. A business community concerned primarily with satisfying its immediate appetite for greater output, more profit, higher dividends, and bigger management bonuses would soon leave our resources depleted, our capital base exhausted, and the economy declining into poverty.

Of course, this is exactly the scenario critics of the market economy see unfolding as a consequence of "rape, ruin, and run" policies allegedly inspired by corporate capitalism. Indeed, this is the same scenario critics of capitalism have seen unfolding ever since the mid-nineteenth century. Unfortunately for their arguments, if not for their persistence, the historical record shows clearly that economic systems based on private markets and free exchange *are* future oriented. It was not until the emergence of market economies that wealth and well-being began increasing steadily from one generation to the next, and economic decision-makers began acting *as if* they were concerned with the distant future. Viewed historically, the charge that markets are myopic is implausible in the extreme. However, there are reasons for fearing that the private sector is becoming less farsighted. Before investigating the basis for this fear, it will be helpful to look at the feature of the market economy that provides current decisions-makers the incentive to consider the long-run consequences of their actions.

PROPERTY AND PATIENCE

Individuals, whether corporate managers or union leaders, shareholders or blue collar workers, will give the appropriate weight to the future consequences of their actions only if it is in their interest to do so. Genuinely farsighted actions always impose near-term costs, since providing more for the future necessarily demands that less be consumed today. And unless those currently in control of resources are in a position to realize some of the distant advantages from current sacrifices, there will be few current sacrifices. It is in this regard that private property rights are crucial to efficient and future-oriented economic decisions. It is the ownership of property that makes it possible for individuals to capture some of the long-run benefits that their current abstinence makes possible.

In one respect, the ability of private ownership to extend one's time horizon is completely obvious. If private property rights are well-defined and respected, then the owner of a resource has confidence that he or she will, by maintaining ownership, benefit from any increase in the future value of the resource. As evidenced by the fact that graffiti are ubiquitous on the walls of public restrooms but seldom seen on the walls of restrooms in private homes, people are more concerned with the future value of property they own than of the property they do not own.

But genuinely farsighted behavior often requires that individuals consider consequences of their decisions that will not be realized until after they are gone. The private ownership of property by itself will not provide the necessary incentive for people to concern themselves with outcomes that extend beyond their own existence. Yet we observe property owners sacrificing current consumption in order to make investments that will not pay off for several generations. For example, many research and development projects will not, at best, pay off for decades. Owners of forest land replant white oak and Douglas fir trees that will not be harvested for sixty or more years. People invest in the production of wines and spirits that will be aged a century or more before they are sold and consumed. The explanation for this behavior lies in the fact that private ownership rights are generally transferable.

The owner of forest land that has been recently clear cut may be old and heirless and personally not care beyond, at most, five to ten years into the future. But, with transferable, rights, such an individual will find it in his interest to replant young trees that will not be ready for harvesting for many decades. Since these young trees will grow at a rate that exceeds the market interest rate, the decision to plant them will cause the present value of his property to increase more rapidly than would alternative investment choices. With the possibility of selling his property to the highest bidder, this increase in present value can be converted into immediate wealth, no matter how long it takes the trees to mature. The current wealth of elderly resource owners is tied directly to the value young men and women who do care about the future place on the long-run value of resources and are therefore willing to pay for them. As long as property is privately owned and transferable, the incentive to value the future will be strong. Through competition in the marketplace, resources will tend to flow to those who best accommodate the tensions between present and future demands.

The above argument makes a compelling case for the farsightedness of owner-operated and -controlled firms. But what about corporations, where decisions are not made by the owners of the corporations (the thousands, and in some cases millions, of shareholders), but by professional managers? Through their voting rights shareholders are nominally in charge of management decisions, but as a practical matter they are seldom active in the making of those decisions. The typical shareholder owns but a tiny fraction of a corporation's outstanding shares. With each share carrying one vote, this means that the typical shareholder's voting impact on corporate decisions will be minuscule. For most shareholders of a large corporation, then, the rational attitude to take toward the policy decisions of corporate management is one of apathy. Rational behavior requires becoming informed in matters where not only are outcomes important to one's well-being, but also where one's decisions will have a significant impact on the outcomes.

It would appear that shareholders are not in a position to exert much control over corporate management. What then, if anything, prevents management from taking advantage of the wide discretion they apparently have to enrich themselves during their relatively brief tenures at the expense of the long-run wealth of the corporation and its shareholders? The answer is, well-defined and transferable ownership claims on the outcomes of corporate decisions. The existence of corporate stock that can be readily bought and sold on organized exchanges exerts far more influence on the time perspective of corporate managers than does the length of their tenure. With corporate stock easily transferable, management decisions that reduce the long-run wealth position of the corporation will be reflected quickly and unmistakably by a decline in the market price of its stock. All it takes is for a few people to recognize the long-run consequences of shortsighted corporate policy. A consequent decline in the price of a corporation's stock transmits information about the performance of management that even the most uninformed shareholder will notice and understand. Furthermore, it provides information that the shareholder can respond to in a completely decisive way by simply picking up the telephone and calling his or her broker.

This connection between the way a corporation is managed and the price of its stock makes it very difficult for management to survive, much less prosper, by maximizing short-run returns while ignoring long-run consequences. If, for example, the management of an otherwise viable corporation decided to deplete the corporation's future capital base in order to finance exorbitant dividends, stockholders would immediately recognize that they were worse off. The value of their stock would, in response to the long-run wealth effects of the dividend policy, decline by more than the value of the additional dividends.

The same would be true if management attempted to realize short-run gains by paying wages that failed to cover the opportunity cost of competent employees. The savings from such a substandard wage policy could support additional dividends or management "perks" for a while, but the long-run effect would be a work force without the skills necessary to keep the company competitive. The destructiveness of such a wage policy to the future potential of the corporation to generate wealth would be reflected immediately in the price of the corporate stock. Similarly, an overly generous wage policy that paid workers greatly in excess of the amount required to attract a competent work force would impose downward pressure on the corporate stock. And the existence of stock that is undervalued because of myopic mis-mangement creates both the incentive and the ability for a more fu-ture-oriented management team to assume control through a takeover bid, a proxy fight, or (more likely) a merger.[7]

When examining the impact of transferable stock on corporate time horizons, two additional features should be mentioned. First, the transferability of corporate stock allows interests in the present value of the corporation to be concentrated. A large percentage of a cor-poration can be, and often is, owned by a relatively small number of the shareholders. This means that the dominant shareholders will have both the incentive and the means to keep management (1) focused on the present value consequences of their decisions and therefore (2) responsive to the long-run as well as the short-run concerns of all shareholders.[8]

Second, privately owned corporate stock allows for compensation schemes that tie managerial self-interest to concern for the future. In most corporations a significant portion of the compensation received by corporate managers is based on the price performance of the cor-porate stock. This compensation takes the form of payment in stock, dividends, and capital gains. Wilbur Lewellen compared this stock-related compensation with wage compensation for managers in fifty of the largest manufacturing corporations over a twenty-three-year pe-riod beginning in 1940. The average stock-related compensation for top executives, according to Lewellen's findings, was over four times larger than their average after-tax wages. This ratio of stock to wage compensation was even larger when only the top five executives were

7. See Henry G. Manne, "Mergers and the Market for Corporate Control," *The Journal of Political Control* 73 (April 1965): 110–20.

8. Ironically, many of those who criticize corporate decision-making for being myopic, at the same time find fault with the concentrations of stock ownership and voting rights that serve to lengthen corporate time horizons. Imposing the "corporate democracy" reforms ad-vocated by these critics would, by diluting ownership interest in corporate wealth, weaken the connection between the long-run concerns of shareholders and decisions of corporate man-agers. For a discussion of the advantages to shareholders from the traditional arrangement of one vote–one share, see Frank H. Easterbrook and Daniel R. Fischel, "Voting in Corporate Law" *The Journal of Law and Economics* 26 (June 1983): 395–427.

considered in each corporation.[9] The advantage realized by share-holders from these types of compensation arrangements should be obvious. With the wealth of managers being held hostage to the willingness of stockholders to continue holding their stock at existing or higher prices, managers will be reluctant to undermine the long-run profitability of the corporation in order to achieve short-run gains.

Moreover, the labor market for managers imposes costs on those managers who might yield to opportunism and be tempted to act against the interest of the corporate organization. The present value of a manager's future earnings, possibly from other corporations, will not be independent of his performance in his current position. The manager who attempts to gain short-run benefits by imposing long-run inefficiencies on the organization can expect some after-the-fact "settling up" through future salary adjustments. This not only provides a motivation for individual managers to concern themselves with the long-run interests of the corporation, it also motivates internal monitoring arrangements for imposing discipline on the entire management team, since the performance of individual members of the team depends on the performance of the other members.[10]

None of this is meant to imply that corporate arrangements work perfectly to solve the agent-principal problem. Agents will always have some latitude in realizing personal gains by acting against the wishes of their principals. In general this will mean agents capturing short-run advantages by imposing both short-run and long-run losses on principals. Certainly this is true in the case of corporate managers, as agents, versus corporate shareholders, as principals. Many cases can no doubt be cited of corporate decisions that serve the short-run interests of top management while reducing both the long-run interests of the shareholder and economic productivity.[11] But it should also

9. See Wilbur G. Lewellen, "Management and Ownership in the Large Firms," *Journal of Finance* 24 (1969): 299–322. Also see Harold Demsetz, "The Structure of Ownership and the Theory of the Firm," *The Journal of Law and Economics* 26 (June 1983): 375–90.

10. For more on this aspect of management control, see Eugene Fama, "Agency Problems and the Theory of the Firm," *The Journal of Political Economy* 88 (April 1980): 288–307.

11. The possibility that government policy is a factor in such cases should never be dismissed. The interaction between corporate tax law and inflationary monetary policy during the seventies and into the eighties imposed an enormous tax burden on corporate income from capital investment. See, for example, Martin Feldstein and Lawrence Summers, "Inflation and the Taxation of Capital in the Corporate Sector," *National Tax Journal* 32 (Dec. 1979): 445–70, as well as other chapters in this volume. In effect the government is taxing farsighted investment decisions. Also, government restrictions on the ability of firms to merge serve to protect myopic corporate managers from the discipline the market would otherwise impose on them.

be recognized that the corporate form has emerged as the dominant form of business organization as a consequence of voluntary contractual arrangements. This ability to survive in a setting of relatively free and open competition furnishes strong evidence for the view that corporations have been responsive to the long-run interests of consumers, employees, and shareholders. Not perfectly responsive, of course, but as a vehicle for conducting a significant amount of our business activity, corporations have proved more responsive than alternative forms of business arrangements.

The important thing to emphasize, however, is the role of privately owned and transferable property rights in providing the incentive for future-oriented decisions. Possibly the best way to appreciate the importance of property rights in this regard is to consider a situation in which while agents are supposedly responsive to the long-run concerns of their principals, transferable property rights do not exist. Transferable property rights to the value of political decisions, as such, do not exist. Politicians do not possess a claim, which can be sold at the end of their tenure, on the long-run economy-wide value generated by their political decisions. Not surprisingly, politicians are seldom concerned with consequences that can be postponed until after the next election. We commonly observe government policies that seek out ways to capture immediate gains by shifting burdens to the future, policies analogous to paying excessive dividends currently by depleting productive capital. For example, the federal government has followed a policy of persistent budget deficits in order to finance expenditures far beyond the level that citizens are willing to fund through their taxes.[12] This policy allows the government to provide currently appropriable benefits at the expense of crowding out private investment, thus reducing the country's future wealth.

That politicians can, over a long period of time, get away with such a policy is evident from the record. Since 1960 the federal budget has been in surplus exactly once, with the almost unbroken string of deficits escalating upward at a rapid rate. This record reflects a degree of myopic mismangement that would soon be rooted out in a private corporation. The difference is not that politicians are inherently more myopic than corporate managers, but rather that the latter

12. The government has pushed hard on the tax margin, possibly close to the point of diminishing returns, as evidenced by the underground economy. See Dan Heldman, *Entrepreneurs and Regulators: A Study in Social Impulses* (Dallas: Fisher Institute, 1982).

are subject to the discipline imposed by the market exchange of private property, while politicians are not.

UNION MYOPIA

We now turn attention to the time perspective of employees, and the impact of this time perspective on investment decisions. As with managers, politicians, or any other groups of decision makers, workers will appropriately weigh the future when it is in their private advantage to do so. Again, private ownership plays an important role in providing the proper set of incentives. Workers own the future income streams their human capital allows them to generate. As a result, they willingly sacrifice current income in order to invest in their human capital by going to college, taking training courses, and working at low-paying jobs that provide opportunities for valuable experience and future advancement. Empirical studies on the rate of return from educational expenditures indicate that the future is not heavily discounted when people are investing in their own human capital.[13]

As far as individual workers are concerned, however, sacrificing current income in the form, say, of a lower current salary in order to invest in the future productivity of the firm for which they work is an entirely different matter. In the first place, each worker would incur personally the entire cost of his or her lower salary while realizing that the future benefits from increased productivity would be spread over everyone with a financial stake in the firm. Each worker would have an obvious motivation for resisting a reduction in his or her salary in order to make such an investment. Secondly, in their roles as workers, individuals will perceive no benefit from improved firm productivity beyond the point in time when they sever their employment connection with the firm. Given the mobility of the work force and the significant percentage of the work force that at any point in time is within a few years of retirement, it is clear that socially productive capital investments with extended pay-back periods will offer little attraction to a large number of workers.[14]

13. See Christopher Jencks, et al., *Inequality* (New York: Basic Books, 1972), for a discussion of many of the empirical studies on the return to education.

14. It should be pointed out that worker ownership of stock in the company they work for will lengthen their time horizon with respect to the firm's productivity. But as a practical matter, for most employees their return from salary will dominate what they can expect to receive from dividends and capital gains; therefore employee time perspectives, as they relate to the firm's capital decisions, will not be appreciably affected by stock ownership.

It can be argued that organizing workers through a union is a means whereby these problems can be mitigated. Unions supposedly make it possible for workers to acquire collective benefits that they would not be able to obtain if required to negotiate with their employees as individuals.[15] For example, when wages are determined collectively, each worker will be more willing to sacrifice current wages for future increases in productivity and wages, since the sacrifice of one worker will be accompanied by the sacrifice of all others. Therefore, it can be argued that workers, voicing their preference through a union organization, will apply a lower discount rate to the future than would be the case in a nonunion setting. Also, unions have an organizational existence that extends beyond the working lifetime of its individual members. This, it can be argued, provides an additional reason for believing that wage and salary demands transmitted through unions will reflect a longer-term perspective than would otherwise be the case.

Two responses to this line of argument need to be considered. First, under traditional arrangements, the time horizon of business decisions depends very little on the time perspective of workers with respect to the trade-off between current wages and long-term business investment. In all aspects of economic activity, specialization is important. Those who are residual claimants to the present value of the firm's profit stream, or those who are agents for these claimants, are in the best position to specialize effectively in making decisions that affect the firm's long-run wealth and productivity. These decisions are guided, of course, by market information on relevant interest rates, the revenue potential of particular product choices, and the value of different input mixes in alternative employments. Workers specialize best in this process by staying informed on their opportunity cost, increasing this cost within limits determined by their individual abilities and preferences, and refusing employment with firms that refuse to cover this cost. Employees have a strong motivation to do all of these things.

---

15. Unions have recently been defended as efficiency-increasing organizations with the argument that many features of the workplace are accurately characterized as public goods, and that unions allow workers to collectively, and therefore effectively, communicate their demand for these public goods. See Richard B. Freeman and James L. Medoff, "The Two Faces of Unionism," *The Public Interest* 57 (Fall 1979): 69–93. For a summary statement, and critical evaluation, of this perspective on unions, see Morgan O. Reynolds, *Power and Privilege: Labor Unions in America* (New York: Universe Books, 1984), pp. 71–72 and 77–80.

Just as few workers have to extend themselves beyond their narrow specialties and worry about agricultural decisions as a means of putting food on the table, neither do they have to concern themselves with the long-run consequences of business investment decisions in order to ensure that the capital base, upon which their real wages depend, continues to grow.

The appropriate response to the argument that unions last beyond the time horizon of workers is that this is largely irrelevant. It is not the longevity of an organization that is important to the discounting of the future, but rather the incentives built into the organization's structure. After all, the fact that corporations commonly outlive their shareholders provides no basis for denying that corporate arrangements are less than ideal at motivating decision makers to apply the appropriate discount to the future. And the same is true for union arrangements. Indeed the incentives built into union organizations are less conducive to weighing the future adequately. Any move in the direction of substituting union control for traditional control over a firm's decisions will only shorten the time horizon for business decision-making.

The comparison to which our discussion has led us is between the organizational incentives of unions and those of corporations, especially as they affect future-oriented decisions.[16] The important distinction between unions and corporations in this regard centers around arrangements involving property rights. In the previous section we examined the importance of transferable property rights, in the form of stock, as a means of reflecting the future consequences of corporate decisions and in providing both the means and the motivation to take those consequences into consideration. The myopia of unions relative to corporations is explained by the fact that unions do not come with comparable property rights, and therefore the long-run wealth effects of current decisions are not clearly registered in a way that feeds back into union decisions. Several implications of this fact are pertinent to our discussion.

Without transferable property rights reflecting the present value of employment opportunities in a firm or industry, the control of union

---

16. It should be pointed out that the problem of motivating agents to remain responsive to the long-run concerns of their principals is, in the case of business organizations, at its most troublesome in corporations. Therefore, this comparison is, if anything, biased against viewing business organizations as being farsighted relative to labor unions.

members over the management of the union is quite limited. It is true that union members may have the right to vote on some levels of their leadership and on some of the recommendations made by that leadership. To this extent, the control of union members over union management is the same as the control of shareholders over corporate management. Well-informed and politically active voters can collectively keep management from deviating too far from their interests in both cases. The problem, of course, is that each voter, as a voter, has little motivation to be either informed or active since his or her individual vote is unlikely to have an impact on the decision being made. It is here that we can recall a major advantage of stock ownership that gives shareholders more control over their agents than union members have over theirs. The shareholder has an additional margin on which to exercise choice both conveniently and decisively, and that margin comes from the ability to buy and sell corporate stock. The member of a union is in a much inferior situation in this regard. The union member would have to be prepared to change employers, and possibly occupations, in order to protect himself against the negative effects of poor management decisions as effectively as the shareholder can by simply selling his stock.

This means that union leaders will have more latitude in maximizing their personal advantages and promoting their own agendas than will corporate managers. The preferences of the union membership will not serve to constrain the decisions of those in union hierarchies as effectively as is the case of shareholder preferences vis-à-vis the managers of corporations.

Also, little control can be exerted over union leaders through the sort of market for managers that does serve as a partial control mechanism in the case of corporations. Union managers typically work up from within a given union organization; seldom is a union leader brought in from the outside. With less opportunity for union leaders to profit financially from a reputation for promoting the interests of their membership, the connection between the self-interest of union management and the welfare of union members is further weakened. Thus, those in a position of power in the union hierarchy have a further degree of freedom to ignore membership concerns in favor of promoting their own.

One can expect, then, with respect to many issues, that union decisions will not be representative of the interests of the rank-and-file member. This is particularly evident when the positions unions take on political issues are contrasted with the political preferences of their members. Researchers have found, for example, that in a majority of questions posed to union members in national opinion polls, their positions differed (sometimes diametrically) from the positions for which their union leaders were lobbying in Congress.[17] It is also of interest to note that union management is able to continue with political activities that are increasingly at variance with the views of their membership.

However, even if union leaders were perfectly responsive to the concerns of their worker members, they would still be relatively insensitive to the future consequences of current wage and salary decisions. Workers, not owning transferable "employment stock" that reflects the long-run value of their jobs, have little motivation to take the long view when balancing current wage demands against the long-run gains from maintaining and expanding a productive capital base. Arranging for the ownership of such "employment stock" would require that workers quite literally own their jobs, with the right to sell them to whomever they please. Such an arrangement would effectively remove all control over employment decisions from those who supplied capital to the industry and would therefore greatly increase the cost of raising large amounts of capital.

There is really little reason to expand on the infeasibility of such an employee job-ownership plan. The point is that, under reasonable property rights arrangements, workers will be less sensitive to the long-run employment effects of current salary, wage, and investment decisions than will corporate managers whose current compensation is directly tied to the price of stocks.[18] If there is an issue upon which workers do focus, and which comes closest to being used as a monitor of the effectiveness of union leadership, it is the issue of current compensation. The quickest way for a union leader to incur the disapproval of the membership, and put his leadership position at risk, is

17. See Dan Heldman and Deborah Knight, *Unions and Lobbying: The Representation Function* (Washington, D.C.: Foundation for the Advancement of the Public Trust, 1980).

18. For an interesting discussion of the myopic investment decisions that result when workers are in charge of management decisions, see Eirik G. Furubotn and Svetozar Pejovich, "Property Rights and Economic Theory: A Survey of Recent Literature," *Journal of Economic Literature* 10 (Dec. 1972): 1137–62.

to demonstrate an inability to negotiate current wage and benefits increases from employers.[19]

GOVERNMENT POLICY AND UNION POWER

Union myopia with respect to business investment and capital formation would pose no threat to economic productivity and growth in the traditional U.S. setting, where government is confined to a rather limited role in economic affairs. The economic role of government as envisioned by the Founding Fathers, though limited, was crucially important. Government was to create an economic environment of stability and confidence in which the rules of the game rewarded productive activity, where people knew what those rules were and had confidence that they would not be constantly assaulted by political whimsy. The primary economic responsibility of the government in this regard involved protecting private property rights against both domestic and foreign violations, and enforcing voluntary contracts. In other words, the task of government was to serve as a referee, making sure the game was being played in accordance with constitutionally agreed-upon rules. It was emphatically not to be the government's role to become an active participant in the economic game in order to determine outcomes favoring some participants at the expense of others.

Although the ideal of the minimal state has never been fully realized in this country, or in any other, there can be no doubt that for almost 150 years of U.S. history, decisions on the allocation of business income between wages and capital investment were left almost entirely to the discretion of capital owners or their corporate agents. It is equally true that the exercise of this discretion—subject as it largely was to the constraints imposed by respect for private property, voluntary exchange, and open competition—resulted in a level of economic progress that served the long-run interests of workers as well as capital owners. To the superficial observer, it may have ap-

19. Although a few unions have recently agreed to take small pay cuts in the face of the threatened bankruptcy of a major employer, the attention received by these concessions attests to their infrequency. It is clearly the case that union leaders have been willing to sacrifice a large number of jobs rather than accept wage and benefit cuts. And the concessions that are made are seen as only temporary, even if, as in the case of the Chrysler Corporation, the long-run financial prospects of the employer remain tenuous. The United Auto Workers entered wage negotiations after their concessions to Chrysler with the slogan, "Restore and More in 84."

peared that the rule of property favored the interests of capital over those of the worker. The fallaciousness of this view is apparent to anyone who examines, even casually, the growth of wealth through U.S. history and how this wealth has been distributed between capital and labor.

Nonetheless, the view that rules of property and free exchange put workers at a disadvantage relative to capital owners has persisted and, over the last half of this century, has been increasingly influential politically.[20] The result has been an obvious shift in the role of government away from that of the impartial enforcer of neutral rules to that of an active participant in the game, promoting outcomes favorable to the interests of workers.[21] Of course, the tilting of the playing field in favor of labor unions is not acknowledged as such. The impression given, as expressed by economists Bennett, Heldman, and Johnson, is that laws regulating labor relations provide "little more than a general framework within which labor exchanges take place largely in response to traditional market pressures."[22] These authors go on to show that this impression is completely false.

One of the more blatant examples of the government overriding market forces in the interest of particular workers is given by minimum wage legislation. Politically determined minimum wages, along wih maximum hour restrictions, as provided for by the Fair Labor Standards Act (FLSA) of 1938, obviously deny both workers and employers opportunities to enter into mutually advantageous exchanges. Over 70 percent of the nonagricultural work force is currently covered by either federal or state wage and hour standards. And this surely understates the extent of government control, since it does not include those who, while not covered by FLSA-type legislation, are restricted by the Davis-Bacon, Walsh-Healey, or O'Hara-McNamara Acts.[23] It

20. Seldom is the notion of the disadvantage of labor challenged. It is simply accepted as a self-evident truth by most, including economists who are normally proud of their professionally honed skepticism. Economist William H. Hutt has, however, carefully examined the implications of the disadvantaged-worker assertions and has called into serious question their validity. See W. H. Hutt, *The Theory of Collective Bargaining* (London: King, 1930). For a concise discussion of Hutt's insights in this regard, see Reynolds, *n*. 15, pp. 26–27.

21. More accurately, the interests of the minority of workers who are members of labor unions.

22. See James T. Bennett, Dan C. Heldman, and Manuel H. Johnson, *Deregulating Labor Relations* (Dallas: The Fisher Institute, 1981), p. 3. Much of the remaining discussion in this section draws from Chapter 3 of the above book.

23. See Bennett, et al., *n*. 22, p. 43

is not the purpose of this paper to elaborate on the unfortunate effects on nonunion and minority workers stemming from these restrictions on the labor market.[24] For our purpose, it suffices to point out that the above acts represent direct government action that shifts control over employment decisions away from capital owners and toward union leaders by denying market opportunities to nonunion workers.

With the enactment of the National Labor Relations Act (Wagner Act) in 1935, the government created another instrument for granting unions power to distort market decisions in favor of organized workers. Although the impact of the Wagner Act was moderated to some extent in 1947 with the passage of the Taft-Hartley Act, the history of the National Labor Relations Board (NLRB), established by the Wagner Act, shows a consistent pattern of decisions favoring union power.

If during a certification election to determine if a union is to be the *exclusive representative* of the employees, the NLRB decides that the employer has committed an "unfair labor practice," the board can order the employer to grant recognition to the union. This has been done even when the union clearly failed to win the support of a majority, not of the employees, but of the employees voting. To avoid an unfair labor practice ruling, the employer has to, among other things, be very circumspect in responding to union charges, assertions, and accusations during the period leading up to a certification election. The employer who threatens (predicts) "loss of employment . . . closing of plant or going out of business . . . moving of plant to new location . . . loss or reduction in pay or overtime,"[25] is seen to be in violation of fair labor practices by engaging in a "threat of force or reprisal." The board is much more tolerant of union communications to employees. Furthermore, if a union is found to have engaged in unfair labor practices, the board will seldom reverse an election that the union has won.

The NLRB has ruled that an employer is violating employee rights if he is "engaged in conduct which, it may reasonably be said, tends to interfere with . . . employee rights under the Act."[26] Neither the

24. The interested reader is refered to Walter E. Williams, "Government Sanctioned Restraints That Reduce Economic Opportunities for Minorities," *Policy Review* 2 (Fall 1977): 1–24.

25. NLRB, *Annual Report* 27 (1963): 89.

26. 154 NLRB at 503, *Cooper Thermometer Co.* (1966). Also quoted in Bennett, et al., n. 22, p. 50.

intent behind nor the success of an employer's supposed violation of employee rights is relevant, according to NLRB rulings—rulings that have defined employee rights, as contained in Section 7 of the NLRA, very broadly. Although the Taft-Hartley Act attempted to provide employees the same protection against unions as the Wagner Act had provided against employers, in practice the unions are given much more latitude than are employers in this regard. For example, the refusal of an employer to bargain with a certified union constitutes a "per se" violation of employee rights. This is seldom the case if a union refuses to bargain with an employer.[27]

Even without the threat of unfair labor practice charges, the deck has been stacked in favor of unions by NLRB rulings, rulings which in some cases override the obvious intent of Congress. Congress clearly stated in Section 9 of the NLRA that in a union certification election, it is the number of employees in the unit that is relevant in determining whether or not a majority favors the union. Yet, over the years the board has chosen to ignore this express language and has ruled that it only requires a favorable vote from a majority of those voting in order for the union to win. It is not hard to find examples of the union being certified the exclusive representative of all the employees when as few as 20 percent of the employees actually voted for the union.[28]

Even the seemingly innocuous requirement, imposed by the Wagner Act, that the employer "bargain collectively with representatives of his employees," has been used to favor the short-run interests of union officials and organized workers. First, it was not even suggested that a corresponding requirement applied to unions until, twelve years after it was enacted, the Wagner Act was amended by the Taft-Hartley Act. But more important than what the legislation actually says is how it has been interpreted and used. The congressional debates over the Wagner Act indicate that congressmen either did not intend, or were reluctant to admit they intended, that the collective bargaining requirement aimed at any particular pattern of outcomes.

27. Bennett, et al., *n.* 22, p. 50.
28. Bennett, et al., *n.* 22, pp. 54–55. Several recent appointments to the NLRB have resulted in some reversals of excessively pro-union precedents, a process that is fragile at best, given the history of the past half-century. See, for example, *Neufeld Porsche-Audi* (Case 20-CB-5272, 1984), where the Board reversed *Dalmo Victor II* (115 LRRM 2972, 1984) and decided that a union may not lawfully restrict the right of members to resign during a strike or penalize any member who does so.

Rather, the stated intent was that of establishing a process to facilitate bargaining between employers and employee representatives. This is reflected in the statement in 1935 by Senator Walsh to the effect that the intent was to "escort representatives to the bargaining door, not control what goes on behind the door."[29] Unfortunately, the impartiality suggested here is not in the least indicative of how the collective bargaining requirement has in fact been interpreted.

For example, bargaining is supposed to take place in "good faith."[30] While few will fault the spirit of good-faith bargaining, fewer yet have any idea of how to operationally define such a nebulous concept in an impartial way. Imprecision breeds on itself: The NLRB determined that ascertaining whether or not good-faith bargaining has been violated requires looking at the "totality of circumstances reflecting respondent's bargaining frame of mind."[31] The reality, as opposed to the rhetoric, has been a wide latitude for the board to rule that bad faith has occurred when bargaining does not proceed in ways that members of the board find agreeable. That this latitude has been used primarily against employers can hardly be considered debatable, even by committed advocates of unions. For example, unable to reach agreement with a union's international negotiators, a company made a proposal instead to the union locals, and as a consequence was found to have acted in bad faith. The firm that has reached an impasse in bargaining with a union is still "obligated to make some reasonable effort in *some* direction to compromise his differences with the union. . . . "[32] Employers have learned through sad experience that this means yielding to union wage demands beyond the point warranted by the long-run interests of all concerned, since doing so is often less costly than facing the "remedies" the NLRB is prepared to impose on those with an "anti-union animus."

Government has gone far beyond its traditional, and proper, role in the area of labor relations. Rather than refereeing a process that, in the long run, serves to benefit workers (unorganized as well as organized), investors, and consumers alike, the government has in effect decided that workers are the underdogs and, therefore, the sub-

29. Bennett, et al., *n*. 22, p. 62.

30. This language did not appear in the statutes until the Taft-Hartley Act, but the NLRB preceded the Taft-Hartley Act in using and interpreting this malleable concept.

31. Quoted in Bennett, et al., *n*. 22, p. 59.

32. *NLRB v. Reed & Prince Mfg. Co.*, 205 F 2d 131, at 134–135. Emphasis in original. Quoted in Bennett, et al., *n*. 22, p. 60.

set of these workers who are organized should receive privileges not available to others. The short-run effect of this perversion of the rule of law is to benefit a small minority of the work force at the expense of all other actors in the productive process. The long-run effect is to reduce the time horizon relevant to investment decisions and to reduce the economic well-being of all our citizens.

POLITICAL ACTIVITY OF UNIONS

Political actions in support of labor unions both reinforce and are reinforced by labor union support of particular political actions. Unions have been very effective in influencing the political process in support of legislation that increases the control of organized labor over business decisions.

The explanation for the political influence of organized labor is twofold. First, labor unions are organized around a few major concerns, higher wages and fringe benefits in the short run being one of the most important. It is well known that narrowly focused groups (typically those oriented around an occupational or professional interest) tend to be more easily organized and more effective politically than are those with a multitude of dispersed interests (e.g., consumers). Secondly, political action is most successful when organized self-interest is able to masquerade behind the rhetoric of a noble purpose. And it would be difficult to find any group that has been more adept than organized labor in disguising narrow self-interest with the mask of public interest. Unions have been very successful at using the political process to increase the incomes of their members at the expense of workers in general, while maintaining the pretense that unions are struggling for the well-being of all workers.

The success of this pretense is derived largely from the fact that organized labor has been able to project the image of a movement dedicated to the protection of workers' rights against the arbitrary power of big business.[33] Union-supported legislation that restricts the

---

33. In fact, the real battle that unions wage for their members is not against business, big or otherwise, but against other workers who are anxious to work in union jobs for less than union scale. See Reynolds, *n.* 15, pp. 47–54. Indeed, in the political arena, organized labor and established business interests are often working on the same side of the fence, both supporting legislation that restricts the options of unorganized workers and potential competitors to existing firms. The support that "domestic content" legislation received from both the UAW and the major U.S. automobile firms is a case in point.

discretion of capital owners, or their representatives, is often politically popular because it is perceived as a justifiable means of curtailing exploitive business practices. Surely, this explains much of the political appeal of minimum wage laws, maximum hour restrictions, and other legislation that limits the ability of employers to contract with employees. The distrust of big business has also been an important factor in much of the regulation government has imposed on business, beginning with the Interstate Commerce Act in 1887 and continuing through to the myriad regulations that characterize the current business environment. But regardless of why such legislation has been enacted, the result has been the same. It has created a setting in which nonunion workers are restricted from competing with union workers, either directly by offering to work for less or indirectly through the emergence of nonunion competitors to existing firms. This increases the ability of unions to extract short-run wage and salary concessions at the expense of long-run considerations of capital investment and productivity.

Organized labor has also been active in support of political measures to limit corporate practices that motivate corporate managers to pay attention to the long run. As we have previously discussed, arrangements that facilitate takeovers and mergers increase the pressure on management to consider the future consequences of current decisions. Also, compensation schemes such as stock options and bonuses perform the same function. Such innovative arrangements have evolved over time, as firms providing the most effective incentives for maintaining long-run productivity find their viability enhanced and their mode of operation imitated.[34] Not surprisingly, organized labor has generally supported legislation that restricts mergers and hampers takeover attempts. Union leaders are also quick to make a political issue out of bonus or stock-option plans for corporate executives. That "fat cat" corporate managers are arbitrarily confiscating money that could, would, and should otherwise go to more deserving recipients

---

34. A recent example of such an innovation is the compensation of executives whose jobs are terminated as a result of a successful takeover or merger. It has been argued that these "golden parachutes" provide incentives for corporate executives to take risks more in line with what their diversified shareholders would consider appropriate, and not to fight takeovers that would be in the shareholders' interest. See William J. Karney, "Pols Poking Holes in Golden Parachutes," *Wall Street Journal,* 16 April 1984, p. 32. But independent of whether or not golden parachutes do improve incentives, the important point is that they, like any innovation, are best evaluated in the marketplace. The value of new corporate arrangements will certainly be more accurately assessed by competition in markets than by politics in Congress.

(preferably unionized workers) is a politically attractive albeit zero-sum fiction. Consider the Deficit Reduction Act of 1984, which singles out for an extra tax burden executive pay resulting from a change in corporate ownership.[35] The degree of influence exerted by organized labor in support of any particular provision of this tax bill is, of course, debatable. But union support for political restrictions on management compensation clearly exists—and is influential.

The effect of union-supported restrictions of this type on corporate management is to reinforce the myopic thrust of union bargaining by shortening the time horizon of corporate management. Anything that reduces the incentive for corporate managers to value the future has the effect of lowering their resistance to union demands and increasing the vulnerability of capital to these demands. The tax that the shortsighted demands of unions imposes on business capital is just as destructive of economic productivity as are the taxes that government imposes on capital.

UNIONIZE NOW, STAGNATE LATER

The effect of union myopia on future productivity can be expected to show up in two ways. First, in anticipation of a union's negative impact on the return to capital, one would predict that the projected equity value of a newly unionized firm, or one threatened with unionization, will fall. Secondly, in those industries in which union power is strongest, one would expect that wage demands will eventually reduce the industry's competitiveness and, in the absence of government bailouts and protections, push it into serious decline.

The best measure of the future profitability, appropriately discounted, of a firm is given by the value of that firm's stock, assuming it is being bought and sold in an organized and open market. If a current decision is expected to reduce the future profitability of a firm, this will be reflected in an immediate decline in the price of the firm's stock. Two Massachusetts Institute of Technology economists, Richard Ruback and Martin Zimmerman, accordingly examined the impact on the price of a firm's stock caused by the filing of a union election petition and then by the results of that election. Based on data from 1962 to 1980, Ruback and Zimmerman concluded that, on

---

35. See Graef S. Crystal, "Congress Thinks It Knows Best About Executive Compensation," *Wall Street Journal*, 30 July 1984.

average, a successful union drive against a firm lowers the price of the firm's stock by 3.84 percent. This corresponds to an average loss of $46,800 per worker employed by the unionized firms.[36] This evidence reflects clearly the ability of unions to impose a tax on capital.

There are no economically neutral taxes, whether government imposed or union imposed, and investors will respond to the union confiscation of capital returns. This investor response will necessarily reduce the efficiency of the unionized firm, or industry, although the exact form of the response is difficult to predict a priori. On the one hand, the reduction in returns to current and potential investors reduces the industry's investment appeal. This consideration suggests that capital formation will be retarded by the effects of unionization. Also, with profitability affected adversely by unions, internal financing of capital will be hampered. On the other hand, one way to reduce the burden of union wage-demands is by substituting capital for labor. And, indeed, one can be sure that the *ratio* of capital to labor will, over time, increase in response to excessive wage requirements. Whether or not this substitution effect will motivate an absolute increase in the amount of capital is not clear a priori. If, as is likely, the industry declines, or fails to grow as rapidly as otherwise, because of the union, then the capital-labor ratio can be increasing while the level of capital formation is being retarded. But even if the amount of capital in the industry actually increases, it will be the result of a union-induced distortion in the capital-labor mix, which will reduce both the efficiency of the industry and its ability to compete.

Certainly the evidence strongly suggests that an industry that becomes subject to a virtual union monopoly over labor is on its way to becoming a sick industry. When a union has the power to do so, it will obtain wage and benefit packages for its current members that cannot be sustained and, indeed, will mean less opportunity for future employees. The U.S. steel and automobile industries are notable examples. Both industries require large amounts of long-lived and immobile capital, which are subject to exploitation by powerful unions. Not surprisingly, these industries have been confronted with industry-

---

36. Even the threat of unionization in the form of an unsuccessful union effort results in a 1.32 percent decline in a firm's stock price, or a $7,400 loss for each employee. See Richard S. Ruback and Martin B. Zimmerman, "Unionization and Profitability: Evidence from the Capital Market" (NBER Conference Paper, Cambridge, Mass., May 1983).

wide unions that, for several decades, have presented management with an effective labor monopoly. The result has been labor costs that when measured against productivity, have been and are substantially higher than those faced by most other U.S. industries or by foreign automobile and steel producers. For example, U.S. auto firms face wage and benefit costs of about $22 to $23 per hour for assembly line workers. This is approximately 70 percent higher than the national average for U.S. factory workers. And it exceeds by a wide margin the $12 to $14 that Japanese auto workers cost their employers. Similar disparities are seen when the salaries of U.S. steelworkers are compared with those of their domestic and foreign counterparts.

The long-run impact of these excessive wages is perfectly predictable. Capital formation has lagged in the U.S. steel industry, with outdated and inefficient equipment and techniques still being widely used. Without political protection against foreign competition (provided through such devices as direct import restrictions, tariffs, or "domestic content" requirements), the technologically backward U.S. steel industry would be in even worse shape than it already is. The U.S. automobile industry has managed to maintain a technologically more current capital base than has the steel industry, although car makers have also lagged behind foreign competition in important ways in this regard. Sales of U.S. auto manufacturers were far below their previous peaks even in the strong recovery year of 1984, and the industry has reversed its traditional stand in favor of free trade and has now joined its erstwhile union opponents in pushing for stronger trade restrictions.[37] Despite trade restrictions and the Chrysler bailout, 170,000 auto industry jobs (approximately 23 percent of the total industry work force) have been lost since 1978, and the prognosis is that even with a good recovery, more jobs will be irreversibly lost over the next decade. The auto and steel industries are unfortunately not the only example of shortsighted union demands contributing to the decline of basic industries and to shrinking employment opportunities for union members in those industries. The railroad and the

37. The United Auto Workers supported free trade for a long time. This was a sensible position for them to take when the U.S. auto industry was dominant in the world market and a major exporter. As the competitiveness of the U.S. auto industry eroded, however, the UAW became a political force for domestic-content legislation, import quotas, and other trade restrictions designed to protect their noncompetitive wage structure at the expense of the consumer.

rubber industries might also be cited as evidence of the long-run effect of strong labor unions on economic productivity.[38]

The union myopia that motivates excessive wage demands has been detrimental to the long-run well-being of all sections of the economy—consumers, providers of capital, and employees alike. But this economically destructive shortsightedness is the completely predictable consequence of political action that increases the power of unions over business decisions and over the allocation of business profits. Political attempts to rescue unions from the plight in which they find themselves, attempts that ordinarily involve granting them yet more power and imposing yet more restrictions on business decisions, will prove just as self-defeating in the long run as have previous attempts.

CONCLUSION

We have examined a form of capital taxation that is seldom recognized as such. Government, by granting privileges to the minority of workers who are organized into unions, imposes a tax that is just as pernicious in its effect on capital formation as is any explicit tax. This is explained by the fact that the incentive structure of union organizations motivates myopic decisions, in contrast to the incentives built into the structure of private firms and corporations—incentives that reward those who give appropriate attention to the long-run consequences of current decisions. As long as owners and managers of private businesses are free to allocate revenues between shareholders, employees, and capital investment in response to market forces, decisions will be made that promote capital formation and lead to long-run economic growth. Unfortunately, government regulation of labor relations has increasingly usurped business control over decisions relevant to capital investment and has passed that control to union officials. The result has been to lessen the attention business decisions pay to the future, to substitute excessive wages for appropriate capital investment, and to reduce the competitive vitality of major U.S. industries—a result that has harmed many of the very workers unions purport to help.

---

38. Obviously union demands are not the entire explanation for the decline of heavily organized industries. The myopia of labor organizations imposes a heavy tax on these industries. As is clear from other chapters in this volume, however, this is only one source of the tax burden that U.S. business must shoulder. But it should further be recognized that many of the tax burdens discussed elsewhere in this volume enjoy the active political support of unions and their allies.

12

COMMANDING RESOURCES: THE MILITARY SECTOR AND CAPITAL FORMATION

Lloyd J. Dumas

INTRODUCTION

The economy is an intriguing, intricately interconnected web of human activity and institutions. There is the fascinating process by which the efforts of human beings are combined with the tools they have created to transform raw materials of little apparent value into goods and services much more attuned to the satisfaction of wants and needs. There are the complex decisions that must be made, decisions that affect the mix of goods and services produced and the patterns of distribution of the means for acquiring them—decisions that touch all members of the society during every day of their lives.

It is much too easy, whether theorizing or empirically investigating, to become so wrapped up in all of this as to forget that there is a rather simple, yet overriding purpose of this complicated beehive of activity—a purpose that sets the context within which economic analysis must proceed. The central purpose of economic activity is to enhance the quality of human life by providing the material standard of living.

The mere act of producing a good or service does not guarantee that economic activity is taking place. Economic value is generated only when the good or service produced adds to the standard of living. Not all goods and services do this. For example, make-work activity, such as the classic case of digging holes then immediately refilling them, provides a service that clearly adds nothing to the standard of living. No economic value is generated.

Beyond this, there are activities that produce goods or services of value, but not of *economic* value in any material sense. Building a new church, for example, may add spiritual value to the life of the community. Yet it adds nothing to the material standard of living— it is not intended to. Building an apartment house, on the other hand, may be considerably less uplifting, yet it clearly increases material well-being by adding to the available housing stock. It is not that the church is without value, or even of lesser value than the apartment house. It is simply that the apartment house provides *economic* value, while the value provided by the church lies outside the economic realm.

There is, of course, a great deal of subjectivity inevitably involved in the determination of human wants and valuations. And all categorical definitions are to some extent arbitrary. Yet the above distinctions are especially useful in understanding the structural impact of military spending on the functioning of the economy in general and on the process of capital formation in particular. Thus, they are worth highlighting here.

Whatever its direct contribution to our security, military spending is *noncontributive* economically, in the sense that it adds nothing to the material standard of living. On the other hand, producing ordinary consumer goods (such as food, clothing, furniture) is clearly contributive, as is producing capital goods that increase the economy's productive capacity (such as metalworking machinery, oil refining equipment, industrial furnaces). Consumer goods add to the immediate standard of living, while capital goods serve as tools, adding directly to the standard of living that the economy is capable of generating in the future.

The activity of producing military goods and services, however, is an entirely different matter. Fighter planes, battle tanks, cruise missiles, nuclear warheads, etc., add nothing to the present standard of living. They do not provide the nourishment, entertainment, housing, transportation, and the like that are the hallmark of ordinary consumer goods. Nor do they increase the economy's capacity to produce— they are not the means of further production. Thus while they may have military value, political value, or perhaps other forms of value, they do not have economic value.

Though military goods do not have economic value, they do have economic cost. The production of these noncontributive goods and services requires the same basic economic inputs that are necessary for the production of goods and services that do have economic value. This value forgone, this opportunity cost of military production, is not adequately captured by the usual short-term "guns or butter" trade-off that has been so often discussed. To this must be added a "guns or machine tools" trade-off that has much deeper, longer lasting, more structural impact on the economy.

To the extent that economic resources are diverted from contributive consumer goods production, there is an immediate and possibly painful sacrifice in terms of the present living standard. But to the extent that this diversion of resources comes at the expense of contributive capital formation and persists for prolonged periods, a process of long-term economic deterioration may be set in motion that may eventually cripple the economy. This latter possibility is the focus of this analysis.

THE MILITARY–INDUSTRIAL COMPLEX AS A NONCONTRIBUTIVE COMMAND SECTOR

Whether or not a product has economic value depends upon the nature of the good or service itself. Therefore, money cost or price is not necessarily an accurate reflection of economic value. The fact that a church, a missile, and an apartment building might have precisely the same money price in no way establishes that they are of equivalent *economic* value. Nevertheless, to the extent that the price of a good or service is set by the unfettered forces of supply and demand in a free market, neoclassical microeconomic theory maintains that the price reflects the marginal value of the product to its purchasers. The value may not be economic (in a materialistic sense), but price is still a meaningful reflection of whatever form of value the good or service has to those who buy it.

However, this assurance of a connection of price and value no longer necessarily exists when the product's price is determined by non-market processes. In such a situation, money price does not establish even the existence of value, economic or otherwise, let alone its magnitude. This is precisely the case in the American military sector.

The system of military production in the United States does not operate by free market principles. It is the closest thing to centrally planned socialism in the American economy. The Pentagon essentially plays the role of central management of this system.[1] The nature and quantity of output, as well as its price, are not set by impersonal market forces. For the vast majority of products, they are set by the interaction of the central planning authority in the Pentagon and the managers of military-industrial firms. In facilities wholly owned by the government (such as the nuclear weapons facilities of the Department of Energy), the military central planners have even more complete control.

Military-industrial firms operate in a peculiar world characterized perhaps more than anything else by the existence of only one customer. Even when they sell their product to the governments of other countries, they sell equipment first produced for the American military and do so only under federal government authorization. In terms of economic theory, they seem to be operating in a monopsonistic market. Yet their situation does not really fit the standard case of monopsony. Contracts are not, on the whole, let by this single buyer through the mechanism of competitive bidding by the group of firms vying for this business. They are instead largely negotiated.

For many years, law and regulation have explicitly stated that the DoD is to award contracts on the basis of competitive bidding. However, the Armed Services Procurement Regulation provides for exceptions to this rule under specified conditions, and this is one case where the exceptions have apparently become the rule. According to J. Ronald Fox, former Assistant Secretary of the Army for procurement,

> Prior to World War II, virtually all defense procurement was accomplished by formal advertising; during the 1960's and early 1970's by far the largest part of defense procurement has been accomplished through negotiation. In every year since the beginning of the Korean War, more than 80% of all military procurement dollars have been awarded through negotiation.[2]

In 1980, more specific data were provided by Jacques Gansler, an analyst with long experience at high levels of both the DoD and military industry. According to Gansler, as of 1976,

> . . . only around 8 percent of DoD business is done through formally

1. S. Melman, *Pentagon Capitalism* (New York: McGraw Hill, 1970).
2. J. R. Fox, *Arming America: How the U.S. Buys Weapons* (Cambridge: Harvard University Press, 1974), pp.253–54.

advertised price competitions. Most of the other 92 percent fits under
. . . exceptions to the general rule. . . .[3]

In a masterpiece of understatement, he goes on to point out,

When over 90 percent of the business is done under "exceptions" to the
normal practices, it is appropriate to consider alternative regulations rather
than to continue to believe that the normal practice is in operation.[4]

In short, there is little that resembles a free marketplace in operation here.

The microeconomic consumer theory that gives rise to the proposition that transactions prices represent (a lower bound on) the value
of product rests on the assumption that the individuals whose money
is being spent are the same individuals who are deciding on what to
buy. In ordinary markets, this is a reasonable thing to assume. But
in the case of the demand for military goods, those whose money is
being spent, i.e., present and future taxpayers, have very little direct
influence on demand decisions. With generalized congressional oversight, it is the DoD bureaucracy that makes specific demand decisions.

It is generally assumed that these procurement decisions are made
with the objective of maximizing national security, subject to budgetary constraints. Even if this were true, the operational vagueness of
this objective leaves plenty of room for widely varying judgments as
to how it might be achieved. In such a situation, what should be
extraneous considerations, such as interservice rivalry, political influence, the possibility (often realized) of moving into lucrative positions in military industry in the future, etc., may unduly color
purchasing decisions. As a result, prices paid by taxpayers for these
products need have no necessary relation to their real security value
to those taxpayers.

Beyond this, the mechanism through which actual transactions prices
are established for these products further separates these money prices
from any normal concept of a market price. In contracting with a
military-industrial firm, the DoD establishes a payment formula that
specifies the way in which final purchase price will be determined.
Commonly used generic types of payment formulas include "cost plus
fixed fee," "fixed price," "fixed price incentive," and "cost plus in-

3. J. Gansler, *The Defense Industry* (Cambridge: MIT Press, 1980), p. 75.
4. Ibid., p. 76.

centive fee." Some of these formulas are explicitly designed to provide financial incentives for least-cost production.

In practice, however, regardless of specific contract language, virtually all major military contracts have operated as if they were "cost plus." That is, the producing firms have eventually been reimbursed whatever it cost them to produce the equipment, plus an additional amount for profit. Operating under a cost-plus contract provides no incentive for efficient production. In fact, to the extent that managers are concerned with expanding the size of the company by enlarging revenues as well as earning profits, there is every incentive to drive costs as high as possible. This process of cost escalation is not subject to the restraint that would be exerted in a free market. It is instead restrained only by what could be called a political "what you can get away with" constraint.

The failure of these payment formulas to encourage efficient, low cost production is partly a result of flaws in their design, as I have argued elsewhere in some detail.[5] But it is perhaps even more a result of an unwillingness to rigidly enforce the terms of the original contract. The strong propensity to renegotiate contracts so that revenues will cover whatever "cost overruns" have developed makes nonsense of any contractual incentives for efficiency. Until the DoD is ready to use effective incentive formulas and refuse to adjust contracts after the fact, even if this bankrupts the contractor and/or delays the weapons program, cost-plus will be the operational rule.

For its part, the DoD has little incentive to introduce such discipline. To do so could easily disrupt the production plans that the Pentagon's central planners had established. Perhaps more important, rising weapons costs provide the DoD with a built-in argument for expanded military budgets, an argument that has been extremely effective politically. There is little evidence that the escalation of weapons costs has produced any real disadvantage to the Department of Defense. The DoD is a very large bureaucracy, and like any other large bureaucracy, it is fertile ground for any process that provides effective arguments for the maintenance and expansion of its budget.

There is thus a combination of military-industrial firms operating under an incentive system that encourages inefficiency, a central planning bureaucracy set up to achieve an operationally vaguely defined

---

5. L. J. Dumas, "Payment Functions and the Productive Efficiency of Military-Industrial Firms," *Journal of Economic Issues* 10 (no. 2, June 1976): 454–74.

objective and unwilling to discipline the producers under its control, and a Congress only too willing to open wide the public coffers. The effect of this powerful combination is to create an environment that invites waste and excess. The "$500 hammer" and "$7,000 coffee pot" stories of excessive payments made by the Pentagon for simple items and spare parts represent only the leading edge of a system in which value and price have become completely disconnected. The point is that they are neither isolated cases nor the result of some bizarre aberration. The "$500 hammer" and the "$7,000 coffee pot" may be more extreme than most, but they are natural outcomes of the context in which America's system of military production operates.

The military-industrial complex is not a market sector. It is a command sector. It is insensitive to the usual market forces. Military-industrial firms service a large well-funded customer willing to cover whatever costs they incur. They do not bid for the labor, machinery, and other productive resources they require on the same basis as do firms whose operations are subject to a market test. Rather, they are in a position to pay whatever they need to pay to obtain the resources they want. Thus, in the military production system, in effect political decisions are made to provide whatever funds are necessary to acquire whatever resources are necessary at whatever price must be paid. The practical result is as effective a preemption of productive resources from the commercially oriented private sector as if the government were diverting these resources by decree.

Over the period since the end of the Second World War, the military sector has in fact preempted substantial quantities of productive resources of all kinds: raw materials, fuels, land, capital equipment, buildings, and labor of many grades. In terms of long-run economic impacts, the most important resources diverted to this form of non-contributive activity have been capital equipment and human capital.

On the whole, the diversion of human capital has been quite direct. Highly trained individuals have been attracted to military-oriented work by higher pay, and in some cases higher prestige and the opportunity to work with more advanced equipment as well. The economically most significant form of this internal "brain drain" into the military sector has undoubtedly been the diversion of engineers and scientists.

The diversion of physical capital has sometimes been direct and sometimes indirect. Direct diversion involves the taking of physical capital for military-serving uses, as for example through the purchases of metalworking machines by military industrial firms. Indirect diversion occurs when financial capital is taken for noncontributive purposes to such an extent that contributive investment is starved for lack of the ability to finance it. More will be said about this shortly.

The process of capital formation clearly exerts strong influence on the future prospects of any economy. But it is not capital formation per se that is so economically important; it is the formation of capital that supports contributive activity. The diversion of capital into a military support role, whether direct or indirect, impedes this crucial process.

Though the diversion of human capital is far too important to be ignored, the emphasis of this analysis will be on the diversion of physical and financial capital. It is to this matter that we now turn.

THE MILITARY SECTOR AND CAPITAL RESOURCES

As a noncontributive command sector, it is clear that the military can and does preempt a substantial amount of capital resources. However, trying to produce an accurate comprehensive estimate of the extent of this diversion is quite a large and complex problem. Part of the difficulty lies in the problem of finding and aggregating all the pieces of the vast interconnected network that is the military sector. An accurate estimate would have to add to the capital directly used by the military agencies of the federal government all of the capital taken by the 20,000 or so prime military contracting firms and the more than 100,000 subcontractors. If all the data were readily available in the proper form, one could conceptually use techniques such as input-output analysis to derive reasonable estimates. Even so this would be a major project.

However, the data are not readily available in the proper form. For example, though it is relatively easy to obtain data that allows identification of firms serving as prime military contractors and the value of their contracts, data on such matters as capital equipment investments and number of engineers and scientists employed by the military-serving divisions of these firms is much harder to come by. Furthermore, it is no easy task even to fully identify all of the subcontracting firms, let alone get these data for them. Beyond this, often data that are available are published in a form that tends to obscure rather than clarify the extent of diversion.

In some cases it is argued that the necessary information is proprietary; in others, that matters of secrecy and security prevent disclosure; in still others perhaps, that the cost of making the information available may be excessive. Whether there are legitimate or illegitimate reasons for these data difficulties, the net effect is to make the task of producing even reasonable estimates of the extent of the military sector claim on these resources much more difficult than it otherwise would be.

A thoroughgoing attempt at untangling these data is simply beyond the scope of the present analysis. Consequently, the estimates presented here are unavoidably rougher and less complete than would be desirable. Nevertheless, they should present a sufficient picture of the extent of capital diversion to convey an appreciation for the seriousness of the military sector's impact on capital formation.

Physical Capital

It was earlier argued that the mode of organization of the system of military production in the United States is the closest thing to centrally planned socialism in the American economy. To the reasons given earlier, another can now be added—government ownership of the means of production. Much of the physical capital used in military industry is at least formally privately owned, though its use is in practice largely controlled by government contracting decisions. However, the various military agencies of the federal government do directly own quite a substantial amount of physical capital.

Some of this government-owned capital is in the form of landholdings, some in the form of structures, and some is in the form of highly specialized maintenance or test facilities. But there is also a substantial amount of direct production equipment, such as metalworking machine tools.

Table 12–1 provides data on the stock of physical capital owned by the Department of Defense and its various subagencies, as of the end of September 1983. At that time, the total reported value of all physical capital owned by the military was $474.9 billion. That there may be some understatement involved here is indicated by the fact that, for example, the nearly $300 million value of the roughly 12.2 million acres owned by the U.S. Army implies an average land value of under $25 per acre.[6] Nevertheless, it will be assumed that the re-

---

6. This may well be the result of valuing the land at acquisition cost. The same approach is applied in valuing buildings and other long-lived equipment, such as ships.

Table 12–1. Department of Defense Holdings of Physical Capital as of 30 September 1983 (Billions of $).

	Dep't of Defense[a] (Total)	Army	Navy[b]	Air Force	Defense Logistics Agency
ALL PHYSICAL CAPITAL	474.9	114.6	213.4	131.6	14.3
REAL PROPERTY	57.4	18.8	17.6	21.0	—
Land Cost (Million Acres)	—	0.3 (12.2)	—	0.2	—
Buildings	—	13.1	—	13.3	—
Other Structures	—	5.5	—	7.5	—
CONSTRUCTION IN PROGRESS	9.3	4.3	3.0	2.0	—
OTHER PHYSICAL CAPITAL	408.2	91.5	192.8	108.6	14.3
Weapons & Other Military Equipment in Use	267.1	45.7	153.2	68.3	—
Equipment, Material & Supplies in Stock	114.0	37.4	30.3	35.7	10.6
Plant Equipment	20.2	7.9	8.2	2.4	0.6
Excess, Surplus Property	5.6	0.4	0.6	1.6	3.0

SOURCES: *Department of Defense Real and Personal Property* (30 Sept. 1983) (Washington Headquarters Services, Directorate for Information, Operations and Reports, U.S. Department of Defense). Department of the Army, "Cost and Rentals of Military Real Property Controlled (30 Sept. 1983)" and "Acreage of Military Real Property Controlled and Located at Installations (30 Sept. 1983)," unpublished. Department of the Air Force data provided to author in correspondence from Chief, Policy Control Branch, Real Property Division, Directorate of Engineering and Services, Office of the Assistant Secretary, Department of the Air Force, unpublished.

[a]Includes Army, Navy, Marines, Air Force, Defense Logistics Agency, and other defense agencies.
[b]Includes Marine Corps.

ported values are essentially accurate. To the extent that they may be understated, the analysis will then be conservative.

Not surprisingly, the largest single category of capital in this summary is "Weapons and other military equipment in use," valued at $267.1 billion or more than 56% of the total. These are the "tools" with which the military works in carrying out its main functions. The vast majority—perhaps nearly all—of this type of capital is frozen into a form specialized to noncontributive use. The second largest category, inventories of equipment, materials and supplies, valued at $114 billion, makes up another 24% of total capital. It is likely that much of this category is also specialized to noncontributive use. Thus, the largest part—more than $380 billion, or roughly 80%—of the physical capital owned by the military may have been cast into forms essentially without contributive use. The economically valuable services of vast quantities of productive resources embedded in this capital have consequently been permanently lost to the contributive sector.

Real property, in the form of land, buildings, utilities and other structures accounts for $57.4 billion, or some 12% of the total. Though it is less than 5% of the total, the $20.2 billion of plant equipment directly owned by the military represents a large stock of equipment with considerable productive capacity. It is sufficiently important to warrant further attention later.

In absolute terms, the huge amounts of capital diverted to this noncontributive command sector are impressive enough. But it is also worth comparing this claim on capital to that of sectors that do generate economic value, in order to get a feeling for the relative capital drain.

At the end of 1983, the value of the net stock of all capital equipment, structures, and inventories owned by all manufacturing establishments in the United States combined was $1,011.9 billion.[7] This stands against the $474.9 billion value of the stock of all physical capital owned by the Department of Defense as of September 30 of that year.

These two numbers are not precisely comparable, since they are not for the same point in time and since the Department of Defense figures include landholdings. However, unless the Department of Defense physical capital inventories were decreasing during the last quarter of 1983 (which is highly unlikely, given the huge military buildup that the Reagan administration was pursuing at the time), using the September 30 Department of Defense figure as an estimate for year-end 1983 would be conservative. Furthermore, land costs are very small in comparison with other forms of physical capital for the Army and Air Force (for which separate data on landholdings are presented in Table 12–1), less than 0.3% of the capital stocks held by those services. To be conservative, it will be arbitrarily assumed that land costs for the Department of Defense as a whole are more than three times that high, or 1% of the total.

The adjusted Department of Defense capital stock figure for 1983 is thus $470 billion, as against the $1,011.9 billion value of the net

---

7. U.S. Bureau of the Census, *Statistical Abstract of the United States, 1985* (Washington, D.C.: U.S. Government Printing Office, 1985), p. 758 (Table 1350).

stock of capital equipment, structures, and inventories in manufacturing industry. Thus, the stock of physical capital preempted by the noncontributive military sector was more than 46% as large as the stock of physical capital owned by all manufacturing establishments in the United States combined! This is even more striking when you consider that all of the physical capital owned by privately owned military-industrial firms is included in the manufacturing industry figure. Were estimates available of the value of this military-industry-owned physical capital (which after all is part of the noncontributive military production sector), it would be subtracted from the denominator and added to the numerator in this calculation. With that adjustment, the revised estimate of the relative amount of physical capital diverted would be still higher. Therefore, it seems reasonable to estimate that the military sector has preempted from the civilian economy a stock of capital whose book value is roughly half that of the capital stock held by all manufacturing establishments in the United States combined. Looked at another way, if there had been no diversion of capital, U.S. manufacturing industry could have a 50 percent larger stock of physical capital (in quantity and/or quality) with which to work, without there having been any increase in the book value of the nation's capital.

The comparisons just presented are intended to convey only a rough overall picture of the military sector's physical capital drain. They are subject to some serious limitations. For one thing, the structural inefficiency and nonmarket character of the present system of military production in the United States disconnects price from value, as I have argued earlier. Consequently, to the extent that the book value of items included in the military capital stock reflects excessive prices paid, these values are distorted. The result will be a substantial overestimate of the true dollar value of this capital stock as compared to the capital stock in manufacturing industries that do operate in a market setting. It could be argued that the capital drain has therefore been overstated.

On the other hand, the financial capital used inefficiently to purchase the overpriced items in the military capital stock, had it been available to market-oriented enterprises, could have been used to finance investment in capital goods that were more efficiently produced and more appropriately priced. Thus it could be argued that the book value of items in the military capital stock does represent a reasonable picture of capital drain, in the sense of investment opportunities lost to market-oriented manufacturers. In other words, a billion dollars of greatly overpriced items in the military stock of physical capital still represents a billion dollars of purchasing power that could have been used by market-oriented manufacturers to buy more reasonably priced items of capital goods. The fact that the military spent that billion dollars very inefficiently does not alter the fact that its diversion cost the market-oriented manufacturers a chance to spend the billion more efficiently to expand their capacity qualitatively or quantitatively.

It might also be argued that it is inappropriate to include weapons in the military capital stock since they are not capital goods in the same sense that factory buildings, metalworking machines, and the like are capital goods. On the other hand, weapons are without question created by the military system as an important class of "tools" with which that system attempts to produce its "product," national security. In that sense, weapons are capital goods of the military in the same way that furnaces are capital goods of the steel industry.

These considerations are sufficiently important to caution us to use the earlier military-sector/manufacturing-industry capital stock comparisons only as rough general indications that the diversion of physical capital is substantial. However, it is possible to look more closely at the issue of physical capital drain in ways that avoid some of the objections raised above. In particular, we can focus on the diversions of industrial plants and industrial plant equipment.

As shown above in Table 12–1, the DoD held inventories of plant equipment valued at $20.2 billion as of September 30, 1983. According to the DoD, the book value of this stock of plant equipment had increased by $3.3 billion over fiscal year 1982.[8] In 1982, net capital investment in equipment *and* structures by all manufacturing establishments in the U.S. was only $1.4 billion.[9] Of course, 1982 was a deep recession year, with unemployment rates rising halfway to those prevailing during the Great Depression of the 1930s. The following year, during the "recovery," the situation was far worse, with net investment in plant and equipment in manufacturing industries dropping well below zero, to −$6.6 billion.

Rather than comparing the 1982 figures directly, it would be more

8. *Department of Defense Real and Personal Property (September 30, 1983)*, Washington Headquarters Services, Directorate for Information, Operations and Reports, U.S. Department of Defense, p. 7.

9. See *n.* 7.

reasonable to compare the military sector rate of net investment in plant equipment with an average rate of net investment in plant equipment alone by manufacturers. The average net investment in plant equipment by all U.S. manufacturing over the three-year period 1980–82 was $8.8 billion. The 1982 net investment in plant equipment by the DoD was, as previously stated, $3.3 billion. Thus, in 1982 the DoD alone invested in plant equipment to the extent of nearly 38 percent of the average annual net investment in plant equipment by all manufacturing establishments in the United States combined! And again, the data on manufacturing establishments' investment is overstated because it includes military industrial manufacturers. Thus, this comparison is conservative.

The physical capital directly owned by the military in the form of industrial plants and plant equipment is operated under a variety of arrangements. Facilities owned *and* operated by the military are referred to as GOGO plants ("government-owned, government-operated"). In many cases, government-owned plant equipment and even entire industrial plants are operated by private contractors. Such facilities are designated as GOCO plants ("government-owned, contractor-operated"). There are also a few JOCO plants ("jointly owned, contractor-operated").

As shown in Table 12–2, the DoD directly owned a total of 113 industrial plants. These were located in nearly three-quarters of the

Table 12–2.   Industrial Plants Owned by the U.S. Armed Forces, 1984.

	Army	*Navy*[c]	*Air Force*	*Combined*
Production Facilities	37	21	12	70
GOGO[a]	6	2	0	8
GOCO[b]	31	19	12	62
Maintenance Facilities (all GOGO)	10	27	6	43
Total Plants	47	48	18	113

SOURCE: U.S. Department of Defense, *Defense Industrial Reserve Report,* transmitted to the President of the Senate and the Speaker of the House 18 April 1985.

[a]Government-owned, government-operated.
[b]Government-owned, contractor-operated.
[c]Includes Marine Corps.

states throughout the country. The government operated 51 of these plants itself, contracting out the operation of the remaining 62 plants to privately owned military-industrial firms. All of this latter group of GOCO plants were production facilities, while only16 percent of the GOGO plants were used for production activities.

Table 12–3 focuses on only those industrial plants both owned *and* operated by the armed forces. The total reported value of the real property and plant equipment associated with these 51 GOGO plants in 1984 was nearly $7.4 billion. Eight of these plants were actual production facilities, involving physical capital with a reported value approaching a billion dollars, as shown in Table 12–4. The remaining 43 maintenance facilities involved reported value of physical capital of nearly $6.5 billion (see Table 12–5).

Table 12–6 presents data for the 62 industrial production facilities that are owned by the Armed Forces but operated by private contractors. The combined value of physical capital in these GOCO facilities was reported at more than $5.3 billion in 1984.

Aside from entire industrial production plants owned by the military, there is a great deal of government-owned physical capital in the hands of many private military contractors. As of September 30, 1984, the DoD reported that more than 900 contractors possessed such

Table 12–3. Total Government-Owned, Government-Operated (GOGO) Military-Industrial Plant Facilities and Related Equipment, Fiscal Year 1984 (10/1/83–9/30/84).

	Army	*Navy*[a]	*Air Force*	*Combined*
Number of Plants	16	29	6	51
Real Property ($ Millions)	$1,334.9	$2,615.1	$ 379.1	$4,329.1
Industrial Plant Equipment ($ Millions)	$ 265.1	$ 505.2	$ 301.5	$1,071.8
Other Plant Equipment ($ Millions)	$ 256.3	$1,057.6	$ 651.8	$1,965.7
Total Physical Capital ($ Millions)	$1,856.3	$4,177.9	$1,332.4	$7,366.6

SOURCE: U.S. Department of Defense, *Summary of Departmental Industrial Reserve Plants/ Maintenance Facilities Reports*, FY 1984, unpublished.

[a]Includes the Marine Corps.

Table 12–4.   Government-Owned, Government-Operated (GOGO) Military-Industrial Production Plants and Related Equipment, Fiscal Year 1984 (10/1/83–9/30/84).

	Army	*Navy*[a]	*Air Force*	*Combined*
Number of Plants	6	2	0	8
Real Property ($ Millions)	$459.4	$ 34.8	—	$494.2
Industrial Plant Equipment ($ Millions)	$209.6	$ 56.6	—	$266.2
Other Plant Equipment ($ Millions)	$116.3	$ 42.3	—	$158.6
Total Physical Capital ($ Millions)	$785.4	$133.7	—	$919.1

SOURCE: U.S. Department of Defense, *Summary of Departmental Industrial Reserve Plants/ Maintenance Facilities Reports,* FY 1984, unpublished.

[a]Includes the Marine Corps.

government property. Half of these were large businesses, nearly 40 percent were small businesses, and the remainder were nonprofit organizations. Together, they hold DoD physical capital valued at a total of more than $9.7 billion. Nearly 60 percent of this reported dollar value was plant equipment, including almost 42,000 items clas-

Table 12–5.   Government-Owned, Government-Operated (GOGO) Military-Industrial Maintenance Facilities and Related Equipment, Fiscal Year 1984 (10/1/83–9/30/84).

	Army	*Navy*[a]	*Air Force*	*Combined*
Number of Plants	10	27	6	43
Real Property ($ Millions)	$ 875.5	$2,580.3	$ 379.1	$3,834.9
Industrial Plant Equipment ($ Millions)	$ 55.5	$ 448.6	$ 301.5	$ 805.6
Other Plant Equipment ($ Millions)	$ 140.0	$1,015.3	$ 651.8	$1,807.1
Total Physical Capital	$1,070.9	$4,044.2	$1,332.4	$6,447.6

SOURCE: U.S. Department of Defense, *Summary of Departmental Industrial Reserve Plants/ Maintenance Facilities Reports,* FY 1984, unpublished.

[a]Includes the Marine Corps.

Table 12–6.   Government-Owned, Contractor-Operated (GOCO) Military-Industrial Production Plants and Related Equipment, Fiscal Year 1984 (10/1/83–9/30/84).

	Army	Navy[a]	Air Force	Combined
Number of Plants	31	19	12	62
Real Property ($ Millions)	$2,389.6	$345.4	$509.3	$3,244.3
Industrial Plant Equipment ($ Millions)	$ 674.0	$169.2	$151.6	$ 994.8
Other Plant Equipment ($ Millions)	$ 757.8	$ 75.5	$285.4	$1,118.7
Total Physical Capital	$3,821.5	$590.1	$946.3	$5,357.9

SOURCE: U.S. Department of Defense, *Summary of Departmental Industrial Reserve Plants/Maintenance Facilities Reports*, FY 1984, unpublished.

[a]Includes the Marine Corps.

sified as industrial plant equipment.[10] Though it is unclear from the relevant DoD sources, it is possible that some or all of the GOCO facilities are included in these data.

The Department of Defense has special plant equipment packages in storage at various locations. According to DoD,

> A plant equipment package (PEP) is a complement of active and idle machine tools and other industrial manufacturing equipment held by and under the control of DoD to produce particular defense materiel or defense supporting items at a specific level of output in the event of an emergency. PEP's may include a few machine tools to supplement a particular planned emergency producer's facilities, or may consist of a complete production line of machine tools that is either retained in place, or in a contractor's plant or in Government storage.[11]

In 1984, there were 162 PEPs containing more than 27,000 items of industrial plant equipment with a reported value of over $1 billion.[12]

More details on at least part of the military's industrial plant equip-

10. U.S. Department of Defense, *Report of Government (DoD) Facilities in Possession of Contractors (DAR & APP B/C-311, FAR/DFARS 45.505-14) as of 30 September 1984 (Report No. 3400625, DoD Summary)*, Dec. 1984, p. 117.

11. U.S. Department of Defense, *Defense Industrial Reserve Report (January 1984–December 1984)*, p. 3.

12. Ibid.

Table 12–7.   Defense Industrial Plant Equipment Center (DIPEC) Inventory of Active and Idle Industrial Plant Equipment, as of 2 March 1985.

Type of Equipment	Items	Value ($Millions)
Metalworking-Cutting	44,611	$1,501.5
Metalworking-Forming	9,102	$ 303.9
Metalworking-Other	6,106	$ 105.0
Measuring and Testing	16,665	$ 316.9
General Plant	16,713	$ 535.0
TOTAL	93,197	$2,762.3

SOURCE: Letter to author from Director, Office of Planning and Financial Management, DIPEC (28 March 1985).

Note: DIPEC is part of the Defense Logistics Agency, not the individual armed forces, and is located at Memphis, Tennessee.

ment inventories are given in Table 12–7. As of March 2, 1985, the Defense Industrial Plant Equipment Center (DIPEC) at Memphis, Tennessee (operated by the Defense Logistics Agency), listed a total of more than 93,000 pieces of such equipment valued at nearly $2.8 billion in its active and idle inventory. The average value of an item in this inventory was thus nearly $30,000. Metalworking equipment accounted for almost two-thirds of the inventoried items and nearly 70% of the reported value. Such equipment, most assuredly, has valuable alternative use in contributive manufacturing industry.

In addition to all of this, the Department of Defense operates a special program of advanced contingency purchase agreements with the machine tool industry, known as the "Machine Tool Trigger Order Program." According to DoD,

> This is a program that utilizes stand-by agreements with machine tool builders for the purchase and production of long lead-time machine tools in an emergency. The reason for having these agreements is to speed up delivery of essential machine tools for defense production. The scope of the program when completed will encompass 120 machine tool builders with tools valued at $1.5 billion.[13]

As of the end of 1984, 97 agreements had been signed with 75 companies. These agreements cover about 9,000 machine tools with a

13. Ibid., p. 4.

reported value of $1.2 billion.[14] These numbers imply an average price of more than $133,000 for each of these machine tools.

Presumably, the "emergency" that would trigger this preplanned additional preemption of the nation's machine tool capacity would not be the outbreak of nuclear war. In such a war, industrial production capability would be of absolutely no consequence. Nor does it seem likely that the "emergency" could be the outbreak of a massive purely conventional World War III, comparable to World War II. The nature and deployment of military forces and their equipment, as well as present tactical and strategic doctrine, virtually guarantee that any such war would either be over fairly quickly or would escalate into nuclear war. Thus, unless we are planning to fight World War II again (which involves serious elements of fantasy) the "emergency" that would activate this Machine Tool Trigger Order Program must be limited but obviously quite protracted conventional war, on the order of the war in Vietnam.

Apart from the political implications of gearing up to tread such a path once more, the economic implications are quite striking. Our engagement in such a war will more quickly block the access of commercial market-oriented firms to the productive capacity of the machine tool industry. Thus, the next version of the Vietnam war will more quickly send shock waves through American industry. That we are ready to do this in the name of fighting another Vietnam war says something about the lack of understanding of the crucial relationship between the health of American industry and the nation's security.

There are two possible exceptions to the shock wave effect of this sudden preemption of the machine tool industry. One is if the U.S. machine tool industry had become so inefficient that American manufacturers were satisfying nearly all of their demand for this equipment from foreign sources. The other is if American industry was so flat on its back at the time of the "emergency" that it was doing very little investing. Neither of these exceptions is all that pleasant to contemplate.

Cross-checking the various official published and unpublished sources on DoD-owned physical capital reveals various problems with the data. In some cases, it is difficult to reconcile figures for components of this capital stock with overall figures from equally legitimate sources provided elsewhere. It is often unclear what degree of overlap there

14. Ibid.

is in various of the data categories, as between differing official DoD reports.

In trying to pursue this matter further, I contacted various staff people in the Department of Defense. One apparently thoroughly knowledgeable source, in the office of an Under Secretary of Defense confirmed that there were many inaccuracies and inconsistencies in the data. This source indicated that the data on "industrial plant equipment" were probably most accurate and reliable, but that the data for "other plant equipment" and, in general, data on GOGO physical capital were severely understated. It was further indicated that the DoD was, at the time of this writing, preparing to contract for studies and recommendations as to how to correct this situation. It was rather explicitly stated that no existing sources of aggregate data of this sort in the DoD were free of such problems and that any serious attempt to gather such data would require a great deal of "legwork" at the more or less grass-roots level in the military organization.

As they stand, these officially reported figures reflect a very substantial diversion of physical capital by the military sector. We have seen that (1) the total reported value of the stock of physical capital directly owned by the Department of Defense in 1983 was roughly half of that owned by all U.S. manufacturing establishments combined and (2) during 1982 net investment by the DoD in plant equipment was nearly 40% as large as the average annual net investment (1980–1982) by all of American manufacturing industry. In 1984, the DoD directly owned more than a hundred industrial plants in almost three-quarters of the states, with nearly $7.4 billion worth of associated capital.

Yet these data are seriously understated because they do not include any of the physical capital owned by private military-industry firms themselves—which is obviously a very real part of the physical capital preempted by the military sector. And internal DoD sources indicate that serious data problems are also likely to have resulted in understatement of reported government-owned physical capital.

It is clear that the diversion of so much capital to serve the military sector cannot help but have very serious negative effects on the rate of capital formation in the private commercial, market-oriented economy.

Financial Capital

When financial capital is taken for noncontributive purposes, a less direct but very real form of capital diversion occurs. It is less direct because no physical capital need be shifted or preempted. Yet financial capital represents purchasing power and in a market economy conveys considerable control over the allocation of productive resources. Thus a substantial diversion of financial capital can impede the contributive economy's access to the productive resources needed to create new physical capital (or to maintain, and thus slow depreciation of, existing physical capital). The result is therefore very similar to that of the direct diversion of physical capital—a slowed rate of contributive capital formation.

In a market economy, the government acquires financial capital, and hence command over the resources and goods and services it needs to perform various functions, by means of taxation, money creation, or borrowing. Taxation amounts to direct confiscation of private wealth. Money creation can, by generating inflation, indirectly shift purchasing power involuntarily from private organizations and individuals to the government. Borrowing takes private wealth voluntarily in exchange for the promise to return more than is borrowed in the future by shifting wealth from the general population to the lenders. While it is true that these differing approaches have different economic implications, they all share the common feature of removing wealth from private hands.

The removal of this wealth does reduce the availability of the means of contributive investment to private, market-oriented commercial producers. However, not all contributive investment results from the actions of the private sector. The government can and does add to the stock of capital needed for efficient economic activity through contributive investments of its own. Most prominently, the various levels of government in the United States have been major investors in infrastructure capital—the roads, dams, bridges, airports, sewage treatment facilities, electric power plants, etc., that provide the crucial underpinnings of the economy.

Whether or not the government is the most efficient creator of infrastructure is not the issue here. Both historically and potentially, government investment in the nation's economic infrastructure surely constitutes contributive activity. Thus, if the private wealth shifted to the government is used for such purposes, an important class of contributive capital formation still takes place.

But when financial capital taken by the government is put to non-contributive use, there is no contributive investment by government to wholly or partially offset the effects of reduced access to the means of investment by market-oriented producers. The financial capital used in support of the military system thus tends to deflect government-sector as well as private-sector efforts from the kinds of capital formation that strengthen the economy. Just how extensive has this drain of financial capital been?

There are basically two ways in which the total annual amount of military expenditure is officially measured in the United States: "budget authority" and "outlays." Budget authority is the money the Congress appropriates to the military each fiscal year. Some of these funds are spent in the year they are appropriated. Appropriations for military pay and other operations and maintenance typically fall into this category. However, other appropriations, such as those designated for weapons development and production, are typically only partly spent in the year of appropriation. The rest of these funds may be obligated at that time, but they are actually paid out over a number of years—from the initial placement of the order to the final delivery of the weapons system. Outlays, on the other hand, are funds actually spent during a given fiscal year. They may have been appropriated during that year, or they may result from budget authority of previous years.

In a sense, budget authority may be the more relevant measure for the purposes of analyzing the drain of financial capital. Once the budget authority has been granted, financial capital in that corresponding amount has been committed and so is, in a manner of speaking, already tied up. However, it could be argued that until the money is actually spent, contracts involved might be subject to cancellation or renegotiation. Therefore, the outlays measure should be used.

In practice the situation is not so straightforward as this latter argument implies. Nevertheless, since outlays are normally significantly smaller than budget authority, outlays are used here to assure that any bias is a conservative one. For the past three fiscal years (1982–84), for example, budget authority has been between 14 and 16 percent greater than outlays in each year. Of course, budget authority would be expected to be higher than outlays during periods of military buildup and would not necessarily be so in periods of military budget reductions. Since at least some thirty of the past forty years have seen escalating military budgets, and since most of the other years have seen relatively minor reductions quickly reversed, the general downward bias from using outlays clearly predominates.

In terms of current dollars, narrowly defined national defense outlays over the period 1946–84 have totaled $2,830 billion.[15] This as-

15. Bureau of the Census, U.S. Department of Commerce, *Historical Statistics of the*

tronomical sum is difficult to comprehend. A continuously running printing press printing a thousand-dollar bill each second would take well more than twice as long to print that much money as it took the United States to spend it! Such a machine would require about a decade less than a century to print that sum. This seems all the more remarkable, in light of the fact that the press will have printed $10,000 or so in the time it would take an average reader to read this example.

During the past five fiscal years alone (FY 1979–84), the United States has spent more than one trillion dollars on the military ($1,060 billion). What might such a quantity of financial capital have done if it had instead been applied to contributive capital formation? As of 1983, the latest data available, the entire net stock of physical capital owned by all U.S. manufacturing establishments combined (including all structures, equipment and inventories) was valued at $1,011.9.[16] Thus, the financial capital spent on the military in only those five years would have been more than enough to purchase the entire stock of physical capital held by U.S. manufacturing industry at its book value.

As of 1983, the book value of equipment and structures held by all U.S. manufacturers (i.e., excluding inventories) totaled $672.4 billion. Nearly that much financial capital was spent on the military in just the three years 1982–84 ($647.6 billion). Looked at another way, if the 1983 book value underrepresented their actual market value by as much as 50 percent it still would have been possible to repurchase all of the equipment and structures held by all U.S. manufacturing establishments combined with the amount of financial capital expended on the military during the five years FY 1979–84.

Looking forward, the Reagan administration's projections for military outlays during the *four* years of its second term, FY 1985–88 are nearly 35% higher than actual outlays have been over the *five* years, FY 1979–84, we have been considering. Suppose we assume that the purchase price of the stock of structures and equipment in the hands of all of U.S. manufacturing industry was actually twice its 1983 book value. Even so, if the financial capital we are planning to spend on the military during the Reagan administration's second term

---

United States, *Colonial Times to 1970* (Washington, D.C.: U.S. Government Printing Office, 1975), p. 1114; and Bureau of the Census, U.S. Department of Commerce, *Statistical Abstract of the U.S., 1984* (Washington, D.C.: U.S. Government Printing Office, 1983), p. 343.

16. See *n.* 7.

were applied to capital formation instead, there would be enough financial capital available to replace *all* of the buildings and machinery owned by *all* manufacturers in the U.S. by the end of the 1980s.

While all of the individual financial capital comparisons presented here have their limitations, the basic picture is clear. There is no question but that the military sector has been a huge drain on the nation's pool of financial capital.

A Note on Human Capital.   The diversion of human capital into the military sector, particularly in the form of engineering and scientific skills, has been substantial. I have elsewhere estimated—quite conservatively—that at least 30 percent of the nation's engineers and scientists are engaged in military-oriented work, and that this level of human capital drain has been going on for decades.[17] This large-scale preemption of the efforts of American scientists and engineers has seriously retarded the stream of innovation directed to the purposes of improving the equipment and techniques of manufacture available to the nation's market-oriented commercial producers.

What "spinoff" there has been from military research and development to application in civilian areas has been far too small to make up for the direct removal of so many engineers and scientists from civilian-oriented technological development.[18] In 1980 Simon Ramo, one of the founders of TRW, estimated the civilian technological lag created by the military diversion of technology in the U.S. at about two decades—a very long time in terms of the rapidity of technological change in modern societies:

> In the past thirty years, had the total dollars we spent on military R&D been expended instead in those areas of science and technology promising the most economic progress, we probably would be today [1980] where we are going to find ourselves arriving technologically in the year 2000.[19]

RESOURCE DIVERSION AND CAPITAL FORMATION

The military sector claim on American capital resources—physical, financial and human—has been substantial throughout most of the

---

17. See, for example, Dumas, L. J., "University Research, Industrial Innovation and the Pentagon," in J. Tirman, ed., *The Militarization of High Technology* (Cambridge, Mass.: Ballinger, 1984).

18. Ibid., p. 143–45.

19. S. Ramo, *America's Technology Slip* (New York: Wiley and Sons, 1980), p. 251.

post–World War II period. And it is unquestionably large today. How has this claim affected capital formation in the contributive economy?

Physical Capital

The military diversion of physical capital has clearly had a strong effect on commercial capital formation. Insofar as various production equipment and facilities used for military-related production have potential alternative use in commercial, market-oriented production, the contributive economy has been directly deprived of the use of this capital. The vast majority of the billions of dollars worth of metal-working equipment and other plant equipment (along with many industrial production facilities themselves) fall into this category, whether owned by the government or private military-industrial firms.

Other forms of military-sector physical capital, not directly usable for civilian production, can interfere with contributive capital formation indirectly. The labor, machinery, etc., used to produce this military capital could potentially be turned to creating contributive capital instead.

There is even a more subtle interference with market-oriented capital formation. Since the military production system is a very large and lucrative market for some particularly important classes of industrial equipment and machinery, the peculiar requirements of this system can distort the nature of this capital. As one example, American producers of metalworking machine tools—a very crucial class of industrial machinery—have directed considerable effort to producing equipment capable of machining very large workpieces to extremely high accuracy. Such equipment is suited to the special requirements of military aerospace producers, but it is also extremely expensive. In the cost-plus world of military aerospace, this is no particular problem. However, very few commercial producers really need this kind of machining capability, and in any case they could not pay such prices and stay competitive.

Over time the products of American machine tool manufacturers have shifted in directions that have made them somewhat less adapted to the needs of commercial, market-oriented producers than they once were. As this has happened, and to the extent this has happened here and in other capital goods industries, the attractiveness of these products to contributive producers has diminished, thus reducing their incentives to invest in new capital.

Financial Capital

The military sector's claim on financial capital is achieved through taxation and government borrowing. Consider each of these in turn.

The largest part of the tax burden on most of the U.S. population is the federal income tax. The great taxpayer revolt of 1978 began with the passage of Proposition 13 in California, aimed at slashing the property tax. Yet in 1977 the average U.S. taxpayer paid roughly $2.50 in federal income tax for every dollar of property tax.[20] Furthermore, assuming that federal individual income taxes were spent on the military in the same relative proportions as were total federal budget outlays, the "military tax" burden on individuals alone was at least 10 percent (and perhaps nearly 60%) higher than their property tax burden at that time.[21]

In any given society at any point in time, there is a certain limited tax potential—only a certain amount that government at all levels is able to extract in taxes without creating a serious backlash. The use of a large part of this tax potential by the federal government for the nourishment of the military sector has left that much less for its non-military functions, as well as for all of the functions of state and local government.

Among the contributive activities of government in the United States, one of the most economically important has historically been investment in public infrastructure. In the light of the heavy government use of financial capital for military purposes, it is not surprising that the American infrastructure has fallen into an advanced state of decay.

In 1981, the Council of State Planning Agencies published a report entitled *America in Ruins* detailing this problem:

> American's public facilities are wearing out faster than they are being replaced. . . . In hundreds of communities, deteriorated public facilities threaten the continuation of basic community services such as fire protection, public transportation, water supplies, secure prisons and flood protection. The United States is seriously underinvesting in public infrastructure.[22]

20. L. J. Dumas, "Taxes and Militarism," *The Cato Journal* 1 (no. 1, Spring 1981): 278.
21. Ibid., pp. 278–80.
22. P. Choate and S. Walter, *America in Ruins: Beyond The Public Works Porkbarrel* (Washington, D.C.: The Council of State Planning Agencies, 1981), p. 1.

More specifically, the study points out that nearly one-fifth of the interstate highway system is beyond its designed service life and in need of rebuilding, that 20 percent of the nation's bridges require major rehabilitation or reconstruction, and that a large number of the 43,500 dams in the United States have hazardous deficiencies. Later stories in such journals as *Newsweek* and the *New York Times* in the early 1980s echoed this same basic theme.[23]

Public borrowing to support military spending is interest-insensitive and tends to "crowd out" private borrowing on financial markets. Private borrowing by military-industrial firms will also be relatively interest-insensitive for the same reasons these firms are insensitive to other costs. Consequently, private contributive producers whose borrowing *is* sensitive to interest rates, are doubly squeezed.

Historically, much of the national debt has been war-related. The Reagan administration's deficit spending has been clearly related to sharply expanded military spending. At the rate at which these recent deficits have been run, the United States will have added as much to the national debt in the first six years of the 1980s (i.e., 1980–85) as in the preceding 200-plus years of its history.[24]

All this borrowing has caused real interest rates to surge. Adjusting the prime rate charged by banks by the consumer price index, the real interest rate more than quadrupled in 1981. It rose still higher in 1982, and though it declined somewhat in the next two years, as of 1984 the real rate still stood at more than double the 1959 peak.[25] These high real interest rates clearly do not encourage capital investment by interest sensitive commercial market-oriented producers.

Human Capital

Civilian technological progress has always been a major stimulus to contributive investment. To the extent that improvements in the techniques of manufacture were embodied in the improved design of manufacturing equipment, commercial producers had strong incentives to buy this new and better machinery. As the diversion of large numbers of engineers and scientists persisted, the rate of civilian technological

23. For example, the cover story on the August 2, 1982, issue of *Newsweek* was entitled "The Decaying of America: Our Bridges, Roads and Water Systems Are Rapidly Falling Apart."

24. *Economic Report of the President* (February 1985), Appendix B, Table B-79, p. 325.

25. Ibid., calculated from Table B-66, p. 310 and Table B-56, p. 296.

progress slowed, and this incentive began to disappear. Put simply, if the new equipment available offered very little, if any, improvement compared to existing, still functioning equipment, why buy it? Thus, the military-induced retardation of civilian technological progress in the United States has played a major role in hampering contributive capital formation. This effect has severely exacerbated the capital formation problems caused by the preemption of physical and financial capital on which the major part of this analysis has focused.

IMPLICATIONS AND CONCLUSIONS

The military production system, unaffected by the constraints that face market-oriented producers, operates as a command sector that asserts and enforces its claim to the productive resources of the society through the special political priority it has been accorded. It has taken and continues to take large quantities of physical, financial, and human capital out of the hands of the contributive economy, with strongly negative effects on the nation's rate of formation of economically productive capital.

The removal of this burden on the economy could open the door to an unprecedented industrial renaissance in this country, as the huge quantities of capital locked up in the military sector were freed for productive use. But what of the nation's defense? Can this capital be freed without endangering the nation?

To the extent that the military forces are required to provide for the nation's security, it is clear that it is not the amount of money spent, but the nature and capability of the military force assembled that matters. Aside from the extraordinary waste and inefficiency inherent in present military procurement practices, large parts of U.S. military expenditures are oriented to the defense of other nations whose real income levels are comparable to those in the United States. By one estimate, some 42 percent of the Reagan administration's 1985 defense budget authorization request was for the defense of Europe.[26] While it may have been true that the nations of Europe were in no position to defend themselves or contribute much to their own defense in the immediate post–World War II period, it is certainly not true today. As one indication, average industrial wages in 1980 were sub-

---

26. E. C. Ravenal, *Defining Defense: The 1985 Military Budget* (Washington, D.C.: Cato Institute, 1984), p. 16.

stantially higher in eight European nations than they were in the United States.[27]

Beyond this, a large fraction of current military expenditures is not required (and not designed) for the protection of either the United States or its major allies. Instead, such expenditures are associated with so-called "power projection" and global policing functions, or they provide massively redundant destructive power in our nuclear arsenals.[28] It is perfectly possible, by restructuring forces, to provide the military component of the nation's security with a substantially reduced military budget. For example, a detailed 350-page study published by New York Times Books in 1979 described such a restructuring, arguing that the result would be a stronger, more effective military force with a nearly 40 percent lower military budget.[29] And since then, military expenditures in these areas have increased even more dramatically, implying that even larger percentage reductions in current budgets are warranted.

Even without success in reaching verifiable international agreements on arms reduction, it is possible to greatly reduce the economic burden of the military sector. Eliminating the tremendous waste and inefficiency built into the American system of weapons procurement could hardly be looked upon as a weakening of our defenses, yet it could potentially unlock a substantial amount of the capital that is presently diverted. For example, the extensive report of the Grace Commission (President's Private Sector Survey on Cost Control) found that by subjecting DoD to the kind of sound management practices essential in the private sector, a minimum total of $165.7 billion could be made in cost reductions over three years.[30] Both the reduction of pure waste and the restructuring of U.S. military forces to increase effectiveness and reduce cost is well within our grasp and could greatly increase the nation's security.

27. S. Melman, *Profits Without Production* (New York: Knopf, 1983), p. 309 (unpublished Department of Labor, Bureau of Labor Statistics, data prepared April 1982).

28. The excess of nuclear weaponry and associated systems is not simply useless overkill but actually degrades our security. For analyses of some military/technical reasons why this is so, see L. J. Dumas, "National Insecurity in the Nuclear Age," *Bulletin of the Atomic Scientists,* May 1976; and L. J. Dumas, "Human Fallibility and Weapons," *Bulletin of the Atomic Scientists,* November 1980.

29. Boston Study Group, *The Price of Defense* (New York: New York Times Books, 1979).

30. President's Private Sector Survey on Cost Control, *War on Waste* (New York: Macmillan Publishing Company, 1984).

If instead we allow the military sector to continue its parasitical erosion of the productive economy and its undermining of the crucial process of capital formation, the reindustrialization of America will remain beyond our reach. If we do not undertake this rebuilding, the long-term prospects for the American economy will remain poor. And it is wise to remember that no nation whose economy continues to deteriorate can long remain secure.

SELECTED BIBLIOGRAPHY
PART II

Anderson, Terry L., and Peter J. Hill. *The Birth of a Transfer Society*. Stanford, Calif.: Hoover Institution Press, 1980.

Ando, Albert, and Franco Modigliani. "The 'Life Cycle' Hypothesis of Saving: Aggregate Implications and Tests." *American Economic Review* 53, no. 1 (1963): 55–84.

Barro, Robert J. "Are Government Bonds Net Wealth?" *Journal of Political Economy* 82, no. 6 (1974): 1095–118.

———. "Reply to Feldstein and Buchanan." *Journal of Political Economy* 84, no. 2 (1976): 343–50.

Belloc, Hilaire. *The Servile State*. London: P. N. Foulis, 1913. Reprint. Indianapolis: Liberty Press, 1977.

Bennett, James; Dan Heldman; and Manuel H. Johnson. *Deregulating Labor Relations*. Dallas: Fisher Institute, 1981.

Browning, Edgar K. "Why the Social Security System is Too Large in a Democracy." *Economic Inquiry* 13 (September 1975): 373–88.

Browning, Edgar K., and William R. Johnson. *The Distribution of the Tax Burden*. Washington: American Enterprise Institute, 1979.

Buchanan, James M. *Public Principles of Public Debt: A Defense Restatement*. Homewood, Ill.: Irwin, 1958.

———. "The Samaritan's Dilemma." In E. Phelps, ed., *Altruism, Morality, and Economic Theory*, pp. 71–85. New York: Russell Sage, 1975.

Buchanan, James M.; Robert D. Tollison; and Gordon Tullock, eds. *Toward a Theory of the Rent-Seeking Society*. College Station: Texas A & M Press, 1980.

353

Buchanan, James M., and Richard E. Wagner. *Democracy in Deficit.* New York: Academic Press, 1978.

Campbell, Colin, ed. *Financing Social Security.* Washington, D.C.: American Enterprise Institute, 1979.

Choate, Pat, and Susan Walter. *America in Ruins: Beyond the Public Works Pork Barrel.* Washington, D.C.: Council of State Planning Agencies, 1981.

Darby, Michael R. *The Effects of Social Security on Income and the Capital Stock.* Washington, D.C.: American Enterprise Institute, 1979.

Denison, Edward F. *Accounting for Slower Economic Growth in the 1970s.* Washington, D.C.: Brookings Institution, 1979.

Diamond, Peter. "A Framework for Social Security Analysis." *Journal of Public Economics* 8 (1977): 275–98.

Drazen, Allan. "Government Debt, Human Capital and Bequests in a Life-Cycle Model." *Journal of Political Economy* 86, no. 3 (1978): 505–16.

Dumas, Lloyd J. *The Overburdened Economy: Uncovering the Causes of Chronic Unemployment, Inflation and National Decline.* Berkeley: University of California Press, 1986.

———. "Payment Functions and the Productive Efficiency of Military-Industrial Firms." *Journal of Economic Issues* 10, no. 2 (June 1976): 454–74.

———. "Taxes and Militarism." *Cato Journal* 1, no. 1 (Spring 1981): 277–92.

———. "University Research, Industrial Innovation and the Pentagon." In J. Tirman, ed., *The Militarization of High Technology,* ch. 7, pp. 123–51. Cambridge, Mass.: Ballinger Publishing Co., 1984.

Easterbrook, Frank H., and Daniel R. Fischel. "Voting in Corporate Law." *Journal of Law and Economics* 26, no. 2 (June 1983): 395–427.

Fama, Eugene. "Agency Problems and the Theory of the Firm." *Journal of Political Economy* 88, no. 2 (April 1980): 288–307.

Feldstein, Martin S. "Social Security, Induced Retirement, and Aggregate Capital Accumulation." *Journal of Political Economy* 82, no. 5 (1974): 904–26.

———. "Does the United States Save Too Little?" *American Economic Review* 67, no. 1 (1977): 116–21.

———. "Perceived Wealth in Bonds and Social Security: A Comment." *Journal of Political Economy* 84, no. 2 (1976): 331–36.

———. "Social Security and Private Saving: Reply." *Journal of Political Economy* 90, no. 3 (1982): 630–42.

Ferguson, James, ed. *Public Debt and Future Generations.* Chapel Hill: University of North Carolina Press, 1964.

Ferrara, Peter J. *Social Security: The Inherent Contradiction.* Washington, D.C.: Cato Institute, 1980.

———. "The Prospect of Real Reform." *Cato Journal* 3, no. 2 (1983): 609–21.

Flowers, Marilyn R. "The Political Feasibility of Privatizing Social Security: Comment on Butler and Germanis." *Cato Journal* 3, no. 2 (1983): 557–62.

Fox, J. Ronald. *Arming America: How the U.S. Buys Weapons*. Cambridge: Harvard University Press, 1974.

Freeman, Richard B., and James L. Medoff. "The Two Faces of Unionism." *Public Interest* 57 (Fall 1979): 69–93.

Friedman, Milton. "Choice, Chance, and the Personal Distribution of Income." *Journal of Political Economy* 61 (August 1953): 277–90.

Fuchs, Victor. *How We Live*. Cambridge: Harvard University Press, 1983.

Furubotn, Eirik G., and Svetozar Pejovich. "Property Rights and Economic Theory: A Survey of Recent Literature." *Journal of Economic Literature* 10, no. 4 (December 1972): 1137–62.

Gansler, Jacques. *The Defense Industry*. Cambridge: MIT Press, 1980.

Gilder, George. *Wealth and Poverty*. New York: Basic Books, 1981.

Glicken, Morley D. "Transgenerational Welfare Dependency." *Journal of Contemporary Studies* 4 (Summer 1981): 31–41.

Heldman, Dan, and Deborah Knight. *Unions and Lobbying: The Representative Function*. Washington, D.C.: Foundation for the Advancement of the Public Trust, 1980.

Himmelfarb, Gertrude. *The Idea of Poverty*. New York: Alfred A. Knopf, 1983.

Hochman, Harold M., and James D. Rodgers. "Pareto Optimal Redistribution." *American Economic Review* 59 (September 1969): 542–57.

Lebergott, Stanley. *The American Economy*. Princeton, N.J.: Princeton University Press, 1967.

Leffler, Keith B. "Minimum Wages, Welfare, and Wealth Transfers to the Poor." *Journal of Law and Economics* 21 (October 1978): 345–58.

Leimer, Dean R., and Selig Lesnoy. "Social Security and Private Saving: New Time Series Evidence." *Journal of Political Economy* 90, no. 3 (1982): 606–29.

Manne, Henry G. "Mergers and Markets for Corporate Control." *Journal of Political Economy* 73, no. 2 (April 1965): 110–20.

Melman, Seymour. *Pentagon Capitalism*. New York: McGraw-Hill, 1970.

Modigliani, Franco, and Richard Brumberg. "Utility Analysis and the Consumption Function: An Interpretation of Cross Section Data." In K. Kurihara, ed., *Post Keynesian Economics,* pp. 388–436. New Brunswick, N.J.: Rutgers University Press, 1954.

Munnell, Alicia. *The Effect of Social Security on Personal Saving*. Cambridge, Mass: Ballinger Publishing Co., 1974.

Murray, Charles. *Losing Ground*. New York: Basic Books, 1984.

Nozick, Robert. *Anarchy, State, and Utopia*. New York: Basic Books, 1974.

Paglin, Morton. "The Measurement and Trend of Inequality: A Basic Revision." *American Economic Review* 65 (September 1975): 598–609.

Parsons, Donald O., and Douglas R. Munro. "Intergenerational Transfers in Social Security." In M. Boskin, ed., *The Crisis in Social Security: Problems and Prospects*, ch. 4, pp. 65–86. San Francisco: Institute for Contemporary Studies, 1978.

Pechman, Joseph A., and Benjamin A. Okner. *Who Bears the Tax Burden?* Washington, D.C.: Brookings Institution, 1974.

Prest, Alan R. "The Statistical Calculation of Tax Burdens." *Economica* 22 (August 1955): 234–45.

Rawls, John. *A Theory of Justice*. Cambridge: Harvard University Press, 1971.

Reynolds, Morgan O. *Power and Privilege: Labor Unions in America*. New York: Universe Books, 1984.

Roberts, Russell D. "A Positive Model of Private Charity and Public Transfers." *Journal of Political Economy* 92 (February 1984): 136–48.

Ramo, Simon. *America's Technology Slip*. New York: John Wiley & Sons, 1980.

Samuelson, Paul A. "An Exact Consumption-Loan Model Interest, With or Without the Social Contrivance of Money." In J. Stiglitz, ed., *The Scientific Papers of Paul Samuelson*, vol. 1, p. 219. Cambridge: MIT Press, 1966.

———. "Optimum Social Security in a Life-Cycle Growth Model." *International Economic Review* 16, no. 3 (1975): 539–44.

Sowell, Thomas. *Ethnic America*. New York: Basic Books, 1981.

Tullock, Gordon. "The Rhetoric and Reality of Redistribution." *Southern Economic Journal* 47 (April 1981): 895–907.

———. *The Economics of Income Redistribution*. Boston: Kluwer-Nijhoff, 1983.

Wagner, Richard. "Funded Social Security: Collective and Private Options." *Cato Journal* 3, no. 2 (1983): 581–602.

Weaver, Carolyn. *The Crisis in Social Security*. Durham, N.C.: Duke University Press, 1982.

Williams, Walter E. *The State Against Blacks*. New York: McGraw-Hill, 1980.

PART III

ENTREPRENEURSHIP IN THE PRIVATE AND PUBLIC SECTORS

13

TAXES AND DISCOVERY: AN ENTREPRENURIAL PERSPECTIVE

Israel M. Kirzner

Israel M. Kirzner

The central theme of this chapter will take the form of a rather basic criticism of an unstated premise of the accepted theory dealing with the economic effects of taxation. If this criticism is accepted as sound, it will raise serious questions concerning the completeness (if not the very validity) of the conclusions arrived at through application of the standard theory. In order to reformulate the theory of taxation to take adequate account of our basic criticism, a significant array of new theoretical challenges will have to be grappled with. This paper therefore implies not only a broad attack on orthodox taxation theory, but also an extensive positive agenda for its reconstruction. This paper by no means attempts to undertake the required reconstruction. (In fact it must be freely confessed that it is not clear that economics yet possesses the conceptual and analytical tools necessary for this task.) It confines itself to the far more modest (and, it is to be hoped, achievable) objectives of articulating the basic insight underlying our criticism and identifying some of the theoretical issues raised by awareness of this basic insight.

THE PREMISE OF ORTHODOX THEORY

Underlying the standard theory that assesses the economic consequences of taxation is the premise that *taxes are introduced into a*

359

world in which available opportunities for gainful actions are given and known (in the sense to be defined below) to relevant decision-makers. Acceptance of this premise has meant that the economic impact of a tax is explored only insofar as it may affect the relative preferability for the decision maker of already-perceived alternative courses of action (the fully known benefits of which may be affected unequally by the tax). No consideration is given to the possibility that the tax may perhaps have significant impact upon the very perception by the prospective taxpayer of what array of opportunities are available for his choice, or of what their pretax benefits for him may in fact be. In other words, no consideration is given to the possibility that taxation may affect what it is that decision makers *discover* to be the situation in which they act. The effect of taxation upon incentives has been explored on the premise that the degree to which the taxpayer can successfully discover the true state of affairs surrounding him is left unaffected by all taxation patterns (and it is often assumed, in fact, that the taxpayer is able to discover this state of affairs with *complete* success under all circumstances). We shall argue that, in general, this basic premise is likely to be unfounded. Once we recognize the possibility of a linkage between what a person is to be taxed and what opportunities that person discovers to be available for his taking, we must recognize further the need to modify substantially the conclusions reached by standard theory (on the basis of this challenged premise) concerning the effect of specific taxes upon what prospective taxpayers decide to do. Let us elaborate briefly on two quite different senses in which the notion of *incentives* may be relevant to the economic analysis of taxation.

INCENTIVES AND INCENTIVES

Economists ordinarily treat the concept of an incentive as referring to the provision of an encouragement for a decision maker to select a particular alternative out of an array of *already perceived alternatives*. What is already perceived about these alternatives is taken to be not only the possible courses of action themselves, but also key elements, at the very least, concerning the respective consequences one might reasonably expect from pursuing these courses of action. To provide an incentive to encourage the decision maker to select course of action *A*, rather than courses of action *B*, *C*, . . . , means to seek to modify the consequences of these various courses of action in such a manner as to render the perceived consequences of A more desirable than those of B, C, ... Typically this is likely to take the form of arranging an enhancement of the value to the decision maker of the perceived consequence of A itself. In other words, the way to induce the decision maker to adopt course of action A is, to use the economists' opportunity-cost phraseology, to overcome the cost of sacrificing B, C, ... Whereas absent this inducement, course of action B might have been judged to promise greater rewards than action A, the provided incentive (enhancing the total value of A's consequences) renders A more desirable than B. The high cost of rejecting B has been met by increasing the payoff on action A. It is easy to understand how taxes (and subsidies) may be deployed in this way to provide the incentives designed to encourage taxpayers to pursue courses of action that the taxing authorities would like them to pursue.

To encourage work rather than leisure, it may be deemed necessary to increase after-tax labor income (without affecting the desirability of relevant forgone leisure); to encourage saving rather than the immediate consumption of income, it may be deemed necessary to offer tax exemptions on that portion of income directed toward saving (while leaving unchanged the severity of the tax bite on other income). These tax measures provide tax-based incentives to encourage work, or saving, through modifying the rewards of working, or saving, in such a way as to outweigh the perceived costs of working, or saving. Let us call this kind of incentive, an *incentive of the first kind*. We wish to draw attention to an altogether different notion of an incentive that will be of critical importance for the theme of this chapter.

This second, entirely different, incentive concept does not operate by way of overcoming the cost, to the decision maker, associated with his adoption of the to-be-encouraged option, A; it does not operate by enhancing the value of A's consequences in order to make these consequences appear more valuable, all in all, than those of B, C, ... Rather this second kind of incentive operates to encourage the adoption of A by making A more likely to be *noticed* by the decision maker. In other words it may be the case that even *without* any new incentives, course of action A may *already* have in fact involved consequences more desirable than those of B, C, . . . , but that this preferred action A would, in the absence of new incentives, *not* have been adopted *simply because it would have failed to be noticed as a possibility by the decision maker*. Here the incentive takes the form, not of altering the *relative* attractiveness of the payoffs to A, B, C,

. . ., but of somehow enhancing the potential of action *A* to *attract attention*. It is not essential to offer incentives in order to overcome the opportunity cost of rejecting course of action *B*. *A* is *already* offering greater rewards than *B*. Thus, in this situation, if the authorities wish to structure taxes in order to provide taxpayers with incentives to pursue course of action *A*, any tax-policy-generated sweetening (for the taxpayer) of the anticipated value of the consequences of undertaking *A* would not necessarily affect action through the enhancement of (the relative) desirability of *A*. Rather the incentive to undertake *A* operates, under the specified assumptions, *through its inducement to discover* the possibility and/or the attractiveness of *A*. We will refer to this kind of incentive as an *incentive of the second kind*.

It should perhaps be pointed out that an inducement to discover *A* is not at all the same as an inducement *deliberately to undertake the search effort* (involving possibly significant search costs) that might reveal the existence and value of *A*. A decision maker might indeed be convinced that by the expenditure of a specified degree of search effort, he could locate a superior course of action, but that the cost of the necessary search effort was so high as to make the whole search not worthwhile. And tax authorities might indeed then be able to provide sufficient enhancement of the value of the to-be-searched-for course of action as to make the expensive search appear worthwhile after all. But *this* kind of inducement to search is evidently no different from any of the incentives of the first kind, discussed earlier. This kind of inducement is designed to overcome the costs of undertaking an already-perceived course of action, viz., that of deliberately searching for a superior course of action (to be undertaken subsequent to the search). This kind of inducement operates (as do all incentives of the first kind) by enhancing the relative desirability of an already-perceived (and already correctly evaluated) course of action (viz., the act of searching). The sense in which incentives of the second kind can be said to serve as inducements for discovery is quite different.

Discovery may be induced by incentives of the second kind, not by rendering an already-perceived possibility of costly search worthwhile, but by sparking interest in a possible, but hitherto *unnoticed* course of action (or at least, a course of action the net desirability of which had not been noticed). One cannot deliberately search for an opportunity whose existence—or even the very possibility of whose existence—one is totally unaware of. (One of the avenues through which incentives of the second kind may spark interest in hitherto unnoticed possibilities may of course take the form of sparking interest in the possible worthwhileness of deliberate search itself. But then the reason why the search would not have been undertaken deliberately, absent these new inducements, had nothing to do with the costliness of the search effort. The to-be-expected results of a search would, in such cases, be sufficient to render the cost well worthwhile; the search would not have been undertaken because the very possibility of such a search (or of its likely outcome) was somehow—in the absence of the new incentives—not perceived).

The theme of this chapter can now be concisely stated in terms of the two kinds of incentives described above: The standard theory of the economic effects of taxation proceeds exclusively through the analysis of the incentive (or disincentive) effects of taxation in the context of the first kind of incentive concept; what needs to be introduced is an analysis of taxation that takes into account the role of incentives (and disincentives) of the second kind.

THE INCENTIVE OF PURE PROFIT

The foregoing suggests rather clearly that the reconstruction of the economic theory of taxation that we are calling for must proceed through a reconsideration of the theory of the economic effects of the taxation of pure entrepreneurial profit. That this is so emerges immediately from the insight that the incentive role of pure ("economic") profit is *entirely* that of the *second* kind of incentive discussed in the preceding section. Although the disincentive effects of taxation upon profit have been frequently referred to in the tax literature, it appears that these references have had only the *first* kind of incentive effect in mind. We shall argue in this section that this latter understanding of the incentive effect of profit (and hence of the disincentive effect of profit taxes) is valid only to the extent that *accounting* profit (upon which taxes may be levied) includes elements other than pure entrepreneurial profit. With respect to the *pure* (economic) profit component, we shall maintain that the *only* relevant incentive category is that which we have labeled the second kind.

Pure profit is captured by the entrepreneur when he succeeds in selling an item (a good or a service) at a price that exceeds the price for which he purchased that item (or the total of the outlays incurred in producing that item and making it ready for sale). Pursuing this definition we observe that all payments necessary to command the services of relevant productive factors have *already* been included in

the outlay total to be subtracted from the sales proceeds. By definition, therefore, pure profit is a sum that cannot be described as necessary for the production of the item sold (or for its availability for
sale at the relevant selling price). Pure profit contains no element
needed to ensure the availability of the item to be sold. All necessary
costs of production, including all outlays (such as selling costs, delivery costs, and the like) needed to ensure that the item to be sold
will be forthcoming at the appropriate time and place, are included
in the total deducted from sales revenues in arriving at the profit amount.
Pure profits are therefore not needed to provide the economic incentives necessary to evoke relevant productive effort. Notice that this
means, of course, that even without the presence of pure profits, sales
revenues are, by being sufficient to cover all the service outlays for
necessary factors, sufficient to overcome the pull exercised by the
bids of entrepreneurs in other industries competing to secure the services of these factors for other productive uses. Any incentive role
that may be ascribed to pure profit can therefore not take the form of
the first kind of incentive role identified earlier (in which an income
receipt provides the incentive to the decision maker to undertake a
given course of action by rendering the consequences of that course
of action preferable to those of alternate courses of action). Here the
course of production action (undertaken in the profitable line of production) would have, we have seen, been worthwhile even if the pure
profit amount was not forthcoming from the sales revenues. The possibility that pure profit fulfills an incentive role can, therefore, exist
only in the *second* of the senses that we have identified earlier (in
which an income receipt provides the incentive for a course of action
to be undertaken by enhancing the potential of that course of action,
and of its worthwhileness, to attract entrepreneurial attention).

That this indeed may be an incentive role provided by pure entrepreneurial profit follows from the very concept of entrepreneurship
and from the theory of pure entrepreneurial profit. The very possibility of the emergence of pure entrepreneurial profit rests, after all,
on the circumstance that worthwhile opportunities may simply not be
noticed. Were all worthwhile opportunities to be noticed at all times
(i.e., were all opportunities for producing items the prospective sales
revenues of which fully covered necessary costs of production, to be
immediately noticed), then we could hardly expect that sales revenues
would ever exceed costs of production. No buyer would pay for an

item a sum larger than the perceived minimum outlay sufficient to obtain the availability of that item. The possibility of sales revenue exceeding cost of production arises solely out of the possibility that desirable courses of action may not be noticed (or that their desirability may not be noticed).

The incentive role of pure entrepreneurial profit therefore fits in naturally with the theory accounting for its very existence. Profit is generated by earlier failures of market participants to notice worthwhile possibilities. The profit thus generated sparks interest in these overlooked possibilities. The incentive of profit thus works not to affect the relative attractiveness of already-perceived opportunities; rather it is to attract notice to the most desirable (but possibly not yet perceived) of the existing opportunities. The concept of entrepreneurship is closely linked to that of alertly noticing hitherto unnoticed opportunities. As we shall see, there is every reason to recognize the possibility of pure profit as providing the incentive that inspires entrepreneurial discovery of such hitherto unnoticed opportunities. *These insights certainly hold considerable relevance for understanding the impact of profit-taxation.*

We note, in concluding this section, that accounting profit may, of course, not conform at all closely with this pure entrepreneurial profit that we have been discussing here. As is well known, accounting profit figures may contain very significant components of a variety of different analytical categories, especially interest, and wages of management. To the extent that interest must be paid in order to compete for capital with other branches of production, or to dissuade potential investors from succumbing to the lure of more immediate consumption possibilities, or to the extent that wages of management must be paid in order to attract talent away from other pursuits, accounting profits may well be needed to secure the availability of the resource services for these, as against competing, branches of production. To this extent accounting profits may certainly be held to perform the first kind of incentive role identified earlier. The effects of the taxation of accounting profit must certainly, as standard theory does, deal with the *first* kind of disincentive effect of such taxation. (Our contention is that such analysis covers only part of the full effects of such taxation.) The discussion in this section has referred *only* to the pure profit element.

At the same time we must not forget that just as accounting profit is likely to embrace elements other than pure entrepreneurial profit, so also may other accounting categories, such as wages or interest, include elements of pure profit. We turn to elaborate briefly on this theme.

THE UBIQUITY OF PURE PROFIT

We have argued that the reconstruction of the theory of taxation called for in this paper must proceed by way of a reconsideration of the economic effects of the taxation of pure entrepreneurial profit. This does not mean, however, that such reconstruction would leave unaffected the theory dealing with the effects of the taxation of income categories other than accounting profit. The truth is that pure entrepreneurial profit is a ubiquitous economic phenomenon, present in a variety of economic circumstances and captured by a variety of economic agents. As Ludwig von Mises wrote, "In any real and living economy every actor is always an entrepreneur."[1]

What this means is that each and every action in the market economy reflects the actor's alertness to aspects of his situation that might otherwise have escaped attention. In a changing, open-ended world, acting man is never exempt from the self-generated pressure to ensure that his decisions not overlook available opportunities. Action never does consist merely in selecting the highest-valued of a given array of opportunities; it always embraces the simultaneous *identification* of what the relevant opportunities (and their values) really are at the moment of action. While we usually think of pure entrepreneurial profit as generated by the independent businessman through acts of purchase and sale, the truth surely is that an element of profit is captured whenever, say, a worker moves out of an industry where his (marginal productivity and therefore his) wages are low and obtains a job in another industry (or location) where compensation for similar skills is higher. This wage differential is the incentive that attracts the worker to change jobs; it can hardly be described as an incentive of the first kind—only a small fraction of it may be needed to render the new job more attractive than the old. Clearly the wage differential acts as an incentive for workers to become aware of the most desirable employment opportunities, in exactly the same way as price differentials attract potential entrepreneurs to buy at low prices and sell at

---

1. Ludwig von Mises, *Human Action* (New Haven: Yale University Press, 1949), p. 252.

higher prices. The role of incentives of the *second* kind (as we have called them in this paper) is a ubiquitous one. Hence the reconsideration of the economic theory of taxation that we call for in this paper is by no means confined to taxes explicitly levied on profit receipts. The reconstruction and the reconsideration that we call for have implications that extend to most kinds of taxes, to a greater or lesser degree.

Nonetheless, having recognized the entrepreneurial element in all human action, and having asserted the possibility of incentives of the second kind playing roles in almost every kind of economic receipt, we must acknowledge that the adviser on tax policy can hardly be as great a purist as the present section might appear to demand. Assertions concerning the impact of taxation upon analytical categories must, for the purposes of tax policy, be translated into assertions that relate, broadly if not precisely, to empirically identifiable classes of receipts. It is for this reason that most of the subsequent discussion is directed toward the impact of taxation upon accounting profit, insofar as a significant element in it is likely to be pure entrepreneurial profit in the more obvious sense. By "pure profit in the more obvious sense" we mean the difference between the amounts paid and received by an entrepreneur in buying and selling transactions (including in the buying transaction the purchase of all factor services needed to make possible a subsequent selling transaction of a produced item).

PURE PROFIT THAT PROVIDES NO INCENTIVES FOR DISCOVERY?

We have discussed some of the pitfalls surrounding attempts to identify empirical expressions of the analytical category of pure entrepreneurial profit. Our discussion was conducted on the basis of our insight into the special character of the incentive provided by pure entrepreneurial profit, viz., that this represented the *second* kind of incentive that we distinguished earlier in the paper. It was this insight into the special character of the pure profit incentive that suggested that the impact upon entrepreneurial discovery exercised by the taxation of profit urgently needs to be taken into account. We must now consider the possibility that the winning of pure entrepreneurial profit—in the form of a surplus of sales revenues over total relevant purchase outlays—may be accompanied by *no* incentive effects whatsoever.

This possibility was raised, in a somewhat different context, by

Professor Shackle many years ago.[2] Shackle distinguished between two possible sources of pure profit: (a) "imagination and knowledge," (b) "luck." In Shackle's view of a goal for tax policy should be to avoid discouraging the exercise of imagination and knowledge; but he believed that the taxation of lucky gains involved no such disincentives. The problem remaining for Shackle was then a practical one: "How are we to determine when a high rate of profit is due to luck and when to instructed imaginative enterprise?"[3] Only if such a determination can be made is it possible to hope to answer positively the central questions Shackle poses for tax policy in regard to profit: "Is it possible to devise a form of tax by which the majority of actual ventures will be caused to yield some revenue, but which will leave the incentive to enterprise, that is, the *ex ante* attractiveness of every venture, entirely unaffected? Can such a tax be so fashioned that actual gains realized *ex post* are taxed at lower rates when they accrue to those who have been able rather than merely lucky?"[4]

Shackle's understanding of the incentive role that pure profit plays in evoking "instructed imaginative enterprise" on the part of the "able" is perhaps not quite the same as our interpretation of pure profit as providing incentives "of the second kind." But the questions that he has posed are of direct relevance for our inquiry, as well. May it not, after all, perhaps be the case that a realized difference between sales revenue and purchase outlay corresponded to nothing that provided any incentive (of the second kind) for discovery, but was instead merely the outcome of a lucky break? To point out that the emergence of pure profit is evidence of hitherto overlooked opportunities is by itself not sufficient to establish that the entrepreneur who captures such pure profit was inspired to his discovery *ex ante* by the incentive effect of that prospective profit. May it not, in any particular situation, perhaps be the case that the entrepreneur was the fortunate beneficiary of pure and simple good luck, independent of his own entrepreneurial alertness? And in addition may it not perhaps be that the nature of the changes that generated the profit margin were so drastic as to have

2. Our critical discussion here of Professor Shackle's position pertains only to the one paper cited (first published in 1949). We certainly do not wish to suggest that that paper adequately represents the comprehensive view on pure profit developed by Professor Shackle in the course of a number of later works.

3. G. L. S. Shackle, *Expectations in Economics* (Cambridge: Cambridge University Press, 1952), p. 96.

4. Ibid., pp. 95–96.

been clearly beyond the scope of possible human anticipation, making it idle to speculate on the incentive power that the prospect of profitability might have had on the entrepreneur's decisions?

If indeed a significant fraction of realized pure profits is to be ascribed to sheer luck and therefore held to have played no incentive role whatsoever, then much of our concern in this paper would appear to be beside the point. Theorists claiming to account for the consequences of the taxation of profit might well be held responsible for considering the special kind of incentive role—the "second" kind—that may be played by pure profit in inspiring discovery. But they might be deemed justified in ignoring the second kind of incentive if it turns out that that category of income receipt exemplifying this second kind of incentive is in fact largely a matter of sheer luck, in no way responsive to, or a result of, "instructed imaginative enterprise." Were we to believe that pure entrepreneurial profit is indeed mainly a matter of sheer good luck—were we to believe that the successful entrepreneur, looking back on his wise decisions, can honestly state that the prospect of the profit eventually reaped played no incentive role in inspiring those decisions—then we would seem to have great difficulty in claiming that the taxation of pure profit operates to discourage alert decision-making. And it might appear that our critique of orthodox taxation theory could safely be ignored.

Professor Shackle's own suggestion for distinguishing between lucky profits and profits won through shrewd entrepreneurial judgment depends heavily on his own ("focus-value") theory of decision making under uncertainty. His suggestion involves the identification of "that one rate of profit which [the entrepreneur] had most vividly in mind when he decided that the venture was sufficiently attractive to warrant his embarking on it."[5] It should be observed that this way of putting the matter makes it clear that the emergence of a profit rate other than the one most "vividly in mind" would be (in Shackle's terminology), not the emergence of an "unexpected" course of events, but of a "counterexpected" course of events.[6] The profit that might emerge would, even if far above that "most vividly in mind," represent an outcome that had at least been considered. Moreover, the framework of Shackle's discussion is one in which "the venture" was clearly defined at the moment of decision, quite apart from the rate of profit

5. Ibid., p. 99.
6. Ibid., p. 73*n*, and p. 96.

to be associated with it. The sense in which the vividly anticipated rate of profit served as an incentive to undertake the venture is thus quite different from that which we have identified as "incentive of the second kind." Perhaps our appreciation of this difference between Professor Shackle's frame of reference and that developed in this paper may permit us to see through somewhat different spectacles the nature of (what Professor Shackle considers to be) profit-due-to-luck.

THE COUNTEREXPECTED AND THE UNEXPECTED

As we have seen, Shackle identifies a portion of realized pure profit as merely the result of luck by showing it to have been "counterexpected." Viewing matters from this perspective, it is difficult not to agree with Shackle that the taxation of this portion of profit can have no disincentive effect on entrepreneurial action. But it must be submitted that this understanding of the scope for "imaginative enterprise" seems far too narrow. It may be suggested that a broader view of the entrepreneurial role would permit us to see that what is important is not so much the distinction between the expected (in Shackle's sense of the prospect "most vividly in mind") and the counterexpected, but rather the distinction between that which has been considered as a possible contingency and that which has somehow not been considered at all. (The latter is what Shackle calls the "unexpected event," i.e., the "contingency which has entirely escaped attention.")[7] This distinction will permit us to recognize the possible incentive character of profit resulting from sheer luck at several distinct levels.

For us, to choose entrepreneurially calls for more than merely identifying, out of an array of conceivable outcomes perceived as available, that which appears most vivid. To choose entrepreneurially must include also the step of "discovering" those courses of action, and those arrays of potential outcomes, that one believes to be relevantly conceivable. Now we know very little about how "incentives of the second kind" operate; we know little about how the attractiveness of an outcome (or an array of possible outcomes) of a course of action stimulates the discovery of the possibility of this course of action. But we do know, if only in a very general way, that potentially at-

7. Ibid., p. 73.

tractive outcomes somehow do tend to stimulate attention.[8] We do seem to notice what we are personally interested in more than we notice what holds no interest for us. From the perspective of our analysis of "incentives of the second kind," the profit incentive is not called for to stimulate *adoption* of perceived courses of action. Were we to be concerned with what stimulates the entrepreneur to *undertake* a risky, already perceived course of action, we would have to agree that (considered, but) counterexpected outcomes can have played no role in stimulating the relevant assumption of risk by the entrepreneur.[9]

Our concern, however, in the context of incentives of the second kind, is with the discovery of possibilities *worthy of consideration*. Consider the following set of imagined circumstances:

1. Very attractive potential outcomes help call attention to a relevant course of action that may be available.
2. After consideration of this possible course of action, it turns out that those particular outcomes are indeed, in the end, counterexpected.
3. Nonetheless, the course of action is adopted because of other more vivid, if not quite as attractive, outcomes.

Surely, in the above circumstances, we must concede that those very attractive outcomes have played their incentive role in the discovery of the adopted course of action. These insights are already sufficient for us to recognize that at least some portion of apparently "lucky" profits (viz., that portion which entrepreneurial foresight had rendered "counterexpected" but not "unexpected") may yet have played an incentive role in stimulating adoption of the profitable course of action (by rendering that course of action sufficiently noticeable to have been discovered). But we can go even further.

The insights contained in the preceding paragraphs do not, after all, affect our understanding of profits that were in fact not merely counterexpected but indeed totally unexpected. Outcomes of an adopted

8. On this, see B. Gilad, "An Interdisciplinary Approach to Entrepreneurship: Locus of Control and Alertness" (Ph.D. dissertation, unpublished, New York University, 1981).

9. It should be noted in this respect that since *other* courses of action do not involve this riskiness, the incentive needed to render this risky course of action the preferred course must be that of "the first kind."

course of action that were so far from the decision maker's field of vision as to have escaped his notice altogether must surely, even according to these insights, appear to have totally lacked any incentive role in the fortunate adoption of that course of action. Yet we shall argue that the distinction between the counterexpected and the unexpected permits, in the light of our identification of incentives of the second kind, a different view even of this character of the entrepreneurial decision-making context.

INCENTIVES IN AN OPEN-ENDED WORLD

Although we have made frequent reference to what we have called "incentives of the second kind" (those that encourage *discovery* of courses of action, or their desirable outcomes, that might otherwise escape attention), we have not yet given attention to the paradox inherent in the very notion of this second kind of incentive. How, one must surely ask, can an enhancement of the desirability of a particular course of action that (by the very definition of this kind of incentive) *has not yet been noticed* inspire its discovery? How can an *unnoticed* potential outcome, no matter how attractive, affect behavior? How can the attractiveness of an unknown opportunity that awaits one around the corner possibly inspire one to peer around that corner?

It would be presumptuous and misleading to suggest that we know how to answer these questions. We do not know (and this appears to hold true not only for economists but for psychologists as well) precisely how human beings are inspired by the attractiveness of unknown opportunities. But there can be no doubt that such inspiration has been of enormous importance throughout recorded human history. The sources of entrepreneurial energy and alertness are still urgently in need of very basic research. Yet we know that the driving force behind this energy and this alertness is firmly rooted in the nature of the unknown—precisely the opposite of the economic motivations that govern nonentrepreneurial endeavor. Ordinary, nonentrepreneurial economic motivation operates within a given (real or assumed) closed set of circumstances. Under such circumstances the drive to succeed is motivated by the visible outcomes promised by success (in relation to the perceived necessary sacrifices required by the given, closed framework). The drive that spurs entrepreneurial energy and alertness, on the other hand, appears to take its source from the very open-endedness of the entrepreneurial context.

What activates the entrepreneurial antennae appears to be the potential entrepreneur's awareness that the situation holds unknown possibilities unhampered by known constraints. It is the entrepreneur's awareness of the *open-endedness* of the decision-context that appears to stimulate the qualities of self-reliance, initiative, and discovery.[10] It is here that we encounter once again, in a different context, the distinction between what Professor Shackle called the "counterexpected" and what he called the "unexpected."

That which is counterexpected, relates to the given, closed decision-context. The decision maker knows enough, or at least thinks he knows enough, to be convinced that a considered outcome or event is not to be expected. Even if the counterexpected character of this outcome or event derives from an assessment of the probability of its occurrence (also including in the notion of probability any relevant notion of "subjective probability," or of Shackleian potential surprise, that one may wish to invoke)—the conviction not to expect it resides, under these circumstances, in the set of given constraints viewed as governing the relevant probabilities. For the stimulation of entrepreneurial alertness, on the other hand, what is needed is the awareness of the *open* character of the situation one is confronting.

From this perspective, the truly unexpected character of an outcome or an event emerges—paradoxically, perhaps—as an aspect of it that is related, possibly in an essential manner, to that which inspires successful entrepreneurial decision-making. Entrepreneurial talent consists in peering into an unknown future and arriving at an assessment of relevant features of that future. The circumstance that this assessment occurs against the background of the realization that this future that one is assessing is, after all, an unknown future—is at the heart of what stimulates shrewd entrepreneurial assessments. In peering at the future one is aware that *nothing* is known with certainty about it, not the parameters of any probability functions, not the potential surprise functions, nor anything else.

From this perspective a profit component that emerges from a "lucky" entrepreneurial decision—in the sense that it would be wholly unreasonable to believe that the decision maker seriously entertained any expectation that this particular profit component might emerge—is not all to be dismissed as having played no incentive role. While this particular result was certainly wholly "unexpected" (in Shackle's sense,

10. See Gilad, *n.* 7.

particularly), it is precisely the entrepreneur's awareness of the potential that the situation held for the wholly unexpected that may have stimulated action and discovery.

To announce in advance to potential entrepreneurs that "lucky" profits will be taxed away, is to convert open-ended situations into situations more and more approximating those of a given, closed character. The complete taxation away of pure entrepreneurial profit can, it is clear, only succeed in removing all incentive for potential entrepreneurs to pay attention to anything but the already known (with the "already known" to be interpreted as including that which is known concerning the possibilities for costly, deliberate search, in the context of a given stochastic environment).

THE TAXATION OF ENTREPRENEURIAL DISCOVERY: REMARKS ON MORAL ASPECTS

As we have seen earlier, the taxation of pure profit involves none of the disincentives ("of the first kind") usually discussed in the economic theory of taxation. Without the insights argued in this chapter concerning the "second kind" of disincentive that may be associated with the taxation of pure profit, therefore, there would appear to be no purely economic reasons whatever not to tax away pure profit. (It should be remembered that pure profit is calculated, for our purposes, after deducting from gross revenues an amount sufficient, prospectively, to counterbalance the related risk of economic loss.) Now this conclusion, that the taxation of pure profit entails no undesirable allocative consequences—a conclusion this paper wishes to deny—turns out to reinforce a widely held view of the morality of profit. In this section we take note of this circumstance. We will, further, show in this section that the insights of this chapter (pointing out the economic disincentives involved in the taxation of pure profit) permit us to draw attention to moral aspects of pure profits that are not widely appreciated. Thus the questions raised in this paper, about the economic desirability of the taxation of profit, at the same time, weaken the moral grounds for considering such taxation as wholly justified.

In popular judgment, economic profit has frequently been held morally inferior to wage remuneration. This moral inferiority attached to profit appears to be derived from its *surplus* character: Profit is a receipt over and above the portion of output needed to ensure the maintenance of existing productive potential. From this perspective many critics of the capitalist system (and perhaps some of its defenders as well) have seen the theories advanced by economists to account for economic profit as somehow seeking to redeem the moral questionability of profit. The late Joan Robinson put this point of view most bluntly by asserting that the "unconscious preoccupation behind the neo-classical system was chiefly to raise profits to the same level of moral respectability as wages. The labourer is worthy of his hire. What is the capitalist worthy of?" [11]

Now whatever the moral justification that may be provided by economic theory for the share of profit received by the *capitalist,* it should be noticed that such justification does not yet extend to the category of pure entrepreneurial profit. By definition such profit consists of the surplus after the returns to *all* necessary factors of production, including interest on invested capital, have been set aside. No penny of pure entrepreneurial profit can be justified as *needed* to ensure the availability of any necessary productive service. Nor, by the same token, can any penny of pure profit be justified as being the *reward* of any necessary productive effort.

It may be observed that this apparent lack of moral justification for pure profit parallels with precision our discussion of how the category of pure profit possesses no incentive character (of the "first kind") whatsoever. Everything that is being done, in the course of the profitable productive activity, would be done even without one penny of profit. The circumstance that removes any incentive character (of the first kind) from pure profit is the same circumstance that, in the popular view, seems to render it morally unjustified. In that way economic reasoning arguing for the economic innocuousness of profit taxation is closely related to the reasoning that upholds the moral justification of such taxation.

The reasoning in this paper concerning the disincentive effects of profit taxation impinges on these considerations with obvious significance. On the one hand our reasoning supports, of course, the insight that pure profit fulfills no incentive role (of the first kind). But, more importantly, we have seen that an altogether different incentive role (that of the second kind) is fulfilled by pure profit. Understanding this incentive role for entrepreneurial discovery that is fulfilled by pure profit does not, of itself, invalidate the reasoning that we have cited questioning the moral justifiability of pure profit. After all, it

11. Joan Robinson, *Economic Philosophy* (New York: Penguin Books, 1962), p. 57.

still remains the case that no penny of pure profit was *necessary* to be paid in order to make it worthwhile for the owner of a productive service to put that service to work for this profitable undertaking; no penny of profit represents the *reward* for productive effort.

Nonetheless our emphasis upon the (second kind of) incentive role played by pure profit does have several possible moral implications. (1) Pure profit is indeed not necessary, in the narrow meaning of the word, to ensure availability of relevant productive services, *given widespread awareness of the worthwhileness of this productive undertaking*. But it may yet be, as we have seen, that the incentive role of pure profit was a crucial factor in attracting the attention of the successful entrepreneur. It could well be that without such pure profit, this productive undertaking would *not*, after all, have been undertaken. (2) Pure profit is, indeed, not received *in exchange for* any necessary productive service rendered. It is captured by entrepreneurs who were inspired to undertake courses of action the profitability of which was "unexpected" by the market at large. This circumstance permits us to recognize profits as having been "created" or, at least, "found," by the insightful entrepreneur. In this way it may be possible to defend the moral justifiability of pure profit on what has been called the "finders-keepers" ethic.[12]

Thus the question this paper asks concerning the economic desirability of the taxation of pure profit does tend to dovetail, in a clearly specified sense, with the related questions concerning the moral justifiability of such taxation.

THE ECONOMICS OF TAXATION: THE SCOPE FOR RESEARCH

In this chapter we have critically questioned the unstated premise of the standard theory of taxation. Our criticism rested on our insights into what we have described as incentives of the second kind. But to offer these questions and state these insights is not yet to formulate an economic theory of taxation (or even of the taxation of pure profit); far less is it to develop theoretically sound and administratively practical tax policy. A number of difficult theoretical and practical problems block the way, at least for the time being, to these goals. We

---

12. For more discussion of the "finders-keepers" ethic and its relevance for entrepreneurial profit, see Israel M. Kirzner, *Perception, Opportunity, and Profit, Studies in the Theory of Entrepreneurship* (Chicago: University of Chicago Press, 1979), chaps. 11 and 12.

may organize our listing of some of these problems under two main headings: (1) problems arising out of our ignorance concerning the precise disincentive impacts of different patterns of profit taxation; (2) problems arising out of the practical and empirical difficulties of identifying the pure profit components that are part of more conventional accounting categories, and hence the difficulties in identifying which taxes may in fact involve disincentive effects (of the second kind).

1. Unsettled Issues Related to the Disincentive Impact of Profit Taxation

We have pursued the insight that the pure profit inherent in economic opportunities may play an incentive role in inspiring the entrepreneurial discovery of those opportunities. This suggested strongly that the taxation of pure profits involves a disincentive not discussed in the standard literature on the economics of taxation. We linked this kind of disincentive to the circumstance that the taxing away of pure profit tends to convert an "open-ended" situation (that inspires entrepreneurial alertness) into the closed situation in which the alert, wide-awake, resourceful entrepreneur reverts into the routinely consistent, optimizing decision-maker within the given, perceived constraints. What is left unclear after these insights are acknowledged is the extent to which the *partial* taxation of profits affects the incentives for discovery. One the one hand it might appear that if profits provide incentive, then *any* reduction in the profit received must be presumed to weaken the incentives for discovery. On the other hand, however, it might be argued that a given percentage tax on prospective pure profit does not significantly erode the *open-endedness* of the situation. It is not, it may be held, the *absolute* levels of pure profit that confer the *open-ended* character upon the entrepreneurial situation. Thus at least moderate taxation of profit may perhaps only slightly affect its incentive power.

Research into the extent of the disincentive exercised by this kind of partial taxation of profit might consider the example of the entrepreneurial *partnership*. In such a partnership, too, each entrepreneurial partner can expect only a portion of the pure profits that the partnership may win through his own alertness. To what extent, one wonders, is the individual entrepreneur likely to be better motivated, more likely to perceive opportunities for pure gain, than the entrepreneur who is aware that whatever his own entrepreneurial insight perceives must be shared with a partner, or with the government?

Again, although we have emphasized the importance of pure profits as providing incentives of the second kind, we possess little knowledge of the possible different degrees in which these incentives operate in different contexts. The circumstance of "open-endedness" may perhaps operate quite differently in different concrete situations. Such differences in context appear to be distinguishable along several different dimensions.

It is well known that entrepreneurial endeavor (and thus pure entrepreneurial profit) may find scope at three distinct levels:[13] (1) the level of pure arbitrage, where paired buying and selling transactions are simultaneous (so that what the successful arbitrageur must "see" is entirely in the virtual present); (2) the level of pure speculation, where simultaneity is absent, so that entrepreneurial alertness must assess the future (but where that which is to be sold is physically identical with that which was bought); (3) the level of productive *creativity,* where not only is simultaneity absent, but the entrepreneur must also, so to speak, "be alert to" the possibility of combining given inputs into novel forms of product, or of obtaining given forms of product from novel combinations of input. At each of these levels the incentive for the entrepreneur to "see" correctly is to be attributed to the open-endedness of the environment. But to see a *present* price differential may call for human qualities different from those that make for shrewd speculation regarding the future. And the qualities of mind and character that stimulate "alert" creativity in production may be altogether different from those that inspire shrewd speculative vision into the future. Research into the sources of entrepreneurial alertness and into the incentive effects of pure profit must, presumably, treat each of these different kinds of entrepreneurial visions separately.

Or, again, in modern capitalism a good deal of entrepreneurial vision is exercised *within* complex organizations. In the large modern corporation, for example, there may be many levels at which alert corporate executives may enjoy sufficient discretionary scope, and be stimulated by sufficiently significant opportunities for pure gain for themselves, to require us to recognize these possibilities as representing important examples of entrepreneurial activity. There is every

---

13. I am indebted to Professor L. M. Lachmann for drawing my attention to this classification.

reason, however, to believe that the personal qualities undergirding successful entrepreneurship *within* the modern corporation may fail to overlap entirely with those qualities making for successful entrepreneurship in more conventional contexts. The impact of the taxation of the "pure profit" component in corporate executive rewards may turn out to be significantly different from the impact of taxation on other kinds of entrepreneurial profit. (One possibility for relevant research is suggested by the insights contained in Professor Henry Manne's thesis that legal prohibitions on "insider trading" operate to block the incentives to entrepreneurial discovery on the part of corporate executives.[14])

2. The Identification of Pure Profit

The second main heading under which we organize our listing of urgent research needs (in the area of entrepreneurial incentives) is that of the empirical identification of pure profits. For policy purposes, any propositions concerning the disincentive effects of the taxation of pure profits must be translated into corresponding statements referring to measurable accounting categories. But we have already seen that accounting profits are both wider and narrower than the category of pure entrepreneurial profit to which our discussions (concerning the "second kind" of incentives) have pertained. Accounting profits are wider than the category of pure profits, since the former may include implicit interest on invested capital and other nonentrepreneurial categories. Accounting profits are narrower than the category of pure profits insofar as the latter may include elements of entrepreneurial receipts won by the owners of resources, including labor.

All of this means that the empirical identification of the profit base, with respect to which our policy pronouncements are to be made, calls for careful and insightful research. Professor Shackle was concerned, we saw, with the practical problem of measuring the portion of pure profit attributable to entrepreneurial imagination (as distinct from that attributable to sheer luck). For us, as noted earlier, Shackle's problem need not perhaps appear to hold significant relevance for practical tax policy. But, as we see, measurement difficulties are likely to be severe even if no attempt is made to separate out elements (within the overall category of pure profit) attributable to sheer luck.

---

14. See Henry G. Manne, *Insider Trading and the Stock Market* (New York: Free Press, 1966).

But the measurement problem touches on deeper theoretical as well as policy issues. The category of pure profit is, after all, one that is linked essentially to *decisions*. Accounting categories, on the other hand, are linked specifically to *periods of time*. Where a long-run decision has been a profitable one (for example, a shrewd decision to build a plant capable of producing what turns out later to be a product in high demand), the entrepreneur may reap immediate accounting profit (e.g., by selling the plant to eager manufacturers when the strong demand has become apparent to all). But the entrepreneur's profitable decision may not be translated into accounting profits until later periods (e.g., when the entrepreneur operates the plant himself, in a market for which the profitability of this line of production has not yet become widely apparent). Within any given accounting period, therefore, the bare amount of accounting profit recorded reveals little that is definitive concerning the timing and the nature of the entrepreneurial decisions inspired by these profits.

The problems listed in this section certainly do not exhaust the research agenda that our position in this chapter seems to call for, if meaningful tax policy is to take account of our concerns. Nor, again, does our position in this chapter itself hold promise of any straight-forward solutions to these problems. Nonetheless, the questions raised with respect to orthodox tax theory do appear to demand the attention of theorists and policy analysts. It is for this reason that, inconclusive as our explorations have been, it seems necessary to offer them for consideration.

14

MONOPOLY POWER, TAXATION, AND ENTREPRENEURSHIP

E. C. Pasour, Jr.

INTRODUCTION

> The entrepreneurial function, the striving of entrepreneurs after profits, is the driving force in the market economy. . . . If the methods of taxation . . . restrict the accumulation of new capital, the capital required for marginal employments is lacking. . . . The wants of consumers are satisfied to a lesser extent. . . .[1]

Investment in capital goods hinges on expected productivity and profitability. The importance of profits in capital formation in the United States is stressed in the business community as well as the financial press. However, the role of profits in conventional neoclassical theory is not consistent with the importance of expected profits in investment decisions. When the norm of "perfect competition" is used as a benchmark, any firm facing a less than perfectly elastic demand is considered to be producing "too little." In this approach, any economic profits are considered to be "economic rents" serving no beneficial purpose.[2] The focus of public policy is then on taxation, marginal

---

1. Ludwig von Mises, *Human Action*, 3d ed. (Chicago: Henry Regnery Company, 1966), pp. 809–10.

2. This paper contrasts two theories of competition. The "structuralist" approach emphasizes the importance of "perfect competition." The "behaviorist" approach, in contrast, is concerned with how firms *act*. Donald Armstrong, *Competition versus Monopoly* (Vancouver:

cost pricing, and other economic regulation schemes to improve resource allocation.

Insights from the entrepreneurial market process approach provide
a much different perspective on competition and monopoly. Specifically, competition is concerned with entrepreneurial behavior or how
firms act, and the competitive market is considered to be a *process*
directed by profit and loss signals rather than a static situation in which
demand is perfectly elastic. In the nonequilibrium market process approach, returns commonly labeled "monopoly profits" *might* more
appropriately be viewed as returns to entrepreneurship rather than
"economic rents" that serve no useful function.

The major purpose of this chapter is to describe the adverse effects
of taxation and other economic regulations on the entrepreneurial market
process. The limitations of the concept of monopoly and monopoly
power in conventional neoclassical theory are first described. Monopoly power is then related to entrepreneurship—the driving force
of the market economy. Problems of identifying examples of resource
misallocation and entrepreneurial inefficiency, under real world conditions of uncertainty and imperfect information, are stressed. Entrepreneurial profit is contrasted with "economic rent," and it is shown
why taxes on "windfalls" and other profits adversely affect entrepreneurial incentives. Since profits and losses are the best indicators of
how well producers have accommodated consumer demands, it is argued, taxing profits is equivalent to taxing success in best serving the
public. Finally, it is held that there are ethical as well as economic
reasons for reducing the role of government, including restrictions on
entrepreneurship.

The policy implications of the analysis for taxation and capital formation are shown to be straightforward. Taxation adversely affects
entrepreneurial profits and, consequently, investment and capital formation. The entrepreneurial market process approach, however, reveals that capital formation hinges not only on taxation and expected
profitability but more broadly on market coordination. Since the production process occurs over time, intertemporal plan coordination is
necessary for savings to be converted into the most highly valued
investments. Expected product and input prices, profits, and interest

---

The Fraser Institute, 1982). In this chapter, these approaches are generally referred to as the
conventional neoclassical approach and the entrepreneurial market process (or profit and loss)
approach, respectively.

rates are all considered to be important in this coordination process. Consequently, the importance of political and economic conditions that hamper increased entrepreneurial activity is stressed.

MONOPOLY IN CONVENTIONAL NEOCLASSICAL THEORY

Monopoly in conventional theory is viewed as a market *situation,* but there is no consensus as to what that situation is. For Friedman and Becker, monopoly is taken to be a situation where demand is not perfectly elastic.[3] Glahe and Lee define monopoly as a situation in which there is a single seller of a product for which there are no close substitutes.[4] Hirshleifer considers monopoly to be the situation that exists when an industry consists of a single firm.[5]

In this traditional neoclassical approach, monopoly power may arise from several sources. Economies of scale is perhaps the most widely discussed basis of monopoly power. However, the theory of the so-called "natural monopoly," where average cost of production falls throughout the relevant region of output, presupposes a problem, at least to some extent, by assuming the presence of large economies and the lack of good substitutes. Increasingly, questions are being raised about the practical significance of the "natural monopoly" as a source of monopoly power. First, Demsetz argues that the competitive result can be obtained through bidding by rival potential monopolists even if there are economies of scale that limit production of the good or service to a single firm.[6] This argument holds that scale economies in production need not lead to "monopoly power" in the market place if the productive inputs are available to many potential bidders and rival producers do not collude. Entrepreneurial competition can be expected to eliminate "excess profits" as long as entry does not depend on prior possession of a particular resource. The problem of *rebidding* when one firm has capital facilities in place, however, raises questions about the feasibility of this bidding ap-

3. Milton Friedman, *Price Theory* (Chicago: Aldine Publishing Co., 1976), p. 126. Gary S. Becker, *Economic Theory* (New York: Alfred A. Knopf, 1971), p. 94.

4. Fred R. Glahe and Dwight R. Lee, *Microeconomics: Theory and Applications* (New York: Harcourt, Brace, Jovanovich, Inc., 1981), p. 287.

5. Jack Hirshleifer, *Price Theory and Applications,* 2d ed. (Englewood Cliffs, N.J.: Prentice-Hall, 1980), p. 232.

6. Harold Demsetz, "Why Regulate Utilities?" *Journal of Law and Economics* 11 (April 1968): 55–65.

proach. Moreover, if government selects only one supplier for a particular service, there is an incentive for firms to engage in bribery and other "rent seeking" activities, and for public officials to compromise themselves to some extent.

Second, regardless of the feasibility of the Demsetz proposal, it is becoming increasingly clear that direct competition is feasible in the case of many services traditionally labeled "natural monopolies." In more than twenty cities throughout the United States, for example, producers now face direct competition in providing electric utility services.[7] Savas cites evidence that private companies relative to government agencies can provide fire protection, mail service, garbage collection, health care and many other services at lower cost.[8] Such results raise questions about the theory of "natural monopoly" as a basis of monopoly power and the rationale for "public utility" regulation.

Restrictions on the access to productive factors is another alleged basis of monopoly power. The control of oranges, for example, might be expected to give a firm a monopoly position in the production of orange juice.[9] However, two questions immediately arise in the case of an alleged resource monopolist. First, how would a producer achieve such a position? The conventional wisdom appears to be erroneous concerning perhaps the most frequently cited historical example of monopoly based on control of inputs. The Aluminum Company of America (Alcoa) is alleged to have "controlled practically every source" of bauxite essential in the production of aluminum.[10] In fact, Alcoa owned less than half the bauxite in the United States at the time, and the supply outside the country was found to be "practically inexhaustible."[11]

The Alcoa example illustrates the problem facing any would-be monopolist—the problem of limiting entry and eliminating domestic and foreign competition. How would a producer of orange juice, for example, obtain control over oranges? The cartel model suggests that

7. Jan Bellamy, "2 Utilities Are Better Than One," *Reason* 13 (Oct. 1981): 23–30.

8. E. S. Savas, *Privatizing the Public Sector* (Chatham, N.J.: Chatham House Publishers, Inc., 1982).

9. Israel M. Kirzner, *Competition and Entrepreneurship* (Chicago: University of Chicago Press, 1973), p. 99.

10. Edwin Mansfield, *Microeconomics: Theory and Applications* (New York: W. W. Norton and Company, 1979), p. 281.

11. Dominick Armentano, *Antitrust and Monopoly: Anatomy of a Policy Failure* (New York: John Wiley and Sons, Inc., 1982), p. 105.

the free-rider incentive is likely to cause participating firms to cheat on agreements to restrict competition. Each firm has a financial incentive to secure an agreement to reduce sales in the aggregate and then to secretly break the agreement—to "free ride" on the other members. The orange example is a timely example of the approach commonly used by producers to achieve and maintain monopoly power. Orange producers in California are able to control the market flow of fresh oranges only because oranges are marketed under federal marketing orders—a *legalized* cartel system that uses the sanctions of government to supress the free-rider incentive of domestic producers and importers. Without such sanctions, voluntary cartel arrangements are typically short-lived.

There is also another shortcoming of resource control as a basis of monopoly power. If resources are defined narrowly enough, *every* producer has a resource monopoly—including Grandma Moses or the owner of the corner drugstore. Yet, it is obvious that such resource monopolies do not imply harmful monopoly power in any meaningful sense. There are good substitutes for the services of the corner drugstore or for the paintings of Grandma Moses.[12] Consequently, it is important to distinguish between the monopoly power arising because of government intervention and the so-called monopoly power of firms that face less than perfectly elastic demand curves achieved through entrepreneurial alertness. This distinction is generally not made in conventional neoclassical theory.

The orthodox view holds that monopoly involves resource misallocation because output in the industry directly affected is too small. In the example of the price searcher depicted in Figure 14–1, output is said to be reduced from OQ_c to OQ_m and price is increased from OP_c to OP_m. The alleged inherent inefficiency of monopoly involves a "transfer" of area A from consumers to producers. The efficiency loss of area B, the "welfare cost" or "deadweight loss," is due to the decrease in "consumer surplus" arising from the lower quantity of output (OQ_m rather than OQ_c). Thus, the monopolist is said to produce "too little" and to charge a price that is "too high" when contrasted with perfect competition. Monopoly in the situation depicted is deemed

---

12. E. C. Pasour, Jr., "Monopoly Theory and Practice—Some Subjectivist Implications: Comment on O'Driscoll," in I. M. Kirzner, ed., *Method, Process and Austrian Economics: Essays in Honor of Ludwig von Mises*, (Lexington, Mass.: D. C. Heath and Company, 1982), ch. 17, pp. 215–23.

Figure 14–1.   Monopoly—Equilibrium Price and Output in the Conventional Approach.

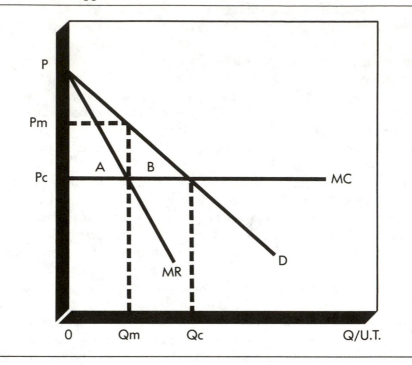

to be socially harmful because it leads to output restriction and price that is higher than marginal cost.[13]

There is, however, a basic difficulty with the presumed monopoly equilibrium depicted in Figure 14–1. This equilibrium presupposes that there is no price discrimination, or to put it another way, that the transactions costs of engaging in price discrimination—which are *not* depicted in the figure—make discrimination unprofitable. If unlimited price discrimination *is* profitable, the marginal revenue schedule becomes coincidental with the demand curve, and profit-maximization entails production where the marginal revenue schedule intersects a revised marginal cost schedule that considers the costs of price discrimination. In either this case or the case in which price discrimination is *not* profitable, the relevant policy question is whether there

13. Richard H. Leftwich and R. D. Eckert, *The Price System and Resource Allocation* (Chicago: The Dryden Press, 1982), p. 331.

exist alternative institutional arrangements that economize on trans-action costs sufficiently to produce an output level superior to that which will result from the market process.[14]

In conventional analysis, the economic profit (area A in Figure 14–1) is considered to be a Ricardian economic rent—a return perform-ing no useful economic function from the standpoint of a static anal-ysis. If this is correct, it follows that "a lump sum tax must be borne entirely out of the monopolist's profit."[15] In this approach, all traces of monopoly represented by less than perfectly elastic demand are branded socially harmful, and it is held that "monopoly profits" can be taxed away without adversely affecting resource allocation or the production process.

There are at least two problems with the approach just depicted. First, if every firm facing a negatively sloped demand curve is re-garded as having a monopoly, many sellers operating under compet-itive conditions (under any practically meaningful definition of the term) will be erroneously classified as monopolists—including the 10-year-old entrepreneur operating a lemonade stand. Buyers of a par-ticular product lack alternatives only if demand is perfectly inelastic. Since there are substitutes for *all* goods and services, however, no seller faces a perfectly inelastic demand. Thus, since closeness of substitutes is a matter of degree, any demarcation concerning how inelastic demand must be for the seller to be considered a monopolist is somewhat arbitrary. A second and even more fundamental reason why production is not socially harmful when demand is less than per-fectly elastic is emphasized in the market process approach.

MONOPOLY AND ENTREPRENEURSHIP IN THE MARKET PROCESS APPROACH

In the conventional equilibrium framework typically used to analyze monopoly, all economic profit is due to some degree of monopoly. In long-run competitive equilibrium the decisions of all market par-ticipants dovetail perfectly. There are no opportunities for gain and, consequently, neither profits nor profit opportunities. Within this framework profits are viewed as an imperfection.[16]

---

14. Gerald P. O'Driscoll, Jr., "Monopoly in Theory and Practice," in Kirzner, *n.* 12, p. 200.

15. Leftwich and Eckert, *n.* 13, p. 342.

16. Ludwig von Mises, *Planning for Freedom,* memorial ed. (South Holland, Ill.: Lib-ertarian Press, 1974).

The alternative suggested by the Austrians is to focus not on equilibrium states, but on the market process. The existence of high profits by one firm (or many firms) will attract competing producers as long as the market process is at work. The central theoretical issue to be solved by any monopoly theory is therefore the problem of a firm's entry into the market process.[17] In this view, competition is a *process,* and the lack of effective market competition (or the presence of monopoly) is not because a particular market situation (perfectly elastic demand or a large number of firms) doesn't prevail. It hinges instead on something that prevents market participants from competing in the market.[18] Restrictions on competition other than those of a short-run nature, however, are almost invariably the result of government intervention.[19] Thus, it is argued here, the unhampered market tends to be a competitive market, and competition in the market-process sense is likely to be present as long as there exist no arbitrary state-imposed impediments to entry.

The entrepreneurial profit-and-loss approach places conventional monopoly theory in a new light and raises a key question. If a seller achieves a supranormal profit, why does the entry of new firms not occur? If, as Kirzner suggests, entrepreneurial activity is always competitive, one would expect entry as long as there are economic incentives and entry is not legally restricted.[20] Although the individual entrepreneur may achieve an "above normal" rate of return in the short run, competition erodes the advantage, given time for adjustment and freedom of entry by other firms.[21] That is, in an unhampered market there is an inherent tendency over time for profits (and losses) to disappear.

Another shortcoming of conventional monopoly theory is that it

17. O'Driscoll, *n.* 14, p. 189.

18. Even if market competition between firms is restricted by government, there is still likely to be competition by firms in the political arena. The theory of "rent seeking" suggests that individuals and firms compete in attempts to use the power of the state to enhance their own economic interests. James M. Buchanan, R. D. Tollison, and Gordon Tullock, *Toward a Theory of the Rent-Seeking Society* (College Station: Texas A & M University Press, 1980).

19. Benjamin A. Rogge, *Can Capitalism Survive?* (Indianapolis: Liberty Press, 1979), p. 147.

20. Kirzner, *n.* 9.

21. As Mises stresses, it should be recognized that "there is nothing 'normal' in profits and there can never be an 'equilibrium' with regard to them. Profit and loss are, on the contrary, always a phenomenon of a deviation from 'normalcy,' of changes unforeseen by the majority." See *n.* 1, p. 297.

does not fully reflect the long-run nature of the entrepreneurial market process. Where monopoly power is not the result of government intervention, the welfare consequences of monopoly cannot be appraised strictly in terms of the immediate allocation of resources. A downward sloping demand curve doesn't necessarily imply a harmful restriction on output when the nature of the competitive entrepreneurial process is taken into account. A particular firm may acquire a short-run advantage over competing firms through earlier entrepreneurial alertness or ingenuity. Consequently, entrepreneurial profits may be due to an awareness of arbitrage opportunities in time or space, or they may arise from the development or sale of a new product. Olson, in a recent study of the effects of specialized pressure groups, suggests that above-normal short-run rates of return due to innovation are of crucial importance in economic growth and progress.[22]

The preceding discussion suggests a shortcoming of the competitive equilibrium model in identifying or measuring "monopoly profits." The role of profits in stimulating entrepreneurial activity is ignored, since all profits are necessarily taken to imply market imperfections.[23] Thus, this approach, which deemphasizes the scope of beneficial profits, downplays the crucial role of profits in the market system.[24] Profits, in reality, provide the entrepreneurial incentive to produce goods and services consumers most urgently want and to direct resources into the hands of those most competent in producing and bringing goods to market. Moreover, since profits and losses reflect the success or failure of the entrepreneur in adjusting production to consumer demand, the profits of a competitive (in the Austrian sense) industry can never be said to be "too high" or "too low." In the words of Rogge: "The abnormally high profits in some industries are the signals that consumers are calling for more firms to enter those industries. The below-normal profits or outright losses in other industries are the signal that consumers are calling for some firms to get out.

---

22. "In the short run . . . there are often supranormal . . . rates of profit for some firms even with free entry. . . . What gives rise to these temporary profits? Most notably, innovations of one kind or another—discoveries of new technologies, previously unsatisfied demands of consumers, lower cost methods of production, and so on. And the greater the extent of the profits due to difficulties of entry and imitation, the greater the reward to the innovations that mainly explain economic growth and progress!" Mancur Olson, *The Rise and Decline of Nations* (New Haven: Yale University Press, 1982), p. 61.

23. S. C. Littlechild, "Misleading Calculations of the Social Costs of Monopoly Power," *The Economic Journal* 91 (June 1981): 348–63.

24. Mises, *n.* 16 r, p. 19.

. . . The above-normal profits then are not 'too high' in any value sense, nor are the below-average profits 'too low.' They are simply signals and very, very important signals as well."[25]

The entrepreneurial market process approach, in contrast to that of long-run competitive equilibrium, stresses the necessity of using a model that permits above-average returns to entrepreneurship. The relevant alternative to output OQ_m in the situation depicted in Figure 14–1 may not be OQ_c but rather no output at all—at least during the time period under consideration. Consequently, the entrepreneur's action in producing the product is likely to generate a net *social gain* rather than a net social cost.[26] It is inappropriate and inconsistent with the very nature of the competitive market process to consider returns to entrepreneurship as socially harmful.

The concept of the market as a competitive process stresses the importance of taking a longer-run view of what from a shorter-run view may appear to be excessive profits or losses; such a concept also suggests that the most meaningful way to define monopoly is as a governmental grant of special privilege.[27] If one considers the important cartels in the United States today, virtually all are rooted in government power. Occupational licensing, restrictions on imports of autos and steel, agricultural marketing orders and other agricultural price support programs, labor cartels, the Post Office, and various firms operating under government franchise are examples of state-sanctioned and -enforced restrictions on competition. Government restrictions on entry in these and other areas have the effect of stifling initiative and the creative discovery process of the competitive market. Yet, discussions of monopoly profit seldom distinguish profits due to entrepreneurship from profits rooted in state power. The failure to make this distinction appears to be closely related to the general neglect of entrepreneurship in neoclassical theory.

The entrepreneur is seldom encountered in neoclassical theory as

25. Rogge, *n.* 19, p. 143–44.
26. Littlechild, *n.* 23, p. 358; Dean A. Worcester, Jr., "On the Validity of Marginal Analysis for Policy Making," *Eastern Economic Journal* 8 (April 1982): 87.
27. "The charge . . . that capitalism is doomed by the growth of monopolies is unfounded. Few monopolies would survive if it were not for protective government policies. The tremendous progress in transportation and communication technology, the rapid spread of technological knowledge, the development of new industrial centres in different parts of the world . . . and the resulting rapid growth of world trade in manufactured goods have undermined monopoly positions." Gottfried Haberler, "Schumpeter's Capitalism, Socialism and Democracy after Forty Years," in A. Heertje, ed., *Schumpeter's Vision*, (New York: Praeger, 1981), p. 83.

presented in economic theory texts.[28] In the words of Baumol, "The theoretical firm is entrepreneurless—the Prince of Denmark has been expunged from the Discussion of Hamlet."[29] Kirzner suggests that the neglect of entrepreneurship can be traced to the general preoccupation of neoclassical theory with final equilibrium positions.[30] The focus on equilibrium masks the role of the entrepreneur, since the plans of different individuals are mutually compatible when markets are in equilibrium.[31] Stated differently, the decisions of all market participants dovetail completely in equilibrium so there is no scope for profit-seeking entrepreneurship. There is no explanation of how market participants obtain the knowledge required; it is merely assumed that information and transactions costs "are such as to provide the conditions that are required for economic equilibrium."[32]

In the conventional Robbinsian approach to the theory of the firm, entrepreneurial problems are largely assumed away. It is implicitly assumed that the decision maker has the necessary information on costs and returns of alternative production strategies—that is, means and ends are assumed to be *given*. In this approach, where the entrepreneurial problem consists of selecting from among known alternatives, entrepreneurship is reduced to calculation.[33] In the real world, of course, the entrepreneur is *not* given perfect information on means or ends, and the decision maker must deal with the uncertain future.[34] In this setting where all decisions are shrouded in uncertainty, entre-

28. "It may be said quite categorically that at the present time there is no established economic theory of the entrepreneur." Mark Casson, *The Entrepreneur: An Economic Theory* (Totowa, N.J.: Barnes and Noble, 1982), p. 9.

29. W. J. Baumol, "Entrepreneurship in Economic Theory," *American Economic Review* 58 (May 1968): 69.

30. Israel M. Kirzner, *Perception, Opportunity, and Profit* (Chicago: University of Chicago Press, 1979).

31. F. A. Hayek, *Individualism and Economic Order* (Chicago: University of Chicago Press, 1948), p. 41.

32. T. W. Schultz, "The Value of the Ability to Deal with Disequilibrium," *The Journal of Economic Literature* 13 (Sept. 1975): 829.

33. "Conventional economics is not about choice, but rather about acting according to necessity." G. L. S. Shackle, *Decision, Order and Time in Human Affairs* 2d ed. (London: Cambridge University Press, 1969), p. 272. Buchanan explains why this is so: "Once the format has been established in allocation terms, some solution is more or less automatically suggested. Our whole study becomes one of applied maximization of a relatively simple computational sort." James M. Buchanan, *What Should Economists Do?* (Indianapolis: Liberty Press, 1979), p. 24.

34. Loasby indicates why choice is rooted in uncertainty. "If choice is real, the future cannot be certain; if the future is certain, there can be no choice." Brian J. Loasby, *Choice, Complexity and Ignorance* (New York: Cambridge University Press, 1976), p. 5.

preneurial mistakes are far more likely to be due to an erroneous assessment of present and future conditions rather than to errors in calculation.[35]

As suggested above, there are no entrepreneurial opportunities when markets are in equilibrium. The real world decision-making arena, however, is one of disequilibrium—a situation characterized by incomplete market coordination, which gives rise to profit opportunities. That is, since the decisions of market participants never perfectly dovetail when economic conditions are constantly changing, alert entrepreneurs are able to perceive or create new market opportunities that have not been noticed or taken advantage of by other decision makers.[36] Thus, the competitive market process is set in motion by disequilibrium conditions.

There is no consensus about the nature of the entrepreneurial process. Kirzner considers the entrepreneur important in moving markets toward equilibrium by discovering and profiting from arbitrage across markets.[37] In this view, the entrepreneur is not required to own any productive resources; there *is* the necessity, however, to be alert in perceiving and exploiting price differences. In contrast, the entrepreneur is a disequilibrating force in the Schumpeterian analysis. Temporary monopoly profits are the rewards to entrepreneurs who introduce successful innovation. It is a basic premise of Schumpeter's analysis that such rewards are necessary to induce entrepreneurs to engage in innovative activity. Indeed, this is the economic logic of the patent system—a state-imposed restriction on competition.[38] Olson, also stressing the importance of innovation in economic progress, suggests that an innovative firm may achieve short-run profits through delays in entry and imitation by competitors even when the firm is a price-taker.[39] The conclusion is that a firm may achieve short-run profits

35. Kirzner, *n*. 30.

36. T. W. Schultz, "Investment in Entrepreneurial Ability," *Scandinavian Journal of Economics* 82 (no. 4, 1980): 437–48.

37. Kirzner, *n*. 9.

38. Brian J. Loasby, "The Entrepreneur in Economic Theory," *Scottish Journal of Political Economy* 29 (Nov. 1982): 241.

39. "Suppose that a . . . firm in any purely competitive industry discovers a new method of production that is significantly less expensive than any previously known, but suppose also that increasing costs . . . ensure that the innovator will not take over the industry. The innovative firm has no monopoly power . . . but until others can successfully initiate the innovation it has supranormal profits. So it is disequilibrium rather than monopoly itself that is emphasized here as the reward to innovation." Olson, *n*. 22, p. 61.

from innovative activity regardless of whether it has "monopoly power." Thus, it is argued, entrepreneurial profits are socially beneficial whether or not the seller is a price-taker and regardless of whether entrepreneurial activity is equilibrating.

It is significant that the theory of perfect competition and market equilibrium is rooted in the assumption of perfect knowledge. In the market process approach, in contrast, emphasis is placed on how information is brought to bear on decisions by market participants and how it directs relevant information to those who make the best use of it. In this sense, then, the competitive market is a discovery process.[40] Different people have different information about production and market conditions, and markets enable individuals to communicate this information to other people and to learn about information that other people have. The "economic calculation debate" of the 1920s and 1930s was fundamentally about the importance of decentralized markets in organizing production.[41] Since that time, a great deal of effort has been spent analyzing the efficiency of competitive markets. Economic efficiency has a well-defined meaning based on the norm of perfect competition. However, as shown in the following section, the competitive norm is of little (if any) value in identifying inefficiency under real world conditions of uncertainty and costly information.

PERFECT COMPETITION AND MONOPOLY WASTE—MEASURING INEFFICIENCY

Efficiency in welfare economics is defined in terms of the competitive norm. Perfect competition assumes price-taking behavior in buying and selling and "perfect markets"—including perfect communication, instantaneous equilibrium, and costless transactions.[42] No real-world market, of course, can match this "ideal." Thus, real-world markets will *always* fall short when measured against the competitive norm. Price-taking, for example, implies that demand is perfectly elastic. Yet, as suggested above, many sellers operating under highly competitive conditions will be considered "imperfectly competitive" on the basis of this criterion. Thus, when perfect competition is the benchmark, monopoly profit, monopoly power, and resource misal-

40. Hayek, *n.* 31.
41. F. A. Hayek, *New Studies in Philosophy, Politics, Economics and the History of Ideas* (Chicago: University of Chicago Press, 1978).
42. Hirshleifer, *n.* 5.

location inevitably will appear to be serious problems in real-world markets.

Similarly, the stress on the "perfect market" masks the real-world contribution of individuals who would have no role to perform in "perfect markets." If there were perfect communication, for example, there would be neither the need to advertise nor a role for advertisers. Similarly, if there were no transaction costs and markets achieved instantaneous equilibrium, neither middlemen nor speculators would have productive roles. Uncertainty and imperfect information, however, are features of all real-world markets. Demsetz has labeled the procedure of comparing existing imperfect arrangements with an unattainable ideal, the "nirvana" approach.[43] Thus, although analytically useful for some purposes, the competitive norm is not appropriate for evaluating the economic effciency of the real-world activities.[44] Furthermore, no one has discovered an appropriate benchmark for evaluating the efficiency of actual entrepreneurial decisions that are necessarily rooted in uncertainty and imperfect information. It is clearly inappropriate, however, to use a model that assumes away problems facing the entrepreneur in assessing entrepreneurial efficiency.

Economizing in the use of information is an important problem in entrepreneurial decisions. Whether it is economical for an individual to acquire more information before acting hinges on expected costs and benefits. The rational decision maker will attempt to acquire additional information only as long as the expected benefits exceed the costs.[45] What are the implications for measuring efficiency? The cost of any action is the value of the highest sacrificed alternative, and the value placed on the forgone alternative never actually experienced is inherently subjective.[46] Consequently, the outside observer cannot measure choice-influencing opportunity costs. This means that in making empirical efficiency measurements, the outside observer's own

43. Harold Demsetz, "Information and Efficiency: Another Viewpoint," *Journal of Law and Economics* 12 (April 1969): 1–22.

44. "But the critical question is, not what should the pattern of resource allocation look like, but how is it to be achieved; and the perfectly competitive model . . . provides no recipe for achieving anything." Loasby, *n.* 34, p. 190.

45. "Ignorance is like subzero weather: by a sufficient expenditure its effects upon people can be kept within tolerable or even comfortable bounds, but it would be wholly uneconomic entirely to eliminate all its effects." George J. Stigler, "The Economics of Information," *Journal of Political Economy* 69 (June 1961): 224.

46. James M. Buchanan, *Cost and Choice* (Chicago: Markham Publishing Co., 1969).

standard of value must be imposed to identify waste in the actions of other people.[47]

There is an important distinction between the *existence* and the *measurement* of inefficiency.[48] The subjective nature of data upon which decisions are based means that outside observers cannot identify and measure inefficiency on the part of others. This does *not* imply that there is no scope for improvement on the part of individual decision-makers. Kirzner defines an action as inefficient if the entrepreneur places himself in a position viewed (by himself) as less desirable than an equally available state.[49] Inefficiency from this standpoint implies an error or incorrect move in the sense that the decision maker fails to notice profit opportunities. We can be confident that genuine opportunities exist because the decisions of market participants are never perfectly coordinated.[50] The problem of measuring waste and inefficiency is closely related to that of windfalls and taxation addressed in the following section.

WINDFALLS, TAXATION, AND CAPITAL FORMATION

The concept of the market as a competitive entrepreneurial process, as suggested above, casts a different light on the role and importance of profits. If long-run equilibrium is used as a benchmark, all observed profits are due to some degree of monopoly, are considered to be permanent, and imply a welfare loss. In marked contrast, the entrepreneurial profit-and-loss approach stresses the importance of profits and the importance of taking a long-run view of what may seem from a short-run perspective to be excessive profits.[51] A major function of profit is "to shift the control of capital to those who know

---

47. Buchanan, *n*. 33, p. 63.

48. E. C. Pasour, Jr., "Economic Efficiency and Inefficient Economics: Another View," *Journal of Post Keynesian Economics* 4 (Spring 1982): 454–59.

49. Kirzner, *n*. 30, p. 120.

50. "At each instant, because the market is in a state of disequilibrium, genuine allocative inefficiencies remain to be removed simply because entrepreneurs have not yet noticed the profit opportunities these inefficiencies represent." Kirzner, *n*. 30, p. 135.

51. "A longer run view of what may seem to be excessive profits or losses is appropriate because every successful penetration of the unknown successful because of artful foresight, scientific estimation, or plain luck gives the entrepreneur an edge . . . that can be classified as a monopoly return." Worcester, *n*. 26, p. 87.

how to employ it in the best possible way for the satisfaction of the public."[52]

The treatment of profits in the long-run equilibrium framework reflects the neglect of the entrepreneurial aspects of productive activity.[53] Moreover, if entrepreneurs are risk-averters, what appear to be "unreasonably" high returns to the lucky or insightful may be necessary to evoke high levels of entrepreneurial activity.[54] Stated somewhat differently, what often appear to be excessive profits provide the "bait that lures capital on to untried trails."[55]

The profits of entrepreneurs who are most successful in coping with changing economic conditions cannot be taxed without adversely affecting entrepreneurial incentives and resource use. That is, taxes on "windfall profits," "speculative profits," and so on, will inevitably hamper entrepreneurial activity. Consequently, taxation reducing entrepreneurial returns is tantamount to an attack on the means used to cope with economic change. Taxes on entrepreneurship often come in disguise, as in the case of the Carter administration's "windfall profits" tax on the oil industry. In a dynamic economy, however, "windfalls" are the norm rather than the exception and are closely related to property rights and entrepreneurial expectations. Property rights, in a broad sense, refer to the entire set of people's expectations about what they can and may do.[56] A windfall, defined as the difference between the outcome expected and that actually realized, is commonly associated with pure luck. However, profit achieved by predicting the future more accurately than do others is not a windfall but a return to entrepreneurship. Moreover, in reality there is no objective way to separate windfalls from profits due to entrepreneurial

52. Mises, n. 16, p. 123.

53. What are the reasons for this neglect? Worcester suggests three reasons. "Perhaps most important is that there is virutally no theory of entrepreneurial activity. . . . Secondly, each generation seems to expect the stationary state to emerge. . . . Should this happen, entrepreneurs would have little or nothing to do. . . . Finally, there is the matter of self-interest. . . . [I]f the 'centralized computational way of finding efficient patterns' is, in principle, equivalent to the 'decentralized, atomistic way' professional advantage combines easily with social usefulness if some way can be found to reduce the costs of the centralized procedure below the costs of decentralized procedures." Worcester n. 26, pp. 85–86.

54. Ibid., p. 87.

55. Joseph A. Schumpeter, *Capitalism, Socialism, and Democracy*, 3d ed. (New York: Harper and Brothers, 1947) p. 90.

56. Paul Heyne, *The Economic Way of Thinking*, 4th ed. (Chicago: Science Research Associates, Inc., 1983), p. 199.

skills. Was the individual who invested in the petroleum industry in the early 1970s, for example, farsighted or merely lucky? In a market economy, the entrepreneur can expect to reap the rewards if future economic conditions are favorable and to bear the losses if economic conditions prove to be unfavorable. In the haste to tax windfalls, it is often forgotten that windfalls may be losses instead of gains. If entrepreneurs expect that losses will not be subsidized and profits will be taxed away, they have incentives to minimize risk.[57] Thus, any tax on windfalls is tantamount to an attenuation of property rights and will inevitable adversely affect entrepreneurial incentives.

The conclusion that there will be less risk-taking and innovative activity with an increased expectation that any future windfalls will be taxed away implies that the supply of entrepreneurial activity is upward sloping—the higher the expected return, the greater the amount of entrepreneurship. Conversely, the lower the expected return (e.g., due to taxes), the lower the amount of entrepreneurial activity. This view that entrepreneurship is a function of expected profitability is inconsistent with statements frequently made during the past decade suggesting that taxes levied on "windfall profits" of oil firms would not adversely affect production. "Monopoly profits" or "windfall profits" cannot be distinguished from entrepreneurial returns and, consequently, are *not* (purely) Ricardian economic rents. Economic rent, as conventionally defined, can be taxed away without adversely affecting production.[58] In contrast, taxes on profits arising from competitive entrepreneurial activity will inevitably have an adverse affect on expected returns, resource allocation, and entrepreneurship.

Entrepreneurial profits may be taken as the best indicator of the extent to which the decision maker has anticipated and accommodated the demands of the market. Even if entrepreneurial profits are due to luck rather than foresight, the end result of the entrepreneurial activity is no less beneficial. In the words of Mises: "Specific entrepreneurial profits and losses are not produced by the quality of physical output.

---

57. Ibid.

58. "*Economic rent* is defined as that portion of the payment to the supplier of an input that is in excess of the minimum amount necessary to retain the input in its present use." Edgar K. Browning and J. M. Browning, *Microeconomic Theory and Applications* (Boston: Little, Brown and Co., 1983), p. 434. In order for the return to entrepreneurial activity to be an "economic rent," the supply of entrepreneurship must be perfectly inelastic so that quantity available does not respond to changes in the expected return.

. . . What produces them is the extent to which the entrepreneur has succeeded or failed in anticipating the future—necessarily uncertain—state of the market."[59]

In summary, if it is acknowledged that the supply of entrepreneurial activity is upward sloping, it follows that taxes on entrepreneurial profits inevitably affect resource allocation and future production. That is, there are *no* profits or entrepreneurial returns that can be taxed away without affecting resource allocation and capital formation. A recognition of the crucial nature of the entrepreneurial role in the market process means that the quest for a "neutral" tax is futile. That is, a tax that will leave the market exactly the same as it was without taxation "must always be a chimera."[60]

INFLATION AND ENTREPRENEURIAL ACTIVITY

The interaction of the tax laws and inflation can be devastating for entrepreneurial activity. During the past decade, the corporate sector in the United States was taxed at nominal rates up to 46 percent and individuals were taxed at rates up to 70 percent.[61] After taking inflation into account, however, the real tax burden on capital was frequently greater than 100 percent.[62] One important factor has been the bracket creep associated with progressive income tax rates. During the 1970s, even when workers received pay raises enough to offset inflation, real after-tax wages often decreased because of bracket creep. Whereas only 3 percent of U.S. taxpayers faced marginal tax rates of 30 percent or more in 1960, by 1981 the number of taxpayers in the 30 percent (or higher) tax bracket had reached 34 percent.[63] Real

59. Mises, *n.* 1, pp. 292–93.

60. Murray N. Rothbard, *Power and Market: Government and the Economy* (Menlo Park, Calif.: Institute for Humane Studies, 1970), p. 65.

61. The Economic Recovery Tax Act (ERTA) of 1981 reduced the highest nominal marginal tax rate from 70 percent to 50 percent.

62. "In the decade of the 1970s . . . the real tax rate on investment income . . . was not 70 percent, but 70 percent of a nominal amount of earnings that was mostly inflation, combined with a decline in the value of principal equal to the rate of inflation. . . . On a $10,000 certificate of deposit earning 10 percent interest, for example, pretax earnings would be $1,000, taxation would be $700, exclusive of state levies, and the loss in principal due to an inflation rate of 7 percent would be $700. The *real* tax, therefore, would be $1,400 on earnings of $1,000, or 140 percent. . . ." George Gilder, *Wealth and Poverty* (New York: Basic Books, Inc., 1981), p. 175.

63. Thomas Humbert, *Tax Indexing: At Last a Break for the Little Guy* (Washington, D. C.: The Heritage Foundation, 1983), p. 1. ERTA provides that all tax rate brackets and personal exemptions are to be indexed for inflation beginning in 1985. There was, however,

tax burdens, on average, increased about 15 percent from 1975 to 1981 as a result of bracket creep.[64] The interaction of tax laws and inflation during the past decade also led to earnings being overstated because of understated depreciation expenses, since depreciation for tax purposes is based on the original purchase price rather than opportunity cost. Thus, in view of bracket creep, overstated earnings, and public policies that decrease savings, it is not surprising that there was a relatively low level of saving and investment during the 1970s.[65] Moreover, environmental, safety, and other government regulations also have increased costs and reduced the expected profitability of business activity. These regulations are, in effect, hidden taxes on business enterprise.

At a time when there is widespread concern about unemployment and the competitive position of U.S. industry, the relationship between capital formation and productivity warrants additional emphasis. In the words of Mises, "There is only one way that leads to an improvement of the standard of living for the wage-earning masses, *viz,* the increase in the amount of capital invested."[66] There can be little doubt that the rate of capital formation in the United States during the past decade has been adversely affected by taxes, inflation, and government regulations.[67]

---

a political attempt in 1983 to repeal tax indexing before it became effective. The future of tax indexing remains uncertain as of March 1984.

64. Joseph A. Pechman, "Anatomy of the U.S. Individual Income Tax," in S. Cnossen, ed., *Comparative Tax Studies: Essays in Honor of Richard Goode* (New York: North-Holland Publishing Co., 1983), p. 81.

65. A number of policies that have discouraged saving are identified in the following section.

66. Mises, *n.* 16, p. 152.

67. Lachmann has stressed that there is an inherent problem of measuring capital, since the concept "capital" as used by economists has no clear and unambiguous meaning. Sometimes the term "capital" is used to denote material resources, sometimes their money value. The basic problem is that since capital resources are heterogeneous both physically and in use, the "best" use of capital is not *given* but is instead an entrepreneurial decision. In the words of Lachmann: "The generic concept of capital without which economists cannot do their work has no measurable counterpart among material objects; it reflects the entrepreneurial appraisal of such objects. Beer barrels and blast furnaces, harbour installations and hotel room furniture are capital not by virtue of their physical properties but by virtue of their economic functions. Something is capital because the market, the consensus of entrepreneurial minds, regards it as capable of yielding an income." Ludwig M. Lachmann, *Capital and Its Structure* (Kansas City: Sheed Andrews and McMeel, Inc., 1978), p. XV.

MARKET SIGNALS, SAVING, AND CAPITAL FORMATION

In the entrepreneurial market process, where expectation of gain is the propelling force of action, capital formation hinges on savings and productive investment.[68] In this profit-and-loss system, information is coordinated and transmitted through the price system, which helps ensure that the right things will get produced. Prices provide accurate signals to consumers and producers; they do so, however, only when they are free to change in response to changing economic conditions. When price supports raise prices of agricultural products above the market clearing level, for example, producers are encouraged to produce "too much," whereas consumers are induced to consume "too little" at the artificially high price. Such programs not only increase domestic production but also inhibit shifts in production between different production regions. In this sense, price controls served to stifle the discovery process of the market.[69]

Similarly, expected profits provide incentives for entrepreneurs to use effectively the information conveyed by prices. As suggested above, however, entrepreneurship is not an either/or phenomenon—instead, the amount of entrepreneurial activity hinges on the expected profitability. Therefore, an increase in taxes, *ceteris paribus*, inevitably has an adverse impact on profitability and hence induces producers to produce "too little" in most cases.

Consider next the relationship between entrepreneurship and saving and its implications for capital formation. Saving is a necessary condition for a high level of capital formation. In Keynesian analysis, however, capital accumulation as opposed to aggregate demand is downplayed and saving is often viewed as positively harmful.[70] A major conclusion of Keynesian theory is that unemployment during the Great Depression was caused by a low level of spending—reflecting the desire of households to save more than firms wished to invest. The importance of maintaining a high level of aggregate de-

---

68. "Profit hoped for, profit deemed possible, drives the market. . . . *Investment* in long-lasting and complex equipment is also in essence an operation decided on under market influences, under the hope of profit." G. L. S. Shackle, "Means and Meaning in Economic Theory," *Scottish Journal of Political Economy* 29 (Nov. 1982): 233.

69. Hayek, *n*. 41.

70. Martin Feldstein, "The Retreat from Keynesian Economics," *The Public Interest* (Summer 1981): 97.

mand in Keynesian theory provided justification for a wide variety of public policies designed to encourage spending and to discourage saving.[71] What has been the result? "Unfortunately, our policies have been very successful in depressing the rate of saving. . . . And since the amount of saving that any nation does effectively limits the amount of investment that it can make, these low saving rates have caused correspondingly low rates of investment."[72]

The theory of entrepreneurship further demonstrates why the Keynesian animus toward saving is misdirected. The accumulation of capital hinges on savings that provide the resources necessary for investment. Yet saving is not sufficient, since there must be intertemporal plan coordination for savings to be converted into the most highly valued investments. Prices, profits, and interest rates all play key roles in decisions concerning production over time.

Capital formation is also affected by redistribution and related "rent seeking" activities. Rent-seeking is the term applied to efforts by individuals and groups to achieve income transfers through the aegis of the state.[73] Special-interest groups in some cases seek to increase their incomes by lobbying directly for income transfers. The increase in rent-seeking activities and the resulting income transfers have reduced the profitability of entrepreneurial activity because of increased tax burdens. In other cases, organized groups seek legislation to raise some price or wage. Gains to particular groups from government-sanctioned and -enforced cartels in agriculture, labor, and other markets have been achieved by restricting output to obtain higher prices. Regardless of the particular form of government-enforced restriction on competition, the effect is to increase income to small groups at the expense of overall productivity and output. In short, the economy is made less dynamic.[74]

71. ". . . our low saving rate does not reflect any single policy but rather a whole range of policies that affects every aspect of economic life: tax rules that penalize saving; a social security program that makes saving virtually unnecessary for the majority of the population; credit market rules that encourage large mortages and extensive consumer credit while limiting the rate of return available to the small saver; and perennial government deficits that absorb private saving and thereby shrink the resources available for investment." Ibid., p. 101.

72. Ibid., p. 99.

73. Buchanan, et al., eds., *n.* 18.

74. "The growth of coalitions with an incentive to try to capture a larger share of the national income . . . and the increased bargaining . . . that cartels create alter the pattern of incentives and the direction of evolution in a society. The incentive to produce is diminished; the incentive to seek a larger share of what is produced increases." Olson, *n.* 22, p. 72.

Incentives, information, and coordination are all important aspects of entrepreneurial activity and of capital formation. This suggests that taxation directly affecting savings and capital formation cannot be considered independently of government intervention in general.[75] Stated differently, the coordination of economic activity (including capital formation) is affected not only by tax policies but also by numerous other market distortions, including those rooted in monetary and regulatory policies. The effects of monetary policies on inflation, interest rates, and investment, although highly important, are beyond the purview of this chapter.

Capital formation hinges on the extent to which key market signals—prices, profits, and interest rates—are free to perform their coordination roles in the market process. Consequently, the removal of tax disincentives alone may not be sufficient to significantly increase capital formation when prices, profits, and interest rates are distorted by such factors as price controls, inflation, and economic regulations. However, tax disincentives can be great enough to impede entrepreneurial activity significantly, even in an otherwise unhampered market. Moreover, tax disincentives are always a deterrent to entrepreneurship, whether or not there are other distortions.

IMPLICATIONS AND CONCLUSIONS

Although antitrust policies are ostensibly designed to foster competition, numerous governmental agencies and activities deliberately restrict competition. These activities hamper or prohibit the operation of decentralized markets, thereby impeding the discovery process of the market. The competitive entrepreneurial market process approach, focusing on how firms act, stresses the importance of bona fide competition, which "requires not large numbers of buyers and sellers but simply *freedom of entry*."[76] There is a great deal of casual evidence

75. ". . . even if supply-side tax policies are instituted and the level of savings and investment increases dramatically, the informational problems associated with distorted prices and interest rates that guide the channeling of this investment remain. . . . Tax cuts do not address the problem of determining which specific capital goods should be bought, where should new plant and equipment be located, how capital-intensive should any given production process be and how do these investment plans dovetail with the plans of other producers and with consumers. These problems can be solved only by removing the distorting influences on prices and other market signals." Richard H. Fink, *Supply-Side Economics: A Critical Appraisal* (Frederick, Md.: University Publications of America, Inc., 1982), p. 392.

76. Israel M. Kirzner, *The Perils of Regulation: A Market Process Approach* (Coral Gables, Fla.: Law and Economics Center, 1978), p. 9.

that unhampered markets are inherently competitive and that, in practice, effective restrictions on competition are almost always rooted in the power of the state.[77]

Since the market is a competitive discovery process, government intervention to tax away windfall profits or to initiate "antitrust policies" is unlikely to foster increased competition. In reality, government attacks on "monopoly power" are often attacks on firm advantages achieved through alert entrepreneurship. Moreover, effective restrictions on competition and taxation are similar in that both are rooted in state power. This raises the question: How can the harmful effects of state-supported monopoly power and taxation be reduced? Or, alternatively: What can be done to increase capital formation and productivity? The conclusion of Hayek concerning the dangers of economic planning appears to be fully applicable to government policies affecting entrepreneurship and capital formation. "If man is not to do more harm than good in his efforts to improve the social order, he will have to learn that . . . he cannot acquire the full knowledge which would make mastery of the events possible. He will therefore have to use what knowledge he can achieve, not to shape the results as the craftsman shapes his handiwork, but rather to cultivate a growth by providing the appropriate environment, in the manner in which the gardener does this for his plants."[78]

The effect of taxation and other market impediments on capital formation is clearly related to the size and scope of government. Policies that reduce taxation, government regulations, and "rent seeking" by special-interest groups will also increase entrepreneurial incentives, improve economic coordination, and thereby promote capital formation and productivity. Possible modifications of the political process to reduce the scope and magnitude of rent-seeking behavior is addressed by other papers of this volume. Regardless of the merits of particular alternative institutional reforms, Mitchell's conclusion appears apt: "While collective choice stands in the sharpest contrast to the market, marginal improvements are possible. But of all improvements the most effective is a steady diminution of the scope of government."[79]

---

77. Rogge, *n.* 19, p. 47.

78. Hayek, *n.* 41, p. 34.

79. William C. Mitchell, "Efficiency, Responsibility, and Democratic Politics," in R. Pennock and J. W. Chapman, eds., *Liberal Democracy* (New York: New York University Press, 1983), pp. 367–68.

In the final analysis, all taxes adversely affect entrepreneurial activity—the key element in capital formation. The level of taxation is closely related to the scope of government. Consequently, a decrease in taxes implies a diminution in the scope of government. This implies that an increased understanding of the entrepreneurial market process is an important step in achieving the political and economic environment necessary for investment and capital formation.

Although an "economic education revolution" is a necessary precondition in limiting the role of government, economic theory does not provide an objective procedure for determining the level of taxation or other public policies. Since costs and benefits are inherently subjective and cannot be aggregated across individuals to determine social costs and benefits, public policies cannot be determined on strictly economic grounds.[80] Consequently, economic theory is not a substitute for political and ethical analysis in resolving policy problems.[81] If freedom is accepted as an ethical standard, individuals have the *right* to engage in voluntary mutually beneficial exchange. Free enterprise or economic freedom means the right of anybody to compete—not the right of existing firms to maintain their markets. Income transfers obtained through state-imposed restrictions on competition are not consistent with economic freedom. In this light, state-sanctioned and -enforced restrictions on competition are inherently coercive and, thus, raise ethical issues.

A recognition of the importance of entrepreneurship in the market process shifts the focus away from the conventional economic approach, which emphasizes maximization techniques, equilibrium conditions, and perfect competition. In the entrepreneurial market process approach, much less emphasis in economic analysis is placed on determining the optimal allocation of resources, the most profitable pattern of production, or the proper distribution of income. In considering monopoly, taxation, entrepreneurship, and other economic issues, the

---

80. Although economic analyses often purport to measure "social costs" and "social benefits," the subjective nature of cost and value means that ". . . net social benefit is an artificial concept of direct interest only to economists." S. C. Littlechild. "The Problem of Social Cost," in Louis M. Spadaro, ed., *New Directions in Austrian Economics* (Kansas City: Sheed Andrews and McMeel, Inc. 1978), p. 92. Although economic theory provides knowledge useful to policy choices, it is not sufficient to enable the economist to advocate any public policy, since policy decisions ultimately rest on ethical or value judgments. Murray N. Rothbard, *The Ethics of Liberty* (Atlantic Highlands, N. J.: Humanities Press, 1982), p. 212.

81. G. Warren Nutter. *Political Economy and Freedom* (Indianapolis: Liberty Press, 1983).

focus of attention rather is on the framework of institutions and rules within which people can effectively cooperate in pursuing their own diverse ends.[82] The payoff from additional work on this "morally relevant" approach to political economy is potentially great.[83] This reorientation of economics will lead to both an increase in the range of individual choice and a decrease in the scope and power of government.

---

82. Leland B. Yeager, "Economics and Principles," *Southern Economic Journal* 42 (April 1976): 559–71.

83. James M. Buchanan, "The Related but Distinct 'Sciences' of Economics and of Political Economy," *British Journal of Social Psychology* 21 (1982): 175–83.

15

CAPITAL FORMATION AND INTERSTATE TAX COMPETITION

Bruce L. Benson and Ronald N. Johnson

INTRODUCTION

Conclusions derived from a large body of empirical evidence have fostered the belief that state and local taxes do not significantly affect the geographic allocation of investment and economic activity across the United States. This evidence appears to imply that state and local taxes do not affect capital formation or economic growth in the aggregate. The contention here is that such empirical studies have missed an important element and are therefore misleading. We argue that taxes at the state and local level do adversely affect capital formation and economic development.

Two primary explanations are offered here for why empirical studies have failed to find a consistent and significantly negative relation between various measures of state economic activity and state and local taxes. First, *interstate competition for tax base* tends to keep states' taxes in line with one another. Thus, there appear to be insufficient differences in taxes across states to allow detection of an impact of taxes in purely cross-sectional studies. Second, most studies of the impact of state and local taxes have failed to consider that investment and economic activity are likely to respond with a *lag* to changes in tax rates. Introducing a distributed-lag specification provides results that show a negative relation between taxes and capital

formation. However, we emphasize that interstate tax competition re-
strains states from dramatically increasing taxes. Since interstate tax
competition constrains political behavior, we anticipate and explore
actions on the part of states to reduce that competition.

The first section of this chapter offers a review of the literature
dealing with the impact of state and local taxes. The second develops
the concept of interstate tax competition, while a third provides empirical evidence showing the lag effect of taxes on investment. Section four considers actions by the states to reduce competition for the
tax base.

DO STATE AND LOCAL TAXES MATTER? A REVIEW OF THE EVIDENCE

A substantial portion of the literature indicating that state and local
taxes do not matter explores factors that influence interregional business location choices. Empirical investigations of this type exist in
sufficient numbers to have induced two comprehensive review articles: one in 1961[1] and another in 1981.[2] The conclusion drawn from
the literature did not change during the twenty years separating the
two surveys. As Wasylenko reported, " . . . empirical evidence that
taxes affect interregional business location decisions is almost nonexistent."[3] A recent empirical examination of location choice appears
to lend further support to Wasylenko's observation.

Dennis Carlton has examined the relative importance of a number
of factors in the location choice of new firms and new branch plants
in the plastic products, electronic transmitting equipment, and electronic components industries.[4] Carlton's procedure involves predicting the probability of location choice. Independent variables included
wage rates, various energy costs, a measure of potential agglomeration economies, labor force variables (e.g., unemployment, the num-

---

1. John F. Due, "Studies of State-Local Tax Influences on Location of Industry," *National Tax Journal* 14 (June 1961): 163–73.

2. Michael Wasylenko, "The Location of Firms: The Role of Taxes and Fiscal Incentives," in R. Bahl, ed., *Urban Government Finance: Emerging Trends*, vol. 20 of Urban Affairs Annual Review (Beverly Hills, Calif.: Sage, 1981), pp. 155–96.

3. Ibid., p. 186.

4. Dennis Carlton, "Why New Firms Locate Where They Do: An Econometric Model," in W. Wheaton, ed., *Interregional Movements and Regional Growth* (Washington, D.C.: The Urban Institute, 1979), pp. 13–50; Carlton, "The Location and Employment Choices of New Firms: An Econometric Model with Discrete and Continuous Endogenous Variables," *Review of Economics and Statistics* 65 (Aug. 1983): 440–49.

ber of engineers), and four different tax variables—the local property tax rate, the state personal income tax rate, the state corporate income tax rate, and an index representing the number of fiscal and financial incentives available from government units. Wage rates, energy costs, the agglomeration measure, and labor force variables were all found to be significant factors. However, the tax variables were generally found to be insignificant. Personal income taxes and property taxes were insignificant, while the corporate income tax rate was significant in two cases, but it was *positively* related to the probability of locating. The incentives index was usually insignificant, although the direction of influence was negative. These results correspond closely to findings in virtually every location study.[5]

The conclusion, drawn from econometric studies, that taxes do not have a substantial impact on location is also supported by survey results. Morgan reviewed seventeen survey and seven interview studies done before 1964.[6] Taxes were often mentioned by respondents as a location factor but were consistently ranked in the bottom one-fifth to one-tenth of influential factors. Only one of the seventeen surveys concluded that taxes were a primary location factor, while three concluded that they were of some significance and the remaining thirteen found them to be of little significance. The seven interview studies all concluded that taxes were of little significance.

There have also been several more recent survey-type studies. Stafford's interviews with firms that had recently located in Ohio, for example, ranked the relative importance of fourteen factors.[7] Taxes were the least frequently mentioned of the factors and appeared to be unimportant in determining either the choice of region or the actual site. Kieschnick surveyed independent firms that had established new locations and firms that had chosen locations for branches.[8] Only 14 percent of the new establishments considered that taxes had an influence on their location decision, but 35 percent of the plant-location choices for branches were said to be influenced by taxes. Kieschnick

5. See Wasylenko, *n.* 2; and Due, *n.* 1.

6. W. Morgan, "The Effects of State and Local Taxes and Financial Inducements on Industrial Location" (Ph.D. dissertation, University of Colorado, 1964).

7. H. Stafford, "The Anatomy of the Location Decision: Content Analysis of Case Studies," in F. E. Ian Hamilton, ed., *Spatial Perspectives on Industrial Organization and Decision-making* (New York: John Wiley, 1974).

8. Michael Kieschnick, *Taxes and Growth: Business Incentives and Economic Development* (Washington, D.C.: Council of State Planning Agencies, 1981).

concluded that business taxes do not assume any major importance except for branch plant locations.[9]

The few survey results indicating that taxes do matter are often treated with skepticism. As Washylenko pointed out, even unbiased surveys do not provide very precise information on the magnitude of a variable's impact on a location decision. Moreover, respondents may bias their answers in order to lobby for lower taxes or other fiscal inducements. If survey results therefore overstate the importance of taxes, they would appear to have only a minor influence on location choices.[10]

Carlton found it "difficult to understand why taxes do not matter more strongly in influencing location choice especially in view of the frequent public clamorings of business against taxes."[11] He offered several "possible" explanations for the results, and since these explanations appear frequently in the literature, they are worth reviewing. One argument is that the immobility of certain factors of production means that taxes are fully born by those factors through lower prices. Another widely proposed explanation for the apparent lack of a tax impact is that the benefits the firm receives from public expenditures offset the taxes that are paid. Carlton discounts this argument, however, because a large portion of state and local taxes are not used to provide business services.

The failure of many empirical studies to demonstrate that taxes have a significant impact on firm locations has also been attributed to the lack of variability in taxes across states.[12] Taxes do vary, of course, but perhaps not enough to overcome other differences (e.g., labor costs, energy costs). Furthermore taxes are not a large share of a firm's total costs.[13] On a composite basis, taxes represent only around 3 percent of annual total costs.[14] Since labor costs, for example, are

9. Ibid., p. 74.

10. Wasylenko, n. 2, p. 164.

11. Carlton, "The Location and Employment Choices of New Firms: An Econometric Model with Discrete and Continous Endogenous Variables," n. 4, p. 447.

12. Wasylenko, n. 2, p. 168; and see W. D. Morgan and W. E. Brownlee, "The Impact of State and Local Taxation on Industrial Location: A New Measure for the Great Lakes Region," Quarterly Review of Economics and Business (Spring 1974): 67–77.

13. However, as Wasylenko (n. 2. p. 170) notes, tax differentials may be a large share of a firm's total profit, and it is profit maximization rather than cost minimization that is expected to provide the motivation for a location choice.

14. Advisory Commission on Intergovernmental Relations (ACIR), Regional Growth: Interstate Tax Competition (Washington, D.C.: ACIR, 1981), pp. 32–34.

many times larger than state and local taxes, a very small differential in wages can outweigh a very large tax difference. The impact of the interstate tax differentials is also reduced by the deductibility of state and local taxes from federal taxes.[15]

Carlton further stressed that his findings—that location choice in the three industries he studied does not appear to be influenced by taxes—should *not* be interpreted to mean that taxes do not affect state (or regional) growth. He pointed out that taxes could have indirect effects (e.g., on the location choice of labor), which in turn can have an impact on the location choice of firms.[16] There are other reasons to be cautious in extrapolating the implications of studies of location choice of new firms or plants to conclusions about regional capital formation. The birth of new firms or plants, or the relocation of existing firms, is only a relatively small part of the economic growth (decline) of a state. For instance, between 1969 and 1976 only 554 major manufacturing firms out of the estimated 140,093 establishments that existed in 1969 changed their primary location.[17] Furthermore, only 35,988 new establishments, including new firms, branches, and subsidiaries, came into existence over the same period, for an average of about 5,000 interstate location decisions a year. This led the Advisory Commission on Intergovernmental Relations (ACIR) to conclude that "the low average number of industrial location decisions in relation to the total number of major manufacturing establishments supports the view that, everything else being equal, major manufacturers are predisposed to expand at their present location, rather than branch—much less pick up and move."[18] A substantial portion of the economic growth that occurs in a state is associated with expansion of existing plants.[19] It would seem more appropriate, then, to focus on aggregate measures of growth.

Several empirical studies of regional growth have been performed, using a wide variety of growth measures, including employment, income, and capital investment. The earliest statistical effort to relate

15. Ibid., pp. 19–22.
16. Carlton, "Why New Firms Locate Where They Do: An Econometric Model," *n*. 4, p. 37.
17. ACIR, *n*. 14, p. 34.
18. Ibid., p. 37.
19. James P. Miller, "Manufacturing Relocations in the United States, 1969–75," in R. McKenzie, ed., *Plant Closings: Public or Private Choices?* (Washington, D.C.: Cato Institute, 1982), pp. 19–35.

taxes to state growth was the oft-cited examination of differences in state manufacturing employment growth in two-digit industries over the 1947–1954 period by Thompson and Mattila.[20] Several explanatory variables were employed in their multiple regression analysis, including state and local taxes as a percentage of personal income. Taxes were found to be insignificant in all industry equations except the apparel industry. In fact, as Kieschnick noted, the Thompson-Mattila results are widely cited to demonstrate that state and local taxes do not have a significant impact.[21] After reviewing much of the empirical and survey literature on the impact of state and local taxes on growth, and conducting further studies of his own, Kieschnick concluded, "In most industries, the general level of business taxation has an undetectable effect on investment patterns. In those industries where an effect can be detected, it is quite small." [22]

In a recent comprehensive study of state industrial growth, Plaut and Pluta[23] examined three growth measures: the percentage change in a state's real value added; the percentage change in manufacturing employment; and the percentage change in real capital stock. An attempt was made to explain each growth measure by factors such as measures of total tax effort, corporate taxes, personal income taxes, sales taxes, and property taxes. Plaut and Pluta found that a high tax effort, measured by total state and local taxes as a percentage of revenue capacity,[24] had a significant and negative impact on both employment and capital stock growth but not on real value added. However, the effect of other tax measures was not significantly negative (the effect of property taxes was significantly *positive* in some cases). Still, the results do imply that some aspect of taxes might have an impact on state growth.

The occasional finding that taxes have had some impact on state growth is not restricted to regional growth studies. Miller has provided results indicating that location decisions are influenced by changes

20. W. Thompson and J. Mattila, *An Econometric Model of Postwar State Industrial Development* (Detroit: Wayne State University Press, 1959).

21. Kieschnick, *n.* 8, p. 47.

22. Ibid., p. 83.

23. Thomas Plaut and Joseph Pluta, "Business Climate, Taxes and Expenditures, and State Industrial Growth in the United States," *Southern Economic Journal* 50 (July 1983): 99–119.

24. The "revenue capacity" concept is defined by the ACIR to be "the total amount of revenue that would result by applying, within the area, the national average rate of each of the numerous kinds of state-local revenue sources." See *Measuring the Fiscal Capacity and Effort of State and Local Areas* (Washington, D.C.: ACIR, 1971), p. 7.

in tax burdens rather than currently observed tax levels.[25] He pointed out that during the 1969–1975 period, the movement of firms was largely from states with relatively high growth in tax burden to states with relatively low growth in tax burden. Such moves were made by 520 firms, while only 77 moved to states with higher growth in tax burden than the state of origin. However, even if there were absolutely no statistical or survey evidence in the literature discussed here that state and local taxes are negatively related to state growth, the conclusion that taxes do not matter is inappropriate. Such a conclusion ignores the fact that competition among the states for the location of business investment exists.

In its report on state and local taxes and industrial location, the ACIR notes that

> . . . there appears to be no clear relationship between industrial growth trends and tax differentials. This lack of relationship can be attributed in no small measure to the fact that States are constantly taking steps to insure that their taxes do not "get out of line" with those of their neighboring jurisdictions. A State usually moves into this competitive arena armed with many tax options and sufficient political support to enable it to go a long way toward neutralizing any tax differential advantage possessed by a neighboring state.[26]

Accordingly, competition can be expected to play a role in keeping state and local taxes close enough so that business firms will not be enticed to alter their locations and investment plans. Major shifts in relative growth due to taxes should occur only when a state gets too far out of line with the others.

INTERSTATE COMPETITION FOR BUSINESS ACTIVITY

Interstate competition takes two primary forms. First, some states follow a "direct matching" approach wherein they attempt to stay in line with neighboring states on a tax-by-tax basis.[27] Alternatively, states can stay in line with their neighbors under a "trade off" system that involves the offsetting of one unfavorably high tax rate with a relatively low tax rate in some other tax category. Second, states have

25. Miller, *n.* 19.
26. ACIR, *State-Local Taxation and Industrial Location* (Washington, D.C.: ACIR, 1967), p. 70.
27. Ibid., p. 66.

numerous special tax and nontax inducements they can employ on a case-by-case basis to offset tax disadvantages: "In the competition to attract or hold manufacturing industry, states can and do pursue various strategies, ranging from passivity in the face of provocation to defensive reaction and even aggressive offense."[28]

The concept of tax competition among states does not, however, imply that states will have identical overall tax rates. Rather, it implies that state taxes will tend toward an equilibrium in which whatever tax differentials exist are not sufficient to give any state a locational advantage. That is, tax differentials should not be sufficient to overcome the other locational factors over which states have little or no control, e.g., factors like population density, energy costs, and proximity to ports and established institutions.

The implications of interstate tax competition for most statistical and survey results may be quite different from those that are often drawn. If, for example, the results are interpreted as saying that immobile resources absorb the entire impact of tax differentials, or that other locational factors simply overwhelm *any* existing tax differentials, then one can conclude that taxes do not matter and the fear of lost state growth potential should not deter state or local politicians in their taxing decisions. However, *if competition prevents taxes from varying sufficiently to have a statistically measurable impact on relative economic growth, then the conclusion that taxes do not matter is not supported by any of the evidence* referred to earlier.

There is evidence to support the contention that interstate competition plays a major role in relative tax level determination. Consider Table 15–1, for instance, which shows the average ratio, for 48 states, of state and local tax revenue to total state personal income for the years 1960–81. That ratio is often considered as a measure of a state's aggregate tax rate. Note that the standard deviation about the mean is relatively small, indicating that most states have similar aggregate tax rates. Furthermore, states like New York with higher tax rates (.17 in 1978) and states with the lower rates, like Ohio (.10 in 1978), have tended to remain in their respective high/low categories over time. As state and local taxes rose nationally, most states paralleled the national trend.[29] There are, of course, states that altered their rel-

---

28. ACIR, *n*. 14, p. 23.

29. Taxes have been trending upward and this may suggest to some that competition does not characterize tax setting policies. However, prices rise in competitive markets, too, when

Table 15–1. Mean and Standard Deviation of Tax Rates for 48 States, 1960–1981.

Year	Mean	Standard Deviation	Year	Mean	Standard Deviation
1960	.097	.014	1971	.117	.014
1961	.098	.012	1972	.122	.015
1962	.101	.012	1973	.123	.015
1963	.100	.011	1974	.118	.016
1964	.103	.011	1975	.116	.015
1965	.105	.012	1976	.120	.016
1966	.106	.012	1977	.121	.017
1967	.105	.012	1978	.121	.017
1968	.107	.013	1979	.117	.015
1969	.110	.013	1980	.112	.015
1970	.114	.014	1981	.111	.015

SOURCES: Tax revenue data are from U.S. Dept. of Commerce, Bureau of the Census, *Governmental Finances,* various years. State personal income is from U.S. Dept. of Commerce, Bureau of Economic Analysis, revised data, August 1983.

Note: The tax rate is defined as total state and local revenue divided by state personal income.

ative rankings, but none of the forty-eight states has moved from the highest five to the lowest five or, conversely, from the lowest five to the highest five. Parallel action by itself does not imply a competitive framework, but this brings us to the second piece of evidence concerning the existence of interstate tax competition.

If taxes do matter then, anytime a state gets too far out of line with competing states, that state will undergo substantial reductions in relative economic growth. Thus, evidence of the significance of interstate tax competition in keeping tax rates relatively similar can be obtained by observing what happens to a state that gets out of line with its neighbors. According to the ACIR, New York and Massachusetts tax burdens have gotten out of line relative to their neighbors.[30] New York's public sector outlay per dollar of personal income,

demand increases. According to Borcherding, government growth has occurred primarily as a consequence of increasing demand. We shall suggest below that some supply-side considerations may also be relevant in light of changing institutional constraints that have reduced the incentives for interstate competition. See T. E. Borcherding, ed., *Budgets and Bureaucrats* (Durham, N.C.: Duke University Press, 1977).

30. ACIR, *n.* 14, p. 27.

for example, is about 30 percent higher than such outlay for the rest of the nation. What has happened to New York and Massachusetts in terms of firm location and economic growth? Among the 303 major manufacturing establishments in food, textiles, apparel, fabricated materials, machinery and electrical equipment industries that moved between 1969 and 1976, a total of 91 left New York.[31] Of those, 29 moved to other states in the Mideast region. Massachusetts lost 25 major manufacturing establishments to states within the New England region alone (17 moved to New Hampshire). As the ACIR concluded, Massachusetts and New York were vulnerable to interstate tax competition.[32] This goes beyond simply the loss of several firms, however. New York is the only state in the country to have actually lost substantial numbers of manufacturing jobs. New York had 2,042,200 employees in manufacturing in 1956. This number had fallen to 1,760,600 by 1970 and had reached 1,432,000 in 1981. Massachusetts also incurred declining manufacturing employment, but the decline was considerably less substantial—711,000 in 1956, 640,000 for 1970, and back up to 666,800 by 1981.[33] The experience of New York and Massachusetts does indeed suggest that if a state government were to raise taxes without regard to tax levels in other states, that state would probably find itself growing at a substantially slower rate within a few years.

How have New York and Massachusetts reacted to their competitive disadvantage? Both have taken steps to move back in line by reducing the rate of spending growth and the associated level of taxation. In 1979, New York Governor Hugh L. Carey wrote, "During the past four years, New York State has demonstrated that the way to provide tax relief (other than the state's very substantial tax concession program) and revive the economy is to control the growth in

31. Ibid., pp. 46–47.
32. Ibid., p. 47.
33. Other states with modest declines (relative to New York) in manufacturing employment in recent years include Illinois (a state suggested by ACIR as being out of line for its region), Maryland, Michigan, New Jersey, Pennsylvania, Rhode Island, and West Virginia. All of these states had relatively high tax rates in the early 1970s. The employment information was obtained from Bureau of Labor Statistics, *Employment and Earnings, State and Areas, 1939–78* (Washington, D.C.: U.S. Dept. of Labor, 1979); Bureau of Labor Statistics, *Supplement to Employment and Earnings, States and Areas, 1977–1981* (Washington, D.C.: U.S. Dept. of Labor, 1982), and selected Bureau of the Census, *Statistical Abstracts of the United States* (Washington, D.C.: U.S. Dept. of Commerce). The source for relative tax rate data is given in Table 1.

spending. Spending increases have been held far below the rate of inflation, making tax cuts possible three years in a row." [34] Indeed, the rate of increase in New York's state and local tax burden (1.1%) was below the national average (1.2%) for the 1975–78 period, and perhaps more important, it was considerably lower than both Connecticut's (2.5%) and New Jersey's (2.3%) increases. However, the ACIR concluded that New York would actually have to make much larger spending or tax cuts to shield itself from interstate competition. [35]

Another evidence of the intensity of interstate competition for growth-generating capital investment is the substantial increase in the use of tax and financial incentives by states to attract or hold firms. Between 1966 and 1980 virtually every state introduced at least one new financial incentive, tax exemption, or special service in an effort to attract or retain industry. [36] Thirty-four states added at least ten new direct-assistance programs during that period, and the number of such activities more than doubled in twenty-eight states. Initially these programs tended to be directed at attracting new firms or branches, but recently they have been used to encourage expansion of firms already located in the state. Figure 15–1 details the upward trend in such activities by census region.

The spread of such programs follows the same competitive process as does the tax level competition described above, although the impetus is likely to be a little different. It is commonly recognized that firms in a market where the reaction of their competitors must be considered would generally prefer not to compete in terms of price. Firms do, on occasion, engage in nonprice forms of competition in an effort to avoid price competition. The same can be said for state governments in terms of tax rate competition. The incentives of state politicians to avoid competition are discussed in detail later, but these incentives must be recognized now in order to explain the growth in special tax concessions. Politicians would prefer not to lower overall tax rates for existing residents and firms in order to attract or retain a relatively small number of new or potentially mobile firms. Thus, state governments have strong incentives to devise policies that can be selectively applied in cases where they may make a difference.

34. ACIR, *n.* 14, p. 29.

35. Ibid., p. 58.

36. James P. Miller, "Interstate Competition for Business: Changing Roles of Federal and State Initiatives," Economic Research Service Staff Report No. AGES 831012, Economic Development Division, U.S. Dept. of Agriculture, Washington, D.C., December 1983.

Figure 15–1. Growth of State Financial and Tax Incentive Programs by Census Region.

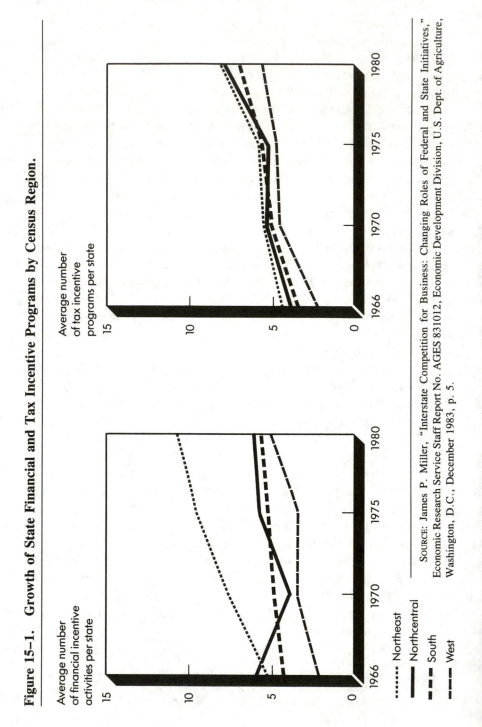

Average number
of financial incentive
activities per state

Average number
of tax incentive
programs per state

Northeast

Northcentral

South

West

SOURCE: James P. Miller, "Interstate Competition for Business: Changing Roles of Federal and State Initiatives," Economic Research Service Staff Report No. AGES 831012, Economic Development Division, U.S. Dept. of Agriculture, Washington, D.C., December 1983, p. 5.

But, once one state introduces such a policy instrument, its neighbors meet the competitive pressure with an instrument of their own to offset their competitive disadvantage. In this way, the competitive action of one state spreads throughout the country. The ultimate consequence is that states are unable to avoid tax level competition, since each state keeps its tax concession and financial inducement program in line with its competitors. Nominal state tax levels may be higher than they would be without these programs but they still will have to be in line. The programs of states need not be identical to be competitive. They simply must be sufficient to offset a potential competitive advantage that could exist. The ACIR concluded that, indeed, "widespread state enactment of incentives to businesses in the 1960s and the 1970s has tended to neutralize their pulling power." [37]

Interstate competition implies that state and local tax levels, tax concessions, and financial inducements should not *appear* to be important determinants of location choice and state growth in cross-section studies. There is another reason to expect that the often performed cross-section analysis would fail to detect a significant tax impact. The economic activity that takes place during a particular year is likely to have been stimulated by occurrences in previous years. In particular, businesses need time to respond to tax changes. In other words, there is reason to expect that taxes should have a lagged impact on location choice, capital formation, and hence state growth.

One reason for expecting a lag comes from the firm location literature. Since the location decision underlies regional and state economic growth theory, it is appropriate to turn to this literature first. Analysts of location decision-making contend that the location process involves several stages. [38] First, some impetus for considering a new location for a move, for expansion, or for a new establishment must occur. The impetus could involve rising taxes at a current site, deteriorating capital, growing demand for the firm's product, or any number of other factors. Then a search begins. Information about the relevant characteristics of alternative sites is usually not readily available. Such factors as access to markets, labor market conditions, energy costs, the availability and prices of other inputs, and construction

37. ACIR, *n*. 14, p. 5.
38. See, for instance, David Mulkey and B. L. Dillman, "Location Effects of State and Local Industrial Development Subsidies," *Growth and Change* 7 (April 1976): 37–43; or Roger W. Schmenner, *The Manufacturing Location Decision* (Cambridge: Harvard-MIT Joint Center for Urban Studies, 1978).

costs dominate the early search. After potential sites are narrowed down to a few, state and local taxes and the availability of tax or financial incentives are likely to be compared. Once a site choice is made and construction contracted for, there is still a period of time before plant construction actually begins.

Similarly, site abandonment is rarely immediate. In-place physical capital is not likely to be abandoned in the face of a large tax increase until that capital is deteriorated to the point where the additional revenue it can generate is no longer sufficient to cover the additional costs of maintaining it, including further tax payments. In fact, Schmenner found that gradual "organizational control" shifts, in which companies open new branch operations or merge and shift emphasis on expansion to different locations while gradually phasing out operations at another site, contribute much more to the disparity of growth between regions than do outright relocations.[39]

The ACIR has noted that "economic development—the basic rationale for interjurisdictional tax competition—is a long-term process. The results of forgoing business taxes or providing incentives are generally neither noticeable nor measurable until long after the fact."[40] Indeed, the embodiment of a lag effect has long been a vital part of statistical aggregate investment models for the U.S. economy.[41] Nevertheless, the concept and utilization of a distributed-lag model appears to be absent in studies of state and local tax impacts. Some studies have used measures of state or regional growth over a given period and related it to past tax rate levels or changes, but these are not distributed-lag models.[42] They are not designed to capture the impact of a change in current tax rates on current and future investment, nor do they trace out a time profile. In the following section we offer evidence on the impact of state and local taxes and show that introducing a lag specification is critical.

39. Roger W. Schmenner, *The Location Decision of Large, Multiplant Companies* (Cambridge: Harvard-MIT Joint Center for Urban Studies, 1980).

40. ACIR, *n.* 14, p. 11.

41. See, for example, Gary Fromm, ed., *Tax Incentives and Capital Spending,* (Washington D.C.: The Brookings Institution, 1971).

42. See, for example, Robert J. Genetski and Young D. Chin, "The Impact of State and Local Taxes on Economic Growth" (Harris Trust and Savings Bank, 1978). (Mimeo.) Their study essentially presents simple correlations of economic growth with changes in tax rates in past periods. No attempt was made to account for locational advantages across states or other factors that could influence growth.

THE LAGGED EFFECT OF STATE AND LOCAL TAXES

The purpose of this section is to discuss empirical evidence (detailed in the Appendix to this chapter) on the importance of a distributed-lag effect in determining the impact of state and local taxes on economic activity. As the major theme of this book centers on capital formation, the measure of economic activity used here is the U.S. Department of Commerce estimate, by state, or annual expenditures for new plant and equipment.[43] The basic approach requires both cross-sectional and time-series data. Individual state data were collected for the period 1966–78. The Department of Commerce ceased publishing individual state data after 1978.

To determine whether state and local taxes do affect capital formation, a consistent and meaningful definition of each state's tax rate must first be determined. The question as to which state and local taxes should affect location-specific business decisions is not without controversy. Some researchers contend that only those state and local taxes that businesses pay directly should be considered in analyzing location decisions.[44] However, this presumes that an adequate distinction can be made between taxes that fall primarily on business establishments and taxes paid by consumers. While there have been some attempts at identifying taxes directly affecting businesses, they are controversial, and necessary data are available only for a few and intermittent time periods. More important, it is recognized that "because wage and salary payments may need to be higher in one state than another to compensate for higher personal tax rates, managers are increasingly concerned about their own, as well as their associates', personal tax situation."[45] Hence, taxes on labor are at least partially shifted onto firms in the form of higher wages. A similar response can also be expected to occur with sales and property taxes. Such considerations have led the ACIR to conclude that "in considering the total tax bill differential, little attention is paid to the type of tax. Businessmen seem to feel that if a particular jurisdiction lacks

---

43. U.S. Dept. of Commerce, *Survey of Manufacturers*, various years.

44. For example, see William C. Wheaton, "Interstate Differences in the Level of Business Taxation," *National Tax Journal* 36 (March 1983): 83–94; and Kieschnick, *n.* 8.

45. ACIR, *n.* 14, p. 26.

a given type of tax—for example a state corporate income tax—it will have other taxes whose burden will be sufficient to make up for the absence of a particular levy." [46] Accordingly, we defined each state's tax rate as the total tax revenue collected at the state and local level divided by total state personal income. [47]

Consideration of total taxes, including those which businesses do not pay directly, appears to be particularly relevant in the context of distributed-lag analysis, since taxes may affect the movement of population, which in turn can influence the movement of industry. Labor market and output market factors have both proven to have important influences on location choices. Thus, if low taxes attract people and a population center in turn attracts firms, nonbusiness taxes would be a significant determinant of capital expenditures in the long run.

As argued previously, tax competition among states is prevalent. But, it was also noted that states with higher taxes can experience similar rates of growth compared to low tax states if other factors such as particular locational advantages are present. What matters, then, is how a state's tax policy is altered relative to that of other states.

The empirical results of our analysis account for interstate tax competition by use of a relative tax rate measure. In addition, we control for many of the interstate differences that might influence relative levels of capital formation across states. Our estimating procedure is designed to reflect the possibility of a lagged impact of taxes on capital formation and detail the time profile of that lag. As with many cross-section studies of the impact of state and local taxes on economic activity, we find *no immediate* or current effect of a change in relative state and local taxes on capital expenditures. However, our results do indicate a statistically significant negative lagged response in capital formation due to a change in relative tax rates. Not surprisingly, businesses apparently cannot react immediately to a change in a state's tax policy; but given sufficient time, they do react. The major portion of the long-run effect of relative tax changes occurs within four to five years of the change.

The estimates obtained indicate that the long-run elasticity of a change in relative tax rates on relative capital expenditures evaluated at the sample means (in this case all means are equal to unity) is equal to

46. ACIR, *n.* 26, p. 62.
47. See Table 1 for data sources.

−0.769. That is, for every 1 percent change in a state's tax rate relative to other states, capital expenditures relative to those in other states fall 0.769 percent. (See Appendix Table 15–3.) The relatively inelastic response suggests that states can vary taxes *somewhat* without experiencing massive capital influxes or decreases in formation rates. While we have argued that interstate tax competition is a prevailing force, it does appear that states have power within a narrow range. This finding, along with the significant distributed-lag effect, is a vital ingredient to an argument recently advanced by Lee and Buchanan.[48]

Lee and Buchanan argue that political decisions are made on the basis of a limited time perspective. Politicians are seen as having little motivation to consider consequences much beyond their expected period of tenure. These incentives are heightened by the notion that voters tend to be *rationally ignorant* about the long-run consequences of tax policies. In the context of the findings presented here, politicians who argue that increases in tax rates (in order to provide additional benefits to their supporters) will not affect investment will have a short-run advantage over those who argue that higher taxes will have a significantly negative impact on economic activity. By the time the evidence is accumulated, the politician with a long-run view may not be around. Indeed, he can be proven wrong in the short-run. As Buchanan and Lee note, "so long as government makes its fiscal decisions on the basis of a time horizon shorter than that period required for full taxpayer adjustment to tax rate changes, observed tax rates will be higher than those that a far-seeking or 'enlightened' government would impose."[49]

In one major respect the argument advanced by Buchanan and Lee is more applicable to the federal government's tax policy than it is to state and local governments. It is far more costly to give up one's citizenship or move production out of the United States than it is to move from New York to Texas. Interstate tax competition can be expected to moderate the tendency toward excessively high state and local taxes. But to the extent that interstate tax competition interferes with the objectives of politicians, we anticipate attempts by public officials to reduce it. The following section considers these attempts.

48. Dwight R. Lee and James M. Buchanan, "Tax Rates and Tax Revenues in Political Equilibrium: Some Simple Analytics," *Economic Inquiry* 20 (1982): 344–54.

49. Ibid., p. 354.

THE ACTIONS AND ABILITY OF STATES TO REDUCE INTERSTATE TAX COMPETITION

The desire to avoid competition that can be harmful to one's own interest appears to be universal. In the process of attempting to alter the rules and impose constraints, arguments are often put forth that, on the surface at least, seem plausible. This appears to be particularly true of behavior in the public sector, with the issue of interstate tax competition being one example. Advocates of restricting interstate competition contend that tax competition, tax concessions and financial inducements (1) are ineffective development tools because they cannot outweigh other locational factors and (2) distort decisions made by firms and inefficiently shift industry locations among states without contributing to national economic expansion.[50]

First note that the two arguments are logically inconsistent. If such competition is ineffective, then it cannot shift industry location among states. However, our empirical results indicate that state and local taxes do matter. It is competition that keeps states in line with their competitors and thus prevents substantial tax-induced redistribution of economic activity among regions. Since the first argument is not correct, perhaps the second *is,* given that they are logically inconsistent. However, interstate tax competition implies that the only firms likely to choose a location because of tax differences or inducements offered by a particular state are those firms which are relatively indifferent between two locations in terms of production cost and marketing factors. Therefore, neither location could have a significant comparative advantage, nor could the location choice be influenced by the relatively slight differences in taxes that competition allows. Consequently, tax competition is not likely to shift industry inefficiently.

A second component of argument 2 above is that state and local taxes do not influence national economic development except, according to the argument, that they may reduce growth if inefficient locations are chosen. In other words, interstate tax competition is a zero- or perhaps negative-sum game, according to this argument. But if competition does anything, it will lower taxes, not raise them. Accordingly, interstate competition keeps state and local taxes lower than they otherwise would be. Hence, tax competition appears to be a positive-sum game.

50. ACIR, *n.* 14, pp. 5–6.

Having apparently accepted the above two arguments for restricting interstate tax competition, some policy analysts have argued that "as a first reform, then, states must begin to develop regional economic pacts that would allow the elimination of competing incentives and equalize state business burdens."[51] Like business firms, state governments have an incentive to avoid competition.

Some evidence of the efforts to avoid tax competition has already been discussed: the growth of nontax forms of competition (e.g., individual tax concessions and financial inducements). In addition, there have been attempts to collude. The governors of six Great Lakes region states have discussed the possibility of "calling a truce on attempts to pirate industry from each other's states."[52] However, the six governors have been unable to reach an agreement. Minnesota's governor took the lead, and after unsuccessful attempts to convince Iowa and North and South Dakota to reduce competition for industry, he reached an agreement with Wisconsin; the two states' governors publicly pledged not to initiate any state-sponsored business recruiting in the other's state, although contacts by firms from the other state will be pursued. Indiana and Illinois refused to join such a pact, however, despite interest by Michigan and Ohio. Even with an agreement, it is doubtful that a no-raid pact can make much difference.[53] Firms that are actually considering branching or moving can initiate contact, and negotiations for tax concessions or financial inducements can follow. Furthermore, this suggested "no-raid" agreement does not put any limits on tax competition nor is it an agreement to set taxes. It is revealing to note that even this extremely limited agreement has not been achieved. Private sector cartels are very tenuous arrangements because all cartel members have strong incentives to try to evade them. The same appears to hold for public sector cartels. As Kleine noted, "At the state level, tax competition could be reduced by the cooperative efforts of regional economic planning groups such as the Southern Growth Policies Board (SGPB). Neither the SGPB or any

51. Sandra Kanter, "A History of State Business Subsidies," *Proceedings of the Annual Conference of the National Tax Association—Tax Institute of America* 70 (Nov. 1977): 152. Also see Andrew Reschovsky, "New Strategies for Metropolitan Area Cooperation: Sharing Rather than Competing for Business Tax Base," in the same publication, pp. 155–62. In fact, the ACIR study, *Regional Growth: Interstate Tax Competition,* was commissioned to evaluate these issues.

52. Eugene Carlson, "Great Lakes Governors Split over Truce on Industry Raids," *Wall Street Journal,* 12 July, 1983, p. 31.

53. Ibid.

of the other regional groups currently in existence, has taken steps to reduce competition among member states [however]." [54]

Under the right circumstances we might anticipate some sort of tacit collusion even when a formal cartel arrangement does not arise. For instance, Montana and Wyoming have huge deposits of low sulfur coal. It is by far the cheapest coal in the United States to produce, so even when transportation costs are added, the coal competes very favorably in the midwestern and southern markets of the United States.[55] When Montana raised its severance taxes on surface-mined coal to 30 percent, it could have given Wyoming a substantial competitive advantage. However, Wyoming responded by raising its taxes as well, although not to the level established by Montana.

Apparently, even in cases where the tax base is highly immobile and residents outside the state can be expected to absorb most of the tax, states have difficulty in setting revenue-maximizing collusive tax rates. Kolstad and Wolak contend that Montana and Wyoming could actually charge substantially higher rates on coal than they do. The actions of one state may affect those taken by another, but existing rates appear to be much closer to those of a noncooperative ("Cournot-Nash") environment than a collusive one. In the case of Montana-Wyoming coal taxing, Kolstad and Wolak conclude that there are "substantial losses in market power as a result of interregional competition, but despite these losses, producing regions can still individually . . . capture sizable amounts of rent." [56]

The point is that even when there is considerable potential for collusion (at least, in the short run), states do not appear to be able to take full advantage of it. Taxes tend to be higher under such circumstances than they might be in a more competitive environment, but they do not approach collusive levels. This should not be surprising to anyone who has studied private sector efforts to form and maintain cartels. The only successful private sector cartels over long periods

54. Robert J. Kleine, "State and Local Tax Levels and Economic Growth—A Regional Comparison," *Proceedings of the Annual Conference of the National Tax Association—Tax Institute of America* 70 (Nov. 1977): 170.

55. Charles D. Kolstad and Frank A. Wolak, Jr., "Competition in Interregional Taxation: The Case of Western Coal," *Journal of Political Economy* 91 (June 1983): 449.

56. Ibid., p. 455. For other estimates of cartel tax rates that substantially exceed actual rates, see M. B. Zimmerman and C. Alt, "The Western Coal Tax Cartel," Hoover Institution, Stanford University Working Paper E-80-9, March 1981; and Albert M. Church, *Taxation of Nonrenewable Resources* (Lexington, Mass.: Lexington Books, 1981).

of time appear to be those backed by government's coercive power through regulation or government franchising. Thus, private sector firms that are able to organize cartels, but unable to prevent cheating by members, typically turn to the government for help.[57] That is precisely what state (and local) governments appear to be doing.

Several organizations of state and local governments are now in existence for the primary purpose of lobbying the federal government. For example, the Northeast-Midwest Economic Coalition, made up of 213 congressmen from eighteen states, "seeks to inform its members about regional implications of federal policies and influence those policies wherever possible." Furthermore, it "neither seeks nor encourages confrontation with other regions of the nation. In [its] view, economic problems of regions must be addressed in the context of national policy because economic difficulty in one part of the country weakens the nation's entire economic structure."[58] Many groups of this nature exist: the Western Governors Association, a lobbying organization representing fourteen states and three territories; the National Governors' Association; the U.S. Conference of Mayors; the National League of Cities; and other similar organizations.

Of course, constitutionally there is little that the federal government can do directly to reduce interstate tax competiton. Congress and the courts rarely interfere with the taxing powers of sovereign states. Still, there are institutional arrangements instigated by the federal government that can significantly curtail the impact of interstate tax competition or reduce the incentives to compete. Two factors of this type stand out above all others. One, deductibility of state and local taxes from federal taxes, was instituted some time ago for reasons unrelated to interstate competition. The other, the growing share of state and local expenditures covered by federal revenues, has arisen largely as a consequence of intensive lobbying by state and local governments. Both appear to have a substantial impact on the incentives to compete. We consider each in turn.

---

57. For example, see George Stigler, "The Theory of Economic Regulation," *Bell Journal of Economics and Mangement Science* 2 (Spring 1971): 3–21; and Richard A. Posner, "Theories of Economic Regulation," *Bell Journal of Economics and Management Science* 5 (Autumn 1974): 335–58.

58. Shelley Amdur, Samuel Friedman, and Rebecca Staiger, *Investment and Employment Tax Credits: An Assessment of Geographically Sensitive Alternatives* (Washington, D.C.: Northeast-Midwest Institute, 1978). p. 4.

Federal deductibility of state and local taxes.   The allowance of state and local tax payments as business expenses for federal taxes, and the deductibility of state and local income, property, and sales taxes from federal income taxes effectively reduced real state and local tax rates to well below their nominal rates. In addition, such deductibility generally narrowed the actual tax differentials between states substantially. Table 15–2 provides some evidence of this. In 1977 the range of total personal taxes relative to the average, when state and

Table 15–2.   Comparison of 1977 Personal Taxes in Selected States, $50,000 Income.

States	State and Local Taxes As Percent of Income	Index	State, Local and Federal Taxes As Percent of Income	Index
Arizona	7.7%	.74	27.9%	.95
California	12.0	1.14	30.4	1.03
Colorado	8.7	.83	28.5	.96
Connecticut	8.5	.81	28.4	.96
Georgia	9.2	.88	28.7	.97
Illinois	8.0	.76	28.0	.95
Indiana	8.8	.84	28.5	.97
Kentucky	9.6	.91	29.0	.98
Maine	12.0	1.14	30.4	1.03
Massachusetts	14.4	1.37	31.8	1.08
Michigan	9.2	.88	28.8	.97
Minnesota	14.8	1.41	32.0	1.08
New Hampshire	7.0	.67	27.5	.93
New Jersey	13.3	1.26	31.1	1.05
New York	17.1	1.63	33.4	1.13
North Carolina	8.3	.79	28.2	.96
Ohio	8.1	.78	28.2	.95
Pennsylvania	11.8	1.12	30.2	1.02
Rhode Island	12.6	1.21	30.8	1.04
Texas	5.6	.53	26.7	.90
Vermont	10.0	.95	29.2	.99
Wisconsin	14.1	1.34	31.6	1.07
Average	10.5	1.00	29.5	1.00

SOURCE: Advisory Commission on Intergovernmental Relations (ACIR), *Regional Growth: Interstate Tax Competition* (Washington, D.C.: ACIR, 1981), p. 20.

Note: Figures in Index columns represent total personal taxes relative to the average.

local taxes alone are considered, is from .53 in Texas to 1.63 in New York. However, when federal taxes are added in, the range narrows from Texas' .90 to New York's 1.13. The deduction of state and local taxes substantially diminished the cross-state variation in taxes by transferring much of the tax burden in high tax states to the federal tax base.

Earlier it was pointed out that New York appeared to be out of line in terms of interstate tax competition. Given the figures in Table 15–2, New York was only 13 percentage points above the average, after federal taxes are considered. If federal deductibility of state and local taxes were not allowed, New York would have been 63 percentage points above the average. We might then expect that New York would be forced to make tremendous tax cuts to prevent substantial economic decline. In other words, without federal deductibility the high tax states would probably have been forced to lower their taxes.

On the other side of the coin, Texas had about half the average tax rate, but this apparently extremely competitive tax policy actually only reduced personal taxes to 10 percent below the average because Texas citizens have had fewer deductions from their federal taxes. In other words, federal deductibility substantially reduces the competitive impact of a low tax policy and reduces the incentives to compete in terms of tax rates. For every dollar in revenue a state gives up, its citizens and businesses gain less than a dollar in overall tax relief.

Of course, federal deductibility of state and local taxes was not designed to mute interstate tax competiton. Its primary purpose supposedly was to guarantee that individuals' total tax rates remain below 100 percent. However, this did not prevent states from taking advantage of the situation and shifting their tax burden onto the federal tax base. Nor did it eliminate the disincentives to compete, in terms of taxes, that arose as a consequence.

Fiscal federalism.   The portion of state and local revenues that are simply transfers from the federal government have been increasing for some time, though the trend may have been reversed by Reagan administration policies. In 1961, for example, 11.1 percent of total state and local revenues came from the federal government. By the 1965–66 fiscal year this value had grown to 13.4 percent, and it reached 15.7, 18.2 and 18.4 percent in 1970–71, 1975–76 and 1979–80 respectively.[59] Total federal transfers to state and local governments have grown from 1.4 percent of GNP in 1959 to 3.3 percent of GNP in 1980. This growing portion of revenues coming from the federal government should be considered in the context of the growing state and local tax burden shown in Table 15–1. State and local government lobbying has played a major role in the development of this system wherein federal tax revenues are used to cover state and local expenditures. There have been several reasons put forth to explain the lobbying for such federal financing of state and local expenditures. For instance, "By divorcing expenditure from revenue, what people want is separated from what they are willing to give. Revenue sharing distorts state citizenship and state responsibility. No longer is it possible for citizens to determine what they would have wanted (if they had to pay for it directly) or to hold states accountable for what they have done with (federal) funds." [60]

There are, of course, "public interest" explanations for state and local government lobbying efforts. For example, it is argued that economies of size in tax collection and administration exist. Thus, low-cost federal collection followed by federal transfers (e.g., revenue sharing, grants-in-aid) to state and local governments will allow those governments to lower taxes. However, there is a very substantial body of empirical and theoretical evidence indicating that tax abatement is only a secondary use of such federal dollars. *The primary use has been to increase state and local expenditures.* For example, a study of revenue sharing, which is actually a relatively small component of the total federal transfer of revenues to state and local governments, concluded that more revenue-sharing dollars are used to maintain or expand programs than to stabilize or reduce taxes.[61] Only 20 to 25 percent of revenue-sharing funds go toward tax abatement uses. Similarly, a study of the impact of grants-in-aid concluded

59. These percentages are calculated from revenue figures obtained from various U.S. Dept. of Commerce, Bureau of the Census, publications titled *Government Finances,* (various years).

60. Aaron Wildavsky, "Birthday Cake Federalism," in R. B. Hawkins, Jr., ed., *American Federalism: A New Partnership for the Republic* (San Francisco: Institute for Contemporary Studies, 1982), pp. 186–87.

61. Thomas Juster, ed., *The Economic and Political Impact of General Revenue Sharing* (Ann Arbor: Survey Research Center, Institute for Social Research, University of Michigan, 1977), p. 5.

that only 15 percent of the grants are used for tax relief.[62] The obvious implication is that *total* taxes from federal, state, and local sources collected to cover state and local expenditures are substantially higher than they would be without such federal transfers. Over $90 million in such transfers were made in 1981, implying that total taxes to cover state and local expenditures were probably $65 to $75 million higher than they would be if the federal moneys were not available to states, counties, and cities.

But the implication of the availability of large amounts of federal funds for state and local use goes beyond the immediate impact that studies such as those noted above are able to detect. As the tax collecting function has increasingly been performed by the federal government, effective state and local government tax differentials have shrunk owing to federal deductibility. Interstate tax competition has been further muted, and the incentives to lower state and local taxes for competitive purposes have declined.[63]

On June 30, 1981, President Reagan told the National Conference of State Legislatures that the ultimate objective of his federalism policy initiatives "is to use block grants as a bridge leading to the day when you will have not only the responsibility for program that properly belong at the state level, but you'll have the tax sources now usurped by Washington returned to you—ending that round trip of the people's money to Washington and back minus carrying charges."[64] Indeed, the share of state and local revenues coming from the federal government fell from the 18.4 percent reached in 1979–80 to 17.8 percent in 1980–81. But, the reductions achieved by the Reagan administration were part of a political deal wherein reduced federal revenues were accompanied by substantial reductions of federal controls on state use of funds. With the reductions in federal controls, state and local governments were more willing to accept a decline in federal moneys. However, given the incentives that state and local

62. Martin C. McGuire, "The Analysis of Federal Grants into Price and Income Components," in Peter Mieszkowski and William H. Oakland, eds., *Fiscal Federalism and Grants-in-Aid*, (Washington, D.C.: The Urban Institute, 1979), pp. 31–50.

63. Richard B. McKenzie and Robert J. Staaf, "Revenue Sharing and Monopoly Government," *Public Choice* 33 (1978): 93–97. See also, David D. Friedman and Michael M. Kurth, "Revenue Sharing and Monopoly Government: A Comment," *Public Choice* 37 (1981): 365–70; and McKenzie and Staff, "Revenue Sharing and Monopoly Government: A Reply," *Public Choice* 37 (1981): 371–75.

64. As quoted in the *National Journal* 22 Aug. 1981, p. 1492.

politicians face, there are limits to increasing federalism since state and local governmental entities will find it more difficult to raise taxes in a competitive environment and maintain spending levels. As Stubblebine has noted, "The major effect of federal grant reductions . . . will tend to be a general decline in the share of state personal income going to state and local spending, inclusive of federal grants." [65] The incentives of state and local governments to support federalism are largely absent. Simply granting states and local governments more control over remaining federal moneys has its limits. Accordingly, a prognosis of significantly increasing federalism would probably be proven wrong.

CONCLUSIONS

It is not surprising that in the political arena individuals are willing to argue that taxes do not have a negative impact on economic activity. What is somewhat disturbing, however, is the vast amount of research that appears to support the notion that state and local taxes do not matter. In this chapter we have argued that those studies are misleading. Our empirical results indicate that state and local taxes do have a negative effect on capital formation. Of importance, however, is the fact that interstate tax competition has kept state and local taxes relatively close to one another. Competition in the political sector appears to operate much like it does in the private sector: It constrains behavior. But as in the private sector, there are those who wish to reduce competition. State governments have attempted to reduce interstate tax competition, and while apparently unsuccessful on their own, they do appear to utilize the offices of the federal government with some success. The existence of federally established institutions, such as deductibility of state and local taxes from federal taxes, mutes the impact of interstate tax competition. Thus, the likelihood of state and local taxes being too high is increased.

APPENDIX

To incorporate the concept of competition into the empirical analysis, the tax rate variable in time period t for each state i is defined in relative terms as follows:

65. Wm. Craig Stubblebine, "Revenue Reallocation in the Federal System: Options and Prospects," in R. B. Hawkins, Jr., ed., *American Federalism: A New Partnership for the Republic* (San Francisco: Institute for Contemporary Studies, 1982), p. 148.

$$RELTAX_i = \left(\frac{TR_i}{PI_i}\right) \div \left(\frac{1}{48}\sum_{j=1}^{48}\frac{TR_j}{PI_j}\right).$$

Here, TR_i is total state and local tax revenue, and PI_i is state personal income. Each state's tax rate is divided by the average of the 48 continental states. While the constructing of a relative measure will alter the variance of an explanatory variable, it also permits the capture of a change in a state's relative tax position over time.

The dependent variable is each state's per-capita capital expenditure divided by the same average measure derived across 48 states. A relative measure is used here to neutralize any aggregate trend effect due to the business cycle or other factors that could influence total U.S. investment over time. It also allows inference about a state's changing relative ranking over time as regards capital formation. The relative capital formation variable was regressed on a free-form distributed-lag specification of the variable *RELTAX* going back six years. The use of a free-form distributed-lag is particularly unconstraining as to the form of the lag.[66] The sum of the coefficients of the *RELTAX* variables yields an estimate of the long-run response to a change in the relative tax rate of a typical state.

In addition to the distributed-lag specification, three other explanatory variables were included: the relative wage in manufacturing (*RELWAGE_{it}*), a relative measure of welfare expenditures as a percentage of total state and local expenditures (*RELWELFARE_{it}*), and a relative measure of state and local long-term debt as a percentage of state personal income (*RELDEBT_{it}*).[67] The three variables are relative to their corresponding average across 48 states. The wage variable was included because a large number of survey studies indicated the wage rate as an important determinate of business location. The variable *RELWELFARE* was included to account for the distributional orientation of state and local expenditures and to act as a proxy for business "climate." *RELDEBT* reflects the effect of future tax liabilities. The expected sign on *RELDEBT* is negative. We note that the price of capital is not included, as we assume that the market rate of interest is similar across all states.

66. See G. S. Maddala, *Econometrics* (New York: McGraw-Hill Book Co., 1977), p. 388.

67. Data on state and local expenditures and long-term debt are from U.S. Dept. of Commerce, *Government Finances*, various years. Wage data was obtained from the sources listed in *n*. 33.

While inclusion of the variables *RELWELFARE, RELDEBT,* and *RELWAGE* is designed to capture differences across states that can influence capital formation, a more important ingredient of the analysis is the use of individual state dummy variables in the regression equation. As mentioned, many of the studies attempting to measure the impact of state and local taxes on economic performance have relied strictly on cross-sectional data. Those studies suffer from a lack of controlling variables, since it is almost impossible to account for the numerous factors influencing relative economic performance across states. However, many of these same factors, e.g., population density, climate, and natural resources, will be relatively constant over time within a state. The inclusion of state dummy variables will essentially allow for the capture of much of the cross-sectional variation and allow inference about the effect of changing relative tax rates in a dynamic context.

Table 15–3 shows the results of regressing relative per-capita capital expenditures on the three controlling variables and a free-form distributed-lag specification for the relative tax rate measure. While the coefficients on *RELWELFARE, RELDEBT* and *RELWAGE* are all negative, none is significant at the 5 percent level.[68] On the other hand, the sum of the coefficients of the variables *RELTAX* is $-.769$ and is significantly different from zero with a t-statistic equal to -2.352. The mean lag is slightly over two years, indicating that half the effect of a change in the relative tax position of a typical state is felt two years after the initial period. Because of high multicollinearity between the *RELTAX* variables, interpretation of each coefficient individually is cautioned against. Setting the six lagged components of *RELTAX* equal to zero, however, yielded a coefficient of $-.039$ on $RELTAX_t$ with a t-statistic of only $-.213$. Progressively adding lagged components of *RELTAX* increased the negative sum of the coefficients until the fourth period lag. These results indicate that the current effect of a change in relative state and local taxes on capital expenditures is essentially nonexistent, but the lagged response is significantly negative—with the major proportion of the long-run effect occurring within four to five years.

---

68. Setting the coefficients in *RELWELFARE, RELDEBT,* and *RELWAGE* to zero does not alter the basic results reported for the *RELTAX* variables. Furthermore, as New York is often considered an outlier, a run was made excluding it. The results reported are not altered by the inclusion or exclusion of New York.

Table 15–3.   Capital Outlays and Relative State and Local Taxes, 1966–1978.

Independent Variables[a]	Coefficient
RELWELFARE$_t$	−.1080
	(−1.4639)
RELDEBT$_t$	−.0325
	(−.6125)
RELWAGE$_t$	−.3027
	(−.8452)
RELTAX$_t$	.1521
	(.7849)
RELTAX$_{t-1}$	−.4862
	(−2.5307)
RELTAX$_{t-2}$	−.0563
	(.2935)
RELTAX$_{t-3}$	−.5304
	(−2.8928)
RELTAX$_{t-4}$	.1187
	(.6454)
RELTAX$_{t-5}$	.0432
	(.2329)
RELTAX$_{t-6}$	−.0098
	(−.0538)
Sum of coefficients	
$\sum\limits_{i=0}^{6}$ RELTAX$_{t-i}$	−.769
	(−2.352)
SE of Sum	.327
$\bar{R}^2$	.642
Number of Observations[b]	.611

[a]The results were obtained after correcting for first-order autocorrelation. The estimated rho was .42. It was assumed that each state had the same rho. Individual state dummies were included in the regression but omitted here for brevity. The figures in parentheses are *t*-statistics.

[b]To avoid the problem of a singular disturbance covariance matrix, observations on one state (Minnesota) were dropped.

Although the use of relative measures has its advantages, such as negating underlying trends that in the absence of standardization of the variables could lead to spurious results, interpretation of the coefficients is no longer straightforward. Consider that the sum of the coefficients on the *RELTAX* variables is a −.769. That would imply that if a state were to decrease (increase) its relative tax rate by say .10, its relative position as regards per-capita capital expenditures would increase (decrease) by .0769. How much of an actual tax rate increase (decrease) is required to change the state's relative tax rate by .10 is not explicit. The reason is that as the state alters its tax rates, other states can be expected to react. The coefficients on the *RELTAX* variables capture this effect, but it cannot be separated out from the total effect. In addition, attempts at extrapolating are cautioned against. The range of the *RELTAX* variable over the entire time period 1966–78 was .68 to 1.47, and the range for the dependent variable was .09 to 2.62. No state, however, has even come close to changing its relative tax rate position from the bottom to the top. Accordingly, the results obtained are reliable only for small changes in relative tax positions. Larger changes can invoke a response not currently detectable in the data and hence not reflected in the estimated coefficients. Despite these drawbacks, the results do indicate a significantly negative effect of taxes on capital formation.

16

AMERICA'S VERSION OF THE MELANESIAN CARGO CULTS: THE NEW INDUSTRIAL POLICY

John Baden, Tom Blood, and Richard L. Stroup

Wealth creation is central to improved well-being. It does not start with investment bankers, nor is it primarily caused by them. They may, however, play an important role in some innovative and productive ventures. Generally, productive new wealth-creating enterprises are conceived, directed, and initially managed by entrepreneurs who often have relatively little wealth. Instead, they have human capital in the form of the alertness and imagination to see new opportunities, and the salesmanship required for financial backing. This support comes from many sources: friends, relatives, partners, the sale of penny stocks, and even investment bankers and major equity markets. The successful entrepreneur must also have the enthusiasm and fortitude necessary to carry the project through bad times, and will do so if his or her vision indicates that success is attainable.

Truly new wealth is created only by truly new ideas, or truly new applications of old ideas. Thus, the entrepreneur is normally a strong-minded individualist who resists the current of conventional wisdom. Fortunately, in the private economy only a small minority of all potential financial backers need be convinced by the entrepreneur-salesman. Those few can share the vision, the opportunity, and the risk by their personal investment decision. The vast majority can remain unconvinced and uncommitted while the project develops. Only the few need monitor the progress or lack thereof—it is their investment that is at stake. They have strong incentives to support promising projects and to stop supporting those whose payoff is negative. From this perspective on wealth creation, we easily see why the private sector spawns nearly all successful entrepreneurial ventures, and why the best-intended collective "investment banks" back so few successful entrepreneurial projects. Political-bureaucratic calculus is such that only private individuals are likely to think "against the current" and to act on their convictions when the majority opposes an idea. Moreover, individuals who have their own resources on the line will monitor them responsibly. They face strong incentives to swallow their pride and fold an unpromising venture or, when merited, to grit their teeth and give additional support in difficult times.

The government has a constructive role to play in fostering innovation and production. Its contribution comes from enforcing contracts and defining and protecting property rights to the resources used by entrepreneurs and producers. Only with secure, exchangeable property rights can a market system work well. When rights are undefined or difficult to protect, a resource is likely to be abused or difficult to use. Clean air is an example of a resource abused owing to failures to establish property rights. If labor, land, and capital goods were similarly unprotected from misallocation, the entire economic system would malfunction; entrepreneurship would be far less productive. Wealth creation requires secure and exchangeable rights, and government's role here is crucial.

This chapter compares two flawed movements intended to duplicate or to cause capital formation and economic growth. One movement is described in the ethnographic literature of anthropology and goes by the term "Cargo Cult." The other, described in current newspapers and news magazines, is called "The New Industrial Policy." The two movements differ substantially in their apparent level of sophistication, but each contains the same fundamental flaw: They look backward to existing conventional wisdom. Both ignore the role of innovative entrepreneurs capable of visionary leadership, operating in small niches while supported by a tiny minority of voluntary and personally responsible backers. By ignoring the critical role of these people, both movements subvert rather than foster progress.

THE MELANESIAN CARGO CULTS

In the vast openness of the Pacific Ocean lies a group of islands inhabited by tribes known collectively as Melanesians. For thousands of years, these tribes existed in a primitive state, depending primarily on domestic pigs, gardens, and copra (dried coconut meat) as staples, and producing no important commercial product. During the early 1900s, the German government attempted to build copra and rubber industries on the larger islands. These efforts were unsuccessful. Moreover, they caused a series of increasingly costly social movements among the natives, movements that anthropologists have called "cargo cults." Like most peoples, the Melanesians had a strong desire to acquire wealth. The ethnographic records indicate that the Melanesian culture awarded social and political status to those hosting the biggest feasts from their surplus pigs and garden stores. As a result, secret and highly involved rituals developed to increase pig fertility, control the weather, and influence other factors that contributed to the size of the food supply.[1]

After the Europeans arrived, the natives observed that great quantities of cargo arrived by ship and, later, by airplane. Since the exercise of ritual was the only wealth-generating strategy that the Melanesians had known, they assumed that the whites had discovered especially powerful magic rituals. Surely such vast quantities of wealth must be from the gods themselves; if the natives were to acquire cargo, they had to discover the appropriate ritual and imitate it. The Melanesians subsequently developed a variety of cargo rituals, none of which produced positive results.

On several occasions, Melanesian tribes constructed airports, having observed that U.S. soldiers "attracted" loaded planes out of the sky with their landing strips and control towers.[2] The natives spent weeks preparing and building so that they too might attract cargo-laden planes. With the "airport" ready, tribe members gathered in prayer circles on the hacked-out airstrip. The prophet sat in the rickety bamboo flight tower issuing prayers and commands into a wooden microphone, watching for signals on the bamboo instrument panels, and listening for replies over his bark earphones.[3]

Despite repeated failures, the underlying belief in the effectiveness of the ritual was seldom questioned. Cargo cults continued to spring up among groups of natives. As each ritual failed to bring cargo, its failure was explained as a result either of inappropriate ritual or prophet error. Somewhere there was a ritual that would supply cargo, and in

1. Peter Worsley, *The Trumpet Shall Sound* (London: MacGibbon & Kee, 1968).
2. Ibid.
3. R. F. Mettler, "Cargo Cult Mentality in America," *Business Week,* 20 Sept. 1980, p. 22.

accord with their model of the way the world works, the Melanesians' task was to find it. Thus, their desperate search continued. Natives participating in the rituals abandoned gardens, ignored their livestock, and bypassed employment opportunities in the European settlements. Many cult rituals called for the deliberate destruction of house and garden and the butchering of pigs, and required that European money be given to leaders to be thrown into the sea.[4] Thus, because of a failure to understand the creation of wealth, counterproductive investments were undertaken. The Melanesians, however, have no monopoly on misunderstanding.

NATIONAL INDUSTRIAL POLICY

Before the cargo cults are written off as a topic suitable only for discussion with an anthropologist over a leisurely lunch, the Melanesian/ U.S. link deserves closer attention. The Melanesians devised policies intended to create wealth, but were ignorant of the real wealth-creation process. Similarly, some Americans are recommending policies for our nation that are incompatible with the entrepreneurship needed for wealth creation in America. The goals are laudable, as were the goals of the Melanesians. But because they ignore the critical processes of successful entrepreneurship, the results of these well-intended policies will almost certainly be different from their stated goals, just as they were in Melanesia.

The issue remains very much alive today. Proponents of industrial policy call for tougher laws to restrict plant closings, expand protection against foreign imports, and increase governmental spending on unemployment compensation and worker-retraining programs. Bills before Congress spell out plans to create a Reconstruction Finance Corporation designed to allocate low-interest loans and subsidies for both sunrise and ailing industries, while providing workers with federal subsidies to purchase their closed plants.[5]

These proposals vary widely in type and extent of governmental involvement. The only point of agreement seems to be that industrial policy must be specific and well defined. The following views are but a few examples:

● *The "accelerationists"* are concerned with how capital is invested. Their aim is to accelerate changes already signaled in the mar-

4. Worsley, *n*. 1.
5. "Industrial Policy: Is It The Answer?" *Business Week*, 4 July 1983, p. 54.

ketplace by identifying promising industries and supplying them with government funds to foster product development, thus enabling these industries to move quickly into competitive markets.

- *The "adjusters"* simply promote governmental support by subsidizing ailing industries so that they may upgrade their performance and regain competitiveness.
- *The "targeters"* advocate support of economic development by targeting "promising" industries in *all* areas rather than certain trade industries. These targeted industries can then provide the impetus for economic development and growth. The targeters also emphasize the importance of refurbishing the country's neglected and deteriorating infrastructure.
- *The "central planners"* are oriented toward using macro policies. Gar Alperovitz of the National Center for Economic Alternatives proposes to

> go beyond identifying leading growth sectors and identifying other sectors as well that could become bottlenecks and engines of inflation once you start to grow. It's a mistake to write off an industry like steel. By throttling down its capacity too much, we could quickly run into shortages in a high-growth situation and excessive dependency on foreign steel.[6]

Though the specifics differ, the basic objective of all industrial policy is to revive the industrial economy by duplicating the processes that created wealth in the past. Thus, industrial policies accelerate the progress of sunrise industries such as robotics, and shore up ailing industries such as steel and autos, all the while trying to promote the welfare of workers who become misplaced, replaced, or sidelined through economic evolution.

To be sure, this philosophy is not new. America has a history of various kinds of industrial policy. What is new is its expanded scope.

> In the 19th century, federal support helped build the nation's railroads, canals, and university systems as well as protect growing industries with high tariffs. In the 20th century, a paternalistic government created or bankrolled a large part of the nation's highways, synthetic rubber, computers, integrated circuit industries, as well as a host of other projects, products, and industries.[7]

Yet many view even these policies less than enthusiastically. Nobel Laureate George J. Stigler exclaims, "Look at the splendid triumphs

---

6. Ibid., pp. 55–56.
7. Ibid., p. 55.

of government: it subsidized the railroads into bankruptcy, destroyed interurban transportation with regulation, and regulated thousands of banks out of existence in the 1930s."[8]

When government is responsible for distributing capital, decisions must be controlled politically. To survive at election time, the politician must allow influence by special interests, anointed experts, and bureaucrats, each of whom is buffered and insulated from the long-range effects of his or her actions. Industry's attention is necessarily diverted from the market process where greater efficiency, increasing productivity, and lowering costs lead to success. Instead, it is focused to a large extent on the political arena, where allocations of capital are decided. Firms must work hard to court governmental favor; to intensify lobbying efforts; to increase time and resources spent to capture subsidies, tax breaks, import protectionism; and to obtain other politically determined favors.

In terms of wealth *generation,* this activity is little different from Melanesian natives abandoning productive gardening and hunting activities in order to gain wealth through rituals. Unfortunately, in both cases the outcome is the same: Huge amounts of resources are wasted as both cultures regress from positive- to negative-sum societies. The similarities become more apparent as the two operations are examined in greater detail.

Japanese Industrial Policy

> During the Yali movement, a Cargo cult that arose in New Guinea around the middle of this century, . . . [it] was observed that the white people liked to keep vases of fresh flowers in their dwellings, and that they would have fresh flowers when they gathered together for dinner. Thinking there might be some esoteric significance in this, the natives proceeded to decorate not only their houses, but even whole villages, with enormous amounts of flowers. Then, perhaps, kago [cargo] might come to them as well.[9]

The natives who belonged to the Yali cult arrived at a common logical fallacy: If two events occur at the same place and time, a cause and effect relationship must exist. Europeans receive cargo. They decorate their houses and dinner tables with flowers. Therefore, decorating with flowers produces cargo.

---

8. Ibid., p. 57.
9. T. Merton and N. B. Stone, "Cargo Cults in the South Pacific," *America,* 27 Aug. 1977, p. 95.

Advocates of national industrial policies have made a similar mistake. For example, they quickly credit Japan's Ministry of International Trade and Industry (MITI) for the recent successes in the Japanese economy. As Katsuro Sakoh, Director of International Economics at the Council for Competitive Economy has said:

> It is clear that many observers of Japan have committed the classic fallacy of elementary logic—*post hoc ergo propter hoc* (false association). Since Japan has something those observers choose to call an industrial policy and since the country's industrial capacity has been growing dramatically, they conclude that there must be a causal relationship between the two. Yet other concurrent factors just as easily could be selected to explain Japan's successes. There is, for example, Japan's generous tax treatment of investment income—similar to supply-side economics. There is Japan's determination to improve quality control. And there is, of course, the "uncorking" of Japanese entrepreneurship due to the explosion of political and social freedom after 1945. Strangely, these factors are ignored by advocates of an American industrial policy.[10]

If a cause-and-effect relationship exists between MITI and economic growth, it should not be difficult to uncover. A comparison of the success of MITI-backed industries to those left relatively untouched should determine if the ministry has had a positive or negative influence.

In a report compiled for the Heritage Foundation, several relevant questions about a Japanese industrial policy were examined:

1. Do governmental expenditures dominate the economy?
2. Is governmental aid a major contributing factor to the phenomenal growth of Japan's most successful industries?
3. How successful have the targeted industries been?[11]

First, Sakoh discovered that the amount of resources allocated by government is *inversely* related to the economic success of the country. Government-funded research and development (R & D) in Japan was lower than in both West Germany and the United States by the late 1970s. If one looks at government-funded research and development as a percentage of total R & D, one finds 50 percent in the United States, 40 percent in West Germany, and 30 percent in Japan,

10. Katsuro Sakoh, "Industrial Policy: The Super Myth of Japan's Super Success," *Asian Studies Center Backgrounder* (Washington, D.C.: Heritage Foundation, 13 July 1983), p. 2.
11. Ibid., pp. 1–2.

where only 5 percent went into private industrial research. This indicates the relatively limited influence of Japan's governmental investment program.[12]

When specific Japanese industries currently experiencing substantial growth are examined, it is evident that there was also an inverse relationship between MITI's involvement with any specific industry and the growth of that industry.[13]

When one conjures up images of Japanese industrial strength, computers, automobiles, and electronic products come to mind. Yet, the machine and information industries receive a meager 0.8 percent of Japan's Fiscal Investment and Loan Program's (FILP) total annual investment from special loans.[14] Technological development as a whole received considerably less than what was lent to ocean shipping, urban development, or energy resource sectors. Technological development, in fact, places second to last on FILP's priority budget list.[15] Perhaps this helps explain its phenomenal growth.

It is also useful to examine those industries with which MITI has been most heavily involved. Areas targeted for financial assistance by the government have included agriculture, coal mining, ship building, petroleum refining, and petrochemicals.[16] Agriculture is by far the most inefficient of Japan's significant industries. The coal mining industry, despite large influxes of government capital, has steadily declined since 1972, and production has fallen off to more than half of its 1962 level. Both U.S. and Japanese shipbuilding receive a great deal of government support. Until the oil shock in 1973, when the Japanese shipping industry was decimated, shipbuilding had been cushioned with subsidies. Since then, nineteen companies have closed, 46,000 workers have been laid off, and output has fallen by 65 percent.[17]

The Japanese aluminum industry has also suffered. Government misdirection created excess capacity, which has led to a structurally depressed industry. Soon, however, Japanese aluminum producers may suffer no longer; this heavily supported industry threatens permanently to go out of business, leaving Japan to import all of its aluminum.[18]

12. Ibid., p. 3.
13. Ibid., p. 10.
14. Ibid., p. 5.
15. Ibid., p. 7.
16. Ibid., pp. 10–12.
17. Ibid., pp. 10–11.
18. Ibid., pp. 11–12.

Before the public follows the Pied Piper prophets of national industrial policy schemes, let them first realize that MITI's success has been in what it has *not* done, rather than in what it has done. MITI's program is a cargo ritual that does not work.

Reconstruction Finance Corporation

The Reconstruction Finance Corporation (RFC) provides an excellent example of cargo cult thinking in America. The RFC was an experiment that failed to allocate resources efficiently; yet there are those who want to recreate it, altering various parts to match new ideas concerning governmental policy or theory. Some still hold the ritualized idea that bureaucrats manage resources more effectively than do entrepreneurs or their individual backers. New variations on political direction and bureaucratic management are considered new ways to get cargo.

Missionaries living among the Melanesians observed behavior fundamentally similar to that of policy makers intent on rebuilding an RFC. Sacred houses were constructed and spiritually purified with pig's blood so that they might be filled with cargo, but the cargo did not appear. Old churches were torn down and rebuilt. Whole communities prayed fervently for days and nights. The houses remained empty. Obviously, there was a defect. If it wasn't in the ritual, then it was in the people. Sin was "rooted" out of the people through punishment and confession. Even this activity failed to bring cargo. "The villagers now went to their gardens, stripped them bare and ate all the food, killed their pigs and hens, and implored the ancestors and the spirits of dead missionaries that were buried nearby to help them."[19]

In March 1984, at least seven bills were before Congress proposing the resurrection of the RFC, a bureaucracy that will be asked to pump billions of tax dollars into both sunrise and ailing industries.[20] This will be done at the expense of prosperous businesses and successful ventures.

In 1932 when President Hoover signed the original RFC into law, he promised, "It is not created for the aid of big businesses or banks. Such institutions can take care of themselves."[21] But wealth and po-

19. Worsley, *n.* 1.

20. Gregory L. Klein, "Industrial Policy: A Summary of Bills Before Congress," *Issues Bulletin* (Washington, D.C.: Heritage Foundation, 1983).

21. Sheldon Richman, "Let Sleeping Failures Lie: The Reconstruction Finance Corporation," *Policy Report* 2 (no. 11, 1980): 3.

litical power are positively related in all societies. As we should expect, the RFC eventually came to the aid of big business. At a U.S. Chamber of Commerce dinner, humorist Will Rogers noted that as each big businessman stood up during the ceremonies, Jesse Jones, president of the RFC, "would write on the back of the menu card just what he had loaned him from the RFC." In fact, loans to small businesses accounted for only 5.3 percent of the RFC's total funds.[22]

Not only did the RFC provide lucrative subsidies eagerly sought by powerful business lobbyists, but the allocation of public money was greatly influenced by political considerations. For example:

- Charles G. Dawes received a $90 million loan that went to the Central Republic Bank in Chicago, a bank with deposits of only $95 million. Dawes was honorary chairman of the bank's board and president of the RFC.
- Union Trust Company of Cleveland received $14 million from the RFC. Union Trust's board chairman was the treasurer of the Republican National Committee.
- The Guardian Trust Company received $12.3 million from the RFC. Atlee Pomerene, one of Guardian Trust's directors, was president of the RFC.[23]

As time went on, the situation worsened. Clark Nardinelli, professor of economics at Clemson University, has noted that "despite its nominal independence, the RFC lost its bipartisan nature after the war and became embroiled in a series of bribery and corruption scandals." According to a 1951 Senate investigation, "securing an RFC loan through the Democratic National Committee became a common practice."[24]

It is possible that projects such as the RFC could fail simply because some element was poorly planned or executed. If that were the case, major changes might correct the problem. But the problems with the RFC were not the result of a design error. There is a fundamental flaw in the premise upon which the RFC was founded. As with all government bureaus, RFC personnel are more attentive to the political concerns of legislators and special interest lobbyists than to the move-

22. Ibid., p. 4.
23. Ibid.
24. Clark Nardinelli, "The Reconstruction Finance Corporation's Murky History," *Heritage Foundation Backgrounder* (Washington, D.C.: Heritage Foundation, 1983), p. 3.

ment of resources to more highly valued uses. Political profits are not measured by dollar earnings made through the most efficient use of resources. Instead, politicians and bureaucrats are rewarded by allocating resources to those who can return the favor in the form of votes, increased budgets, and campaign contributions.

Even if bureaucrats are able to ignore political considerations and survive, they still have no means of determining where money is most efficiently employed. They must make decisions based on information provided by outside sources—lobbyists—all of whom have a stake in a particular outcome. While effective lobbyists must not be dishonest if they are to remain effective, they have virtually no incentive to provide balanced information to decision makers.

An entrepreneurial venture-capital institution controlling private deposits does not have these problems. It prospers by allocating resources to parties who place the highest value on the resources, using information and signals provided through the marketplace. Success is measured through profit margins, not political results. In governmental institutions, general efficiency enjoys no constituency, while specific actions, though leading to inefficiencies, normally have strong and well-organized constituencies.

Advocates of RFC are quick to point to the recent Chrysler bailout and claim that the once troubled corporation is back on its feet, producing cars that are revitalizing sales and turning a profit. The corporation, they argue, was pulled from the brink of bankruptcy by $1.5 billion in government loan guarantees. They proudly boast that it has already managed to pay those loans off, costing the government and the American people nothing.

This sounds like a convincing case for a new RFC. However, a closer examination reveals that the bailout of Chrysler was more apparent than real. Indeed, many analysts claim that Chrysler in effect went through the equivalent of bankruptcy. For instance, Chrysler was allowed to pay off $600 million worth of debt at 30 cents on the dollar, and its creditors were forced to undergo a loss of $420 million. Chrysler converted another $700 million in debt to preferred stock, which has paid *no* dividends.[25] This $1.3 billion was transferred to Chrysler from other industries and stockholders, implying that there was no industrial improvement and probably an overall loss in the

---

25. James Hickel, "The Chrysler Bail-Out Bust," *Heritage Foundation Backgrounder* (Washington, D.C.: Heritage Foundation, 1983), p. 2.

economy. Further, a large part of the profits currently claimed by Chrysler resulted from carrying tax losses forward. According to James Hickel,

> Chrysler's massive losses in 1979, 1980, and 1981 have given the company large tax deductions to cut its tax bills almost to zero throughout the 1980s. Of the $170 million "earned" by Chrysler in the first quarter of 1983, only half actually represents operating profit; the other half is attributable to Chrysler's large loss carry-forward.[26]

Additionally, sacrifices were forced on Chrysler stockholders. Many sold their stock prior to the government's intervention. Those with inside knowledge or an understanding of political economy gambled and bought the stock while it was near the bottom, profiting when the government overrode the information provided by the market.[27]

Moreover, even though government policy-makers thought that leaving Chrysler intact would make the American auto industry more competitive with foreign automakers, Chrysler's gains came at the expense of General Motors, Ford, and AMC, rather than at the expense of the Japanese or Europeans. A glance at the before-and-after figures shows that before Chrysler received the government loans, its share of all U.S. registered cars was 7%, with other domestic producers accounting for 65% and imported cars accounting for 28%. After receiving the loans, Chrysler's share rose to 9%, but the share of other domestic producers fell to 62%, while that of imported cars rose one percentage point to 29%.[28] Not only did GM and Ford workers and stockholders help keep Chrysler alive with their tax dollars, they jeopardized their own welfare in the process.

In summary, consumers told Chrysler through market signals that they no longer wanted so many of the automaker's cars and that they wanted Chrysler to shift its assets toward other uses. These signals were transmitted to Chrysler via decreased car sales. But government policy makers chose to ignore them.

Protectionism

In order to revive traditional customs, cargo cult followers repeatedly blocked European efforts to transfer tools, knowledge, and skills to

26. Ibid., p. 5.
27. Ibid., pp. 2–3.
28. Ibid., p. 6.

the islands. The natives refused to adopt superior farming techniques, for example, and would not use European currency for many transactions. Oftentimes, when cults were active, money was tossed into the ocean. The natives felt that abandoning the old ways insulted the ancestral spirits, thus making them unworthy of cargo.[29] Protectionists are taking a similar tack when they attempt to close American markets to foreign sellers; they also believe that money is the source of wealth, not just a tool that facilitates wealth creation through gains from trade. Coddling does not lead to recovery. Uncompetitive business should not be protected from the necessity of improving its competitive position in the market.

For example, the U.S. government began protecting the steel industry in the late 1960s by forcing the Japanese into an agreement that involved "voluntary" restrictions on its exports to the United States. And in 1977, the Japanese accepted even more restrictions through the Carter administration's trigger-price mechanism. But the capital expenditure growth in the American steel industry has been a meager 4 percent per year since then.[30] Rather than retooling and upgrading capital and technology during the breathing space provided by the restrictions (as originally promised), the industry diversified into other, more promising areas.

In 1979, for example, U.S. Steel sold thirteen steel and fabricating plants while building a shopping center near Pittsburgh, purchasing the Marathon Oil Company for $6.4 billion, and constructing a chemical plant in Texas. In 1975, steel assets made up 63 percent of the company's total assets; today, they comprise only 40 percent. Other steel companies have followed suit, investing in savings and loan corporations, acquiring insurance companies, and merging with other unrelated firms. Today, the steel industry still claims to be more than $1 billion short of the capital necessary to regain competitiveness, even though it has been able to afford these other expenditures.[31] This is not to suggest that such diversification should *not* occur, but rather that protection has not produced the claimed results. Even with pro-

29. Ron Brunton, "The Origins of the John Frum Movement: A Sociological Explanation," in Michael Allen, ed., *Politics, Economics and Ritual in Island Melanesia* (New York: Academic Press, 1981), p. 357.

30. Robert B. Reich, "Playing Tag With Japan," *New York Review,* 24 June 1982, p. 38.

31. Robert B. Reich, *The Next American Frontier* (New York: Times Books, 1983), pp. 182–83.

tection, the steel industry remains severely uncompetitive relative to the steel industries of Japan and other countries.

The scenario is frighteningly similar in U.S. automobile manufacturing, consumer electronics, and the footwear, textile, and apparel industries. All have been protected through tariffs and export agreements, yet none consistently used the protection to improve competitiveness. Despite recurrent promises to Congress that the assisted firms would restructure, retool, and streamline in exchange for the "necessary" protection, almost without exception the actual progress made through such protectionism falls short of the original promises.[32]

Despite its emphasis on free trade, the Reagan administration has been developing a policy of trade reciprocity. Under this policy, still ill-defined, other industrialized nations will be forced to lower their own trade barriers and tariffs or face the matching of such protectionist policies by the United States.[33]

> In April 1981 the Reagan administration forced Japan to restrict its auto exports to America. At about the same time the administration quietly imposed duties on $3.8 billion worth of imports from Hong Kong, South Korea, Taiwan, Brazil, and Mexico, thereby substantially increasing the protection accorded American manufacturers of car parts, electrical goods, fertilizer, and chemicals. The Reagan administration even put quotas on imported clothespins. There are now special duties on 132 products, ranging from South Korean bicycles to Italian shoes. . . .[34]

This policy may simply be a smokescreen to raise tariffs. Even if it is not, we should recognize that this announced strategy has seldom worked in the past. Instead, it will almost surely raise tariff barriers. Consumers, along with producers who buy in these markets, will suffer as a consequence of the higher duties. Higher prices and lower productivity are the long-range result of political protection of special-interest sellers of import-competing goods. The arguments in favor of protection simply imitate cargo cult rejection of preferred benefits from abroad.

MARGINAL TAX RATES

Just as the cargo cults diverted effort and attention from productive activities, government subsidies and the taxing needed to provide them

---

32. Ibid., p. 180.

33. Murray L. Weidenbaum, "Is Protectionism Back in Style?" *Policy Report* 5 (no. 12, 1983): 3.

34. Reich, *n.* 3, p. 178.

cause people to divert their attention and their resources to seeking governmental favors and avoiding their part of the tax burden. Government taxes have the same power to destroy wealth as did the cargo cults.

Reactions to the Increased Role of Government

Just how serious these costs of adjustment and avoidance are can be seen in the work of James Gwartney and Richard Stroup.[35] They have shown that as governmental regulation, subsidization, and taxation have all exploded in recent decades, so too have the efforts of Americans to cope with the added restrictions, burdens, and pressures to replace productive activities with conniving. For example, data on the number of law and accounting degrees conferred has increased dramatically relative to the number of engineers graduating in the same years. Accountants and lawyers help people cope with the increased levels of taxation and regulation. Engineers work primarily for production rather than to help people to avoid the effects of regulations and taxes. Such changes in strategy by individuals, though helpful to them personally in managing their affairs, direct attention and energy away from the production of wealth. Note the large declines over time in the ratios in columns 4 and 6 of Table 16–1.

Table 6–2 further illustrates the effects of rising tax rates. Shown there are responses to very large increases in income tax rates from

Table 16–1. Total Degrees Conferred in Engineering, Law, and Accounting.

Year	Engineering	Law	Ratio E/L	Accounting	Ratio E/A
1960	45,624	9,240	4.94	10,769	4.24
1965	50,664	11,583	4.37	15,012	3.37
1970	63,753	14,916	4.27	21,354	2.99
1975	65,308	29,296	2.23	31,600	2.07
1977	68,114	34,104	2.00	39,200	1.74

SOURCE: *Statistical Abstract of the U.S.*, various years, cited in James Gwartney and Richard L. Stroup, "Cooperation or Conniving: How Public Sector Rules Shape the Decision," *Journal of Labor Research* 3 (no. 3, 1982): 247–57.

35. James Gwartney and Richard L. Stroup, "Cooperation or Conniving: How Public Sector Rules Shape the Decision," *Journal of Labor Research* 3 (no. 3, 1982): 247–57.

Table 16–2. Net Income Losses Compared to Net Income Gains for Selected Sources of Income, 1965 and 1978.

Source of Income Gain or Loss	1965 Returns			1978 Returns		
	Net Income Gain	Net Income Loss	Ratio	Net Income Gain	Net Income Loss	Ratio
	($ billions)	($ billions)	(%)	($ billions)	($ billions)	(%)
Rent	4.02	1.57	39.1	20.98	17.84	71.4
Business and Professional	26.31	1.73	6.6	61.41	7.87	12.8
Farm	5.22	1.85	35.4	11.03	7.47	67.7
Partnership and Small Business Corporations	11.96	1.35	11.3	29.30	11.97	40.9
TOTAL	47.51	6.50	13.7	112.72	35.15	31.2

SOURCE: Internal Revenue Service, *Statistics of Income: Individual Tax Returns* (1965 and 1968), cited in James Gwartney and Richard L. Stroup, "Cooperation or Conniving: How Public Sector Rules Shape the Decision," *Journal of Labor Research* 3 (no. 3, 1982): 247–57.

1965 to 1980. As Gwartney and Stroup point out,[36] the income and Social Security tax load for a typical American family rose more than 60 percent between 1965 and 1980. Taxpayers confronting a 25% or larger tax burden on every extra dollar of income rose from 19.2% of all taxpayers in 1965 to 61.6% in 1977, the last year of their data on that topic. Those facing rates of 40% or higher more than doubled, from 5.9% in 1965 to 14.8% in 1977. Table 16–2 indicates part of the result. The sharp increases in ratios of losses to gains reported reflect the dramatic change in incentives facing taxpayers. Paper losses became very profitable as tax rates shot up. Again, the energy and ingenuity of people have been diverted from productive, entrepreneurial activity resulting in taxable income toward conniving to manipulate reported income figures and minimize individual tax burdens.

CARGO CULTS, CONNIVING, AND TRANSFER ACTIVITY

Cargo cults provide rewards to those individuals who invent the most convincing cargo story. Therefore, even though society as a whole suffers, people devote time and energy to creating and maintaining a cargo cult rather than engaging in entrepreneurial activities and ordinary production that create and maintain wealth.

Consider the Red Box Cult on the island of New Guinea. In 1971 a ritual ceremony was held; the cult leaders, Ru and Tipuka, made their appearance just as a lively, spectacularly colorful dance began. As the evening wore on and the dancers grew exhausted, the natives became absorbed by some red boxes that had only recently been taken out of concealment. Ru and Tipuka had charged almost $200 apiece for each box, nearly a third of each native's annual income. Each box was filled with carefully selected items: empty cigarette cartons, broken bottles, and bits of rock and grass. Ru and Tipuka had then performed secret rituals to transform the junk into large bundles of cash. When the boxes were opened, the natives would at last become as rich as the Europeans with whom they had been sharing the island. As the lids were pried loose, there were cries of disappointment, and Ru and Tipuka claimed that the money had been changed back into rubbish.[37] In a sense, Ru and Tipuka had transformed garbage into

36. Ibid., pp. 251–56.
37. Andrew Strathern, "The Red Box Money Cult in Mount Hagen 1968–71," *Oceania* 50 (no. 2, 1979): 99.

money—not through magic, but through a simple fraudulent transfer, benefiting only themselves. From the natives' viewpoint, their money *had* been transformed into garbage.

In the same way, governmental interferences in the form of industrial policy and high marginal tax rates encourage activities that, rather than generating wealth, transfer existing wealth. In a society that concentrates benefits among transfer recipients while diffusing the costs over a large taxpaying society, incentives are very strong for individuals and interest groups to seek wealth through political transactions.

As governmental involvement in the economy increases, so does the proportion of resources to which the controlling government has access. Consequently, special interests accelerate their efforts to secure those resources. As Terry Anderson and Peter J. Hill wrote in *The Birth of a Transfer Society,*

> The range of empirical estimates of transfer activity is broad and continues to grow. From forestry to fishing, from airlines to trucking, and from welfare programs to political campaigns, the evidence is clear: we do invest considerable resources in transfer activity.[38]

A glance at European economic history produces useful insight into factors contributing to different rates and types of economic growth. Why, for example, did the Industrial Revolution occur in England rather than in France? Aside from different cultural backdrops, which perhaps played a role, England and France had vastly different institutional frameworks. While England still had protective and productive government, France had already evolved into a predatory state by the time of the Industrial Revolution.

The French relied heavily upon the tax structure as a means of redistributing income and "promoting" industrial growth. As a result, geographic and economic regions developed through the efforts of businesses and individuals vying for governmental favor. These individuals and businesses learned how to lobby effectively for the highest payoff. They became adept at pie-rearranging, and high returns channeled human capital into careers of playing transfer games. Unfortunately, this human capital usually consisted of highly creative and talented minds.

---

38. Terry L. Anderson and Peter J. Hill, *The Birth of a Transfer Society* (Stanford: Hoover Institution, 1980), pp. 89–90.

On the regional level, this system may have seemed efficient, but France *as a country* suffered tremendously in terms of forgone economic growth. As the predatory state evolved, heavy industrial regulation and nationalization stifled industrial revolution possibilities.

Conversely, the English, through Coke's common law, operated under institutions that allowed for definable, enforceable, and transferable property rights. These enabled individuals to capture increases in values resulting from improved economic coordination. This was true in the manufacturing sector where profits from progress in technology, increased production, and more efficient utilization of labor were *captured* by producers rather than taxed away. The institutional setting was such that private rates of return approximated social rates of return, thus providing the incentive stimulus which sparked the Industrial Revolution.

During the past hundred years, however, the United Kingdom has experienced relatively little growth. The government has nationalized many industries, changing from a protective, productive state into a "predatory" one, and stifling economic growth.[39] In the United States, we face proposals for an industrial policy that would bring *this* nation closer to such a predatory state. A Reconstruction Finance Corporation, designed to promote industry through strategically guaranteed loans, would compound current transfer games by encouraging tax-dodging schemes and inviting firms to invest resources in efforts to capture RFC largess. This would divert resources and time from productive activities on both the *giving* and the *getting* side. It is the predictable consequence when the government attempts to sell Chrysler cars by coercing the American public away from buying from Japanese and European competitors.

Along with the growth in transfers have come the underground economies that flourish in the European industrialized countries and in the United States. Adrian Smith, a British government economist, has estimated that the underground economy "accounts for 10 percent of the gross national product in France; 8 to 10 percent in Germany, the low countries, and Scandinavia; 7.5 percent in Britain and an astonishing 15 percent in Italy."[40] The underground economy in the

---

39. Terry L. Anderson and Peter J. Hill, "Economic History in the United States" (Lecture delivered at Montana State University, Bozeman, Montana, February 1984).

40. David Fairlamb, "Europe's Thriving 'Black' Economies," *Dun's Business Month* 120 (no. 2, Aug. 1982): 70.

United States involves an estimated $700 billion annually—more than the total GNP of France.[41]

If an individual cannot survive by seeking transfers, he faces powerful incentives to pursue a partial livelihood in the unmonitored, underground economy. When one conjures up an image of the underground economy, drug dealers, Mafia hitmen, and other riffraff come to mind. Such undesirables are certainly part of the underground system. But John Q. Public's tax evasion or cash payments to his garage mechanic also contribute. Unlike John Q., however, drug dealers and pimps are outlaws because society has ruled their actions both illegal and undesirable. However, overrestrictive laws tend to drive John Q. Public and many like him into the black market. Consider, as extreme examples, some of the underground market activities that have evolved in Peru as the result of its restrictive laws:

> Illegal buses provide 85% of Lima's public transportation, and illegal taxis provide 10% more. Underground activity accounts for 90% of the clothing business and 60% of housing construction, including relatively sophisticated structures up to six stories high. Underground entrepreneurs assemble cars and buses, build furniture and make high precision tools.[42]

Perhaps it is useful to separate the two kinds of underground activities without making any moral judgments in the process. Let us call them gray and black economies. Activities in the black economy are deemed undesirable by society and are outlawed. Gray economies develop as a result of high marginal tax rates, overregulation, excessive red tape, and other legal, bureaucratic restrictions on the marketplace. One is the *cause* of legal restrictions; the other is the *effect* of legal restrictions.

In the 1920s when federal marginal tax rates were cut by nearly 50 percent, reported income rose so much that tax revenues remained nearly constant. For those earning more than $100,000 per year, the marginal tax rate fell from 75 percent to 25 percent. Yet their reported income more than quadrupled, so that tax revenues actually increased substantially! High marginal tax rates encourage taxpayers to shift resources away from the formal economy into the gray economy. Hence, marginal tax revenues drop as the tax base is eroded, and the government finds that it must milk its existing tax base to maintain

41. Ibid.

42. Claudia Rosett, "How Peru Got a Free Market Without Really Trying," *The Wall Street Journal*, 27 Jan. 1984, p. 27.

revenue levels. Those milked are individuals who, facing incentives to cheat, refuse to do so and individuals who, facing incentives to lobby for lower tax rates, do not receive favorable tax treatment because they do not possess the necessary voice and resources.

The statistics generated by the U.S. government have become increasingly unreliable as the gray economy grows. *The Wall Street Journal* asked, "Inflation roars on—or does it? Unemployment persists at intolerable levels—or does it? Productivity sags—or does it? . . . The economic patient is much healthier than we imagine. The trouble . . . is that the thermometer by which the economy's health is judged has gone awry."[43] With all the unrecorded activity taking place in the gray economy, unemployment is much lower and production undoubtedly much higher than the government estimates, while savings and income levels are grossly underestimated. Our economy is more robust than the statistics indicate.

It is a vicious cycle. In Melanesia, the cargo cults are caught in a similar whirlwind of waste. Their bizarre beliefs, dances, and rituals may be more exciting than picking coconuts, but they waste large amounts of resources. Failures only breed more outlandish attempts to make wealth materialize from nowhere, while resources evaporate.

Government programs encourage the diversion of resources into the gray economy by raising marginal tax rates and tightening regulations. Deficits and distorted statistics result, and political candidates build platforms embracing industrial revival ideologies by which our country can, they claim, be nursed back to health.

CONCLUSION

Wealth creation is seldom centrally directed. "Planned" economies are notable these days by their slow rates of growth. Entrepreneurship—individuals pursuing specific projects, usually against the advice of conventional thinkers—is instead the fountain of wealth.

The cargo cults, which failed to recognize the true origins of wealth, failed to prosper. So also will U.S. efforts to generate wealth via the standard wisdom, central planning, and bureaucratic control. Instead, the individual liberty of individuals to dream, build, cooperate, and produce is required. That freedom cannot exist without individual responsibility. Only when the dreamer and the entrepreneur are held

43. Alfred L. Malabre, "Underground Economy Grows and Grows," *The Wall Street Journal,* 20 Oct. 1980, p. 1.

fully accountable for their actions can society give them the liberty to act. In turn, this requires private property rights, defensible and exchangeable. The owner of a resource, and those contracting to buy or use it, are accountable in the most direct way for the use (and misuse) of that resource. The owner who takes a resource to a lower-valued use suffers the loss of value personally—his wealth declines. Conversely, one who creates new value captures its benefit.

A centralized plan, seeking consensus support from society, is almost certain to lack the creativity, enthusiasm, and careful monitoring necessary to generate truly new capital formation and wealth. Harking back to old formulas or old patterns is unlikely to be productive. Further, the subsidies, taxes, and regulations needed to implement any "new industrial policy" are guaranteed to undermine the freedom and the private property base necessary to allow and encourage entrepreneurship. The same measures undermine the ordinary production process as well. They divert time, resources, and attention from purely cooperative production to the more devious wealth-destroying activities designed to help the individual escape the impacts of regulation and taxation and obtain politically controlled favors.

17

CAPITAL TAXATION AND INDUSTRIAL POLICY

Richard B. McKenzie

The national industrial policy debate has focused public policy discussion on the growing mobility of capital, the obverse of which is the growing inability of unions to negotiate wage increases and of governments, especially local governments, to tax capital. Barry Bluestone and Bennett Harrison pose the emerging dilemma faced by the threat of growing capital mobility:

> Management found [in the 1970s] that it could no longer afford the social contract and maintain its accustomed level of profit. Instead of accepting the new realities of the world marketplace, one firm after another began to contemplate fresh ways to circumvent union rules and to hold the line on wages. Of course, labor was not initially ready to concede its hard-won victories; therefore, to accomplish its goal of reasserting its authority, management had to find some mechanism for disarming organized labor of its standard weapons: the grievance process, various job actions, and work stoppages. The solution was capital mobility. . . .
>
> The capital mobility strategy is not merely aimed at organized labor. The newly enhanced ability to move capital between regions within the same country provides corporate management with the necessary economic and political clout to insist upon reductions in local taxation, and therefore cuts in community services and the social safety net.[1]

1. Barry Bluestone and Bennett Harrison, *The Deindustrialization of America* (New York: Basic Books, 1982), pp. 17, 18.

An important purpose of this chapter is to explain why, and how, many industrial policy proposals—such as protectionism, plant closing restrictions, and so-called "unitary tax" systems—slow down the mobility of capital and how such policies can be expected to lead to higher tax rates extracted by governments. Of course, this is very likely what is intended. The net effect of such policies, if they are ever enacted as a part of an industrial policy agenda, will be a tendency of governments to "exploit" the capital base, which means charging tax rates that are "too high" to maximize the *long-run* revenues of governments, as well as the long-run growth rate of the economy.

The central lesson of this chapter is that capital taxation offers governments (and their constituencies) the opportunity to increase current consumption by draining the capital base of its income-generating potential (without making provision for renewal), thus shifting the tax burden to future generations through reduced capital stock and income flows. Many proposed industrial policies can be seen as disguised methods of capital taxation. In order to support these claims, however, we must first note some of the reasons why governments tend to "overtax" the capital base.

THE TENDENCY TOWARD EXCESSIVE CAPITAL TAXATION

A common presumption in discussions of tax policies is that government is intent upon acquiring only so much revenue, perhaps only enough to finance a given set of public goods and services. Such analysis, in other words, does not generally assume that government will extract all the revenue it can. With such premises, government can be expected to choose the tax base that will minimize the extent to which tax rates distort the allocation of resources. If government were truly like that, we would not want to restrict its tax base. Indeed, we would want to give the government total flexibility in choosing its tax base, because the definition of the tax base would not, by assumption, affect the amount of taxes collected. Flexibility in defining the tax base could only reduce the inefficiency in the taxes collected.

Suppose, however, that government is viewed as a revenue maximizer, a "Leviathan" (Thomas Hobbes's characterization—now being reconsidered by public finance theorists—for a model of government). That is to say, government tries to collect all the taxes it can. Indeed, such a revenue-maximizing government, constitutionally unconstrained in its revenue sources, aside from the restrictions imposed by the rules of democracy, can be expected to seek capital as an important source of taxation, a point that has been developed in detail and with considerable precision by public choice economists James Buchanan and Dwight Lee.[2] The key to their argument is the distinction between the long- and short-run desires for income (as opposed to leisure, or other commodities). The short-run demand for income is more inelastic (i.e., unresponsive) with respect to tax rates than are long-run demands. This is because the human or physical capital stock held by taxpayers cannot be immediately altered when tax rates are either raised or reduced. It takes time to increase the capital stock in response to a tax rate reduction, and there is no necessary reason for the capital stock to be reduced at a rate faster than its natural depreciation rate in response to a tax rate increase. Workers who are paid for the "sweat of their brow" can, however, alter the number of hours worked with relative ease if taxes on labor income are increased.

This distinction between the long- and short-run demands for income by taxpayers is important because of the institutional constraints of competitive politics that force politicians to devise tax policies in the short run with an eye on being elected or reelected in the short run—say, in two, four, or, at most, six years. Current tax rate increases may lower the capital stock and the revenue received by government; similarly, current tax rate reductions may lead to an increase in the capital stock, along with an increase in government revenues. However, it needs to be stressed that the effects of capital taxation on the capital stock, national income, and tax revenues are realized in the long run, and many politicians can understandably reason that many of these effects will not be realized until some time beyond their tenure in office.

For that matter, a policy course directed toward maximizing future income and future tax revenues can shorten the political careers of politicians who vote in favor of a long-run tax-maximizing policy course. A politician, argue Buchanan and Lee, who votes for tax rate reductions may be faced with the charge of fiscal irresponsibility, as

---

2. James M. Buchanan and Dwight R. Lee, "Politics, Time, and the Laffer Curve," *Journal of Political Economy* 90 (no. 4, 1982): 816–19.

were supporters of the 1981 Reagan three-year tax-cut package, since the tax rate reductions translate in the short run to lower tax revenues and higher budget deficits. They may also be caricatured as lacking a social conscience, because their focus on the long-run, rather than the short-run, health of the economy can mean that they oppose tax rate increases currently that could generate the needed revenues to finance current welfare programs.

In other words, politicians interested in maximizing the government benefits that go to their constituencies will choose tax rates that may maximize short-run tax revenues but will hold long-run tax revenues below the maximum that could be had. This is, again, because taxpayers' short-run demand for income is more inelastic than their long-run demand for income. The capital stock, which is responsible for a growing portion of people's income in industrial societies, cannot be, in the short run, changed very readily in response to tax rate changes.

These points can be explained more carefully with the use of examples and graphs. The revenue received by the government is necessarily related to the tax rate and the amount of income earned. However, because the income earned is inversely dependent on the tax rate, total tax collections can move up or down, depending upon the relative magnitudes of the tax rate and income changes. For example, a 10 percent tax rate applied to an income base of $10 billion yields total tax revenues of $1 billion (.10 × $10 billion); if the tax rate is raised to 20 percent and the income earned falls to $8 billion (which describes the inverse relationship between tax rates and collections pictured in a downward sloping demand curve in Figure 17–1), total tax revenues rise to $1.6 billion (.20 × $8 billion). However, total tax revenues would have fallen if the income earned had fallen to $4 billion when the tax rate was increased to 20 percent. Again, total tax collections may rise or fall, given the tax rate change; it all depends upon the extent to which people respond to the tax rate change.

For example, consider the income demand curve in Figure 17–1, which relates the amount of income earned (demanded) to the tax-price, stated as a percentage. Such a downward sloping curve is based on the intuitively plausible and empirically supported assumption that a lower tax rate will induce people to work harder and save and invest more to obtain more earned income. After all, the after-tax reward is greater as the tax rate falls. At a tax rate of zero in Figure 17–1, taxpayers may earn a lot of income, I_4, but the government will still

Figure 17–1.   The Income Demand Curve.

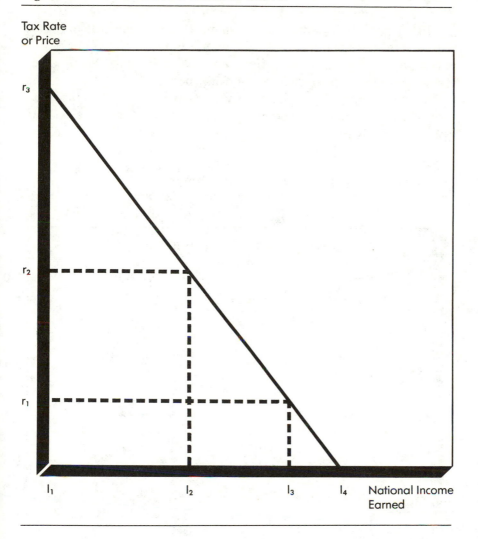

get no revenue ($0 \times I_4 = 0$). However, if the tax rate is raised to r_1, income may fall, but a tax rate of r_1 times the income level of I_3 will yield total tax collections above zero. If the tax rate is raised above r_1, the total tax collections of government may, for a while, rise. At some point, on the other hand, we know that total tax collections must fall. This is because at a tax rate of r_3 (the point at which the income demand curve intersects the vertical axis of Figure 17–1), total tax collections again fall to zero ($r_3 \times 0 = 0$).

In short, a plotting of all tax revenue levels against all tax rates will yield a curve that looks like the one in Figure 17–2, a curve that is popularly known as the "Laffer curve." All this curve does is describe the normal, expected relationship between tax rates and tax collections deduced from the highly plausible proposition that taxpayers will earn more income at low tax rates than at high ones. The peak of the Laffer curve in Figure 17–2 occurs at a tax rate of r_2,

Figure 17–2.   The Laffer Curve.

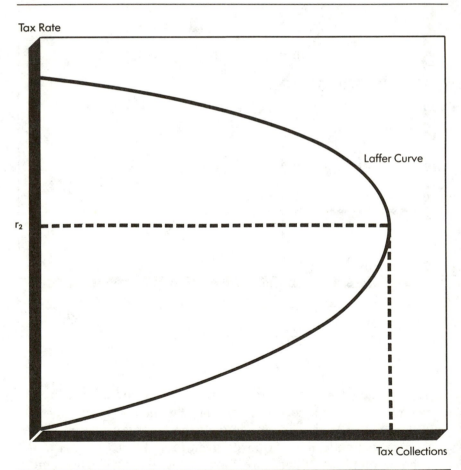

which is the tax rate in the middle of the income demand curve in Figure 17–1.[3]

Because it is derived from demand curve analysis, few economists dispute the *general* shape of the Laffer curve. What has caused a great deal of controversy among economists, however, is the argument made by "supply side" economists that a reduction in tax rates will necessarily lead to more (not less or the same level of) tax revenues. In other words, supply-siders claim the government is on the upper half of the Laffer curve. The credibility of supply-side theory became suspect when supply-siders were unable initially to explain why this would necessarily be true for the economies of California and Massachusetts, where the first supply-side tax battles were fought, much less the whole United States.

On the surface, it appears silly for government to be on the upper half of the Laffer curve. At such "high" tax rates, taxpayers earn less income and enjoy life less than at lower rates. Politicians, who must vote on tax rates, must suffer the consequences of a dissatisfied electorate, and the government has less money than it could have to spend on its constituencies. Fortunately, Buchanan and Lee have devised a theory of politics that explains why the political process results in tax rates that are "too high," meaning above the point where the Laffer curve starts to bend backward. Their theory is founded on the distinction between the long-run and short-run demand for income.

To see their explanation, consider Figure 17–3, in which the representative taxpayer's *long-run* demand curve for income with respect to tax rates is the more elastic (or flatter) darker income curve labeled D_{lr}.[4] That curve indicates that if tax rates are adjusted downward, taxpayers will demand more future income through greater investment. In the long run investors have enough time to reduce their capital stock in response to a tax increase, and vice versa. Given the long-run demand curve D_{lr} in Figure 17–3, long-run revenue is maximized at a tax rate of r_1 (which, because the curves are linear for

---

3. Why the Laffer curve starts bending backward at the midpoint of the straight-line income demand curve requires a mathematical digression that will unnecessarily complicate our discussion. See Buchanan and Lee, *n.* 2.

4. Following Buchanan and Lee, *n.* 2, I assume (for expository reasons) that the optimum tax level is unaffected by the cost of government goods and services. Such an assumption does not disturb the central conclusion of their analysis, which is that governments will tend to "overtax."

Figure 17–3.   The Long-Run and Short-Run Income Demand Curves.

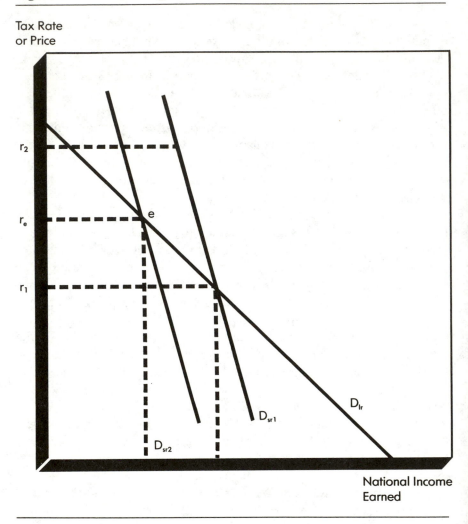

purposes of illustration, is necessarily the midpoint of D_{lr}). However, if the short-run demand curve is more inelastic, because of the tax-payer's inability to adjust readily his capital stock, then there is a short-run demand curve (D_{sr1}) that cuts the long-run demand curve (D_{er}) at the midpoint of the long-run demand curve. The midpoint of this short-run demand curve is up and to the left of the midpoint of the long-run curve. Short-run tax collections are maximized at the midpoint of the short-run demand curve, at a tax rate of r_2, not r_1.

The tax revenues will not, however, remain over the long run at the maximum that will be achieved at a rate of r_2 in Figure 17–3. This is because in the long run, a tax rate of r_2 will discourage saving and investment. The capital stock will, therefore, contract in response to r_2, reducing the ability of future generations to earn income. The short-run demand for income curve in the future will, as a consequence, shift inward, reflecting the reduced capital stock. Operating with a short-run political perspective will, however, still attempt to maximize short-run revenues of government and will move to the midpoint of the then short-run income demand curve—a move that should lower tax rates, since a demand curve closer to the origin will have a midpoint that is at a lower tax rate.

Ultimately, the tax rate will be adjusted (and the capital stock will adjust to the tax rate) until the midpoint of the short run income demand curve lies on the long-run income demand curve. At such a tax rate (which is at the midpoint of the short-run demand curve and on the long-run demand curve) the capital stock will be stable. Accordingly, the income level will be stable. This stable or "equilibrium" tax rate occurs at r_e in the figure. Such an equilibrium tax rate will be at the turning point of the short-run Laffer curve (since it is at the midpoint of the short-run income demand curve) but it will be at a point above the turning point of the long-run Laffer curve. (Notice that the r_e is above the midpoint of the long-run income demand curve, which is where the turning point of the long-run Laffer curve occurs. The midpoint of the short-run, more inelastic income demand curve will necessarily lie up and to the left of the long-run, more elastic income demand curve.)

The central point of the Buchanan/Lee model of a short-sighted political process is that politicians have a tendency to vote for tax rates that tend to be on the upper half of the long-run Laffer curve—that tend to hold tax collections below the long-run maximum that could be achieved.

Buchanan/Lee's argument is developed in terms of income taxation and the residual effects of such taxation on the capital stock. Their argument would appear to be all the stronger if, or when, government has the authority to tax capital directly. Short-sighted politicians would then have an incentive to exploit the immobility of capital and drain away future income.

Embedded in the mechanics of the Buchanan/Lee analysis is a case for restricting, by constitutional means, the ability of government to tax capital, which is to say that the institutional framework within which capital taxation is permitted should be made congruent with the productive life of capital assets. Such congruency between political time horizons and the productive life of capital assets may dictate a prohibition of capital taxation. Barring such a stringent restriction, congruency may mean that capital taxation may be permitted only by local governments, which are constrained by the forces of competing local governments in the tax rates that can be imposed. Clearly, the Buchanan/Lee perspective suggests that the case for constitutional restrictions on capital taxation is stronger than the case for such restrictions on income taxation.

Capital taxation, either directly or indirectly, inevitably poses a problem for policy makers. Unless the tax revenues are used for equally productive public capital projects, taxation of capital transfers the burden of current government programs from the present to future generations. Greater consumption in the current time period is made possible by a diversion of resources away from capital formation and reduced income flow in future time periods.

Because of the accumulating effects of capital taxation on the size of the capital stock available in future time periods, a tax rate reduction on capital will necessarily, at some point, increase future income sufficient to increase future tax revenues. However, the inherent political problem consists in ensuring that the political process will allow capital tax rates to be set so that long-run revenues may be maximized.

Constitutional restrictions on capital taxation, or social norms that restrict the appetite of political leaders to impose capital taxes, may be necessary, but such restrictions can be expected to weaken with the passage of time. This is because as the capital stock grows over time in response to zero or constitutionally restricted tax rates, the temptation to tax capital can grow. With growth in the capital stock, there is simply more for the voting population to extort from future generations. Even Marx praised capitalism, an economy with little government intervention, for its ability to build a capital stock so huge that a communist society, in which people would be subsidized according to their needs, would be feasible.

Interest in capital taxation has been partially a product of social attitudes, not present in the past, that seek greater goods and services produced by government. Recent attitudes can be linked to shifts in taxpayer tastes, increases in consumer income, and expansions in the population, all of which have led to an increase in demand for publicly delivered goods and services. However, such factors are not the whole story. There is more capital now than in the past; the temptation to tax capital has simply been greater of late. In addition, past generations of citizens were simply prohibited by constitutional means and social norms from expanding government intervention in the economy.[5] The breakdown of these constitutional barriers to expanded government have effectively given recent generations of voters greater freedom to tax the capital stock—and to force future generations to share the cost of their consumption. Greater reliance on a democratic process, unconstrained by fiscal restrictions, is apt to reduce the growth of the capital stock.

THE DEMOCRATIC BIAS AGAINST CAPITAL

Advocates of expanded taxation often contend that such decisions should be left to the democratic political process. After all, democracy is a "fair" political game in the sense that everyone—through the power of the vote—is given equal standing in the political process. Therefore, to the extent the political setting in which the taxing decisions are made is "fair," tax rates higher than the turning point of the long-run Laffer curve may be deemed "just." This philosophical position may appear on the surface to be supported, at least to a limited degree, by the work of Harvard University philosopher John Rawls, who contends that behind the "veil of ignorance," a methodological device that effectively cuts people off from information on their absolute and relative social and economic status, people would choose to give everyone an equal vote on such social policies as taxation.[6] As Richard Wagner, a Florida State University economist, has stressed, however, real-world democracies do not meet the stringent fairness tests set forth by Rawls.[7] People in the real world, out from behind the veil of ignorance, know their positions in life (they know, for

5. See Terry Anderson and Peter J. Hill, *The Birth of the Transfer Society* (Stanford: Hoover Institution Press, 1980), for a discussion of the breakdown in constitutional restrictions on taxation. See James M. Buchanan and Richard E. Wagner, *Democracy in Deficit: The Destructive Legacy of Lord Keynes* (New York: Academic Press, 1977), for an account of the breakdown in the "balanced budget norm," which permitted an expansion of government activities.

6. John Rawls, *A Theory of Justice* (Cambridge: Harvard University Press, 1971).

7. Richard E. Wagner, "Politics, Bureaucracy, and Budgetary Choice: The Brookings Budget for 1971," *Journal of Money, Credit and Banking* (Aug. 1974): 367–83.

example, that they exist in the current generation) and will vote their interests—a fact that robs democracy of much of its ethical claims, especially with regard to transfer policies, which tend to dampen incentives to save and invest.

Unrestrained democracy is "unfair" for another, more fundamental reason: Voting rights are usually restricted to the present generation. Future generations do not have a vote, simply because most of them do not exist. Granted, the current generation of voters may have an interest, because of their children, in the welfare of future generations. But there is no reason to believe (and every reason to assume the contrary) that current voters will be as concerned about the welfare of future generations, especially the ones far removed, as will future generations be concerned about their own welfare.

A basic problem of democracy has been the tendency of political interest groups to use their political clout to redistribute income from others to themselves. That tendency is reflected in such transfer programs as import protection, support prices for agriculture goods, and Social Security. Such a redistributive tendency should be just as frequently, if not more frequently, observed in the willingness of the current generation to redistribute income from future generations—who are precluded from voting—to themselves, the people who have all of the votes. The essential means of making such a transfer is through the taxation of capital, which has income consequences that will not manifest themselves until the very long run.[8] Taxes that discourage current capital formation free up resources for the production of a greater quantity of currently consumed consumer goods and increase the welfare of current consumers, many of whom would not have lived to benefit from the capital. In short, because of who is allowed to vote, democracies have a built-in bias against capital formation, especially capital with a long pay-out period.[9]

Seen from this perspective, studies that show, for example, that Social Security has reduced the nation's capital stock and income stream

8. One may reasonably surmise that the current generation will be tempted to tax capital according to how far in the future the benefits are received.

9. Markets have built-in means of handling, albeit imperfectly, the demands of future generations; these means are interest rates and prices. Interest rates and prices rise to reflect the anticipated demands of future generations. But when economic decisions are moved from markets to politics, the demands of the future generations are discounted, simply because the intent of the shift is largely to override the dictates of market-determined interest rates and prices.

of future generations are ones that reveal that the program has, perhaps, had the desired consequence: a redistribution of consumption from future to current generations. To the extent that deficits crowd out private investment, deficit spending is a means of taxing future generations for the benefit of the current generation, which has the votes. To the extent that capital, especially physical capital, becomes a progressively more important source of people's income, as must be the case in developing economies, we should anticipate that current voters will progressively attempt to tax capital as a means of redistributing income from future to current generations. This inference leads to the conclusion that to the extent that deficit spending actually affects capital, it will tend, over time, to become a more prominent means of financing government expenditures.

CAPITAL MOBILITY AND CENTRALIZATION OF TAXING AUTHORITY

The theory of competitive government teaches that tax rates among local governments will tend to be lower than tax rates among states, and state tax rates will tend to be lower than the tax rates imposed by the federal government, assuming everything else held constant. This is because the elasticity of demand for living in any given local government jurisdiction, by virtue of the narrowness of the governmental jurisdiction, will tend to be higher than the elasticity of demand for living in any given state; and the elasticity of demand for living in any given state will tend to be higher than the elasticity of demand for living within the federal tax jurisdiction, the entire country. There are a greater number of alternative places to live and escape taxation at the local level than at the state level, and a greater number of substitutes at the state level than at the federal level. As is to be expected in markets for private goods, the greater the number of alternatives, the greater the competition—and the closer will tax rates move toward the marginal costs of the goods and services provided.

The ability of people to escape increases in tax rates is dependent upon the cost of moving out from under the tax rates, and the moving cost is a function of the distance that must be traveled and the cost of physical movement, i.e., the transportation costs. The lower the cost of movement, generally speaking, the more difficult it is for the governmental unit to charge monopoly tax rates. Therefore, it stands to reason that reductions in transportation costs (or any other change that increases capital mobility) will tend, *ceteris paribus,* to lower tax rates from what they otherwise would be.[10]

Increases in capital mobility enhance the competition among governments and impair the ability of governmental units to extract monopoly rents through the rates they impose. It follows that beneficiaries of government transfer programs will tend to maintain their benefits by working, in times of growing capital mobility, for centralization of taxing authority, first in state governments and then in the federal government. Tax rates that are imposed by the more inclusive government will be imposed across a broader jurisdiction, resulting, in turn, in an increase in the transportation costs that must be incurred to escape the higher taxation.

Centralization of taxation can, from this perspective, be seen as a governmental-institutional device for overriding the tax rate consequences of the growing mobility of capital.[11] To a growing extent in a developed economy such as the United States, this mobility is embodied in people (in the form of human capital) and is due to improvements in transportation and communication systems. Protectionism may be seen as a device for offsetting the advantages of moving capital abroad (and importing the goods back to the United States). Proponents of plant closing restrictions, which would increase the cost of shutting down plants, argue that the growing mobility of capital enables firms to pit communities (and countries) against one another in the struggle for jobs and tax bases at stake. They effectively argue that plant closing restrictions are a means of holding firms hostage and thereby keeping tax rates (as well as wages) up.[12]

From the perspective of this section, the growing hostility of government officials to the emergence and proliferation of multinational corporations becomes more understandable. Multinationals are a form

10. Reductions in mobility costs are likely to affect the revenue-raising capacity of states more than that of local government, since the latter's tax rates are more likely to be closer to the competitive tax rates.

11. Of course, growth in capital mobility may, on the margin, be inspired by growth in government tax rates.

12. For a presentation of the case for plant closing restrictions, see Bluestone and Harrison, *n.* 1. For a critique of the Bluestone/Harrison arguments for plant closing laws, see Richard B. McKenzie, *Fugitive Industry: The Economics and Politics of Deindustrialization* (San Francisco: Pacific Institute for Public Policy Research, 1984); and Richard B. McKenzie, ed., *Plant Closings: Public or Private Choices,* 2d ed. (Washington, D.C.: Cato Institute, 1984).

of business organization that reduces mobility costs and therefore reduces the ability of governments, at all levels, to extract monopoly rents through capital taxation. Multinationals can more readily move work from plant to plant across more tax jurisdictions, in response to tax rate changes, than can firms bound to a given area. As a consequence, the multinational can achieve tax and benefit concessions that cannot be acquired by companies bound by the taxing authority of given countries or communities. To this extent, the capital tax burden imposed at jurisdictional levels below the national level can be disproportionally borne by firms that do not have the capacity to shift work among tax jurisdictions. The lesson of this example is that capital taxation can alter the rational structure of business; it can induce firms to spread out among tax districts to a much greater extent than they would otherwise (in the absence of capital taxation) choose, and perhaps to maintain a higher degree of excess capacity than could otherwise be justified. The cost of the excess capacity and added flexibility would be financed by way of capital tax concessions obtained through movement or, perhaps more important, the threat of movement.

Similarly, elements of proposed national industrial policy agendas may be interpreted as concessions that must, or should, be made by governments in response to the growing mobility of capital. Clearly, the growing mobility of capital is a frequent complaint by industrial policy proponents who are concerned about the growing economic power of business. Industrial policy proponents want to establish national boards and banks that would have the authority to allocate capital by way of grants, interest subsidies, and loan guarantees across industries and regions, principally to save so-called "basic industries." Translated into the terms of this chapter, such government programs are a means of granting concessions to capital in face of growing capital mobility and the threat of plant closures.

Protectionist measures can be seen as devices for increasing the profits of domestic firms, profits that can then be divided up among their workers (through higher wages), the governmental units that support and provide the protection (through higher tax rates), and owners (through higher retained earnings). In short, protectionism may be as much a means of *increasing* capital taxation, in terms of both the tax base and the tax rates, as it is a means of raising the prices, payrolls, and profits of the protected industry. Clearly, protectionism can, by diverting resources away from a country's comparative advantages, reduce the country's future capital stock and tax revenues. Nevertheless, the transfer of income from future to current generations can be what is intended.

Furthermore, protectionism can redistribute the capital stock, enabling well-identified local governments to increase their tax revenue by way of an increase in *their* capital stock and tax rates. In an unrestrained democracy, the state of Pennsylvania can fully support its steelworkers' union in the latter's drive for protection against steel imports on the grounds that such restrictions will permit greater investment in steel capacity in Pennsylvania and, as a consequence, higher tax rates on capital across the industrial board in that state. Similarly, the state of South Carolina can support textile protectionism on the grounds that its taxing capacity will be enhanced. If all states engage in a competitive struggle for protection of their industries, all can lose, even in the short run. However, so long as states are not constitutionally prevented from seeking protection, then all can reason that they each had better seek protection, or else become even worse losers in the competitive protectionist game. If all other states seek and obtain protection for their industries, those states that refrain from doing so will become losers.

Finally, the points raised in this section may explain the growing interest of states in "unitary taxation," meaning the taxation of the worldwide income of corporations that have plants inside and outside their geographical jurisdiction. Unitary taxation may be viewed as a means of reducing the effective mobility of national and multinational companies. Such taxing authority not only allows states to increase their tax base but to raise their tax rates (to the extent that all states adopt such taxing methods). Without question, states that permit unitary taxation will, because of the competition from nonunitary tax states, be interested in having federal tax laws requiring unitary taxation in all states.

CONCLUSION

The subject of capital taxation has tended to be considered by economists in technical terms—how capital taxation affects the capital stock and how capital taxes are distributed among owners, workers, and consumers. Little has been written on the interdependence of capital taxation and the political decision-making process. A recurring theme of this chapter is that capital taxation provides voters with an opportunity to extort the income of people who have saved, or refrained from consumption, in anticipation of future income. Because of the disincentive effects of taxes on capital formation, capital taxation offers current generations of voters the opportunity to transfer consumption goods, via reductions in income growth, from future generations to themselves. Voters in future generations are simply not around to defend themselves politically. Many proposed industrial policies can be seen as hidden means of increasing current tax rates on capital and transferring income from future to current generations.

Economists have also spent much professional energy considering how political operatives attempt to use their command over votes to redistribute income from others to themselves. The focus of these studies has implicitly been on redistributive schemes within the current voting population. The lesson of this chapter is that more attention should be given to how the current generations of voters can—under, for example, the guise of national industrial policy—use their political clout to redistribute income to themselves from future generations. More attention should be devoted to understanding how the political process can be effectively constrained to restrict the ability of the current generation to exploit their favored political position. One reason industrial policy advocates should be feared is that they propose to do what they say they want to do: reduce the mobility of capital in order that capital can be more heavily taxed by governments at all levels, and in order that capital can be more easily exploited by worker groups.

SELECTED BIBLIOGRAPHY
PART III

Advisory Commission on Intergovernmental Relations (ACIR). *State-Local Taxation and Industrial Location*. Washington, D.C.: ACIR, 1967.

————. *Measuring the Fiscal Capacity and Effort of State and Local Areas*. Washington, D.C.: ACIR, 1971.

————. *Regional Growth: Interstate Tax Competition*. Washington, D.C.: ACIR, 1981.

Amdur, Shelly; Samuel Friedman; and Rebecca Staiger. *Investment and Employment Tax Credits: An Assessment of Geographically Sensitive Alternatives*. Washington, D.C.: Northeast-Midwest Institute, 1978.

Anderson, Terry L., and Peter J. Hill. *The Birth of a Transfer Society*. Stanford, Calif.: Hoover Institution Press, 1980.

————. "Economic History in the United States." Lecture delivered at Montana State University, Bozeman, Montana, February 1984.

Armentano, Dominick. *Antitrust and Monopoly: Anatomy of a Failure*. New York: John Wiley & Sons, 1982.

Armstrong, Donald. *Competition versus Monopoly*. Vancouver, British Columbia: Fraser Institute, 1982.

Baumol, William J. "Entrepreneurship in Economic Theory." *American Economic Review* 58 (May 1968): 64–71.

Becker, Gary S. *Economic Theory*. New York: Alfred A. Knopf, 1971.

Bellamy, Jan. "Two Utilities Are Better Than One." *Reason* 13 (October 1981): 23–30.

Borcherding, Thomas E., ed. *Budgets and Bureaucrats*. Durham, N.C.: Duke University Press, 1977.

Browning, Edgar K., and Jacquelene M. Browning. *Microeconomic Theory and Applications*. Boston: Little, Brown and Co., 1983.

Brunton, Ron. "The Origins of the John Frum Movement: A Sociological Explanation." In M. Allen, ed., *Politics, Economics, and Ritual in Island Melanesia*. New York: Academic Press, 1981.

Buchanan, James M. "Positive Economics, Welfare Economics, and Political Economy." *Journal of Law and Economics* 2 (October 1959): 125–38.

———. *Cost and Choice*. Chicago: Markham Publishing, 1969.

———. *What Should Economists Do?* Indianapolis: Liberty Press, 1979.

———. "The Achievement and the Limits of Public Choice in Diagnosing Government Failure and in Offering Bases for Constructive Reform." Paper presented at International Symposium on Anatomy of Government Deficiencies. Dissen am Ammersee, Bavaria, July 1, 1980.

———. "The Related but Distinct 'Sciences' of Economics and of Political Economy." *British Journal of Social Psychology* 21 (1982): 175–83.

Buchanan, James M., and Alberto di Pierro. "Cognition, Choice, and Entrepreneurship." *Southern Economic Journal* 46 (January 1980): 693–701.

Buchanan, James M., and Dwight R. Lee. "Politics, Time, and the Laffer Curve." *Journal of Political Economy* 90 (1982): 816–19.

Buchanan, James M., and George F. Thirlby, eds. *L. S. E. Essays on Cost*. London: Weidenfield and Nicolson, 1973.

Buchanan, James M.; Robert D. Tollison; and Gordon Tullock, eds. *Toward a Theory of the Rent-Seeking Society*. College Station: Texas A & M University Press, 1980.

Carlson, Eugene. "Great Lakes Governors Split Over Truce on Industry Raids." *Wall Street Journal*, 12 July 1983, p. 31.

Carlton, Dennis. "Why New Firms Locate Where They Do: An Econometric Model." In W. Wheaton, ed., *Interregional Movements and Regional Growth*, pp. 13–50. Washington, D.C.: Urban Institute, 1979.

———. "The Location and Employment Choices of New Firms: An Econometric Model With Discrete and Continuous Endogenous Variables." *Review of Economics and Statistics* 65 (August 1983): 440–49.

Casson, Mark. *The Entrepreneur: An Economic Theory*. Totowa, N.J.: Barnes and Noble Books, 1982.

Church, Albert M. *Taxation of Nonrenewable Resources*. Lexington, Mass.: Lexington Books, 1981.

Demsetz, Harold. "Why Regulate Utilities?" *Journal of Law and Economics* 11 (April 1968): 55–65.

———. "Information and Efficiency: Another Viewpoint." *Journal of Law and Economics* 12 (April 1969): 1–22.

Dorn, James A. "Trade Adjustment Assistance: A Case of Government Failure." *Cato Journal* 2 (Winter 1982): 865–905.

Due, John F. "Studies of State-Local Tax Influences on Location of Industry." *National Tax Journal* 14 (June 1961): 163–73.

Fairlamb, David. "Europe's Thriving 'Black' Economies." *Dun's Business Month* 120, no. 2 (August 1982): 69–70.

Feldstein, Martin S. "The Retreat from Keynesian Economics." *Public Interest* 64 (Summer 1981): 92–105.

Fink, Richard H., ed. *Supply-Side Economics: A Critical Appraisal.* Frederick, Md.: University Publication of America, 1982.

Friedman, David D., and Michael M. Kurth. "Revenue Sharing and Monopoly Government: A Comment." *Public Choice* 37 (1981): 365–70.

Friedman, Milton. *Price Theory.* Chicago: Aldine Publishing Co., 1976.

Fromm, Gary, ed. *Tax Incentives and Capital Spending.* Washington, D.C.: Brookings Institution, 1971.

Genetski, Robert J., and D. Chin Young. "The Impact of State and Local Taxes on Economic Growth." Harris Trust and Savings Bank, 1978. (Mimeo.)

Gilder, George. *Wealth and Poverty.* New York: Basic Books, 1981.

Glahe, Fred R., and Dwight R. Lee. *Microeconomics: Theory and Applications.* New York: Harcourt Brace Jovanovich, 1981.

Gwartney, James, and Richard L. Stroup. "Cooperation or Conniving: How Public Sector Rules Shape the Decision." *Journal of Labor Research* 3, no. 3 (Summer 1982): 247–58.

Haberler, Gottfried. "Schumpeter's Capitalism, Socialism, and Democracy After Forty Years." In A. Heertje, ed., *Schumpeter's Vision,* chap. 4, pp. 69–94. New York: Praeger, 1981.

Hayek, Friedrich A. *Individualism and Economic Order.* Chicago: University of Chicago Press, 1948.

————. *New Studies in Philosophy, Politics, Economics, and the History of Ideas.* Chicago: University of Chicago Press, 1978.

Heyne, Paul. *The Economic Way of Thinking.* 4th ed. Chicago: Science Research Associates, 1983.

Hickel, James. *The Chrysler Bail-Out Bust.* Washington, D.C.: Heritage Foundation, 1983. Heritage Foundation Backgrounder, no. 276.

Hirshleifer, Jack. *Price Theory and Applications.* 2d ed. Englewood Cliffs, N.J.: Prentice-Hall, 1980.

Humbert, Thomas. *Tax Indexing: At Last a Break for the Little Guy.* Washington, D.C.: Heritage Foundation, 1983. Heritage Foundation Backgrounder, no. 255.

"Industrial Policy: Is It the Answer?" *Business Week* (4 July 1983): 54–62.

Juster, Thomas, ed. *The Economic and Political Impact of General Revenue Sharing.* Ann Arbor: Survey Research Center, Institute for Social Research, University of Michigan, 1977.

Kanter, Sandra. "A History of State Business Subsidies." *Proceedings of* the Annual Conference of the National Tax Association, Tax Institute of America* 17 (November 1977): 147–55.

Kieschnick, Michael. *Taxes and Growth: Business Incentives and Economic Development*. Washington, D.C.: Council of State Planning Agencies, 1981.

Kirzner, Israel M. *Competition and Entrepreneurship*. Chicago: University of Chicago Press, 1973.

———. *The Perils of Regulation: A Market-Process Approach*. LEC Occasional Paper. Coral Gables, Fla.: Law and Economics Center, 1978.

———. *Perception, Opportunity, and Profit*. Chicago: University of Chicago Press, 1979.

Klein, Gregory L. *Industrial Policy: A Summary of Bills Before Congress*. Washington, D.C.: Heritage Foundation, 1983. Heritage Foundation Issues Bulletin, no. 96.

Kleine, Robert J. "State and Local Tax Levels and Economic Growth—A Regional Comparison." *Proceedings of the Annual Conference of the National Tax Association, Tax Institute of America* 17 (November 1977): 162–72.

Kolstad, Charles D., and Frank A. Wolak, Jr. "Competition in Interregional Taxation: The Case of Western Coal." *Journal of Political Economy* 91 (June 1983): 443–460.

Lackman, Ludwig M. *Capital and Its Structure*. Kansas City: Sheed, Andrews and McMeel, 1978.

Lee, Dwight R., and James M. Buchanan. "Tax Rates and Tax Revenues in Political Equilibrium: Some Simple Analytics." *Economic Inquiry* 20 (July 1982): 344–54.

Leftwich, Richard H., and Ross D. Eckert. *The Price System and Resource Allocation*. Chicago: Dryden Press, 1982.

Littlechild, Stephen C. "The Problem of Social Cost." In L. Spadaro, ed., *New Directions in Austrian Economics*, pp. 77–93. Kansas City: Sheed, Andrews and McMeel, 1978.

———. "Misleading Calculations of the Social Costs of Monopoly Power." *Economic Journal* 91 (June 1981): 348–63.

———. *The Fallacy of the Mixed Economy*. London: Institute of Economic Affairs, 1978.

Loasby, Brian J. *Choice, Complexity, and Ignorance*. New York: Cambridge University Press, 1976.

———. "The Entrepreneur in Economic Theory." *Scottish Journal of Political Economy* 29 (November 1982): 235–45.

Maddala, G. S. *Econometrics*. New York: McGraw-Hill, 1977.

Malabre, Alfred L. "Underground Economy Grows and Grows." *Wall Street Journal*, 20 October 1980, p. 1.

Mansfield, Edwin. *Microeconomics: Theory and Applications*. New York: W. W. Norton, 1979.

McGuire, Martin C. "The Analysis of Federal Grants Into Price and Income Components." In P. Mieszkowski and W. Oakland, eds., *Fiscal Federalism and Grants-in-Aid*, pp. 31–50. Washington, D.C.: Urban Institute, 1979.

McKenzie, Richard B. *Fugitive Industry: The Economics and Politics of Deindustrialization*. San Francisco: Pacific Institute for Public Policy Research, 1984.

McKenzie, Richard B., and Robert B. Staaf. "Revenue Sharing and Monopoly Government." *Public Choice* 33 (1978): 93–97.

———. "Revenue Sharing and Monopoly Government: A Reply." *Public Choice* 37 (1981): 371–75.

Merton, T., and N. B. Stone. "Cargo Cults in the South Pacific." *America* 137, no. 5 (27 August 1977): 94–99.

Mettler, R. F. "The Cargo Cult Mentality in America." *Business Week* (20 September 1980): 22.

Miller, James P. "Manufacturing Relocations in the United States, 1969–75." In R. McKenzie, ed., *Plant Closings: Public or Private Choice*, pp. 19–35. Washington, D.C.: Cato Institute, 1982.

———. "Interstate Competition for Business: Changing Roles of Federal and State Incentives." Economic Staff Research Report No. AGES 831012. Washington, D.C.: U.S. Department of Agriculture, Economic Development Division, December 1983.

Mitchell, William C. "Efficiency, Responsibility, and Democratic Politics." In R. Pennock and J. Chapman, eds., *Liberal Democracy*, ch. 13, pp. 343–73. New York: New York University Press, 1983.

Moldofsky, Naomi. "Market Theoretical Frameworks—Which One?" *Economic Record* 58 (June 1982): 152–68.

Morgan, Douglas W. "The Effects of State and Local Taxes and Financial Inducements on Industrial Location." Ph.D. dissertation, University of Colorado, 1964.

Morgan, Douglas W., and Elliot W. Brownlee. "The Impact of State and Local Taxation on Industrial Location: A New Measure for the Great Lakes Region." *Quarterly Review of Economics and Business* 14 (Spring 1974): 67–77.

Mulkey, David, and B. L. Dillman. "Location Effects of State and Local Industrial Development Subsidies." *Growth and Change* 7 (April 1976): 37–43.

Nardinelli, Clark. *The Reconstruction Finance Corporation's Murky History*. Washington, D.C.: Heritage Foundation, 1983. Heritage Foundation Backgrounder, no. 317.

Niskanen, William A., Jr. *Bureaucracy and Representative Government*. Chicago: Aldine-Atherton, 1971.

Nutter, G. Warren. *Political Economy and Freedom*. Indianapolis: Liberty Press, 1983.

O'Driscoll, Gerald P., Jr. "Monopoly in Theory and Practice." In I. Kirzner, ed., *Method, Process, and Austrian Economics: Essays in Honor of Ludwig von Mises*, ch. 16, pp. 189–213. Lexington, Mass.: D. C. Heath, 1982.

Olson, Mancur. *The Rise and Decline of Nations*. New Haven, Conn.: Yale University Press, 1982.

Pasour, Ernest C., Jr. "Economic Efficiency: Touchstone or Mirage?" *Intercollegiate Review* 17 (Fall/Winter 1981): 33–44.

———. "Economic Efficiency and Inefficient Economics: Another View." *Journal of Post Keynesian Economics* 4 (Spring 1982): 454–59.

———. "Monopoly Theory and Practice—Some Subjectivist Implications: Comment on O'Driscoll." In I. Kirzner, ed., *Method, Process, and Austrian Economics: Essays in Honor of Ludwig von Mises*, ch. 17, pp. 215–23. Lexington, Mass.: D. C. Heath, 1982.

Peacock, Alan. "On the Anatomy of Collective Failure." *Public Finance* 35 (1980): 33–43.

Pechman, Joseph A. "Anatomy of the U.S. Individual Income Tax." In S. Cnossen, ed., *Comparative Tax Studies: Essays in Honor of Richard Goode*, ch. 3, pp. 61–84. New York: North-Holland, 1983.

Plaut, Thomas, and Joseph Pluta. "Business Climate, Taxes and Expenditures, and State Industrial Growth in the United States." *Southern Economic Journal* 50 (July 1983): 99–119.

Posner, Richard A. "Theories of Economic Regulation." *Bell Journal of Economics and Management Science* 5 (Autumn 1974): 335–58.

———. "The Social Costs of Monopoly and Regulation." *Journal of Political Economy* 83 (August 1975): 807–27. Also published in J. Buchanan, R. Tollison, and G. Tullock, eds., *Toward A Theory of the Rent-Seeking Society*, ch. 5, pp. 71–94. College Station: Texas A & M University Press, 1980.

Reich, Robert B. "Playing Tag With Japan." *New York Review* (24 June 1982): 37–39.

———. *The Next American Frontier*. New York: New York Times Book Co., 1983.

Reschovsky, Andrew. "New Strategies for Metropolitan Area Cooperation: Sharing Rather than Competing for Business Tax Base." *Proceedings of the Annual Conference of the National Tax Association, Tax Institute of America* 17 (November 1977).

Richman, Sheldon. "Let Sleeping Failures Lie: The Reconstruction Finance Corporation." *Policy Report* 2, no. 11 (1980): 3.

Robbins, Lionel. "Economics and Political Economy." *American Economic Review* 71 (May 1981): 1–10.

Rogge, Benjamin A. *Can Capitalism Survive?* Indianapolis: Liberty Press, 1979.

Rosett, Claudia. "How Peru Got a Free Market Without Really Trying." *Wall Street Journal,* 27 January 1984, p. 31.

Rothbard, Murray N. *Power and Market: Government and the Economy.* Menlo Park, Calif.: Institute for Humane Studies, 1970.

———. *The Ethics of Liberty.* Atlantic Highlands, N.J.: Humanities Press, 1982.

Sakoh, Katsuro. *Industrial Policy: The Super Myth of Japan's Super Success.* Washington, D.C.: Heritage Foundation, 13 July 1983. Asian Studies Center Backgrounder.

Savas, Emanuel S. *Privatizing the Public Sector.* Chatham, N.J.: Chatham House Publishers, 1972.

Schmenner, Roger W. *The Manufacturing Location Decision.* Cambridge: Harvard-MIT Joint Center for Urban Studies, 1978.

———. *The Location Decision of Large, Multiplant Companies.* Cambridge: Harvard-MIT Joint Center for Urban Studies, 1980.

Schultz, Theodore W. "The Value of the Ability to Deal With Disequilibria." *Journal of Economic Literature* 13 (September 1975): 827–46.

———. "Investment in Entrepreneurial Ability." *Scandinavian Journal of Economics* 82 (1980): 437–48.

Schumpeter, Joseph A. *Capitalism, Socialism, and Democracy.* 3d ed. New York: Harper and Brothers, 1947.

Shackle, George L. S. *Decision, Order and Time in Human Affairs.* 2d ed. London: Cambridge University Press, 1969.

———. *Epistemics and Economics: A Critique of Economic Doctrines.* London: Cambridge University Press, 1982.

———. "Means and Meaning in Economic Theory." *Scottish Journal of Political Economy* 29 (November 1982): 223–34.

Sowell, Thomas. *Knowledge and Decisions.* New York: Basic Books, 1980.

Stafford, Howard. "The Anatomy of the Location Decision: Content Analysis of Case Studies." In F. Hamilton, ed., *Spatial Perspectives on Industrial Organization and Decision-Making.* New York: John Wiley & Sons, 1974.

Stigler, George J. "The Economics of Information." *Journal of Political Economy* 69 (June 1961): 213–25.

———. "The Theory of Economic Regulation." *Bell Journal of Economics and Management Science* 2 (Spring 1971): 3–21.

Strathern, Andrew. "The Red Box Money Cult in Mount Hagen 1968–71." Parts 1, 2. *Oceania* 50, nos. 2 and 3 (December 1979, March 1980): 88–102, 162–75.

Stubblebine, William Craig. "Revenue Reallocation in the Federal System: Options and Prospects." In R. Hawkins, Jr., ed., *American Federalism: A New Partnership for the Republic*. San Francisco: Institute for Contemporary Studies, 1982.

Thompson, Wilbur R., and John M. Mattila. *An Econometric Model of Postwar State Industrial Development*. Detroit: Wayne State University Press, 1959.

Von Mises, Ludwig. *Human Action*. 3d ed. Chicago: Henry Regnery Co., 1966.

————. *Bureaucracy*. New Rochelle, N.Y.: Arlington House, 1969.

————. *Planning for Freedom*. Memorial ed. South Holland, Ill.: Libertarian Press, 1974.

Wasylenko, Michael. "The Location of Firms: The Role of Taxes and Fiscal Incentives." In R. Bahl, ed., *Urban Government Finance: Emerging Trends,* (vol. 20 of *Urban Affairs Annual Review*), ch. 7, pp. 155–96. Beverly Hills, Calif.: Sage Publications, 1981.

Weidenbaum, Murray L. "Is Protectionism Back in Style?" *Policy Report* 5 (December 1983): 1–3.

Wheaton, William C. "Interstate Differences in the Level of Business Taxation." *National Tax Journal* 36 (March 1983): 83–94.

Wildavsky, Aaron. "Birthday Cake Federalism." In R. Hawkins, Jr. ed., *American Federalism: A New Partnership for the Republic*. San Francisco: Institute for Contemporary Studies, 1982.

Wolf, Charles, Jr. "A Theory of Nonmarket Failure: Framework for Implementation Analysis." *Journal of Law and Economics* 22 (April 1979): 107–39.

Worcester, Dean A. "On the Validity of Marginal Analysis for Policy Making." *Eastern Economic Journal* 8 (April 1982): 83–88.

Worsley, Peter. *The Trumpet Shall Sound*. New York: Schocken Books, 1968.

Yeager, Leland B. "Economics and Principles." *Southern Economic Journal* 42 (April 1976): 559–71.

Zimmerman, Martin B., and Christopher Alt. "The Western Coal Cartel." Stanford University Working Paper E-80-9. Hoover Institution, March 1981. (Mimeo.)

PART IV

TAXATION AND INDIVIDUAL RIGHTS

18

THE ETHICS OF TAXATION: RIGHTS VERSUS PUBLIC GOODS

Eric Mack

INTRODUCTION

This chapter commences with a fairly brief account of a moral philosophical perspective on the basis of which all taxation has been condemned. This perspective is essentially Lockean and focuses on each individual's moral status as a possessor of sovereignty over his own person and not, to any degree, over any other person. The portions of this perspective that immediately speak to the ethics of taxation are its theory of private property rights and justice in economic holdings. It will not be argued that all existing holdings are just and hence should be immune from governmental seizure. Indeed in light of the libertarian doctrine, which will be outlined, many existing holdings are not just. But no existing or pending tax scheme targets for confiscation precisely those holdings that should be judged unjust. All existing or pending tax schemes, in fact, deprive many individuals of holdings to which, in the libertarian perspective to be developed, those individuals have every right. If this is correct, then all such schemes are morally unacceptable, and alternative means must be found for financing the relatively few projects currently financed through taxation and worthy of continuation.

While the second section of this chapter attempts a plausible rendition of the ethics of tax-condemnation, the third and fourth sections examine one important attempt to circumvent this antitax ethic. The general idea beyond this attempt is that the Lockean/libertarian argument most plausibly and forcefully strikes against redistributivism, i.e., belief in taxation to alter patterns of wealth or patterns of what wealth sometimes brings (opportunity, utility, etc.) in order to bring about a socially better pattern of wealth (or opportunity, utility, etc.). The libertarian argument strikes against redistributivism by denying the validity, and perhaps even the meaningfulness, of the notion of *socially better*. It denies the validity, or even the meaningfulness, of positing some extra-individual perspective from which a redistributive alteration can be pronounced a social improvement. But if the libertarian argument strikes specifically, or with most force, against redistributive schemes, then a program is suggested for outflanking this libertarian critique. The program consists of looking for modes of justification for coercive takings that are not based on some redistributist ideology.

Sections three and four of this chapter deal with the sort of non-redistributivist justification most obvious to an economic way of thinking, *viz.*, a public-good justification.[1] If each individual subject to a forcible seizure of some of his wealth on balance benefits (in comparison to his other opportunities) because of the value to him of the good thereby financed, no individual can claim to have had a loss imposed on him for the sake of another's benefit or to have been sacrificed on the altar of the public's (i.e., other people's) interests. If the right that the libertarian argument yields is simply the right not to be subject to redistributivism, then there seems to be a strong case that seizures for the financing of public goods do not violate libertarian strictures. The public-goods argument occurs at the ethical margin in that its advocate may accept the basic moral vocabulary and spirit of the libertarian critique. This advocate simply argues that this critique does not yield a right against all forced yet nonredistributive takings and that, in the absence of such a precluding right, there are good reasons for those nonredistributive forced takings that finance (certain) public goods. Section four of this chapter is devoted to defending the libertarian moral critique against this flanking attack.

Such a defense can take a more or less aggressive form. The phil-

---

1. An alternative strategy for identifying taxlike schemes that are not redistributive and do not violate libertarian strictures is to construe taxlike forced takings as rectifications of past violations of those very strictures.

osophically more aggressive form would so fortify the foundations of this moral perspective that anything at all contrary to this perspective, e.g., any tax scheme, could be dismissed out of hand. This form would insist that, of course, the right that people possess is one against any forced taking and, of course, that right settles the matter. The more modest approach taken here sees that right as a moral *presumption* against forced takings, a presumption that might, at least in principle, be overcome in special cases—specifically, cases that do not fit the paradigm of unjustified forced *redistributions*. But it is maintained that when we think through the various specific bases for overthrowing the presumption against forced takings, we find no sufficiently plausible basis for actually overthrowing this presumption. Thus, the flank attacked by the public-goods argument is strong enough to resist this campaign on behalf of nonredistributive taxation. Perhaps it is morally significant that, by not being redistributivist, certain tax schemes, e.g., taxation structured to finance true public goods, *come closest to being permissible*. Perhaps it could be argued that being closest to permissible equals being minimally permissible. But this issue will not be pursued.

It remains only to note that, for the most part, the argument of this chapter bears only indirectly on the connection between taxation and capital formation. There is here no concern with what specific effects on *voluntary* capital formation this or that particular tax scheme would have. There is only the moral that people should have vastly greater choice over the disposal of their justly achieved holdings. The satisfaction of this prescription is compatible with vastly greater capital formation or with none—depending on people's free decisions. Of course, insofar as public-goods arguments are seen as arguments for coercive, governmental capital formation, the bearing of this essay is quite direct.

THE LIBERTARIAN PERSPECTIVE

As noted in the introduction, the moral philosophical perspective from which this essay proceeds is essentially Lockean.[2] Among individuals there are no natural moral slaves and no natural moral sovereigns. No one's purposes or goals take moral precedence over the purposes and

---

2. In this section I draw on portions of my paper, "In Defense of 'Unbridled' Freedom of Contract," *American Journal of Economics and Sociology* 40 (Jan. 1981): 1–15.

goals of any other person in a way that would justify the complete or partial subordination of any individual to any other individual or to any group of individuals. There is a moral equality among persons. But this moral equality does not merely consist of an equal presence in a morally empty universe—a universe in which acts of aggression and subjugation, while not right, are also not wrong. The moral equality of persons includes the equal ultimacy of the value of each person's life. Each individual's life is an ultimate value to that individual. For each person that which is of fundamental value and is the rational goal of his action and planning is the fulfillment of his best (available) plan of life, i.e., the most harmonious lifetime satisfaction of his desires, interests, and capacities. The value of the fulfillment of a rational life plan or of the elements contributing to such a plan is objective, but it is also agent-relative or positional.[3] It is for the person who stands in relationship to a fulfilled rational plan of life as its agent and subject that this fulfillment is ultimately valuable. It is objectively the case that the fulfillment of any given rational plan of life is of ultimate value to someone (and quite possibly of nonultimate value to other individuals). But the someone for whom it is fundamentally desirable is the person in the position of living and undergoing that life.

This individualistic conception of the equally (but noncommensurably) ultimate value of each person's respective harmonious fulfillment of his desires, interests, and capacities has crucial implications for how individuals must act (or refrain from acting) toward others. These implications constitute a person's fundamental natural rights and obligations. In maintaining that each person's well-being is an ultimate value, *the* ultimate value with respect to *that* agent, one is not only maintaining about persons that they constitute a multiplicity of points or even receptacles in which value can be achieved and lodged. For the "receptacles" themselves, i.e., these individuals, respectively occupy moral space not merely as depots for the storage of well-being but as embodied, active, choosing beings having the achievement of their well-being as their respective rational purposes. Having a specific and separate rational end of his own, each person's faculties and capacities for choice and action—and his choices and

---

3. For a recent account of this conception of objective, albeit relational, value from a perhaps surprising source, see Amartya Sen, "Evaluator Relativity and Consequential Evaluation," *Philosophy and Public Affairs* 12 (Spring 1983): 113–32.

actions—are not like natural resources that are equally morally available to whoever desires to put them to use. Rather, the possession of a separate moral purpose removes each person as an embodied, active, choosing being from the domain of objects that simply exist as possible material for the use of other individuals.

Morally speaking, a person's faculties and capacities are therefore uniquely means to an end, that person's well-being. One cannot coherently affirm that the well-being of each is his separate and distinctive end without affirming also that some things stand as distinctly means to that end, and hence, as means not available to others. On the most fundamental level, it is the person himself, his existence as an embodied, living, purposive being, that stands as a means to the end (which is his well-being) and hence as material that is morally out of bounds for another's exploitation.

Since each person is an end-in-himself in the sense that the most cohesive realization of his person, desires, capacities, etc., is the distinctive rational ultimate value (for him), each person is a means to that separate ultimate value which is his successful life; therefore, no person is a means for anyone else's life or purposes. This is our reading and explication of the Kantian slogan that because each is an end-in-himself, each has a moral immunity against being treated as a means.[4] A person's moral sovereignty over himself involves claims, i.e., rights, to life and liberty, to property in his own body, and to other property permissibly acquired. There are correlative obligations in all others not to (nonconsensually) deprive him of life, liberty, and legitimate property. These (natural) moral rights and obligations exist independent of and prior to any agreements among persons and independent of the social utility or positive legality of recognizing these rights and obligations.

This doctrine of people's propriety over themselves and their legitimate possessions must be fleshed out with at least a minimal account of property rights in extrapersonal objects. Following Robert Nozick's discussion in his *Anarchy, State and Utopia*,[5] we can see these rights being determined by three principles: a principle of initial ownership; a principle of just transfer; and a principle of rectification. Initial property rights in any object come about through the creation

---

4. But this is not intended as an explication of what Kant himself actually meant.

5. Robert Nozick, *Anarchy, State and Utopia* (New York: Basic Books, 1974), especially pp. 149–82.

of that object. Creation, of course, will not be *de novo*. Rather, he who intentionally and identifiably transforms some material, through acts that do not themselves violate anyone's rights, in order to render that material a more serviceable and controllable instrument of his purposes, acquires a right to the transformed object. Such a party, in Locke's phrase, "mixes his labor" with some previously unowned material. The transforming agent acquires a right to the created object in virtue of his antecedent right to his labor, because that labor is now so intermixed with the created object that to deprive him of the object would be to seize his labor, to treat him at least in part as the natural servant or slave of the expropriator. As Nozick puts it:

> Seizing the results of someone's labor is equivalent to seizing hours from him and directing him to carry on various activities. If people force you to do certain work, or unrewarded work, for a certain period of time, they decide what you are to do and what purpose your work is to serve, apart from your decisions. This process whereby they take this decision from you makes them a *part-owner* of you; it gives them a [legal, but morally unjustified] property right in you. Just as having such partial control and power of decision, by right over an animal or inanimate object would be to have a property right in it.[6]

A property right to a given object includes the right to dispose of that object, and one form of disposition involves the transfer of the very right to that object. So, once a property right is established in any object, a party other than the creator of that object can acquire a right to it by eliciting the transfer of the title to him. The transfer of title will be valid whenever the process eliciting the transfer involves no violation of rights. A given individual's possession of a particular object will be just if and only if each of the "moves" actually leading to his possession satisfies either the initial ownership principle or the transfer principle.[7] The only essential amendment to this claim is the rectification principle, viz., another acceptable move preserving valid title is the repossession by an individual of an object (or its equivalent) from the individual or group who has seized it.

---

6. Nozick, *n.* 5, p. 172.

7. The doctrine as stated needs modification. Not any past unrectified injustice in the holding of a given object renders its current possession unjust. Sufficiently distant past injustices, whose effects have been washed out by time and the complexities of human affairs, will not undercut the validity of current holdings. But what "sufficiently distant" and "washed out" mean has to be worked out.

This theory of justice in holdings is what Nozick calls a "historical non-patterned" theory. What a given individual has property rights to depends on how he has acted and how others have acted toward him. If he has created much or elicited much in the way of gifts or payments, he will have just claims on much. If he has created little and elicited little from others in the way of gifts or payments, he will have just claims on little. And there is no antecedently specifiable pattern, such as equality or proportionality to intelligence or proportionality to virtue, that the profile of just holdings across individuals will fit. A just "social distribution" is whatever distribution is created by individuals engaging in acquisition in accordance with the constraints laid down by the three principles. Insofar as individuals' just holdings are seized by bandits or by governments, rights are impermissibly violated. It does not require wild empirical premises about how people have actually acquired their current holdings to conclude that all existing and prospective tax schemes of the U.S. government and its political subdivisions do involve many such impermissible seizures—seizures that, from the perspective developed here, have the same moral status as banditry.

There are two common philosophical replies to this sort of condemnation of taxation. The first is that the taking carried out as taxation at least sometimes is, contrary to appearances, carried out under the consent of its subjects. A belief in some sort of voluntary background consent was, after all, the basis for Locke's having accepted taxation. But here the appearances have far more veracity than the alleged underlying reality. There has been no actual consent for most people. Nor can the most plausible candidates for actual consenters— naturalized citizens, for example—be said to have consented to particular taxes with the degree of specificity normally required for legally binding consent. And even their oaths can be construed as being made under duress, under threat of being denied freedoms (e.g., the freedom to move unencumbered across the "state's" boundaries) that the state has no right to deny peaceable individuals.

Similarly, the existence of democratic electoral processes does very little to legitimize coercive taxation. It cannot legitimize the impositions upon those who do not vote, those who vote against the taxes in question and/or against the champions of those taxes, or those who voted for the taxes in question and/or for the tax champions on the basis of lies and false promises. That leaves, at most, very few people who can reasonably be said to have incurred obligations to pay taxes

494 TAXATION AND THE DEFICIT ECONOMY

on the basis of their electoral participation. Nor is there any other type of electoral or even more mystical control exercised by the "people," either individually or collectively, over our rulers that constitutes a morally significant consent to coercive taxation or that shows taxation to be really only something "we" do to "ourselves." As J. S. Mill pointed out, against such Rousseauistic fantasies, ". . . such phrases as 'self-government' and 'the power of people over themselves' do not express the true state of the case."[8]

Certainly mere continued residence within the state's boundaries cannot be interpreted as free consent to its exercise of taxation. For one thing, individuals obviously have many motives for maintaining residence other than signifying their allegiance to some political institutions. For another thing, the state has no right to make people's residence within the geographical area it controls (and *claims* to rule legitimately) contingent upon submission to its takings. A private owner may stipulate that occupants of his property must agree to a certain schedule of payments as a condition of remaining on his property. But to suppose that the state may make comparable stipulations is to presuppose what is supposed to be established, viz., that the state owns the country, that it has property rights in "the country's" wealth which override individual rights. Finally, we should note that if one waters down what counts as binding consent to a point where everyone subject to taxation in the United States can be said to have consented to this subjugation, one's notion of consent will be so encompassing that almost all people under almost all regimes, no matter how grotesque and brutal, will count as having consented to their being so ruled.

The second common philosophical line of reply to the libertarian perspective and antitax conclusion developed here invokes some overarching, extra-individual, social goal. The greater realization of such a goal is supposed to justify the infringement upon individual entitlements. The proposed social goal may be the greatest good for the greatest number, or the most (feasible?) equality of wealth and social position, or the greatest possible "compensation" to the wretched, or any other of many competing "social ideals." One level of response to such a social goal proposal denies any positive basis for believing that any such goal, having the status of imposing enforceable obli-

8. John Stuart Mill, *On Liberty*, in *Utilitarianism, Liberty and and Representative Government*, ed. A. D. Lindsay (New York: E. P. Dutton, 1950), p. 88.

gations on nonconsenting individuals, exists. A full version of this response would consist of a systematic critique of all positive arguments for each of these overarching goals. Such a systematic critique would be easy, but very lengthy.[9] Here we will only cite a passage from Nozick which, in effect, combines the premise that at least some presumption against violating Lockean rights has been established with an all-purpose debunking of the social goal approach. Why not, Nozick rhetorically asks, require "that some persons have to bear some costs that benefit other persons more, for the sake of the overall social good?" This is his answer:

> But there is no *social entity* with a good that undergoes some sacrifice for its own good. There are only individual people, different individual people, with their own individual lives. Using one of these people for the benefit of others, uses him and benefits the others. Nothing more. . . . Talk of an overall social good covers this up. (Intentionally?)[10]

Two brief rejoinders to social goal proposals that go beyond the debunking of these purported goals are also possible here. The first of these rejoinders is that, insofar as the rights that would be infringed by forced allegiance to this or that social goal are well established, we have structural reasons to disbelieve in the social goal. For, given a well-founded belief in individual natural and property rights, the additional endorsement of a countervailing social goal would leave us in a theoretical morass of conflicting claims of different sorts, claims that somehow were supposed to be measured against one another. And since there would be no rational method for weighing these competing claims, to accept the addition of such a countervailing social goal would be to surrender the possibility of rational judgments about people's rights.

The deeper brief positive rejoinder refers back to the agent-relative or positional conception of value, in terms of which the separate and equal (yet noncommensurable) value of each person's life-fulfillment

---

9. One powerful critique of the rationality of utilitarianism is to be found in John Rawls, *A Theory of Justice* (Cambridge: Harvard University Press, 1971). Rawls rejects utilitarianism for insufficiently taking account of the importance of the separateness of persons and their rational plans of life. But instead of concluding that all proposed principles of "social choice" must be rejected (where the alternative is the adoption of a set of interpersonal rules that merely define people's rights and do not specify what is "socially" better or worse), he simply advocates an alternative principle of social choice. For a critique of Rawls's proposals and of egalitarianism, see Nozick, *n.* 5.

10. Nozick, *n.* 5, pp. 32–33.

was explicated. If ultimate value is agent-relative, then there can be no overarching, extra-individual value of the sort posited in any social goal theory. There can be no goal whose value transcends particular individuals and their lives and establishes an enforceable claim on them to serve it. Individuals are, of course, free to choose to devote their respective lives to the greatest good of the greatest number, or to equality, or whatever. But in such cases they are merely making a choice for themselves, a choice of a certain type of life. They are not responding to a mandate from the transcendent value of greatest utility or greatest equality. They are not responding to a mandate that may be enforced upon nonconsenting parties.

However, this reassertion of the agent-relativity of value, against theories that suppose the existence of overarching, extra-individual values, suggests a type of individualistic, indeed Hobbesian, argument for the coercive imposition of sacrifices on some people. The argument, quite simply, asks us to consider those cases of fundamental conflict of interest in which great losses for many can only be prevented by imposing lesser costs on some smaller number of people. Imagine, for instance, that five people will starve unless a sixth person is forcibly deprived of his pet pig. (The five are so disadvantaged that they will never be able to compensate the pig lover. Their inability to get the pig through voluntary exchange is not due to transaction costs.) Would it not be rational and at least *not impermissible* for those finding themselves in such an emergency to save themselves by forcibly seizing that delicious pet pig? And if so, would not the government, as the agent of these endangered five be acting permissibly if it were to seize that pig on their behalf—and engage in many other comparable acts of redistribution? According to this argument, the government's seizure is legitimized in terms of the individual benefits to the endangered five and not in terms of any alleged "higher" extra-individual value.

One reply to this sort of argument is to insist that justice must be done, that (even) property rights must be respected, though the heavens fall or the five starve. This (sometimes) satisfying reply insists that everyone must continue to abide by the basic principles of social interaction, even when this requires that some submit to (undeserved) catastrophe. But it is arguable that when people are confronted with situations in which there are fundamental conflicts of interests, i.e., in which there is no room for beneficial cooperation, the interpersonal principles of justice no longer apply. Fortunately, in reality, such catastrophe/conflict-of-interest situations are extremely rare—especially within (generally) just and free societies. We are usually too quick to conclude that, for example, the starving five have nothing to offer the pig lover. But cases of absolute conflict of interest can exist—the proverbial lifeboat cases, for instance. The question is how we should interpret such circumstances.

Under such circumstances we revert, morally speaking, to a Hobbesian state of nature in which the notions of justice and rights no longer have significance. And that is why it would be *not impermissible* for the starving five or even some agent of the five to "steal" the pig. But to say that it would be not impermissible is not to say that it would be right or just. Indeed it would be precisely as "not impermissible" for the pig lover forcibly to resist the five. For they are *all,* by hypothesis, in a Hobbesian state of nature. Thus, even under the hypothesized circumstances, one should not conclude that a governmental seizure of that loveable pig would be legitimate. It would be no more legitimate than for the government to protect the pig lover's possession of his pet. And it would *not* be impermissible for the pig lover to resist such a governmental taking. Governmental seizure would simply constitute a preferential use of force on behalf of some of the conflicting parties. It could not be justified by any interpersonal principles binding on all the parties concerned. It could not be represented as an act of government neutrally pursuing the rational or the good or the just among its citizens. Fanatical pig lovers should, however, be on notice that they would not have a right to governmental protection against the (unjustly) starving. And they would probably be well advised to avoid the Hobbesian situation by offering their fellows simple humanitarian aid.

Social goal objections to the antitax ethic described here are objections from far outside the libertarian moral landscape. And the Hobbesian argument turns out not to be a moral argument at all. But, as indicated in the introduction to this chapter, there may be objections from the periphery of the libertarian's position—objections from the ethical margin. The theory of individual rights proposed here seems to rule out infringements upon an individual's right even if such an infringement would leave its "victim" no worse off (except for being a "victim"). But much of its rhetorical force may come from its association with the less extensive demand that individuals not suffer infringements of rights *which leave them worse off,* that no individual's well-being be sacrificed (without his consent) to enhance the well-being of others. Note, for example, that in the passage from Nozick last considered, the argument is, strictly speaking, directed against justifications for imposed sacrifice. So perhaps the core of the libertarian argument, or the underlying intuitions that give it plausibility, leave room at the ethical margin for infringements on (what the argument takes to be) individual rights when those infringements are not sacrifice-imposing. The most obvious candidate for such an infringement is a taking for the sake of financing a public good. Whether the libertarian perspective must leave room for such coercive takings is, then, the topic of the next two sections.

THE PUBLIC-GOODS ARGUMENT

A public good can be defined as some state of affairs, condition, or activity that significantly benefits every individual within some interestingly large group and is of such a nature that it is impossible or economically infeasible to exclude any significant number of its members from receipt of its benefits should the public good come into existence. Any given public good is a public good only with respect to its class of potential beneficiaries. The standard and useful example is, of course, an effective system of national defense (anarchists can substitute "national-scale" defense). Seemingly, given the existence of such a system, it would be impossible or infeasible to exclude any significant number of citizens from the benefits of the system.

What is crucial about this inability to exclude potential beneficiaries is the way it might effect the noncoercive, rights-respecting, market-financing of the public good. The entrepreneur who seeks to finance his production of such a good will encounter potential customers who will reason as follows: Even if I do not contribute, I will enjoy the benefits of the good anyway if it actually comes into existence. True there is a range of purchase prices such that I would be better off paying any price along this range and receiving the good than I would be not paying and not enjoying its benefits. But I am better off yet not signing up and still receiving the good. Furthermore, the action I take (signing the contract or not) will not significantly affect the chances of these different alternatives being realized. So my signing up will not be in my interest. It is rational for me to attempt to be a free-rider.

Now some moralists, at least, are disturbed about free-ridership *per se*. They claim that a free-rider would be acting unfairly or taking improper advantage of those who did sign up. Often it is claimed that if others have (or would have) contributed to funding the good, our calculating hero owes a like contribution.[11] But this objection to free-ridership *per se* is not very plausible. We are all free-riders with respect to all sorts of different social institutions. That is one of the general advantages of social life. As long as the contributions others make are made freely and in accord with their own chosen purposes, they have no basis for requiring the free-rider to improve *further* the terms of their voluntary and already beneficial arrangements. Suppose, for example, that I eat at a fancy restaurant only once a year. Fortunately for me lots of people in New Orleans dine out more often, and this sustains a large number of excellent restaurants. Their existence is a public good and I free-ride on this when I indulge once a year. For, although I pay for my meal, I could not get such a meal at that price were it not for others' more extensive patronage. Yet, clearly, it does not follow that I should subsidize *their* eating habits.

The problem is not the immorality of free-ridership but, rather, the possibility that enough individuals will pursue the free-rider strategy so that the potential producer of the public good will never raise the financing necessary for its production. So many people may seek the most preferred alternative of enjoying a good while not paying for it that everyone will end up in the least preferred alternative of not having the good at all.[12] Here we would, by hypothesis, have a case of rational individuals, being left to their own devices, *not* entering into mutually advantageous arrangements. The core of the public-goods argument for taxation for the financing of public goods is that this coercive taking would cut through the self-defeating strategic maneuvering involved when many seek to be free-riders and would leave everyone better off than they would be were this self-defeating maneuvering allowed to take its course.

Before proceeding further with a moral philosophical analysis of this argument, two points should be recorded. The first point is that it does not at all follow from the fact that a good is public in the specified sense that it will not be financed noncoercively. Indeed the

---

11. See the discussions of the "principle of fairness" in H. L. A. Hart's "Are There Any Natural Rights?" *Philosophical Review* 64 (1955): 175–91; and in Rawls, *n.* 8, and Nozick, *n.* 5.

12. Some would say we are in the worse yet situation of paying for public goods and getting very little of them.

very fact that there are free-riders all over the place entails that some public goods are financed without their beneficiaries being forced to support them. As long as there are some people who benefit *enough* from, or who *strongly enough* feel that they should provide support for, the public good, it will to some degree be financed without coercion. The second point is that much of what, for example, the U.S. government currently taxes for is not for the financing of public goods. Were taxation to be restricted to the financing of public goods, with the taxes imposed on each given individual for each of the goods *that is a public good for him* being less than the value to that individual of his enjoyment of that good, taxation and government would exist on a vastly smaller scale than they now do.

Let us proceed using the example of national-scale defense. I shall assume that there can be and that we are talking about some significantly effective system of defense against unjust national-scale aggression and coercion. And, (although there may be many such possible systems), I shall further make the highly unrealistic assumption that there is only one such possible system. So, for now, the problem of how to choose between the competing public goods, system *A* or *B* or *C*, does not arise. And, of course, we continue our assumption that this system is such that at least most of its beneficiaries could not feasibly be excluded from enjoying its benefits. (The system does not, for example, consist of many person-sized invulnerable shields.) But it must immediately be noted that the class of persons for whom this nonindividualized defensive system would be a public good would not include everyone within our nation. Presumably there are lots of individuals who would prefer to live under Soviet hegemony. And there are lots of individuals who would just make out better under such circumstances—certain types of aspiring bureaucrats and ballet dancers, for example. There are pacifists and masochists who are deeply disturbed by the idea of instruments of war being readied in their defense. And there are those who are simply completely indifferent to what sort of political regime they live under. These people do not withhold their participation in a voluntary scheme for financing our hypothesized effective defensive system because they are strategically maneuvering to become free-riders. They withhold their participation because, by their lights, no such payments would be worth it.

A tax scheme that seized wealth from both beneficiaries of effective defense and these nonbeneficiaries *would* be redistributive. It would impose net sacrifices on some to increase the net advantages enjoyed by others. Allowing interpersonal utility comparisons, the scheme as a whole might increase total utility in our society. The scheme might even increase total utility moreso than any nonredistributive scheme for financing defense, for it might avoid the costs of discriminating between beneficiaries and nonbeneficiaries. (Similarly, a particular system of deterrence against ordinary crime might produce the greatest net utility by sometimes avoiding the costs of discriminating between the guilty and the innocent.) Morally speaking, nothing can be said in favor of such a scheme except that it satisfies utilitarian ambitions. And this moral defense is readily rejected on the basis of the position developed in section two of this chapter.

At the very least people's rights over their own lives creates a moral presumption against imposing sacrifices (in particular, sacrifices comprising infringements on their rights) in order to benefit others. The only thing that could overcome such a presumption would be a showing that the goal achieved through the imposed sacrifice, which in this case is the enhancement of aggregate utility, is an overarching, "higher" goal that each person affected may be forced to serve. But no such showing is available. Nor is the idea of such a "higher" transcendent goal plausible in light of the agent-relative conception of value.

So, for the public-goods argument to get off the ground, we have to assume that we can pick out at least most of the individuals who would benefit from the public good in order to target them for taxation. But even this will not ensure avoidance of redistributivism. We must further assume that the amount of taxation to be imposed on each given individual is less than the benefit to him of the public good to be financed. There is the further problem for the public-goods argument of assigning a tax to each individual such that the distribution of net benefits among the good's consumers will itself be fair. So we must further assume knowledge of the extent of each individual's benefit from the public good, and knowledge of some moral rule about fair distribution of net benefits, e.g., that net benefits should be equal or that net benefits should be proportional to taxes paid, etc. Let us, for the moment, make the first two assumptions and ignore the further need for the last two assumptions. Thus we are allowing ourselves to imagine that we have at hand a tax scheme that, if imposed, will leave everyone on whom it was imposed better off than the status quo.[13] How strongly can the libertarian object to the imposition of precisely such a scheme?

The libertarian cannot object that favoring the coercive imposition of this scheme involves a commitment to utilitarianism as such and, therefore, to all the injustices and moral blindnesses associated with utilitarianism. Acceptance of this tax scheme on the grounds that, on net, it advances the interests of each who is subject to it, clearly does not involve acceptance of sacrifice-imposing *redistribution* whether that redistribution be of the standard economic sort, or of bodily parts, or involve, for example, the framing of innocent people to assuage public passions. The libertarian might offer the objection that this tax scheme is a case of many-personed paternalism. Each is forced, contrary to his current will and inclination, to do what is in his own best interest. Of course, were basic Lockean side-constraints limited to a right against redistribution, those rights would not proscribe paternalistic interventions. But paternalism does violate the broader Lockean rights over oneself and one's life. Nevertheless, the defender of coercive takings for public goods might respond that the paternalism involved in his scheme is of a particularly benign sort. Malign paternalistic interventions coerce individuals in the name of a conception of their own good that, no matter how correct, they do not share. But in the scheme under examination, the position of each individual is improved *as judged by that individual's own current conception of his good*. For it is not ignorance of their own (true) good that poses a problem for these individuals, but rather it is the danger that too clever strategic negotiation will (by hypothesis) leave them worse off by their own lights.[14]

Let us pursue two further ways to fortify the public-goods argument. Once any particular vindication for taxation is accepted, and authoritative and coercive mechanisms are established for the assignment and collection of taxes, there will be great institutional pressure toward wider and wider use of these mechanisms and more and more sophistical, but politically effective, arguments about how the funding

---

13. Note the further *assumption* that the status quo is the failure of voluntary means of financing public goods.

14. But how benign is paternalism that coercively advances its subject's interest as he currently conceives it? Such a paternalism would allow forcing people to avoid perversely chosen self-harm. It would allow us to require that a person act rationally, at least by the lights of his own actual conception of the good.

of this or that newly discovered "public good" falls under the accepted vindication. A defender of the argument, therefore, will benefit from there being a nonarbitrary limitation on the type of alleged public good coercive financing that the argument seeks to justify. And, perhaps, there is such a nonarbitrary line. There are public goods that secure people's rights. National defense is of this sort. And there are public goods that advance their public's interests in some other way. Mosquito abatement, dams, and city parks might be included in a list of public goods of this latter sort.

Now the defender of the public-goods argument as flanking action around the libertarian position might argue as follows: Forced takings for public goods do not have certain of the morally offensive marks typical of rights violations. As we have seen, they are not redistributive and they are not malignly paternalistic. Still, they remain *arguably* in violation of valid Lockean rights. And we should eschew violating what are even *arguably* a person's rights, no matter what the ordinary benefits to that person or to others would be. Similarly, we should eschew violating what are even *arguably* that person's rights for the sake of securing someone else's rights. But it is reasonable to (arguably) violate what are merely *arguably* a person's rights when performance of the act in question will more secure that person's unquestioned rights. So not every taking for public goods that would leave the taxpayer better off is endorsed by this newly fortified public-goods argument. Rather, and more modestly, only those takings are endorsed which leave the taxpayer better off in his enjoyment of his rights, even if the taking as such turns out to be a violation of his rights.

The second fortification of the public-goods argument involves a revisionist account of what is entailed by a person's having a right to some particular thing, e.g., the stack of coins the government seizes to help finance a particular public good. This account is drawn from, but is not intended as an explication of, several discussions in Nozick's *Anarchy, State and Utopia*.[15] On the ordinary notion of the right to that stack of coins, for example, an individual's right to those coins entails that they may not be taken without his consent, even if the

---

15. See especially chapter 4, "Prohibition, Compensation and Risk," of Nozick's *Anarchy, State and Utopia*, no. 5. For a detailed account of the argument of this chapter, see Eric Mack, "Nozick on Unproductivity: The Unintended Consequences," in Jeffrey Paul, ed., *Reading Nozick* (Totowa, N.J.: Rowman and Littlefield, 1981).

taker were subsequently to make due compensation for their loss. In a complex discussion, Nozick rejects this simple entailment. He raises the question of whether A's right to the coins justifies his prohibiting B's taking them or merely requires that B duly compensate A for the taking of those coins. Nozick's answer to this question, roughly, is that a policy of allowing takings of rightful holdings (and conditions) while requiring that the "boundary crossers" make due compensation to the rightholders is to be preferred in certain circumstances over a policy of simply prohibiting all boundary crossings. But it would be preferred only for those cases in which subsequently identifying and carrying out due compensation for a right infringement would be feasible. We should require A's *prior* consent to the taking of his coins, i.e., we should *prohibit* B's seizing them (even when accompanied by attempts at subsequent due compensation), if and only if there is no feasible method of identifying and instituting posterior due compensation.

Nozick maintains, however, that in most cases a policy of allowing the seizure as long as it is accompanied by subsequent due compensation is *not* feasible. Suppose that B seizes o from A. Due subsequent compensation cannot be merely that payment which would return A to a point on his previous indifference curve. For a policy of allowing the seizure of o while merely requiring that B bring A back to a point on this curve would allow B to capture all the benefits of the exchange (which he has forced). It seems that the correct posterior compensation would be what A would have accepted from B in exchange for granting B permission to take o. But it is not feasible to determine this market compensation after the fact of the seizure. If due compensation is market compensation, the way to identify and institute due compensation is to forbid B from taking o without A's permission. B must bargain with A before the fact. Then, having struck a deal with A and having arranged for the agreed upon payment, there is no right infringement in his taking o.[16] The revisionist conception of a

16. Here I discuss only the broadest of Nozick's arguments in favor of prohibiting over allowing boundary crossing with compensation, *viz.*, what he calls the argument from the division of the benefits of exchange. Another important argument centers on the fact that many boundary crossings are feared. If these crossings are allowed, how are people to be compensated for their fears? And who is to be compensated—only those whose rights are actually infringed or also those who (reasonably) feared such infringements? These are further reasons for favoring the prohibition of such crossings. But I assume that the takings for financing public goods are not, in Nozick's sense, fearful takings. So this secondary argument for prohibiting takings does not apply.

right, then, can be summed up as the view that A's right to o is a right of A to require that he consent to any taking of o if and only if a process of consent is feasible. If a process of consent is not feasible, then o may be taken as long as A subsequently receives due compensation.

The greater feasibility of determining market compensation directly through antecedent negotiation, rather than subsequent counterfactual reasoning, justifies broad application of the policy of prohibiting infringements of rights rather than allowing them as long as due compensation is made afterwards. But this reason may not apply in all cases. And where it does not apply, A's right to o may only require that any taker of o subsequently, duly, compensate A. What is crucial for our present topic is that the reason for favoring prohibition of taking does not apply to takings for the financing of public goods.

For, it can be argued, the peculiar bargaining incentives had by individuals negotiating about the purchase of a public good make antecedent bargaining a relatively poor method for determining market compensation. (Here we are speaking of compensation for money taken which is to come in the form of enjoyment of some public good.) Each individual, noting the prospect of being a free-rider, will have reasons to refuse offered terms that have nothing directly to do with his valuation of what is asked of him or what is offered to him. In such cases someone may reject offered terms even though he would benefit from the proposed exchange, and his refusal would not show that the offer did not constitute true market compensation. Since, in these cases, antecedent negotiation is not preferable, A's right to o entails only that a taker of o must make due subsequent compensation to A. In the case of A for whom national defense is a public good, his right to the coins seized to help finance national defense is *not* violated as long as that national defense is produced, since his enjoyment of national defense, under the hypothesis that is a public good for him and that he benefits on net from this coercive financing of it, duly compensates him for the seizure.

THE PUBLIC-GOODS ARGUMENT: A CAUTIOUS CRITIQUE

The philosophical reply to the public-goods argument may begin with a rejoinder to this second, revisionist, fortification. It should be noted that there is a tension between this fortification and the first one. For *if* the second fortifying argument is correct, then no rights are infringed when takings occur for the financing of *any* public good. If the second argument is correct, no line can be drawn that allows takings only for rights-securing activities. This, of course, will not bother the advocate of the expansionist state. But it will disturb anyone strongly sympathetic with the original libertarian perspective—even sympathizers who would like to see *some* loopholes in the antitax ethic. For such a line is needed as a device for firmly blocking taxation for progressively more extensive funding of politically useful pseudo public goods.

But there is a deeper tension within this revisionist conception of rights. I have presented the revisionist as emphasizing our inability, in the typical case, to identify due posterior compensation. But the revisionist cannot push this very far, for he will probably want to hold that, should a prohibited crossing occur, we *will* be able to say something plausible about the compensation due to its victim. Furthermore, the revisionist wants to be able to say, on a case-by-case basis, whether posterior compensation in the form of enjoyment of some public good duly compensates individuals forced to help finance that good. Yet we should be just as good at counterfactual identification of subsequent due compensation in typical boundary-crossing cases as in seizure of funds for public goods cases. So the revisionist's emphasis must be on the claim that in the typical case, we can do pretty well at identifying due posterior payments. In the typical case, however, we can place even more confidence in prior negotiations.

But if we are pretty good at determining appropriate posterior payments, then surely there are a significant minority of *typical* (i.e., nonpublic goods) cases in which seizure accompanied by subsequent payments would have to be allowed. Consider the case of the coercive wholesaler of, for example, Chrysler mini-vans. Let us suppose that in the free market such vans, moderately equipped, sell for about $11,000. Let us also suppose that our wholesaler could make lots of money selling such mini-vans for $10,000 if only he could sell 1,000 of them. Let us then imagine that our wholesaler has a method for identifying serious potential purchasers and that for each serious potential purchaser an exchange of $10,000 for a mini-van is advantageous. But our wholesaler must sell 1,000 units and, let us add, must do so quickly. Yet the potential buyers are (irrationally) leery about the wholesaling of such products, it is difficult or very costly to communicate with them, or they are slow decision-makers. It seems that under the revisionist conception, it would be permissible for our wholesaler to seize $10,000.00 from each of the serious potential purchasers as long as he duly compensates them with the delivery of one of the mini-vans. (Indeed, he might well claim that relative to this set of potential purchasers his existence as a 1,000-unit "seller" is a public good which, of course, each of them may be forced to help finance!)

The moral problem here is not that these forced exchanges would be disadvantageous. The case is set up so that they are beneficial. Rather, the problem *for the revisionist* is that these forced sales are justified by his doctrine and yet, at the same time, are clear violations of the "purchasers" rights. Many such cases can be imagined—all of which turn on some excellent deal being available only if the purchasers' actions are better coordinated than they will be if the purchasers are allowed to decide freely. And other embarrassing cases exist. The revisionist seems to be committed to its being permissible to appropriate anything owned by another, even in nonemergency situations, as long as it would be difficult or impossible to negotiate with the owner and as long as the appropriator leaves the owner what he would have agreed to sell for had he been asked. Such takings would avoid the normal transactions costs, some of which would fall on the appropriator. Thus, it would often be wise and permissible for a potential buyer to wait until the seller is unable to negotiate, seize the property in question, leave the amount of money that would have been agreed to, and save himself his normal share of the transaction costs.

Finally and more generally, the revisionist conception of rights seems untrue to the core idea of rights. If A has a right to a certain object or condition, e.g., some tool he has fashioned or his very life, then it is wrong for others to take or destroy that object or condition, and A may prohibit such acts in the name of his rights. A's prohibition need not appeal to the idea that only by forbidding these takings or acts of destruction can he (in ordinary circumstances) ensure that he will be duly compensated for these acts. Persons who desire to take or destroy any of those objects or conditions must negotiate with A, not because this is the best way of ensuring that A's loss of such an object or condition will be duly compensated, but simply because, being A's by right, others may take or destroy them only with A's permission.

Let us move back to a consideration of the first fortifying argument. This argument rests on two premises. The first is that A only *arguably* has a right to the coins which, if seized from him, would help finance the public good. The second is that a taking of a merely arguable right is justified if this taking is necessary for and conducive to preventing that very rightholder from suffering a more extensive loss of unquestioned rights. Both premises are dubious. With regard to the first, on what basis is A's claim to those coins merely *arguably* a right? If the permissibility of taking those coins were already well established, then A's right to those coins would indeed be arguable at best. But this permissibility is precisely the issue at hand. It cannot be presupposed in an argument that seeks to undercut that right to the coins.

If A's claim cannot be demoted to the status of merely arguable, then the defender of the coercive financing needs a stronger version of the second premise. This is the assertion that, since rights are to be understood as especially valuable *goals,* the proper response to A's rights is to perform the act conducive to the greatest possible realization of those rights. This stronger version of the second premise would justify violating A's rights to the coins if, in fact, this was necessary for and conducive to preventing a more extensive violation of A's rights (by somebody else). But the libertarian endorses a different and more plausible conception of rights. Rights are moral sideconstraints on all other persons' actions. Both B and C are morally constrained not to take A's coins and not to take his life. And the fact that B could prevent C from taking A's life by his (i.e., B's) taking A's coins does not free B from his obligation not to take A's coins. Of course, A can release B from this obligation. But if he does not, A retains (however foolishly) his full and unarguable right against B's taking his coins.

Finally, suppose we do allow that A's right to the coins is merely arguable. So, apparently, all that is needed to draw the protax conclusion is the second premise as originally stated. But is this premise plausible in itself? The case against its bolder variant at least casts doubt on the second premise itself. Moreover, if we accept the predicate "arguable," we might also have to accept that there are degrees of arguability. Perhaps, then, what is true is a more modest than original version of the second premise, *viz.,* that, if A's right to the coins is *highly* arguable, then the coins may be taken to secure more extensive nonarguable rights. But then what the protax advocate has to show, by some independent argument, is not simply that A's right is arguable but rather that it is at least as highly arguable as this modest version of the second premise requires. As the creator of the first fortifying argument, I can see no way to refortify it against this problem.

Having disposed of the fortifications for the public-goods argument, we can turn to our core criticism. Simply put, it is that the assumptions needed to get it morally off the ground are highly unreasonable. These are the assumptions about it being known which individuals are included in that subset of individuals for whom some activity or object is a public good and to what extent each of these individuals benefits from the activities or objects that, respectively, are public goods for them. The latter assumption, it will be recalled, is needed so that a tax schedule can be drawn up which, if imposed, would still leave *each* member of the subset a net beneficiary. Indeed, the most attractive vision of the argument would have it that there is some sort of equity in the distribution of net benefits. And this would require quite precise information, somehow acquired in the absence of a market, about the value of the given public good for *each* relevant individual.

If the taxing authorities do not have such information available to them, then it is a practical certainty that a considerable number of individuals will have rightful property seized for the financing of something that is not, for them—at least at the prices imposed upon them—a public good. And it is also a practical certainty that a considerable number for whom the activity or object *as such* is a public good will end up net losers from the financing scheme. In both cases large numbers of people will be subjected to the coercive redistribution of their rightful belongings. They will be hurt, not merely subjected to paternalism no matter how benign. If we allow interpersonal utility comparisons in principle and commonsensical comparisons in practice, we might still expect such a scheme to increase net social utility (over the nonfinancing of the public good). But this expectation is not enough to justify the numerous violations of rights committed—unless, of course, one retreats to utilitarianism. But, on the basis of the rejection in section two of transcendent social goals such as general happiness, such a retreat constitutes *not* getting the argument morally off the ground.

Even this utilitarian "justification" assumes, for example in the case of national defense, that a public good financed by taxation will be provided in an efficient manner—though even if social utility were thereby greatly enhanced, many *individuals* would be worse off and would experience a greater loss of rights than with attempts to finance the good in a noncoercive fashion. There are, of course, many reasons for doubting that the good would be provided in an efficient manner even if the government's legitimate mandate were restricted to the provision of public goods. It is not even obvious that the aggregate social utility in the world that actually results from authorizing coercive governmental provision of public goods is greater than a world in which individuals would remain free to dispose of their wealth in their most preferred private pursuits. For, after all, there are good reasons to believe that a government empowered to finance public goods coercively will not provide anything like what would really sell to rational purchasers (putting aside the problem of consummating the sale). And there are good reasons to believe that, whatever the government actually provides, its imposed charges will often be sufficiently high to ensure very little net benefits of exchange, if any, to its captive clients.[17]

Where, then, are we left? Notice that were the knowledge available to us that must be assumed to get the public-goods argument morally off the ground, we might not be in bad shape at all. For a major part of the difficulty in obtaining voluntary agreement from individuals for the financing of public goods is the absence of this knowledge. It we utterly lack this knowledge, too many potential beneficiaries can convincingly say, "It's no use your telling me that unless I sign up, or unless 90 percent of the members of my group sign up, there'll be no public good—because I could not (or could hardly) care less." But *if* we had knowledge of who would benefit from a particular public good and how much, then it does not seem impossible to design a complex conditional contract that if offered (with minor revisions) to people repeatedly, would eventually be agreed to by enough individuals for it to come into effect and for it to generate the needed revenues. Indeed, if we knew *precisely* where the benefits lay and to what extent, we could announce to each person what his proposed fee was, indicate that unless each person agreed to pay his assigned fee the public good would not be provided, and be sure that the proposed fees would be acceptable to all these individuals.

---

17. We might speak of the great likelihood of defense (and other public goods, both real and alleged) being overproduced were it reasonable to judge the amount of defense by the amount spent on it by a tax-imposing government. But it would be more accurate to speak of the overfinancing of defense—with that being perfectly consistent with its actual underproduction.

But what can be done in our actual world of highly imperfect knowledge? While potential solutions to the problem may be rather complicated, at least a very informal approach suggests some basis for hope. To begin with, consider a genuinely defensive system, one truly protective of our lives, liberties, and property; it would seem to be of immense value for most people. Perhaps one can estimate that, for many people, the value of being so defended is in the same ballpark as the current cost to them of the federal government. The argument for this estimate is as follows:

1. The sort of defensive system that would appeal to a rational purchaser of defense (and that would have to be offered by a "government" seeking voluntary funding) would be very much more valuable to most people than the current military structures.
2. The difference in value between this rational system and the current system is at least as great as the other benefits people (*think they*) get from the federal government.
3. Very few people, if presented with a magic button that would save them their current federal taxes at the cost of all their supposed current federal "benefits," including current defense, would push that button.
4. Hence, very few people would push a magic button that would relieve them of costs equivalent to their current federal taxes if they would thereby forgo the benefits of a rational rights-protecting system of national defense.

But, presumably very much less need be spent on the sort of defensive system a rational purchaser would be voluntarily attracted to than is spent currently by the federal government.

There is thus *a lot* to be gained by the voluntary purchase of public goods (over their nonfunding). There is a great deal to be lost if voluntary funding schemes fall through. Moreover, it is probably possible to know enough about *the vast majority* of people (and other possible fee-payers) to draw up a schedule of proposed payments such that, for a high percentage of these people, as individuals there is a lot to be lost if voluntary funding is not approved. Finally, one needs clever conditional contracts that do three things. They must leave room for those who, in fact and contrary to the supplier's estimates, would not benefit from receiving defense for the fee proposed. But they must not leave so much room as to tempt potential beneficiaries with the prospect of free-ridership. And they must give potential beneficiaries some incentive to sign up early (within a given offering or within a series of repeated offerings). This last condition is to counteract the temptation to free-ride by squeezing in to the room left for whoever are the true nonbeneficiaries.

Such contractual offers would presumably (1) assign to each likely beneficiary a fee considerably below the estimated benefits to him of the public good in question; (2) indicate that individuals will be bound to pay their proposed fees only if, for example, 90 percent of them sign up; and (3) include discounts for early sign-ups and/or add-on charges for later sign-ups. The presentation of such contracts could be accompanied by many forms of permissible social (and economic) pressure on individuals to join up, e.g., appeals to people's community or national pride, to the importance of not being seen as a parasitic free-rider, by threats of social ostracism or economic boycott against nonsigners, and so on.[18] Looked at informally at least, if the contracts and the (nonforcible) social incentives are well designed, individuals will not to any huge extent forgo valuable public goods. Indeed, many foundations have developed conditional contracts of the sort outlined above for potential donors.

The foregoing optimistic projection is consistent with the recognition that with voluntary funding, public goods may receive less than their "optimal" funding (in the sense of neoclassical economics). Of course, to know what the optimal funding would be in any particular case, we would need to actually have all the knowledge involved in the original unrealistic assumptions. But it is plausible to imagine the noncoercive seller of a public good cautiously proposing to individuals fees that are well below what he estimates they would be willing to pay for a similarly valued private good. So the optimistic projection should be qualified with the realization that voluntarily funded public goods might be underfinanced, perhaps substantially. Recent theo-

---

18. Tibor R. Machan suggests that the government preclude national defense free-riders from purchasing other governmental services that are not public goods, e.g., the enforcement of their contracts. The proposal is to create a package of legitimate governmental services that itself will be a private good. This strategy requires that the government be allowed to bar other agencies from competitively providing these further services without any add-on charge for the public good. See "Dissolving the Problem of Public Goods: Financing Government without Coercive Measures," in T. R. Machan, ed., *The Libertarian Reader* (Totowa, N.J.: Rowman and Littlefield, 1982).

retical work in schemes for getting people to reveal their willingness to pay for public goods, combined with the potential of two-way cable television and other communications technologies, suggests, however, that much optimism is justifiable. Not surprisingly, the most controversial area of discussion involves public goods with large numbers of beneficiaries, where the transactions costs of negotiating conditional contracts are presumably high.[19]

If certain public goods would not to any significant degree be voluntarily financed, the costs of refusing to allow taxation would clearly be very high. As I have argued, however, in the real world allowing taxation does not benefit all. It is redistributist. It does impose sacrifices on some for the sake of the greater sum of benefits to others. And morally speaking, there is no way to distinguish this from the many other rights-violating impositions of sacrifices in which utilitarian doctrines would have us indulge. Fortunately, the more likely real-world voluntary outcome would be one of significant provision of public goods, albeit at somewhat "suboptimal" levels of funding. This, however, does not necessarily mean that the actual quantities provided would be any less than with coercive and superoptimal funding: The noncoercive provider (of, for example, an environmental preserve funded through the Nature Conservancy) must offer a product that convinces its buyers of its value in a way in which coercive financers of public goods rarely have to convince their customers, and has greater incentives to maximize output per unit of input. But let us acknowledge that significantly lesser (noncoercive) funding might mean reduced quantities of public goods. The worst plausible cost, then, of the libertarian refusal to allow forced takings for public goods would be a *heightened risk* of suboptimal levels of provision. In light of the argument in section two of this chapter, however, incurring this cost satisfies what is at least a moral presumption against any

19. See T. Nicolaus Tideman and Gordon Tullock, "A New and Superior Process for Making Social Choices," *Journal of Political Economy* 84 (Dec. 1976): 1145–59; and "Some Limitations of Demand-Revealing Processes: Comment," *Public Choice* 29 (no. 2, 1977): 125–28. See also, Earl R. Brubaker, "On the Margolis 'Thought Experiment' and the Applicability of Demand-Revealing Mechanisms to Large-Group Decisions," *Public Choice* 41 (no. 2, 1983): 315–19. For another approach, see Michael Taylor, *Community, Anarchy and Liberty* (Cambridge: Cambridge University Press, 1982), chap. 2. It should be noted that the "Clarke taxes" referred to in the Tideman/Tullock literature do not necessarily have to be viewed as "taxes" in the coercive sense; they might instead be viewed as charges to which some people will be subject under the rules of a game they have voluntarily elected to play.

forced taking. And it is far from clear that the deviations from optimality occurring from the voluntary provision of public goods would
be greater than what *actually* occurs under coercive government-fi-
nanced schemes. Thus the libertarian's principled rejection of coercive taxation—even against advocates of forced financing solely for
(what are supposed to be) rights-protecting public goods—may turn
out to be rational as well as moral.

SELECTED BIBLIOGRAPHY
PART IV

Ackerman, Bruce. *Social Justice and the Liberal State*. New Haven, Conn.: Yale University Press, 1982.

Arthur, John, and William Shaw, eds. *Justice and Economic Distribution*. Englewood Cliffs, N.J.: Prentice-Hall, 1978.

Axelrod, Robert. *The Evolution of Cooperation*. New York: Basic Books, 1984.

Fried, Charles. *Right and Wrong*. Cambridge: Harvard University Press, 1978.

Friedman, David. *The Machinery of Freedom*. New York: Harper & Row, 1973.

Hayek, Friedrich A. *The Mirage of Social Justice*. Vol. 2 of *Law, Legislation and Liberty*. Chicago: University of Chicago Press, 1976.

Miller, Fred; Ellen Paul; and Jeffrey Paul. *Social Philosophy and Policy*. Vol. 1, no. 1 (Autumn 1983).

Nozick, Robert. *Anarchy, State and Utopia*. New York: Basic Books, 1974.

Osterfeld, David. *Freedom, Society and the State*. Lanhan, Md.: University Press of America, 1983.

Rawls, John. *A Theory of Justice*. Cambridge: Harvard University Press, 1971.

Rothbard, Murray. *Power and Market*. 2d ed. Kansas City, Ks.: Sheed, Andrews and McMeel, 1977.

Taylor, Michael. *Community, Anarchy and Liberty*. Cambridge: Cambridge University Press, 1982.

INDEX

517

ABOUT THE EDITOR

Dwight R. Lee is professor of economics and holder of the Bernard B. and Eugenia A. Ramsey Chair of Private Enterprise at the University of Georgia. Professor Lee received his B.A. from San Diego State College, and his Ph.D. from the University of California at San Diego. Most recently, Professor Lee was associate professor and research fellow at the Center for Study of Public Choice at George Mason University, and at the Virginia Polytechnic Institute and State University. He has also served on the faculties of the economics departments at the University of Colorado, United States International University, and San Diego State College. Professor Lee received the Brython P. Davis Fellowship at the University of California at San Diego and was second-prize winner of the N. Goto Essay Contest at the meetings of the Mont Pelerin Society in 1982.

Professor Lee is the coauthor of three economics textbooks, and his articles have appeared in a variety of scholarly and popular publications, including *The American Economist, Atlantic Economic Journal, Australian Economic Papers, Canadian Journal of Economics, Cato Journal, Chicago Tribune, Economic Inquiry, Finance Quarterly, The Freeman, Heritage Foundation Backgrounder, International Journal of Transport Economics, Kyklos, Journal of Contemporary Studies, Journal of Economics, Journal of Energy and Development, Journal of Environmental Economics and Manage-*

541

ment, *Journal of Law and Economics, Journal of Political Economy, Journal of Public Finance and Public Choice, Land Economics, Management Science, Public Choice, Public Finance Quarterly, Quarterly Review of Economics and Business, Reason, Review of Economic Studies, St. Louis Post Dispatch, Southern Economic Journal,* and *Wall Street Journal.*

Professor Lee's articles have been published as monographs, including *The Inflationary Impact of Labor Unions; Economics, Politics and the All Volunteer Army; The Political Economy of Social Conflict; Environmental vs. Political Pollution;* and *Inflation and Unemployment.*

ABOUT THE AUTHORS

John Baden is president and chairman of the Political Economy Research Center and director of the Maguire Institute at Southern Methodist University. He received his B.A. from Wittenberg University and his Ph.D. from Indiana University. Dr. Baden has taught at Utah State University, Oregon State University, University of Oregon, Montana State University, and Indiana University. His articles have appeared in *Cato Journal, Environmental Law, Journal of Law and Economics, Literature of Liberty, Policy Review, Public Choice, Reason, Taxing and Spending,* and *Western Wildlands.* He is the author of *Earth Day Reconsidered, Managing the Commons* (with G. Hardin), *Rationing Wilderness Lands* (with G. Stankey), and *Politics, 'Progress' and Environmental Quality.*

James Bennett is an Eminent Scholar at George Mason University and holds the William P. Snavely Chair of Political Economy and Public Policy in the department of economics. He received his B.S. and M.S. from Case Institute of Technology and his Ph.D. from Case Western Reserve University. Professor Bennett is editor of the *Journal of Labor Research* and has published more than fifty articles in professional and popular journals such as the *American Economic Review, Canadian Journal of Economics, Cato Journal, Inquiry, Journal of Economics and Business, Journal of Environmental Economics*

543

and Management, Journal of Labor Research, Journal of Money, Credit and Banking, Journal of Regional Science and Urban Economics, Journal of Social, Political, and Economic Studies, Land Economics, Policy Review, Public Choice, Public Finance Quarterly, Review of Economics and Statistics, and *Wall Street Journal.*

He is the author of *Better Government at Half the Price* (with Manuel H. Johnson); *Deregulating Labor Relations* (with Dan C. Heldman and Manuel H. Johnson); *The Political Economy of Federal Government Growth* (with Manuel H. Johnson); and with T. DiLorenzo, *Labor Unions and the State; Tax-Funded Politics;* and *Underground Government: The Off-Budget Public Sector.*

Bruce L. Benson received his Ph.D. in economics from Texas A&M University. He is currently associate professor of economics at Florida State University, having previously taught at Texas A&M University, Pennsylvania State University, and Montana State University. He is an associate of the Center for Political Economy and an F. Leroy Hill Fellow of the Institute for Humane Studies.

Professor Benson has contributed articles to *American Economic Review, American Journal of Agricultural Economics, Antitrust Bulletin, Canadian Journal of Agricultural Economics, Cato Journal, Economic Inquiry, Harvard Journal of Law and Public Policy, Industrial Organization Review, International Journal of Industrial Organization, Journal of Consumer Affairs, Journal of Contemporary Studies, Journal of Industrial Economics, Journal of International Economics, Journal of Legal Studies, Journal of Libertarian Studies, Journal of Urban Economics, Public Choice, Public Finance Quarterly, Regional Science and Urban Economics, Review of Regional Studies,* and *Southern Economic Journal.* Among other projects, he is presently at work on the forthcoming volume from Pacific Research Institute, *Privatizing Law and Order.*

Tom Blood received his B.S. from Purdue University and was Murdock Fellow at the Political Economy Research Center. He is currently pursuing his masters degree in economics and journalism at the University of Washington. Mr. Blood's articles have appeared in *The Denver Post, National Wetlands Newsletter, The Oregonian, Orvis News, Reason,* and *Western Wildlands.*

Edgar K. Browning is professor of economics at Texas A&M

University. He received his B.A. from the University of Virginia, and his Ph.D. from Princeton University. He was previously professor of economics at the University of Virginia. Professor Browning was a Woodrow Wilson Fellow, National Science Foundation Fellow, Charles Grovesnor Osgood Fellow, Princeton University Fellow, and is listed in *Who's Who in Economics*. His books and monographs include *The Distribution of the Tax Burden* (with W. R. Johnson), *Microeconomic Theory and Applications* (with J. M. Browning), *Public Finance and the Price System* (with J. M. Browning), and *Redistribution and the Welfare System*.

Professor Browning's articles have appeared in *The American Economic Review, Atlantic Economic Journal, Economic Inquiry, The Humanist, Journal of Law and Economics, Journal of Political Economy, Kyklos, National Tax Journal, Public Choice, Public Finance Quarterly, The Public Interest, Social Science Quarterly*, and *Southern Economic Journal*.

James M. Buchanan received his B.S. from Middle Tennessee State College, his M.A. from the University of Tennessee, and his Ph.D. from the University of Chicago. He has been University Professor and General Director of the Center for Study of Public Choice at George Mason University since 1983. Professor Buchanan was University Distinguished Professor at Virginia Polytechnic Institute and State University, professor of economics at UCLA, professor and chairman of the economics department and director of the Thomas Jefferson Center for Political Economy at the University of Virginia, professor and chairman of the economics department at Florida State University, and professor at the University of Tennessee. He was Fulbright Visiting Professor at Cambridge University, and Fulbright Research Scholar in Italy, and has received an honorary doctorate from the University of Giessen, West Germany, and honors from the Freedom Foundation, and the Virginia Social Science Association.

Professor Buchanan is president of the Mont Pelerin Society and past president of the Western and Southern Economic Associations. He is a member of advisory boards for many organizations, including Pacific Research Institute for Public Policy, Law and Economics Center at the University of Miami, Commission for a Competitive Currency, Center for Libertarian Studies, Graduate School of Business at the University of Dallas, Fraser Institute, International Center for Economic Policy Studies, Domestic Studies Program at the Hoover

Institution, Public Interest Law Project, and Institute of Economic Affairs. Professor Buchanan is a member of the board of directors of the Foundation for Research in Economics and Education, Joint Council on Economic Education, and the executive committee of the International Seminar in Public Finance.

Professor Buchanan is the author of over twenty books, many of which have been translated into five languages, including *The Calculus of Consent: Logical Foundations of Constitutional Democracy* (with G. Tullock); *Cost and Choice: An Inquiry in Economic Theory; Demand and Supply of Public Goods; Democracy in Deficit: The Political Legacy of Lord Keynes* (with R. Wagner); *The Limits of Liberty: Between Anarchy and Leviathan; The Public Finances* (fourth and fifth editions with M. Flowers); *Toward a Theory of the Rent-Seeking Society* (edited with R. Tollison and G. Tullock); and *What Should Economists Do?*

Professor Buchanan has contributed articles to *American Economic Review, Antitrust Law and Economics Review, Atlantic Economic Journal, Canadian Journal of Economics and Political Science, Cato Journal, Economica, Economico, Economic Inquiry, Ethics, History of Political Economy, Il Politico, Journal of Conflict Resolution, Journal of Economic Issues, Journal of Law and Economics, Journal of Legal Studies, Journal of Monetary Economics, Journal of Political Economy, Journal of Public Economics, Kyklos, National Tax Journal, Natural Resources Journal, Public Choice, Public Finance, Quarterly Journal of Economics, Review of Economic Studies, Southern Economic Journal, University of Chicago Law Review, Virginia Law Review,* and *Western Economic Journal.*

Professor Buchanan has testified numerous times before congressional committees, including the House Ways and Means Committee, the Joint Economic Committee, and the Interstate Commerce Commission.

Thomas DiLorenzo is associate professor of economics at George Mason University. He received his B.A. from Westminster College and his Ph.D. from Virginia Polytechnic Institute and State University. Professor DiLorenzo previously taught at Wittenberg University and the State University of New York at Buffalo, and is on the academic advisory board of the National Center for Policy Analysis. He is the author (with J. Bennett) of *Labor Unions and the State; Tax-Funded Politics;* and *Underground Government: The Off-Budget Public Sector.*

Professor DiLorenzo's articles have been published in *American Economic Review, Cato Journal, International Review of Law and Economics, Journal of Economic Affairs, Journal of Labor Research, Journal of Public Finance and Public Choice, Journal of Social, Political, and Economic Studies, Policy Review, Public Choice, Public Finance, Public Finance Quarterly,* and *Southern Economic Journal.*

Lloyd J. Dumas received his B.A. from Columbia College, and his M.S. and Ph.D. from Columbia University. He was on the faculties of the City University of New York and Columbia University before joining the University of Texas at Dallas where he is professor of political economy.

Professor Dumas has been a member of technical and editorial advisory boards for organizations such as American Association for the Advancement of Science, the Governor of Colorado's Blue Ribbon Citizens Committee, Council on Economic Priorities, and the Cato Institute. He has submitted testimony to the Department of Energy, the U.S. House of Representatives, and various state legislative committees on planning, investment, and development in California, Colorado, Connecticut, and Massachusetts. Professor Dumas is active in international conferences of scientists, economists, physicians, teachers, historians, and political scientists and has discussed the policy implications of his work on numerous television and radio programs in North America and Europe.

Professor Dumas's articles have appeared in nine languages in scholarly and professional publications including *American Historical Association Proceedings, American Institute of Industrial Engineers Transactions, Annals of the New York Academy of Sciences, Bulletin of the Atomic Scientists, Cato Journal, Cincinnati Post, Dallas Morning News, Economic Forum, Journal of Economic Issues, Journal of Economic Studies, Journal of Peace Science, Journal of Sociology and Social Welfare, Los Angeles Times, New York Times,* and *Technology Review.*

He is the author of *The Conservation Response: Strategies for the Design and Operation of Energy Using Systems; The Overburdened Economy: Uncovering the Causes of Chronic Unemployment, Inflation and National Decline;* and *Reversing Economic Decay: The Political Economy of Arms Reduction.*

Marilyn R. Flowers received her B.A. from the University of Iowa, her M.A. from UCLA and her Ph.D. from Virginia Polytechnic Institute and State University (VPI). She has taught at VPI, Montana State University, and the Australian National University in Canberra. She is currently associate professor of economics at University of Oklahoma.

Professor Flowers's articles have been published in *Cato Journal, Economic Inquiry, Public Choice, Public Finance, Public Finance Quarterly,* and *Western Economic Journal.* Her research on regulation and urban transit was part of a study, *Economic Characteristics of the Urban Public Transportation Industry,* prepared for the U.S. Department of Transportation by the Institute for Defense Analyses. Professor Flowers collaborated on the fourth and fifth editions of *The Public Finances* with James M. Buchanan.

James D. Gwartney is professor of economics at Florida State University. He received his B.A. from Ottawa University and his M.A. and Ph.D. degrees from the University of Washington.

Professor Gwartney has written several textbooks including, *Economics: Private and Public Choice, Microeconomics: Private and Public Choice, Macroeconomics: Private and Public Choice,* (all with R. Stroup), *An Economic Handbook for the Turbulent Seventies* (with M. Maxfield), and *Essentials of Economics* (with R. Stroup and J. Clark). His articles have appeared in *American Economic Review, Encyclopedia of Economics and Business, Industrial and Labor Relations Review, The Intercollegiate Review, Journal of Human Resources, Journal of Labor Research, Journal of Political Economy, Mercurio, Notre Dame Lawyer, Social Science Quarterly, Southern Economic Review,* and *World Research Ink.*

Ronald N. Johnson is professor of agricultural economics and economics at Montana State University. He received his B.S. from Utah State University, his M.A. from California State University at Long Beach, and his Ph.D. from the University of Washington. Dr. Johnson specializes in natural resources and property rights as well as applied price theory and industrial organization.

Professor Johnson's articles and reviews have appeared in *American Economic Review, American Journal of Agricultural Economics, Economic Inquiry, Explorations in Economic History, Journal of Economic History, Journal of Labor Research, Journal of Law and Economics, Journal of Political Economy, Natural Resources Journal, Review of Economics and Statistics,* and *Southern Economic*

Journal. In addition, Dr. Johnson has contributed to the volumes, *Bureaucracy vs. Environment, Water Rights: Scarce Resource Allocation, Bureaucracy, and the Environment,* and *Forestlands: Public and Private.*

Israel M. Kirzner is professor of economics at New York University. He received his B.A. from Brooklyn College and his M.B.A. and Ph.D. degrees from New York University.

Professor Kirzner is the author of *An Essay on Capital; Competition and Entrepreneurship* (translated into four languages); *Discovery and the Capitalist Process; The Economic Point of View; Market Theory and the Price System;* and *Perception, Opportunity and Profit: Studies in the Theory of Entrepreneurship;* editor of *Method, Process, and Austrian Economics,* and *Subjectivism, Intelligibility, and Economic Understanding.* Professor Kirzner's articles have appeared in popular and professional journals such as *Atlantic Economic Journal, Eastern Economic Journal, The Freeman, Il Politico, The Intercollegiate Review, Journal of Economic Affairs, Journal of Political Economy, National Review, New Individualist Review,* and *Southern Economic Journal.*

James E. Long received his A.B. from Erskine College and his M.A. and Ph.D. from Florida State University. He is professor of economics at Auburn University. Professor Long is the coauthor of *Women and Part-Week Work,* a study prepared for the U.S. Department of Labor, and articles appearing in *American Economic Review, Industrial and Labor Relations Review, Journal of Human Resources, Journal of Industrial Economics, Journal of Labor Research, Journal of Political Economy, National Tax Journal, Policy Report, Public Finance Quarterly, Review of Economics and Statistics, Social Science Quarterly,* and *Urban Studies.*

Eric Mack is associate professor of philosophy at Newcomb College, Tulane University. He received his B.A. from Union College, and his M.A. and Ph.D. degrees from University of Rochester. He has previously taught at Hunter College, Queens College, and Eisenhower College. Professor Mack is editor of *The Right and Wrong of Compulsion by the State and Other Essays,* and *The Man versus The State,* and his articles have appeared in *American Journal of Economics and Sociology, Canadian Journal of Philosophy, Ethics, Jour-*

nal of Libertarian Studies, The Personalist, Philosophy and Public Affairs, Philosophical Studies, Reason, and Southwestern Journal of Philosophy and in numerous anthologies.

Richard B. McKenzie is currently professor of economics at Clemson University. He was recently John M. Olin Visiting Professor of American Business at Washington University. He received his B.S. from Pfeiffer College, his M.A. from the University of Maryland, and his Ph.D. from Virginia Polytechnic Institute and State University (VPI). Professor McKenzie has taught at Appalachian State University and Radford College, and was visiting research associate at the Center for Study of Public Choice at VPI. He is also Senior Fellow at the Heritage Foundation.

Professor McKenzie is the author or editor of over a dozen books and monographs, including *Bound to Be Free; Competing Visions; An Economic Theory of Learning* (with R. Staaf); *Fugitive Industry: The Economics and Politics of Deindustrialization; The Limits of Economic Science; Modern Political Economy; The New World of Economics* (with G. Tullock, translated into three languages); *Plant Closings;* and *Restrictions on Business Mobility.*

Professor McKenzie's articles have appeared in professional and popular publications such as *Christian Science Monitor, Ethics, Journal of Economic Education, Journal of Economic Issues, Journal of Labor Research, Journal of Legal Studies, Journal of Political Economy, National Review, New York Times, Policy Review, Public Choice, Public Finance Quarterly, Reason, Regulation, Review of Social Economy, Social Science Quarterly, Southern Economic Journal,* and *Wall Street Journal.*

Morgan O. Reynolds is professor of economics at Texas A&M University. He received his B.S., M.S., and Ph.D. degrees from the University of Wisconsin. He has taught at the University of California at Riverside, University of California at Davis, and has been research associate and fellow at the Institute for Research on Poverty, and staff economist at the Free Enterprise Center.

Professor Reynolds is the author of *Crime by Choice; Public Expenditures, Taxes, and the U.S. Distribution of Income; Power and Privilege;* and *Unions and Productivity.* His articles have been published in *American Economic Review, American Journal of Econom-*

ics and Sociology, Cato Journal, Challenge, Economic Journal, Environmental Affairs, Journal of Economic History, Journal of Economic Theory, Journal of Labor Research, Journal of Political Economy, Journal of Social and Political Studies, Policy Review, Public Finance Quarterly, World Research Ink, and other journals.

Paul Craig Roberts holds the William E. Simon Chair in Political Economy at the Center for Strategic and International Studies, Georgetown University. He received his B.S. in industrial management from Georgia Technical University, and his Ph.D. in economics from the University of Virginia. He did post-graduate work at the University of California at Berkeley and at Merton College, Oxford University. He is a senior research fellow at the Hoover Institution at Stanford University, and has held academic appointments at Virginia Polytechnic Institute and State University, Tulane, and other universities.

Dr. Roberts served as Economic Counsel to Representative Jack Kemp, Staff Associate with the Defense Appropriations Subcommittee, Chief Economist with the Minority Staff of the Committee on the Budget, and Economic Counsel to Senator Orrin Hatch. Dr. Roberts managed the tax-cut movement in the U.S. Congress in 1975–78, and drafted the original version of the Kemp-Roth bill. During 1981–82 he was Assistant Secretary of the Treasury for Economic Policy. He is a consultant to the U.S. Department of Defense and to various private financial institutions, and he is on the board of directors of the Value Line Investment Funds.

Dr. Roberts has held distinguished appointments in U.S. journalism, including associate editor of the editorial page of the *Wall Street Journal,* contributing editor to *Harper's,* and author of the "Economic Watch" column for *Business Week.* He is the author of *Alienation and the Soviet Economy; Marx's Theory of Exchange, Alienation, and Crisis;* and *The Supply-Side Revolution.* Dr. Roberts's articles have been published in popular and scholarly journals such as *Business Week, Ethics, Fortune, Harper's, Journal of Law and Economics, Journal of Monetary Economics, Journal of Political Economy, New York Times, Oxford Economic Papers, Public Choice, Public Finance Quarterly, The Public Interest, Slavic Review, Soviet Studies, Wall Street Journal, Washington Post,* and other U.S. and European publications.

Richard L. Stroup is professor of economics at Montana State University, and research director for the Political Economy Research Center. He received his B.A., M.A., and Ph.D. from the University of Washington. Professor Stroup has taught at Seattle University, and Florida State University, and from 1982 to 1984 he was director of the Office of Policy Analysis for the U.S. Department of the Interior.

Professor Stroup's articles have been published in *Cato Journal, Economic Inquiry, Journal of Law and Economics, Literature of Liberty, Montana Business Quarterly, Policy Review, Public Choice, Reason, Southern Economic Journal,* and others. He is the author of *Economics: Private and Public Choice* (with J. Gwartney), *Natural Resources: Bureaucratic Myths and Environmental Management* (with J. Baden), and co-editor (with J. Baden) of *Bureaucracy vs. Environment: The Environmental Costs of Bureaucratic Governance.*

Gordon Tullock is professor of economics at the Center for Study of Public Choice at George Mason University. He received his J.D. from the University of Chicago Law School, and spent several years studying Chinese at Yale and Cornell Universities. Professor Tullock spent nine years in the Foreign Service, most notably, two years in Mainland China, including the seizure of the city of Tientsin by the Communists in 1949. He was later transferred to the Consulate General in Hong Kong, and to the U.S. Embassy in Korea. He was University Distinguished Professor of economics and public choice at Virginia Polytechnic Institute and State University, and has also served on the faculties of the University of Virginia, University of South Carolina, and Rice University.

Professor Tullock is a founding member of the board and past president of the Public Choice Society, and past president of the Southern Economic Association, and former elected member of the Council of the American Political Science Association. Professor Tullock is the author of over twenty books and monographs, including *The Calculus of Consent* (with J. Buchanan); *The Economics of Redistribution; The Logic of the Law; Modern Political Economy* (with R. McKenzie); *The Politics of Bureaucracy; Private Wants, Public Means* (translated into Spanish); *The Social Dilemma: The Economics of War and Revolution* (translated into Japanese); and *Trials on Trial: The Pure Theory of Legal Procedure.* He is the editor of over eight books, including *Towards A Theory of the Rent-Seeking Society* (with J. Buchanan and

R. Tollison); *Frontiers of Economics* (three volumes); and *Explorations in the Theory of Anarchy*, among others.

Professor Tullock is the author of over 100 articles that have appeared in professional publications, including *American Economic Review, Atlantic Economic Journal, Bell Journal of Economics, Economic Inquiry, Economic History Review, Il Politico, International Review of Law and Economics, Journal of Money, Credit and Banking, Journal of Law and Economics, Journal of Political Economy, Journal of Theoretical Biology, Kyklos, Modern Age, National Review, New Individualist Review, Oxford Economic Papers, Public Administration Review, Public Choice, The Public Interest, Quarterly Journal of Economics, Social Science Quarterly, Southern Economic Journal, Theory and Decision*, and *Western Economic Journal*.

Richard K. Vedder is professor of economics at Ohio University. He received his B.A. from Northwestern University, and his M.A. and Ph.D. from the University of Illinois. He has been an Earhart Fellow and a Liberty Fund Fellow. Professor Vedder was research associate for the Illinois State Commission on Revenue, and Economist for the Joint Economic Committee of the U.S. Congress (1981–1982).

Professor Vedder is author or co-editor of *The American Economy in Historical Perspective, Essays in Nineteenth Century Economic History*, and *Variations in Business and Economic History*. His articles have appeared in domestic and international publications, such as *Agricultural History, Atlantic Economic Journal, Business History Review, Canadian Journal of Economics, Economic Inquiry, Explorations in Economic History, Journal of Austrian Economics, Journal of Contemporary Studies, Journal of Economic History, Journal of Regional Science, Scottish Journal of Political Economy, South African Journal of Economics, Swedish Journal of Economics, Western Economic Journal*, and other publications.

Richard E. Wagner is professor of economics at Florida State University. He received his B.S. from the University of Southern California, and his Ph.D. from the University of Virginia. He has served on the faculties of the University of California at Irvine, Tulane University, Virginia Polytechnic Institute and State University, Auburn University, in addition to spending one year as senior research associate at The Urban Institute. Professor Wagner has been a visiting fellow at the Institute for Humane Studies, and visiting professor at the University of Konstanz (West Germany).

Professor Wagner has been on the editorial boards of *Policy Report, Policy Studies Journal,* and *Cato Journal.* He is the author or editor of over fifteen books and monographs, including *Balanced Budgets, Fiscal Responsibility, and the Constitution* (with R. Tollison); *The Consequences of Mr. Keynes* (with J. Buchanan and J. Burton); *Democracy in Deficit: The Political Legacy of Lord Keynes* (with J. Buchanan, translated into three languages); *Perspectives on Tax Reform; Public Finance: Revenues and Expenditures in a Democratic Society;* and *Myth, Reality, and the Welfare State* (forthcoming from Pacific Research Institute), and others.

His articles have been published in *American Economic Review, Atlantic Economic Journal, The Banker, Cato Journal, Journal of Contemporary Studies, Journal of Law and Economics, Journal of Monetary Economics, Journal of Money, Credit and Banking, Kyklos, National Tax Journal, Policy Review, Policy Studies Journal, Public Choice,* and other journals.

PACIFIC STUDIES IN PUBLIC POLICY

RESOLVING THE HOUSING CRISIS
Government Policy, Decontrol, and the Public Interest
Edited with an Introduction by M. Bruce Johnson

OFFSHORE LANDS
Oil and Gas Leasing and Conservation on the Outer Continental Shelf
By Walter J. Mead, et al.
Foreword by Stephen L. McDonald

ELECTRIC POWER
Deregulation and the Public Interest
Edited by John C. Moorhouse
Foreword by Harold Demsetz

TAXATION AND THE DEFICIT ECONOMY
Fiscal Policy and Capital Formation in the United States
Edited by Dwight R. Lee
Foreword by Michael J. Boskin

THE AMERICAN FAMILY AND THE STATE
Edited by Joseph R. Peden and Fred R. Glahe
Foreword by Robert Nisbet

FORTHCOMING

DEALING WITH DRUGS
Problems of Government Control

CRISIS AND LEVIATHAN
Critical Episodes in the Growth of American Government

THE NEW CHINA
Comparative Economic Development in Hong Kong, Taiwan, and
Mainland China

POLITICAL BUSINESS CYCLES
The Economics and Politics of Stagflation

RATIONING HEALTH CARE
Medical Licensing in the United States

HEALTH CARE IN AMERICA: PUBLIC AND PRIVATE

CRIME, POLICE, AND THE COURTS

MYTH AND REALITY IN SOCIAL WELFARE

RENT CONTROL IN SANTA MONICA

UNEMPLOYMENT AND THE STATE

For further information on the Pacific Research Institute's program and a catalog of publications, please contact:

PACIFIC RESEARCH INSTITUTE FOR PUBLIC POLICY
177 Post Street
San Francisco, California 94108
(415) 989-0833